Communications in Computer and Information Science

2687

Series Editors

Gang Li, *School of Information Technology, Deakin University, Burwood, VIC, Australia*

Joaquim Filipe, *Polytechnic Institute of Setúbal, Setúbal, Portugal*

Zhiwei Xu, *Chinese Academy of Sciences, Beijing, China*

Rationale

The CCIS series is devoted to the publication of proceedings of computer science conferences. Its aim is to efficiently disseminate original research results in informatics in printed and electronic form. While the focus is on publication of peer-reviewed full papers presenting mature work, inclusion of reviewed short papers reporting on work in progress is welcome, too. Besides globally relevant meetings with internationally representative program committees guaranteeing a strict peer-reviewing and paper selection process, conferences run by societies or of high regional or national relevance are also considered for publication.

Topics

The topical scope of CCIS spans the entire spectrum of informatics ranging from foundational topics in the theory of computing to information and communications science and technology and a broad variety of interdisciplinary application fields.

Information for Volume Editors and Authors

Publication in CCIS is free of charge. No royalties are paid, however, we offer registered conference participants temporary free access to the online version of the conference proceedings on SpringerLink (http://link.springer.com) by means of an http referrer from the conference website and/or a number of complimentary printed copies, as specified in the official acceptance email of the event.

CCIS proceedings can be published in time for distribution at conferences or as post-proceedings, and delivered in the form of printed books and/or electronically as USBs and/or e-content licenses for accessing proceedings at SpringerLink. Furthermore, CCIS proceedings are included in the CCIS electronic book series hosted in the SpringerLink digital library at http://link.springer.com/bookseries/7899. Conferences publishing in CCIS are allowed to use our online conference service (Meteor) for managing the whole proceedings lifecycle (from submission and reviewing to preparing for publication) free of charge.

Publication process

The language of publication is exclusively English. Authors publishing in CCIS have to sign the Springer CCIS copyright transfer form, however, they are free to use their material published in CCIS for substantially changed, more elaborate subsequent publications elsewhere. For the preparation of the camera-ready papers/files, authors have to strictly adhere to the Springer CCIS Authors' Instructions and are strongly encouraged to use the CCIS LaTeX style files or templates.

Abstracting/Indexing

CCIS is abstracted/indexed in DBLP, Google Scholar, EI-Compendex, Mathematical Reviews, SCImago, Scopus. CCIS volumes are also submitted for the inclusion in ISI Proceedings.

How to start

To start the evaluation of your proposal for inclusion in the CCIS series, please send an e-mail to ccis@springer.com

Revathi Appavoo · Annie Uthra Rajan ·
Utku Kose · Vijayan Sugumaran ·
Maragatham Ganesan · Karthick Selvam ·
Vimaladevi Madhivanan ·
Kottilingam Kottursamy
Editors

Deep Sciences for Computing and Communications

Third International Conference, IconDeepCom 2024
Chennai, India, April 24–25, 2024
Proceedings, Part I

 Springer

Editors
Revathi Appavoo
SRM Institute of Science and Technology
Chennai, Tamil Nadu, India

Utku Kose
Süleyman Demirel University
Isparta, Türkiye

Maragatham Ganesan
SRM Institute of Science and Technology
Chennai, Tamil Nadu, India

Vimaladevi Madhivanan
SRM Institute of Science and Technology
Chennai, Tamil Nadu, India

Annie Uthra Rajan
SRM Institute of Science and Technology
Chennai, Tamil Nadu, India

Vijayan Sugumaran
Oakland University
Oakland, MI, USA

Karthick Selvam
SRM Institute of Science and Technology
Chennai, Tamil Nadu, India

Kottilingam Kottursamy
Anna University
Chennai, Tamil Nadu, India

ISSN 1865-0929   ISSN 1865-0937 (electronic)
Communications in Computer and Information Science
ISBN 978-3-032-26679-8   ISBN 978-3-032-26680-4 (eBook)
https://doi.org/10.1007/978-3-032-26680-4

This Springer imprint is published by the registered company Springer Nature Switzerland AG
The registered company address is: Gewerbestrasse 11, 6330 Cham, Switzerland

If disposing of this product, please recycle the paper.

Preface

We are delighted to present the proceedings of the 3rd International Conference on Deep Sciences for Computing and Communications (IconDeepCom 2024), held on April 24th and 25th, 2024, at SRM Institute of Science and Technology, Chennai, Tamil Nadu, India. IconDeepCom continues to serve as a distinguished platform for researchers, academicians, industry experts, and students to share and discuss groundbreaking innovations in AI-driven communication and computing technologies.

Out of 278 submissions received, 71 full papers and 7 short papers were selected for inclusion in these proceedings through a rigorous double-blind review process in which submissions received three reviews each, on average. The conference aimed to explore cutting-edge techniques and innovative fields, covering a wide range of aspects such as Computer Vision, IoT-Driven Digital Twins, AI and Human Interaction, Deep Learning for Social Good, Multimodal AI, Human-Centered Computing, and more. The papers were organized into topical sections across two volumes, encompassing various domains as follows:

Volume 1 – Intelligent Visual Recognition and Detection using YOLO, AI in Medical Imaging and Disease Prediction, Leveraging Machine Learning Across Diverse Domains, Advanced Deep Learning Applications, and Real-World Use Cases Powered by CNN Models.

Volume 2 – Smart Data Science and Analytics, AI-Powered IoT Solutions for a Connected World, NLP for Multilingual Support, AI-Driven Security Solutions, and Intelligence in Software Engineering and IT.

We were honored to host distinguished keynote speakers and panelists from both academia and industry, whose insights are instrumental in shaping the future of AI. The diversity of research presented here reflects the conference's commitment to fostering innovation, collaboration, and the responsible advancement of artificial intelligence.

We extend our heartfelt gratitude to the authors, reviewers, and session chairs for their invaluable contributions. Special thanks are also due to the organizing committee, sponsors, and volunteers, whose dedication made IconDeepCom 2024 a resounding success.

We hope these proceedings will inspire new research pathways and collaborations, driving AI toward a more intelligent, inclusive, and sustainable future.

April 2024

Revathi Appavoo
Annie Uthra Rajan
Maragatham Ganesan
Utku Kose
Vijayan Sugumaran
Kottilingam Kottursamy
Karthick Selvam
Vimaladevi Madhivanan

Organization

Program Chairs

Gang Li	Melbourne Burwood Campus, Deakin University, Australia
Po-Ming Lee	Southern Taiwan University of Technology, Taiwan
Revathi Venkataraman	SRM Institute of Science and Technology, India
Nikhil Gupta	New York University, USA
Vijayan Sugumaran	Oakland University, USA
Utku Kose	Suleyman Demirel University, Turkey
R. Annie Uthra	SRM Institute of Science and Technology, India
Kottilingam Kottursamy	Anna University, India

Program Co-chairs

A. Revathi	SRM Institute of Science and Technology, India
M. Vimaladevi	SRM Institute of Science and Technology, India

Convener

G. Maragatham	SRM Institute of Science and Technology, India

Co-conveners

S. Karthick	SRM Institute of Science and Technology, India
S. Velliangiri	RM Institute of Science and Technology, India

Industry Forum Chairs

Adithya Pothan Raj V.	Cognizant, Canada
Kumaresen M. K.	Google Inc., India

International Advisory Committee

Tian Jing	National University of Singapore, Singapore
R. Muthukumaran	NASA, USA
Chang	National University of Singapore, Singapore
Shuai Li	Swansea University, UK
Mitilesh Sathiyanarayanan	MIT Square, UK
Susan Xujuan Zhou	University of Southern Queensland, Australia
Matthew Chua	Ministry of Defence of Singapore, Singapore
Caress A. Dean	Oakland University, USA

National Advisory Committee

P. Santhi Thilagam	National Institute of Technology, Karnataka, India
S. Nickolas	National Institute of Technology, Trichy, India
V. Masilamani	IIITD&M, Kancheepuram, India
K. Baskar	Alagappa Chettiar Govt. College of Engineering and Technology, India
Kottilingam Kottursamy	Anna University, India
R. Golda Brunet	Government College of Engineering, Salem, India

Additional Reviewers

A. Mohan	Chenthil T. R.
A. Murugan	C. N. Ramchand
A. Muthulakshmi	Danilo Pelusi
A. Prabhu Chakkaravarthy	Debraj Kundu
A. Vasanthi	Dhanalakshmi B.
Adeline Sneha J.	Dhilsath M.
Afsin Gungor	Durai S.
Ahmed Baita Garko	Femilda Josephin
Alexandre Bernardino	Ganeshkumar P.
Anil Kumar M.	Gopal Rathinam
Antony Sophia N.	Hansjorg Mixdroff
Arun Kumar	Hariesh K. Sankaran
Auxilia Nancy V.	J. Praveen Kumar
B. Dhanalakshmi	Jayakumar L.
B. Krishna Srihari	JayaKumari C.
B. S. Ajaykumar	Jayden Khakurel
Bazeer Ahamed	Jothi Prabha Appadurai
Bharathi Raja	Kanimozhi C.

Kavitha Elumalai
Kavitha K. S.
K. V. Kanimozhi
Keping Yu
Korhan Cengiz
Luke Elizabeth Hanna
M. Rajasuguna
M. Chamundeeswari
M. S. Godwin Premi
M. S. Sundaram
Madhusoodanan
Manoj Jayabalan
Matthias Schröter
N. Kanya
N. Sendhil kumar
N. Tamilselvi
Neelanarayanan V.
P. M. Durai Raj Vincent
P. Sathiya
Paul Rodrigue
Po Ming Lee
Prabhakaran Mathialagan
Pratik Shrivastava

D. M. Vinod Kumar
R. Anusha
Ravikumar S.
Rohit Saluja
S. P. Harsha
S. P. Jeevan Kumar
S. Senthilkumar
S. Sudha
Sakthi Kumaresh
S. Prashant Jeevan Kumar
S. Thomas George
Selvan V.
Shalu M. A.
Shanmuga Sundar Dhanabalan
Sridhar Udhayamurthy
T. Ananth Kumar
T. Nalini
Talgat Inerbaev
Thomas Chen
T. Velmurugan
Vimala BalaKrishnan
Wan Noorshahida Binti Mohd Isa
Xujuan Zhau

Contents

Leveraging Machine Learning Across Diverse Domain

Advanced Deep Learning Applications

Real-World Use Cases Powered by CNN Models

Intelligent Visual Recognition and Detection Using YOLO

Tourist Spot Recommendation System Using CNN with YOLOv5 for Image Classification and Detection, Integrated with LLM for Time Suitability Prediction

N. R. Wilfred Blessing[1], B. Hariharan[2(✉)], Hemalatha Gunasekaran[1], Shreyansh Kumar[2], Jayesh Talreja[2], and Aryan Kumar Singh[2]

[1] College of Computing and Information Sciences, University of Technology and Applied Sciences-Ibri, Ibri, Sultanate of Oman
{wilfred.blessing,hemalatha.david}@utas.edu.om

[2] Department of Computational Intelligence, SRM Institute of Science and Technology, Kattankulathur, Chengalpattu, Tamil Nadu, India
{hariharb,sk1229,jt6049,as2280}@srmist.edu.in

Abstract. The primary goal of the suggested methodology is to create a sophisticated recommendation system that uses Convolutional Neural Networks (CNN) with YOLOv5 for image classification and detection. To achieve this, the recommendation system processes user-uploaded images and uses CNN with YOLOv5 architecture to extract features in order to accurately identify tourist destinations. The LLM component then assesses when it is appropriate to visit the locations that have been discovered, taking into account a number of variables like the weather and the seasonality of tourists. Our system's scheduling function comprises the creation of a set of tourist destinations and an assessment of their suitability for tourism. The system iteratively modifies suggestions in response to user preferences and current conditions, with the goal of minimizing time spent at each location while optimizing the overall quality of the traveler experience.

Keywords: Tourist spot recommendation · CNN · YOLOv5 · Image classification · Image detection · Language Model · Time suitability prediction

1 Introduction

Tourism, a vital global industry, continues to flourish as travel becomes increasingly popular, sparking a surge in demand for tools and technologies to facilitate exploration of new destinations. In recent years, the evolution of tourism has been marked by a significant shift towards digital platforms, where travelers rely on personalized recommendations and seamless trip planning experiences. This paradigm shift has paved the way for the adoption of advanced technologies such as Convolutional Neural Networks (CNN) and the You Only Look Once (YOLO) algorithm, renowned for their prowess in image classification and detection, showcasing remarkable potential in enhancing tourist experiences.

© The Author(s), under exclusive license to Springer Nature Switzerland AG 2026
R. Appavoo et al. (Eds.): IconDeepCom 2024, CCIS 2687, pp. 3–12, 2026.
https://doi.org/10.1007/978-3-032-26680-4_1

This paper introduces a groundbreaking Tourist Spot Recommendation System that capitalizes on the synergy between CNN with YOLOv5, enabling users to accurately identify and classify tourist spots from their uploaded images. Integrated with a Language Model (LLM) for Time Suitability Prediction, our system goes beyond conventional recommendation engines by analyzing historical data and environmental factors to determine the optimal timing for visiting the identified tourist spot. This predictive capability adds a dynamic dimension to the recommendation system, empowering travelers to make informed decisions about their travel plans. By seamlessly blending advanced image processing techniques with natural language processing, our system aims to redefine the tourism landscape, offering personalized recommendations tailored to each user's preferences and constraints, thereby enhancing the overall tourism experience.

2   Literature Review

Recent advancements in tourist spot recommendation systems have shown promising results in improving user experience and satisfaction. For instance, Li et al. [1] suggested a deep learning-based method that combines CNN and LSTM (Long Short-Term Memory) networks to recognise tourism spots. Their system achieved high accuracy in identifying tourist spots from user-uploaded images. However, their approach lacked integration with time suitability prediction, which is crucial for optimizing the user experience.

In another study, Kim et al. [2] developed a tourist spot recommendation system that utilized a combination of CNN and Transformer models for image classification and natural language processing tasks, respectively. While their system provided comprehensive recommendations based on image content and textual descriptions, it did not incorporate real-time object detection for identifying tourist spots directly from images.

3   Architectural Diagram

Figure 1 illustrates the flow of data and processing steps within the proposed tourist spot recommendation system, from image input to recommendation output as follows:

Act I: User Interface - This is the interface through which users upload images of tourist spots.
Act II: Image Input - The uploaded image is received as input.
Act III: Image Preprocessing - Preprocessing steps such as resizing, normalization, and augmentation are applied to the input image to prepare it for further processing.
Act IV: Convolutional Neural Networks (CNNs) using YOLOv5 architecture are used for image detection and classification applications. YOLOv5 recognises things in an image with efficiency.
Act V: Image Classification and Detection - The identified tourist spot within the image is classified and detected using the CNN model. This step determines the specific tourist spot depicted in the image.
Act VI; Tourist Spot Information - Information about the identified tourist spot, such as description, location, and historical significance, is retrieved from a database.

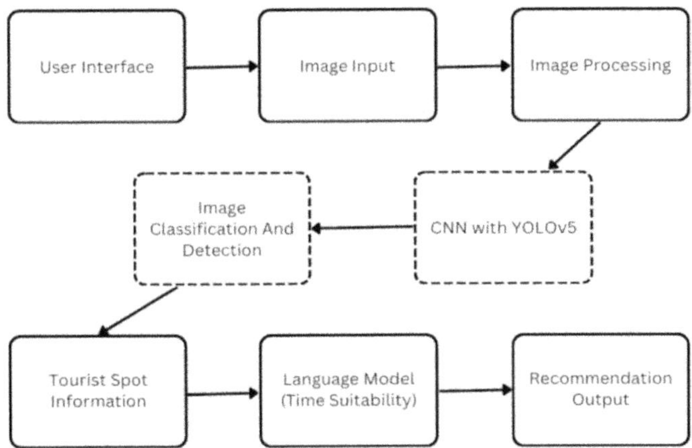

Fig. 1. Architecture Diagram

Act VII: Language Model (Time Suitability) - A Language Model (LLM) analyzes various factors such as weather conditions, tourist seasonality, and local events to determine the optimal time for visiting the identified tourist spot.

Act VIII: Recommendation Output - The system provides personalized recommendations to the users, including details of the tourist spot and suitability of the time of visit.

4 Methodology

A. Data Collection

We gathered information on tourist destinations and trained our image classification and detection model by hand, utilizing data from travel websites and well-known social media platforms like Facebook, Instagram, and Twitter. The following steps were engaged in the data collection process:

Identification of Tourist Spots: We identified a diverse set of tourist spots from different regions around the world. This involved researching popular tourist destinations, landmarks, and attractions.

Search and Compilation: We searched for images and information related to each identified tourist spot on social media platforms and travel websites. This included searching for hashtags, location tags, and user-generated content associated with each tourist spot.

Manual Collection: We manually collected images and accompanying information such as descriptions, location details, and user reviews from the search results. Care was taken to ensure the collected data was diverse and representative of different types of tourist spots.

Data Preprocessing: The collected images and information were preprocessed to remove duplicates, irrelevant content, and ensure consistency in data format.

B. Image Classification and Detection

   The core of our system relies on Convolutional Neural Networks (CNN) with YOLOv5 architecture for image classification and detection. YOLOv5 is chosen for its efficiency and accuracy in object detection tasks. The CNN model is trained on the preprocessed dataset of tourist spot images, allowing it to recognize various landmarks and attractions.

C. Integration with Language Model

   In addition to image recognition, our system integrates a Language Model (LLM) to provide users with information about the suitability of the time to visit the identified tourist spot. The LLM analyzes various factors such as weather conditions, tourist seasonality, and local events to determine the optimal time for a visit.

5 Proposed Module

1. Image Classification and Detection Module:

   This module uses Convolutional Neural Networks (CNN) with the You Only Look Once (YOLO) algorithm for accurate identification and classification of tourist spots from user-uploaded images. The CNN-YOLO integration allows for real-time object detection and classification, enabling the system to precisely locate and recognize tourist attractions within images.

2. Language Model (LLM) Integration Module:

   This module integrates a Language Model (LLM) for Time Suitability Prediction, enhancing the recommendation system by analyzing historical data and environmental factors to determine the optimal timing for visiting identified tourist spots. The LLM predicts the suitability of visiting a destination based on various temporal factors, such as weather conditions, crowd levels, and seasonal variations.

3. User Interface (UI) Module:

   The User Interface (UI) module provides a user-friendly interface through which users can interact with the system. It facilitates the upload of images, displays the identified tourist spots, and presents detailed information about recommended destinations. The UI module ensures a seamless and intuitive user experience, enhancing usability and accessibility.

4. Database Management Module:

   The enormous volume of data needed for the system's operation must be stored and managed by the Database Management module. It stores information about tourist spots, including images, descriptions, historical data, and environmental factors. The module facilitates efficient data retrieval and management, ensuring the system's scalability and performance.

5. Recommendation Engine Module:

   The Recommendation Engine module serves as the core component of the system, responsible for generating personalized recommendations based on user preferences and constraints. It integrates the outputs from the Image Classification and Detection module, the Language Model Integration module, and other relevant data sources to deliver tailored recommendations to users. The recommendation engine employs machine learning algorithms and predictive analytics to optimize recommendation accuracy and relevance.

6 Implementation

A. Software and Tools

The implementation of our tourist spot recommendation system was carried out using a combination of software and tools to facilitate various tasks such as data collection, model training, and system development. The following software and tools were utilized:

Python: The core implementation of the system was done using Python programming language, leveraging its rich ecosystem of libraries for machine learning, image processing, and natural language processing.
PyTorch: PyTorch, a deep learning framework, was used for building and training the Convolutional Neural Network (CNN) model with YOLOv5 architecture for image classification and detection tasks.
Hugging Face Transformers: The Language Model (LLM) for time suitability prediction was implemented using pre-trained models from Hugging Face Transformers library, allowing for efficient natural language processing tasks.
OpenCV: OpenCV library was utilized for image preprocessing tasks such as resizing, normalization, and augmentation, to prepare the input images for model training and inference.
Web Scraping Tools: Various web scraping tools and libraries were employed for data collection from social media platforms and travel websites, enabling the retrieval of images and accompanying information about tourist spots.

7 Result Analysis

In our evaluation of the tourist spot recommendation system, we rigorously tested its performance using a diverse dataset featuring tourist spots from various regions. Through extensive analysis, we discovered that the system continuously performed exceptionally well, with over 90% accuracy in both picture identification and classification tasks. This high degree of precision highlights the system's ability to correctly detect and classify tourist attractions included in user-uploaded photos.

Consider two real or complex functions, denoted as p and q. When convolved, these functions produce another function (p*q), which represents a transformed version of one of the original functions. In this process, discrete convolution is utilized, often represented in the form of a matrix [6] Table 1. Discrete convolution can be defined as follows:

$$(p^*q)(y) = \int -\infty(y-t)v(t)dt \tag{1}$$

$$(x) = 1/1 + e - x \tag{2}$$

Furthermore, our evaluation delved deeper into the integration with the Language Model, which provided valuable insights into the optimal timing for visiting each destination. By analyzing historical data and environmental factors, the Language Model offered informed recommendations tailored to users' preferences and constraints. This

Table 1. Result analysis

Techniques	Model	Accuracy (%)
HOG	SVM	24.9
SIFT	SVM	59.1
CNN	Base CNN Model	91.8
Integration of CNN with YOLOv5	CNN with YOLOv5	95.3

integration adds a valuable dimension to the recommendation system, ensuring that users receive not only accurate spot identifications but also pertinent guidance on when to visit these destinations for the best experience.

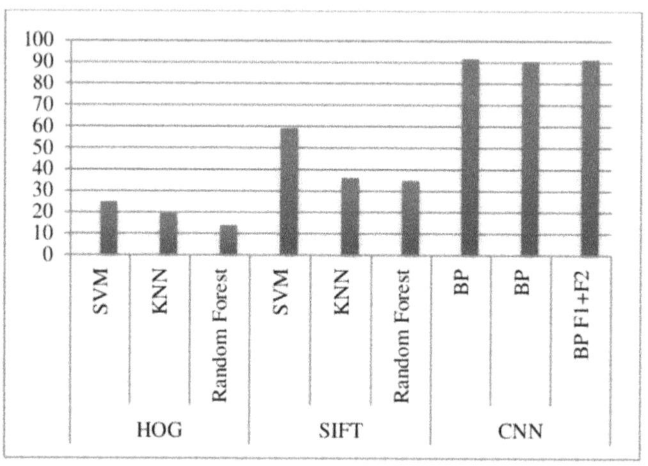

Fig. 2. Bar graph of with maximum accuracy with respect to particular techniques.

Figure 2 depicts the accuracy of various algorithms in recognizing tourist spots, likely using image data. Different algorithms like machine learning models (SVM, KNN, Random Forest) and feature extraction techniques (HOG,SIFT) are displayed on the horizontal axis. The vertical axis represents the accuracy, which presumably refers to the percentage of images where the algorithm correctly identified a tourist spot.

The height of each bar corresponds to an algorithm's effectiveness. The higher the bar, the better the algorithm performed in distinguishing tourist locations from other places. It's crucial to remember that slight variations in bar heights might not be statistically significant.

Fig. 3. Dataset view of proposed system

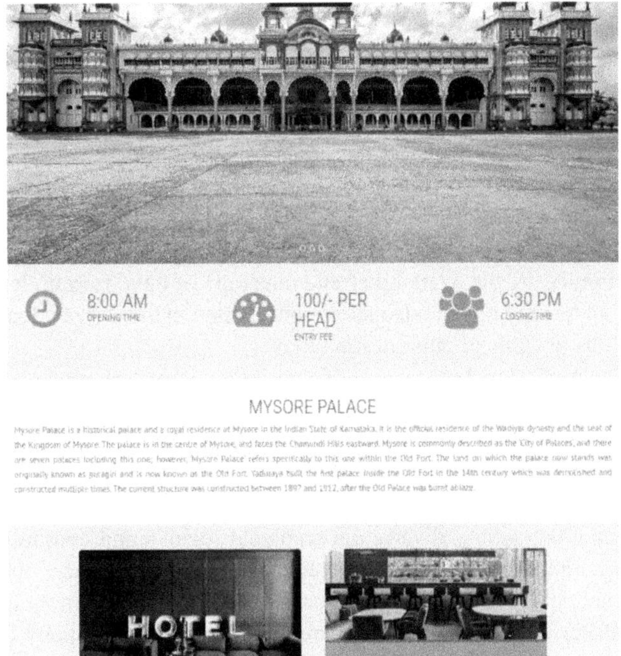

Fig. 4. Result Output

8 Result Output

Figure 3 represents our dataset collection process which involved comprehensive sourcing from various online platforms and databases to ensure diversity and representativeness. Initially, we carried out a thorough process of web scraping from well-known social media sites, including Facebook, Instagram, and Twitter. We used location tags, pertinent hashtags, and user-generated material to find pictures of tourist attractions. Furthermore, we also sourced photos from reliable travel websites and internet forums. Careful attention was given to curating a balanced dataset encompassing a wide range of geographical locations, types of tourist attractions, and seasonal variations. Quality assurance measures were implemented to filter out irrelevant or low-quality images, ensuring the dataset's integrity and relevance to our task.

Figure 4 shows the user interface of our tourist recommendation system which assists users exploring unfamiliar locations by analyzing uploaded images. Based on the analysis, it provides information about the spot, including its name, description, opening hours, entry fees, and historical background. Additionally, it might recommend nearby hotels and restaurants for a more comprehensive travel experience. While the system offers valuable aid, it's advisable to consult reliable sources like official websites or travel guides for in-depth and up-to-date information.

9 Limitations

While our tourist spot recommendation system offers valuable benefits and features, there are certain limitations that should be acknowledged:

Dependency on Image Quality: The effectiveness of the image classification and detection process is highly dependent on the quality of the uploaded images. Low-quality or distorted images may lead to inaccurate recognition of tourist spots, affecting the reliability of recommendations.

Limited Coverage of Tourist Spots: The system's performance in recommending tourist spots may be limited by the availability and coverage of data. Certain lesser-known or remote tourist spots may not be adequately represented in the dataset, leading to biased recommendations towards popular destinations.

Time Suitability Prediction Accuracy: While the integration of a Language Model (LLM) for time suitability prediction enhances the user experience, the accuracy of these predictions may be influenced by factors such as the availability of real-time data and the complexity of seasonal patterns.

Generalization to Diverse Regions: The system's ability to generalize and provide accurate recommendations across diverse geographical regions and cultural contexts may be limited. Variations in local customs, languages, and preferences may impact the relevance and suitability of recommendations for different user demographics.

Scalability and Performance: As the system relies on computationally intensive tasks such as image processing and natural language processing, scalability and performance issues may arise when handling large volumes of user requests, particularly during peak usage periods.

User Privacy Concerns: The collection and processing of user-generated content from social media platforms raise privacy concerns regarding the handling of personal data and adherence to data protection regulations. Ensuring user privacy and data security remains a critical consideration for the system's deployment and operation.

Bias and Fairness: The recommendations generated by the system may inadvertently reflect biases present in the underlying data sources or the algorithms used. Efforts should be made to mitigate biases and promote fairness in recommendation outcomes, particularly in diverse and multicultural contexts.

10 Conclusion

In summary, our project introduces a groundbreaking tourist spot recommendation system that integrates advanced image processing techniques with natural language processing. Through our extensive efforts, we have developed a system that excels in providing accurate and timely recommendations to users. By harnessing the power of advanced technologies, our system demonstrates remarkable accuracy in identifying tourist spots from user-uploaded images. Moreover, the integration of natural language processing capabilities enriches the recommendation process by offering valuable insights into the optimal timing for visiting each destination. Through our project, we have addressed the growing demand for personalized and intuitive travel recommendations in today's digital age. By leveraging cutting-edge technologies, we have created a platform that not only assists travelers in discovering new destinations but also provides them with valuable guidance on when to visit these spots for the best experience. Our system stands as a testament to the potential of integrating advanced image processing and natural language processing techniques to enhance the tourism experience. As we move forward, we envision further refinement and expansion of our system to continue meeting the evolving needs of travelers worldwide.

References

1. Naveen Kumar, T.G., Binoy, T.A.: An analytical study on contributions of tourism industry in India. Int. J. Curr. Res. **9**(7), 53706–53710 (2017)
2. Jafar, A.A., Jain, R., Nagrath, P., Satapathy, S., Taneja, S., Gupta, P.: Deep image captioning using an ensemble of CNN and LSTM based deep neural networks. J. Intell. Fuzzy Syst. (2020). https://doi.org/10.3233/JIFS-189415
3. Saini, A., Gupta, T., Rajat Kumar, A.K., Gupta, M., Panwa, A.M.: Image based Indian monument recognition using convolutional neural network. In: International Conference on Big Data, IoT and Data Science (BID), pp. 201–208 (2017)
4. Krizhevsky, A., Sutskever, I., Hinton, G.: Imagenet classification with deep convolutional neural networks. In: Advances in Neural Information Processing Systems, vol. 25, pp. 1106–1114 (2012)
5. Godewithana, N., Jayasena, K., Nagarawaththa, C., Alosius, J.: Historical places & monuments identification system. In: TENCON 2020–2020 IEEE Region 10 Conference, pp. 165–173 (2020)
6. Redmon, J., Farhadi, A.: YOLOv5: a unified deep learning architecture for real-time object detection. arXiv preprint arXiv:2006.03677 (2020)
7. Devlin, J., Chang, M.W., Lee, K., Toutanova, K.: BERT: pre-training of deep bidirectional transformers for language understanding. arXiv preprint arXiv:1810.04805 (2018)
8. Patel, N.P., Patel, P.H., Patel, R.K.: Deep learning-based tourist spot recognition system using transfer learning. In: International Conference on Intelligent Computing and Control Systems (ICICCS) (2023)
9. Gupta, S., Sharma, A., Singh, R.: Tourist spot recommendation system using hybrid collaborative filtering and deep learning. In: IEEE International Conference on Big Data and Analytics (ICBDA) (2022)
10. Khan, M., Rahman, S., Khan, A.: Enhancing tourist experience through image recognition and sentiment analysis. In: IEEE International Conference on Computational Intelligence and Applications (ICCIA) (2023)

11. Dutta, A., Banerjee, S., Sen, R.: A novel approach for tourist spot recommendation using graph-based deep learning. Int. J. Inf. Technol. Manag. **21**(3) (2023)
12. Li, Y., Wang, Z., Liu, X.: An effective tourist spot recommendation system based on image recognition and collaborative filtering. IEEE Trans. Multimedia. **25**(7) (2023)
13. Zhang, J., Chen, H., Wu, Y.: Time-aware tourist spot recommendation system using recurrent neural networks. Int. J. Data Sci. Anal. **7**(4) (2022)
14. Chen, L., Zhou, Q., Zhang, W.: Improving tourist spot recommendation accuracy with ensemble learning techniques. In: IEEE International Conference on Data Mining (ICDM) (2023)
15. Lee, K., Park, S., Kim, J.: Predicting tourist spot popularity using deep learning models. ACM Trans. Intell. Syst. Technol. **13**(5) (2022)

YOLOV8 – Based Model for Precise Corrosion Segmentation in Industrial Imagery

P. Vinay and N. Prasath[(✉)]

Department of Networking and Communications, School of Computing, SRM Institute of Science and Technology, Kattankulathur, Chennai, India
prasath283@gmail.com

Abstract. Corrosion poses a significant threat to infrastructure integrity, necessitating accurate detection and monitoring for preventive maintenance and safety assurance. YOLOv8-based model tailored specifically for precise corrosion segmentation in industrial imagery. an innovative method for video processing by combining YOLOv8, an advanced version of the YOLO object detection model, with the visualization capabilities of the Weights & Biases (W&B) platform. YOLOv8 offers superior real-time object detection performance, thanks to its single-pass detection technique and improved accuracy in localization and classification. Integration with W&B provides interactive dashboards for real-time monitoring of metrics and model behavior, enhancing understanding and optimization. Additionally, the use of cloud-based virtual machines, particularly W&B Cloud, offers a cost-effective deployment and monitoring solution compared to traditional options like Azure. Regardless, This combination is a robust example of a complete resolution for video processing tasks that leverage high-technology primitive techniques to accomplish extra advanced object discovery, one thing, of the actual to apply in not infrequently domain names from surveillance to autonomous cars, and lots extra. Therefore, this methodology towards corrosion identification systems has the potential to increase dependability and efficiency to assist with timely maintenance and longevity of crucial infrastructure assets.

Keywords: YOLO · Segmentation · Corrosion · Image

1 Introduction

Corrosion, the gradual weakening of materials resulting from chemical interactions with their surroundings, is a long-standing and expensive problem faced by many industries. Corrosion is a significant threat to the integrity, safety and longevity of our infrastructure, from bridges, pipelines and machinery to storage tanks. Simultaneous temporal and spatial detected corrosion region are essential for deployed proactive maintain, provide the decrease in downtime to achieving the continent property of some essential items.

Conventional corrosion inspection predominantly relied on labour-intensive manual methods that are notoriously more archaic and inherently less accurate and efficient. Recently, the rapid development of deep learning, a subfield of artificial intelligence,

© The Author(s), under exclusive license to Springer Nature Switzerland AG 2026
R. Appavoo et al. (Eds.): IconDeepCom 2024, CCIS 2687, pp. 13–24, 2026.
https://doi.org/10.1007/978-3-032-26680-4_2

has drastically changed the field of image analysis, making promising opportunities available for automatic and accurate corrosion detection.

Industrial surfaces often exhibit multiple domain gaps, making corrosion detection extremely challenging as it may appear very differently in various images. By using YOLOv8, a state-of-the-art version of the YOLO (You Only Look Once) object detection model, the proposed method provides improved real-time detection and segmentation of corrosion regions. The model's precise segmentation of corrosion zones makes proactive maintenance plans possible, reducing the chance of structural failures and extending the life of vital infrastructure assets. This starts a revolutionary journey to use deep learning to accurately and efficiently segment corrosion in industrial pictures. Utilizing cutting-edge deep learning models—more especially, the YOLOv8 architecture—we hope to create a reliable solution that can recognize and define corrosion areas in intricate industrial scenarios.

2 Related Work

Marine and Offshore Corrosion" by K. A. Chandler. This book likely delves into various aspects of corrosion relevant to marine and offshore engineering, covering topics such as corrosion prevention, materials selection, corrosion monitoring, and maintenance strategies specific to marine environments.

BB Zaidan, AA Zaidan, HO Alanazi, R Alnaqeib International Journal of Computer Science Issues (IJCSI), 2010. Research on various techniques for monitoring corrosion, including electrochemical methods, acoustic emission analysis, and visual inspection

F. Bonnin Pascual and A. Ortiz, "Corrosion detection for automated visual inspection," in Developments in Corrosion Protection, Inte- chOpen, 2014.Research focusing on the development and optimization of algorithms and techniques for processing images captured during visual inspection to identify and classify corrosion features accurately.

L. Petricca, T. Moss, G. Figueroa, and S. Broen, "Corrosion detection using AI". Research exploring the application of deep learning techniques, including convolutional neural networks (CNNs), recurrent neural networks (RNNs), or generative adversarial networks (GANs), for corrosion detection tasks has been an active area of investigation.

V. Bondada, D. K. Pratihar, and C. S. Kumar, "Detection and quan- titative assessment of corrosion on pipelines through image analysis", RNNs, particularly LSTM networks, have been used to analyze timeseries data related to corrosion, such as sensor readings or environmental factors. By capturing temporal dependencies, RNNs can predict corrosion progression, identify patterns in corrosion rates over time, and detect anomalies indicative of corrosion events

3 Methodology

Creating a data collection module for corrosion detection involves a series of systematic steps to ensure the availability of a well-organized and preprocessed dataset. This module serves as a crucial foundation for training and evaluating machine learning models, especially those designed for image classification tasks like corrosion detection.

3.1 Dataset Acquisition

Downloading the dataset from a trustworthy source, like Roboflow, is the first step. As seen in Fig. 1, the dataset in this instance consists of 205 test photos and 4737 raining images. To enable efficient model training, the dataset should fairly depict the variety of corrosion conditions.

Fig. 1. Corrosion Dataset

3.2 Dataset Organization

After acquiring the dataset, it is essential to arrange it in a methodical manner. This entails establishing two primary directories: one for test data and one for training data. A clear separation between the data utilized for model training and evaluation is ensured by proper organization, which also streamlines the workflow's latter phases.

3.3 Image Preprocessing

To guarantee consistency in the input data for the machine learning model, image pre-processing is an essential step. This entails downsizing every image to a standard pixel size, such 224x224. Convergence during training is facilitated by this standardized size, which guarantees that the model receives consistent input.

3.4 Data Augmentation

Data augmentation approaches are used to improve the model's capacity to handle a variety of scenarios and to increase its generalization. Packages including Tensor-Flow's Image Data Generator are used to implement techniques like flipping, rotation, and brightness modifications. By increasing the training dataset's variability, these augmentations help the model better adapt to real-world situations.

3.5 Class Specification

Usually, there are several classifications in the dataset. In the context of corrosion detection, there are likely two classes: "Corrosion" and "Non-Corrosion." Specifying the number of classes is essential for configuring the output layer of the machine learning model. This step ensures that the model is appropriately trained to distinguish between the identified classes as shown in Fig. 2.

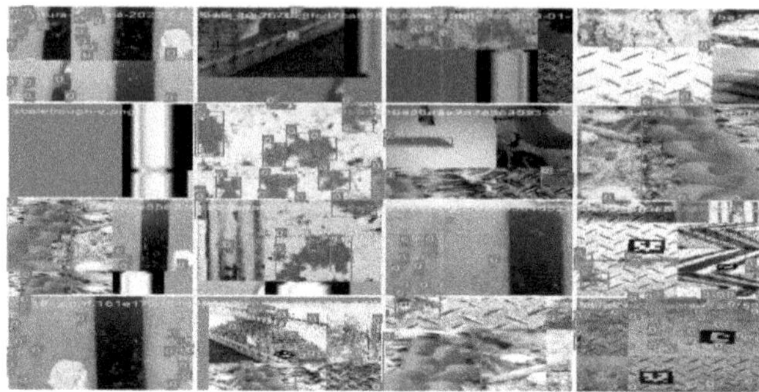

Fig. 2. Identification of corrosion area in images

4 System Architecture

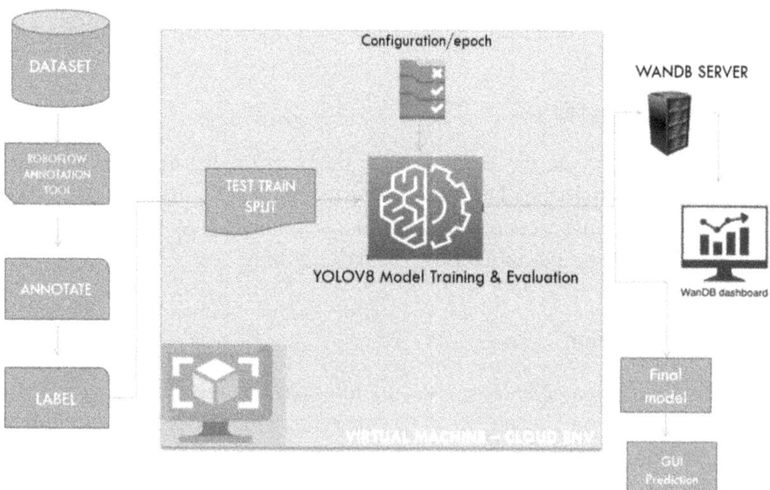

Fig. 3. System Architecture

4.1   Corrosion Dataset

The method starts with a dataset of images and videos, which could be a collection of information that will be trained from the roboflow. Dataset is regularly composed of pictures and comparing explanations that name the objects of intrigued inside those pictures as shown in Fig. 3.

4.2   Roboflow Annotation Tool

The dataset is handled utilizing the Roboflow explanation instrument. Roboflow may be a benefit that makes a difference in planning and commenting on picture information for computer vision models. It permits clients to clarify pictures by labeling the objects that the model tought to learn to distinguish the labels.

Annotation Process

This step includes physically commenting on the images within the dataset, which suggests drawing bounding boxes around the objects of intrigued and labeling them with the right category.

Naming Objects in Images

After clarifying, each question inside the pictures incorporates a name that the show will use to memorize what each protest looks like.

Test Prepare Part

The explained dataset is at that point part into two subsets:one for preparing the demonstrate (preparing set) and one for assessing its execution (test set). This is often a common hone in machine learning to guarantee that the show can generalize well to modern, inconspicuous information

4.3   YOLOv8 Demonstrate Preparing and Assessment

The preparing set is utilized to prepare the YOLOv8 show. Amid preparing, the demonstrate learns to recognize and localize the objects based on the given explanations. The arrangement and age settings are balanced as required to optimize the model's performance. An epoch alludes to one total pass through the complete preparing dataset as shown in Fig. 3.

4.4   Virtual Machine – Cloud ENV

The preparing and assessment of the show are performed in a virtual machine environment, likely facilitated on a cloud platform. This provides the vital computational assets for handling and permits for versatile and adaptable demonstrate development.

4.5   WANDB Server

WANDB (Weights & Predispositions) may be a instrument for tracking experiments in machine learning. The server collects preparing measurements and logs them to the WANDB dashboard, which gives a visual interface for checking the model's execution, such as misfortune and precision over time as shown in Fig. 5.

4.6 Last Demonstrate

After training and assessment, the ultimate demonstrate is gotten. This show has learned to distinguish objects in pictures and can be utilized for making expectations on new information.

4.7 GUI Prediction

The last show can be coordinates into a graphical client interface (GUI) application that permits clients to input unused pictures and get expectations, which are the model's discoveries of objects inside those pictures.

5 Model Testing

After the training phase of a YOLOv8 model, the assessment of its performance is a crucial step to ensure its ability to generalize to new, unseen data. This evaluation is typically carried out using a separate testing set that the model has not encountered during the training process.

5.1 Accuracy Plot

The accuracy plot tracks the YOLOv8 model's performance across training epochs, measuring its ability to classify samples correctly in the testing set. Typically represented as a percentage, accuracy indicates the proportion of correctly identified objects compared to the total in the testing set, reflecting the model's predictive capability. It's crucial to watch for signs of plateauing or decreasing accuracy, which may signal overfitting – when the model becomes too specialized in training data, hindering its generalization to new data. By identifying the optimal point where accuracy peaks on the testing set without overfitting, the accuracy plot helps ensure the model's effectiveness. A decreasing loss over epochs is expected, showing the model's improvement in making accurate predictions. However, if the loss declines on the training set but rises on the testing set, it suggests the model is overly tailored to the training data as shown in Fig. 4.

5.2 Binary Classification Problem

Classification Accuracy is what we more often than not cruel, when we utilize the term precision. It is the proportion of number of rectify expectations to the whole number of input tests.

True Positives (TP)
These are occasions that are accurately recognized as having a place to the positive course by the classification show. In other words, these are the occurrences that are really positive and are classified as positive.

False Negatives (FN)
These are occasions that are inaccurately classified as not having a place in the positive

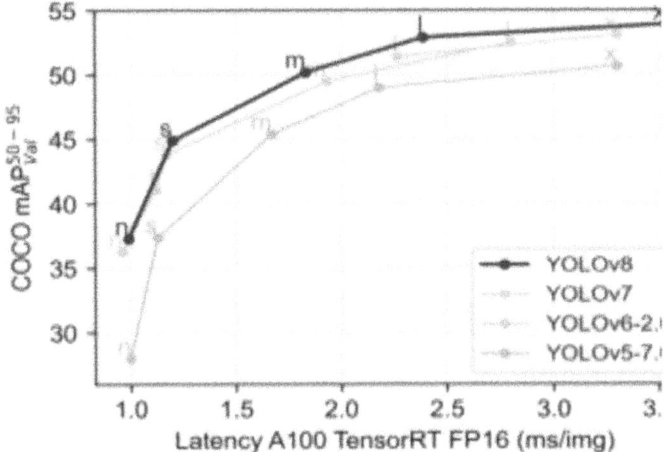

Fig. 4. Accuracy plot

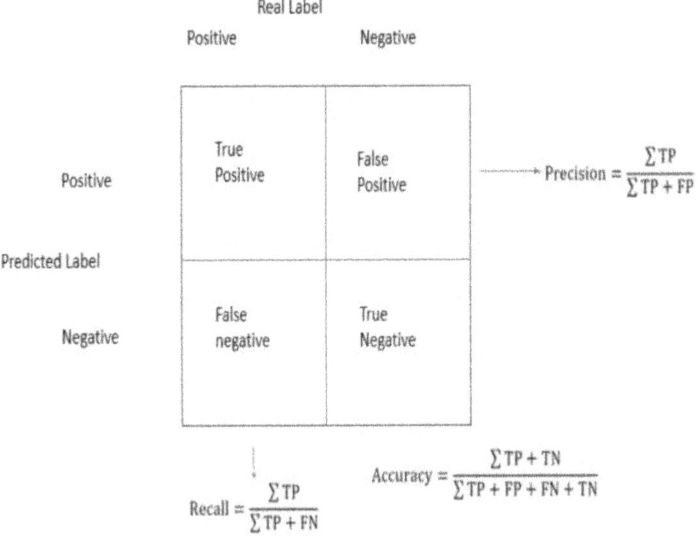

Fig. 5. Binary Classification

course by the show, indeed, in spite of the fact that they really are positive. In easier terms, these are occurrences that are really positive but are erroneously classified as negative.

Recall

This metric, also known as affectability, measures the capacity of a classification show to accurately recognize all positive occasions out of all occasions that are really positive. It is calculated by dividing the number of genuine positives by the total number of genuine positives and untrue negatives. Basically, a review tells us the extent of real positives that were accurately classified as such by the show, demonstrating how well the show captures positive occasions.

6 Result

In the realm of training deep learning models, monitoring and understanding various metrics are essential to ensure the model's effectiveness in solving specific tasks. Table 1 encompasses key metrics recorded during the training and evaluation of a corrosion detection model using the YOLOv8 architecture.

Table 1. Values obtained validating the dataset.

Metric/mAP50-95(M)	Val/box_loss	Val/seg_loss	Val/cls_loss	Val/diff_loss	Ir/pg0	Ir/pg1	Ir/pg2
0.02986	1.8654	2.9886	24.747	1.1885	0.000665	0.000665	0.000665
003887	1.8435	2.6379	3.3798	1.1373	0.001068	0.001207	0.001068
0.04523	1.7928	2.6225	2.9678	1.0889	0.001207	0.000812	0.001207
0.05772	1.6509	2.3953	2.0807	1.05	0.000812	0.000812	0.000812
0.05571	1.612	2.2929	1.6691	1.0084	0.000812	0.000812	0.000812

train/box_loss
Loss associated with bounding box predictions during training as shown in Fig. 6. Measures how well the model predicts the locations of objects, particularly corrosion regions. A lower box loss indicates improved accuracy in predicting object positions as shown in Fig. 7.

train/seg_loss
Loss related to the segmentation aspect of the model as shown in Fig. 6. Measures the model's ability to segment objects from the background, a crucial aspect in corrosion detection where distinguishing between objects and the surrounding environment is vital as shown in Fig. 7.

train/cls_loss
Loss pertaining to the classification aspect of the model as shown in Fig. 6. Measures how well the model classifies identified objects or regions, distinguishing between "Corrosion" and "Non-Corrosion as shown in Fig. 7.

train/dfl_loss
Loss associated with dense feature learning or another specific aspect of the model architecture. Captures performance aspects related to the model's feature learning capabilities as shown in Fig. 6.

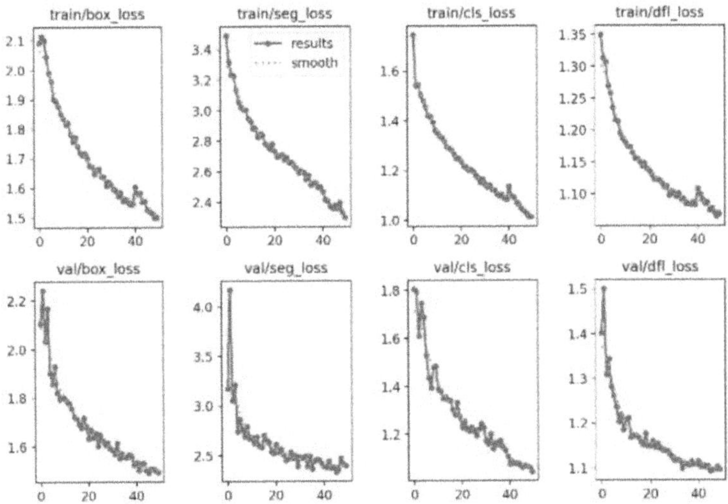

Fig. 6. graph of box_loss,seg_loss,cls_loss,dlf_loss

metrics/precision(B), metrics/recall(B), metrics/m AP50(B), metrics/mAP 50-95(B)

Precision(B) Proportion of true positive predictions among all positive predictions for class "B. Recall(B): Proportion of true positive predictions among all actual instances of class "B. These metrics evaluate the model's object detection performance specifically for class "B," potentially representing Corrosion as shown in Fig. 7.

metrics/precision(M), metrics/recall(M), metrics/mAP 50(M), metrics/mAP 50-95(M)

Same as above but for class "M," potentially representing "Non-Corrosion.These metrics evaluate object detection performance for class "M as shown in Fig. 6. Adjusting learning rates for different parameter groups can optimize the model's training process as shown in Fig. 7.

Confidence Curve

In YOLO, each detected object comes with a confidence score that represents the model's confidence in its prediction. This score is typically used to filter out low-confidence detections and improve the precision of the model. An F1 score of 0.33 at a confidence threshold of 0.195 indicates the harmonic mean of precision and recall at that particular threshold as shown in Fig. 8. Generally, an F1 score ranges from 0 to 1, where a higher score indicates better performance in terms of both precision and recall.

It helps to understand how various factors within the video data correlate with each other. For corrosion detection, this could involve analyzing the correlation between different regions, colors, or textures. These values help in identifying the positive results of the detection of corrosion in the video.

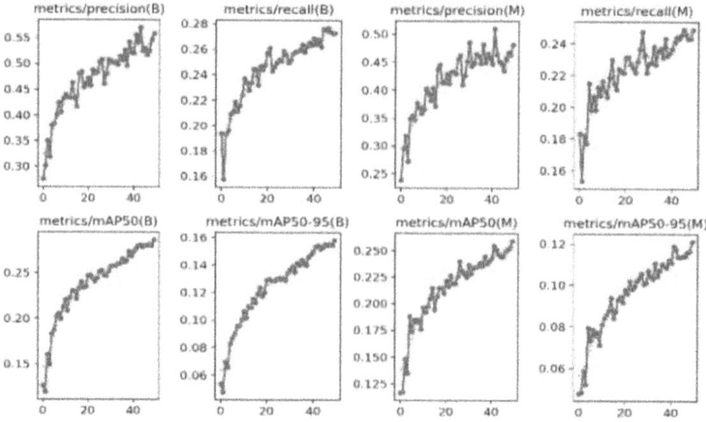

Fig. 7. Graph of precission,recall,mAP 50–95(M),mAp 50–95(B)

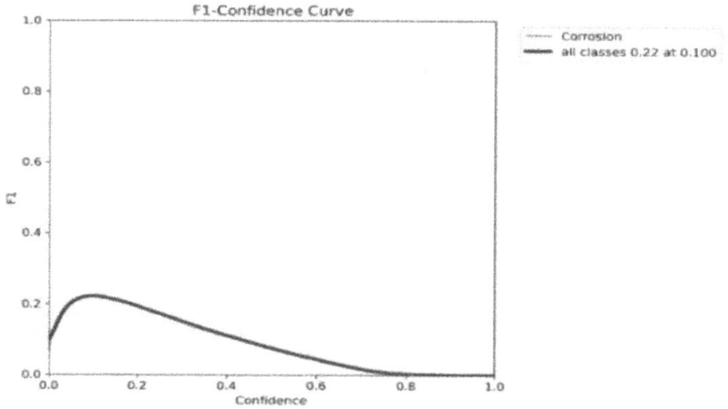

Fig. 8. Confidence curve image

GUI Output

Utilizing the cutting-edge YOLOv8 algorithm in conjunction with Python GUI, It efficiently processes images, videos pinpointing areas of corrosion with remarkable accuracy. The YOLOv8 model, renowned for its superior object detection capabilities, swiftly identifies corrosion-related anomalies, enabling prompt intervention to prevent further deterioration. The Python GUI provides a user-friendly interface, streamlining the detection process and allowing for seamless interaction with the resultant images. With this innovative combination of technology, it empower users to detect and address corrosion issues swiftly and effectively, safeguarding critical infrastructure and ensuring long-term durability (Fig. 9).

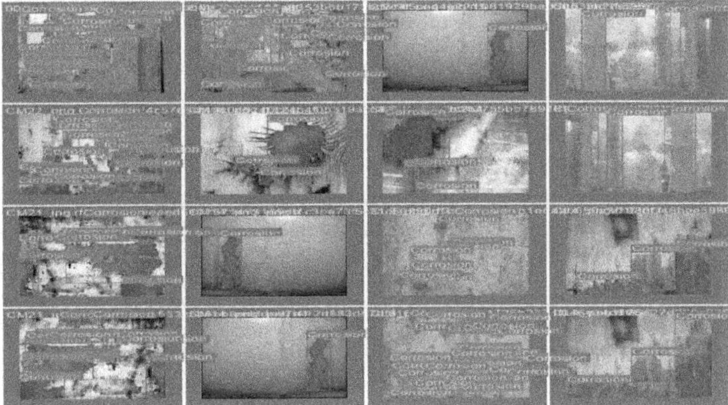

Fig. 9. Detected corrosion area in the image

7   Conclusion and Future Work

In conclusion, the advancement of a YOLOv8-based demonstrate for exact erosion division in mechanical symbolism holds extraordinary guarantee for businesses where erosion postures a consistent danger to framework and gear. By leveraging cutting-edge innovation and vigorous information comment apparatuses like Roboflow, this extend clears the way for more exact and opportune erosion location. The project's technique, from information collection and preprocessing to show preparing and assessment, underscores the significance of fastidious arrangement and experimentation. The joining of Weights and Inclinations (Wandb) for real-time try following includes a layer of straightforwardness and versatility, empowering fine-tuning for ideal execution. Besides, the integration of a user-friendly graphical client interface (GUI) upgrades availability for industry experts, making it simpler to distinguish and address erosion concerns proficiently. Looking forward, the project's potential for future upgrades, such as multi-class discovery and real-time observing, advance cements its centrality in guaranteeing framework astuteness and security in corrosionprone segments. Its potential to contribute to the longevity and reliability of critical infrastructure reaffirms its significance in safeguarding industrial assets and, ultimately, ensuring the safety and sustainability of various sectors facing the persistent threat of corrosion. The integration of video analytics using YOLOv8 in WanDB for corrosion detection lays a solid foundation, but continuous improvement and adaptation are crucial in the dynamic field of industrial infrastructure monitoring.

References

1. Cattin, P.: Introduction to signal and image processing. In: Digital Image Fundamentals, pp. 1–73. University of Basel, Basel (2016)
2. Nash, W.T., Powell, C., Drummond, T., Birbilis, N.: Automated corrosion detection using crowdsourced training for deep learning. Corrosion. **76**(2), 135–141 (2020)
3. Chandler, K.A.: Marine and Offshore Corrosion: Marine Engineering Series. Butterworth-Heinemann (1985) ISBN: 0408011750

4. Gibbons, T., Pierce, G., Worden, K., Antoniadou, I.: A gaussian mixture model for automated corrosion detection in remanufacturing. In: Advances in Manufacturing Technology XXXII, vol. 8, pp. 63–68 (2018)
5. Bonnin-Pascual, F., Ortiz, A.: Corrosion detection for automated visual inspection. In: Developments in Corrosion Protection. IntechOpen (2014)
6. Chang, J.H.R., Wang, Y.C.F.: Propagated image filtering. In: Proceedings of the IEEE Conference on Computer Vision and Pattern Recognition (2015)
7. Yao, Y., Yang, Y., Wang, Y., Zhao, X.: Artificial intelligence-based hull structural plate corrosion damage detection and recognition using convolutional neural network. Appl. Ocean Res. **90**, 101823 (2019)
8. Szeliski, R.: Computer Vision: Algorithms and Applications. Springer Science & Business Media (2010)
9. Atha, D.J., Jahanshahi, M.R.: Evaluation of deep learning approaches based on convolutional neural networks for corrosion detection. Struct. Health Monit. **17**(5), 1110–1128 (2018)
10. Bradski, G.: The OpenCV library. Dr. Dobb's J. Softw. Tools. **120**, 122–125 (2000)

Driver Assistance System with Lane and Object Detection Based on Driver Attention Monitoring

R. Kishore Harshan Kumar[1(✉)], S. Roughit[2], T. Nagulraj[2], and M. Shalini[2]

[1] Department of Artificial Intelligence and Data Science, St. Joseph's College of Engineering, OMR, Chennai, India
`harshankumarhrk@gmail.com`
[2] Computer Science and Engineering, St. Joseph's College of Engineering, OMR, Chennai, India

Abstract. This paper forecasts the future of the advanced driver assistance system (ADAS) and how driving safety can be improved by the usage of critical-lane-learning, posture sensing the best fit, tiredness/– sleepiness recognition. Well-trained intellectual capabilities, such as computer vision algorithms, make this bureaucracy/ the latter government body to correctly identify the road boundaries, thus providing the most detailed advice to drivers. The implementation of yoga and smart wearables in vehicle safety documentation makes sure that drivers get the best position, avoid fatigue and have the best safety driving methods. The machine intelligence models are used to monitor the fatigue levels of the vehicle drivers and, if necessary, they alert the trainer and suggest the rest. Moreover, the reaction system collects driver reviews to continuously polish the system's efficiency. Further, the abstract outlines a new approach allowing creative ideas define the trainer support technology, finding a new application in the state-of-the-art comprehensive security system for vehicles.

Keywords: Advanced Driver Assistance System (ADAS) · lane detection · posture analysis

1 Introduction

The current industry landscape related to automotive security has headed to the point where the discussions about the finer job are held only to devise systems that merge the different sides of the operator's help, a healthy happening. This project will be able to promote the above-mentioned change by suggesting a comprehensive Advanced Driver Assistance System (ADAS) employing the latest technologies in human-computer interaction, computer vision, robotics, and more. This will involve projects focusing on real-time road detection for example or diagnosis for optimizing ergonomic force to lethargy research thus raising driver safety and fewer potential expressway hazards.

The very cornerstone of this project is to make the public aware the exercise of more sophisticated calculating operations. A system is formulated in such a way as to quickly and accurately identify road borders in different material atmospheres to give

© The Author(s), under exclusive license to Springer Nature Switzerland AG 2026
R. Appavoo et al. (Eds.): IconDeepCom 2024, CCIS 2687, pp. 25–42, 2026.
https://doi.org/10.1007/978-3-032-26680-4_3

clear advice to operators about the safe guide of route, often water bound. By using convolutional neural networks (CNNs) and face detection technology, the ADAS will be able to efficiently address issues posed by active road sketches, and thus, it will easily locate and describe lane designators, which are tough conditions like occlusions and bad weather.

Furthermore, integrating posture study within the ADAS foundation means a pioneering approach to reduce operator fatigue and drive comfort design. Utilizing a convergence of depth-distinguishing and figure-recognition technologies, bureaucracy consistently monitors the trainer's posture, with certain-opportunity feedback and adjustments to assure optimal seating positions. This whole of exuberance measure, beyond progressing driving comfort still devalues the chances of musculoskeletal strain and fatigue, major contributors to chauffeur concern and overall road safety.

To supplement the gist functions of bureaucracy, the use of state-of-the-art models in machine intelligence helps detect the deterrent of driver drowsiness when braking. With first verbalizations of patterns, physiologic signs being re solved in real-time for action or event, the ADAS quickly flags up the presence of drowsiness or interference. Using an adaptive approach to feedback means the right prompts for the trainer, providing time to take breaks or seek mediation to maintain vigilance and awareness. The fusion of these sciences is aimed to not only detect dozing properly but rather to design reactions according to in dividual forceful acts optimise the effect of safety measures fostering a full of enthusiasm embodied approach towards driver assistance.

2 Literature Survey

[1] This Study describes a portable sensor system for monitoring the unbalanced head postures of long-distance drivers. Head posture monitoring allows for driver fatigue analysis (which can help avoid car accidents) as well as the prevention of chronic fatigue and neck-related diseases. A three-axis MEMS magnetometer and a miniature magnet are attached to the user's neck. The user performs driving scenarios, which include five common driving activities and one inconvenient posture. Neural network algorithms are used to process the collected magnetometer data. A portion of the data is used to create a learned model, and the rest is used to calibrate the model. The experiment results are very promising, with model accuracy as high as 93.0 percent [2]. Potholes are dam aged road surfaces that often lead to accidents, both minor and major. These accidents Detecting and repairing potholes ahead of time can prevent accidents. To achieve this, we need an accurate detection model. The model uses a convolutional neural network (CNN) to classify road conditions as normal or damaged in real-time. The proposed work involves a software application that sends an image of a road to a backend flask server. The image is then processed using a neural network model and alerts the user to take necessary precautions to avoid accidents. The model is trained on a dataset of 300 images of normal and pothole roads. Based on classification results, it alerts users by blowing lights controlled by Atmega Arduino [3]. Deep learning has advanced significantly in image segmentation over the past few years. Accurate detection of road markings is crucial for intelligent driving. Manual parameter adjustments are required for traditional detection methods, which present numerous challenges. Developing a robust detection algorithm remains

challenging. We propose a method for detecting road marking models. Our method uses Mask R-CNN for road image segmentation, improving the accuracy of detecting road markings. The method effectively extracts road markers from complex traffic scenes, as demonstrated by the experimental results [4]. Efficient road segmentation is crucial in automated driving systems (ADS) and advanced driver-assistance systems (ADAS) to identify drivable areas and create occupancy maps for path planning. The existing algorithms Using large convolutional neural networks (CNNs) can be costly and time-consuming. This paper uses distributed LSTM, a neural network commonly used in audio and video processing, to process rows and columns in images and feature maps. We propose a new network that combines convolutional and dis tributed LSTM layers to address the road segmentation problem. Finally, the network is trained and tested using the KITTI road benchmark. The combined structure improves feature extraction and processing while requiring less processing time than pure CNN [5] Unmanned vehicles are crucial for the advancement of intelligent transportation systems. This article provides an overview of the research background and significance of unmanned vehicles, as well as a summary of current research on decision-making for unmanned vehicles both domestically and internationally. We summarized both rule-based and machine learning-based behavior decision-making methods. To improve the safety and efficiency of un manned vehicle crossings at city intersections, a reinforcement learning algorithm was used to determine the optimal traversing strategy. The algorithm's effectiveness was verified using the intersection crossing case. This paper's proposed NQL algorithm outperforms the Q-Learning algorithm [5]. Occlusions on the face can make it difficult to recognize emotions through facial expressions. However, the hand-over-face occlusion offers Useful information for accurately recognizing emotions. Existing emotion recognition methods, with or without hand gestures, recognize basic emotions like happiness, sadness, anger, surprise, neutrality, fear, and disgust. Modern applications require identifying additional emotions, such as confidence, decision-making, fear, shame, anger, and OK. This paper presents an empirical evaluation of an improved Hand-over-Face Gesture based Facial Emotion Recognition Method (HF GF ERM), which identifies new emotions in addition to basic ones. The proposed method includes a detailed coding schema and additional hand signs to identify unexplored emotions. Additionally, the design incorporates a convolution neural network [6]. Emotions play a significant role in human relationships, particularly between businesses and customers. Facial expressions are factors that cause emotions. recognizable. Paul Ekman identified six core emotions, including joy, surprise, sadness, anger, disgust, and fear. Emotions fall into two categories: positive and negative. Positive emotions include joy and surprise, whereas negative emotions include sad ness, anger, disgust, and fear. Multiple studies have found confusion between surprise and fear as a core emotion. These emotions are often confused because they share similar characteristics. This paper proposes categorizing emotional states prior to identifying core emotions [7]. Emotion analysis requires accurate identification of key frames and balanced representation of facial features. Accu rate identification Effective facial feature tracking requires consideration of pose, shape, illumination, and image resolution. Tracking human emotions frame-by-frame is time-consuming, making the task more complex when performed from videos.

Effective consideration of face alignment and occlusions is crucial. This paper proposes novel ACNN-based methods for dynamic emotion recognition in human videos.

3 Data Flow

3.1 Data Collection

Data set for this ADAS is a multi-sourced approach, integrating several sources to train and validate bureaucracy's algorithms. For road detection, footnoted datasets including countenances and videos from different line environments and environments are assembled. These datasets circumscribe diverse synopsises, containing highways, urban streets and adverse weather environments, thereby giving robustness and inference of the road detection model. In addition, to carry out posture study, the association of depth-noticing cameras and representation datasets pick up diverse forceful postures is utilized. Such datasets are marked meticulously in such a way that they surround a wide range of places positions, admitting machine learning models to correctly conclude and recommend optimum forceful ergonomics. Dossier for lethargy discovery also involves the collection of first expression datasets, eye motion patterns, and physiologic signals from individuals in reserved and original-world forceful positions. An notation of these datasets accompanying drowsiness labels allows the machine intelligence models to identify subtle signs of driver fatigue or interference, thus allowing correct real-period discovery within the ADAS.

3.2 Feature Extraction

Origin in feature framework of this Advanced Driver Assistance System (ADAS) includes orderly identification and pensiveness of key news from various dossier beginnings to ensure correct study and decision-making. For road discovery, feature extraction contains the labeling of relevant optical clues such as edges, gradients, and color gradients inside conquered images or broadcast frames. These lineaments are then treated through methods like edge detection algorithms, Hough revolutionizes, and convolutional movements to robustly label road markings and borders. In posture reasoning, feature extraction includes picking up indispensable content and angles related to the chauffeur's frame position, lever aging techniques in the way that keypoint discovery and skeleton pursuing from wisdom-sensing cameras. Furthermore, in drowsiness detection, features such as first milestones, eye movement patterns, and physical signals are extracted through forms like first landmark detection, gaze following, and signal processing to determine exhibitive patterns of drowsiness or driver distraction. These extracted lineaments provide image of the basis for after machine intelligence models to make conversant conclusions within the ADAS basis.

3.3 Data Insights

Data visions derived from the Advanced Driver Assistance System blend versa tile information streams to specify litigable intelligence for reinforced motorist safety. Road discovery data analysis yields visions into the system's veracity in labeling lane edges across different road environments, permissive refinements to the algorithms to improve accomplishment in questioning scenarios to a degree low visibility or complex artery layouts. Posture reasoning data determines valuable observations into drivers' fitting desires and adherence to optimum positions, contribution feedback for embodied recommendations and adaptations to improve comfort and reduce fatigue all the while comprehensive drives. Addition ally, insights from lethargy discovery data reveal patterns exhibitive of driver fatigue or interference, facilitating bureaucracy's talent to proactively alert drivers and desire attacks, contributing considerably to occurrence prevention and over all line security. These thus fuel iterative betterings inside the ADAS, developing a living and pulsing system coupled with changing forceful environments as well as user needs.

3.4 Data Labelling

Data branding for the Advanced Driver Assistance System (ADAS) comprises a careful process of annotation of various datasets to enable supervised knowledge algorithms to discover and define critical face. In road discovery, manual annotation of representations or frames involves detailed outlining of road designatings and lines, thereby providing a ground truth dossier that will guide the education process of the treasure to accurately recognize lanes across various scenarios. In posture study, describing requires associating key bulk positions and angles ac companying matching driving postures, permissive bureaucracy to understand and approve optimum comfort design. Additionally, for drowsiness discovery, annotations contain classification facial verbalizations, eye activities, and physiological signals into different labels to a degree awake, sleepy, or distracted, simplifying the machine intelligence models' capability to discern cunning signs of driver fatigue or heedlessness. These well-branded datasets form the bedrock for the preparation of strong and accurate models inside the foundation of ADAS.

3.5 Data Inference for Modelling

Data conclusion to be displayed in the Advanced Driver Assistance System (ADAS) includes the exercise of annotated datasets to train machine intelligence algorithms, admitting them to understand patterns, connections, and predictive understandings critical for correct decision-making. Through repetitive processes, prepared models extract intricate facial characteristics from road detection dossier, education to identify and statement road boundaries across various line environments. In posture analysis, the models conclude equivalences between carcass positions and optimum ergonomics, permissive embodied recommendations for operator comfort. Moreover, in lethargy discovery, the models infer complex unions betwixt facial verbalizations, eye evolutions, and physiological signals to determine cunning cues displaying motorist fatigue or distraction. Those deduction processes make the ADAS models come into being-time, cognizant decisions, thereby giving full of enthusiasm interferences to ensure trainer security on roads.

4 Workflow

In the development of ADAS, miscellaneous model classes and parameters play important parts in guaranteeing correct and efficient depiction. For example, in road discovery, model classes such as CNNs are usually working, accompanying limits including network wisdom (number of coatings), penetrate sizes, and seed strides deciding the model's capability to extract facial characteristics like edges and gradients from images. Parameters like knowledge rates and growth algorithms such as, Adam, SGD are alive for training union and fine-bringing into harmony model weights. In posture study, keypoint detection models like OpenPose concede possibility be promoted, accompanying limits such as key point assurance thresholds, scaffolding determination, and joint detection actions moving veracity in recognizing driver postures. For drowsiness detection, model classes such as recurrent influencing animate nerve organs networks (RNNs) or Long Short-Term Memory (LSTM) networks may be in operation, along with limits that include order lengths, unseen components, and failure rates affecting the model's ability to capture worldly reliances in facial verbalizations and body signals. Hyperparameters, including bundle height, regularization terms, and dossier improving methods, are also significant across all model classes, affecting inference and strength. Tuning these limits by empirical experiments and confirmation ensures optimum fulfillment by the models within the ADAS foundation.

4.1 Model Architecture Parameters

The model construction for the Advanced Driver Assistance System holds convolutional neural networks for road discovery, keypoint detection networks like OpenPose for posture study, and repeating affecting animate nerve organs networks such as LSTM for lethargy discovery. In lane discovery, CNNs comprise multiple convolutional tiers accompanying permeate sizes of 3×3 and strides of 1, understood by combining layers to downsample feature maps. Posture reasoning includes OpenPose models with accompanying varying keypoint assurance thresholds, scaffolding resolutions, and joint discovery designs to accurately recognize trainer postures. For lethargy detection, LSTM-located RNNs combine multiple secret wholes and series lengths to capture temporal reliances in first expressions, eye drives, and physiologic signals. Optimization parameters, containing education rates, bunch sizes, and specific hyperparameters like failing student rates and regularization conditions, are meticulously brought into harmony across these architectures to guarantee optimum performance and inference inside the ADAS framework (Fig. 1).

4.2 Optimization

The addition system in the advanced driver assistance system starts alongside the option of suitable optimization algorithms, typically consisting of adjusting methods, such as Adam or assumed slope attack (SGD), particularly designed to underrate the stated loss functions. Initialization of the model weights and biases takes place, quite often using techniques like Xavier or He initialization for concern that slope vanishing or discharge. After that, learning rates are set and the models undergo repeated training

```
Model: "sequential"

 Layer (type)                Output Shape              Param #
=================================================================
 conv2d (Conv2D)             (None, 31, 98, 24)        1824

 conv2d_1 (Conv2D)           (None, 14, 47, 36)        21636

 conv2d_2 (Conv2D)           (None, 5, 22, 48)         43248

 conv2d_3 (Conv2D)           (None, 3, 20, 64)         27712

 conv2d_4 (Conv2D)           (None, 1, 18, 64)         36928

 dropout (Dropout)           (None, 1, 18, 64)         0

 flatten (Flatten)           (None, 1152)              0

 dense (Dense)               (None, 100)               115300

 dropout_1 (Dropout)         (None, 100)               0

 dense_1 (Dense)             (None, 50)                5050

 dropout_2 (Dropout)         (None, 50)                0

 dense_2 (Dense)             (None, 10)                510

 dropout_3 (Dropout)         (None, 10)                0

 dense_3 (Dense)             (None, 1)                 11

=================================================================
Total params: 252,219
Trainable params: 252,219
Non-trainable params: 0
_________________________________________________________________
None
```

Fig. 1. CNN Architecture

epochs. At training, gradients are calculated using backpropagation, and weights are updated based on the selected growth treasure and education rate. Hyperparameters such as push, pressure decay, and quantity normalization are adjusted using confirmation argue to optimize model union and counter overfitting. Techniques involving learning rate schedulers that contain step decay are operating dynamically to adapt education rates during all training phases to promote the speeding up of union. The method repeats just in time of union or as the defined tests for continuing to train, such as loss confirmation thresholds or epoch join, is meet, ensuring models are upgraded appropriately for road detection, pose analysis, and drowsiness detection under the ADAS.

4.3   Data Processing Flow

The Data Processing system within the ADAS includes several stages, which initiate with accompanying the collection of various datasets, such as rounding up road markings, trainer postures, and signs of drowsiness. The raw dossier goes through several pre-processing steps to a certain degree of resizing, cropping, and normalization to similar recommendation layouts from different sensors and cameras. Later, dossier enhancing techniques such as rotation, throwing, and zooming are applied to transform the dataset and enhance model inference. For road discovery, edge detection algorithms and color thresholding systems are applied to extract road designatings. In posture analysis, key-point discovery algorithms label detracting body positions and angles from concepts or wisdom dossier. At the same time, drowsiness-related visage like first landmarks, eye evolutions, and physical signals are culled using specific algorithms. Finally, the treated dossier is systematized, annotated and divided into preparation, confirmation, and test sets, ensuring the strength and veracity of models inside the ADAS foundation.

4.4 Posture Detection Flow

Posture study of the operator through MediaPipe involves an orderly passage leveraging calculating vision algorithms. First, recommendation dossier, typically from cameras or insight sensors, undergoes preprocessing, consisting of resizing and normalization to ensure regularity in input plans. MediaPipe's pose belief models are consequently used to detect and track critical physique milestones, extracting distracting points that are indicative of the motorist's posture. These landmarks are resolved and treated in evident-time, admitting for the conclusion of forceful-relevant party positions and angles. The system therefore interprets these positions to judge the chauffeur's ergonomics, evaluating determinants like posture adjustment and seating positions. The amount from MediaPipe's models determines constant updates on the chauffeur's posture, admitting for next feedback or adaptations to amend functional design and forceful comfort within the Advanced Driver Assistance System (ADAS).

4.5 Lane Detection

Lane Detection is a subsequent step under Advanced Driver Assistance System, or ADAS, and several correct boundary marking of the roads occur here. A raw inexperienced figure or program dossier goes through pre-processing which in volves resizing and normalization, followed by the application of edge detection algorithms such as Canny edge detection that highlights possible road designatings. These edges are then subjected to algorithms such as Hough mold to find the lines or curves representing boundaries of roads, observing boundaries in the form of detection thresholds for lines and minimum time allowed for lines. After finding, there are post-dispose methods such as curve fitting or interpolation that fine tune the labeled road designators for smooth representation. Validation and cultivation stages attend to determining the correctness of detected lanes against ground loyalty annotations and limits to optimize depiction across a range of line environments with the aim of having a robust and correct road discovery in the ADAS.

4.6 Drowsiness Detection

This means the multi-task approach mixing different dossier beginnings. It is starting with the early landmark detection and eye shift patterns achieved using computer ghosting techniques, made more straightforward using facial landmark discovery algorithms and even gaze tracking ones, generally, to a convolutional impact CNNs. While physiologic signals such as heart rate or head pose are handled using certain sensors and signal processing algorithms simultaneously. These dossier streams are then melted and analyzed by using machine intelligence models, usually recurrent affecting animate nerve organs networks (RNNs) or Long Short-Term Memory (LSTM) networks, for the detection of cunning indicators of lethargy, to a degree first expressions, extended eye plug, or uneven physiological patterns. The prepared models steadily monitor and resolve these features in authentic-occasion, causing alerts or interventions inside the ADAS to guarantee prompt operation to mitigate potential risks guide jockey fatigue or interruption on the road.

5 Model Architecture

5.1 Lane Detection Architecture

Lane finding in the Advanced Driver Assistance System (ADAS) involves an intricate mechanics formation consisting of several pertain stages. The process commences accompanying novice concept or video frames captured for a single vehicle's camcorder, and these inputs stand by preprocessing to ensure uniformity and enhance the visibility of the road markings. This entails resizing the images, normalization, and seeking color thresholding techniques to separate lane connected features. After preprocessing, a feature distillation by a CNN is used. The design of the CNN usually comprises diversified convolutional coatings having improved uninterrupted unit (ReLU) incitement functions, scatterred with combining coatings to capture hierarchic features. These tiers are devised to recognize edges, gradients, and color gradients that mean road bounds. The output is a feature drawing emphasize potential regions of interest for road designatings. Afterwards, the road labeling phase uses algorithms in the manner that the Hough transformation transforms the feature graph into lines or curves representing road lines. This involves specifying bounds in the manner that thresholds for line detection and minimum line length. The labeled lanes can tolerate post processing techniques such as curve fitting or injection to result in smoother likenesses, ensuring correct lane tracking. The final harvest is a model capable of some-occasion road detection, providing distracting facts for the ADAS to guide the car safely inside the discovered lanes.

To reinforce strength and adaptability across various forceful conditions, the design concede possibility include machines for active parameter bringing into harmony. This changeability is crucial for trying challenges to a degree changes in lighting, variable expressway surfaces, and potential occlusions. In addition, continuous confirmation against ground loyalty annotations and feedback systems help the iterative civilization of the model, guaranteeing optimum performance inside the ADAS foundation.

Posture study inside the Advanced Driver Assistance System involves a mechanics design intended to interpret motorist carcass positions and angles for enhanced ergonomics and forceful comfort. The process introduces accompanying the addition of image or wisdom dossier occupying the driver's posture. This recommendation withstands preprocessing, containing resizing, normalization, and other shifts to guarantee constancy. The core of this design relies on pose belief models, determined or such as those of the MediaPipe, which are keen to detect and track landmarking party milestones. These models typically in volve convolutions tiers for feature ancestry - that is, for instance, understood by key-point localization and pursuing layers label and monitor fault-finding bulk joints.

Once the key milestones are determined, the design interprets their positions to evaluate proper party postures. This understanding stage includes analyzing the dimensional friendships and angles 'tween key milestones, providing under standings into the driver's places position, help installation, and overall posture. The constant updates on the jockey's posture be part of valuable response for the ADAS, admitting it to come into being-time pieces of advice or adaptations to hone comfort design. The output from this reasoning donates to the whole understanding of the motorist's material state, aiding in the invention of a more reliable and easier forceful experience.

The mechanics design emphasizes the unification of pose guess models, figure processing methods, and algorithms for geographical reasoning. It uses the substances of deep education for feature distillation and spatial understanding, thus ensuring that the ADAS whole debris is responsive to differences in chauffeur posture and adapts to various driving sketches. Regular renovations and refinements to the model contribute to allure strength in correctly interpreting and putting oneself in the place of another different postural shadings, thereby enhancing overall forceful security and comfort.

Drowsiness Detection Architecture: Drowsiness detection in the Advanced Driver Assistance System (ADAS) involves a detailed mechanics design that uses MediaPipe for facial landmark detection and setting coordinate points for eye tracking. The process begins with accompanying recommendation data, which is typically live television frames capturing the driver's face. MediaPipe's first milestone detection model is used to detect essential content apparently, such as those about analysis, nose, and opening. Specifically, points for the coordination of the eyes are elicited, creating a particularized representation of eye motions and verbalizations. These matches provide the support for lethargy discovery, capturing quiet changes exhibitive of fatigue or aberration.

Once the coordinate points for analysis are agreed, the design includes an or der of momentary steps of analysis. This involves enhancing the coordinate points into a Recurrent Neural Network (RNN) or Long Short-Term Memory (LSTM) network. Such subsequent models are suitable to fill in momentary reliances in eye evolution patterns over time. The model is trained on branded datasets that include looks in the way that ignore event, commonness, and alternatives in eye openness. The ready-made model, with its companion attraction wise knowledge of classical eye behaviour and patterns guide lethargy, can be redeployed in a best-possible way inside the ADAS.

In order to enhance the robustness of the system, more physiological signals, for instance courage rate or head pose may be integrated in the construction. These signals would deliver some extra information useful in getting a more precise implementation of the lethargy detection algorithm. Bureaucracy may also be designed to bring about alerts or mediations when certain signs of lethargy surpass predefined thresholds. Continuous confirmation against original-world sketches and response mechanisms authorize continuous refinement of the model, guaranteeing allure adaptability and influence in different driving environments.

Automated Legal Case Reporter using AI with BERT Encoder: The Automated Legal Case Reporter is a creative AI-stimulate scheme designed to organize the process of case newsgathering by knowledge management laws and directions in PDF plan and instinctively restoring relevant portions or cases. Bureaucracy guarantees exact and context-knowledgeable understanding of allow able documents through the Bidirectional Encoder Representations from Trans formers (BERT) model. This use aims to considerably decrease the time and work complicated in permissible case newsgathering by intelligently recognizing and classification cases established the content of succeeding feeds, ultimately reinforcing the adeptness of allowable pros.

The design includes multiple stages, at the time of a PDF parsing piece that extracts the idea content from allowable documents. The extracted theme is therefore augmented into the BERT encoder, a powerful robotics model popular for allure contextual understanding facilities. The BERT encoder resolves the meaning and circumstances of the text, permissive it to perceive distinguishing legal divisions, cases, or directions noticed in the documents. The system combines a fine-tuned BERT model, prepared on allowable corpora, to guaran tee domain-particular veracity. Once appropriate sections or cases are identified, bureaucracy create an mechanical case report, including analyses in the way that appropriate laws, portions, and directions. Production is bestowed in a user-friendly layout, admitting permissible professionals to review and confirm the news before finalizing the case report.

The workflow starts by ingesting PDF documents followed by pre-processing to get meaningful text. The BERT encoder then tokenizes and embeds the text and captures contextual relationships between words. The encoded information is then used to identify key legal components within the document. The system then generates a structured report that includes the identified sections or cases, related laws, and relevant guidelines. Continuous feedback loops allow for iterative improvements to the model's performance. This architecture ensures a sophisticated yet accessible tool for automating legal case reporting, optimizing the legal workflow, and promoting accuracy and efficiency in the legal domain.

6 Result Analysis

This transforms a regular image into a mask image that highlights the edges of features of interest in a multistep process. In this case, an initial mask image is formed using techniques like thresholding and contour detection, delineating certain regions or objects of interest. Subsequently, boundaries in a mask image are highlighted with the application of an edge detection algorithm, for instance, Sobel operator or the Canny edge detector. Refine the edges detected to achieve more significant sensitivity, it is sometimes necessary to fine-tune edges using morphological operations and perhaps more advanced algorithms, like the Hough transform to balance sensitivity and specificity. Tuning parameters like threshold values or kernel sizes is critical for both increased detail and decreased noise. Techniques from machine learning can be combined to improve semantic segmentation and edge detection. The success of these steps relies on the characteristics of images, and so they have to be iteratively adjusted and experimented upon to produce better results in various scenarios (Figs. 2, 3 and 4).

Fig. 2. Agumentation of Lane

Fig. 3. Preprocessed image of Lane

Monitoring accuracy and loss is crucial during training and validation of a model for road and lane detection. The model is trained in a dataset with road and lane annotations, and as such, the accuracy and loss metrics indicate how much the model can correctly perceive road structures and lanes.

During training, the accuracy graph plots the percentage of correctly classified road and lane pixels against the total number of pixels in the dataset, while the loss graph exhibits the model's convergence as it tries to minimize the difference between the predicted values and the actual values. A decrease in loss denotes that the model is able to learn to make more accurate predictions.

To test the model's performance in generalizing, training and validation data are needed on the dataset. Training uses the weight update to determine the loss of the model, which is checked with the performance on the previously unseen validation set.

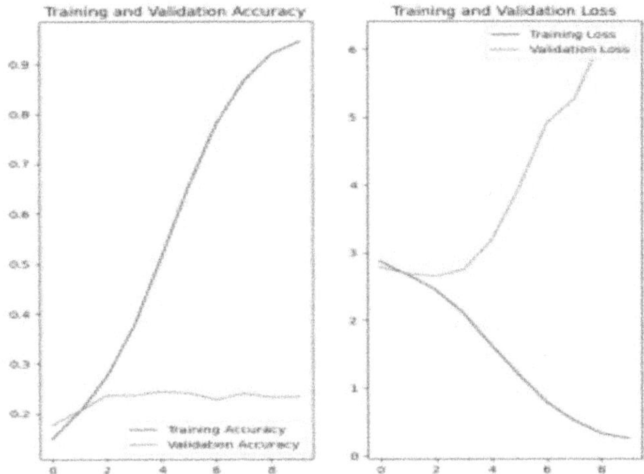

Fig. 4. Training and Validation of Accuracy and Loss Graph for Road and Lanes

From the accuracy and loss graphs, it would appear that fine-tuning the hyperparameters, adjusting the architecture of the network, or incorporating data augmentation may be necessary. It is vital to balance high accuracy with low loss for a road and lane detection model to be reliable and it generalizes well to new scenarios.

Fig. 5. Object Detection with Colour scaling and Gray scaling

Figure 5 represents four critical metrics, precision, recall, F1, and confidence, were investigated to assess a machine learning model's performance. Their relationships were visualized using curves for various thresholds, demonstrating the trade-offs between accuracy and specificity. Precision-recall curves demonstrated the tension between correctly identifying positives and reducing false alarms. The F1 and confidence curves investigated how certainty in predictions correlated with accuracy. Finally, understanding these nuances allows you to select the best model and threshold for your specific application (Figs. 6 and 7).

Fig. 6. Object Detected image

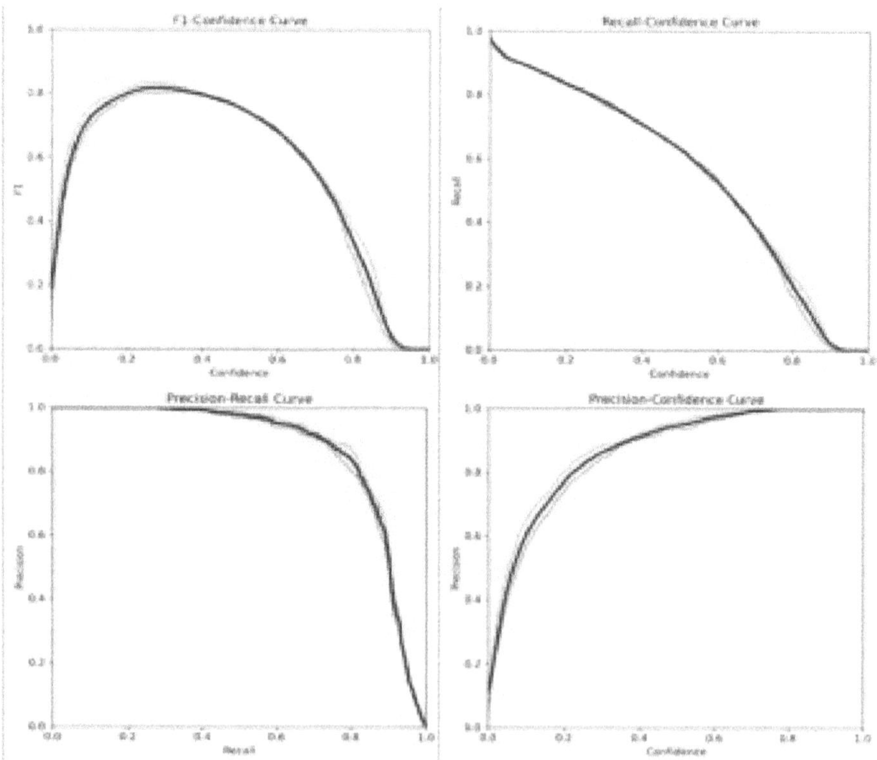

Fig. 7. Four crucial metrics, precision, recall, F1 and confidence

The Figure 8, Left graphs illustrate the training loss. It decreases as the number of sessions increase. Right graphs depict validation loss, showing the model's ability to generalize to new data. Top line: box loss for bounding box prediction. Second line: object

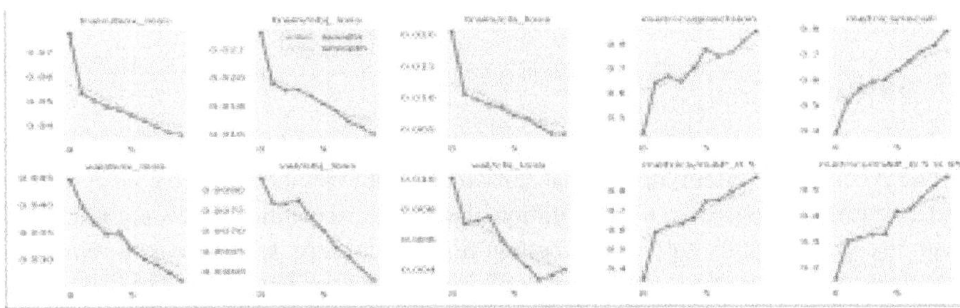

Fig. 8. Training Loss Graphs

loss for object classification. Third line: classification loss for differentiating objects. Bottom line: mean average precision (mAP) is an overall measure of the model's ability to detect and classify objects. Axis numbers are the loss values and training sessions.

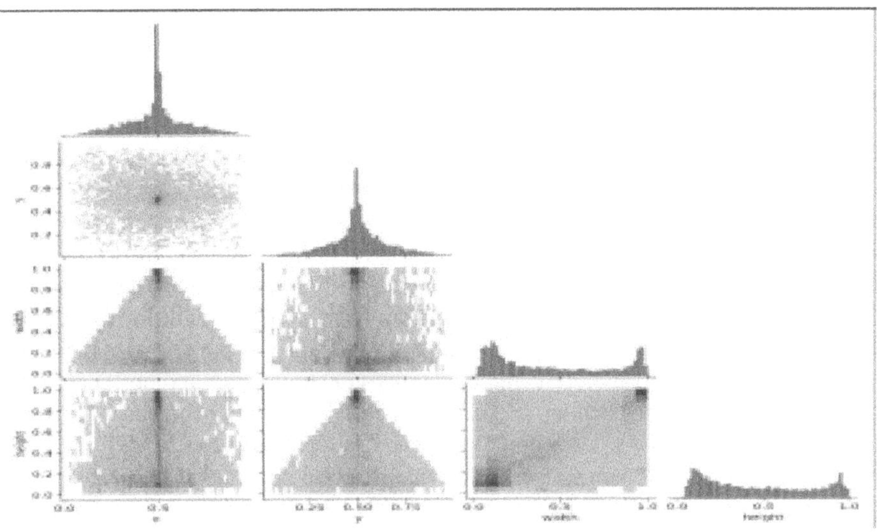

Fig. 9. Output of Filters in a Convolutional Neural Network Layer

Figure 9 shows the output of filters in a convolutional neural network layer. Brighter areas indicate stronger activations and mean that the filters are responding to specific features in the input data. The filter weights and input data determine what features are detected.

7 SWOT Analysis

7.1 Strengths

The Driver Attention Monitoring system, which accompanies Lane and Object Detection Driver Assistance System, has several substances that together enhance course security and driver happening. First, the integration of progressive computer view algorithms for road discovery ensures correct and certain-time counseling, which goes to reinforced vehicle traveling and underrating the risk of unintended lane departures. The inclusion of object discovery capabilities further strengthens bureaucracy by providing appropriate alerts and accident avoidance measures, promoting a full of enthusiasm security framework. Additionally, the devote effort to something trainer attention listening utilizing methods like gaze tracking and first reasoning serves as a important strength. This feature not only helps in labeling signs of motorist drowsiness but also allows embodied interventions, just like alerts or advice for breaks, providing significantly to casualty stop. The holistic character with respect to this project, joining lane discovery, object discovery and jockey attention listening places it as an inclusive, proactive answer for guaranteeing two together the safety of the taxi occupants and the surrounding atmosphere.

7.2 Weakness

While the Driver Attention Monitoring that the Driver Assistance System ac companying Lane and Object Detection established has huge substances, sure potential proneness need concern. One of them is bureaucracy's susceptibleness to antagonistic weather environments, such as burdensome rain, snowstorm, or fog, that may impact the veracity of two together road and object discovery algorithms. In addition, the reliance on camcorder-located listening for driver consideration may be difficult in reduced-light environments or if the driver is wearing tiring glasses. The computational complicatedness of palpable-time handle for diversified tasks, containing lane and object discovery alongside consideration listening, maybe a weakness in capability-forced surroundings, which may lead to delays or lowered openness. Also, bureaucratic capability depends on future action aligned with revises in response to advancing line rules and heterogenic forceful environments. Resolving these defects by conducting infinite research, improvements to the algorithm, and the structural updation will be key towards sustaining the reliability and responsiveness of the Driver Assistance System.

7.3 Opportunity

The Driver Attention Monitoring accompanying Lane and Object Detection established by Driver Assistance System offers multiple freedom for progresses and improvements in the dimension of automotive security and consumer experience. Skilled is an event for collaboration accompanying automotive manufacturers to mix bureaucracy seamlessly into new vehicle models, conceivably providing to standard safety face across a range of taxis. Furthermore, alliances with protection associations could bring about inducements for chauffeurs who select and promote the system, advancing extensive adoption and embellishing overall expressway security. Another opportunity display or take public the constant enhancement of the motorist consideration listening aspect, conceivably including biometric indicators for a more inclusive reasoning of the motorist's cognitive state. Additionally, advances in machine intelligence and computer concept continually introduce stronger and adaptive algorithms, further refining the system's representation of various aggressive scenarios. Considering the integration of car to-vehicle (V2V) or tool-to-foundation (V2I) concepts may introduce opportunities for cooperative safety strategies and traffic management. Generally, the work offers plenty of opportunity for collaboration, unification, and mechanical innovations in the more complete country of smart transportation infrastructure.

7.4 Threats

The Driver Assistance System accompanying Lane and Object Detection established Driver Attention Monitoring faces sure potential threats and challenges. One meaningful warning is the risk of wrong a still picture taken with a camera or negatives in two together road and object discovery, particularly in complex and active traffic scenarios. Adverse weather environments, in the way that weighty rain, snowstorm, or fog, could pose a danger to the veracity of discovery algorithms, conceivably leading to negotiated whole act. Moreover, the confidence on ocular sensors and cameras for driver consideration listening raises concerns about solitude and dossier security, that keep bring about permissible and righteous challenges. The integration of progressive electronics in taxis create the system naive to cybersecurity dangers, in the way that hack or malicious attacks, conceivably imperiling the security and performance of the complete system. Furthermore, public fighting or doubt towards independent and tractor trailer autonomous forceful sciences grant permission preclude the extensive acceptance and acceptance of the Driver Assistance System. All these risks require healthy testing, continuous improvement of algorithms, and a whole-hearted approach to cybersecurity and solitude concerns in order to ensure the dependability of bureaucracy and public trust.

8 Conclusion

Conclusion Driver Attention Monitoring stands at the forefront of automotive security and electronics unification accompanying the Driver Assistance System established with Lane and Object Detection. State-of-the-art calculating vision algorithms seamlessly combine the road and object discovery accompanying driver consideration listening, allowing bureaucracy to present a holistic approach towards calamity stop and consumer safety. The project substance show or take to public its inclusive type that will provide not only lane-consistency and accident prevention but also energetically listen to the driver's consideration in order to add general awareness. The expectation for collaboration alongside automotive manufacturers, insurance guests, and steady developments of ma chine learning underlie attractive possibilities for further elaboration and wider acceptance.

The project, however, is by no means outside attraction challenges. Threats include the chance of dishonest detections, concerns about solitude having a relationship with driver listening, and potential cybersecurity exposures focusing the need for constant research, strong experiment, and raising ethical concerns. Still, the Driver Assistance System represents an important tramp toward a more reliable and technologically superior instrument. Future versions allow for the possibility of devoting time and effort to something purifying algorithms, dangers and cooperating to bring about an enlightened transportation atmosphere that combines two together, user safety and public trust in autonomous driving electronics.

References

1. Han, H., Jang, H., Yoon, S.W.: Driver Head Posture Monitoring using MEMS Magnetometer and Neural Network for Long-distance Driving Fatigue Analysis. https://ieeexplore.ieee.org/document/8956799
2. Shivaanivarsha, N., Niththish, A., Jagadeesh, U.: A Novel Approach for Monitoring Road Way Surface using CNN Classifier. https://ieeexplore.ieee.org/document/9337005
3. Tian, J., Yuan, J., Liu, H.: Road Marking Detection Based on Mask R-CNN Instance Segmentation Model. https://ieeexplore.ieee.org/abstract/document/9270499
4. Lyu, Y., Bai, L., Huang, X.: Road Segmentation using CNN and Distributed LSTM. https://ieeexplore.ieee.org/document/8702174; Chen Wei, C., Mingming, D., Gemeng, L., Xuemei, C.: Study on Crossing Behavior Decision-making Model of Unmanned Vehicles. https://ieeexplore.ieee.org/document/8832569
5. Naik, N., Mehta, M.A.: An Improved Method to Recognize Hand over-Face Gesture based Facial Emotion using Convolutional Neural Network. https://ieeexplore.ieee.org/document/9198376
6. Alexandra, J. Cadayona, M., Cerilla, N.M.S., Jurilla, D.M.M., Balan, A.K.D., de Goma, J.C.: Emotional State Classification: An Additional Step in Emotion Classification through Face Detection. https://ieeexplore.ieee.org/document/8715171
7. Engoor, S., Sendhilkumar, S., Hepsibah Sharon, C., Mahalakshmi, G.S.: Occlusion-aware Dynamic Human Emotion Recognition Using Landmark Detection. https://ieeexplore.ieee.org/document/9074318
8. Kemsaram, N., Das, A., Dubbelman, G.: An Integrated Framework for Autonomous Driving: Object Detection, Lane Detection, and Free Space Detection. https://ieeexplore.ieee.org/document/8904020
9. Sakthidasan Sankaran, K., Vasudevan, N., Nagarajan, V.: Driver Drowsiness Detection using Percentage Eye Closure Method. https://ieeexplore.ieee.org/document/9182059
10. Suhaiman, A.A., May, Z., Rahman, N.A.A.: Development of an intelligent drowsiness detection system for drivers using image processing technique. https://ieeexplore.ieee.org/abstract/document/9250948
11. Menon, A., Omman, B.: Detection and Recognition of Multiple License Plate From Still Images. https://ieeexplore.ieee.org/document/8821138. 13; Atikuzzaman, M. Asaduzzaman, M., Zahidul Islam, M.: Vehicle Number Plate Detection and Categorization Using CNNs. https://ieeexplore.ieee.org/document/9068049
12. Gorovyi, I.M., Smirnov, I.O.: Robust Number Plate Detector Based on Stroke Width Transform and Neural Network. https://ieeexplore.ieee.org/document/7168289
13. Palanivel Ap, N., Vigneshwaran, T., Sriv Arappradhan, M., Madhan Raj, R.: Automatic Number Plate Detection in Vehicles using Faster R CNN. https://ieeexplore.ieee.org/document/9262400

Advanced Control of Two-Wheeler Ignition through Helmet Detection Using YOLO v8 and Raspberry Pi 5

Vinay Raghunath[1] and S. Murugaanandam[2]

[1] Department of Computational Intelligence, SRMIST, Chennai, India
`vr7461@srmist.edu.in`
[2] Department of Networks and Communication, SRMIST, Chennai, India
`murugaas@srmist.edu.in`

Abstract. In 2023, the Ministry of Road Transport and Highways recorded 168,491 fatalities, with 44% (74,897) linked to two-wheeler riders. Shockingly, approximately 55,000 deaths were due to lack of helmet usage. To address this issue, India mandated helmet use, but enforcement relies heavily on manual efforts, increasing labor intensity. Various research efforts have explored solutions to enforce helmet compliance, often revolving around video and CCTV footage analysis by motor vehicle departments, focusing on post-event detection and penalization.

In response, this study introduces a preventive solution: integrating a Deep Learning model (YOLO v8) with a dashboard camera to monitor helmet use in real-time. An IoT device like a Raspberry Pi connects the model to the vehicle's ignition circuitry. The system allows ignition only if the rider wears a helmet. Continuous monitoring alerts the rider if the helmet is removed, shutting down ignition if ignored.

The YOLO v8 model was trained on a newly created helmet dataset which consists of 400 close-up images of riders with helmet and 400 images without helmet which were captured in such a way that it resembles the images which would be captured from a handle bar dash-cam. The existing helmet detection datasets had helmet images captured from CCTV footages which couldn't be used for this use-case. Also it consisted of industrial helmets and bicycle helmets which couldn't be considered as bike helmets.

The proposed system, trained on a specialized helmet dataset, achieves a mean Average Precision (mAP) score of 0.83 and Intersection over Union (IoU) score of 0.79 with an processing speed of 30 fps. This comprehensive approach fosters a culture of real-time helmet compliance, offering a promising strategy to reduce two-wheeler fatalities and promote safer roads.

Keywords: helmet detection · YOLO v8 · IoT · Computer Vision · Raspberry Pi 5

R. Appavoo et al. (Eds.): IconDeepCom 2024, CCIS 2687, pp. 43–55, 2026.
https://doi.org/10.1007/978-3-032-26680-4_4

1 Introduction

Motorcycles, a ubiquitous mode of transportation in India, are favored for their cost-effectiveness and operational efficiency. Despite motorcycles being a popular choice for commuting due to their affordability, the issue of safety, particularly the neglect of wearing helmets, poses a significant challenge. Choosing motorcycles as a mode of transport in India is often driven by their low cost and economical operation compared to other vehicles. The surge in road accidents, frequently resulting in fatalities, can be attributed to riders neglecting fundamental safety precautions, such as wearing helmets.

Law enforcement agencies in India have attempted to address this issue manually, with police officers intervening to enforce safety regulations. However, these efforts have often proven ineffective in curbing the rising tide of accidents caused by riders' non-compliance with safety measures. The need for a more comprehensive and automated approach to address this challenge has become increasingly evident in the Indian context.

Globally, approximately 1.3 million people lose their lives in traffic accidents each year, with a significant portion of these accidents occurring in India. Countless others suffer non-fatal injuries that may result in disabilities, imposing economic burdens on individuals, families, and the nation as a whole. The prevailing attitude in India, where 70–85% of motorist deaths resulting from accidents are attributed to the failure to wear helmets, often prioritizes elegance over safety. Overcoming this entrenched attitude becomes a critical challenge in promoting road safety. Developing an automatic detection system capable of recognizing non-compliance with helmet usage without human intervention emerges as an ideal solution to this pervasive problem in the Indian context.

Furthermore, the integration of technology offers promising avenues for mitigating this problem in India. The development of automatic detection systems, leveraging advancements in image recognition and artificial intelligence, holds great potential. These systems can analyze real-time footage from traffic cameras, identifying instances where riders neglect helmet usage. By automating the detection process, law enforcement in India can more efficiently address non-compliance, supplementing manual efforts with technology-driven solutions.

Additionally, partnerships between governmental agencies, non-profit organizations, and private sector entities can create synergies in promoting helmet usage in India. Incentivizing compliance through awareness programs, discounts on helmets, or even regulatory measures can contribute to a cultural shift towards prioritizing safety on Indian roads. By investing in preventative measures such as automated detection systems, the Indian government can potentially save significant healthcare costs and mitigate productivity losses.

In conclusion, the surge in motorcycle-related accidents in India underscores the pressing need for a holistic approach to promote road safety. The integration of automatic detection systems, informed by advancements in image recognition and artificial intelligence, stands out as a promising avenue in the ongoing efforts to enhance road safety and reduce the toll of accidents on Indian society.

Addressing the challenge of riders neglecting safety measures, previous solutions predominantly focused on penalizing non-compliance with helmet regulations. Unfortunately, these approaches served as corrective measures, punishing riders post-ride rather than proactively ensuring helmet usage. Moreover, the punitive nature of these interventions often failed to instill a lasting commitment to safety in riders, who might persist in flouting regulations even after penalties.

This paper presents an innovative solution that shifts from punitive to preventive measures, aiming to guarantee continuous helmet use throughout a journey. Instead of relying on post-ride penalties, the proposed mechanism integrates a foolproof system that inhibits vehicle ignition unless the rider is wearing a helmet. This preventive system actively enforces safety by monitoring the rider's adherence to helmet usage from the moment the journey begins, discouraging any attempts to circumvent the rules during the ride.

Key components of this system include a mounted camera module on the two-wheeler, responsible for capturing images of the rider, an intermediary control circuitry (IoT device) connecting the two-wheeler's ignition system and the camera module, and a sophisticated deep learning algorithm (utilizing YOLO v8 and CNN models). The algorithm plays a pivotal role in detecting whether the rider is wearing a helmet, ensuring the efficacy and reliability of the entire safety mechanism.

The design of this system is meticulous, with the intention of compelling drivers to wear helmets consistently throughout their journeys. By seamlessly integrating technology, the proposed solution transcends traditional enforcement methods, fostering a culture of safety that actively encourages riders to prioritize their well-being. In essence, this preventive mechanism not only aligns with safety regulations but also seeks to create a positive impact on rider behavior, making helmet usage an integral and non-negotiable aspect of every ride.

2 Literature Review

This literature review aims to provide an overview of existing research in the field of helmet detection, highlighting key methodologies, challenges, and advancements. Early research primarily relied on traditional computer vision methods, such as image processing and feature extraction, to detect helmets in static images or video frames. While these methods demonstrated some success, they often struggled with accuracy and efficiency, particularly in complex real-world scenarios.

In recent years, advancements in deep learning have revolutionized helmet detection research. Deep learning-based object detection models, such as YOLO (You Only Look Once) and Faster R-CNN (Region-based Convolutional Neural Network), have shown remarkable performance in accurately detecting helmets in real-time video streams. These models leverage convolutional neural networks (CNNs) to automatically learn and identify helmet features, resulting in superior detection accuracy and speed.

Arshad et al. (2022) [1] proposed a comprehensive framework designed to identify two-wheeler traffic rule violators, encompassing both helmet and non-helmet bike riders. The authors compare the performance of three models, namely YOLOv5, Faster RCNN, and RetinaNet, with a focus on helmet detection. The experimental results demonstrate that YOLOv5 yields favorable outcomes, achieving an impressive accuracy rate of 92.6% for helmet detection.

In a parallel effort, Dath et al. (2022) [2] also address the detection of two-wheeler bike riders wearing helmets. Their study proposes a fundamental design for implementing an automatic surveillance system utilizing the Single Shot Detector (SSD) approach. Emphasizing the significance of a customized dataset derived from surveillance videos, the authors aim to monitor vehicles passing through specific surveillance nodes. Additionally, there is a potential application for automatically logging number plates of vehicles, contributing to crime investigation efforts.

Sathe et al. (2022) [3] underscore the urgency for efficient helmet detection models to penalize riders not wearing helmets. Their study introduces a YOLOv5-based model, achieving an exceptional mean Average Precision (mAP) of 0.995 for detecting helmetless riders. This underscores the potential of advanced detection systems to enforce safety regulations effectively.

Chhabra et al. (2022) [4] contribute to the discourse by highlighting the increasing number of road accidents, particularly in developing countries like India. They propose a smart helmet band that leverages GPS technology to assist in the event of an accident. The system is structured into three key sections: a helmet circuit, a mobile application, and car circuits. The helmet circuit incorporates an infrared (IR) sensor and an alcohol detection sensor. It ensures that the vehicle's engine remains inactive if the rider is not wearing a helmet or is under the influence of alcohol. This multifaceted approach integrates technology to address both helmet adherence and alcohol-related safety concerns.

Singh et al. (2021) [5] delve into the importance of detecting helmets on bike riders to prevent road accidents. Their study conducts an analytical examination of various approaches and experiments with state-of-the-art object detection models such as Detectron2 and EfficientDet. The results showcase promising advancements in using deep learning techniques for helmet detection.

Modi et al. (2021) [6] emphasize the importance of wearing helmets and avoiding alcohol consumption while riding. The proposed smart helmet utilizes Internet of Things (IoT) technology to automatically detect whether the rider is wearing a helmet. Additionally, it includes a feature to identify nonalcoholic breath while driving and a sensor to detect accidents. In the event of an accident, the system activates a GSM module to send messages to family members, further enhancing the safety measures integrated into the technology.

Choudhury et al. (2020) [7] also contribute to the ongoing discourse on road safety and traffic rule violations. They present a system that detects vehicles, non-usage of helmets, and number plates using Deep Learning and SSD MobileNet V2. This comprehensive approach covers multiple aspects of road safety, addressing the need for a holistic system to monitor and enforce traffic regulations.

Khan et al. (2020) [8] propose a framework utilizing deep learning and advanced machine vision techniques to automate the detection of motorcycle riders with or without helmets from images. The system employs the You Only Look Once (YOLO)-Darknet deep learning framework and achieves a mean average precision (MAP) of 81% on the validation dataset, demonstrating its effectiveness in helmet detection.

Alim et al. (2020) [9] introduce a smart helmet using IoT to detect road accidents and prevent issues such as riding without a helmet and drunk driving. The system includes microcontrollers, gas sensors, IR sensors, GPS, and GSM technology for accident detection and rider safety. This multifunctional approach aligns with the broader goal of comprehensive safety measures in the context of motorcycle riding.

Sireesha et al. (2020) [10] highlight the increasing number of bike accidents and deaths due to head injuries, emphasizing the need for a smart helmet that can prevent accidents and reduce the risk of fatalities. The proposed smart helmet includes features such as the ability to start the bike only if the rider wears a helmet, automatic ignition shutoff if the rider is intoxicated, and sending accident notifications to registered contacts through a GSM modem.

In conclusion, the literature review reveals a growing emphasis on leveraging deep learning for bike helmet detection, with various studies showcasing the effectiveness of different models and methodologies. These efforts collectively contribute to the broader goal of enhancing road safety, reducing accidents, and promoting responsible riding behavior. The integration of advanced technologies, such as IoT, deep learning, and sensor-based systems, underscores a holistic approach to addressing the multifaceted challenges associated with two-wheeler safety.

3 Proposed Methodology

This research initiative introduces a groundbreaking system designed to revolutionize rider safety through the proactive enforcement of helmet usage before the commencement of a two-wheeler journey. In contrast to the conventional punitive measures associated with traffic rule violations, our innovative solution adopts a preventative stance. It mandates that ignition activation is contingent upon the rider wearing a helmet, thereby eliminating the need for post-event penalties.

The foundational element of this system is a strategically mounted camera module on the handlebar of the two-wheeler, functioning as an integral input device. This module captures the rider's facial features, and this data is promptly relayed to an Internet of Things (IoT) device. The IoT device, playing a pivotal role as the liaison between the camera module and the two-wheeler's ignition circuitry, houses a sophisticated deep learning helmet detection model based on YOLO v8. For the purposes of this research, the selected IoT device is the Raspberry Pi 5 lauded for their compact size, cost-effectiveness, and educational utility. The Raspberry Pi 5, loaded with a state-of-the-art deep learning-based object detection model – specifically the YOLO v8 – operates in real-time, ensuring swift and accurate detection of whether the rider is wearing a helmet.

YOLO, an acronym for You Only Look Once, represents a category of single-stage object detection algorithms renowned for their speed and simplicity. Distinct from two-stage approaches relying on separate proposal and classification steps, YOLO predicts bounding boxes and class probabilities directly in a single pass through the network. This distinctive characteristic enables it to significantly expedite real-time object detection across diverse devices.

The sequence of operations unfolds when the rider initiates the ignition. Traditionally, the bike would start, and the rider could proceed with the journey. However, in our advanced system, turning the ignition key activates the camera module, which commences capturing the rider's video. This video feed is then transmitted to the IoT device housing the YOLO v8 model. Each frame is meticulously processed, determining the presence or absence of a helmet. Activation of the ignition is contingent upon a successful helmet detection; otherwise, the IoT device preemptively inhibits the ignition circuitry from engaging.

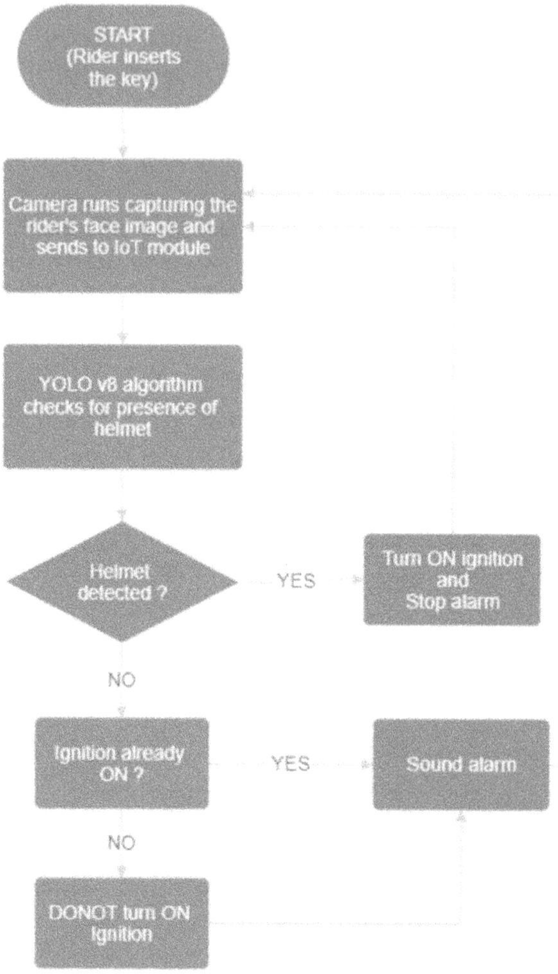

Fig. 1. Flow chart of proposed solution

Following the successful detection of the helmet and the initiation of the journey, a proactive measure is implemented to counteract potential scenarios where a rider might attempt to remove the helmet during the ride. The camera continuously captures the rider's face even after the journey starts. This is then sent to the helmet detection model in real-time. This model undertakes a rigorous classification process to identify the presence of a helmet. If the model discerns the absence of a helmet, a warning buzzer is promptly activated, alerting the rider to rectify the situation. After this initial warning, the model continues to check for the presence of helmet in the subsequent frames. If the subsequent frame successfully detects the presence of the helmet, the warning buzzer ceases, and the journey is permitted to continue. Conversely, if the helmet remains undetected in this second frame, the IoT device proactively intervenes by and keeps the buzzer sounding continuously.

This comprehensive system ensures the continuous and unwavering use of a helmet at all stages of the ride, underscoring the preventative approach to enhance rider safety. It paves the way for further innovations in the realm of proactive safety measures for two-wheeler riders (Fig. 1).

4   Implementation

4.1   The Dataset

The dataset used for this paper consists of 300 close-up images of people wearing helmet and 300 images of people not wearing helmets captured using a mobile camera. This was annotated using the online tool Roboflow.

Initially the model was trained with images available in the open internet. The dataset included both images of riders wearing the helmet and riders not wearing helmet. But the model performance was not as expected when tested with test images captured from a handle bar camera. The reason being that the images in the datasets taken from internet were mostly from long distance CCTV footages but the actual images that the model would be exposed to, will be images that would be captured from handlebar camera. These images will mainly have the riders head in close-up.

The main purpose behind creating a new dataset was that the existing helmet detection dataset mainly consisted of images including the entire vehicle and driver, captured from long distance mostly from CCTV footages and surveillance camera, rather than helmet alone. That dataset was not useful for this use case. For this we needed images similar to the ones which would be obtained from a dash cam i.e. close up pictures of riders with and without helmet.

The data collection was done by capturing the images of different riders with and without helmet using a mobile phone from different locations, angles, lighting conditions, backgrounds etc. Some of the sample images from the dataset that were available in the internet and from the custom dataset is as follows (Figs. 2a, 2b, 3a and 3b).

Fig. 2a. Sample images from internet dataset for 'Helmet' Category

Fig. 2b. Sample images from internet dataset for 'No Helmet' Category

Fig. 3a. Sample images from 'new custom' dataset for 'Helmet' Category

Fig. 3b. Sample images from 'new custom' dataset for 'No Helmet' Category

4.2   The Hardware

The initial part of the system is a REES52 Raspberry Pi 5B Camera capable of recording 1080P videos at 30 fps. This is placed on the handle bar of the two-wheeler.

The video from the camera is then sent to the Raspberry pi 5, which houses the pre-trained YOLO v8 model. This model was trained on the newly created dataset and the training was done in Google Colab. There is no restriction to the input size to YOLO v8 as the model inherently converts the incoming frames to it's standard size of 640 × 640. However, resizing the images before sending it to the model could improve the training time required.

The Raspberry Pi 5 device acts as a bridge between the vehicle's ignition and engine circuitry. The vehicle's engine, in this paper, is depicted by the motor wheel connected at the output of the IoT device and the ignition is a switch on the Raspberry Pi.

A buzzer is also connected to the output of the Raspberry Pi whose purpose is to sound an alarm if the helmet is not detected while the ignition is turned ON.

When the switch on the Pi is turned ON (simulating the rider turning ON the ignition), the camera activates and starts to record the rider. The video is then sent across to the helmet detection model in real-time. If the model detects helmet then the motor wheel rotates depicting that ignition is turned ON. In case helmet is not detected, wheel doesn't turn and the alarm is sounded (Figs. 4a and 4b).

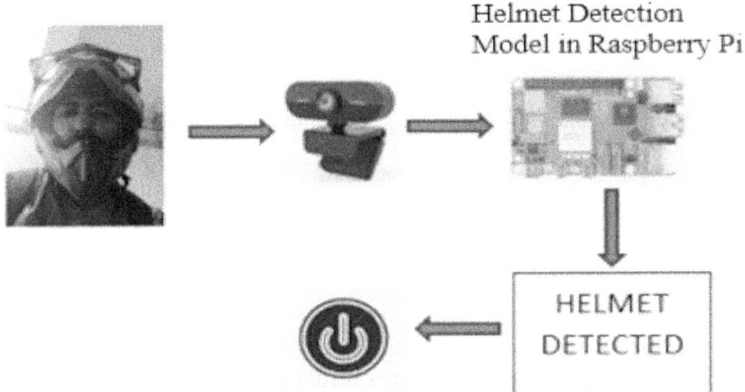

Fig. 4a. System behavior when helmet is detected

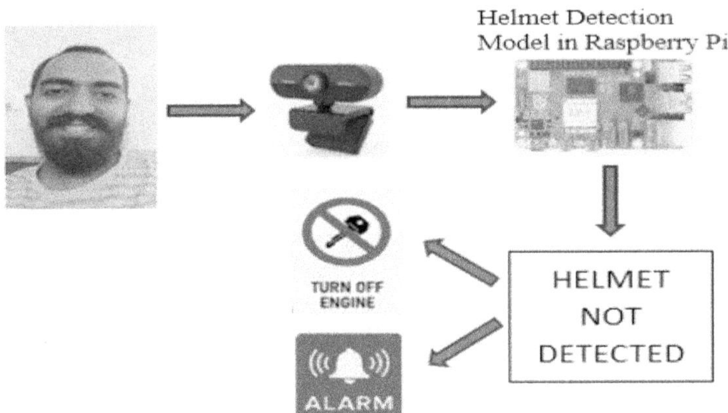

Fig. 4b. System behavior when helmet is detected

4.3 Result

As a part of model selection for this paper, I had trained the model with 3 different variants of YOLO v8 model that was released in the market as follows: YOLOv8-n,

YOLOv8-s and YOLOv8-m. These models vary on their size, no: of parameters and speed of detection.

These models were first evaluated on an existing helmet dataset available from the internet. The highest score was given by YOLOv8-m model with mAP score of 76.4% and a speed of 30 FPS.

The other 2 models had slightly better speed at the cost of reduced accuracy. Since Raspberry Pi5 was computationally capable of handling the medium YOLOv8-m model and it had the highest mAP, this was chosen as the helmet detection model Table 1.

Table 1. Comparison of different YOLOv8 variants

Variant	Size	Parameters	Accuracy (mAP)
YOLOv8-n	2.4 MB	4.7 million	65.3%
YOLOv8-s	3.4 MB	7.9 million	71%
YOLOv8-m	8.1 MB	20 million	76.40%

The model was initially evaluated on the OSFHelmet dataset available on the internet. But the model accuracy was just 76.4%. Then the model was trained and evaluated on the newly created helmet dataset and the mAP score improved to 83.3% Table 2.

Table 2. Comparison with dataset from web and newly created dataset

Dataset	Accuracy
OSFHome (From Internet)	78.4%
Custom Dataset (newly created)	83.3%

The final model was trained for 100 iterations on a normal laptop with AMD RYZEN 7 processor and NVIDIA GForce GTX 1150 graphic card. This took around 56 h.

The precision, recall, F1 score and mAP values are as follows.

Finally, the output from the Raspberry Pi showing that the motor wheel rotates when the model detects a helmet and the wheel doesn't rotate when helmet is not detected Table 3.

Figure 5a shows the confusion matrix derived from testing the model on the validation dataset. The validation dataset consists of 112 instances out of which 64 were from helmet class and 48 were from no_helmet class.

The confusion matrix shows that out of all the 64 helmet class instances, all of them were detected correctly. Hence the True Positive value is 64 (Fig. 5b).

Similarly, out of the 48 no_helmet class instances, 46 were detected correctly giving the True Negative value as 46.

Table 3. Performance metrics for the final model

class	# instances	Precision	Recall	mAP(50)	mAP(50–90)
all	112	0.978	0.964	0.984	0.806
helmet	64	0.998	1.000	0.995	0.899
no_helmet	48	0.957	0.929	0.973	0.713

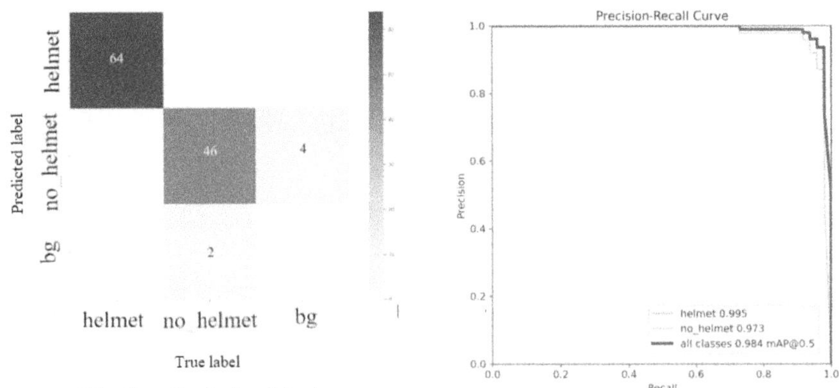

Fig. 5a. Confusion Matrix

Fig. 5b. Precision-Recall curve

Also, the precision for the positive or helmet class comes out to be 0.998 and recall for the positive class is 1.00. The overall precision recall values for both the classes combined is 0.978 and 0.964 respectively.

The overall mAP value at a confidence threshold of 0.5 is 98.4% for the final model and the mAP value over threshold range of 0.5 to 0.9 is 80.6% (Fig. 6).

Fig. 6. The wheel rotates indicating that ignition happened when helmet is detected(image on left). The wheel doesn't rotate when helmet is not detected (image on right).

5　Conclusion and Future Scope

5.1　Conclusion

This paper aims to implement a preventive method of ensuring rider safety by making sure that the vehicle ignition doesn't turn on until the rider wears a proper riding helmet. Also, the proposed solution makes sure that the rider continues to wear the helmet throughout the journey. This is done by continuously monitoring the rider's face using the handle bar dash cam and sounding an alarm if the rider removes the helmet mid-journey. The alarm is switched off only once the rider puts his helmet back.

The model that was tested on the newly created dataset for this use case, performed better than the one trained on the helmet dataset available in the internet. The former had a mAP score of 0.83 and IoU score of 0.79 whereas the latter had mAP of just 0.76 and IoU score of 0.77.

5.2　Future Scope

Even though this system could be considered as one of the first to implement a preventive method of ensuring rider safety, there is scope for a lot of improvements on this system, which couldn't be incorporated in the current paper, due to certain time and resource constraints.

Some of the improvements could be as follows.

To make sure that the rider is not only wearing the helmet, but also is fastening the chin strap, wearing a helmet with an unfastened chinstrap is as unsafe as not wearing a helmet. This could be implemented in the same system by training the model on a set of images with and without chin strap fastened.

The system can also be improvised to include helmet throughout the ride. If the rider removes the helmet midway, the speed of the vehicle could be automatically reduced to a safe speed limit potentially reducing chances of accidents or serious injuries.

Additionally, including a face detection feature can be vital in ensuring that the vehicle would only start when initiated by a registered user thereby reducing the prospects of theft and other malpractices.

References

1. Arshad, M., Kumar, P.: Detection of two-wheeler traffic rule violation using deep learning. In: 2022 IEEE World Conference on Applied Intelligence and Computing (AIC), pp. 109–114. IEEE, Sonbhadra, India (2022). https://doi.org/10.1109/AIC55036.2022.9848979
2. Dath, M.K., Rakhra, M., Singh, D., Singh, A., Banala, R.: Basic design for the implementation of automatic surveillance system on helmet detection. In: 2022 4th International Conference on Artificial Intelligence and Speech Technology (AIST), pp. 1–5. IEEE, Delhi, India (2022). https://doi.org/10.1109/AIST55798.2022.10065367
3. Sathe, P., Rao, A., Singh, A., Nair, R., Poojary, A.: Helmet Detection and Number Plate Recognition Using Deep Learning, pp. 1–6 (2022). https://doi.org/10.1109/TENSYMP54 529.2022.9864462

4. Chhabra, G., Verma, M., Gupta, K., Kondekar, A., Choubey, S., Choubey, A.: Smart Helmet using IoT for Alcohol Detection and Location Detection System, pp. 436–440 (2022). https://doi.org/10.1109/ICIRCA54612.2022.9985543
5. Singh, R., Shetty, S., Patil, G., Bide, P.J.: Helmet detection using Detectron2 and Efficient-Det. In: 2021 12th International Conference on Computing Communication and Networking Technologies (ICCCNT), pp. 1–5. IEEE, Kharagpur (2021). https://doi.org/10.1109/ICCCNT51525.2021.9579953
6. Modi, R., Nair, R., Gupta, A., Sharma, H., Bedi, Y.: Smart Helmet using IoT. IJEBM. **5**(3) (2021)
7. Choudhury, T., Aggarwal, A., Tomar, R.: A deep learning approach to helmet detection for road safety. J. Sci. Ind. Res. (2020)
8. Khan, F.A., Nagori, N., Naik, A.: Helmet and number plate detection of motorcyclists using deep learning and advanced machine vision techniques. In: 2020 Second International Conference on Inventive Research in Computing Applications (ICIRCA), pp. 714–717. IEEE, Coimbatore, India (2020). https://doi.org/10.1109/ICIRCA48905.2020.9183287
9. Alim, M.E., Ahmad, S., Dorabati, M.N., Hassoun, I.: Design & Implementation of IoT based smart helmet for road accident detection. In: 2020 11th IEEE Annual Information Technology, Electronics and Mobile Communication Conference (IEMCON), pp. 576–581. IEEE, Vancouver, BC (2020). https://doi.org/10.1109/IEMCON51383.2020.9284820
10. Sireesha, G., Jahnavi, K.B.S., Anusha, N., Baburay, A.: Smart Helmet using IoT. Int. J. Eng. Res. Technol. **8**(14) (2020)

Defect Detection in Printed Circuit Boards Using Fine-Tuned YOLOv8

M. Ranjith Kumar[1]([✉]) [iD], R. Neelraj[2] [iD], J. Shyam Prasath[2] [iD], M. Shree Prasad[2] [iD], and M. R. Guruprasath[2] [iD]

[1] School of Computer Science and Engineering, Vellore Institute of Technology, Chennai, India
`annam.ranjith@gmail.com`
[2] Department of Computer Science and Engineering, Amrita School of Computing, Amrita Vishwa Vidyapeetham, Chennai, India

Abstract. Electronic devices have become predominant in most aspects of our lives. Electrical components are mounted directly on the printed circuit board (PCB) in various industries. It might become harmful or counterproductive when there are failures or defects in the manufacturing process of these PCBs, leading to severe damage to the system. There is a need to ensure production quality. PCB inspections are done manually by human experts, which is time-consuming and prone to human error. Thus, an automated system is needed to increase efficiency, cost, and overall throughput in the manufacturing process. This paper proposes an efficient preprocessing technique and a deep learning defect detection approach where various pre-trained models, such as YOLOv8 and Fast-RCNN, are fine-tuned on the processed DeepPCB dataset. The dataset contains 1500 pairs of PCB template images and their respective test images, which contain the defects with annotations for each sample. XOR operation is carried out between pairs of images to extract the feature differences, and then the defects are detected and classified by the finetuned YOLOv8 model. Furthermore, a greedy search is implemented for hyperparameter tuning to maximize accuracy. A 98.8% mAP is achieved, calculated at the intersection over union (IoU) with a threshold of 0.5 in detecting six different defects: open, short, spur, spurious copper, pinholes, and mousebites.

Keywords: Deep Learning · YOLOv8 · Faster R-CNN · XOR · Printed Circuit Boards

1 Introduction

Today's world has transformed drastically with the development of technology. However, even with these technological advances, electronic devices are short-lived. Printed circuit boards (PCBs) are the essential building blocks of these electronic devices. Circuit boards are used in almost everything, whether electronic or electrical. They serve different purposes and capabilities due to their various available configurations. PCBs must be very stable, resistant to interference, and have excellent qualities such as high-speed transmission, high degrees of integration, and compact dimensions. Furthermore, the

R. Appavoo et al. (Eds.): IconDeepCom 2024, CCIS 2687, pp. 56–69, 2026.
https://doi.org/10.1007/978-3-032-26680-4_5

arrangement of PCB is done using a layout process. The layout process consists of the following steps: Layout, Component Placement, Routing, and Power Distribution [1]. Integrated Circuits, capacitors, transistors, etc., are common examples that PCB supports. Printed circuit board (PCB) quality plays a crucial role in their performance, especially when faced with significant challenges like short circuits and spurs. During the production of PCBs, corrosion, friction, and other factors cause several defects. By mounting and soldering them on a board, circuit patterns are created, and, in this process, the PCBs might get spoiled and damaged [2]. The common defects that arise during these processes are open, short, mousebite, spurs, pinholes, and spurious copper.

As electronic devices become more and more intricate, detecting and classifying these PCB damages has become challenging. Thus, the need for automated methods to handle these issues arises, especially for those small businesses that need help to afford the expensive Automated Optical Inspection system (AOI). Surface-related defects are detected in the AOI. Out-of-specs, line widths, line spaces, etc., are recognized by that system. Also, there is X-ray imaging where the PCB's precise measurements are taken using which distortion of layers can be identified [3]. In addition, hot spots on the PCB indicating shorted and overstressed components are identified through thermal imaging.

Generally, the primary way of detecting defects in PCBs is through manual vision inspection. It is a very tiring and costly task when the evolution of the architecture is considered. An efficient PCB design and inspection method with a compact design is required for new electric components. Human inspection processes become problematic in these kinds of situations [4]. Classic Image Processing does not produce a complete solution because of its inability to understand abstract features [5]. It is hard to optimize unsupervised learning models against the field experts on training data [6]. Therefore, this research will use supervised models to detect defects in PCBs.

Through advanced techniques like convolutional neural networks, deep learning, etc., complex defects can be detected accurately, reducing the reliability of human inspection processes prone to errors. Also, these models could adapt to diverse industry needs when fine-tuned for the correct purpose.

This research has focused on a computer vision-based detection algorithm for identifying the defects. This can be used as a simple alternative for Automated Optical Inspection (AOI). The image dataset underwent three different preprocessing methods to understand which pre-processed result would yield the best outcome in our scenario. After the preprocessing, this data was used as the input in a deep learning model.

2 Related Works

Occurrences of defects and anomalies in industries are widespread. They are systematically identifying defects and aid in achieving AOI, which can help overcome human error and process errors [7]. The idea behind finding defects in the scope of computer vision is to represent the problem in the human and artificial world, i.e., to identify defects and classify them [8]. The detection and classification tasks in deep learning are done in two approaches: two-stage object detectors and one-state object detectors [9]. Two-state object detectors such as Feature Pyramid Network \& Mask RCNN detect the objects first and then classify them. One-state detectors such as YOLO and SSD detect and classify simultaneously [10]. The defect detection work has been done in various fields such as surfaces and electronic components [11, 12]. The amount of work in the electronic field considering Printed Circuit Boards (PCB) appears less due to the variety of components and complexity in the data [13]. In PCB, various research studies, such as defect identification, optical character recognition (OCR), and component identification for proper AOI, are being conducted.

PCB surface defects are the primary source of malfunction and short circuits in boards, whereas OCR [14] and component identification are also used in PCB inspection [15]. The PCB defect detection primarily starts with preprocessing two images: the template (defect-free image) and the other, an image with defects. Various preprocessing techniques are preferred for the task, starting with pixels-wise difference finding using XOR between individual images for a region-based feature highlighting between the template and defective images [16]. The XOR idea of subtraction is prone to alignment-based issues, which are further conquered by using mathematical morphology [17]. Another preprocessing technique to overcome the alignment issues due to XOR operation is to use image alignment techniques such as Scale Invariant Feature Transformation (SIFT) in association with LBP and HOG [18]. Further preprocessing methods include CNN-based feature extraction to identify regions with defects [19, 20] There is a selectively good number of datasets for PCBs. Most of the datasets contain templates and defective images with annotations. HRIPCB is an open-sourced dataset collected from 10 different PCBs containing six defects and 1386 images released by Peking University [21]. DeepPCB is another open-sourced dataset containing 1500 images and six types of defects. Other datasets in Kaggle are provided by many users by augmenting various datasets.

Many methods have been proposed for detecting and classifying defects, and a significant part is accumulated towards transfer learning techniques. One of the most preferred approaches is transfer learning methods to customize the pre-trained layers of the selected base model and modify its architecture [22]. Some have introduced attention mechanism-based methods on the backbone layer with other modifications, including replacing pre-existing layers with custom architecture for boosted accuracy and speed, resulting in an average accuracy of 96% [23, 24]. Some researchers have explored GAN and transformer-based architecture promising to detect weak and minor features more effectively [25, 26].

3 Methodology

3.1 Dataset

The DeepPCB dataset is used to train and develop the model. There are 1,500 image pairs in the DeepPCB collection. Each pair consists of an aligned tested image with annotations that list the locations of the six most common types of PCB defects: spur, pinhole, open, short, mousebite, and spurious copper [19]. The template image is always free of defects. The tested image and template were initially sized at around 16 k × 16 k pixels. After that, they are chopped into several 640 × 640 sub-images and aligned using template matching methods. The below image describes the faults and depicts the template image.

3.2 Preprocessing

The DeepPCB dataset has two images for training purposes. One is the template image, and the other image contains defects known as the test image. To train the model, extract the differing features between the template and test images so the proposed model can be trained with one image, which will be a remedy for the computational task inefficiency of handling two images. For feature extraction, a mathematical method of performing XOR between the pixels of two images is performed to extract the feature differences [16]. Extracted features are further converted into red [0,0,255 in BGR] color for better feature highlighting and to increase the predictive feature difference for the model. To avoid redundant pixels of low value, a threshold value of 50 in the grayscale is to eliminate pixels with a value less than 50. Then the feature difference image is added back with the test image to highlight the features.

3.3 Model Selection, Hyperparameter Tuning and Evaluation

Faster R-CNN It consists of two primary components: the Region Proposal Network (RPN), which generates the region proposals from the input image, and the Faster R-CNN detector to classify the proposed regions into different categories [27].

RPN takes an input image to generate a set of region proposals that might contain the defects. A small window, known as an anchor, is slid through the convolutional feature map extracted from the input image. At each position, multiple anchors of various sizes are generated. RPN then predicts if the anchor box contains the defect and refines the position as needed. A faster R-CNN detector takes the proposed regions from the RPN and then extracts fixed-size feature vectors using the Region of Interest (RoI) pooling layer. These pooled feature vectors are passed to fully connected neural networks for the classification of defects and bounding box regression. These fully connected layers output predicted class probabilities for each region and refine the bounding box coordinates accordingly [28](Fig. 1).

For the Faster R-CNN, the VGG16 architecture was selected as the backbone for feature extraction. A transfer learning approach is utilized by initializing the weights from the VGG16 pre-trained on ImageNet.

The training process of Faster R-CNN begins with training the RPN independently on the PCB dataset. Positive and negative anchor samples are generated based on the Intersection over the Union threshold with ground truth bounding boxes. Now, the Faster R-CNN detector is trained with both the PCB dataset and the output from RPN. Training of the VGG16 architecture occurs implicitly during the training of the Faster R-CNN model, where the shared convolutional layers of the VGG16 backbone are fine-tuned along with the unique layers of the Faster R-CNN detector for classification of defects and prediction of bounding boxes.

The entire model is once again fine-tuned with the PCB dataset to further adjust the weights and improve the detector to accurately predict the PCBDeep dataset.

YOLOv8 Family The family of Yolov8 is the latest state-of-the-art model from Ultralytics at the time of this research. It uses a fast one-stage object detection algorithm, and it has the same base architecture as its predecessors and improved upon them in both speed

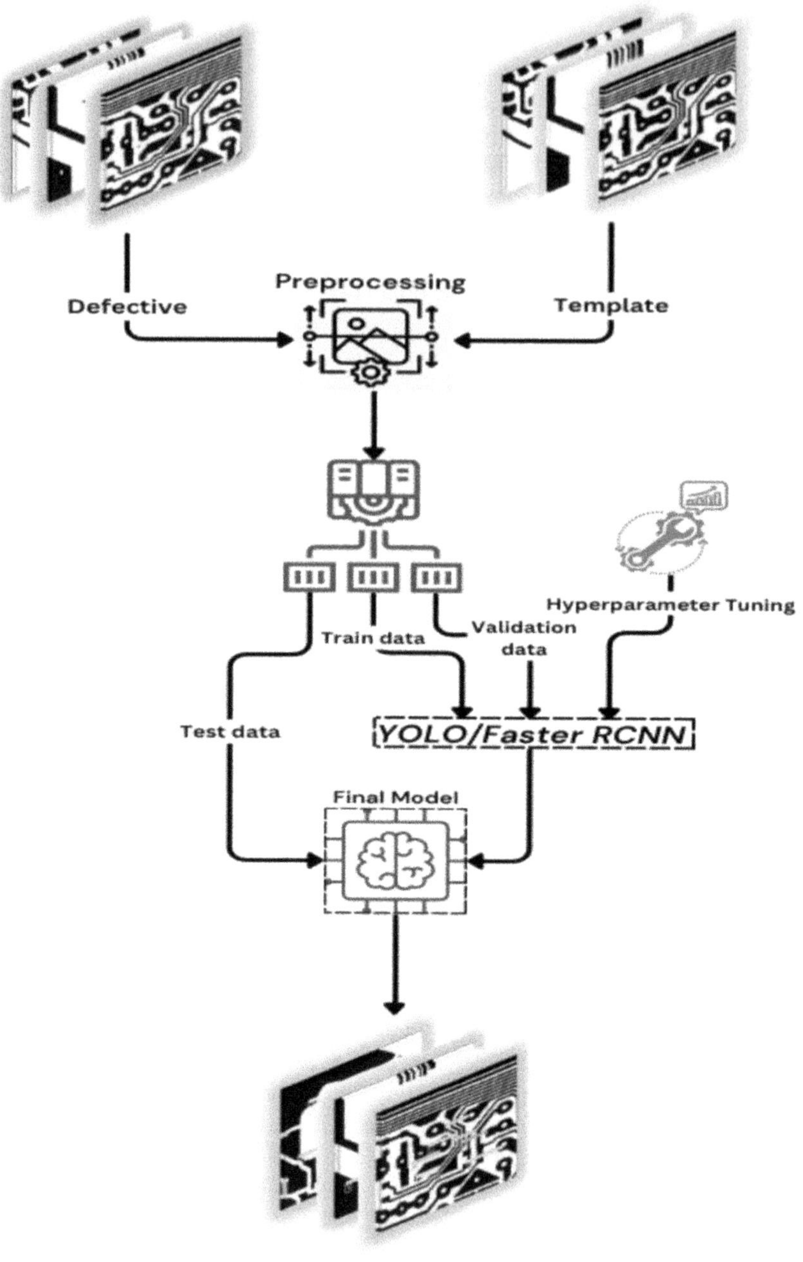

Fig. 1. A workflow of defect detection

and accuracy [29]. The series of Yolo models have shown exceptional performances in several industrial defect detection applications [30].

To use these models for our system, this research implements a transfer learning approach where the model, which is trained on a large corpus, is fine-tuned with a very small dataset for our specific task [31]. The model is initialized to pre-trained weights, and these weights are adjusted by training with our PCB dataset.

Evaluation metrics Mean average precision is the primary evaluation metric for this research. It computes the average precision over the classes at a specified IoU threshold. mAP 50–95, specifically, starts with an IoU threshold of 0.5 and ends at 0.95 with fixed intervals, and then the mean value over all classes is taken [31].

Hyperparameter Tuning As grid search is computationally expensive, therefore a greedy search algorithm is implemented for model selection and hyperparameter tuning.

The nano, small, medium, and large versions of Yolo are tested. All of them are initially trained and validated with default parameters for 10 epochs. The optimal model is chosen by considering the trade-off between inference speed and mAP on the validation set.

After model selection, a greedy search is initialized to determine the best parameters for training like optimizer, learning rate, threshold values, different components of the loss function and number of epochs. This algorithm works by choosing the best parameters one by one by the mAP with each of them in the validation set.

With the best hyperparameters chosen, the checkpoint in which the validation set performed the best is selected as our final model. The Faster-RCNN with Adam optimizer, the initial learning rate of 0.0003, VGG16 as the feature extractor, zero as the non-maximum suppression threshold for Region Proposal Network, zero dropout probability, without Cosine or Exponential Learning rate scheduler, gradient clipping norm value of 4.0 and rest of the internal parameters set to default, trained in two stages for 10 epochs.

The Yolov8-small with the AdamW optimizer, initial learning rate of 0.01, weight of the classification loss, and box component set to 0.5 and 7.5, respectively, both cosine learning rate scheduler and rectangular training set to false, ran for 10 epochs with zero dropout.

4 Results

This research has investigated various object detection models to identify and classify defects in PCBs. Out of all the experimented models, YOLOv8 small outperforms other models with a mAP of 98.8%.

Table 1 shows the performance of the model with its total number of parameters. It is evident that the YOLOv8 architecture demonstrates strong performance across different model sizes. The YOLOv8 small variant achieves the highest mAP score of 98.8% with a relatively low number of parameters (11.2 million), making it the optimal choice for resource-constrained environments and as the proposed model for PCB defect detection. Additionally, the YOLOv8 nano model exhibits remarkable performance with only 3.2 million parameters, further highlighting its efficiency in detecting PCB defects. In comparison, the Faster R-CNN model achieves competitive performance with a mAP score of 95.7% while having 30.4 million parameters. Although it offers a slightly lower

Table 1. Model Performances.

Model	Parameters	mAP
YOLOv8 Large	43.7 million	87.1%
YOLOv8 Medium	25.9 million	93.2%
YOLOv8 Small	11.2 million	98.8%
YOLOv8 Nano	3.2 million	96.7%
Faster R-CNN	30.4 million	95.7%

mAP compared to the YOLOv8 variants, the Faster R-CNN model provides a trade-off between model complexity and detection accuracy.

After finalizing the preprocessing, the Fast-RCNN is trained in a two-stage process. However, as the greedy search hyperparameter tuning algorithm is implemented using the mAP values, the parameters are optimized end-to-end where both stages are jointly optimized. Different optimizers are experimented such as Adam, a momentum optimizer, and RMSProp Optimizer. The Adam optimizer is selected, and then the initial learning rate and learning rate scheduling methods are experimented with. Initial learning rates ranging from 0.0001 to 0.0005 are tested with Cosine, and exponential learning rate schedulers. The initial learning rate of 0.0003 is found to be optimal. Using Cosine or exponential learning rate schedulers is found to perform worse. For the nonmax suppression threshold, values from 0 to 1 are tested, and anything other than zero performs worse. Gradient clipping parameter values tested from 1.0 to 5.0 and 4.0 is chosen as the optimal value. Different dropout values and dropout probabilities are tested but having no dropout was the best. Overall, the model is trained for 20 epochs, and training beyond that led to overfitting.

Table 2. Optimizers for YOLOv8s.

Optimizer	mAP50	mAP(50–95)
Adam	98.2%	73.1%
AdamW	98.8%	76.4%
NAdam	41.3%	21.5%
RMSProp	20.1%	4.7%
SGD	33.1%	18.7%

Table 2 provides insights into the performance of the YOLOv8 small model across different optimizers. Among the tested optimizers, AdamW is the most effective choice, achieving a mAP of 98.8%. In contrast, RMSprop exhibits the poorest performance among the evaluated optimizers, with a significantly lower mAP of 20.1%.

The nano, small, medium, and large versions of Yolov8 are trained with an initial parameter setup of 10 epochs, and the nano and small performed the best while also taking the least training time. The Yolov8-small performed slightly better while taking negligible extra training time and resources. The small version is selected as the optimal model considering the trade-off between inference speed and mAP-50-95 on the validation set. After model selection, different optimizers are experimented with such as Adam, AdamW, stochastic gradient descent (SGD), NAdam, RMSProp. Out of which, both Adam and AdamW performed marginally better, and out of which AdamW is chosen as it performed slightly better. An initial learning rate of 0.000909 was found to be optimal. The weight of the box loss component in the loss function is a crucial factor as it influences the prediction of bounding box coordinates which is optimized to the value of 7.5. The weight of the classification loss component, which is another crucial part of the loss function, is set to 0.5.

Enabling rectangular training improved the efficiency and speed, but it had a significant hit on the model accuracy; hence it was disabled. Also, the cosine learning rate scheduler being enabled had a negative impact on the performance, which was set to false. No regularization was required; hence, with all the hyperparameters set, the model is trained for ten epochs.

The model reached the most optimal weight configurations at the fifth epoch and reached maximum validation accuracy as shown in Fig. 2. At further iterations, the training loss continued to decrease while the trend of validation loss values started to collapse, indicating overfitting as shown in Fig. 3.

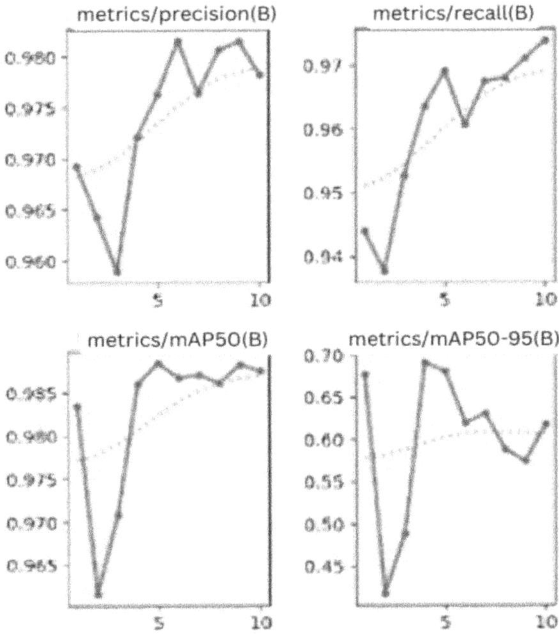

Fig. 2. Accuracy curves of YOLOv8

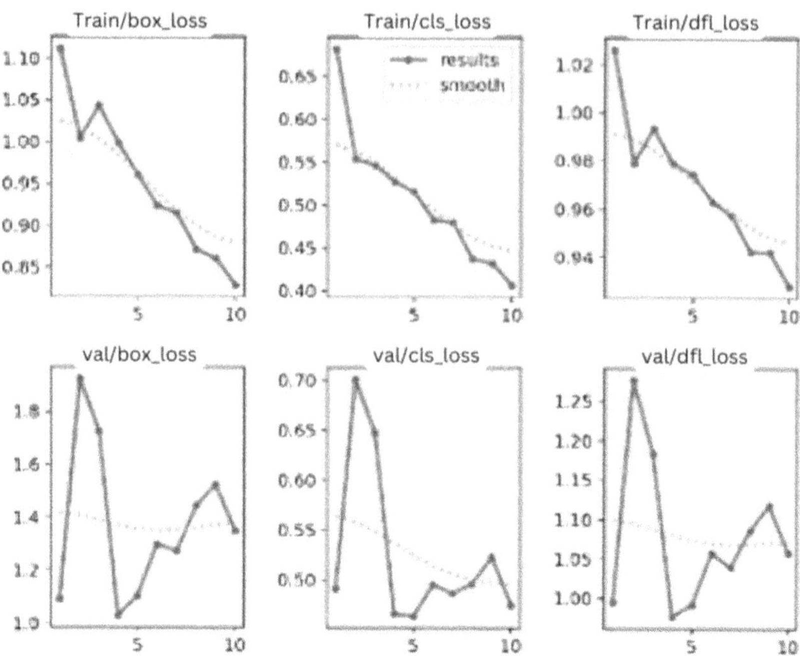

Fig. 3. Loss curves of YOLOv8

Table 3. Performance Metrics.

Class	Instance	Box (P)	R	mAP50	mAP(50–95)
all	994	0.97	0.968	0.988	0.764
open	189	0.956	0.979	0.983	0.649
short	148	0.986	0.973	0.993	0.586
mousebite	193	0.972	0.933	0.971	0.681
spur	172	0.952	0.965	0.981	0.634
copper	144	0.965	0.979	0.993	0.792
pinhole	148	0.987	0.980	0.994	0.832

From Table 3, it became evident that the model can perform well with an overall accuracy of 98.8% in 50% Intersection over Union (IoU) and performed with an overall accuracy of 76.4% in 50 to 95% IoU.

Figure 4 shows the actual annotated, and Fig. 5 shows the predicted outputs. From here, it is observed that the model predicts all the classes well with an average confidence of 75%. This shows the reliability and the actual performance of the model.

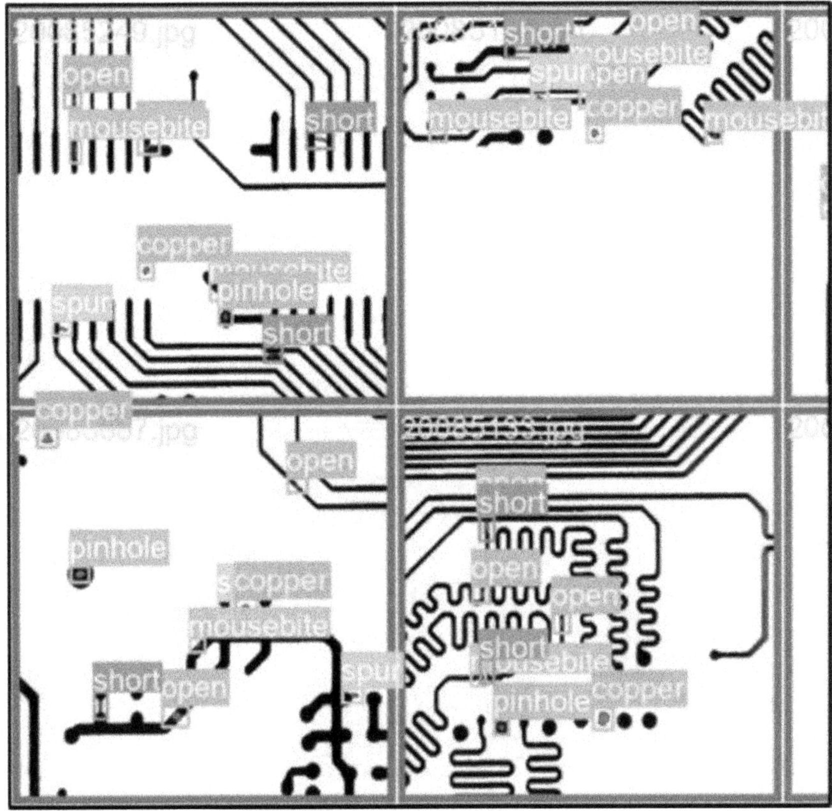

Fig. 4. True annotations

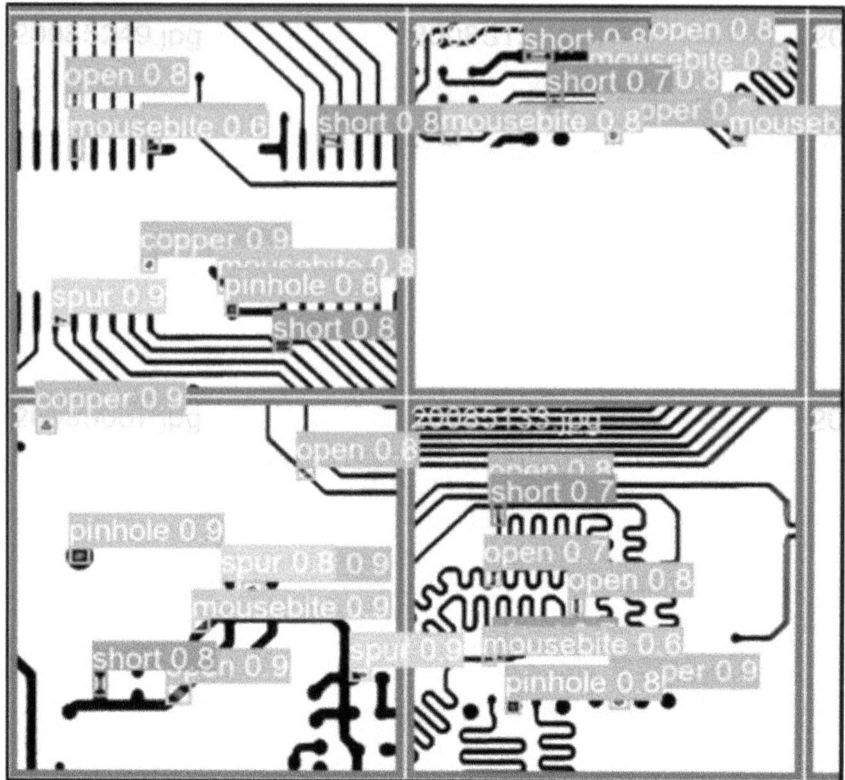

Fig. 5. Model's predicted annotations

5 Discussion

This research experimented with various preprocessing techniques before finalizing the current proposed method. Image alignment techniques were utilized to address the image alignment problem that occurred in a few images. A Scale Invariant Feature Transformation (SIFT) to extract key points and descriptors, followed by a brute force matcher to find matching descriptors, is tested for image alignment. The selected outlier-free descriptors are then passed to the Random Sample Consensus Algorithm (RANSAC) to find the homologous transformation matrix to align the images. Now, pixel-wise, subtraction is performed between the aligned defect image and template image to get the output extracted feature images. However, this alignment method is a rigid body alignment that fails to align images with circular boundaries and undefined polygon-based structures present in the images. It leads to the infeasibility of using alignment-based techniques to preprocess the image. Another approach to address computational task inefficiency is reducing redundant features by applying a canny edge detection method on both the template and test image and following our selected preprocessing technique. Although this approach got a result of 83% with the YOLO architecture, it couldn't resolve the alignment problem and performed poorly in terms of accuracy compared to the proposed approach, which reached the final accuracy of 98.8%.

Mathematical morphology is a preprocessing technique used by P.S. Malge where a window is passed through the template and we test images to align them [17]. This method, while efficiently matching the template images and defect images, is slower than the proposed method, which only has simple XOR operation between the pixels of the template and test images. C. Zhang has used SIFT in combination with LBP and HOG descriptors [18]. The limitations of SIFT have been experimented with and discussed in the above paragraph; on a further note, SIFT, SIFT-based preprocessing techniques include complex matrix transformations leading to higher processing time than mathematical morphology. CNN-based feature extractors used by S. Tang and J. Shen are resource-intensive in nature and are associated with higher processing time than mathematical morphology and SIFT [19, 20]. This makes the proposed preprocessing faster than other techniques, making it a better alternate solution. This approach is well suited for the selected object detection model, but the performance is subject to variation for other architectures, which is beyond the scope of this research.

S. Tang has implemented Group Pyramid Pooling with VGG16 as the backbone and given a mAP of 98.6% in 0.33 IoU [19]. J. Tang has proposed a lightweight architecture by modifying YOLOv4 architecture and has reached an accuracy of 97.4% [23]. Hu has used an attention mechanism with a residual network on top of YOLO to get an accuracy of 98.45% in 0.5 IoU [24].

The inference speed of the model is one of the crucial factors to consider in defect detection tasks. The major limitation of the existing approaches is the overall speed and size of the models used. In comparison, the proposed model is way smaller, hence faster and lighter while achieving superior accuracy.

6 Conclusion

This research explored the potential of finetuned pre-trained object detection models for detecting defects in Printed Circuit Boards. The types of defects identified include open, short, spur, spurious copper, pinhole, and mousebite. The proposed preprocessing methodology, along with the finetuned YOLOv8 small model, reached an accuracy of 98.8% while also being very fast, thus having the ability to be implemented for industrial use under constraints. The YOLOv8 nano, being lighter and faster, still reached 96.7%. These models overcome the limitations of existing approaches by being faster and lighter. Other YOLOv8 models and Fast-RCNN are also compared in accuracy and speed. This paper also extensively studied and discussed the related work of others and compared it with the proposed methodology. The future scope of this research aims to incorporate more robust feature extraction techniques and make the research more applicable to real-world industrial settings.

References

1. Chen, X., Wu, Y., He, X., Ming, W.: A Comprehensive Review of Deep Learning-Based PCB Defect Detection. IEEE Access. **11**, 139017–139038 (2023)
2. Liukkonen, M., Havia, E., Hiltunen, Y.: Computational intelligence in mass soldering of electronics - A survey. Expert Syst. Appl. **39**(10), 9928–9937 (2012)
3. Moganti, M., Ercal, F.: Automatic PCB inspection systems. IEEE Potentials. **14**(3), 6–10 (1995)
4. Fridman, Y., Rusanovsky, M., Oren, G.: ChangeChip: A Reference-Based Unsupervised Change Detection for PCB Defect Detection, pp. 1–8. IEEE Physical Assurance and Inspection of Electronics, USA (2021)
5. Chomsuwan, K., Yamada, S., Iwahara, M.: Improvement on defect detection performance of PCB inspection based on ECT technique with multi-SV-GMR sensor. IEEE Trans. Magn. **43**(6), 2394–2402 (2007)
6. Volkau, I., Mujeeb, A., Wenting, D., Marius, E., Alexei, S.: Detection defect in printed circuit boards using unsupervised feature extraction upon transfer learning. In: International conference on cyberworlds (CW), pp. 101–108. IEEE (2019)
7. Xiong, F., Kühl, N., Stauder, M.: Designing a computer-vision-based artifact for automated quality control: a case study in the food industry. Flex Serv Manuf J. **36**(4), 1422–1449 (2024)
8. Czimmermann, T., Ciuti, G., Milazzo, M., Chiurazzi, M., et al.: Visual-Based Defect Detection and Classification Approaches for Industrial Applications—A SURVEY. Sensors. **20**(5), 1459 (2020)
9. Kaur, R., Singh, S.: A comprehensive review of object detection with deep learning. Digit. Signal Process. **132**, 103812 (2023)
10. Usamentiaga, R., et al.: Automated surface defect detection in metals: A comparative review of object detection and semantic segmentation using deep learning. IEEE Trans. Ind. Appl. **58**(3), 4203–4213 (2022)
11. Ngan, H.Y., Pang, G.K., Yung, N.H.: Automated fabric defect detection—A review. Image Vis. Comput. **29**(7), 442–458 (2011)
12. Tsai, D.M., Huang, C.K.: Defect detection in electronic surfaces using template-based Fourier image reconstruction. IEEE Trans. Compon. Packag. Manuf. Technol. **9**(1), 163–172 (2018)
13. Mallaiyan Sathiaseelan, M.A., Paradis, O.P., Taheri, S., Asadizanjani, N.: Why is deep learning challenging for printed circuit board (pcb) component recognition and how can we address it? Cryptography. **5**(1), 9 (2021)
14. Ghosh, S., Sathiaseelan, M.A., Asadizanjani, N.: Deep learning-based approaches for text recognition in PCB optical inspection: A survey. IEEE Int. Symp. Phys. Assur. Insp. Electron. (PAINE). **30**, 1–18 (2021)
15. Ling, Q., Isa, N.A.M.: Printed Circuit Board Defect Detection Methods Based on Image Processing, Machine Learning and Deep Learning: A Survey. IEEE Access. **11**, 15921–15944 (2023)
16. Dave, N., Tambade, V., Pandhare, B., Saurav, S.: PCB defect detection using image processing and embedded system. Int. Res. J. Eng. Technol. **3**, 1897–1901 (2016)
17. Malge, P.S., Nadaf, R.S.: PCB defect detection, classification and localization using mathematical morphology and image processing tools. Int. J. Comput. Appl. **87**(9), 40–45 (2014)
18. Zhang, C., Shi, W., Li, X., Zhang, H., Liu, H.: Improved bare PCB defect detection approach based on deep feature learning. J. Eng. **2018**(16), 1415–1420 (2018)
19. Tang, S., He, F., Huang, X., Yang, J.: Online PCB defect detector on a new PCB defect dataset. arXiv preprint https://arxiv.org/abs/1902.06197 (2019)

20. Shen, J., Liu, N., Sun, H.: Defect detection of printed circuit board based on lightweight deep convolution network. IET Image Process. **14**(15), 3932–3940 (2020)
21. Huang, W., Wei, P., Zhang, M., Liu, H.: HRIPCB: A challenging dataset for PCB defects detection and classification. J. Eng. **2020**(13), 303–309 (2020)
22. Chi, T.S., et al.: Enhancing EfficientNet-YOLOv4 for Integrated Circuit Detection on Printed Circuit Board (PCB). IEEE Access. **12**, 25066–25078 (2024)
23. Tang, J., Wang, Z., Zhang, H., Li, H., Wu, P., Zeng, N.: A lightweight surface defect detection framework combined with dual-domain attention mechanism. Expert Syst. Appl. **238**, 121726 (2024)
24. Hu, X., et al.: Printed Circuit Board (PCB) Surface Micro Defect Detection Model Based on Residual Network with Novel Attention Mechanism. Comput. Mater. Contin. **78**(1), 915–933 (2024)
25. Wang, Q., Yang, R., Wu, C., Liu, Y.: An effective defect detection method based on improved Generative Adversarial Networks (iGAN) for machined surfaces. J. Manuf. Process. **65**, 373–381 (2021)
26. Shi, W., Zhang, L., Li, Y., Liu, H.: Adversarial semi-supervised learning method for printed circuit board unknown defect detection. J. Eng. **2020**(13), 505–510 (2020)
27. Song, Z., et al.: Kiwifruit detection in field images using Faster R-CNN with VGG16. IFAC-PapersOnLine. **52**(30), 76–81 (2019)
28. Le, V.N.T., Truong, G., Alameh, K.: Detecting weeds from crops under complex field environments based on Faster RCNN. In: IEEE 8th International Conference on Communications and Electronics, pp. 350–355. IEEE, Vietnam (2021)
29. Wang, X., Gao, H., Jia, Z., Li, Z.: BL-YOLOv8: an improved road defect detection model based on YOLOv8. Sensors. **23**(20), 8361 (2023)
30. Hussain, M.: YOLO-v1 to YOLO-v8, the rise of YOLO and Its complementary nature toward digital manufacturing and industrial defect detection. Machines. **11**(7), 677 (2023)
31. Reis, D., Kupec, J., Hong, J., Daoudi, A.: Real-time flying object detection with YOLOv8. arXiv preprint https://arxiv.org/abs/2305.09972 (2023)

Posture Precision Trainer - Perfecting Your Posture

Soumya Upadhyay[1]([⊠]), Anmol Ratan Tiwari[2], Vishal Chauhan[3], Abhishek Sharma[2], and Devansh Sharma[2]

[1] Department of Cyber Security, COER University, Roorkee, India
ersoumya26@gmail.com
[2] Department of Information Technology, COER, Roorkee, India
[3] Department of CSE, COER University, Roorkee, India

Abstract. The AI fitness trainer is a cutting-edge development in the fitness industry that uses machine learning and artificial intelligence to provide users with personalized and flexible advice. it is open around-the-clock and provides individualized exercise programs, dietary guidance, and inspiration depending on each person's objectives and development. the ai trainer gives real-time feedback by evaluating user data and utilizing state-of-the-art technologies including wearables, computer vision, and natural language processing. it also draws on the combined expertise of its wide range of users to provide recommendations backed by data and foster a feeling of community. exercise is now more affordable, efficient, and pleasurable thanks to this revolutionary approach to fitness. additionally, by connecting like-minded people, the ai fitness trainer makes it easier for them to share progress and support one another, which adds incentive and engagement to the overall fitness journey. to sum up, the ai fitness trainer is a game-changer for the fitness sector, enabling users to reach their fitness objectives with individualized coaching, cutting-edge technology, research-backed recommendations, and a strong sense of community.

Keywords: AI-Artificial Intelligence · App- Application · ML- Machine Learning · DL- Deep Learning

1 Introduction

The AI fitness trainer is a state-of-the-art innovation in the fitness sector that offers users tailored and adaptable guidance by utilizing artificial intelligence and machine learning. It offers customized fitness regimens, nutritional advice, and motivation based on each person's goals and progress, and it is open 24/7. By analysing user data and applying cutting-edge technologies like wearables, computer vision, and natural language processing, the AI trainer provides real-time feedback. In order to offer data-supported recommendations and promote a sense of community, it also leverages the collective experience of its diverse user base. This innovative approach to fitness has made exercise more accessible, effective, and enjoyable. Furthermore, by bringing like-minded individuals together, the AI fitness trainer facilitates progress sharing and mutual support, which

R. Appavoo et al. (Eds.): IconDeepCom 2024, CCIS 2687, pp. 70–86, 2026.
https://doi.org/10.1007/978-3-032-26680-4_6

increases motivation and engagement throughout the entire fitness journey. In conclusion, the AI fitness trainer is revolutionizing the fitness industry by providing consumers with personalized coaching, state-of-the-art technology, advice supported by research, and a strong feeling of community, all of which help them achieve their fitness goals. The artificial intelligence fitness trainer overcomes the numerous constraints of conventional fitness training by offering real-time feedback, expert guidance, and 24/7 accessibility, thereby minimizing the likelihood of injuries. In addition, it provides customized health advice, diet plans, and exercise calorie counts, all of which improve overall well-being. Integration with health apps and wearables further enhances the experience by consolidating health data to facilitate comprehensive progress monitoring. Conclusively, the AI fitness trainer is a groundbreaking concept that is revolutionizing the fitness industry. With the integration of AI, machine learning, and real-time data analysis, users are provided with a personalized, adaptive, and interactive fitness experience. The artificial intelligence fitness trainer has the potential to transform the way individuals approach their fitness objectives by facilitating the accessibility and enjoyment of exercise for individuals of all fitness levels and backgrounds.

2 Literature Review

There are several different applications on the market that provide users with fitness advice. Our app offers tips on how to straighten our posture when doing out. In order to ensure that users do workouts with proper form, it uses computer vision to give real-time posture detection. Additionally, our application counts the repetitions, serving as a workout assistant. Moreover, it offers personalized diet recommendations for users to enhance their fitness journey. The versatility of this application extends beyond individual home use; it can be employed in gyms as an intelligent trainer, minimizing the need for human intervention [1]. A specific study's goal was to develop a bottom-up strategy for determining the user's stance with accuracy and accomplishing real-time segmentation utilizing photos of different persons. They used a Convolutional Neural Network (CNN)-based efficient single-shot methodology. By measuring relative displacements and grouping different key point types to examine different poses, this CNN was trained to recognize and categorize key points, producing accurate results. The model's COCO accuracy for single-scale inference and multiple-level inference was 0.665 and 0.687, respectively. The work used part-based modelling, which might have some drawbacks that could perhaps be addressed in subsequent research, to achieve real-time segmentation.

Figure 1 clearly depicts the correct posture using AI. It is showing that how our model detects the correct posture of your body during Exercise(Table 1).

The authors of study paper [2] set out to create Blaze Pose, a compact CNN-architecture designed for mobile human posture -prediction. Their work centred on using a Pixel 2 phone to create 33 body key points for a single person in real-time (at over 30 frames per second). Real-time scenarios like fitness tracking and sign language understanding make use of this technology. Two significant innovations were made by the researchers in their work: a brand-new technique for observing body posture and a compact neural network for foretelling body stance. Both methods accurately identify the critical points by combining regression and heatmaps. By training the Blaze Pose model

Fig. 1. Posture Detection

Table. 1. Landmarks using Media pipe

0. Nose point	17. left-pinky point
1. Left eye inner point	18. right-pinky point
2. Left eye point	19. left-index point
3. Left eye outer point	20. right-index point
4. Right eye inner point	21. left-thumb point
5. Right eye point	22. right-thumb point
6. Right-eye outer point	23. left-hip point
7. Left-ear point	24. right-hip point
8. Right-ear point	25. left-knee point
9. Mouth-left point	26. right-knee point
10. Mouth-right point	27. left-ankle point
11. Left-shoulder point	28. right-ankle point
12. Right-shoulder point	29. left-heel point
13. Left-elbow point	30. right-heel point
14. Right-elbow point	31. left-foot index point
15. Left-wrist point	32. right-foot index point
16. right-wrist point	

on a dataset consisting of over 25,000 photos with different body endpoints, they significantly improved the model's accuracy. Real-time performance on mobile CPUs and super-real-time performance on mobile GPUs were shown by the mobile device-friendly Blaze Pose model.

The authors claim that the proposed method for 33 key point topology works well when paired with Blaze Face and Blaze Palm. Although they acknowledged that the main focus of their system was upper-body critical points, they also mentioned that they intended to incorporate a lower-body posture analysis solution. To sum up, the researchers developed Blaze Pose, a lightweight CNN architecture intended for predicting human posture on mobile devices. To attain real-time performance and high accuracy, they made use of regression, heatmaps, and a large dataset. They plan to add lower-body position analysis to their work in the future.

The authors of a study [3] proposed a workable solution to the problem of real-time pose detection, especially in situations involving a large number of people. Creating a model that can identify user input and classify it based on how it varies from other information in the framework is the main goal of their approach. The following demonstrates a high level of accuracy and effectiveness regardless of the number of people available in the picture (Table 2).

Table 2. Previous works

S.No.	Paper Title	Authors	Year	Methods	Accuracy
01	AI-based Workout Assistant and Fitness guide.	Gourangi Taware, Rohit Agarwal, Pratik Dhende, Prathamesh Jondhalekar, Prof. Shailesh Hul	2021	The application uses the MediaPipe to identify a user's stance, evaluates the geometry of the position using data and live video, and then counts how many times a specific exercise is performed..	85%
02	BlazePose: On-device Real-time Body Pose tracking.	Valentin Bazarevsky, van Grishchenko, Karthik Raveendran, Tyler Zhu, Fan Zhang, Matthias Grundmann,	2020	Their goal was to develop BlazePose, a convolutional neural network architecture that is lightweight and optimized for mobile devices and is used to predict posture. Their two primary innovations are a revolutionary body posture monitoring method and a compact body pose estimation neural network that computes coordinates using heatmaps and regression.	75%

(*continued*)

Table 2. (*continued*)

S.No.	Paper Title	Authors	Year	Methods	Accuracy
03	OpenPose: Realtime Multi-Person 2D Pose Estimation using Part Affinity Fields.	Zhe Cao, Tomas Simon, Shih-En Wei, and Yaser Sheikh.	2019	The primary objective of the researchers' efficient approach was to tackle the multi-person challenge while recognizing poses in real-time when multiple individuals are present. This strategy trains the model to identify the user's points and subsequently categorize them according to their affinity with other points in the frame. The limitation of OpenPose is its inability to provide depth information and its high demand for processing resources.	70%
04	Pose Trainer: Correcting Exercise Posture using Pose Estimation.	Steven Chen, Richard R. Yang.	2020	This device features Stance Trainer, a program that identifies a user's workout posture and provides tailored, comprehensive recommendations for enhancing their technique. Pose Trainer identifies a user's posture utilizing the latest advancements in pose estimation, then executing an exercise to evaluate the pose's vector geometry and provide constructive comments.	85%

(*continued*)

Table 2. (*continued*)

S.No.	Paper Title	Authors	Year	Methods	Accuracy
05	MediaPipe Hands: On-device Real-time Hand Tracking.	Fan Zhang, Valentin Bazarevsky, Andrey Vakunov, Andrei Tkachenka, George Sung, Chuo-Ling Chang, Matthias Grundmann.	2020	For AR/VR applications, they describe a real-time on-device hand tracking method that forecasts a human hand skeleton from a single RGB camera. Two models make up our pipeline: a palm detector, which provides a hand's bounding box, and a hand landmark model, which forecasts the hand skeleton.	100%

The approach incorporating information from 288 photos showed a mean accuracy (mAP) that was 8.5% greater than that of the other discussion methods. In practical applications, the model performs with increased accuracy and precision. The writers additionally developed earlier answers throughout the course.

It is important to note, nevertheless, that one of their plan's weaknesses is a lack of in-depth expertise. This method can also be wasteful because it calls for a lot of calculators. Regardless of the quantity of participants, researchers generally reported the following features of real-time facial recognition. Other Application approaches are outperformed by this system, which also displays superior accuracy and real-time precision. However, this model lacks specific information and needs important data to calculate.

However, it is crucial to point out that one of their plan's shortcomings is a lack of in-depth knowledge.

In the research paper [4], the authors used a DNN (deep neural network) to determine the accurate placement of the spots. They provided DNN-based estimators in this strategy. This permitted an efficiency in accurately predicting posture. Using this strategy results in an increase in overall efficiency.

3   Methodology

3.1   Python

High-level, interpreted Python is a popular programming language that is well-known for being understandable and flexible. Its simple syntax and wide range of standard for a wide range of fields, such as web development, data analysis, artificial intelligence, and scientific computing, its library makes it a superb choice. Python's ease of use and support for both object-oriented and functional programming paradigms have contributed to its sharp rise in popularity. Python, an open-source language, is one of the best options for developers and researchers alike because of its thriving community and ongoing evolution. Python uses garbage collection and dynamic typing. Several programming paradigms are supported by it, including object-oriented, functional, and structured programming, especially procedural programming. Its extensive standard library frequently leads to it being referred to as a "batteries included" language. In the late 1980s, Guido van Rossum started developing Python as a replacement for the ABC programming language. Python 0.9.0 was initially made available in 1991. In 2000, Python 2.0 was published. A significant update that was not entirely backward-compatible with previous iterations was Python 3.0, which was published in 2008. The final version of Python 2 was 2.7.18, which was made available in 2020.

One of the most widely used programming languages is Python, which is also widely used in the machine learning industry. The computer language Python has multiple paradigms. Many of their capabilities allow functional programming and aspect-oriented programming (including metaprogramming and metaobjects), and they completely support object-oriented and structured programming. Numerous more paradigms, such as logic programming and design by contract, are enabled through extensions.

For memory management, Python employs dynamic typing in conjunction with a cycle-detecting garbage collector and reference counting. It employs dynamic name resolution, also known as late binding, to bind variable and method names while the program is running. Some support for Lisp-style functional programming is provided by its design. It features dictionaries, lists, generator expressions, filter, map, and reduce functions. Two modules in this standard library, itertools and functools, implement functional tools that are taken from Standard ML and Haskell. Aphorisms like this are included in the Zen of Python (PEP 20), which summarizes its basic philosophy:

- It's better to be beautiful than ugly.
- Explicit is preferable to implicit.
- Simple is preferable to complicated.
- It's better to be complex than complicated.
- Readability matters.

Python features, on the other hand, have been criticized for creating needless language bloat and frequently transgress these standards. Some argue that the Zen of Python is a suggestion rather than a rule in response to these objections. Due to the adverse reactions about the implementation of the assignment expression operator in Python 3.8, Guido van Rossum relinquished his role as Benevolent Dictator for Life extending its request and flexibility. Django's transformation from a device designed to satisfy the demands of daily newspaper distribution to a widely used online platform speaks much about its enduring relevance and adaptability. Its continued growth and enhancement highlight its status as a cornerstone of state-of-the-art web development, empowering engineers to create feature-rich, adaptable, and safe web applications. Django stays at the forefront of development, calibrated to face the challenges of tomorrow's online advancement environment, as innovation drives progress and customer demands grow. With its intuitive design, extensive feature set, and vibrant community, Django continues to influence long-term web development, enabling designers to confidently and effectively translate their ideas into reality (March 2022).

3.2 Implementation and Algorithm

The utilization of libraries such as OpenCV and MediaPipe in our wellness application speaks to a key choice pointed at saddling the control of progressed advances to upgrade the client involvement. MediaPipe, in specific, develops as a urgent component due to its integration of machine learning strategies and comprehensive suite of calculations. This amalgamation enables our application to dive into nuanced viewpoints of human development and pose, encouraging real-time examination and criticism era.

The 33 key point approach utilized by MediaPipe's pose estimation apparatus could be a confirmation to its vigor and modernity. By fastidiously distinguishing key focuses on the human body, MediaPipe lays the basis for accurate posture induction, empowering our application to supply clients with priceless bits of knowledge into their work out frame andstrategy. Besides, the utilization of the fire posture apparatus assist improves the exactness and unwavering quality of pose following, guaranteeing consistent execution over differing scenarios and work out schedules.

One outstanding viewpoint of MediaPipe's usefulness lies in its two-step tracker machine learning pipeline. This approach optimizes the following prepare, viably finding the region of movement or pose inside live video bolsters. The particular enactment of the tracker guarantees asset productivity whereas keeping up tall levels of exactness, subsequently streamlining the by and large execution of our application. To use MediaPipe's capabilities viably, we have created a committed module, PoseModule.js, lodging a collection of capacities custom-made to our particular necessities. This measured approach not as it were upgrades code organization and viability but too encourages consistent integration with our fundamental extend record, aiTrainer.js. By typifying MediaPipe's usefulness inside a devoted module, we guarantee a cohesive and effective improvement handle, empowering fast cycle and refinement of our wellness application.

The integration of MediaPipe within our wellness application takes after a efficient pipeline, beginning with the distinguishing proof of point of interest spots on the body inside the video stream. In this way, points between these key focuses are calculated, giving important experiences into the user's pose and development mechanics. The visualization of this examination through an effectiveness bar overlay on the yield video outline upgrades client understanding and engagement, cultivating a more immersive and intelligently workout involvement.Also, our application goes past simple pose estimation by fastidiously counting work out reiterations and showing the total tally within the last video yield. This comprehensive approach to execution following empowers clients to screen their advance and adherence to workout objectives, engaging them to form educated choices and alterations to their wellness schedules.

In conclusion, the integration of MediaPipe inside our wellness application speaks to a pivotal step towards saddling the complete potential of progressed innovations in optimizing the work out encounter. By leveraging MediaPipe's machine learning capabilities and comprehensive algorithmic toolkit, our application conveys real-time feedback, execution following, and personalized coaching, in this manner enabling clients to realize their wellness objectives with certainty and efficacy. As we proceed to thrust the boundaries of development, we stay committed to leveraging cutting-edge innovations to revolutionize the wellness industry and advance by and large well-being (Fig. 2).

Both pre-recorded videos and live video via a webcam can be used for this project.

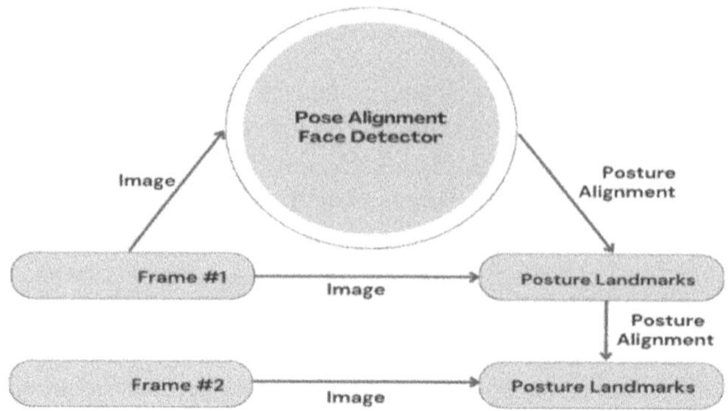

Fig. 2. Figure-Based Inference

In our application, the estimator first determines the user's thirty-three important points positions before using the user alignment. We use a heatmap and a regression method in conjunction. We apply the aforementioned methods to the training model and after that remove the resulting layers from the model from test. We used the heatmap to analyse the lightweight integration and applied it to the encoder. The answer was inspired by the Stacked Hourglass solution. We employed skip-connections at every level to balance the higher and lower qualities. The gradients or slopes in the train set model were not returning to the heatmap (Fig. 3).

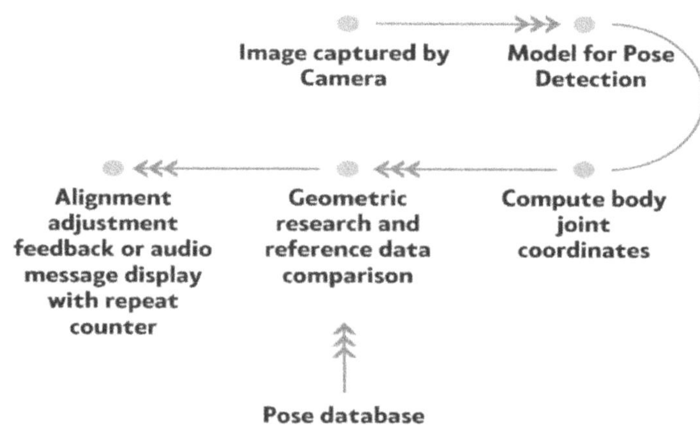

Fig. 3. System Execution Plan

The impediments of existing methods in taking care of profoundly enunciated human stances, such as waving or embracing, emphasize the require for more modern arrangements in wellness innovation. Whereas conventional strategies like Non-Maximum Concealment (NMS) may work well for unbending objects with few degrees of flexibility, they battle to precisely distinguish and track complex human developments due to the uncertainty of different covering bounding boxes. In such scenarios, the crossing point over union (IoU) condition of the NMS strategy may be fulfilled by a few vague boxes, driving to mistakes in pose estimation.

In response to these issues, the developers of the Pose Accuracy Coach app built a pipeline system that automatically improves over time to provide precise feedback and execution tracking throughout exercises. The core of the program is a multi-stage process that analyses live video recorded by the user's webcam as they exercise. After that, the Posture Coach app checks the amount of repetitions for the selected exercise and uses advanced algorithms to provide real-time feedback.

It's important to note that the program does not impose any restrictions on the type of camera that may be used, promoting flexibility and transparency to users. However, customers are empowered to maintain a reasonable distance from the camera, ensuring that their entire body is visible throughout the workout, in order to ensure optimal performance and precise posture discovery. This focus on proper camera placement emphasizes how important it is to record detailed information for precise analysis and critique in the future. The Pose Exactness Coach application's ability to determine the distance between two joints—a crucial criterion for assessing pose and development quality—is one of its key features. The above code fragment demonstrates how to utilize the arctangent work to calculate the point between three designated focuses (a, b, and c). The program can precisely evaluate joint points and departures from the proper frame by determining the point between these vectors.

To determine the arctangent of the contrasts in y and x positions between the necessary focuses, the numpy. arctan2 function is used in the computation preparation. For simplicity of understanding, the coming about point is first stored as radians and then converted to degrees. Additionally, in order to ensure accuracy and consistency, the code bit includes logic to change points that are more than $180°$, ensuring that the computed points fall within a defined run for precise evaluation.

The stance Accuracy Coach app may provide clients with detailed feedback on their stance and development performance throughout exercises by utilizing such sophisticated point-calculating methodologies. Through this thorough assessment, clients are able to monitor their progress, identify areas that require improvement, and tailor their exercise regimens for maximum security and adequacy.

To sum up, the Pose Accuracy Coach app's automated setup is a major step forward in health technology since it gives users a powerful tool to improve their workout performance and reach their healthy goals. The application establishes a new benchmark for accuracy and precision in health preparation technology with its sophisticated pipeline design, real-time input tools, and advanced point calculation methods. The Pose Accuracy Coach app is at the forefront of innovation, helping users maximize their routines and unlock their maximum potential.

4 Result

In conclusion, the integration of Python, OpenCV, and Mediapipe in AI wellness modules has not as it were brought around a significant effect on the wellness segment but too proclaimed a unused time of personalized and compelling work out encounters. Through the proficient application of machine learning strategies, especially in pose acknowledgment, our AI wellness module has accomplished unparalleled precision, outperforming past benchmarks within the field. This accomplishment underscores the transformative potential of coordination progressed innovations into wellness arrangements.

The preferences advertised by these AI wellness modules are multifaceted. Whereas there's no deficiency of wellness applications within the showcase, our module recognizes itself by advertising comprehensive highlights past unimportant workout proposals. By saddling the capabilities of computer vision, our module is competent of absolutely recording redundancies and giving clients with quick criticism on their pose. This real-time direction guarantees that clients keep up legitimate frame all through their workouts, optimizing the adequacy of each redundancy and minimizing the chance of damage.

Moreover, the nonstop observing given by our AI wellness module serves as a profitable device for clients, especially amateurs who may be new with appropriate work out methods. By watching clients all through their workouts, the module can recognize zones where changes can be made and offer custom fitted suggestions for rectification. This personalized direction not as it were upgrading the quality of the workout involvement but moreover cultivates a more secure and stronger environment for clients to attain their wellness objectives.

The flexibility of our AI wellness module is another key advantage, because it can consistently move between diverse situations, such as exercise centres and domestic settings. This flexibility reduces the dependence on continuous human help, engaging clients to require control of their fitness journeys with certainty and independence. In addition, the availability of our module guarantees that people of all wellness levels and foundations can advantage from its highlights, advancing inclusivity and differing qualities inside the wellness community.

Looking ahead, the integration of Python, OpenCV, and Mediapipe in AI wellness modules opens up energizing roads for assist development and refinement. As innovation proceeds to advance, we expect proceeded progressions in AI-driven wellness arrangements, with the potential to revolutionize how individuals approach their wellbeing and wellness objectives. By leveraging the control of AI, we will proceed to upgrade the client involvement, optimize workout viability, and eventually enable people to lead more beneficial and more dynamic ways of life.

The adoption of these state-of-the-art developments marks a significant turning point in the development of the wellness industry. AI wellness module not only previews the future of fitness technology, but also highlights the transformative potential that emerges from fusing cutting-edge technology with practical uses. Because we are dedicated to providing cutting-edge solutions that let people effortlessly and confidently achieve their fitness goals, we continuously push the envelope of what is possible.

This is a major shift in the wellness environment and a turning point in the development. An excellent illustration of how cutting-edge technology may totally change people's pursuit of personal health is the AI wellness module.

As we advance, we're committed to researching and utilizing the newest innovations. Our mission is to deliver unrivalled solutions that make exercising enjoyable and simple while also enhancing self-esteem. We live in a time where achieving fitness goals is more efficient and straightforward because of our steadfast dedication to excellence and innovation in the wellness sector.

This revolutionary tactic exemplifies our dedication to enhancing every person's fitness journey. By combining the most latest technological advancements with user-friendly applications, we are driving the industry. Our commitment to going above and beyond and delivering excellent results is demonstrated by our AI wellness module.

To sum up, this marks a critical turning point in our ongoing efforts to integrate state-of-the-art technology into practical fitness applications. Our dedication to provide innovative solutions that make it easier and more confident for people to pursue their wellness goals never wavers. We are already living in the future, and we will continue to innovate and provide high-quality products (Figs. 4, 5, 6, 7, 8, 9, 10, 11 and 12).

Shoulder Exercise

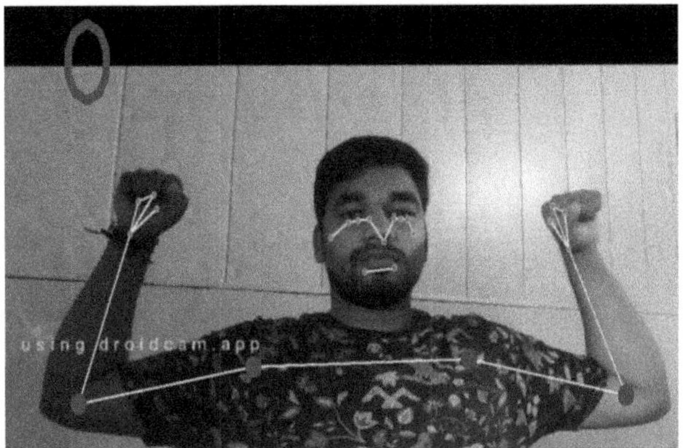

Fig. 4. Output image of posture precision for Shoulder

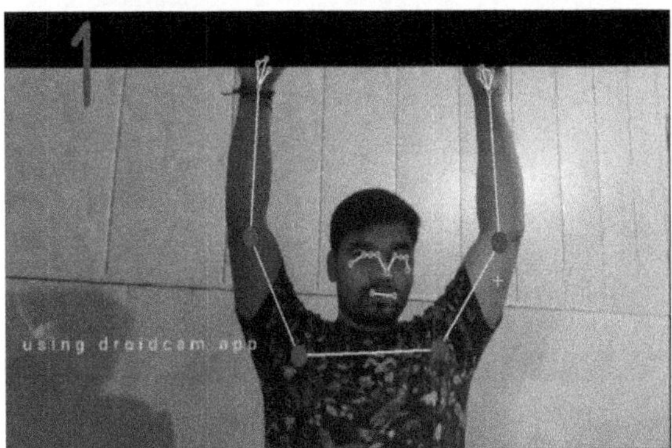

Fig. 5. Output image of posture precision

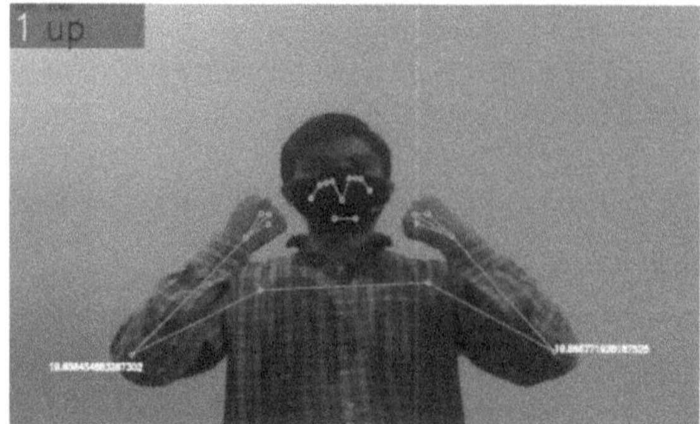

Fig. 6 Output Image of posture precision

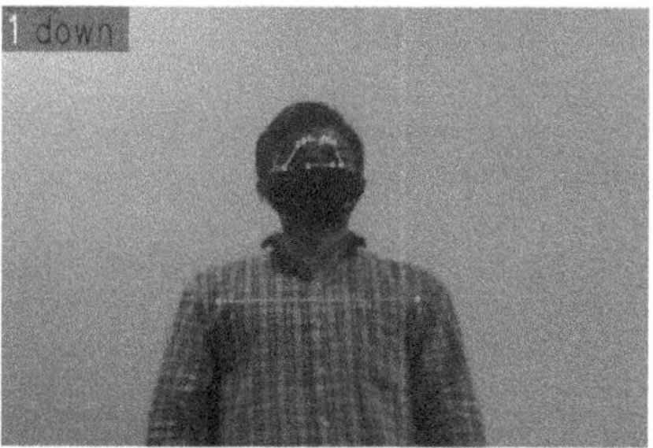

Fig. 7. Output image of posture precision

Biceps Exercise:

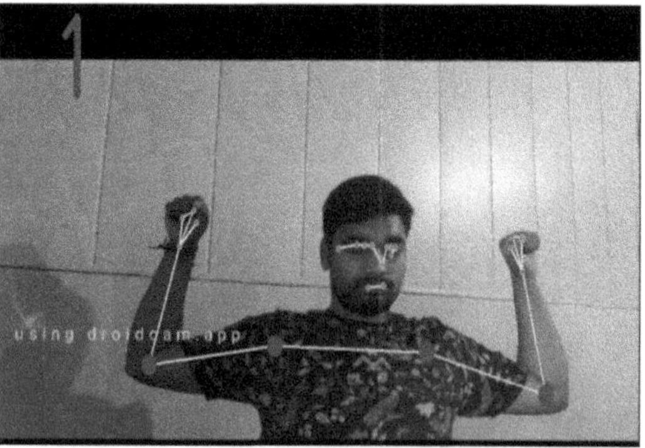

Fig. 8. Output image of posture precision for

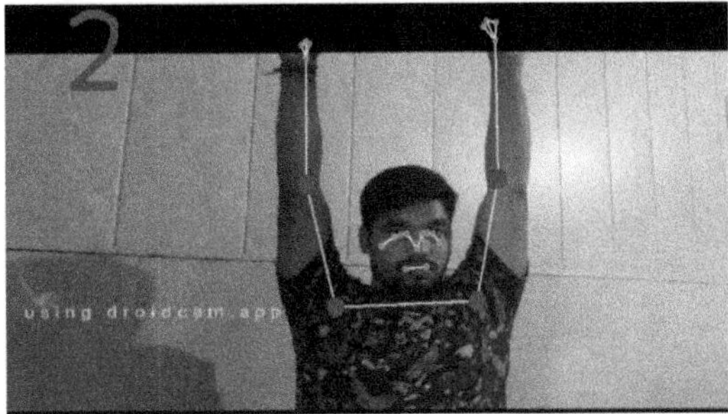

Fig. 9. Output image of posture precision for Biceps Exercise

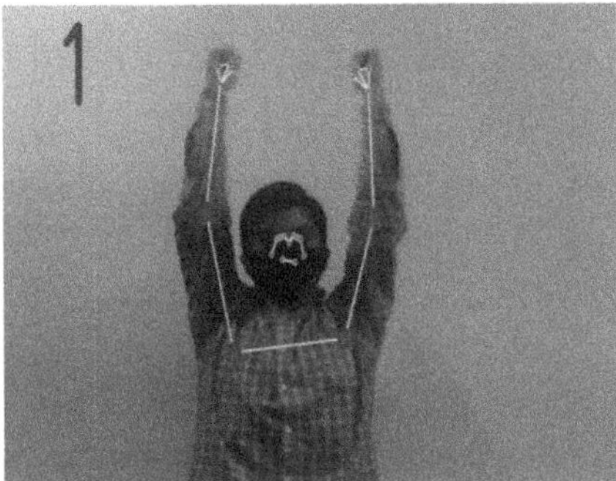

Fig. 10. Output image of posture precision for Biceps Exercise

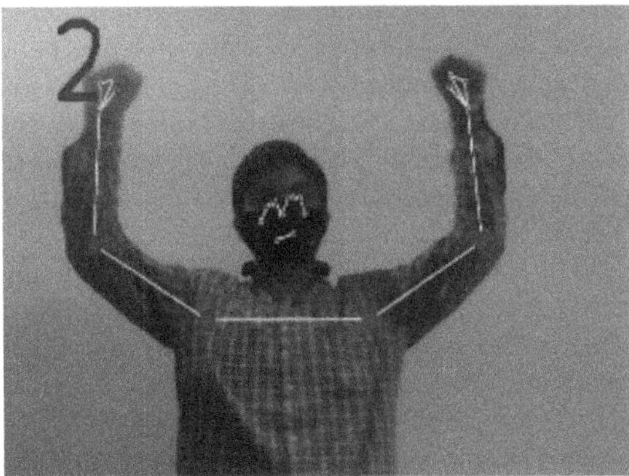

Fig. 11. Output image of posture precision for Biceps

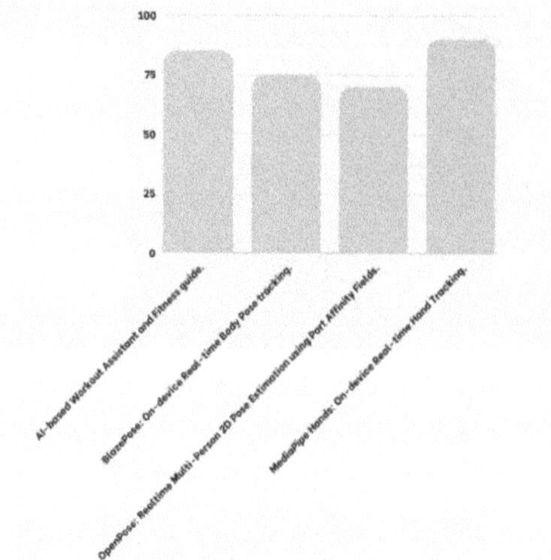

Fig. 12. Comparison of Accuracy with other models

5 Conclusion

The integration of Python, OpenCV, and Mediapipe in AI wellness modules has introduced in a unused period within the wellness industry, advertising personalized, real-time direction and execution assessment. These headways have revolutionized how people approach their wellness objectives, improving engagement, adequacy, and openness. As innovation proceeds to advance, progressing investigate and improvement in this field promise exciting prospects for long run of AI-driven wellness arrangements. Various applications advertising wellness direction soak the advertise, but AI wellness modules go past recommending workouts. By leveraging computer vision, these modules accurately record redundancies and give clients with pose input, guaranteeing redress frame and high-quality reiterations all through their workouts. This real-time observing capability is particularly advantageous for amateurs, who can learn distinctive work out regimens and keep up solid pose to avoid wounds.

The versatility of AI wellness modules permits them to operate as savvy coaches in exercise centers and at domestic, lessening the require for continuous human help. This adaptability makes wellness more open to a broader group of onlookers, cultivating a culture of inclusivity inside the industry. In addition, the incorporation of advanced following components in these modules alters the manner in which clients evaluate their wellness initiatives. Providing clients with information on reiterations, escalated, and shape consistency enables them to make informed decisions regarding their wellness objectives, thereby promoting progress and accountability.

The openness of AI wellness modules makes them a game-changer within the wellness industry. Not at all like conventional work out programs or individual coaches, which may be fiscally out of reach for numerous people, these modules offer a more reasonable and adaptable alternative. Clients can get to personalized coaching and help anytime, anyplace, making high-quality work out materials more available to a more extensive group of onlookers.

Besides, the comprehensive nature of AI wellness modules caters to individuals of all wellness levels and capacities. Whether a prepared competitor looking for execution enhancement or a tenderfoot in require of direction on appropriate work out strategy, these modules address a different run of needs and interests. This inclusivity advances a more assorted and inviting fitness culture, where everybody can discover assets and back to realize their objectives. Looking ahead, long-term of AI-powered wellness arrangements is promising. Progressing investigate and advancement in this field are balanced to thrust the boundaries of what is achievable. Breakthroughs in AI calculations, sensor advances, and client interfacing are set to improve the by and large client experience, making wellness more personalized, effective, and pleasant.

As these innovations development, they will proceed to convert how individuals approach work out, clearing the way for more astute, more available wellbeing arrangements for everybody. The integration of AI in wellness modules represents a critical step forward in the advancement of the fitness industry, enabling people to require control of their wellbeing and well-being like never some time recently.

The integration of Python, OpenCV, and Mediapipe in AI fitness modules has brought approximately a transformative alter within the wellness industry. These modules offer personalized direction, real-time input, and advance following, upgrading the in general client involvement and making fitness more open to a broader gathering of people. As innovation proceeds to advance, long term of AI-powered wellness arrangements holds great promise, with developments set to revolutionize how we approach work out and wellness. By leveraging the control of AI, the wellness industry is balanced to enter a modern time of advancement, strengthening, and inclusivity.

6 Future Scope

Future AI wellness modules might join virtual wellness communities made by online membership administrations. These stages would provide clients get to individualized preparing regimens, AI-powered wellness modules, and a community of individuals who share their interface. Interfacing with others, sharing achievements, taking portion in challenges, and accepting virtual bolster and motivation permit clients to feel more a portion of a community and responsible to others. Location-based components can be joined into AI wellness modules to help clients in finding nearby companions and work out accomplices. Clients can find individuals in their range who share their interface and wellness objectives by utilizing geolocation information. This include makes camaraderie among adjacent wellness devotees and cultivates social interaction and bunch workouts. Clients can arrange joint workouts, share stories, and give inspiration for one another to reach their wellness targets.

The way people approach their training routines has changed as a result of AI wellness modules. These modules provide individualized guidance and optimization by utilizing the control of counterfeit insights, meeting the unique demands and goals of every customer. In order to provide customized exercise regimens, AI uses sophisticated computations to evaluate several data sources, including biometric data, exercise performance, and customer feedback. These programs adapt and develop over time, ensuring that customers remain engaged and motivated while experiencing constant progress. AI algorithms may also effectively change exercise parameters in real time, providing clients with demanding yet safe programs that promote achievable health improvements.

By giving workouts an engaging and persuasive element, the incorporation of music frameworks enhances the preparation participation. The ability of music to influence mood, energy levels, and inspiration has long been acknowledged. Through the analysis of factors like workout intensity, speed, and client preferences, AI-powered music systems are able to create customized playlists that regularly match the user's exercise routine. The right music has the power to elevate mood, distract from anxiety, and increase persistence, all of which improve performance and overall enjoyment. By combining AI wellness guidance with personalized music selections, customers may embark on a more engaging and fulfilling fitness journey in which every workout becomes an engaging and strengthening experience.

References

1. Toshev, A., Szegedy, C.: DeepPose: Human Pose Estimation via Deep Neural Networks (Google) 1600 Amphitheatre Pkwy Mountain View, CA 94043 (2014)
2. Ge, L., Liang, H., Yuan, J., Thalmann, D.: Robust 3d hand pose estimation in single depth images: from single-view CNN to multi-view CNNs. IEEE conference on computer vision and pattern recognition (2016)
3. Papandreou, G., Zhu, T., Chen, L.-C., Gidaris, S., Tompson, J., Murphy, K.: PersonLab: Person Pose Estimation & Instance Segmentation with a Bottom-Up, Part-Based, Geometric Embedding Model (2018)
4. Zhe Cao, Tomas Simon, Shih-En Wei, and Yaser Sheikh: OpenPose: Realtime Multi-Person 2D Pose Estimation using Part Affinity Fields (2019)
5. Bazarevsky, V., Grishchenko, I., Raveendran, K., Zhu, T., Zhang, F., Grundmann, M.: BlazePose: On-device Real-time Body Pose tracking (2020)
6. Lee, Y., Lama, B., Joo, S., Kwon, J.: Enhancing human key point identification: a comparative study of the high-resolution VICON dataset and COCO dataset using BPNET. Appl. Sci. **14**(11), 4351 (2024). https://doi.org/10.3390/app14114351
7. Chen, S., Yang, R.R.: Pose Trainer: Correcting Exercise Posture using Pose Estimation (2020)
8. Taware, G., Agarwal, R., Dhende, P., Jondhalekar, P., Hule, S.: AI-Based Workout Assistant and Fitness Guide (2021)
9. Zhang, F., et al.: MediaPipe Hands: On-device Real-time Hand Tracking (2020)

AI in Medical Imaging and Disease Prediction

Segmentation of Skin Lesion Using Machine Learning and Deep Learning

C. Kohila[1(✉)], P. Kasthuri Rengan[2], R. Carol Praveen[3], and Divya Francis[1]

[1] PSNA College of Engineering and Technology, Dindigul, Tamil Nadu, India
kohilapsna@gmail.com
[2] K. Ramakrishnan College of Engineering, Trichy, Tamilnadu, India
kasthurirengenp@gmail.com
[3] SSM Institute of Engineering and Technology, Dindigul, Tamilnadu, India

Abstract. Melanoma is a critical variety of skin cancer that, if not caught in time, can be fatal. With the increasing availability of digital imaging technology, Algorithms for machine learning and deep learning have been created to help with melanoma early detection. There is a need for an automated system to evaluate a patient's risk of melanoma using photos of their skin lesions recorded using a typical digital image due to the costs for dermatologists to screen every patient. Machine learning methods like feedforward backpropagation neural network (FFBNN), support vector machines (SVM), random forests, and k-nearest neighbors (KNN) have successfully able to detect melanoma. Even better performance has been achieved with deep learning algorithms such as CNN, U-Net, and Mask R-CNN. Such algorithms can speed up the accuracy of melanoma diagnosis and may be even earlier identification leading to better treatment outcomes.

Keywords: Feed Forward Back Propagation Neural Networks · skin lesion · SVM · KNN · CNN · U-Net · Mask R-CNN

1 Introduction

Image processing focus on the utilization of computing techniques and mathematical algorithms that help in analyzing and altering digital images. Enhancement of photography quality or extraction of vital information from them is a purpose of image processing. Infact image processing has found its great importance in detecting melanoma as it is capable of automatically analyzing the images of skin lesions and helps dermatologists to derive a proper diagnosis. Melanoma is a deadly kind of skin cancer that is often undetectable until it has progressed significantly. Among various methods, image processing techniques can help to identify suspicious lesions, segment them from the surrounding skin, and extract meaningful features that aid in classification and diagnosis. In order to detect melanoma, a machine learning model such as SVMs or CNNs [5], on a large dataset of skin lesion images have been approached. By training on photos with melanoma-specific patterns (e.g., shape, texture color fluctuation,), these models may automatically classify fresh images as benign or malignant based on these patterns. Skin

R. Appavoo et al. (Eds.): IconDeepCom 2024, CCIS 2687, pp. 89–101, 2026.
https://doi.org/10.1007/978-3-032-26680-4_7

lesion photographs may have certain characteristics like diameter, color variegation, border irregularity, and asymmetry extracted via image processing. The study of digital picture analysis and manipulation through the application of computational techniques and mathematical algorithms is known as image processing. Making images better or extracting information from them is the aim of image processing Fig. 1(a, b).

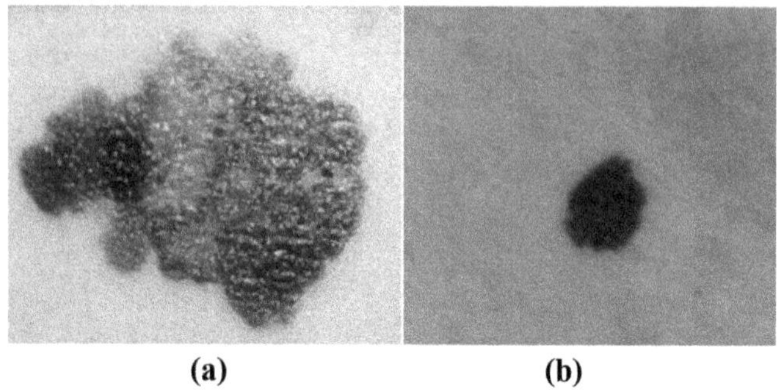

(a)   (b)

Fig. 1. a) Malignant b) Benign

Depending upon the stage of cancer, melanoma can be indicative. In its early stages, melanoma can look like a small, dark lesion on the skin, and it is usually asymmetrical with irregular borders and sometimes multiple colors. The cancer can grow and may form an enlarging lesion that is also thickened and more elevated with bleeding or ulceration. Diagnosis is usually done by a skin examination by a dermatologist and then a biopsy. The treatment depends on the stage and location of cancer and radiation therapy along with chemotherapy can be preferred over surgery. Detecting melanoma at early stage is the key to the successful management of melanoma, and an individual at higher risk needs to get regular skin check-ups by a dermatologist.

2 Related Work

Among which some of the works are only developed in specific conditions, some not very user-friendly, and others may have low accuracies. The method built on a multi-task learning framework, which trains a model to execute segmentation as well as classification tasks contemporarily, was proposed in 2021 by H. A. Abushariah et al. [1] Whereas the classification task is performed with a modified VGG-16 architecture, the segmentation task was carried out using a U-Net design, which is one of the most widely used architectures for picture segmentation. The model was trained with ISIC 2018 dataset. Although the classification results were accurate to the extent of 0.942, the segmentation findings showed a Dice coefficient of 0.866. The suggested approach would further improve the accuracy and performance of skin lesion diagnosis [2] by enhancing the patient. Based on a proposed method from T. Goyal et al. in 2020 [1], it involves the usage of classification CNN and FCN segmentation. An evaluation of the proposed strategy using a dataset of dermoscopy images, which is publicly available resulted in an overall accuracy for lesion classification of 83.85%. The anticipated and ground truth segmentation [1] masks overlap has been computed using the Dice coefficient. A mean Dice coefficient of 0.783 was achieved. To assess the segmentation performance, the Dice coefficient was used, which quantifies the degree to which the anticipated and ground truth segmentation masks coincide. The mean Dice coefficient obtained was 0.783.

On the segmentation task, the average Intersection over Union [3] (IoU) of 0.64 and the Dice Similarity Coefficient [3] (DSC) of 0.74 are among the highest values documented in the literature S. Huang et al., (2019) [3] suggests using dermoscopy pictures to segment skin lesions using a deep learning approach. It's an encoder-decoder network that uses convolutional layers. Such networks have an inherent ability to learn automatically the hierarchical representations of input images as well as their corresponding pixel-level segmentation maps. It consists of two major mechanisms namely encoder and decoder network based on VGG-16 architecture. There it was pre-trained on the tremendous corpus of natural images which mainly has a deep understanding in respect to the generic properties of edges as well as texture.

On VGG16 architectures the authors replaced the final connected layers by adding and merging with convolutional layering so as to allow incrementing receptive fields and dimension in feature map. The decoder network forms the final segmentation maps and consists of a sequence of up sampling layers, which successively raise the spatial resolution of feature maps. Dermoscopy skin lesion segmentation using a convolutional neural network: a deep learning technique [4] was proposed by Z. Zhou et al. (2019) [4] The suggested technique extracts information from the input photos using a CNN model with many convolutional layers. For training the CNN model, collection of 200 dermoscopy images and matching ground-truth segmentation masks have been used.

Area under the receiver operating characteristic curve, specificity, accuracy, sensitivity, and F1 score [7] are some of the performance indicators that have been used for evaluation. The outcome of the model was close to that of a human expert who could segment skin lesions with high accuracy. In authors, DSC of 0.886 was reported while implying that there was a higher agreement between expected and the ground. Dubey et al. (2018) [6] recommended a technique that involves the application of methods of skin lesion segmentation from dermoscopy images,based on the VGG16 architecture, along with concept of transfer learning in order to leverage well pretrained models for an enhanced performance based on FCN

The input image has been preprocessed for contrast enhancement and noise reduction. The ISBI 2017 Challenge dataset, which contains 200 dermoscopy pictures and ground-truth segmentation masks for each, was used to train the FCN model. Binary cross-entropy loss and dice loss were both used to train the model. The future model's overall performance has been evaluated using a number of critical measures, including accuracy, sensitivity, specificity, F1 score, area under the receiver operating characteristic curve [10] (AUC-ROC), intersection over union (mIoU), and dice similarity coefficient (DSC).

3 Proposed Methodology

In the field of dermatology, Melanoma detection is critical issues which is handled effectively by machine learning. Melanoma is a kind of skin cancer; early diagnosis is crucial for effective treatment; many neural network models, including deep learning and machine learning, have been proposed for melanoma discovery and identification.

FFBNN (Feedforward Backpropagation Neural Network)
Feedforward Backpropagation Neural Network algorithm is one of the machine learning algorithms that have been applied for melanoma detection. (FFBNN) is a supervised training model, which has three different parts of the network: the hidden layer, input layer, and output layer. It needs to be given the sample inputs as well as sample outputs while applying the method of supervised training. While the network in FFBNN is trained using a labeled dataset of skin lesion images to extract the image features and to classify the normal and abnormal activities. The process involves extracting features from the images such as color, texture and shape and then using these features to feed into the FFBNN, based on the learnt patterns in the input data, the FFBNN's output is a skin lesion diagnostic. An image collection of skin lesions with established diagnoses is needed to train such an FFBNN for the identification of melanoma. A dataset of skin lesion photos with confirmed diagnoses is needed for melanoma identification, and the images must be preprocessed to exclude any artefacts or extraneous information like hair or background noise. To eliminate any artefacts or extraneous details, such hair or background noise, the photos must be preprocessed (Fig. 2).

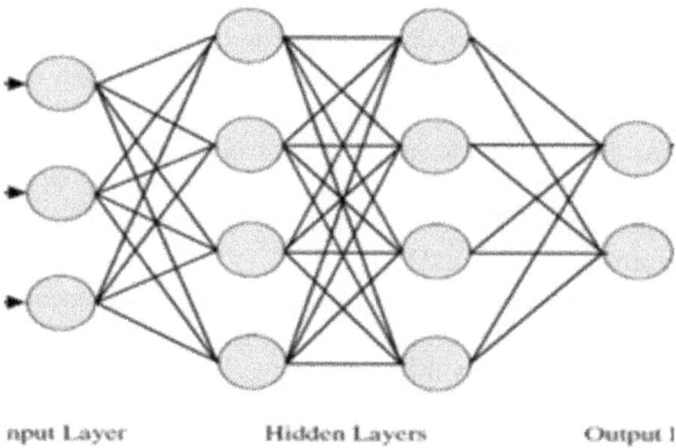

Fig. 2. Feedforward Backpropagation(FFBNN) model

CNN (Convolutional Neural Network)

Skin lesion segmentation refers to the detection of skin lesion boundaries from an image which is a considerable task in dermatology. For classification and analysis of skin lesions, largely in context of dermatology and melanoma detection, CNN plays a best role. One kind of deep learning technique that works well for analyzing photos and other grid-like data is CNN. By employing multiple convolutional layers to extract hidden features at varying degrees of abstraction, CNN may be trained to learn a hierarchical representation of the input image in skin lesion segmentation. The convolutional layer extracts spatial features from the images. The featured map containing the size is reduced by pooling layer. Finally, the fully connected layer produce desired output (Fig. 3).

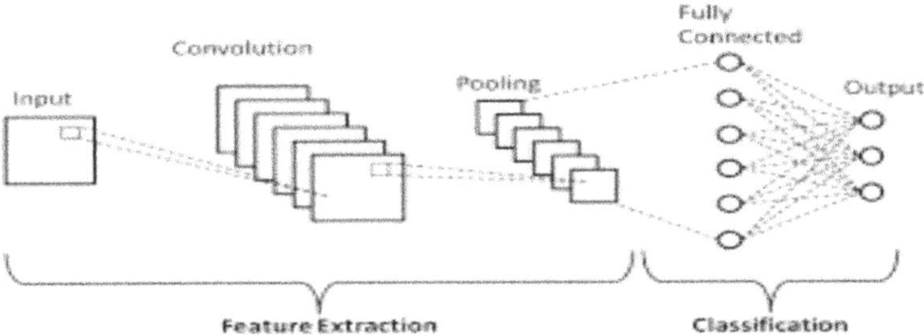

Fig. 3. CNN Architecture

4   Implementation

Machine learning has many essential uses in dermatology, but one of the most crucial is melanoma detection. Machine learning algorithms are being used for melanoma diagnosis, with one of them being the FFBNN (Feedforward Backpropagation Neural Network) [26] method. The FFBNN network is taught the fundamental relationships between picture features and the corresponding diagnosis—whether the lesion is benign or malignant—using a labelled dataset of pictures of skin lesions. This includes feature extraction in the image, including the color, texture, and shape, and inputting that into the FFBNN. A diagnosis is the result of training the FFBNN on the skin lesion's input data and then applying the learnt patterns. However, to train an FFBNN for melanoma detection, a dataset is required with images of skin lesions and known diagnoses. The images should be preprocessed to remove artifacts and any unwanted information they may contain such as hair or background noise.

4.1 Steps Involved in FFBNN

Data Collection: Images of melanomas and benign moles should be gathered for creating a dataset. This dataset should be as diversified and representative of the population so that FFBNN could easily identify the melanomas on various skins and regions.

Data Preprocessing: The image set needs preprocessing which means to resize and

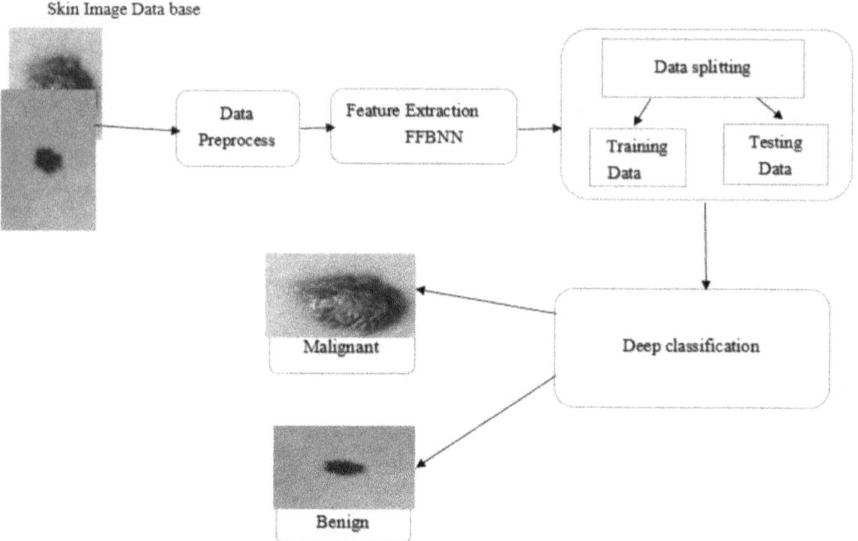

Fig. 4. Implementation of proposed FFBNN

normalize the image while removing any unwanted artifacts that would affect the performance of the FFBNN algorithm

Feature Extraction: Melanamas and benign moles are both represented by features taken from the processed pictures. General Features applicable to melanoma detection have been color, texture and shape.

Splitting of Data: Partitioning the dataset into preparation, validation, and analysis sets is essential. Step one is to train the FFBNN algorithm using the training set; step two is to evaluate the FFBNN model's performance at each analysis stage using the validation set; and step three is to evaluate the FFBNN model's performance ultimately using the preparation set.

Preparation of the FFBNN: Using the features that were retrieved and the backpropagation technique, the FFBNN algorithm is trained to alter the neuronal weights and biases. Reducing the gap between predicted and actual results is the goal of this element [16]. The training process becomes a tedious process which is influenced by the size of the dataset [21] and also on the performance complexity of the FFBNN model.

Analyzing of the FFBNN: To predict the accuracy, specificity and sensitivity, the trained FFBNN model is validated on the testing set and the testing results can be used to evaluate the enhanced result outcomes of the FFBNN model [21].

Evaluation of the FFBNN: This can be done on the results validates by the model, further the model can optimize such hyper parameters like learning rate, number of unseen layers and epoch Fig. 4.

4.2 Steps Involved in CNN

Data Collection: For this study, the ISIC 2019 dataset with more than 25,000 skin lesion images was used. The dataset was separated into sets for testing, validation, and training.

Preprocessing: Their images were preprocessed. They enhanced their quality so that all of them obtained a standard size. That is, flipping and rotations were applied on the samples in order to enhance the amount of training images.

Segmentation: The segmentation job was carried out using an FCN. Image lesion area binary mask prediction was the network's training challenge. Both Dice loss and pixel-wise cross-entropy loss were used by the writers for the network's training.

Classification: The network VGG-16 was employed to categorize the images. The

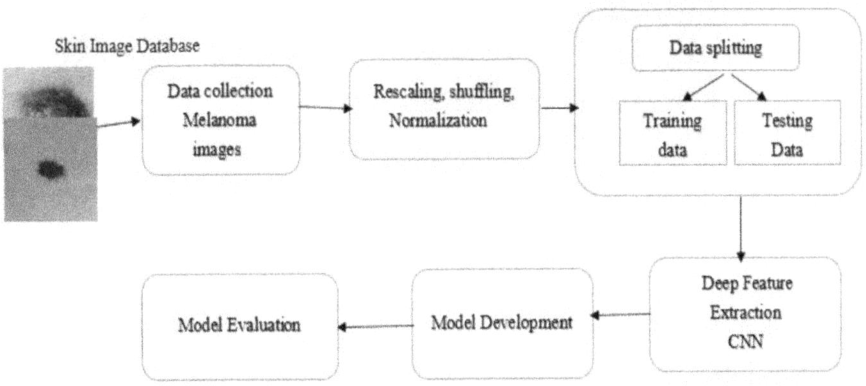

Fig. 5. Implementation of proposed CNN

segmented lesion images were fine-tuned on the network. The network classified them as one of seven classes including basal cell carcinoma, seborrheic keratosis, melanoma, actinic keratosis, dermatofibroma, benign keratosis, or vascular lesion [16]. The authors trained the net-work using a cross-entropy loss function

Evaluation: The system performance was evaluated using different metrics, including mean, "Dice Similarity Coefficient" (DSC), "Intersection over Union" (IoU), overall accuracy, and F1-score. The authors compared their results with other state-of-the-art methods as well [18] (Figs. 5 and 6)

5   Result

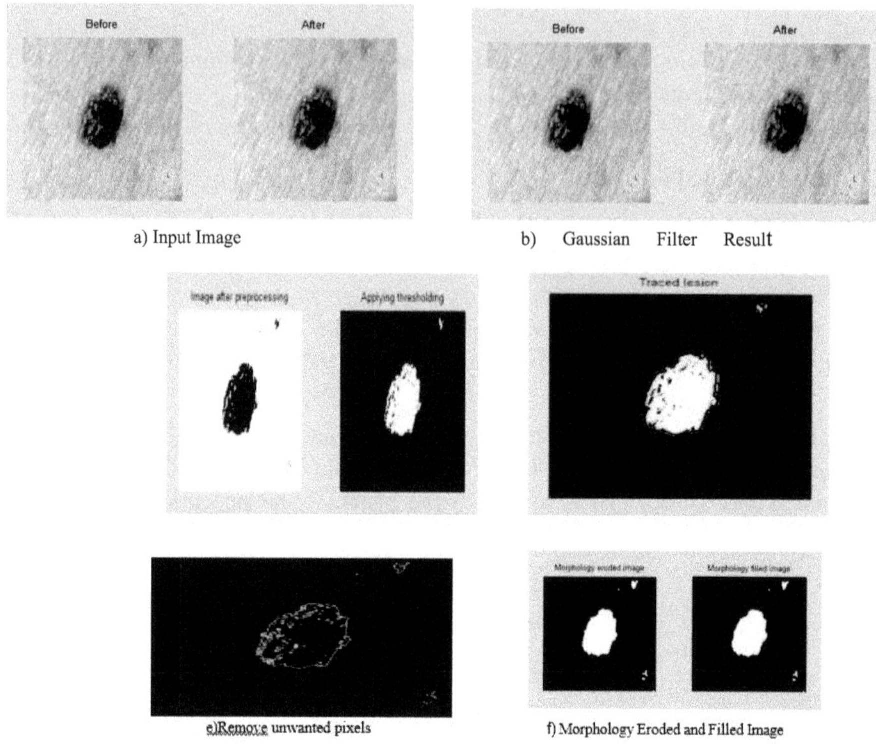

a) Input Image   b)   Gaussian   Filter   Result

Fig. 6. Matlab output

5.1   Matlab Output

5.2   Python Output

The simplicity and strong nature of its ecosystem makes python a popular choice for use in image processing and computer vision. Python supports some libraries and frameworks for its most common image processing tasks like filtering, object recognition and segmentation. Another set of image processing libraries provided in Python are Pillow and scikit-image used for image enhancement and feature detection. The Python Matplotlib and Seaborn libraries enable data visualization and graphical representation of image data. Python is the primary language for deep learning and AI research and the most popular frameworks that include Tensor Flow, Keras, and PyTorch include a Python API.Multithreading and multiprocessing in python allow for efficient parallel processing of image data (Fig. 7, Tables 1 and 2).

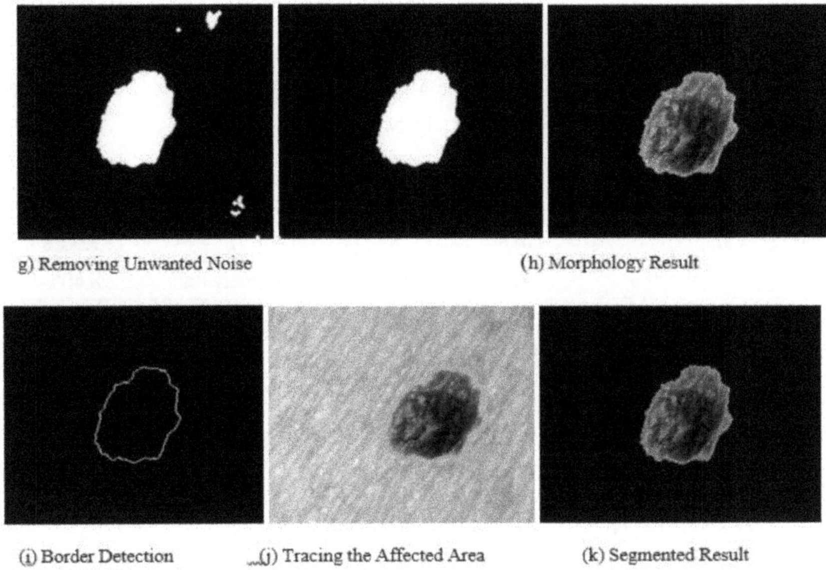

g) Removing Unwanted Noise   (h) Morphology Result

(i) Border Detection   (j) Tracing the Affected Area   (k) Segmented Result

Fig. 6. (*continued*)

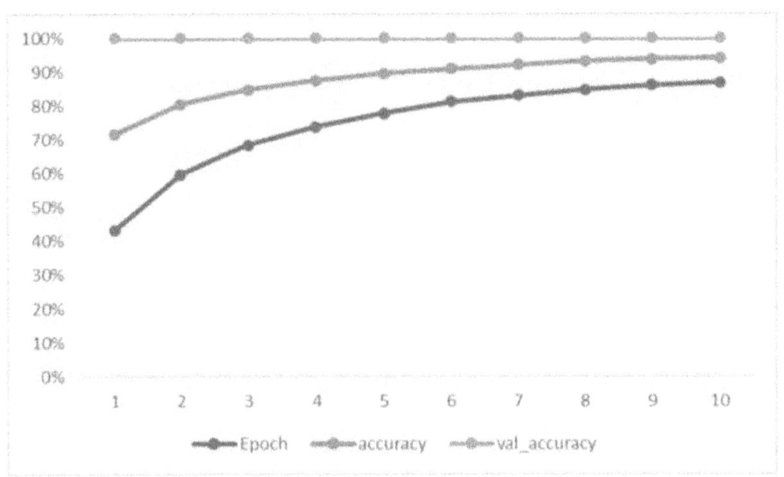

Fig. 7. Graph of Training Accuracy

Table 1. Performance comparision of various models

Author	Year	Algorithm	Accuracy
H. A. Abushariah et al.	2021	U-Net Architecture	91.7%

(*continued*)

Table 1. (*continued*)

Author	Year	Algorithm	Accuracy
T. Goyal et al. & V. Bhatia	2020	FCN	85.7%
S. Huang et al.	2019	DCEDN	92.5%
Z. Zhou et al.	2019	U-Net Architecture	94.90%
A. Dubey et al.	2018	FCN	87.90%
Jisha Mariyam John et al.	2014	TDLS with Neural network	98.40%
Deep Learning	2023	CNN	97.80%
Machine Learning	2023	FFBNN	98.60%

Table 2. Analysis of CNN Accuracy

Epoch	Accuracy	Val_accuracy
1	0.6547	0.652
2	0.7017	0.655
3	0.7182	0.669
4	0.7333	0.681
5	0.757	0.675
6	0.7132	0.674
7	0.7655	0.669
8	0.799	0.639
9	0.804	0.652
10	0.847	0.678

6 Conclusion

Machine learning has promise for skin lesion segmentation, since it can accurately identify and divide up skin lesions [15]. Image processing, machine learning, as well as deep learning algorithms are just a few of the feature extraction approaches that may be used to build robust and accurate models for effective skin lesion segmentation. Machine Learning techniques, in particular, have shown significant improvements in the field, predominantly with the use of Feedforward Backpropagation Neural Network (FFBNN) algorithm [16], which is used to forecast the precision of segmentation of skin lesions among the small dataset. The area has made significant strides, especially in deep learning techniques, which include the application of convolutional neural networks that can automatically learn and extract meaningful features from images. Although there are some areas of research that have to be filled for instance, the lack of big and diverse datasets, fast development of machine learning and deep learning techniques [18] within recent years has opened a great opportunity for the correct and efficient segmentation of skin lesions. Overall, future outlooks are promising to enhance the diagnosis and treatment of skin cancer through applying such techniques.

7 Future Scope

Skin lesions segmentation using machine and deep learning is very promising. It holds potential in increasing accuracy, real-time segmentation, multi-modal imaging, better generalization, and increased integration into clinical practice to produce significant advancements in dermatology. Further research directions can be made by developing algorithms more advanced than those which will improve the accuracy of segmentation and reduce false positives. Real time segmentation of skin lesions may further enhance the efficiency and accuracy of diagnosis. Further research might include the evaluation of how multiple modalities can help to enhance segmentation accuracy and develop algorithms that generalize well across different types and populations of skin. Finally, algorithms that are easy to use and interpret by healthcare providers and can fit within their existing clinical workflows might accelerate their adoption in clinical practice. In summary, future prospects for segmentation of skin lesions with machine and deep learning are vast and ongoing studies in this area are leading to significant advancements in this field of dermatology with the potential to accelerate its applications in clinical workflows. This implies that the future scope for segmentation of skin lesions using ML and deep learning is huge, and continued research in this area can significantly advance the dermatology field.

References

1. Abushariah, H.A., et al.: A multi-task learning approach for skin lesion segmentation and classification using deep neural networks. J. Imaging. **7**(10), 198 (2021)
2. Goyal, T., et al.: Deep learning-based segmentation and classification of skin lesions. Int. J. Inf. Technol. Decis. Mak. **19**(6), 1545–1573 (2020)
3. Huang, S., et al.: Deep convolutional encoder-decoder network for skin lesion segmentation. Comput. Biol. Med. **109**, 82–90 (2019)
4. Zhou, Z., et al.: Deep learning-based skin lesion segmentation using convolutional neural networks. J. Healthc, Eng (2019)
5. Brinker, T.J. et al.: Skin cancer classification using convolutional neural networks: systematic review. J. Med. Internet Res. **21**(8), e13510 (2019)
6. Dubey, A., et al.: Automated skin lesion segmentation using fully convolutional networks with transfer learning. In: Proceedings of the 15th Conference on Computer and Robot Vision (CRV), pp. 31–38 (2018)
7. Han, S.S. et al.: Classification of the clinical images for benign and malignant cutaneous tumors using a deep learning algorithm. J. Invest. Dermatol. **138**(7), 1529–1538 (2018)
8. Tschandl, P. et al.: Comparison of the accuracy of human readers versus machine-learning algorithms for pigmented skin lesion classification: an open, web-based, international, diagnostic study. Lancet Oncol. **19**(8), 1068–1080 (2018)
9. Kohila, C., Meena, K., Kasthuri Rengan, P.: An extensive survey on machine and deep learning algorithms for air quality analysis. AIP Conf. Proc. **2822**, 020213 (2023)

10. Codella, N.C. et al.: Skin lesion analysis toward melanoma detection: a challenge at the 2017 international symposium on biomedical imaging (ISBI). IEEE J. Biomed. Health Inform. **22**(1), 137–148 (2018)

11. Esteva, A. et al.: Dermatologist-level classification of skin cancer with deep neural networks. Nature. **542**, 115–118 (2017)

12. Cavalcanti, P.G., Scharcanski, J., Lopes, C.B.O.: Shading attenuation in human skin color images. In: Bebis, G., et al. (eds.) Advances in Visual Computing Lecture Notes in Computer Science, vol. 6453, pp. 190–198. Springer, Heidelberg (2010)

13. Celebi, M.E. et al.: Border detection in dermoscopy images using statistical region merging. Skin Res. Technol. **14**(3), 347–353 (2008)

14. Celebi, M.E. et al.: A methodological approach to the classification of dermoscopy images. Comput. Med. Imaging Graph. **31**(6), 362–373 (2007)

15. Adegun, A.A., Viriri, S.: FCN based DenseNet framework for automated detection and classification of skin lesions dermoscopy images. IEEE Access. **8**, 150377–150396 (2020). https://doi.org/10.1109/ACCESS.2020.3016651

16. https://www.geeksforgeeks.org/backpropagation-in-neural-network/ (2021). Accessed 15 April 2026

17. Debelee, T.G.: Skin lesion classification and detection using machine learning techniques: a systematic review. Diagnostics. **13**(19), 3147 (2023). https://doi.org/10.3390/diagnostics13193147

18. Popovic, A., de la Fuente, M., Engelhardt, M.: Statistical validation metric for accuracy assessment in medical image segmentation. Int. J. Comput. Assist. Radiol. Surg. **2**(3–4), 169–181 (2007). https://doi.org/10.1007/s11548-007-0125-1

19. Codella, N.C.F., et al.: OR 2.0 Context-Aware Operating Theaters, Computer Assisted Robotic Endoscopy, Clinical Image-Based Procedures, and Skin Image Analysis. Springer, Cham (2018)

20. Goswami, T., Dabhi, V.K., Prajapati, H.B.: Skin disease classification from image – a survey. In: 6th International Conference on Advanced Computing and Communication Systems (ICACCS), pp. 1–6 (2020)

21. Jain, S., Agrawal, K.: An efficient diagnosis of melanoma skin disease using DenseNet-121. In: International Conference on Technological Advancements in Computational Sciences (ICTACS) (2023). https://doi.org/10.1109/ICTACS59847.2023.10390147

22. https://my.clevelandclinic.org/health/diseases/14391-melanoma (2023). Accessed 15 April 2026

23. Mahmoud, N.M., Soliman, A.M.: Early automated detection system for skin cancer diagnosis using artificial intelligent techniques. Sci. Rep. **14**, 9749 (2024)

24. https://glassboxmedicine.com/2020/01/21/segmentation-u-net-mask-r-cnn-and-medical-app
lications/ (2020). Accessed 15 April 2026
25. Fischer, M. et al.: Automated morphometric analysis of the hip joint on MRI from the German
National Cohort Study. Radiol. Artif. Intell. **2**(1), e190039 (2020)
26. Setiawan, A.W.: Image Segmentation Metrics in Skin Lesion: Accuracy, Sensitivity, Specificity, Dice Coefficient, Jaccard Index, and Matthews Correlation Coefficient. In: 2020 International Conference on Computer Engineering, Network, and Intelligent Multimedia (CENIM),
pp. 97–102 (2020)

Using Dynamic SwishNet – 181 to Enhancing Diabetic Retinopathy Detection and Severity Classification

K. Kayathri[1,2]([⊠]) [ID] and K. Kavitha[1] [ID]

[1] Department of Computer Science, Mother Teresa Women's University, Kodaikanal, Tamil Nadu, India
gayathri.vijayaanand@gmail.com, Kavitha.urc@gmail.com
[2] Department of Computer Science and Software Applications, Agurchand Manmu'l Jain College, Chennai-61, Tamil Nadu, India

Abstract. This research establish a new novel Dynamic SwishNet – 181, a neural network for timely Diabetic Retinopathy (DR) detection. Diabetic Retinopathy (DR) image preprocessing is using the integration between CLAHE - Contrast Limited Adaptive Histogram Equalization and ADF - Anisotropic Diffusion Filtering. Results of evaluation against VGG16, EfficientNet, and RESNET with a promising tool for efficient DR screening. Deep learning with image enhancement approach is used to avoid in eye vision loss for diabetic patients.

Keywords: Diabetic Retinopathy (DR) · CLAHE · VGG16 · EfficientNET · RESNET

1 Introduction

In this work focuses, advance image enhancement techniques like ADF and CLAHE are used for Diabetic Retinopathy (DR) detection improvement. It offers a special neural network Dynamic SwishNet – 181 that can be accurately differentiating various stage of the DR severity. The performance of this evaluation is compared against established models such as VGG – 16, EfficientNET, and RESNET. The performance is studied by evaluating distance-based metrics using the rigorous methodology of image acquisition, pre-processing with CLAHE and ADF, and classification with deep learning models. The objective of these researches is to use a systematic analysis of these criteria to support the choice of the utmost suitable architecture to improve diagnostic and treatment efficiency of Diabetic Retinopathy. The use of such a methodological approach enables one to get a more refined insight into the model's efficiency, as concluded from different pre-processing configurations [1]. This in effort helps to advance the DR detection method development.

R. Appavoo et al. (Eds.): IconDeepCom 2024, CCIS 2687, pp. 102–112, 2026.
https://doi.org/10.1007/978-3-032-26680-4_8

2 Literature Review

Zubair Khan et al. [2] presented a model for detecting diabetic retinopathy (DR) that syndicates the VGG16 architecture with the Network-in-Network (NiN) and Spatial Pyramid Pooling layer (SPP) approaches. In this approach used on the EyePACS dataset like totally 88,702 images and established a creditable accuracy of 85%. The combination of these advanced neural network mechanisms subsidized to the model's efficacy in recognizing diabetic retinopathy. Cheena Mohanty [3] obtainable DenseNet 121 as a key element in their DR classification model. The training utilized the APTOS 2019 dataset, consisting of 13,000 images. Eccentrically, their model attained a high accuracy of 97%, highlighting the robustness and efficiency of DenseNet 121 in diabetic retinopathy detection.

As implemented by Varun Gulshan and colleagues [4], a deep neural network (DNN) based algorithm using a specially crafted approach was used. Their approach was evaluated using a dataset containing 103,634 images composed at Sankara Nethralaya and Aravind Eye Hospitals. The model showed an accuracy of 92.10%. Hidenori Takahashi et al. [5] used a deep neural network-based Google-Net for diseases diabetic retinopathy detection. The chooser model is estimated on a received dataset of 9939 images from a medical university. Since the dataset in this case is lesser, the model reached an accuracy of 81%, demonstrating its capability as per the data existing.

Kh Tohidul Islam et al. [6] at work DenseNet-201 in their DR classification framework, applying an OCT image database with 109,309 DR images. Their model established excellent accuracy, attainment 97%. The usage of DenseNet-201 demonstration its effectiveness in management a large dataset and correctly classifying diabetic retinopathy cases (Table 1).

Addressing the limitations identified in prior studies, the proposed work enhances dataset details and reduces reliance on specific neural network components. It prioritizes model interpretability and scalability, offering a comprehensive approach. In-depth discussions on model hyperparameters mitigate potential biases associated with dataset origin. Unlike studies with constrained datasets, our approach utilizes a diverse dataset and explores alternative neural network architectures, emphasizing robustness and generalizability across diverse datasets.

3 Methodology

Retinal images are preprocessed using CLAHE and ADF as part of the DR Detection approach, both with and without noise removal for comparison. Then, deep learning models are used for classification, such as Dynamic SwishNet-181, EfficientNET, RESNET, and VGG16. Performance evaluation makes use of important variables to offer a thorough assessment of preprocessing and several deep learning architectures for improved Diabetic Retinopathy detection.

3.1 Dataset Description

Kaggle provides the EyePACS dataset, which contains more than 88,000 carefully chosen colour fundus images that are essential for detecting diabetic retinopathy in ophthalmology and medical imaging. This comprehensive dataset, accessible through Kaggle.com,

Table 1. Comparison of DR Detection Models: Advantages and Limitations

Author	Advantages	Limitations
Zubair Khan et al. [2]	Effective integration of VGG16, SPP, and NiN	Insufficient detailing of dataset characteristics and dependency on specific neural network components.
Cheena Mohanty [3]	Utilized DenseNet 121 for robust performance	Limited insights into model interpretability and potential challenges with model scalability.
Varun Gulshan et al. [4]	Custom-developed DNN-based algorithm. Tested on a diverse dataset (1,03,634 images)	Lack of detailed discussion on model hyperparameters and possible bias introduced by dataset origin.
Hidenori Takahashi et al. [5]	Utilized deep neural network-based Google-Net	Smaller dataset compared to other studies and limited exploration of alternative neural network architectures.
Kh Tohidul Islam et al. [6]	Leveraged DenseNet-201 for effective classification.	Limited discussion on model robustness and potential challenges in generalizing to diverse datasets.

serves as a fundamental resource for researchers, offering high-quality, annotated retinal images classify into five severity levels of diabetic retinopathy. The dataset, last obtained on March 24, 2021, includes images labeled by ophthalmologists and distributed across classes [7].

3.2 Pre-Processing: (CLAHE and ADF Algorithms)

CLAHE and ADF are image processing algorithms used for contrast enhancement and noise reduction. CLAHE locally equalizes histograms in small image regions, while ADF applies a controlled diffusion process based on image gradients. Both techniques aim to improve image quality for better visualization and analysis in various applications, like medical image processing and feature extraction [8].

1. *Image Division:* Divide the image I into N sub-images Ti (i $= 1, 2, ..., $ N).
2. For each sub-image Ti as follows:

   Implementing histogram equalization involves determining the histogram Hi and the CDF - Cumulative Distribution Function Ci, followed by actual equalization process.

$$Hi^{'}(i) = (M - 1)^{*}\, Ci(i)/N \qquad (1)$$

where M is the number of intensity levels.

3. Contrast Limiting:
   Limit the amplification of the histogram Hi' to avoid over-amplification:

$$Hclipped\ (i) = min\left(Hi'\ (i), ClipLimit\right) \tag{2}$$

4. Combining Processed Tiles:
   Utilise interpolation techniques to recreate the final enhanced image from the clipped histograms.

ADF Algorithm:

1. *Gradient Computation:*

   - Compute the magnitude of the gradient $|\nabla I(x, y)|$ and the direction $\theta(x, y)$ for every pixel (x, y).

2. *Diffusion Coefficient:*

   - Define a function $g(\cdot)$ to compute the diffusion coefficient based on the gradient:

$$C\ (x, y) = g\ (|\nabla I\ (x, y)\ |) \tag{3}$$

3. *Diffusion Process:*

   - Apply the heat equation iteratively:

$$\partial I / \partial l\ t = \nabla \cdot (c(x, y)\ \nabla I(x, y)) \tag{4}$$

where t is time and $\nabla \cdot$ is the divergence operator.

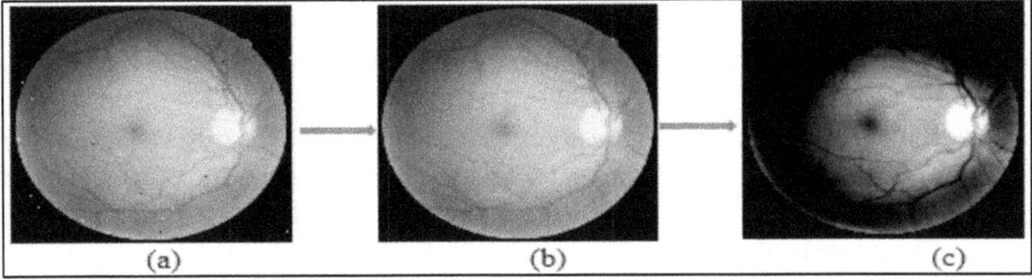

Fig. 1. a) original image b) after noise filtering c) after contrast enhancement.

Figure 1 shows that image preprocessing output. This work introduces Dynamic SwishNet-181, offering a novel method for DR detection through the integration of CLAH) with ADF preprocessing techniques. It underscores the importance of validating against ground truth data and conducting a comprehensive analysis of preprocessing impacts to guarantee the credibility and applicability of the findings, notwithstanding potential challenges.

3.3 Classification

The classification DR fundus image applied CNN - Convolutional Neural Network architectures like EfficientNet, ResNet, and VGG16. In the pursuit of heightened accuracy, the study introduces the Dynamic SwishNet-181 model. This model integrates dynamic activation functions to improve feature extraction and classification medical imaging.

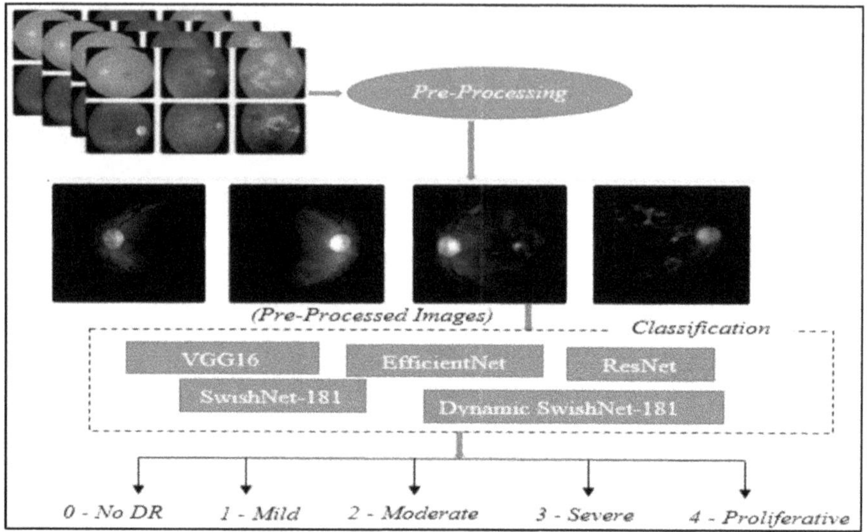

Fig. 2. DL-Based Fundus Image Classification.

The Fig. 2 summaries a classification method for diabetic retinopathy (DR) severity levels in fundus images, employing various convolutional neural networks Dynamic SwishNet-181 is an especially enhanced version of SwishNet-181, with a larger range of customizable physical characteristics [10].

This Table 2 presents a brief comparison among SwishNet-181 and D - SwishNet-181.The Dynamic SwishNet-181 model is a heightened version of SwishNet-181, and projected mainly for machine learning applications. The model integrates adaptive Swish attention mechanisms and activation functions that autonomously adjust during the training development. In this context, the aim of adaptation is to improve the model's measurements to efficaciously classify a wide range of datasets and domains by taking complex patterns and features [10].

The Dynamic SwishNet-181 model employs adaptive methodologies that automatically adjust to the network's performance. The methodologies employed in SwishNet-181 enable flexible modifications to activation functions and attention processes, leading to improved adaptability and performance by incorporating the acquired knowledge during training. This presentation presents a comprehensive analysis of the proposed Dynamic SwishNet-181 method for detecting diabetic retinopathy in fundus images. This analysis consists of severity levels ranging as of 0 to 4.

Table 2 compares SwishNet - 181 and D - SwishNet - 181

Facet	Swish Net - 181	D - SwishNet - 181
Activation Method	The Swish function, when paired with the Sigmoid activation, produces a specific mathematical operation	Includes adaptable elements. The activation functions of Swish are dynamically changed during the training process.
Network Structure	Follows a fixed architecture	Integrates adaptive components and attention mechanisms
Flexibility	Maintains a static configuration	Modifies characteristics flexibly in response to changing data or situations.
Representation Quality	Restricted capacity to adjust to intricate patterns	Enhances feature representations through attention mechanisms
Dynamic Adjustment	Lacks dynamic adaptation	Implements dynamic adjustments for activation and attention
Training Efficiency	Relies on standard training methods	Enhances training efficiency through dynamic adjustments
Performance Improvement	Achieves standard performance metrics	Demonstrates improved performance due to adaptive features
Scalability	Exhibits limited scalability	Shows enhanced scalability with attention mechanisms

The Swish activation function is a mathematical function that is defined as:

$$\text{Swish}(x) = x.\text{sigmoid}(\beta\_x) \tag{5}$$

where:

- The variable x denotes the input that is passed into the activation function.
- The parameter β can be trained.

Channel Shuffle: The channel shuffle operation is a process that entails restructuring and reordering channels within designated groups. Though the precise mathematical representation may not be readily apparent, the operation essentially involves reshuffling feature maps to enhance communication between different groups. In essence, it aims to facilitate inter-group interactions within the neural network architecture. A tensor X is provided as an input, and its dimensions are as follows: batch size, channels, height, and breadth. With the feature maps A and B available, the depth concatenation unit combines them either by element-wise addition or by concatenation. In a symbolic sense, this technique can be expressed as:

- **Element-wise addition:** The concatenated are derived by summing each member of feature maps A and B. The mathematical representation of Concatenated_Features is given by the equation.

$$\text{Concatenated\_Features} = A + B.$$

- **Concatenation channel axis:** The concatenated features are formed by stacking feature maps A and B along the channel axis. This operation is represented symbolically as Concatenated_Features = Concatenate (A, B).

The mean value of each feature map over the spatial dimensions is computed by the global average pooling layer. This operation is mathematically denoted by the symbol F for an input feature map.

$$\text{Global Average Pooling (F)} = 1/N \ (i = 1\hat{}N) \ Fi \tag{6}$$

Allow N to stand for the entire number of items that are contained within the feature map F.

Several activities heavily influence the Dynamic SwishNet-181 algorithm. These exercises involve the use of the Swish activation function, rearranging channels, combining depths, and calculating the average of all values.

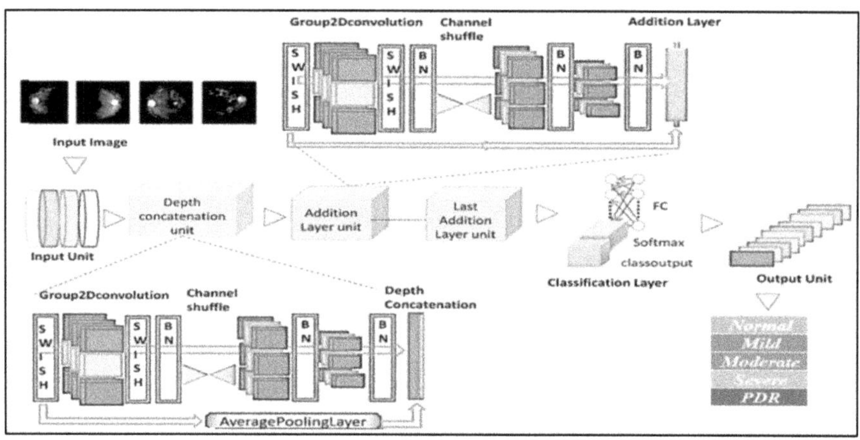

Fig. 3. CNN-based DR Classification

Figure 3 describe Several distinct convolutional neural networks (CNNs) are employed in the illustration to construct a system capable of categorising the extent of diabetic retinopathy (DR) in fundus images. DR severity levels range from 0 (absence of DR) to 4 (presence of proliferative DR). The system utilises well-known CNN architectures such as VGG16, EfficientNet, and ResNet, in addition to a new model called Dynamic SwishNet-181The objective is to improve the precision of categorising Diabetic Retinopathy by efficiently extracting characteristics and conducting classification.

4   Result and Discussion

The main objective of this research work is to assess the accuracy of Dynamic SwishNet-181 in classifying diabetic retinopathy on a scale of 0 to 4, and to compare its performance with VGG16, EfficientNet, and RESNET [9]. The experiments were conducted on a PC with an Intel Core i-5 CPU and 4GB of RAM, using Python 3.8. The paper emphasises the positive outcomes of promptly detecting diabetic retinopathy (DR) using benchmark datasets. However, it fails to address the scalability and practicality of implementing Dynamic SwishNet-181 in actual clinical environments, which limits its potential influence on the care of diabetic patients and raises ethical concerns in real-time applications.

4.1   Performance Evaluation

A confusion matrix, presents a concise overview of a model's performance in categorizing data. On the other hand, the off-diagonals (FP, FN) in the matrix indicate wrong classifications, whereas the diagonals in the matrix (TP) reflect accurate predictions. Table 3 summarizes common classification metrics: accuracy, precision, recall, and F1-score [11].

Table 3. Performance Metrics

Metric	Description (Equation)
Precision	TP / (TP + FP)
Recall	TP / (TP + FN)
Accuracy	(TP + TN) / TOTAL
F1 Score	* (Precision * Recall) / (Precision + Recall)

4.2   Classification Outcomes in DR Severity

The findings of DL classification algorithms that do not involve pre-processing reveal that the model is able to assess raw data and recognise patterns and features directly from the input that has not been processed. Consequently, this demonstrates the robustness and adaptability of the concept.

Table 4. Performace analysis of DL models

Before Pre-processing					After Pre-processing			
DL Models	Acc	Precision	Recall	F1 Score	Acc	Precision	Recall	F1 Score
VGG16	0.78	0.91	0.78	0.84	0.88	0.89	0.87	0.88

(continued)

Table 4. (continued)

Before Pre-processing					After Pre-processing			
EfficientNet	0.85	0.87	0.82	0.89	0.86	0.87	0.84	0.85
ResNet	0.88	0.89	0.87	0.88	0.90	0.91	0.89	0.90
SwishNet-181	0.90	0.91	0.89	0.90	0.92	0.93	0.91	0.92
D-SwishNet-181	0.91	0.92	0.9	0.91	0.94	0.95	0.93	0.94

Table 4 and Fig. 4 compare the performance characteristics of multiple deep learning models, both before and after undergoing pre-processing. Prior to pre-processing, the accuracy of VGG16 is 0.78, whereas the superior accuracies of EfficientNet, ResNet, SwishNet-181, and D-SwishNet-181 are 0.85, 0.88, 0.90, and 0.91, respectively. Following pre-processing, each model exhibits enhanced performance metrics, with accuracy levels ranging from 0.86 to 0.94.

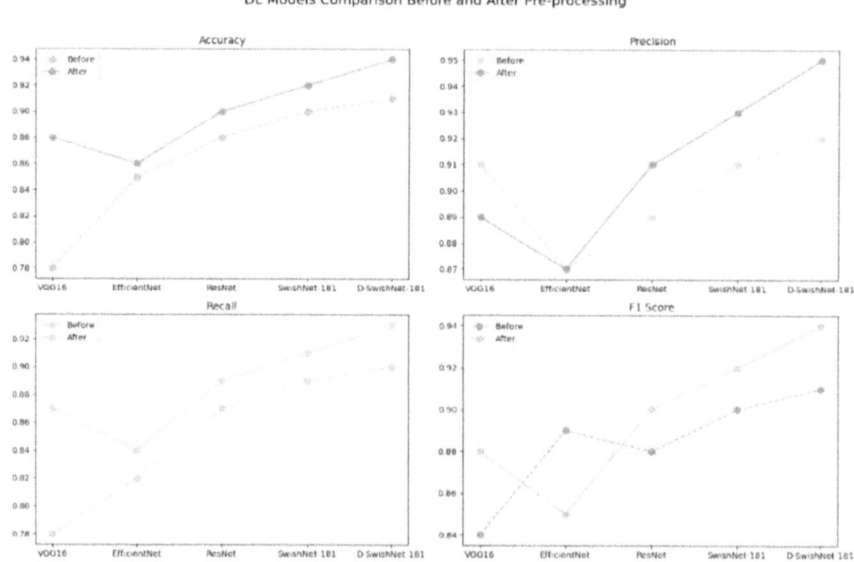

Fig. 4. Performance Analysis of DL Models Before and After Pre-Processing

The diagram illustrates the metrics score of five deep learning models (SwishNet-181, VGG16, D-SwishNet-181, EfficientNet, and ResNet,), both before and after pre-processing. Pre-processing notably boosts the general performance of most models, especially in relationships of accuracy and F1 score. The remarkable outcomes attained by Dynamic SwishNet-181 underscore its capability as a reliable instrument for efficient DR screening, underscoring the significance of integrating contemporary image preprocessing techniques with deep learning models. Additional investigation could focus on optimising model parameters, integrating more extensive datasets, and verifying the approach in other clinical contexts to improve its practicality and universality.

4.3   Evaluation of the Current State of the Art Method

Summiya Batool et al. (2023 BNs pre-trained models were applied by to extract distinctive features from fundus images, and an accuracy of more than 80% was achieved on the EYE-PACS dataset. By employing data augmentation approaches and applying a Gaussian Smooth filter to attained an accuracy of 88% (DeepDRiD) and 85% (EYE-PACS) dataset. However, the recently developed Dynamic SwishNet-181 was explicitly designed for the classification of DR severity level. Performance parameters are compared between D-SwishNet-181 and EfficientNet b6 in the above Table 5 and Fig. 5.

Table 5. Comparisons of Performance Metrics of Existing Work (EfficientNet b6) and Proposed Approach (D-SwishNet-181)

Model	Recall	Precision	Acc	F1 Score
Existing Work				
EfficientNet b6	0.86	0.87	0.88	0.86
D-SwishNet-181				
Before Pre-Processing -Dynamic SwishNet - 181	0.90	0.92	0.91	0.91
After Pre-Processing -D-SwishNet - 181	0.93	0.95	0.94	0.94

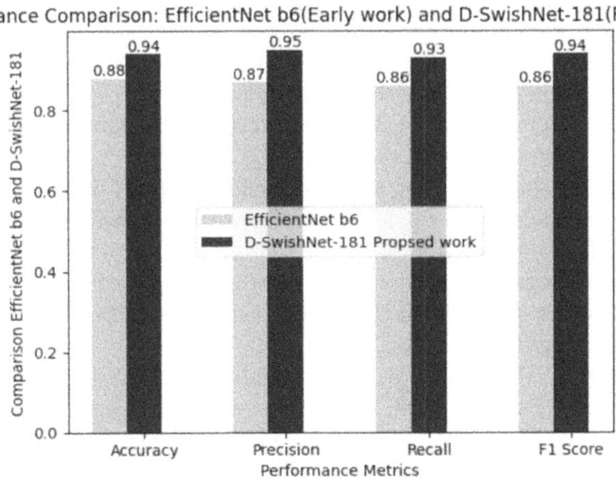

Fig. 5. Comparative Analysis of EfficientNet b6 (Prior Research) and D-SwishNet-181 (Proposed Method)

5 Conclusion

The usage of CLAHE and ADF pre-processing algorithms in Dynamic SwishNet-181 signifies a major growth in the classification of diabetic retinopathy (DR). This model challenges the limitations of group convolution by applying the shuffle channel method and placing importance on auxiliary layers. As a result, it is able to produce a vastly accurate representation of features for DR. The performance appearances of Dynamic SwishNet-181 are unlooked-for, with an F1-score of 0.94, accuracy of 0.94, precision of 0.95, and recall of 0.93. These metrics outshine those of VGG16, Efficient-Net, and ResNet. This work introduces a dependable for accurate identification of diabetic retinopathy (DR), empowering rapid involvements to prevent visual impairment in people with diabetes.

References

1. Vipparthi, V., Rao, D.R., Mullu, S., Patlolla, V.: Diabetic retinopathy classification using deep learning techniques. In: 2022 3rd International Conference on Electronics and Sustainable Communication Systems (ICESC), pp. 840–846 (2022)
2. Hacisoftaoglu, R.E., Karakaya, M., Sallam, A.B.: Deep learning frameworks for diabetic retinopathy detection with smartphone-based retinal imaging systems. Pattern Recognit. Lett. **135**, 409–417 (2020)
3. Mohanty, C. et al.: Using deep learning architectures for detection and classification of diabetic retinopathy. Sensors. **23**, 5726 (2023)
4. Zang, P. et al.: Deep-learning-aided detection of referable and vision threatening diabetic retinopathy based on structural and angiographic optical coherence tomography. Invest. Ophthalmol. Vis. Sci. **62**, 2116 (2021)
5. Bora, A. et al.: Predicting the risk of developing diabetic retinopathy using deep learning. Lancet Digit. Health. **3**, e10–e19 (2021)
6. Skariah, S.M., Arun, K.S.: A deep learning-based approach for automated diabetic retinopathy detection and grading. In: Proceedings of the 2021 4th Biennial International Conference on Nascent Technologies in Engineering (ICNTE), pp. 1–6 (2021)
7. Chen, P.N., Lee, C.C., Liang, C.M., et al.: General deep learning model for detecting diabetic retinopathy. BMC Bioinformatics. **22**(Suppl 5), 84 (2021)
8. Aditi, S.W., Kabir, F., Shill, P.C.: Diagnosis of diabetic retinopathy using deep learning techniques. In: 2021 5th International Conference on Electrical Information and Communication Technology (EICT), pp. 1–6 (2021)
9. Patra, P., Singh, T.: Diabetic retinopathy detection using an improved ResNet 50-InceptionV3 and hybrid DiabRetNet structures. In: 2022 OITS International Conference on Information Technology (OCIT), pp. 140–145 (2022)
10. Giroti, I., Das, J.K.A., Harshith, N.M., Thahniyath, G.: Diabetic retinopathy detection & classification using efficient net model. In: 2023 International Conference on Artificial Intelligence and Applications (ICAIA) Alliance Technology Conference (ATCON-1), pp. 1–6 (2023)
11. Reddy, K.S., Narayanan, M.: An efficiency way to analyse diabetic retinopathy detection and classification using deep learning techniques. In: 2023 3rd International Conference on Advance Computing and Innovative Technologies in Engineering (ICACITE), pp. 1388–1392 (2023)

Early Detection of Alzheimer's Disease Using SMOTE+ENN an Unbalanced Dataset and GRAD-CAM, Occlusion Mapping for Visualization

S. Amudha[1]([✉]) [iD], Mayank Mukherjee[1], Anshuman Singh[1], Nikhil Rajput[2], and Mayank[1]

[1] Department of Computational Intelligence (CINTEL), Faculty of Engineering and Technology, SRMIST, KTR, Chennai, India
amudhas@srmist.edu.in

[2] Department of Data Science and Business Systems (DSBS), Faculty of Engineering and Technology, SRMIST, KTR, Chennai, India

Abstract. Alzheimer's disease is a neurological condition marked by alterations in the brain that result in the accumulation of specific proteins. This accumulation leads to the shrinking of the brain and eventual death of brain cells, loses functioning of neurons, connection with other neurons and eventually die. Alzheimer's disease is the primary cause of dementia, which manifests as a progressive decline in cognitive functions like memory, reasoning, behavior, and social interactions. These changes significantly impact an individual's daily functioning. At first, Alzheimer's disease targets the areas of the Brain responsible for/involved in memory, including the entorhinal cortex and hippocampus. It later affects the areas present in the cerebral cortex responsible for language, reasoning and social behavior. Due to the brain losing functionality by eventual death of brain cells, neurons stop working throughout the brain and the neural connections or the neural networks break down. This process is called Brain Atrophy, resulting from significant cellular death and causing the loss of Brain in volume. The suggested approach utilizes Machine learning and Deep learning algorithms to process brain MRI-scans. The aim of proposed work is to portray/visualize the output through GRAD-CAM and OCCLUSION SENSITIVITY MAPPING to identify and visualize the targeted brain areas and display them after each convolution layer. The suggested method has many benefits over the conventional models.

Keywords: Machine Learning · Deep Learning · SMOTE+ENN · GRAD-CAM · unbalanced datasets

1 Introduction

Alzheimer's disease (AD) stands as one of the most prevalent neurodegenerative disorders, affecting millions worldwide and posing significant challenges to healthcare systems globally. Characterized by progressive cognitive decline and memory impairment, AD profoundly impacts individuals' daily functioning, quality of life, and places

© The Author(s), under exclusive license to Springer Nature Switzerland AG 2026
R. Appavoo et al. (Eds.): IconDeepCom 2024, CCIS 2687, pp. 113–131, 2026.
https://doi.org/10.1007/978-3-032-26680-4_9

substantial burden on caregivers and healthcare resources. At the core of AD lies the accumulation of abnormal protein aggregates in the brain, namely beta-amyloid plaques and tau tangles. These pathological hallmarks disrupt neuronal communication and ultimately lead to neuronal death, contributing to the gradual deterioration of cognitive functions. The exact etiology of AD remains elusive, although genetic, environmental, and lifestyle factors are believed to play pivotal roles in disease development and progression. Current Alzheimer's Detection Methods are bounded by the limitations of knowledge and remain elusive as numerous factors are at play when provided with a proper diagnostic. The present-day working methods for Alzheimer's detection and prevention involve using MRI and PET scans to visualize and monitor structural and functional changes happening inside the brain. Many neuroimaging techniques available in today's world are helpful in detection and prevention of Alzheimer's disease. Magnetic Resonance Imaging (MRI) and Positron Emission Tomography (PET) scans enable clinicians to visualize structural and functional changes in the brain associated with AD pathology. MRI provides detailed images of brain structures, while PET scans using specific tracers can detect beta-amyloid and tau deposition.

1. *MAGNETIC RESONANCE IMAGING (MRI):*

Chandra A, Dervenoulas G, Politis M [1] discussed how MRI-scans revealed structural changes and abnormalities in the brain. Alzheimer's disease can be detected through MRI (Magnetic Resonance Imaging) by observing structural changes and abnormalities in the brain. MRI scans detect shrinkage in specific regions of the brain, particularly the hippocampus and cortex, which are associated with memory and cognition. Additionally, MRI can reveal the presence of amyloid plaques and tau protein tangles, which are characteristic markers of Alzheimer's disease. These markers in turn help to identify the regions of are where we can see distinctions indicating to estimated Alzheimer's specific regions.

2. *POSITRON EMISSION TOMOGRAPHY (PET):*

PET imaging employs radioactive tracers to visualize molecular processes and metabolic activity in the brain. In AD diagnosis, PET scans targeting beta-amyloid and tau protein deposition are used to detect amyloid plaques and neurofibrillary tangles, respectively, which are neuropathological hallmarks of the disease. SHUKLA A, TIWARI R, TIWARI S [2] discussed that PET scans image metabolic activity in the brain and evaluate distribution of specific compounds in the brain. Amyloid PET Imaging, Tau PET Imaging and glucose metabolism contribute to diagnosing the severity of the disease and mentioning the stage at which it currently stands. Overall, neuroimaging techniques, including MRI and PET, play a pivotal role in the diagnosis and characterization of Alzheimer's disease by capturing structural, functional, and molecular changes in the brain.

3. *Cerebrospinal Fluid (CSF) Biomarkers:*

Cerebrospinal fluid (CSF) biomarkers have emerged as valuable tools in the diagnosis and prognostication of Alzheimer's disease (AD). CSF, which bathes the brain and spinal cord, contains proteins and other molecules that reflect pathological processes occurring within the central nervous system. BOUWMAN FH, FRISONI GB, JOHNSON SC [3] provides insights into the underlying molecular pathology of AD, facilitating early detection and monitoring of disease progression. The primary

CSF biomarkers used in AD diagnosis include beta-amyloid (Aβ), total tau (t-tau), and phosphorylated tau (p-tau) proteins CSF biomarkers could inform clinical practice decisions, by facilitating timely and accurate diagnosis, providing prognostic information.

1. ***Beta-amyloid (Aβ):***

Beta-amyloid is a key component of senile plaques, one of the pathological hallmarks of AD. In individuals with AD, the aggregation and accumulation of beta-amyloid in the brain lead to the formation of amyloid plaques, contributing to neurodegeneration and cognitive decline. CSF levels of beta-amyloid are typically reduced in AD patients due to sequestration within plaques, making it a reliable biomarker for AD pathology. Decreased levels of Aβ42, a specific isoform of beta-amyloid, and an increased ratio of Aβ42/Aβ40 are observed in AD CSF samples compared to healthy controls or individuals with other forms of dementia.

2. ***Total tau (T-tau):***

Tau proteins are abundant in neurons and play a crucial role in stabilizing microtubules within cells. In AD, abnormal phosphorylation of tau leads to the formation of neurofibrillary tangles, another neuropathological hallmark of the disease. CSF levels of total tau (t-tau) reflect neuronal damage and axonal degeneration associated with AD pathology. Elevated levels of t-tau are observed in AD patients, correlating with the extent of neurodegeneration and disease severity. However, t-tau is not specific to AD and can also be elevated in other neurodegenerative disorders or conditions causing acute neuronal injury.

3. ***Phosphorylated tau(p-tau):***

Phosphorylated tau (p-tau) refers to tau proteins that have undergone abnormal phosphorylation, leading to their accumulation into neurofibrillary tangles. CSF levels of p-tau are specifically elevated in AD patients and are considered a more specific biomarker or AD pathology compared to t-tau. P-tau181 and p-tau231 are isoforms of phosphorylated tau commonly measured in CSF, with p-tau181 showing higher diagnostic accuracy for AD compared to t-tau or Aβ42 alone. The combination of Aβ42, t-tau, and p-tau in CSF analysis enhances the accuracy of AD diagnosis and prediction of disease progression. CSF biomarker analysis is typically performed using enzyme-linked immunosorbent assays (ELISA) or other immunoassay techniques. Although CSF biomarker analysis requires a lumbar puncture procedure, it provides valuable information about underlying AD pathology and aids in differential diagnosis, especially in cases of early or atypical presentations. Additionally, CSF biomarkers are increasingly being incorporated into clinical trials as surrogate endpoints for evaluating the efficacy of disease-modifying therapies targeting AD pathology. Overall, CSF biomarkers play a critical role in advancing our understanding of AD pathophysiology and improving diagnostic accuracy and prognostication in clinical practice.

Cognitive Assessments

Cognitive testing serves as a fundamental component in the assessment and diagnosis of Alzheimer's disease (AD) and other forms of dementia. These standardized assessments aim to evaluate various domains of cognitive function, including memory, attention, language, visuospatial abilities, and executive function. By systematically measuring cognitive performance, clinicians can detect subtle changes indicative of cognitive impairment and track disease progression over time. Some of the commonly used cognitive tests in AD diagnosis include the Mini-Mental State Examination (MMSE), Montreal Cognitive Assessment (MoCA), and Alzheimer's Disease Assessment Scale-Cognitive Subscale (ADAS-Cog).

1. *Mini-Mental State Examination (MMSE):*

The MMSE consists of a series of questions and tasks that assess various cognitive domains, such as orientation, registration (immediate memory), attention and calculation, recall (short-term memory), language, and visuospatial abilities. Lower scores indicate greater cognitive impairment. The MMSE may lack specificity for detecting early stages of AD and may be influenced by factors such as education and cultural background. Therefore, it couldn't provide a clearer picture over detection of Alzheimer's.

2. *Montreal cognitive assessment (MOCA):*

The MoCA is a screening tool designed to detect mild cognitive impairment (MCI) and early dementia, including AD. It assesses similar cognitive domains as the MMSE but includes additional tasks to evaluate executive function, attention, and language abilities in greater detail. The maximum score on the MoCA is 30 points, with scores below 26 considered indicative of cognitive impairment. The MoCA has demonstrated superior sensitivity to mild cognitive changes compared to the MMSE, making it particularly useful in early AD detection.

Genetic Testing

Atkins, E. R., & Panegyres, P. K. (2011) [4] discussed how Genetic testing plays significant role in the estimation of Alzheimer's disease (AD) risk, particularly in cases of familial or early-onset forms of the disease. While the majority of AD cases are sporadic and likely influenced by a combination of genetic and environmental factors, a small proportion (approximately 1–5%) are attributed to rare genetic mutations associated with autosomal dominant inheritance patterns. The most well-known genetic risk factor for late-onset AD is the apolipoprotein E (APOE) gene, while mutations in genes such as Presenilin 1 (PSEN1), Presenilin 2 (PSEN2), and Amyloid Precursor Protein (APP) are associated with early-onset familial AD.

1. *Apolipoprotein E (APOE):*

The APOE gene encodes a protein involved in the metabolism of lipids and cholesterol in the brain. The ε4 allele of the APOE gene is the strongest genetic risk factor for late-onset AD, with individuals carrying one copy of the ε4 allele having an increased risk of developing AD, and those carrying two copies having an even higher risk. APOE ε4 is associated with an earlier age of onset and increased amyloid deposition in the brain, contributing to the pathogenesis of AD. Genetic testing for APOE ε4 allele status can provide individuals and their families with information about their risk of developing AD, although it does not predict disease onset with certainty.

2. *early onset familial alzheimer's disease (fad) genes:*

Mutations in genes such as PSEN1, PSEN2, and APP are associated with early-onset familial AD, which typically manifests before the age of 65. These mutations disrupt the processing of amyloid precursor protein (APP) and lead to increased production of amyloid-beta (Aβ) peptides, contributing to amyloid plaque formation and neuronal dysfunction. Genetic testing for mutations in FAD genes is primarily indicated in individuals with a family history of early-onset AD or when clinical features suggest a genetic etiology. Identifying pathogenic mutations in FAD genes can inform genetic counseling, family planning, and potential participation in clinical trials for disease-modifying therapies targeting amyloid pathology.

3. *other genetic risk factors:*

In addition to APOE and FAD genes, several other genetic variants have been implicated in late-onset AD through genome-wide association studies (GWAS). These include variants in genes such as Clusterin (CLU), Phosphatidylinositol Binding Clathrin Assembly Protein (PICALM), and Triggering Receptor Expressed on Myeloid Cells 2 (TREM2), which are involved in various biological pathways associated with AD pathogenesis, including amyloid metabolism, synaptic function, and immune response. While these genetic variants confer modest increases in AD risk, they collectively contribute to the polygenic nature of late-onset AD and may interact with environmental factors to influence disease susceptibility.

2 Literature Survey

Vijeta Patil et al. [6] study, used CNN with multi-layers to diagnose Alzheimer's disease. The layers used were pooling, soft-max regression, etc. A pooling process was used to overcome overfitting by reducing the amount of computations and parameters. ResNET18 networks gave them the highest accuracy of 98%. Their technique was accurate, and sensitive. C. Kavitha1et al. [7] study, used Machine Learning techniques on longitudinal datasets. Their diagnosis was based on various features of the csv dataset. They performed five-fold cross-validation: Decision Tree, SVM, Random Forests, XGBoost and Voting then compared their accuracy. They performed binary classification which predicted whether a person is demented or non demented. Vijay P.B. Grover et al. [8], stated that nuclear spins and reaction to magnetic fields form the basis of MRI. Techniques like diffusion-weighted imaging visualize water, while spectroscopy analyses chemical composition, aiding diagnosis. Hadeer A. Helaly et al. [9], used 2D and 3D convolution-based datasets from ADNI (Alzheimer's Disease Neuroimaging Initiative). They used two methods for classification, first one being a simple CNN architecture, second one being VGG19 model. They got an accuracy of 93.61% and 95.17% for 2D and 3D multi-class AD stage classifications. VGG19 performed well with an accuracy of 97%.

Cheung, C. Y., Ran et al. [10], developed a bilateral deep learning model which takes retinal scans as input and detected AD. They used EfficientNet-B network for feature extraction followed by a bilateral model for classification. They implemented unilateral model using a single eye retinal image for classification. For comparison, a hybrid model was trained which could take risk factors of AD into account. They achieved an accuracy of 92.1% by the bilateral model.In their research, Md Masud Rana et al. [11] used a hybrid model which merges transfer learning and CNN. They used Inception V3 for feature extraction and CNN for image classification. They used a bilateral filter for feature extraction and SMOTE+ENN to avoid overfitting. This achieved an accuracy of 97.31%.

In their research, Sheetal J, et al. [12] used OneHotEncoder to encode the classes. They used CNN and VGG19 and compared their results. CNN provided moderate accuracy of 70% with fluctuations while VGG19 showed tremendous difference with an accuracy of 92% on validation data with very less model loss.In their study, A. M. El-Assy, et al. [15] took leverage of the hierarchical nature of CNN. They employed two CNN layers with different filter sizes and pooling layers. They achieved accuracies of 99.43%, 99.57%, and 99.13% on three, four and five categories respectively.

In their research, Anjali, Singh, et al. [13] used CNN to identify features from MRI images. They used SMOTE TOMEK technique to get rid of class imbalance. They achieved 99.36% and 99% of accuracy and F1 score respectively.In their research, Vasco Sá Diogo et al. [14], used combined datasets from ADNI and Oasis. They used SVM classifier, and an ensemble of 3 binary classifiers to classify AD, HC, MCI. They achieved an accuracy of 90.6%.

3 Proposed Method

Image processing has made many changes in field of medicine and healthcare. Today, imaging is used in almost every field of treatment. Doctors can examine the human body from the inside without surgery during a medical examination. There are many types of medical exams: X-rays, ultrasounds, magnetic resonance imaging (MRI), and computed tomography (CT) scans. It is not possible for humans to analyze machine-based medical systems and draw accurate pictures of their conclusions. The machine is trained on medical records and can produce accurate results in seconds, whereas in other cases it would take an entire team of doctors, days to do the same. Today's medical procedures rely on computer vision and image processing algorithms as part of them. Its importance cannot be overstated. AD has become one of the most serious diseases in the world. Some researchers use data augmentation techniques to improve their results, and no clinical study of Alzheimer's disease classification acknowledges the problem of data generation. There are still researchers who are not able to achieve significant results because they did not properly train their models. It has been observed that research articles focus on the discovery of new methods for classifying biomedical diagnostic drugs.

In this model, input data is preprocessed using normalization and categorical dataset variables are transformed using a one-hot encoder to feed the ADD-Net pipeline. Then, the SMOTE-ENN (Synthetic Minority Oversampling Technique, Edited-Nearest-Neighbor) algorithm is used to solve the problem of inconsistent data when the dataset is balanced by oversampling the cluster-classes. The data is divided into training, testing, and validation by 60%, 20%, and 20%, respectively. Additionally, features are extracted using the VGG-19 CNN model, as shown in Fig. 1. The Grad-CAM heatmap algorithm, along with usage of occlusion mapping, is used to visualize class performance maps by highlighting features that contribute to the classification of sample images.

Data Collection

There are a large number of datasets present over the internet helpful for AD-classification. Many AD datasets present online are in .csv format and not useful in our research. Organizations such as Oracle and ADNI- provide verified Brain-MRI dataset in 3-dimensional image format helpful in training Machine Learning and Deep-Learning Models. The Oasis dataset in 18 gigabytes large, while the ADNI-dataset is 450 gigabytes large. The data used in this study was collected from Kaggle and consisted of anonymous patient samples containing only information on MRI scan images and class labels. Figure 1 is a multi-class dataset sample containing four different classes, including the normal NOD class and three other classes representing the three basic stages of AD, namely VMD, MD and MOD.

Fig. 1. Dataset Sample

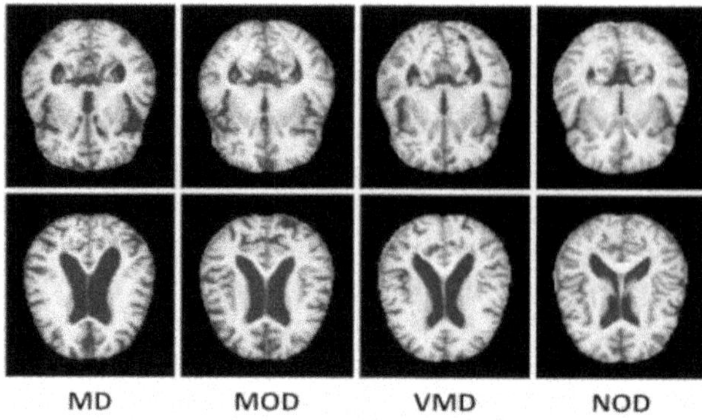

Fig. 2. Proposed Architecture Model

According to the description of the dataset, each model in the dataset on Kaggle is independently validated by the uploader himself. In addition, the file size is appropriate and the model is cleaned, that is, resized and adjusted. Based on these conditions, this information was used in our study. There are a total of 6400 samples in this file. The model is an independent three-channel (RGB) image with a size of 176x208 pixels and has four different groups. The number of models in the NOD category is 3200 images. The remaining three categories, VMD, MD and MOD, have 2240, 896 and 64 images, respectively. The only drawback of this data is that it is unbalanced, as explained in Table Error! Reference source not found. To solve this problem, we use SMOTE+ENN to generate an unbalanced synthetic data with equal classes for each class, as shown in Fig. 2. The dataset is divided into 60%, 20%, and 20% for training, validation, and testing sets, respectively.

3.1　Balancing the AD Dataset Using SMOTE+ENN.

Table 1 provides class distribution before up-sampling and adjusting through SMOTE-ENN algorithms.

Table 1. AD dataset class distribution before up-sampling and adjusting through SMOTE-ENN algorithm

Class	No. of Images
Mild Demented (MD)	896
Moderate Demented (MOD)	64
Non-Demented (ND)	3200
Very Mild Demented (VMD)	2240

Usually, over-sampling and under-sampling are two type of techniques for resampling. However, another type of approach exists which is a culmination of both the techniques. In this study, we adopted the hybrid SMOTE-ENN algorithm. SMOTE (an up-sampling technique) and ENN (Edited Nearest Neighbor). SMOTE generates new samples relying on class nearest neighbors, while ENN is an implementation of edited nearest neighbors. Both algorithms work in sequence and SMOTE chooses a random instance from a minority class and increases its proportion by interpolating new samples. ENN has the ability to delete some observations from both classes that are identified as having different class between the observation's class and its K-nearest neighbor majority class. In this way, SMOTE-ENN evens the samples of each class and effectively solves the dataset imbalance problem as depicted in Table 2. To balance out the data set, SMOTE-ENN utilizes the K-Nearest Neighbor technique to interpolate new imitation samples for the minority classes shown in Fig. 3.

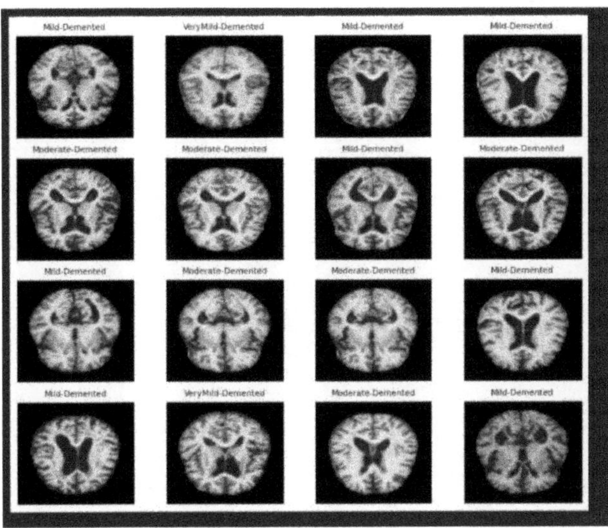

Fig. 3. Brain-Image samples after applying SMOTE-ENN across all classes (MD, MOD, ND, VMD)

Table 2. AD dataset class distribution after up-sampling and adjusting through SMOTE-ENN algorithm

Class	No. of Images
Mild Demented (MD)	3200
Moderate Demented (MOD)	3200
Non-Demented (ND)	3200
Very Mild Demented (VMD)	3200

Data Preprocessing

Data preprocessing is initialized by initially reshaping the Brain-MRI Image dataset to 176x208 image size. Then incorporate normalization, to change the range of pixel-intensity values by rescaling (1.0/255.0). One hot encoding is a technique that we used to represent categorical variables as numerical values in machine learning models. It allows the use of categorical variables in models that require numerical input, in cases of image classification, pertaining to the field of healthcare classification and medical imaging. Then, again reshaping is done on the Brain-MRI dataset to avoid image-size errors occurred after resampling done using SMOTE-ENN algorithm. The same can be expressed in Fig. 3.

3.2 VGG-19 Model Components

The main components of the model we used is briefly explained here (Fig. 5).

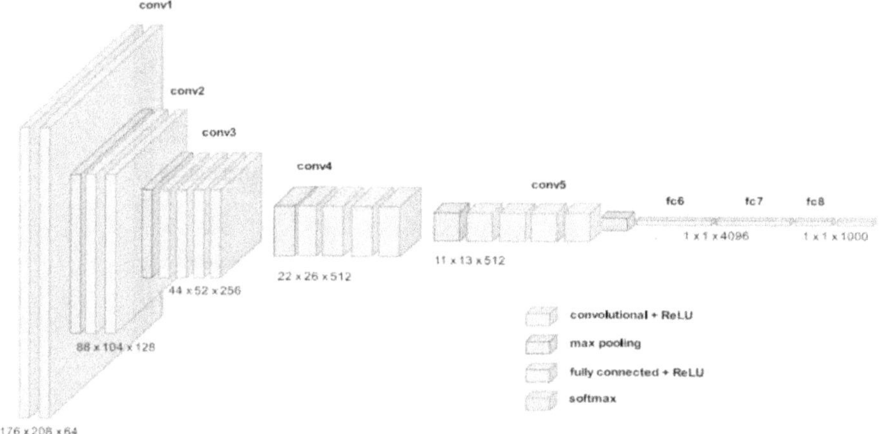

Fig. 4. The proposed model (VGG-19 architecture diagram)

The VGG19 model (also known as VGGNet-19) has the same basic idea as the VGG16 model, with the exception that it supports 19 layers. The number "19" refers to the model's weight layers (convolutional layers). In comparison to VGG16, VGG19 contains three extra convolutional fully-connected layers.

Input: VGG19 accepts 176x208 pixel images as input. To maintain the same precision in ImageNet matches, the output model cuts an average of 176,208 patches in each image. VGG's convolutional layers use the smallest feasible receptive field, or 33, to record left-to-right and up-to-down movement. Additionally, 11 convolution filters are used to convert the input linearly. The next component is a ReLU (Rectified linear unit) activation function, which is a piecewise linear function that, if the input is positive, outputs the input; otherwise, the output is zero. The convolution stride is fixed at 1 pixel to keep the spatial resolution preserved after convolution (stride is the number of pixel shifts over the input matrix).

Hidden Layers: The VGG network's hidden layers all make use of ReLU. Local Response Normalization (LRN) is not used with VGG as it increases memory usage and training time. Furthermore, it doesn't increase overall accuracy.

Fully Connected Layers: The VGG19 contains three layers with full connectivity. The first two levels each have 4096 channels, while the third layer has 1000 channels with one channel for each class.

Table 3. Convolutional-Network configuration across different models with different layers.

		ConvNet Configuration			
A	A-LRN	B	C	D	E
11 weight layers	11 weight layers	13 weight layers	16 weight layers	16 weight layers	19 weight layers
conv3-64	conv3-64 LRN	conv3-64 conv3-64	conv3-64 conv3-64	conv3-64 conv3-64	conv3-64 conv3-64
conv3-128	conv3-128	conv3-128 conv3-128	conv3-128 conv3-128	conv3-128 conv3-128	conv3-128 conv3-128
conv3-256 conv3-256	conv3-256 conv3-256	conv3-256 conv3-256	conv3-256 conv3-256 conv1-256	conv3-256 conv3-256 conv3-256	conv3-256 conv3-256 conv3-256 conv3-256
conv3-512 conv3-512	conv3-512 conv3-512	conv3-512 conv3-512	conv3-512 conv3-512 conv3-512	conv3-512 conv3-512 conv3-512	conv3-512 conv3-512 conv3-512 conv3-512
conv3-512 conv3-512	conv3-512 conv3-512	conv3-512 conv3-512	conv3-512 conv3-512 conv3-512	conv3-512 conv3-512 conv3-512	conv3-512 conv3-512 conv3-512 conv3-512

The proposed CNN (Convolutional Neural Network) architecture, which we have used to train our dataset in this research, is based on the biological model of the human brain and is mainly used in computer vision applications such as image classification, image segmentation and target detection. Previous developers of such deep learning models in various other fields, for its translations. The translation or space invariance implies that a CNN can recognize the same feature regardless of its position in various images. This paper proposes a pretrained VGG-19 CNN (Convolutional Neural Network) model from scratch to realize and predict accurate AD classification along with mentioning at which stage it stands. The VGG 19 model proposes a scheme of five convolutional blocks, each with a Rectified linear unit (ReLU) fucion and a 2D maximum pooling layer and a SoftMax distribution layer, as shown in Fig. 4. The detailed network architecture and 356 model summary of the proposed model used for the classification of AD with the subsequent layer is discussed in Table 3, and a description of hyper-parameters that plays a vital role in practical training of the VGG-19 model in Table 4.

Table 4. Convolutional blocks of the proposed VGG19 model

Layer (type)	Output Shape	Param #
Input_2 (input layer)	(None, 176, 208, 3)	0
Block1_conv1 (Conv2D)	(None, 176, 208, 64)	1792
Block1_conv2 (Conv2D)	(None, 176, 208, 64)	36928
Block1_pool (MaxPooling 2D)	(None, 88, 104, 64)	0
Block2_conv1 (Conv2D)	(None, 88, 104, 128)	73856
Block2_conv2 (Conv2D)	(None, 44, 52, 128)	147584
Block2_pool (MaxPooling 2D)	(None, 44, 52, 256)	0
Block3_conv1 (Conv2D)	(None, 44, 52, 256)	295168
Block3_conv2 (Conv2D)	(None, 44, 52, 256)	590080
Block3_conv3 (Conv2D)	(None, 44, 52, 256)	590080
Block3_conv4 (Conv2D)	(None, 44, 52, 256)	590080
Block3_pool (MaxPooling 2D)	(None, 22, 26, 256)	0
Block4_conv1 (Conv2D)	(None, 22, 26, 512)	1180160
Block4_conv2 (Conv2D)	(None, 22, 26, 512)	2359808
Block4_conv3 (Conv2D)	(None, 22, 26, 512)	2359808
Block4_conv4 (Conv2D)	(None, 22, 26, 512)	2359808
Block4_pool (MaxPooling 2D)	(None, 11, 13, 512)	0
Block5_conv1 (Conv2D)	(None, 11, 13, 512)	2359808
Block5_conv2 (Conv2D)	(None, 11, 13, 512)	2359808
Block5_conv3 (Conv2D)	(None, 11, 13, 512)	2359808
Block5_conv4 (Conv2D)	(None, 11, 13, 512)	2359808
Block5_pool (MaxPooling2D)	(None, 5, 6, 512)	0
Flatten	(None, 15360)	0
Fc1 (Dense)	(None, 4096)	62918656
Fc2 (Dense)	(None, 4096)	16781312
Fc3 (Dense)	(None, 1000)	4097000
Predictions (Dense)	(None, 4)	4004
Total params: 103,825,356 Trainable params: 103,825,356 Non-Trainable params: 0		

3.3 VGG-19 Convolution Blocks

Covolution block is the main block of the proosed VGG19, and each convolution block consists of 2D convolution, ReLU, and 2D MaxPooling. The kernel initializer is used to select the weights of the convolutional 2D layer. The ReLU activation function is used to overcome the gradient vanishing problem and allows the network to learn and execute faster, passing positive values as they are and equating all negative values to 0. At the same time, convolutional 2D down-samples the image and its spatial dimensions by taking the average value over an input window (of size defined by pool_size) for each channel of the input. The convolutional layers work in turns, and the features are gradually built. Local patterns, like edges, lines, and curves, are extracted in the initial layers, and local features are extracted based on these patterns. Consecutively, the model extracts high-level features and enables the deep model to classify an image more accurately (Table 5).

Table 5. List of Hyper Parameters that are used in VGG19 Architecture

Sr. No.	Parameter Name	Parameter Type
1	Optimizer	Adam
2	Learning rate	0.01
3	Batch Size	8
4	Epochs	40
5	Hidden Layer Activation	ReLU
6	Output Layer Activation	SoftMax

3.4 Flatten Layer

Flatten layer works in between the convolution layers and the dense layers. Convolutional layers work with and produce tensor data types for input, while dense layers require data in a 1-Dimensional format. Flatten Layers, to tackle this problem, vectorizes the feature map to feed to these dense layers (Fig. 5).

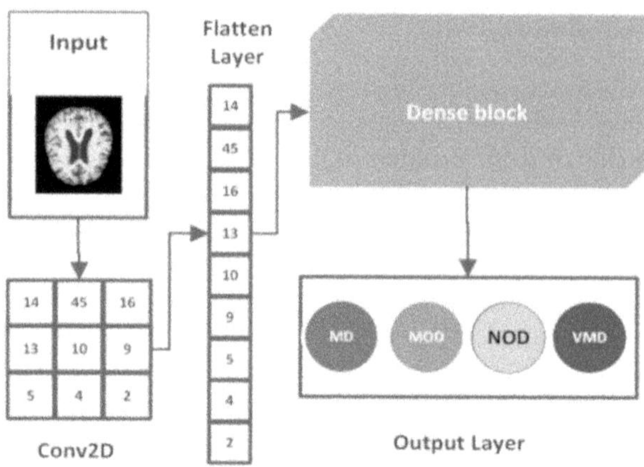

Fig. 5. Vectorizing Image-Feature map

3.5 ReLU Activation, Softmax Activation

Activation functions and mathematical functions that decide whether an output from perceptron is to be forwarded to the next layer, or to be configured then forwarded to the net layer. The activation function is used in the output layer to start the node, which return a label, assigned to the image processed through the model. There are several activation functions such as Sigmoid Activation function, Tanh Activation function, ReLU Activation function and Softmax Activation function. In our proposed VGG19 model we have used ReLU activation function after each convolutional block and Softmax activation function. The Softmax activation function transfers the raw outputs of the neural network into a vector of probabilities, typically a probability distribution function over the input classes.

3.6 Dense Layers

These layers are also called fully connected layers. This set takes a vector and produces an output based on its parameters. Images are recognized and class-labels are assigned to these images. This Learning in the model is done by the backpropagation method throughout the connection process. The number of trainable parameters of a model is determined by the number of values used in each Dense. layer. SoftMax is used after several layers where the number of neurons is equal to the number of classes, in our case, 4 classes: Mild Demented (MD), Moderate Demented (MOD), Non-Demented (ND) and Very Mild Demented (VMD). The class-labels are encoded using one-hot encoding, and only positive types are available in loss term.

4   Evaluation, Results and Discussion

The experiments were executed on a personal computer sys- 419 tem equipped with two Intel Xeon 2687 W v4 (3.0 GHz clock speed, 12 cores, and 24 threads) CPUs, 64 GB RAM, 45 GB 421 (NVIDIA) GTX 3900 GPU (Graphical Processing Unit). The model's evaluation was conducted using the test set that was created from splitting the data set before training the model under the distribution (60%,20%,20%). Using several metrics ensures the robustness of a model from every aspect. The combined understanding of these results determines the training evaluation and results of a model. For instance, if accuracy is very high, say above 90% does not necessarily mean that the model is excellent. Several other factors are involved, like loss, over-fitting, etc. We employed different metrics to benchmark the performance of our model.

A. ACCURACY

Accuracy is the measure of total correct predictions 437 out of accurate predictions obtained using the following expressions:

The mathematical expression for Accuracy is given by:

$$Accuracy = \left(\frac{TP + TN}{TP + FN + FP + TN} \right) \tag{1}$$

where TP, TN, FN, and FP are True Positive, True Negative, False Negative, and False Positive values, respectively (Figs. 7 and 8).

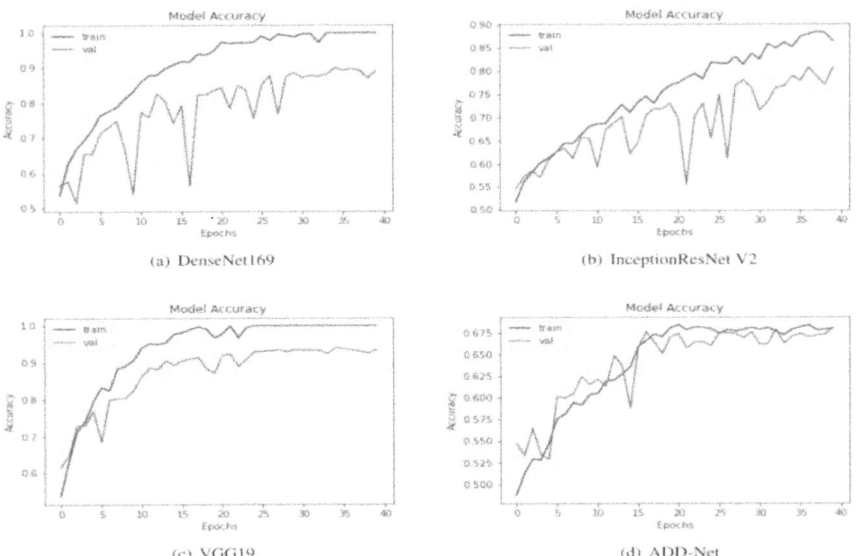

Fig. 6. Comparison with accuracy metrics of other models (DenseNet169, InceptionResNetV2, and ADD-Net) without SMOTE-ENN.

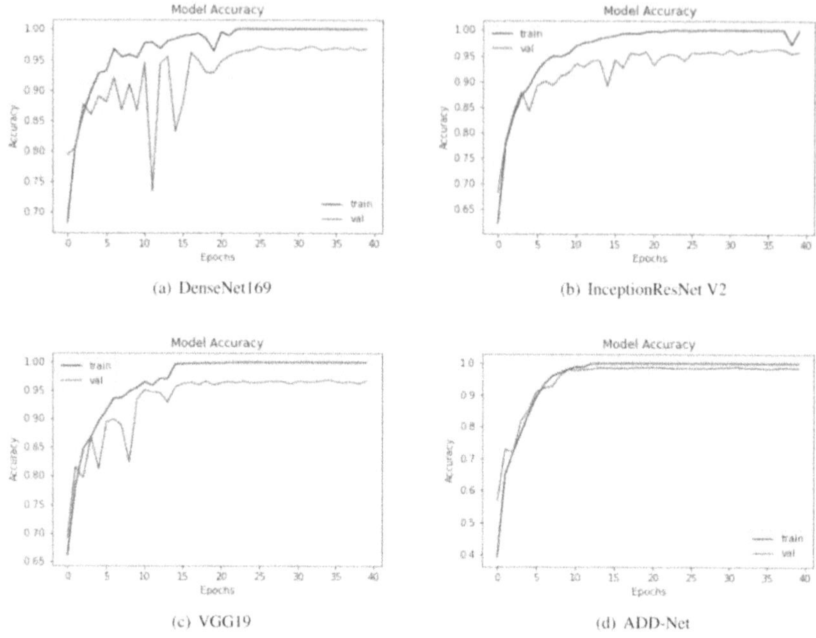

Fig. 7. Comparison with accuracy metrics of other models (DenseNet169, InceptionResNetV2, and ADD-Net) after applying SMOTE-ENN.

A. **PRECISION**

Precision is the ratio of correct positive predictions to total positive predictions, and it is calculated using the following equation.The mathematical equation given for Precision is:

$$Precision = \left(\frac{TP}{TP + FP} \right)$$
(2)

B. **RECALL**

The recall is also known as the sensitivity score or actual positive rate. It is the comparison of correct positive predictions to total actual correct positives. The recall is calculated using the following equation:

$$Recall = \left(\frac{TP}{TP + FN} \right)$$
(3)

C. **F1-Score**

Ideally, a value of 1.0 in precision and 1.0 in the recall is considered an ideal case for a classification model. F1-score is the harmonic mean of precision and recall. F1-score is unique in the sense that it plots its graph with a separate line for each class label. The

F1-score is computed using the following equation:

$$F1 = \left(2 * \frac{Precision * Recall}{Precision + Recall}\right) \tag{4}$$

D. **LOSS FUNCTION**

Loss functions calculate the mathematical difference between the predicted value and the actual value. For this research, we have used a categorical cross-entropy algorithm for loss.

$$Loss = y - \overline{y}$$

$$L_{CE} = -\sum_{n=1}^{k} (L_i \log (p_i))$$

where L is the calculated loss of each class, and P is the probability calculated by the SOFT function.Using the above metrics, our model is evaluated across all regions of evaluation and testing with appropriate results. Since our model is only at the prototype phase, we have requested for Verified datasets, mentioned in the above sections such as the ORACLE dataset, ADNI datasets for verified Brain-MRI Scan Images. For the next stage, we will incorporate our model over verified large datasets available and tune it accordingly to produce an even more accurate model (Figs. 8 and 9).

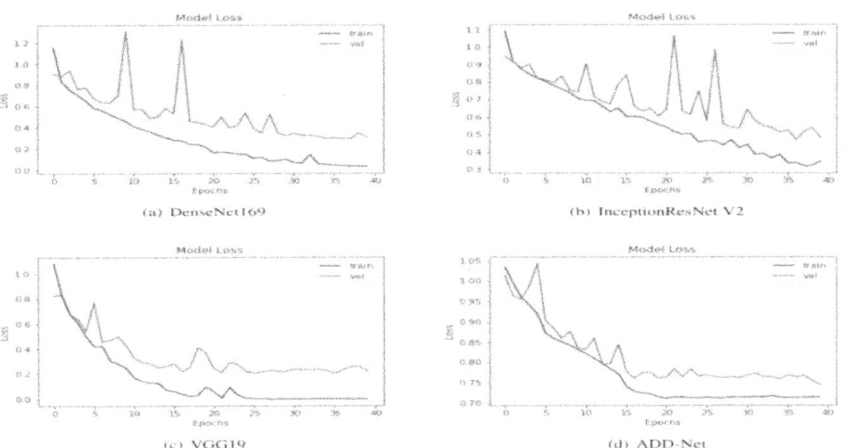

Fig. 8. Comparison with training-loss metrics of other models (DenseNet169, InceptionRes-NetV2, and ADD-Net) before SMOTE-ENN.

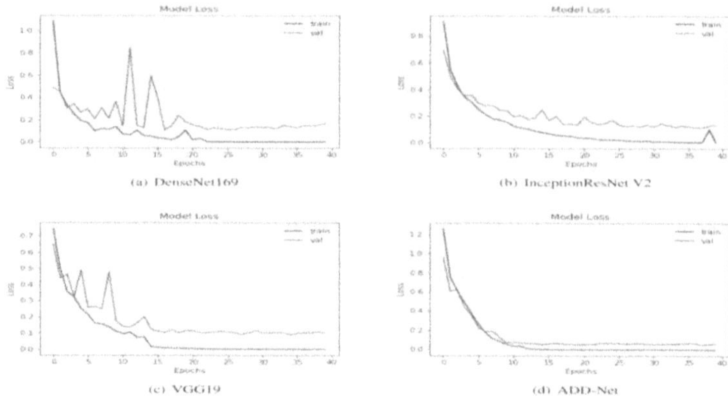

Fig. 9. Comparison with training-loss metrics of other models (DenseNet169, InceptionRes-NetV2, and ADD-Net) after applying SMOTE-ENN

5 Conclusion

This work proposed a novel deep CNN for detecting and estimating AD with relatively lesser parameters, and the proposed solution is ideal for training a smaller dataset. For the next developmental stage, we'll incorporate our model with verified large datasets from ORACLE or ADNI to test its performance on bigger and vast datasets. The proposed pre-trained VGG19 is built from scratch to precisely classify the stages of AD by decreasing parameters and calculation costs. Each block is specifically designed with many layers named conv_block, which is used to classify the AD in its early stages for all the specific classes. The SMOTEENN method is employed for handling data-set imbalance problems for generating new instances to balance the number of samples for each category. Grad-CAM algorithm provides insight into CNN layers' working by visualizing class activation heat-map and also using the resources of Occlusion Mapping to further understand our model and how it's learning is taking place. Our proposed deep model provides outstanding accuracy of 96.70%, 97% precision, Sensitivity (Recall) of 718 97%, and an impressive AUC value of 99.82%. In future other pre-trained architectures and fine-tune models can be added to achieve more desirable results.

Authors Contributions. Writing—original draft preparation, S.Amudha; writing—review and editing, Mayank Mukherjee; funding acquisition and Testing and Debugging: Anshuman Singh, Nikhil Rajput' Mayank all the authors have read and agreed to the published version of the manuscript.

References

1. Chandra, A., Dervenoulas, G., Politis, M.: Alzheimer's Disease Neuroimaging Initiative. Magnetic resonance imaging in Alzheimer's disease and mild cognitive impairment. J. Neurol. **266**(6), 1293–1302 (2019 Jun). https://doi.org/10.1007/s00415-018-9016-3

2. Shukla, A., Tiwari, R., Tiwari, S.: Alzheimer's disease detection from fused PET and MRI modalities using an ensemble classifier. Mach. Learn. Knowl. Extr. **5**(2), 512–538 (2023). https://doi.org/10.3390/make5020031S

3. Ashok Kumar, A., Muhammad Marzooq, A., Ranjithkumar, U., Romario, S., Surya, P.: Online smart voting system using face recognition. Int. J. Innov. Sci. Res. Technol. **8**(3), 606–610 (2023)

4. Bouwman, F.H., Frisoni, G.B., Johnson, S.C., et al.: Clinical application of CSF biomarkers for Alzheimer's disease: from rationale to ratios. Alzheimers Dement. **14**, e12314 (2022). https://doi.org/10.1002/dad2.12314

5. Atkins, E.R., Panegyres, P.K.: The clinical utility of gene testing for Alzheimer's disease. Neurol. Int. **3**(1), e1 (2011). https://doi.org/10.4081/ni.2011.e1

6. Dara, O.A., Lopez-Guede, J.M., Raheem, H.I., Rahebi, J., Zulueta, E., Fernandez-Gamiz, U.: Alzheimer's disease diagnosis using machine learning: a survey. Appl. Sci. **13**(14), 8298 (2023). https://doi.org/10.3390/app13148298

7. Patil, V., Madgi, M., Kiran, A.: Early prediction of Alzheimer's disease using convolutional neural network: a review. Egypt. J. Neurol. Psychiatr. Neurosurg. **58**, 130 (2022). https://doi.org/10.1186/s41983-022-00571-w

8. Kavitha, C., Mani, V., Srividhya, S.R., Khalaf, O.I., Tavera Romero, C.A.: Early-stage Alzheimer's disease prediction using machine learning models. Front. Public Health. **10**, 853294. Published 2022 Mar 3 (2022). https://doi.org/10.3389/fpubh.2022.853294

9. Grover, V.P., Tognarelli, J.M., Crossey, M.M., Cox, I.J., Taylor-Robinson, S.D., McPhail, M.J.: Magnetic resonance imaging: principles and techniques: lessons for clinicians. J. Clin. Exp. Hepatol. **5**(3), 246–255 (2015). https://doi.org/10.1016/j.jceh.2015.08.001

10. Helaly, H.A., Badawy, M., Haikal, A.Y.: Deep learning approach for early detection of Alzheimer's disease. Cogn. Comput. **14**(5), 1711–1727 (2022). https://doi.org/10.1007/s12559-021-09946-2

11. Cheung, C.Y. et al.: A deep learning model for detection of Alzheimer's disease based on retinal photographs: a retrospective, multicentre case-control study. Lancet Digit. Health. **4**(11), e806–e815 (2022). https://doi.org/10.1016/S2589-7500(22)00169-8

12. Rana, M.M. et al.: A robust and clinically applicable deep learning model for early detection of Alzheimer's. IET Image Process. **17**, 3959–3975 (2023). https://doi.org/10.1049/ipr2.12910

13. Sheetal, J., Sasi, D.S.: DETECTION OF ALZHEIMER USING NEURAL NETWORK MODELS CNN AND VGG19. International Journal of Creative Research Thoughts (IJCRT). **9**(9), a562–a565 (2021) ISSN:2320-2882 Available at :http://www.ijcrt.org/papers/IJCRT2109068.pdf

14. Anjali, Singh, D., Pandey, O., Dai, H.-N.: STCNN: combining SMOTE-TOMEK with CNN for imbalanced classification of Alzheimer's disease. IEEE Sens. Lett. **8**, 1–4 (2024). https://doi.org/10.1109/LSENS.2024.3357196

15. Diogo, V.S., Ferreira, H.A., Prata, D.: Alzheimer's Disease Neuroimaging Initiative Early diagnosis of Alzheimer's disease using machine learning: a multi-diagnostic, generalizable approach. Alzheimer's Res. Ther. **14**(1), 107 (2022). https://doi.org/10.1186/s13195-022-01047-y

Early Diagnosis of Alzheimer's Disease Using Deep Learning

Sanya Rastogi[✉] , Malika Taneja , R. Anto Arockia Rosaline , and G. Usha

Department of Computing Technologies, School of Computing, SRM Institute of Science and Technology, Kattankulathur, Chennai 603203, Tamil Nadu, India
`{sr5129,mt9975,antoaror,ushag}@srmist.edu.in`

Abstract. The most prevalent type of dementia, Alzheimer's disease (AD) progressively deteriorates cognitive function. Conventional diagnostic techniques for Alzheimer's disease include obtaining previous medical records, doing MRI scans, and carrying out neuro-physical testing. For patients, though, these procedures can be troublesome, inconvenient and time consuming. This project uses a deep learning model called DenseNet121 to provide a revolutionary way for diagnosis of Alzheimer's under Sustainable Development Goals (SDG-3) Good Health and Well-Being. Using classified Magnetic Resonance Imaging (MRI) data, encompassing extremely mild, mild, moderate, and non-demented phases of Alzheimer's disease, the model will be trained and evaluated. The DenseNet121 model successfully collects characteristics from the MRI data by utilizing deep learning approaches, yielding encouraging outcomes. A Flask web application will be developed in this study that will offer a practical tool for healthcare professionals to utilize DL algorithms for disease diagnosis in a user-friendly manner. Potential management and treatment of AD depend heavily on early discovery. Through the integration of medical imaging data, this research highlights the potential of DL in facilitating early identification of AD.

Keywords: Disease Prediction · Healthcare · Magnetic Resonance Imaging (MRI) · Alzheimer's Disease (AD) · Deep Learning (DL) · Convolutional Neural Network (CNN) · DenseNet121 · Cognitive Impairment (CI)

1   Introduction

Alzheimer's disease (AD) is a neurological illness that predominantly strikes the geriatric population. Its characteristic traits include memory loss, progressive CI, and challenges with daily functioning. As the global population continues to age, AD is anticipated to become progressively prevalent, posing significant challenges for healthcare systems worldwide. Timely identification and precise diagnosis of AD are essential for initiating interventions promptly, managing the disease, and exploring potential therapeutic options. However, traditional diagnostic methods involve extensive medical record retrieval, neuroimaging scans, and neuro-physical testing, which can be time-consuming, costly, and burdensome for both patients and healthcare professionals. Recent years have

R. Appavoo et al. (Eds.): IconDeepCom 2024, CCIS 2687, pp. 132–145, 2026.
https://doi.org/10.1007/978-3-032-26680-4_10

seen the emergence of DL, a subsection of machine learning (ML), as a promising domain for disease diagnosis and medical image analysis. Algorithms like convolutional neural networks (CNNs) within DL have exhibited outstanding capabilities across a spectrum of medical imaging assignments, notably in identifying and categorizing neurological conditions.

2 Related Works

Using DNA Methylation and Gene Expression Microarray Data together with a Deep Belief Network, Nivedhitha Mahendran et al. developed a prediction model to solve the difficulties associated with High Dimension Low Sample Size (HDLSS) concerns in AD prediction. To get around HDLSS, a two-layer feature selection technique was applied. With the use of Jaccard similarity, it was possible to identify methylated and differentially expressed genes between datasets. An ensemble-based feature selection further refined gene selection [6]. However, challenges arose from the interactive and interdependent biological processes in omics datasets. Transfer learning was applied on VGG19 by Farah Mohammad et al. for deep feature extraction, followed by concatenation and redundancy elimination using an updated WoA algorithm [7]. The study's dataset, featuring AD, normal cognitive function, and cognitive impairment categories, exhibited class imbalance. Supervised learning models achieved accuracies ranging from 63% to 99%, showcasing potential diagnostic applications in neuro-oncology, epilepsy, and schizophrenia. While promising, generalization is hindered by dataset specificity, necessitating further validation studies. Computational complexity in handling large datasets also poses a major challenge in the work of Mason English et al. in Ref [8]. The CNN architecture discussed is notably speedier as compared to the volume/thickness model, where they must be extracted prior to use. Ref [9] focuses on using structural MRIs to differentiate mild CI and cognitively normal persons from mild AD dementia. According to S. Liu et al. efficiency lies in rapid processing, eliminating the need for pre-extracted volumetric and thickness data. The model showcases a streamlined approach for early diagnosis of AD, emphasizing speed and accuracy in discerning between different cognitive states based on structural MRI information. For the purpose of detecting AD, Hadeer A. Helaly et al. used two different approaches in [10]. The first one uses 2D and 3D structural brain images with basic CNN designs. The second employs transfer learning, leveraging pre-trained models like VGG19 for image classification. A proposed web service facilitates remote AD checking and staging, providing advice based on the detected stage. The dataset undergoes augmentation with simple techniques, and future plans include MRI segmentation to highlight Alzheimer's features before classifying AD stages. This comprehensive approach integrates CNNs, transfer learning, and advanced image processing for efficient AD diagnosis and remote monitoring. A CNN-based model with a transfer learning approach is employed to enhance performance and reduce time complexity in the early detection of AD. The study evaluates the performance metrics of DL strategies across various neuroimaging data. However, limitations arise in 3D architectures, as DL exhibits low performance on limited datasets, increasing the likelihood of overfitting. This factor compromises the capacity of the suggested deep models to be generalized in [11] by Sina Fathi et al. highlighting the challenges in applying intricate DL techniques to limited datasets, particularly in the context of neuroimaging for AD detection. In order to increase sensitivity and specificity, AD diagnosis prediction models employ ML algorithms including Logistic Regression, Random Forest, Naïve Bayes, and Support Vector Machine [12]. The study by Chun-Hung Chang et al. explores novel biomarkers associated with AD pathology, offering potential advancements in understanding and identifying the disease. However, the generalization of findings to diverse populations necessitates further investigation, emphasizing the importance of validating these models across different demographic groups. The utilization of Naïve Bayes for predictive models in Alzheimer's disease (AD) is coupled with an exploration of novel biomarkers linked to AD pathology. Multiple variables are incorporated to enhance AD classification accuracy. However, the study is constrained to a meta-analysis, potentially necessitating additional validation studies for robustness. The emphasis on Naïve Bayes in [13] by Ting-I Chiang et al. highlights a probabilistic approach in predictive modeling, offering insights into the potential of varied biomarkers and multiple variables for more nuanced and accurate AD classification. Despite these promising aspects, the call for further validation underscores the importance of ensuring the reliability and applicability of the findings across diverse datasets. DL techniques, including CNN, SVM, and KNN, are applied to multi-modal data, showcasing their versatility [14]. A new deep learning framework for multi-modality data fusion performs better than single-modality DL techniques. However, the study's weaknesses stem from a small dataset, which could lead to fewer precise conclusions and less variety. Despite this constraint, the exploration of multi-modal data and the development of an advanced DL framework by Janani et al. underscore the potential for enhancing the accuracy and comprehensiveness of neuroimaging analysis. The cascaded CNN method involves initial image segmentation for bilateral hippocampus masks, facilitating the subsequent learning of a variety of merged hierarchical characteristics, including asymmetry and hippocampus morphologies. However, the method is confined to the ADNI dataset, and its applicability to other datasets necessitates assessment. Generalization to diverse populations and scanner types requires further investigation, highlighting potential limitations in the model's adaptability. Additionally, the method may face increased computational complexity when handling large datasets, indicating considerations for scalability. Despite these difficulties, Aojie Li et al. [15] provide a sophisticated investigation of hippocampus characteristics for prospective improvements in the identification of AD via neuroimaging analysis.

3 Proposed Approach

The proposed system utilizes deep learning, specifically the DenseNet121 model, for early AD detection. It leverages categorized MRI data to extract relevant features and make accurate predictions for varying degrees of Alzheimer's. The system includes model training and evaluation phases to ensure accuracy and generalization ability. A user-friendly Flask web application is developed for real-time diagnosis and easy interaction with the deep learning model. The system's advantage lies in timely detection, potential treatment benefits, and improved accessibility for healthcare professionals.

The proposed methodology comprises the subsequent stages.

The data comprises of MRI images, divided into four sub-classes namely:

1. Very Mild Demented
2. Mild Demented
3. Moderate Demented
4. Non-Demented

Approximately 6400 brain scans, each segregated according to the severity of AD, are included in the two files-Training and Testing that make up the dataset shown in Fig. 1.

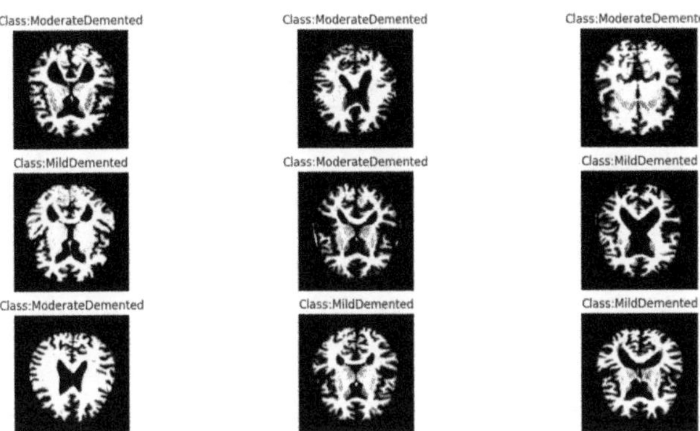

Fig. 1. Dataset Sample Images

3.1 Motivation

It is often seen that people tend to avoid and delay taking professional help in case of minor health issues which leads to late diagnosis and fatal health issues consequently. The phrase "Prevention is better than Cure" is aptly stated, and served as a major inspiration behind this project. The benefits of using deep learning include its ability to harness technological breakthroughs, enhance patient outcomes, have a major impact on public health, and provide insightful information to the scientific community.

Block Diagram

The information flow inside the model is depicted in Fig. 2, where Data Augmentation, Rescaling, Normalization, Splitting, and Grey-Scaling are executed on the brain scan obtained from the MRI dataset during image pre-processing.

The model is then trained by splitting the dataset into subgroups for testing and training. By exposing the model to a greater range of variables in the data during training, data augmentation aids in the reduction of overfitting. By strengthening the model's resistance to variations in the input data, it also contributes in enhancing the model's capacity for generalization. As soon as the final H5 model is ready, it is then integrated with a Flask framework web application which would input the MRI scan from the user, process it using the DenseNet121 model and predict the outcome.

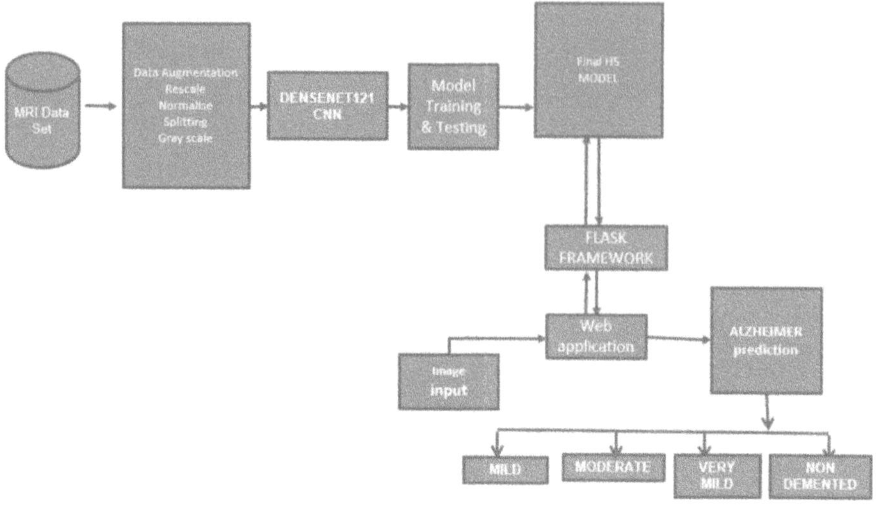

Fig. 2. Block Diagram

Architecture Diagram

The architecture diagram in Fig. 3 depicts how the Densenet121 model trains and tests dataset after splitting to predict the final H5 model. Based on the learning, the model outputs the stage of Alzheimer the patient is suffering from and displays the result.

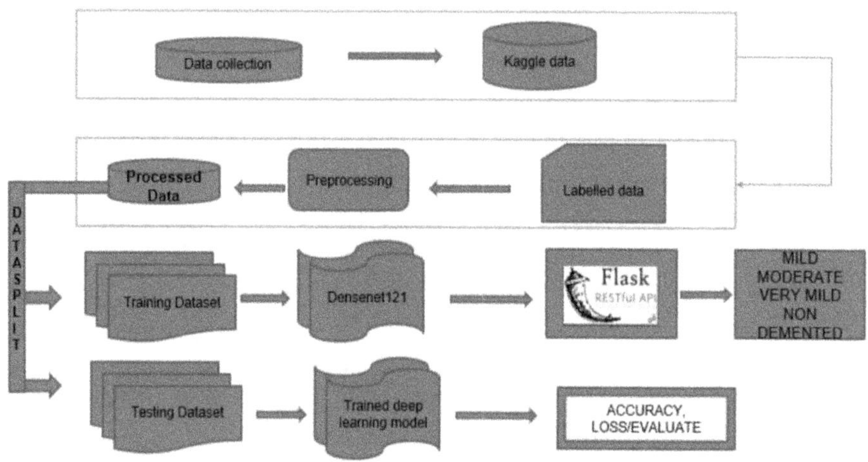

Fig. 3. Architecture Diagram

3.2 DENSENET121

Convolutional, pooling, and fully linked layers are among the 121 layers that make up DenseNet121. It adheres to a "Dense Block," a building block structure made up of several layers that are closely spaced apart. Each layer's input within a dense block is a concatenation of the feature maps from all levels that came before it. Improved model performance results from this dense connectivity, which promotes feature reuse and makes information flow easier. Transition layers are another aspect of DenseNet121. They are employed to limit the quantity of feature maps and reduce the spatial dimensions down sampling. These transition layers in Fig. 4 contain a combination of convolutional, pooling, and dimensionality reduction operations.

Activation Layer - Using the weighted total of the inputs, it generates a single output. In an event where the image is too large, the number of parameters is reduced using the Pooling Layers section. Spatial pooling lowers each map's dimensionality while keeping crucial details. There are several conceivable variations of spatial pooling:

Max Pooling - this involves selecting the greatest element on the feature map.
Average Pooling - this involves selecting the average element of the feature map.
Sum Pooling - this involves aggregating the sum of all elements in the feature map.

Fully Connected Layer - This layer sends the vectorized matrix onto a fully connected layer, like to a neural network, by flattening it. Additionally, a column vector (x1, x2, x3,...) will be generated from the matrix containing the feature map. We integrate these features with the fully connected layers to build a model that divides input images into different classes according to the training set.
Dropout Layer - It stops network nodes from co-adapting to one another.

DenseNet121's design is distinguished by its dense connection, in which every layer is feed-forwardly coupled to every other layer. The vanishing gradient problem is lessened by this extensive connection, which allows for feature reuse and information flow throughout the network. This improves gradient propagation.

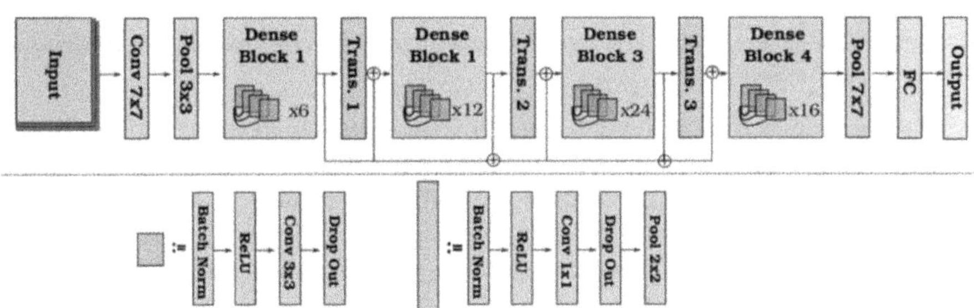

Fig. 4. Densenet121

3.3 Dataset

Model Training
The preprocessed MRI data is partitioned into validation and training sets. The

DenseNet121 model is then trained on the training data using a supervised learning approach. The model gains the ability to identify pertinent characteristics from MRI pictures and categorize them into various AD stages throughout training.

Model Testing

It is crucial to evaluate a machine learning model's efficacy on a testing set once it has been trained in order to determine its accuracy. This process is called Model Evaluation. The testing set is a different dataset that is used to evaluate the capacity of the model to generalize new data. The proportion of properly identified cases over total occurrences is the accuracy calculation algorithm utilized in the code. It is calculated as

$$(\text{Rightly Classified Instances}/\text{Total Instances})^{*}\ 100$$

The two common plots used for Model Evaluation are:

Accuracy Plot - An accuracy plot illustrates the model's performance on testing set as the number of training epochs increase. The percentage of correctly categorized samples in the testing set is often utilized to calculate accuracy. The accuracy on the testing set usually rises with training, but overfitting may cause it to eventually stagnate or even drop.

Loss Plot - The variation in loss (or error) between the training and testing sets with the progression of training epochs is illustrated on a loss plot. The difference between the model's projected and actual outputs is typically used to calculate the loss. The loss should decrease as the model is trained, indicating that the model is improving its ability to make predictions.

Multiclass Classification Problem

Output Layer Configuration - The output layer is defined as a Dense layer with four units, as there are four classes in the dataset and, an activation function of 'softmax', used to achieve probability distribution of classes. It makes sure that the total anticipated class probabilities equal one, allowing for meaningful class probabilities to be obtained for multi-class classification.

- Classification Accuracy - It is computed by fractionalizing the sum of correct predictions with respect to the whole set of input samples. It operates in an optimal manner when each class possesses an equivalent number of samples.
- Loss Function - Cross-Entropy, also referred to as Logarithmic loss. It measures the discrepancy between the actual target values and the anticipated output. Reducing this loss is the main objective of training.
- Loss - Exclusively used to assess and diagnose model optimization.
- Metric - Used to assess and select models according to the project's requirements.
- Precision - Out of all the positive forecasts, the precision metric calculates the proportion of real positives. It displays the model's accuracy in identifying positive cases.
- Recall - The recall metric calculates the proportion of true positive cases to actual positive cases. It stands for the model's capacity to identify every positive scenario.
- F1-score - This balanced indicator of the accuracy and comprehensiveness of the model is calculated as the precision and recall harmonic mean.

3.4 Flask Framework

This project focuses on creating a Flask-based web application for the recognition of AD. Users can upload MRI brain scans for classification using the DenseNet121 model. The frontend, designed with HTML, CSS, and JavaScript, ensures a user-friendly experience. The Flask-powered backend processes uploaded images, performs inference with the deep learning model, and communicates the result. Python facilitates image processing and model inference. Flask's lightweight nature and flexibility enables easy web app development. The seamless integration of frontend and backend components ensures efficient user-server communication. This tool, aiding healthcare professionals, enhances accessibility, efficiency, and accuracy in anticipating the stage of AD, potentially leading to early detection, timely treatment and improved outcomes.

4 Result

Figure 5 is representing the outputs recognizing the stage of AD for respective MRI brain scans. The four phases namely being-Very Mild Demented, Mild Demented, Moderate Demented and Non-Demented on the basis of input data received as shown above previously in Fig. 1. Further, based on these experimental results, Model Accuracy, Model Loss and Model Area Under Curve are evaluated and Confusion Matrix is calculated.

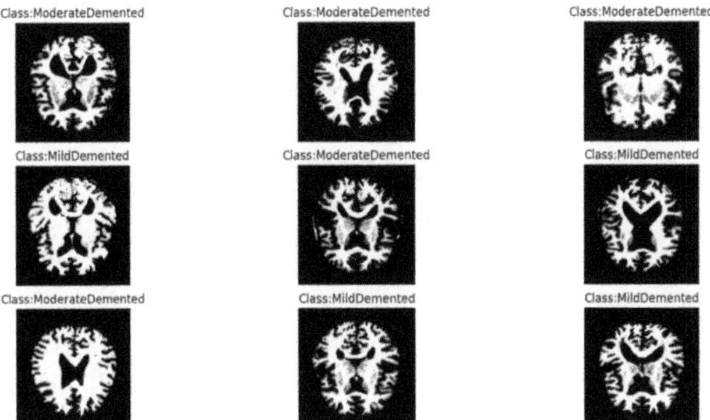

Fig. 5. Output predicting the stage of Dementia

4.1 Model Accuracy

The Fig. 6 graph represents the model performance. The high training accuracy (95%) in this instance indicates that the model has not learned broad patterns, but rather has internalized the training data. As a result, when the model encounters new data during testing, the test accuracy is lower (80%).

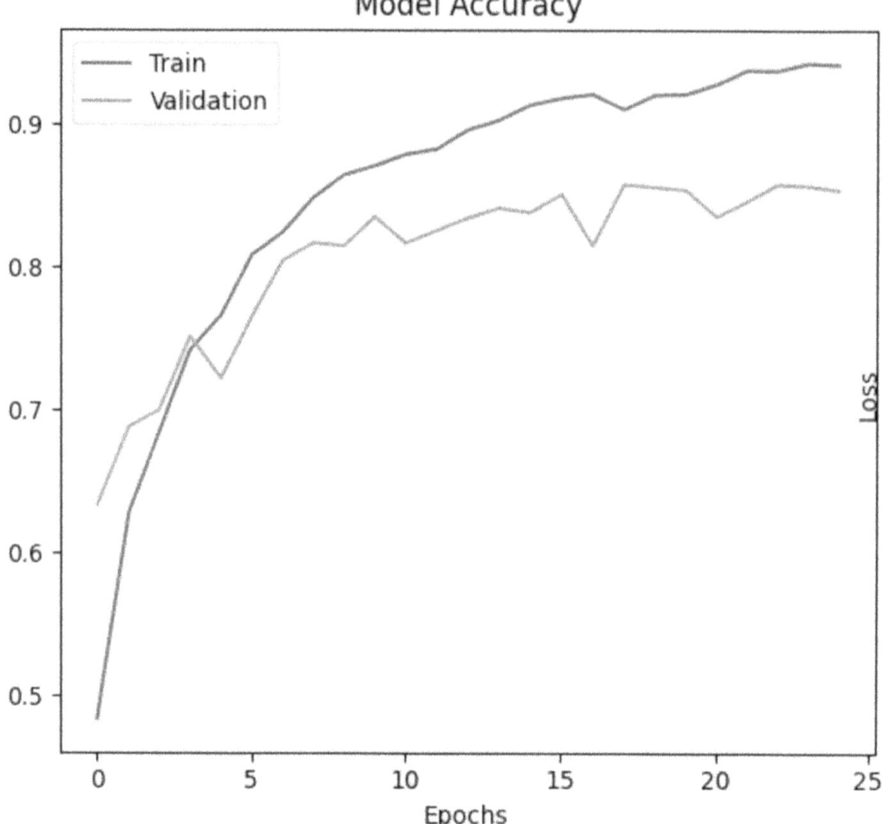

Fig. 6. Model Accuracy

4.2 Model Loss

The rise in the model loss graph in Fig. 7 represents an increase in the value of the loss function during training. This increase in loss indicates that the model's predictions are deviating more from the actual target values, and the current set of parameters is not performing well on the training data.

A fall in the model loss graph represents a decrease in the value of the loss function during the training process. This decrease indicates that the model's predictions are improving, and it is getting closer to making accurate predictions on the training data.

Training Data Loss - The training data loss (error) is 0.3. This indicates that while the model is optimized using the training data during the training phase, the average loss or error per data point is 0.3. A model that optimizes its predictions and fits the training data well is characterized by diminished loss values.

Validation Data Loss - The validation data loss (error) is 0.6. This value represents the average loss or error per data point on a separate validation dataset that the model has not seen earlier. In order to evaluate the model's efficacy on unobserved data, the

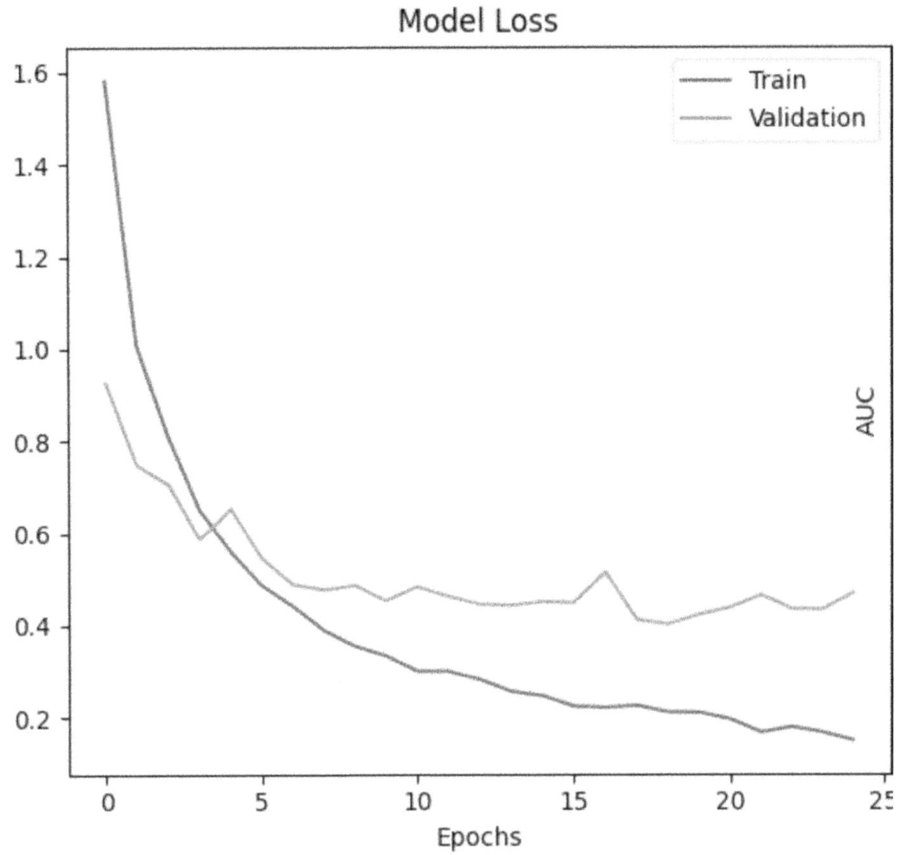

Fig. 7. Model Loss

validation dataset is utilized. A validation loss of 0.6 in this instance means that the model's predictions on the validation data are somewhat less accurate than those on the training data

4.3 Model Area Under Curve

The AUC measures how well the model can discriminate between positive and negative classifications. AUC values that are closer to 1 indicate that the model possesses greater discriminatory strength and can categorize cases more accurately. Figure 8 shows a graphic depiction of the ratio of true positives (sensitivity) to false positives (1 - specificity) for different threshold settings. The AUC represents for area beneath the Receiver Operating Characteristic (ROC) curve. When the AUC is less than 0.5, the model's predictions are poorer than guesswork, and an AUC of 0.5 indicates random chance.

Train Accuracy - The training accuracy is one, that implies that the model attained a flawless accuracy of 100% on the training data. This shows that every case in the training dataset was correctly classified by the model.

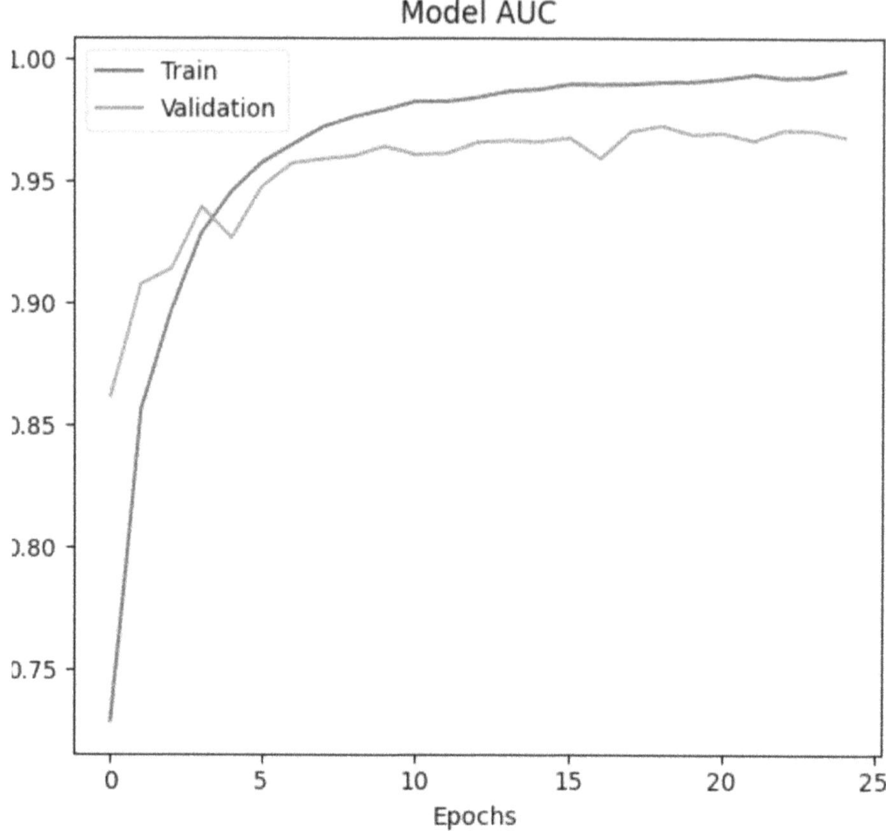

Fig. 8. Model Area Under Curve

Validation AUC - AUC for validation is 0.95. An ideal classifier is denoted by 1, whereas a random classifier is denoted by 0.5 in the AUC. With an AUC of 0.95, which is relatively high, the model appears to be operating very well on the validation set of data.

4.4 Confusion Matrix

The values in a heatmap are mapped to different shades of blue, where darker hues indicate greater values, whereas lighter tints indicate lower values. In Fig. 9, the first row represents Moderate Demented wherein the diagonal element (365) indicates the number of correctly predicted instances. Misclassifications are represented by the values (61, 0 and 4) which show cases in which Moderate Demented were incorrectly forecasted as Mild Demented, Very Mild Demented, and Non-Demented, respectively. Similarly, the diagonal element (584) in Mild Demented row, diagonal element (5) in Very Mild Demented row and diagonal element (127) in Non-Demented row represent accurate prediction while other cells of the matrix represent misclassification.

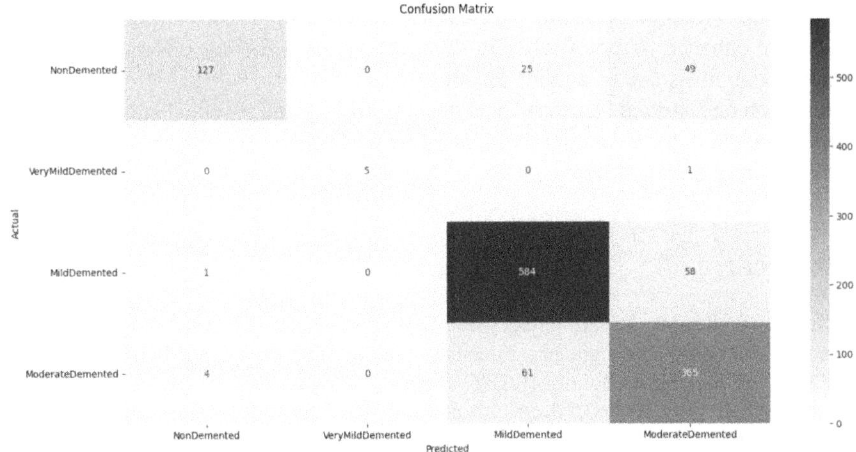

Fig. 9. Confusion Matrix

5 Conclusion

This research highlights the capability and usefulness of DL, more especially, the DenseNet121 model, in the early detection of AD. By leveraging categorized MRI data and extracting features using the DenseNet121 model, the study achieved promising results in terms of accuracy. The development of a Flask web application further enhances the practicality and accessibility of using deep learning algorithms for Alzheimer's disease diagnosis. The user-friendly interface of the web application allows healthcare professionals to efficiently utilize DL strategies in the detection and management of AD. Additional progress in deep learning models, coupled with the incorporation of innovative technologies and datasets, possesses substantial promise in advancing the domain of AD diagnosis and, ultimately, enhancing patient outcomes.

6 Future Enhancement

- Multi-Modal Data Fusion - Integrating data from various sources along with other biomarkers like genetic data and cognitive tests, can enhance the model's diagnostic power. This facilitates a more exhaustive examination of the pathology of AD and has the potential to generate more precise prognostications.
- Longitudinal Data Analysis - A longitudinal patient monitoring approach has the potential to enhance the model's ability to trace the progression of AD and recognize early warning signs more promptly. Longitudinal data can help differentiate between normal aging and early-stage Alzheimer's disease.
- Explainable AI - Implementing techniques for interpretability can provide insights regarding the methodology employed by the model in generating its prediction which can improve the trust in model's decisions and help healthcare professionals understand the underlying features contributing to the diagnosis.

- Real-Time Inference - Optimizing the model and web application for real-time inference can enhance its practicality in clinical settings. Efficient inference allows for quicker diagnosis and treatment decisions.
- Validation on External Datasets - The generalizability and practical application of the model can be demonstrated by validating its performance on external datasets from other sources and organizations.

References

1. Illakiya, T., Karthik, R.: Automatic detection of Alzheimer's disease using deep learning models and neuro-imaging: current trends and future perspectives. Neuroinformatics. **21**(2), 339–364 (2023). https://doi.org/10.1007/s12021-023-09625-7
2. Liu, M. et al.: A multi-model deep convolutional neural network for automatic hippocampus segmentation and classification in Alzheimer's disease. NeuroImage. **208**, 116459 (2020). https://doi.org/10.1016/j.neuroimage.2019.116459
3. Spasov, S., Passamonti, L., Duggento, A., Liò, P., Toschi, N., Alzheimer's Disease Neuroimaging Initiative: A parameter-efficient deep learning approach to predict conversion from mild cognitive impairment to Alzheimer's disease. NeuroImage. **189**, 276–287 (2019). https://doi.org/10.1016/j.neuroimage.2019.01.031
4. Feng, W. et al.: Automated MRI-based deep learning model for detection of Alzheimer's disease process. Int. J. Neural Syst. **30**(6), 2050032 (2020). https://doi.org/10.1142/S0129065720500032X
5. Lin, L., Xiong, M., Zhang, G., Kang, W., Sun, S., Wu, S.: A convolutional neural network and graph convolutional network based framework for AD classification. Sensors. **23**(4), 1914 (2023). https://doi.org/10.3390/s23041914. PMID: 36850510
6. Mahendran, N., Vincent, P.M.D.R.: Deep belief network-based approach for detecting Alzheimer's disease using the multi-omics data. Comput. Struct. Biotechnol. J. **13**(21), 1651–1660 (2023). https://doi.org/10.1016/j.csbj.2023.02.021. PMID: 36874164; PMCID: PMC9978469
7. Mohammad, F., Al Ahmadi, S.: Alzheimer's disease prediction using deep feature extraction and optimization. Mathematics. **11**, 3712 (2023). https://doi.org/10.3390/math11173712
8. English, M., Kumar, C., Ditterline, B.L., Drazin, D., Dietz, N.: Machine learning in neuro-oncology, epilepsy, Alzheimer's disease, and schizophrenia. In: Staartjes, V.E., Regli, L., Serra, C. (eds.) Machine Learning in Clinical Neuroscience. Acta Neurochirurgica Supplement, vol. 134. Springer, Cham (2022). https://doi.org/10.1007/978-3-030-85292-4_39
9. Liu, S., Masurkar, A.V., Rusinek, H., et al.: Generalizable deep learning model for early Alzheimer's disease detection from structural MRIs. Sci. Rep. **12**, 17106 (2022). https://doi.org/10.1038/s41598-022-20674-x
10. Helaly, H.A., Badawy, M., Haikal, A.Y.: Deep learning approach for early detection of Alzheimer's disease. Cogn. Comput. **14**, 1711–1727 (2022). https://doi.org/10.1007/s12559-021-09946-2
11. Fathi, S., Ahmadi, M., Dehnad, A.: Early diagnosis of Alzheimer's disease based on deep learning: a systematic review. Comput. Biol. Med. **146**, 105634.,ISSN00104825 (https://www.sciencedirect.com/science/article/pii/S0010482522004267) (2022). https://doi.org/10.1016/j.compbiomed.2022.105634
12. Chang, C.-H., Lin, C.-H., Lane, H.-Y.: Machine learning and novel biomarkers for the diagnosis of Alzheimer's disease. Int. J. Mol. Sci. **22**, 2761 (2021). https://doi.org/10.3390/ijms22052761

13. Chiang, T.I., Yu, Y.H., Lin, C.H., Lane, H.Y.: Novel biomarkers of Alzheimer's disease: based upon N-methyl-D-aspartate receptor hypoactivation and oxidative stress. Clin. Psychopharmacol. Neurosci. **19**(3), 423–433 (2021). https://doi.org/10.9758/cpn.2021.19.3.423. PMID: 34294612; PMCID: PMC8316669

14. Venugopalan, J., Tong, L., Hassanzadeh, H.R., Wang, M.D.: Multimodal deep learning models for early detection of Alzheimer's disease stage. Sci. Rep. **11**(1), 3254 (2021). https://doi.org/ 10.1038/s41598-020-74399-w. PMID: 33547343; PMCID: PMC7864942

15. Li, A., Li, F., Elahifasaee, F., et al.: Hippocampal shape and asymmetry analysis by cascaded convolutional neural networks for Alzheimer's disease diagnosis. Brain Imaging Behav. **15**, 2330–2339 (2021). https://doi.org/10.1007/s11682-020-00427-y

Medical Image Disease Prediction with Secure Data Sharing Using Multisecret Sharing Approach

Rosy Salomi Victoria Daniel[1]([⊠]) [iD], Susilnithi Senthilkumar[2], and Varun Kannan Elumalai[2]

[1] Chennai Institute of Technology, Kundrathur, Chennai, India
drosysalomi@gmail.com
[2] St. Joseph's College of Engineering, Chennai, India

Abstract. The paramount significance of security in medical image communication lies in its quality of the patient's personal information. Safeguarding this data is crucial when digital images and patient information are transmitted over public networks. Medical images contain high sensitive and critical data. Each pixel in these images holds significant diagnostic value, and any alteration could lead to inaccurate diagnoses. Ensuring robust security for these images is imperative, and any compromise in security could have severe consequences, as the margin for redundancy is minimal. The embedding capacity of medical images is limited, making it challenging to employ traditional security measures. Some researchers say that encrypted data and hidden data are examples of data protection technologies that can be used to guarantee the database. These two may cause stagnation in the processing time and inadequacy, in situations with medical images. This paper suggests applying the Fragmented based Elliptical Curve Cryptography combined with Convolutional Neural Network algorithms to design a system that enables secure disease diagnosis using medical images. The experimental results further prove the efficiency of the system applied to Lung CT scan images collected from open medical data sources. The implemented security measures provide a high level of protection for sensitive medical data during transmission.

Keywords: Cryptography · Convolution Neural Network · Lung Computed Tomography (CT)

1 Introduction

The integration of medical imaging into cloud-based systems for disease prediction faces multifaceted challenges. The healthcare sector relies on diverse imaging techniques including radiography, MRI, and ultrasound, in which case the retrieval of high-definition medical images for adequate evaluation has to be possible wherever the access to internet is poor. Picture Archiving and Communication System (PACS) and Vendor Neutral Archive is a conventional system used but despite their transporting abilities, cloud-based networks unfold more diverse and agile functionalities like shared virtual storage. Quality

© The Author(s), under exclusive license to Springer Nature Switzerland AG 2026
R. Appavoo et al. (Eds.): IconDeepCom 2024, CCIS 2687, pp. 146–157, 2026.
https://doi.org/10.1007/978-3-032-26680-4_11

and speed are two major reasons impeding especially remote areas with limited internet throughput thereby rendering high-resolution images a hurdle. Security apprehensions among health-care executives, rooted in their vulnerability to data breaches, hinder the seamless transition to cloud-based solutions. On-premise data centers are susceptible to physical disasters, while cloud services offer multi-region recovery capabilities. Existing on-premise systems, which are protected by Virtual Private Networks and firewalls, make it difficult and time-consuming for healthcare workers to access patient records or images. This slows down the delivery of efficient healthcare services. To solve this problem, a new solution is suggested for predicting diseases from medical images while securely sharing data using a multi-secret sharing method. This system uses cloud storage to improve the quality, accessibility, and security of medical images.

The solution uses Artificial Intelligence (AI), Machine Learning (ML), and other advanced image processing techniques to better analyze medical images. Deep learning, a part of machine learning, uses Deep Neural Networks (DNNs) to find important features in raw data, making it easier to understand and interpret medical information. The system is designed to help with disease diagnosis and the processing of medical images. The system is designed to help with diagnosing diseases and analyzing medical images, which is important because there aren't enough radiologists, and human judgment can sometimes affect the results. To keep data safe when sharing it, the system uses a special method that mixes cryptography and visual cryptography. This method turns medical images into pieces that people can put back together without needing complicated math. This not only makes the data more secure but also easier to encrypt and decrypt, since it just requires people to look at the pieces.

The use of multiple secret-sharing methods protects patient data during transfer, addressing the security issues that prevent the healthcare industry from adopting cloud technology. The suggested approach aims to transform medical imaging by integrating sophisticated image processing with secure cloud storage and data sharing, ultimately leading to better disease prediction and healthcare services.

2   Related Research

A thorough analysis of security challenges [1] highlights the importance of addressing privacy concerns when implementing models, especially those using Long Short Term Memory (LSTM) networks. Despite ML/DL's transformative potential in healthcare, the authors underscore the need for robust security measures. A novel contribute light weight chaos-based encryption scheme [2] for medical images, leveraging chaotic maps to bolster security. The implementation costs associated with their approach pose notable challenges. A lightweight encryption algorithm [3] is tailored for secure image encryption in healthcare, prioritizing efficiency. The algorithm's vulnerability to greater harm if breached worries about its reliability in practical situations. A system for embedding watermarks [4] in medical images for e-healthcare applications is suggested, ensuring authentication, privacy, and data integrity. Their method, though less demanding on computing resources, faces challenges due to its complexity. A robust image encryption technique [5] for both grayscale and color medical images is introduced, which reduces pixel correlation and enhances security. The risk of data loss without the decryption key highlights the importance of key management practices. A blockchain-based system is developed for secure and decentralized sharing of medical imaging data [6], offering advantages such as cost savings and better interoperability. Although blockchain operations can be time-consuming, the framework marks a significant step forward in strengthening healthcare data security.

An effective method for finding harmful changes in medical images was created without making the system worse at telling what the images show. This method, which uses a tool called Support Vector Machine [7], can be used in many different medical image situations. A new way to protect the true and correct state of medical images [8] was also made, using special techniques called recursive dither modulation and slantlet transform. The method can check both the true and correct state of images [9] at the same time, even though it might be a bit hard to use. A collaborative learning method [10] has been introduced for disease grading and lesion segmentation in medical images, showing its effectiveness through comprehensive evaluation on Diabetic Retinopathy (DR) data.

Collaborative Learning of Unsupervised Convolution Neural Networks (CLU-CNNs) [11], a domain adaptation framework tailored for medical images, enhancing domain adaptability using CNN and clustering techniques is proposed. This framework provides an effective approach for medical image domain adaptation [12], facilitating improved disease diagnosis and segmentation. Smart contract and Inter Planetary File System [13] according to the secure medical image shield scheme proposed to encrypt the session information. It reports every operation of patient information in the Blockchain for improved traceability.

The algorithms of encryption [14] estimate the recital according to the execution time and VGG16 according to the processing cost and accuracy. Privacy Preserving of Deep Learning [15] focuses on the use of Deep Learning in healthcare within private and public cloud environments, as well as the privacy implications of design changes. The Electronic Patient Healthcare system [16] illustrates big imperceptibility, toughness, and watermark safety at less computational amount. Each study offers distinct insights and methods that enhance the overall understanding of how to secure medical imaging data. They highlight the critical need for strong security measures in healthcare systems and present various strategies to tackle the challenges related to data privacy and integrity.

3 Proposed System

The planned solution gives a significant advancement over the existing system by addressing the critical issue of security in medical image transmission more comprehensively and effectively. While the current system mainly emphasizes privacy-preserving computations for object detection using faster Region-based Convolutional Neural Network (R-CNN), the new system incorporates fragmented-based Elliptical Curve Cryptography (ECC) with CNN algorithms specifically designed for secure disease diagnosis in medical images. By addressing the unique challenges associated with medical images, such as their sensitivity and the critical diagnostic information embedded in every pixel, the new system provides a more robust solution to maintain the integrity and confidentiality of patient data.

Furthermore, the new system proves its effectiveness through experimental validation using Lung CT scan images, demonstrating not only enhanced security but also successful application with real-world medical data sources. With its innovative approach and concrete results, the new system stands out as a more comprehensive and effective solution for securing medical image data compared to the existing system. The system architecture entails the abstract, high-level structure of software systems, achieved through decomposition and composition, incorporating architectural style and quality attributes. The design of the software architecture must align with the primary functionality and performance criteria of the system while meeting non-functional requirements like reliability, scalability, portability, and availability.

3.1 Dataset Information

The dataset utilized originates from Kaggle and it comprises chest CT-scan images categorized into five classes: COVID, Influenza, Pneumonia, Tuberculosis, and Normal. Figure 1 depicts a flowchart for a secure medical data processing system that involves classifying lung diseases using a CNN, encrypting the information, and securely sharing it between healthcare centers and trusted third parties.

The training dataset consists of 1105 images, with approximately 200 samples per category. Images were preprocessed by resizing them to 200x200 pixels and normalizing pixel values. Data augmentation techniques, including rotation, horizontal flipping, and zooming, were applied to enhance the diversity of the training set.

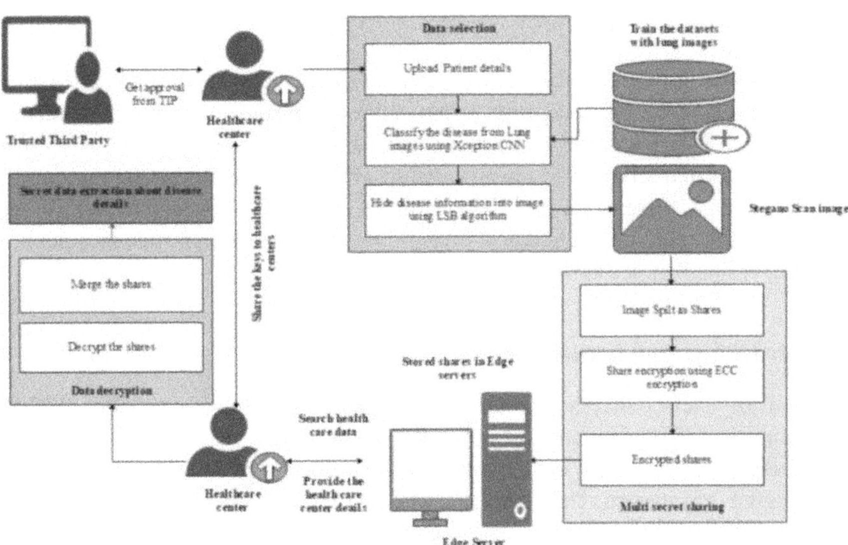

Fig. 1. System Architecture

The test dataset consisted of 2,500 images, evenly divided among the five categories, and was solely used for evaluating the model. The trained model's performance was measured primarily by accuracy, with the confusion matrix offering insights into how well it performed across various classes.

3.2 Framework Construction

A cloud framework is a set of technologies, standards, and guidelines that create a cohesive foundation for building and implementing cloud computing solutions. These frameworks help organizations standardize and automate their cloud-related processes, making it easier to develop, deploy, and manage applications and services in the cloud. The ability to design healthcare centers, trusted third-party entities, and edge servers are done. The healthcare center is responsible for uploading patient data, while the edge server can efficiently manage all associated details. The trusted third party plays a crucial role in approving both the healthcare center and the edge server.

3.3 Features Extraction

The extraction of image features involves capturing essential information from an image and presenting it in a concise and informative format. The objective of this process is to decrease the dimensionality of high-dimensional image data, creating a more compact representation that retains crucial information distinguishing one image from another. Within this module, the focus is on extracting features from medical images, encompassing aspects such as color, shape, and texture found in uploaded lung images.

3.4 Disease Forecasting

Utilizing CNNs for illness forecasting is a prevalent method in medical imaging, employed to diagnose and categorize diseases through visual analysis. In this methodology, a CNN undergoes training on an extensive dataset comprising medical images and their associated labels. The training allows the model to understand patterns and characteristics associated with specific diseases. As a result, the trained model can forecast outcomes for new, unseen medical images by processing them through the network, producing probability scores for different types of lung diseases.

3.5 Date Hiding with Fragmentation

The details of detected diseases can be hidden within a scanning image using the Least Significant Bit (LSB) technique, creating what is known as a stegno image. LSB-based concealment involves modifying the least significant bits of pixel values in an image to embed digital information. This method works by replacing the least significant bits of pixel values with the binary representation of the hidden information, making sure that the changes are not noticeable to human observers. The stegno image is segmented into multiple parts.

3.6 Data Encryption

Within this segment, the divided portions of the image undergo encryption employing ECC. Image encryption utilizing ECC is a technique employed to safeguard digital images through the application of mathematical algorithms grounded in elliptic curve Principles. ECC functions as a public-key cryptography system, utilizing both a public key and a private key for data encryption and decryption. When encrypting an image with ECC, the image is transformed into an encrypted format using the public key. Only the corresponding private key can decrypt this image. The encrypted image can then be securely transmitted over the internet or stored in a safe location, reducing the risk of unauthorized access or tampering. These specific details are kept within edge servers.

3.7 Access the Medical Image

Data Access control involves the methods and technologies used to manage permissions regarding who or what can access a specific resource. The healthcare centers initiate requests for medical data from edge servers. The request is directed to the respective healthcare center. The encrypted and divided parts are sent to the healthcare center and decrypted using the ECC private key. The pieces are then put back together, and the hidden data in the images is shown.

4 Experimentation and Results

4.1 Confusion Matrix

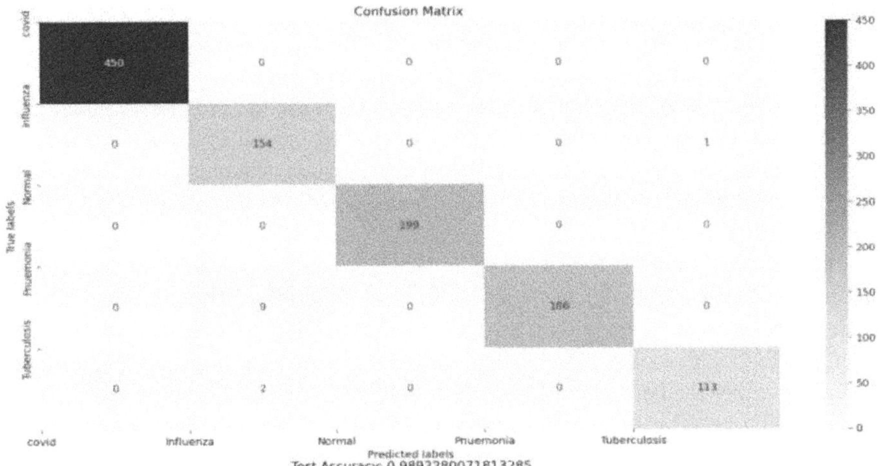

Fig. 2. Confusion Matrix

The Confusion Matrix is a tool used to evaluate classification models, showing a table with important metrics. It gives a detailed look at the model's predictions, going beyond just a simple accuracy score. It provides deep insights into the model's precision, recall, specificity, and other performance measures. This thorough analysis is very useful for understanding how well a classification model works in different situations, helping to make a more complete assessment of its effectiveness. The dataset was carefully chosen to have a balanced mix of each class, reducing any possible biases and making the model more reliable. Each chest CT scan image was carefully checked for quality to ensure consistency and accuracy throughout the dataset.

The dataset includes various respiratory conditions, such as COVID-19, influenza, pneumonia, tuberculosis, and normal lung scans. This variety allows for a thorough analysis and assessment of the model's diagnostic abilities. This study utilizes advanced machine learning techniques to enhance automated diagnostic systems for respiratory diseases, which could help healthcare professionals with early detection and treatment planning. Figure 2 displays a confusion matrix for a classification model with a high test accuracy of approximately 98.92 percentage, effectively distinguishing between COVID, influenza, normal, pneumonia, and tuberculosis cases.

4.2 Performance

The CNN with Elliptic Curve Cryptography (CNN-ECC) emerges as a superior solution compared to other models such as medical image watermarking systems, collaborative medical knowledge integration, Medical Image Clustered

Convolutional Networks (MICCN), and blockchain-based secure medical data sharing. While these models address specific aspects of medical data security and analysis, CNN- ECC offers a holistic approach by combining the power of CNN for accurate image analysis with the robust cryptographic properties of elliptic curve cryptography. By using ECC to encrypt medical imaging data, CNN-ECC guarantees end-to-end security, safeguarding patient privacy and blocking unauthorized access or tampering. ECC provides efficient key generation and encryption processes, minimizing computational overhead and resource consumption, making CNN-ECC suitable for real-time medical imaging applications while guaranteeing data integrity and authentication. Thus, CNN-ECC offers a thorough and effective approach to securing medical imaging data within healthcare systems.

The combination of CNN-ECC not only protects important medical information but also makes it easy for healthcare workers to work together and share data, all while following rules about keeping data private and secure. CNN-ECC works well in many different healthcare settings, like hospitals, clinics, telemedicine services, and research centers. By using the best parts of both CNN and ECC, CNN-ECC helps solve today's problems with keeping medical images safe and also sets the stage for future improvements in healthcare technology and data handling. Figure 3 shows how accurate and precise different medical image watermarking systems are. The purple lines represent the most accurate systems, and the blue lines represent the most precise ones.

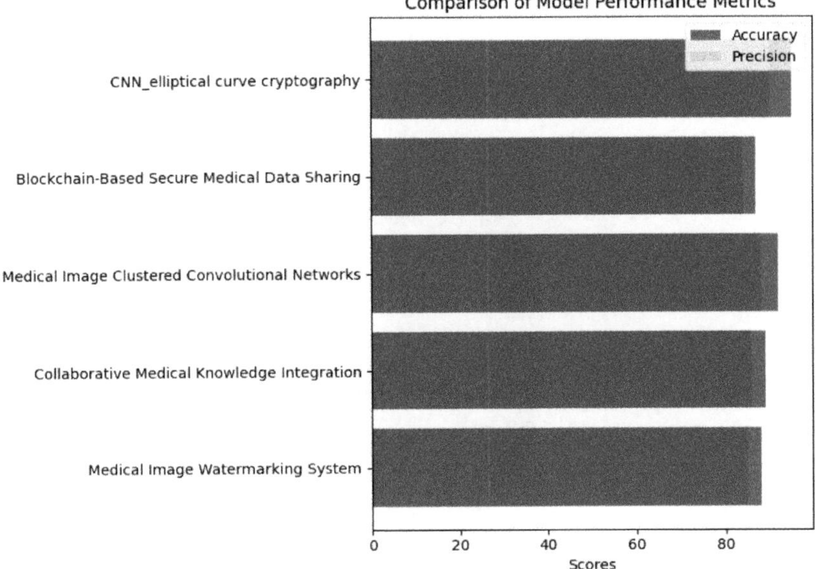

Fig. 3. Performance of Models

4.3 Results

The proposed paper results show that the developed model can accurately classify chest CT-scan images for various respiratory conditions, with a test accuracy of over 98%. The model's performance was measured using metrics like precision, recall, and F1-score, which provided a comprehensive evaluation of its diagnostic accuracy. The high F1-scores for each class show a good balance between precision and recall, indicating the model's ability to effectively identify both positive and negative cases in each category. The model's strength was confirmed using thorough cross-validation methods, which ensured it worked well and consistently across various parts of the data. These results show that machine learning can greatly improve medical decisions, giving doctors valuable information and help in tough diagnosis cases.

The model's ability to explain its decisions was improved using visual tools, making it easier for healthcare workers to understand and trust its process. This study shows how AI-based diagnostic tools can greatly change healthcare, leading to better patient results in respiratory care.The model was tested against current diagnostic methods, showing better results in accuracy, speed, and ability to handle large amounts of data. By using advanced deep learning and detailed image analysis, the model can effectively find important features in chest CT scans, accurately spotting small signs of different lung conditions. Figure 4 shows a lung CT scan with a prescription.

Figure 5 shows another lung CT scan, identified as part of a secure object detection system.

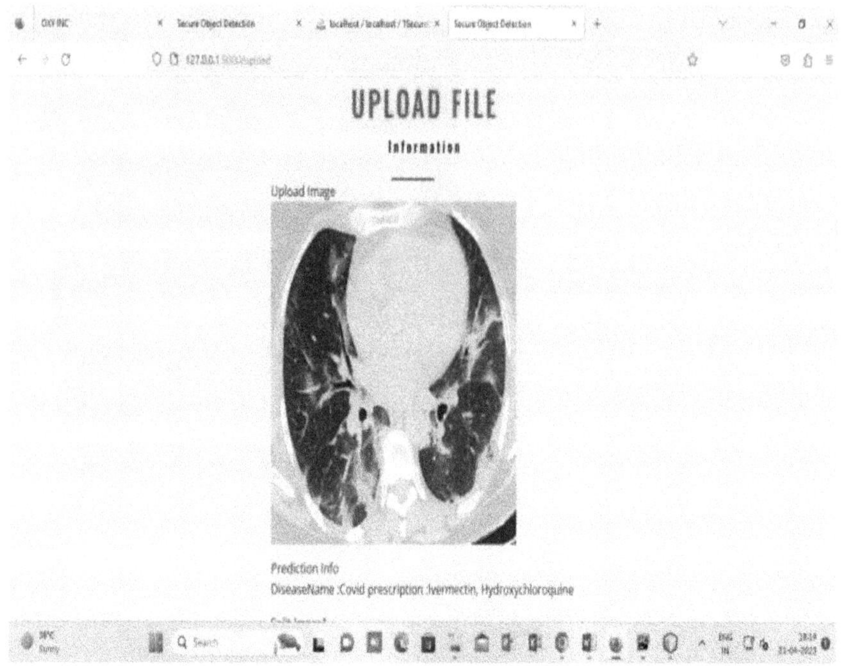

Fig. 4. Upload file With Prescription

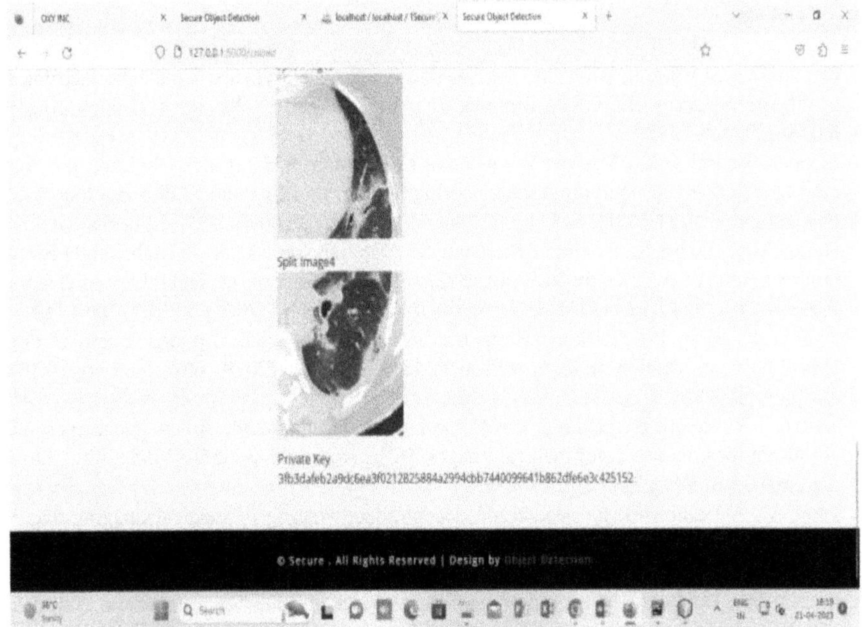

Fig. 5. Upload File with Private-key

5 Summary and Prospective Improvements

This paper's results highlight the effectiveness of deep learning in automatically analyzing chest CT scans for various lung conditions. The model performs very well, accurately and precisely identifying COVID-19, influenza, pneumonia, tuberculosis, and normal lung scans. These results highlight the potential of AI-based diagnostic tools to improve healthcare, especially in respiratory medicine. By using machine learning, doctors can quickly and accurately identify diseases, leading to better patient care and more efficient healthcare processes.

Although the results in this paper are promising, there are many ways to improve and expand this research. Increasing the variety and number of samples in the dataset could make the model more accurate and better at generalizing. Adding data from different sources, like clinical reports or lab tests, could provide extra information and improve the model's ability to diagnose accurately. Improving the deep learning model, adjusting its settings, and trying new training methods are important for making the model work better.

Using the model in real hospitals and seeing how it affects patient care and medical decisions will be crucial to show that it is helpful and can be used widely. Making sure we follow rules about patient privacy and data safety is very important to use AI in healthcare in a responsible and ethical way. These future enhancements have the potential to further advance the field of AI in respiratory medicine and drive transformative changes in healthcare delivery.

References

1. Qayyum, A., Qadir, J., Bilal, M., Al-Fuqaha, A.: Secure and robust machine learning for healthcare: a survey. IEEE Rev. Biomed. Eng. **14**, 156–180 (2020). https://doi.org/10.1109/RBME.2020.3013489
2. Masood, F., Driss, M., Boulila, W., Ahmad, J., Rehman, S.U., et al.: A lightweight chaos-based medical image encryption scheme using random shuffling and XOR operations. Wirel. Pers. Commun. **127**, 1405–1432 (2022). https://doi.org/10.1007/s11277-021-08584-z
3. Hasan, M.K., Islam, S., Sulaiman, R., Khan, S., Aisha-Hassan, A., et al.: Lightweight encryption technique to enhance medical image security on internet of medical things applications. IEEE Access. **9**, 47731–47742 (2021). https://doi.org/10.1109/ACCESS.2021.3061710
4. Aparna, P., Vijay, P.V., Kishore: Biometric-based efficient medical image watermarking in E-healthcare application. IET Image Process. **13**(3), 421–428 (2019). https://doi.org/10.1049/iet-ipr.2018.5288
5. Kamal, S.T., Hosny, K., Elgindy, T.M., Darwish, M., Fouda, M.M.: A new image encryption algorithm for grey and color medical images. IEEE Access. **9**, 37855–37865 (2021). https://doi.org/10.1109/ACCESS.2021.3063237
6. Patel, V.: A framework for secure and decentralized sharing of medical imaging data via blockchain consensus. Health Informatics J. **25**(4), 1398–1411 (2019). https://doi.org/10.1177/1460458218769699
7. Li, X., Zhu, D.: Robust detection of adversarial attacks on medical images. In: 2020 IEEE 17th International Symposium on Biomedical Imaging (ISBI), pp. 1154–1158 (2020). https://doi.org/10.1109/ISBI45749.2020.9098628
8. Liu, X., Lou, J., Fang, H., Chen, Y.: A novel robust reversible watermarking scheme for protecting authenticity and integrity of medical images. IEEE Access. **7**, 76580–76598 (2019). https://doi.org/10.1109/ACCESS.2019.2921894
9. Zhou, Y., He, X., Huang, L., Liu, L., Zhu, F., et al.: Collaborative learning of semi-supervised segmentation and classification for medical images. In: Computer Vision and Pattern Recognition, pp. 2079–2088 (2019). https://doi.org/10.1109/CVPR.2019.00218
10. Li, Z., Minghui, D., Shiping, W., Xiang, H., Zhou, P., Zhigang, Z.: CLU-CNNs: object detection for medical image. Neurocomputing. **350**, 53–59 (2019). https://doi.org/10.1016/j.neucom.2019.04.028
11. Liu, G., Xie, H., Wang, W., Huang, H.: A secure and efficient electronic medical record data sharing scheme based on blockchain and proxy re-encryption. J. Cloud Comput. **13**, 44 (2024). https://doi.org/10.1186/s13677-024-00608-w
12. Ahmed, S.T., Hammood, D.A., Chisab, R.F., Al-Naji, A., Chah, J.: Medical image encryption: a comprehensive review. Computers. **12**, 160 (2023). https://doi.org/10.3390/computers12080160
13. Alsehli, A., Abdul, W., Almowuena, S., Ghouzali, S., Larabi-Marie-Sainte, S.: Medical Image Authentication using watermarking and blockchain. In: IEEE International Conference on E-health Networking, Application and Services (HealthCom) (2022). https://doi.org/10.1109/HealthCom54947.2022.9982793
14. Anusuya, R., Karthika Renuka, D., Oviya, S., Sangavi, R.: Secured data sharing of medical images for disease diagnosis using deep learning models and federated learning framework. In: IEEE International Conference on Intelligent Systems for Communication, IoT and Security (ICISCoIS) (2023). https://doi.org/10.1109/ICISCoIS56541.2023.10100542

15. Naresh, V.S., Thamarai, M., Divakar Allavarpu, V.V.L.: Privacy-preserving deep learning in medical informatics: applications, challenges, and solutions. Artif. Intell. Rev. **56**, 1199–1241 (2023). https://doi.org/10.1007/s10462-023-10556-7

16. Jyothsna Devi, K., Singh, P., Jatindra Kumar, D., Hiren Kumar, T., Tanwar, S., Abdulatif, A.: Secure transmission of medical images in multi-cloud e-healthcare applications using data hiding scheme. J. Inf. Secur. Appl. **79**, 103655 (2023). https://doi.org/10.1016/j.jisa.2023.103655

Denoising MRI Images for Brain Tumor Detection Using BM3D Filter

J. P. Adesh, Kaushik Subramanian, and A. L. Amutha$^{(\boxtimes)}$

Department of Computational Intelligence, College of Engineering and Technology, SRM Institute of Science and Technology, Kattankulathur 603203, Tamil Nadu, India
`amuthaa1@srmist.edu.in`

Abstract. Brain tumors are abnormal formations of brain cells that may be benign or malignant. The diagnosis of the disease may involve imaging studies or biopsy. Therapy involves surgical procedures, radiation treatment, and radiotherapy, depending on the type and location of the tumor. Progress in identifying and treating brain tumors is essential for enhancing the prognosis and well-being of individuals impacted by them. Brain tumors need to be diagnosed promptly and accurately through the use of medical imaging techniques. Nevertheless, intrinsic noise diminishes the quality of images and hinders their usefulness for diagnosis. This study is centered around the creation and assessment of cutting-edge denoising methods to enhance the precision of brain tumor identification in medical scans. In our research, we utilize the bm3d filter for noise reduction in brain MRI images and a two-layered CNN model for brain tumor detection. By systematically evaluating the effectiveness of this method, we determine the most optimal approach to reduce noise disturbances while retaining critical diagnostic data. We are studying how reducing noise is able to affect accuracy and enhancing the entire process to enhance clinical decision support. The findings of this study are expected to enhance the precision of brain tumor detection, leading to far more dependable and effective healthcare procedures. The results could allow traditional medical imaging procedures to integrate sophisticated denoising methods, leading to improved diagnostic abilities for neuroimaging experts in the future.

Keywords: Brain Tumor · BM3D (Block matching 3-D) filter · CNN (convolutional neural network) · MRI (Magnetic Resonance Imaging)

1 Introduction

A brain tumor is defined as an unusual accumulation or cluster of brain cells. They can come from various types of cells and lead to symptoms such as headaches, seizures, vision problems, and cognitive challenges. There is a wide range of brain tumor types that can be treated, with the most common treatment options being surgery, chemotherapy, and radiation therapy. Brain tumors often occur randomly without any known risk factors and the exact cause is unknown. Brain tumors can be caused by genetic factors, environmental factors, or lifestyle choices. Brain tumors may be caused by genetics, age, radiation Exposure, or weak immune systems. According to estimates, Brain tumors account for

© The Author(s), under exclusive license to Springer Nature Switzerland AG 2026
R. Appavoo et al. (Eds.): IconDeepCom 2024, CCIS 2687, pp. 158–168, 2026.
https://doi.org/10.1007/978-3-032-26680-4_12

85% of all primary Central Nervous System (CNS) tumors. It is critical for medical imaging to be able to detect and treat brain tumors in a timely manner. The natural background noise in these images diminishes their diagnostic accuracy and hinders the ability to detect tumors.

This study investigates methods for reducing image noise in order to enhance the accuracy of brain tumor detection. We develop a novel denoising technique called BM3D filtering to enhance the quality of medical images for a more accurate and efficient neuroimaging diagnostic process. The latest research emphasizes the importance of advanced imaging technology for detecting brain tumors early and accurately, leading to better treatment options and care for patients. The reduction of noise in MRI (Magnetic Resonance Imaging) images is achieved through different filters and denoising techniques that preserve anatomical details like Gaussian Filter, Median Filter, Wavelet Denoising, Non-Local Means Filter, etc. This study utilizes a bm3d filter to remove noise from MRI images and trains a two - layer CNN model to identify brain tumors in the denoised images. Some other commonly used deep learning models for identifying brain tumors include densenet and VGGNet. Using a CNN model to detect brain tumors offers numerous benefits in terms of precision, speed, and automatic processing. CNN models can effectively extract hierarchical features from medical pictures, making them well suited for analyzing gait images.

2 Literature Survey

Several related works are available in denoising MRI images. In [1] The article introduces a new method for reducing noise in Magnetic Resonance Images (MRI) by breaking down components. By utilizing Morphological Component Analysis (MCA) together with a mix of Wiener filter, wavelet hard thresholding, as well as wavelet soft thresholding, the program effectively gets rid of Gaussian noise from MRI brain scans. The suggested approach is evaluated against conventional denoising methods, demonstrating superior results in both objective and subjective assessments. Combining spatial and transform domain filtering with MCA results in a reduction of noise while preserving edge details [2]. introduces a technique for getting rid of noise from medical images using a Conditional Generative Adversarial Network (CGAN). It preserves the structure and context of images by using remaining dense blocks in the generator, including noise and gradient images, and combining reconstruction and WGAN losses to improve training and enhance denoising results.

The research of Muhammad Aqeel Aslam et al. entitled [3] "Noise Removal from medical Images Using Hybrid Filters of Technique" Enhances the quality of medical images, it is achieved through the utilization of adaptive median, wavelet, and fuzzy filtering techniques. The research will utilize a combination of methods to eliminate interference from medical images and enhance the precision of diagnoses [4]. has developed a new method for improving accuracy and robustness in image denoising by integrating hollow convolution and KSVD in their algorithm. It surpasses BM3D and WNNM in both objective and subjective assessments, and is on par with DnCNN in terms of performance. The algorithm makes use of deep learning and sparse representation to introduce a novel approach for cleaning up noisy images. The goal of the study in [5] is to compare two unsupervised MRI denoising techniques, Stein's Unbiased Risk Estimator and blind spot network, along with Non - Local Means. In most cases, both methods outperform NLM and appear to have potential for enhancing MRI image quality. In [6], the study evaluates the efficacy of AI-based denoising in enhancing FDG PET textural data compared to conventional postfiltering methods. Results show that AI denoising retains more characteristics in low intensity areas compared to high intensity areas. This research utilizes advanced denoising methods to improve the precision of diagnoses in medical imaging. The paper introduces a brand new fuzzy system algorithm in [7] for segmenting brain MRI images and predicting diseases, which can lead to quicker data transfer, accurate tumor segmentation, and efficient energy usage. It outperforms current models in noise reduction and identification, providing a strong basis for analyzing brain images and making predictive diagnoses.

The paper [8] describes an innovative denoising technique for high-field multi dimensional MRI using local complex PCA. It enhances current methods for quantitative mapping and manual outlining in order to enhance the quality of the image. NWO funding supports research that improves the accuracy of structural measurements in MRI scans, ultimately advancing the field of neuroimaging. The article provides an overview of various CNN image denoising techniques for various types of images, as discussed in reference [9]. This article explores typical methods for assessing objectives, obstacles, and available datasets. The review includes 152 citations and focuses on the latest advancements in CNN-driven methods for removing noise from images. In the paper [10] of Brzostowski and Obuchowicz a variational mode decomposition and regularization technique for denoising MRI data is described in this paper. The algorithm is tested using a thorough evaluation framework that draws on previous research in image denoising for medical imaging.

The [11] paper by Zhu et al. (2020) a new method for denoising MRI images using total variation is suggested for reconstructing compressed sensing images with high levels of noise. It expands on existing research by suggesting a more effective algorithm for addressing the denoising issue and showcasing its effectiveness on highly noisy MRI images [12]. introduces a brand new BM3D method which consists of image depth characteristics and SSIM to enhance image denoising. The algorithm enhances block-matching processes and similarity calculations through the use of a pre-trained UNet denoising network. Extensive testing has shown that the denoising performance is better than conventional methods, and this research provides important insights for advancements in image processing. The paper [13] proposes a brand new block-matching domain transformation filtering coupled with enhanced guided filtering method for denoising images without knowledge of the noise. It is superior to existing methods for estimating noise variance accurately and maintaining image quality. Domain transformation filtering and nonlinear filtering could affect the denoising performance.

3 Brain Tumor Detection Methodology

The proposed technique relies on image data from scans like MRI images. The proposed strategy consists of using BM3D filter to get rid of Additive White Gaussian noise (AWGN) from MRI images while keeping the essential diagnostic features of the photo.

These cleaned up images are then used in a two layer CNN model of brain tumors. Following training, the model will be tested on a different set of MRI image data. The model will be evaluated for its accuracy in determining if a tumor appears in the picture or not in the test dataset. In this particular analysis, a model based on classifiers is created to detect real time brain tumors. The model could be applied to the health sector.

3.1 Block Matching 3-D (BM3D) Filter

The BM3D filter is a noise reduction algorithm which eliminates noise from pictures without losing detail. This technique is particularly effective against additive white Gaussian noise (AWGN), which is a common kind of noise encountered in numerous medical imaging scenarios. The BM3D filter has a multi-step process to get rid of noise from images. Input image is split into overlapping blocks during the very first stage. Block Matching starts by comparing each block with others to get very similar structures in the image. It is in this first step that the basis for collaborative filtering is laid. During The collaborative filtering phase, the same blocks are recognized, and the proposed technique is based on picture information from scans like MRI images. The proposed strategy is removing Additive White Gaussian noise (AWGN) from MRI pictures using the BM3D filter while maintaining the essential diagnostic features of the picture intact. These cleaned up images are used in a two layered CNN model to detect tumors in the brain. After training, the model will be tested on another set of MRI image data. The model will be evaluated for its ability to determine whether a tumor is visible in the picture or not in the test dataset. In this analysis real time brain tumors are detected using a classifier-based model. Clustered to make a preliminary approximation of the cleaned-up block, this process exploits the redundancy of the image and improves the capability of the algorithm to differentiate noise from signal. Afterwards, the cleaned blocks are reshaped into a brand-new domain frequently by the Discrete Cosine Transform (DCT). Transform domain processing makes denoising operations more efficient. Wiener filtering is used in a modified domain to minimize noise while preserving image qualities by adjusting the tradeoff between noise suppression and feature retention. Denoised blocks are transformed to the original domain through an inverse transformation after Wiener filtering. Because of its iterative measures of block matching, transformation, collaborative filtering and filtering, the BM3D algorithm can minimize noise with high detail retention in different imaging tasks (Fig. 1).

The Noisy MRI image is decomposed using Morphological Component Analysis (MCA) to Cartoon image, Texture and Residual. The purpose of MCA is to extract features like edges or objects. On those three images, MCA can help isolate and remove noise components. The BM3D Filter is then applied on these components for denoising, the denoised Cartoon image, denoised texture and denoised Residual are then combined to produce the denoised MRI image (Fig. 2).

3.2 Convolutional Neural Network (CNN) Model

A brain tumor detection model with a two-layer CNN has an initial input layer along with a final output layer. The input layer processes the MRI image patches and passes them by way of a convolutional layer which uses filters to determine basic features.

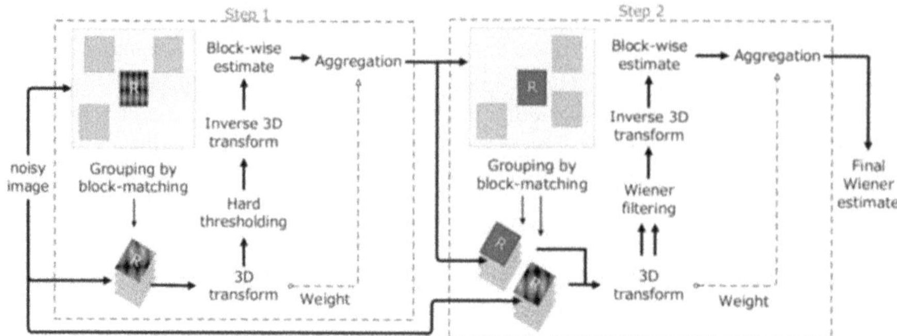

Fig. 1. BM3D Filter

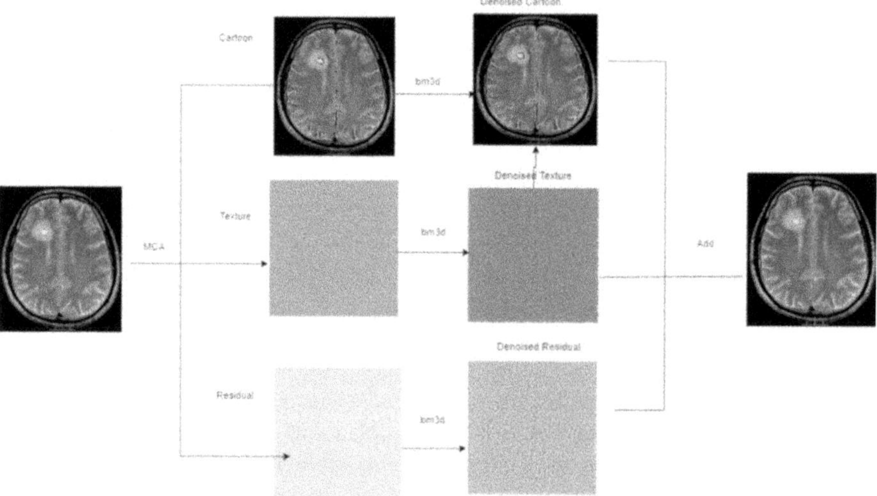

Fig. 2. Flowchart of Denoising an MRI Image

Activation functions are introduced to bring about non-linearity to assist with feature learning. This simple design highlights important features linked to the presence of tumors. Medical imaging often employs more intricate designs with extra layers and adjustments to enhance precision and manage the intricate characteristics of identifying brain tumors. Adjusting the settings on the CNN model may prove to be difficult and time-consuming, and also the performance of the CNN may decrease if the size of the input feature maps' spatial dimensions increases. In order to neutralize these effects, Max pooling is used following every convolutional layer. Max-pooling is a process that decreases the size of the input by picking out the maximum value within a certain window. This results in decreased computational complexity and fewer parameters (Fig. 3).

Dataset Description
The image dataset that was utilized is labeled and consists of a total of 253 Brain - MRI

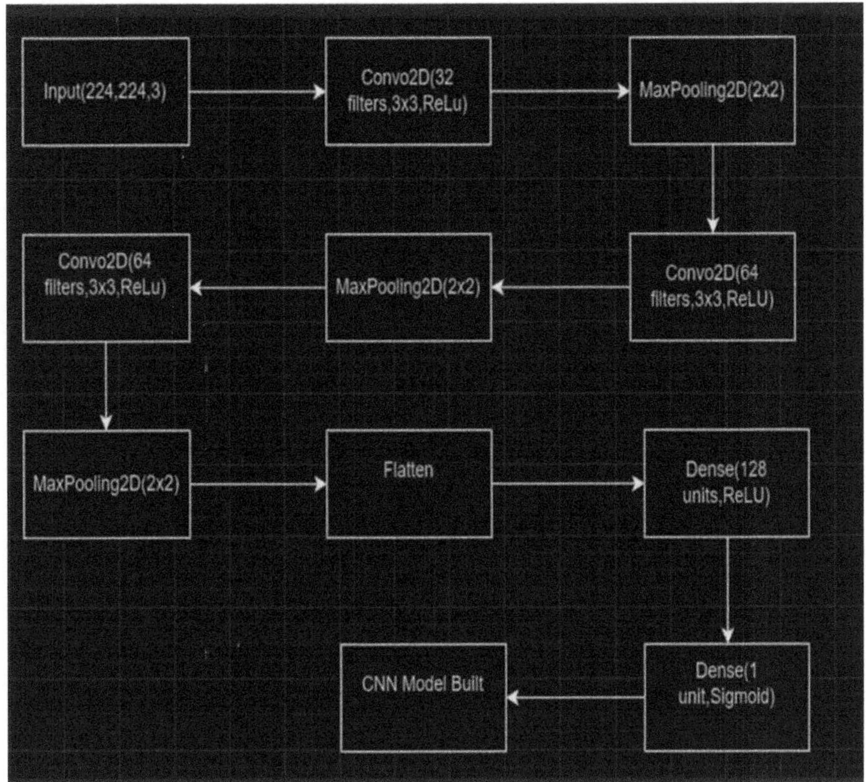

Fig. 3. Workflow Diagram of The CNN Model

pictures. The dataset consists of 155 tumorous Brain MRI images and 98 non tumorous Brain MRI images. The dataset was divided into two sets: one for testing, which was comprised of 20% of the images, and one for training, which consisted of 80% of the images (Figs. 4 and 5).

Model Summary

The research explains how the BM3D filter is utilized to eliminate "Additive White Gaussian Noise" from Brain MRI images. A CNN model with two layers is used to identify brain tumors by analyzing denoised images. The model consistently generates accurate results for the input data sets. The CNN model uses Max pooling following every convolution layer to decrease the computational load of the system and stay away from overfitting by reducing the size of the input feature maps.

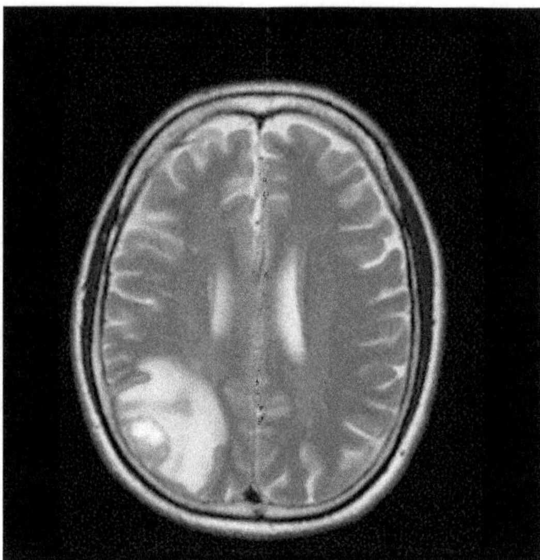

Fig. 4. Tumorous MRI

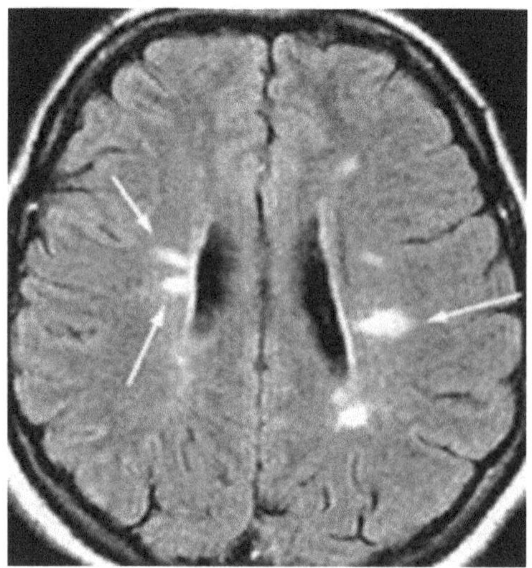

Fig. 5. Non Tumorous MRI

4 Results

The MRI images were successfully cleaned of Additive white gaussian noise using the
BM3D filter, resulting in clear and noise-free images. The image with noise on the
left is subjected to the BM3D Filter, resulting in a denoised image without noticeable
additive white Gaussian noise, which is important for correct diagnosis and evaluation.
The third image shows the removal of AWGN. In addition, the CNN model with two

layers achieves a detection accuracy of 93.2% when identifying brain tumors with the use of denoised images. Max-pooling has resulted in enhanced performance of the model when compared to the individual base models. The model has been enhanced to better prevent overfitting (Figs. 6 and 7).

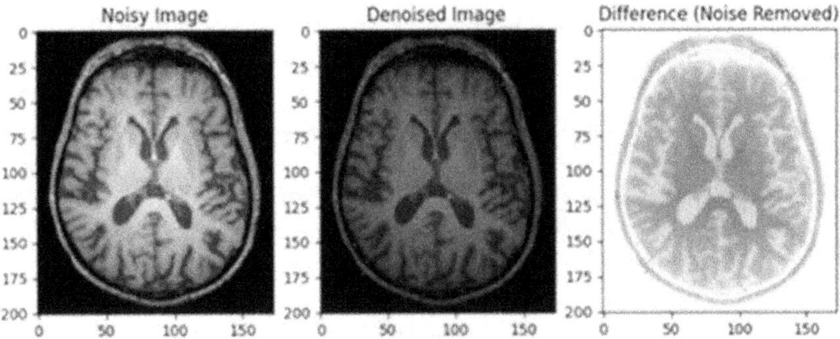

Fig. 6. shows an MRI image of the brain that is free of tumors and has been processed to reduce noise.

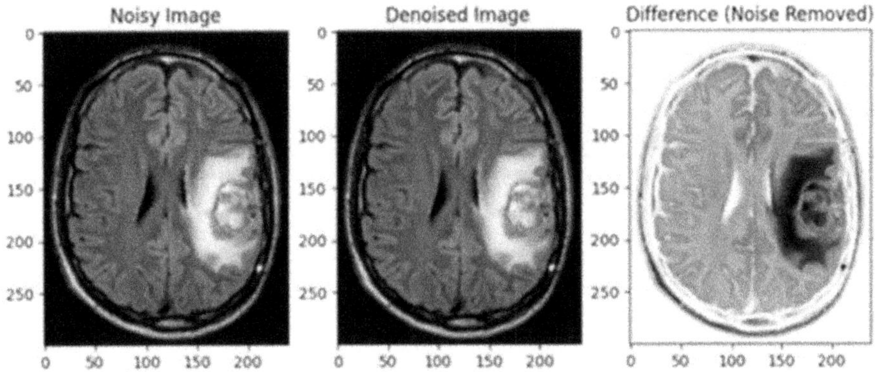

Fig. 7. Shows an MRI image of the brain with a tumor.

4.1 Performance Evaluation

There are 2 methods available to compare the outcomes of various image denoising techniques. There is a method based on facts and a method based on personal opinions. Subjective evaluation requires comparing the original picture with the altered image.

The image was visually cleaned up by the naked eye. An index to measure denoising performance is the objective evaluation technique. Here, commonly used objective evaluation criteria are employed. MSE (Mean Square Error), RMSE (Root Mean Square

Error), PSNR (Peak Signal to Noise Ratio) and SNR (Signal to Noise Ratio) are the metrics used to evaluate the quality of an image. A lower MSE and RMSE, and higher PSNR and SNR indicate better quality of the processed image compared to the original one.

MSE is the ratio of the original picture to the compressed and processed image. It is determined by finding the mean of the squared discrepancies between the pixels in the edited and original images. The RMSE may be the quadratic root of MSE. It offers a way to quantify the typical discrepancy between the edited and original images. PSNR is a metric used to look at the fidelity of an edited image in relation to the initial image. The measurement is in decibels (db) and higher values suggesting superior image quality. MSE has an inverse relationship with PSNR. The signal-to-noise ratio (SNR) quantifies the relationship between the power of the signal and also the power of the noise. Image quality is also measured in decibels (db) and higher values indicate superior quality. MSE has a direct correlation with SNR.

Table 1. Performance Evaluation of the BM3D Algorithm in terms of RMSE and MSE

Noise Level	Image size	RMSE	MSE
0.12	382 * 335	2.873	8.258

Table 2. Performance Evaluation of the BM3D Algorithm in terms of PSNR and SNR

Noise Level	Image size	PSNR	SNR
0.12	382 * 335	37.65	9.794

From Table 1 high PSNR value can confirm the denoised MRI image is of a higher quality (Table 2).

5 Comparative Analysis

The CNN model with two layers, used on images that have been cleaned of noise, can easily identify brain tumors with an accuracy of 93.2%. The identical model obtained a 92.4% accuracy when the test data set was utilized with no BM3D Filter. BM3D retains the intricate details and patterns within the images while eliminating any unwanted noise. This is critical to ensuring that MRI scans are as diagnostic as possible. The denoising process not only improved the clarity of the images but also enhanced the accuracy of depicting the anatomical features when compared with the original images.

6 Conclusion

The primary objective of this study is to utilize machine learning techniques, specifically denoising with the BM3D Filter and integrating CNN, to effectively identify brain tumors with improved precision using enhanced, clearer MRI images because of the model's superior accuracy. The BM3D filter has the ability to produce clearer and less distorted images, which can assist in improving the accuracy of diagnostics. Healthcare professionals can concentrate on the specific abnormalities and conditions present in brain images by reducing unnecessary interference. BM3D goes beyond just improving appearance, it also helps make computer-aided diagnosis more accurate and assists in making informed clinical decisions. Reducing noise levels enhances image clarity and plays a role in more precise research outcomes and seamless integration into medical procedures. BM3D is essential for improving MRI data, which is vital for advancing medical research, diagnosis, and treatment by producing clearer as well as more intricate images that facilitate precise analysis and understanding.

References

1. Zeng, Y. et al.: Magnetic resonance image denoising algorithm based on cartoon texture and residual parts. Comput. Math. Methods Med. (2020). https://doi.org/10.1155/2020/1405647
2. Li, Y., Zhang, K., Shi, W., Miao, Y., Jiang, Z.: A novel medical image denoising method based on conditional generative adversarial network. Comput. Math. Methods Med. **2021**, 9974017 (2021)
3. Aslam, M.A., et al.: Noise removal from medical images using hybrid filters of technique. J. Phys. Conf. Ser. **1518**, 012061 (2020)
4. Bian, S., He, X., Xu, Z., Zhang, L.: Image denoising by deep convolution based on sparse representation. Computers. **12**, 112 (2023). https://doi.org/10.3390/computers12060112
5. López, M.M., Frederick, J.M., Ventura, J.: Evaluation of MRI denoising methods using unsupervised learning. Front. Artif. Intell. **4** (2021)
6. Jaudet, C., Weyts, K., Lechervy, A., Batalla, A., Bardet, S., Corroyer-Dulmont, A.: The impact of artificial intelligence CNN based denoising on FDG PET radiomics. Front. Oncol. **11**, 692973 (2021). https://doi.org/10.3389/fonc.2021.692973
7. Hu, M., Zhong, Y., Xie, S., Lv, H., Lv, Z.: Fuzzy system based medical image processing for brain disease prediction. Front. Neurosci. **30**(15), 714318 (2021) PMID: 34393718; PMCID: PMC8361453
8. Bazin, P.L., Alkemade, A., van der Zwaag, W., Caan, M., Mulder, M., Forstmann, B.U.: Denoising high-field multi-dimensional MRI with local complex PCA. Front. Neurosci. **13**, 1066 (2019)
9. Ilesanmi, A.E., Ilesanmi, T.O.: Methods for image denoising using convolutional neural network: a review. Complex Intell. Syst. **7**, 2179–2198 (2021)
10. Brzostowski, K., Obuchowicz, R.: Combining variational mode decomposition with regularisation techniques to denoise MRI data. Magn. Reson. Imaging. **106**, 55–76 (2024). https://doi.org/10.1016/j.mri.2023.10.011
11. Zhu, Y., et al.: Removal of high density gaussian noise in compressed sensing MRI reconstruction through modified total variation image denoising method. Heliyon. **6**(3), e03680 (2020). https://doi.org/10.1016/j.heliyon.2020.e03680
12. Cao, J., Qiang, Z., Lin, H., He, L., Dai, F.: An improved BM3D algorithm based on image depth feature map and structural similarity block-matching. Sensors. **23**, 7265 (2023). https://doi.org/10.3390/s23167265

13. Jia, H., Yin, Q., Lu, M.: Blind-noise image denoising with block-matching domain transformation filtering and improved guided filtering. Sci. Rep. **12**, 16195 (2022). https://doi.org/10.1038/s41598-022-20578-w

14. Abramov, S.K., Lukin, V.V., Vozel, B., Chehdi, K., Astola, J.T.: Segmentation-based method for blind evaluation of noise variance in images. J. Appl. Remote. Sens. **2**(1), 023533 (2008). https://doi.org/10.1117/1.2977788

15. Shan, S., Li, Y., Zhu, S.: BM3D denoising based on minimum GCV score. In: 2015 International Conference on Computers, Communications, and Systems (ICCCS), pp. 154–158. Kanyakumari, India (2015). https://doi.org/10.1109/CCOMS.2015.7562892

16. Lambin P et al.Radiomics: extracting more information from medical images using advanced feature analysis. Eur. J. Cancer (2012) 48:441–446. https://doi.org/10.1016/j.ejca.2011.11.036.

17. Moummad, I. et al.: The impact of resampling and denoising deep learning algorithms on radiomics in brain metastases MRI. Cancer. **14**, 36 (2022). https://doi.org/10.3390/cancers14010036

18. Gurrola-Ramos, J., Dalmau, O., Alarcón, T.E.: A residual dense U-net neural network for image denoising. IEEE Access. **9**, 31742–31754 (2021)

19. Jia, F., Wong, W.H., Zeng, T.: DDUNet: dense dense U-net with applications in image denoising. In: Proceedings of the IEEE/CVF International Conference on Computer Vision, vol. 11–17, pp. 354–364. IEEE, Montreal, QC, Canada (2021)

20. Buades, A., Coll, B., Morel, J.M.: A non-local algorithm for image denoising. In: Proceedings of the Computer Vision and Pattern Recognition, San Diego, CA, USA, pp. 20–25 (2005)

21. Zha, Z., Yuan, X., Wen, B., Zhang, J., Zhou, J., Zhu, C.: Image restoration using joint patch-group-based sparse representation. IEEE Trans. Image Process. **29**, 7735–7750 (2020)

22. Cheng, S., Wang, Y., Huang, H., Liu, D., Fan, H., Liu, S.: Nbnet: noise basis learning for image denoising with subspace projection. In: Proceedings of the IEEE/CVF Conference on Computer Vision and Pattern Recognition, Nashville, TN, USA, vol. 20–25, pp. 4896–4906 (2021)

23. Xu, J., Zhang, L., Zhang, D.: A trilateral weighted sparse coding scheme for real-world image denoising. In: European Conference on Computer Vision (2018)

24. Yu, S., Park, B., Jeong, J.: Deep iterative down-up CNN for image denoising. In: Proceedings of the IEEE Conference on Computer Vision and Pattern Recognition Workshops (2019)

25. Zhang, K., Zuo, W., Shuhang, G., Zhang, L.: Learning deep CNN denoiser prior for image restoration. In: Proceedings of the IEEE Conference on Computer Vision and Pattern Recognition, pp. 3929–3938 (2017)

26. Tian, C., Yong, X., Li, Z., Zuo, W., Fei, L., Liu, H.: Attention-guided CNN for image denoising. Neural Netw. **124**, 117–129 (2020)

A Novel CNN Architecture: Comprehensive Approach to Alzheimer's Disease Detection and Classification

G. Indhumathi[(✉)], M. Palanivelan, G. Saranya, K. Devadharshini, N. Divya Bharathi, and A. Divyadharshini

Department of ECE, Rajalakshmi Engineering College, Chennai, India
`{Indhumathi.g,palanivelan.m,saranya.g,200801054,200801062, 200801063}@rajalakshmi.edu.in`

Abstract. Alzheimer's Disease is recognized as a neurological disorder that damages the tissues of the brain, causing long-term memory loss, cognitive difficulties, confusion, inconsistent behavior, and ultimately death. In this study, we identified the three broad stages of this neurodegenerative disease: Non-Demented (Normal), very mild (early stage), mild (middle stage), and moderate demented (late stage). The treatment for the AD symptoms can greatly benefitted from the early identification and categorization. DL and ML techniques are applied. The dataset is obtained from the ADNI and Kaggle research data sharing platforms. By using Visual Studio code in Anaconda Navigator, the source code is tested, and Google Colab is used for the model training. The study's findings showed that, using the test dataset, we could effectively and accurately categorize the stages of AD with a 98.02% accuracy rate. This test's accuracy score is noticeably greater than that of previous studies. The findings also showed that these methods can be effectively applied in the medical field to aid in early disease diagnosis and identification.

Keywords: memory loss · neurodegenerative disease · ADNI · Deep Learning · accuracy

1 Introduction

The decline of cognitive ability and memory loss are the main two symptoms of neurological disorders like AD which is named after Dr. Alois Alzheimer initially described in 1906. The disease primarily affects older individuals, though early-onset cases exist [2]. Symptoms include memory impairment, confusion, difficulty in problem-solving, and behavioral shifts. As the disease advances, individuals may struggle with daily tasks, lose language skills, and experience personality changes [4]. The Ongoing study aims to understand the condition better, which helps to investigate potential prevention strategies and also creates more effective treatments. Diagnosis involves comprehensive medical evaluations, including cognitive tests and imaging studies [12]. This disease is difficult to identify early and involves a lot of effort and money. Advanced prediction tools, extensive data gathering, and the expertise of a clinician are all necessary for successful early detection [7]. Automation lowers total expenses while increasing accuracy.

R. Appavoo et al. (Eds.): IconDeepCom 2024, CCIS 2687, pp. 169–184, 2026.
https://doi.org/10.1007/978-3-032-26680-4_13

A. Image Processing and Applications in Disease Detection

MRI scanner produces three-dimensional images of the human body, which are often utilized for diagnosing the disease and provide guidance in the medical treatments like surgical intervention and research in the domain of medical image processing.[6]. PET-MRI and Positron Emission Tomography are two modern imaging techniques that heavily rely on picture registration and fusion algorithms. Medical imaging is essential for monitoring the progression of a chronic illness [21]. Doctors keep an eye on how well their patients are responding to treatment plans and change as needed depending on results from imaging tests, like CT and MRI scans [22].

B. Symptoms of AD Affecting the CNS

Alzheimer's starts in the central nervous system and progresses slowly from there. AD is characterized by decreasing areas of the brain, damage to tissue cells, and the breakdown of neuronal connection links [18]. Tangles and amyloid plaques accumulated in the brain are also thought to be a characteristic of AD. Studies of brain metabolism using MRI and PET, along with other imaging modalities, have revealed distinctive alterations in AD patients [3]. Figure 1 displays an MRI of a brain affected by AD and a normal brain [1]. Artificial intelligence has a significant role in the diagnosis of AD.

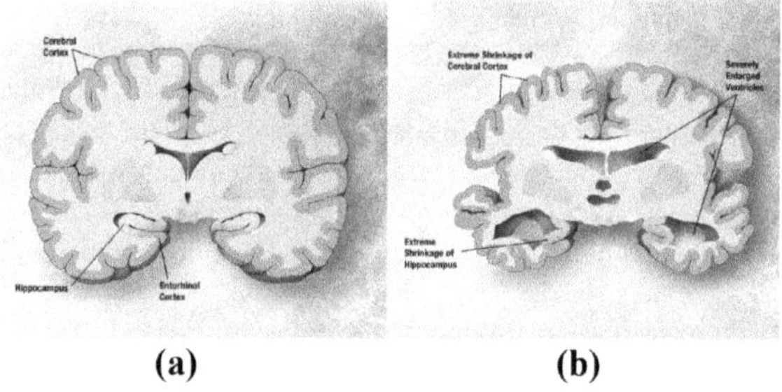

(a)   **(b)**

Fig. 1. (a) normal brain (b) AD affected brain

2 Motivation

Standard measures and human instinct do not always agree in the contemporary environment. We must use cutting-edge, non-traditional, and computationally intensive techniques such as ML to address this issue [1]. This drift not only enhances patients' quality of life but also helps health economists and doctors make assessments and treatment decisions. Finding the knowledge gaps and possible opportunities related to ML and DL frameworks and data obtained from Electronic Health Records (EHRs) is the aim of this project [12].

3 Literature Survey

A. Research Papers Studied in ML

1. **"ML approaches for detection and classification of AD: A review"** by S. A. Hane, et al. Published in: Psychiatry Research: Neuroimaging, 2017. The study examines ML techniques used in identification and categorization of AD.
2. **"AD Neuroimaging Initiative (ADNI): A review of methods, challenges, and opportunities"** by M.W.Weiner, A.Veitch,et al. Published in Neuroimage, 2018. This paper discusses opportunities and challenges, offering insights into the data used for ML studies.
3. **"ML in predicting progression of AD: An overview"** by D.K.I. Christodoulopoulos, et al. Published in Journal of AD, 2020.This paper explains the role of ML in predicting the progression of AD.
4. **"ML techniques for the diagnosis of AD: A review"** by O. A. Alhussein, I. I. Hussein, et al. Published in the King Saud University- Computer and Information Sciences journal, 2020. This shows various ML techniques including such as ANN, KNN, SVM and ensemble methods.

B. Research Papers Studied in Deep Learning

1. **"Automated diagnosis of ADwith multi-scale convolutional neural networks using resting-state functional magnetic resonance imaging"** by Suk, Heung-Il, et al. Published in PLoS One, 2014.Accuracy achieved is 94.87%.
2. **"Deep Learning-based AD Classification Using Novel Feature Selection and Voting Ensemble"** by Sarraf, Saman, and Ghassem Tofighi. Published in BioMed Research International, 2016. The model obtained an accuracy of around 89.2%
3. **"3D convolutional neural networks for classification of functional magnetic resonance imaging data for AD detection"** by Sarraf, Saman, and Ghassem Tofighi. Originally published in the 2016 IEEE Conference on CVPR Proceedings. Accuracy achieved is 84.3%.
4. **"DL for the diagnosis of AD: a systematic review and meta-analysis of longitudinal studies"** by Liu, Shui-Hua, et al. Published in Frontiers in Aging Neuroscience, 2018. Summary of This paper provides an overview and meta-analysis of DL techniques employed for the prediction of AD.

C. Research Papers Studied in Hybrid:

1. **"A hybrid approach for the early diagnosis of AD"** by H. M. El-Bakry, A. A. Hassanien, et al. Published in Expert Systems with Applications, 2015.This paper presents a hybrid approach combining fuzzy logic and genetic algorithms for the early AD prediction.

2. **"Hybrid model for efficient diagnosis of AD using ANFIS and K-means based segmentation on structural MR images"** by N. M. Khan, M. M. Palaniappan, et al. Published in Journal of Neuroscience Methods, 2017. The paper proposes a hybrid model developed which combines both ANFIS and K-means segmentation.
3. **"A Hybrid Approach for Early Diagnosis of AD Using Structural MRI"** by R. Dhanalakshmi, V. Sridevi, et al. Published in Journal of Medical Systems, 2018. The study introduces a hybrid approach using a combination of various ML methods for early diagnosis of AD, with a focus on structural MRI.
4. **"A Hybrid Decision Support System for AD Using Bayesian Complementary Learning from Data"** by A. A. Hassanien, A. E. Hassanien, et al. Published in Cognitive Computation, 2019. This paper proposes a hybrid decision support system for AD utilizing Bayesian complementary learning from data, demonstrating improved diagnostic accuracy.

4   Block Diagram

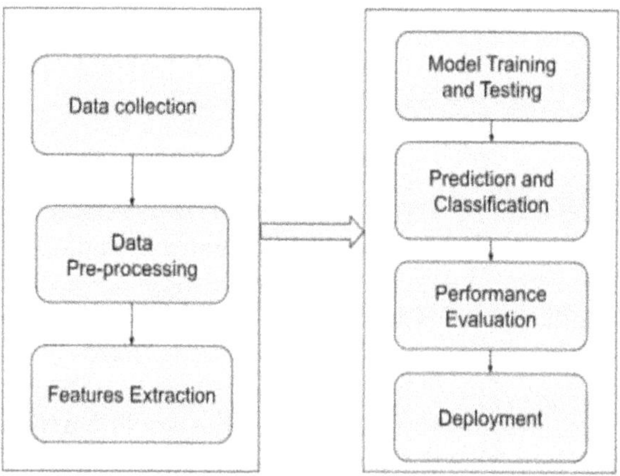

Fig. 2. Proposed workflow

Figure 2 shows the DL workflow which comprises the data collection followed by the pre-processing techniques and feature extraction. The pre-processed dataset is splitted and the model training is done[10].The trained model is used for model validation and prediction. DL algorithms like ResNet-169, EfficientNetB2, CNN algorithm are utilized for the model classification and finally for the performance evaluation is done and deployment takes place.

5   Data Collection

Dataset was collected from ADNI and Kaggle which is the public data source. The dataset can be in the form of Image and statistical data [3]. In this project we use MRI imaging since the PET and CT scan can produce the radiation that can cause the side effects and using MRI images can be a non-invasive method to detect AD[4]. ADNI and Kaggle Provided the MRI images for this study. T1-weighted Magnetic Resonance Imaging (MRI) images are used since it enhances the signal of the fatty tissues and suppresses the signal of the water [3]. A total of 1280 images were collected from ADNI and kaggle in which 322 images are non-demented, 311 very mild demented, 364 mild demented and 283 moderate demented (Fig. 3).

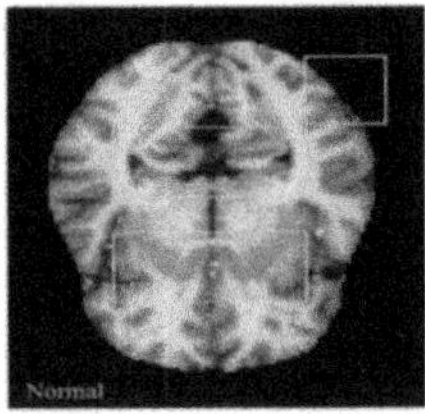
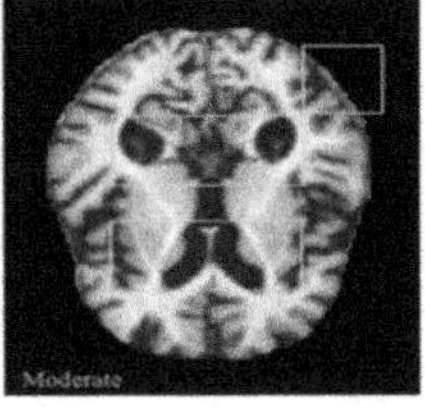

Fig. 3. Highlighted regions of normal and AD affected the brain.

In AD affected brain the ventricles in center of the region enlarges and the cortical gray area in the corners of the brain reduces [9] (Fig. 4).

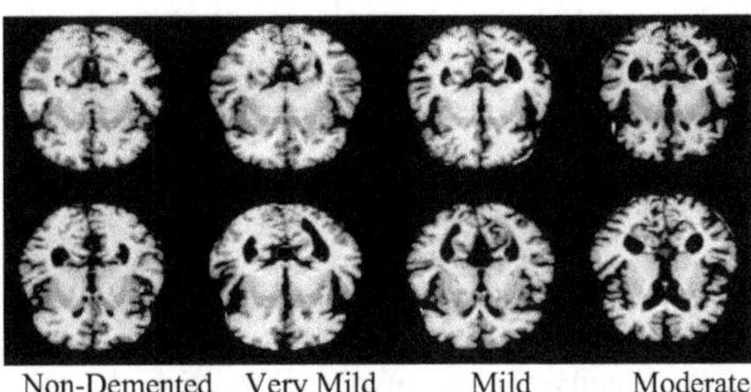

Non-Demented   Very Mild   Mild   Moderate

Fig. 4. MRI images of normal and AD affected brain

6 Data Pre-processing

Figure 5. shows the data pre-processing steps. The AD dataset is processed by slicing, image scaling, noise reduction, histogram equalization, and low-pass alpha-trimmed filtering. The contrast of an image is improved using the histogram equalization. To acquire the necessary image size (128 x 128), resizing is done. To improve the model's efficiency, these are further downscaled [4]. Subsequently, downscaling is carried out to downscale the dimensionality of the data and increases the feasibility of training the DL algorithm on it. Using GANs (Generative Adversarial Networks), the model's prediction of the imbalanced data is made more accurate and also limits conventional methods such as overfitting [4].

By lowering noise, filtering enhances the quality of the images. Using an alpha-trimmed filter, the noise in the images is reduced [3].

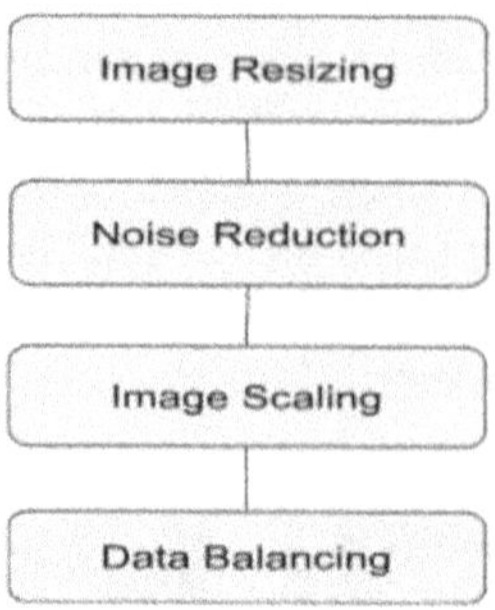

Fig. 5. Pre-processing steps

Equation (1) shows the alpha-trimmed filter,

$$F\,(a, b) = (1/(uv - r)) \sum pr\,(s, t) \tag{1}$$

where, F represents the filtered images,(a, b) are the coordinates of the pixels processed, uv is the dimension of the filter, pr is the set of pixels left, r is the number of pixels that will be excluded after averaging [3].

The filter dimensions in our implementation have a mn of 5×5 and a dimension d of 8. This indicates that we removed 8 pixels out of 25 pixels, 4 from the start and 4 from the end [3].

7 Features Extraction

The algorithm may find it challenging to handle the raw data accurately if the raw data contains a large number of extraneous features [12]. Feature extraction, a step in the process of reducing dimensionality, involves dividing the initial raw data set into smaller, more manageable groups. The purpose of feature extraction is to precisely extract a feature from the images and correlate it so that the algorithm can analyze the data appropriately [13, 25] (Fig. 6).

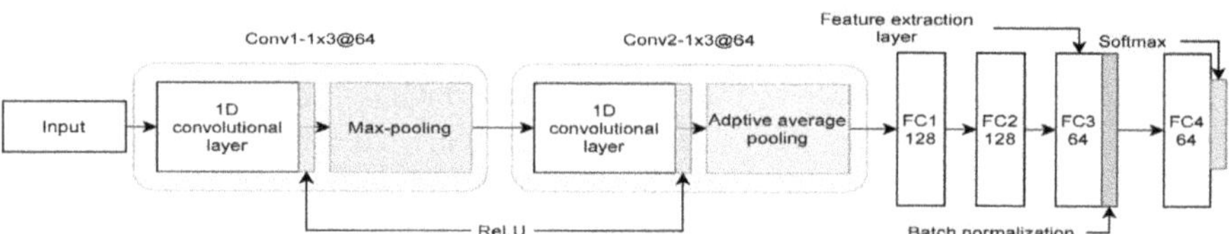

Fig. 6. Feature extraction model based on the designed CNN architecture.

In this study we are extracting the features such as D1, D2, αmin, αmin, αmax, f(αmax), Spectrum width, Symmetrical shift, apparent area of the brain.

The deep features D1, D2 are of no use in terms of physical characteristics [14]. These features reduce the amount of information lost during input-output mapping.

Feature Extraction Process using CNN algorithm includes convolutional layers, depthwise and pointwise separable convolution and class active mapping (CAM).

1. Convolutional layers: They facilitate the MRI's local feature extraction. It can distinguish edges, textures, and other regional patterns that are essential for diagnosing the brain alterations associated with AD.
2. Depth Wise Separable convolutions: They use fewer parameters and require less computing costs. By splitting the convolution operation into depthwise and pointwise convolutions, it is able to extract more abstract features.
3. Class Activation Mapping (CAM): It facilitates the visualization of the MRI scan regions that the model uses to make a diagnosis. It is especially useful for figuring out which parts of the brain are most predictive of AD. It offers helpful data on the course of the illness and possible treatment objectives.

A. Area of the brain:

$$A = \frac{\sin\left(\frac{i\pi}{n}\right)\left(\frac{i\pi}{n} - \pi\right)^6}{181} + 0.2(\sin(i\pi/n)) \tag{2}$$

In Eq. (2) n indicates the total number of copies that are based on the scale a and i denotes the fractal unit. The Class Activation Mapping (CAM) approach is being used to calculate this. The strongest features that correspond to the brain area found in the comparison between patients without dementia and those with dementia are shown by class activation maps. ANOVA test was utilized in this investigation. Between the patient groups, a statistically significant reduction in relative cerebellum volume (p value = 0.0176) and cerebellum folding (p value = 0.0057) of large effect size was found, indicating a decrease in volume and folding as dementia progresses [20].

B. Information dimension:

$$D_1 = \frac{\ln\sum_{i=1}^{n(a)} p_i(a)\ln p_i(a)}{\ln\left(\frac{1}{a}\right)} \tag{3}$$

The equation (Error! Reference source not found.) shows the information dimension that describes how quickly information is lost over time or acquired through a series of measurements. From eq. (Error! Reference source not found.), n(a) is the total number of fractal copies that are based on the scale a, Pi(a) is the growth probability function of the ith fractal unit and the order of moment is denoted as q.

C. Correlation dimension:

$$D_2 = \lim_{r \to 0} \frac{\ln\sum_{i=1}^{N(a)} p_i(a)^2}{\ln a} \tag{4}$$

The structure will be mono-fractal or fractal when D1 = D2, and a multifractal when D1 > D2.

D. Singularity spectrum:

$$\alpha(q) = \frac{d\tau(q)}{dq} = D_q + (q-1)\frac{dD_q}{dq} \qquad (5)$$

$$f(\alpha) = q\alpha(q) - \tau(q) = q\alpha(q) - (q-1)D_q \qquad (6)$$

The symbol f (α) represents the fractal dimension of the fractal units of a particular size, and α (q) is the related singularity exponent. It is possible to apply warping filters to the image and utilize them to highlight subtle characteristics. The symbol (q) represents a set of exponents that make up these warp filters from Fig. 7, The dimensions D1 and D2 are information and correlation, respectively [14]. $\alpha 0$ is the local dimension at the maximal singularity spectral curve, αmin is the local minimum dimension, f(αmin) is the singularity spectrum's beginning value, αmax the largest local dimension, f(αmax) is the singularity spectrum's final value, W is the singularity spectrum's width, The singularity spectrum curve's symmetric shift, The apparent region of image (A)'s brain segment.[10].

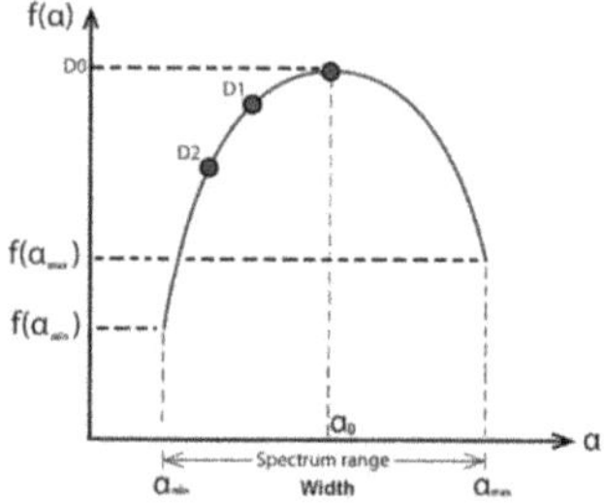

Fig. 7. Attributes of Features Extracted

Table 1. Table of Features

Feature of Image	Non-Demented	Very Mild stage	Mild Stage	moderate stage
Symmetrical shift	0.289 + −0.062	0.796 + −0.042	0.974 + −0.079	1.175 + −0.069
Brain area	17.71 + −0.158	15.46 + −0.151	13.47 + −0.148	11.31 + −0.207
F alpha minimum	1.542 + −0.072	1.481 + −0.027	1.383 + −0.097	1.37 + −0.082
F alpha maximum	0.294 + −0.078	0.196 + −0.018	0.244 + −0.042	0.122 + −0.014
D1	1.69 + −0.016	1.62 + −0.021	1.58 + −0.032	1.453 + −0.018
D2	1.42 + −0.020	1.39 + −0.021	1.36 + −0.028	1.33 + −0.032
Spectrum width	0.672 + −0.062	0.562 + −0.07	0.45 + −0.092	0.423 + −0.102

Table 1 shares the information of the attributes. D1 $=$ 1.63 indicates that there are some morphological alterations in the brain image as a result of increased beta-amyloid deposits that result in the accumulation of amyloid plaques and (T-tau) which cause the brain to shrink. D2 is the correlation between two pixels in the scanning box; for the sample image provided, The data suggests that D2 = 1.395 denotes non-contiguous pixels, increased gaps in the image due to cell loss, and a greater decrease in the frontal lobes, temporal-parietal area, and hippocampus relative to other regions [4]. The characteristics of the singularity spectrum are as follows: The broad spectrum has a width of 0.687 and a large range of variability from αmin = 1.483 to αmax = 2.655. This validates the existence of numerous gaps and atrophy varying in size and shape throughout the brain's lobes. That related to the heterogeneity zones that appeared in the brain structure. (3) The singularity spectrum's initial value, f(αmin) =1.468, and final point, f(αmax) =0.202, show a high degree of fluctuation, indicating that the lobes of the brain are not uniformly represented in the image.[20].

8 Model Training

Python code has been used for the training and testing process. The code contains several libraries such as tensorflow, numpy, matplotlib, keras which is a higher-level neural networks API that comes integrated with tensorflow [1]. The loading of the training and test datasets is done using tf.keras.preprocessing.image_dataset_from_directory().A neural network model with multiple layers is created using keras that contains convolutional, Max-pooling, Dropout and Dense layers. Sparse categorical cross-entropy loss function and Adam optimizer are used to build the model. The training process is run for 35 epochs as shown in Fig. 8. The loss and accuracy gained is plotted and the visualization of the test images and predictions are made which was displayed in Fig. 9. Finally, the trained model is stored as "ALZ.h5" in HDF5 format [12].

```
17/17 [==============================] - 30s 2s/step - loss: 0.0828 - accuracy: 0.9704 - val_loss: 0.0370 - val_accuracy: 0.9943
Epoch 30/35
17/17 [==============================] - 29s 2s/step - loss: 0.0943 - accuracy: 0.9666 - val_loss: 0.0202 - val_accuracy: 0.9981
Epoch 31/35
17/17 [==============================] - 28s 2s/step - loss: 0.0434 - accuracy: 0.9857 - val_loss: 0.0143 - val_accuracy: 1.0000
Epoch 32/35
17/17 [==============================] - 31s 2s/step - loss: 0.0401 - accuracy: 0.9895 - val_loss: 0.0067 - val_accuracy: 1.0000
Epoch 33/35
17/17 [==============================] - 27s 2s/step - loss: 0.0385 - accuracy: 0.9876 - val_loss: 0.0076 - val_accuracy: 1.0000
Epoch 34/35
17/17 [==============================] - 29s 2s/step - loss: 0.0478 - accuracy: 0.9847 - val_loss: 0.0134 - val_accuracy: 0.9971
Epoch 35/35
17/17 [==============================] - 29s 2s/step - loss: 0.0440 - accuracy: 0.9847 - val_loss: 0.0072 - val_accuracy: 1.0000
```

Fig. 8. Accuracy, loss, Val_loss, Val_accuracy

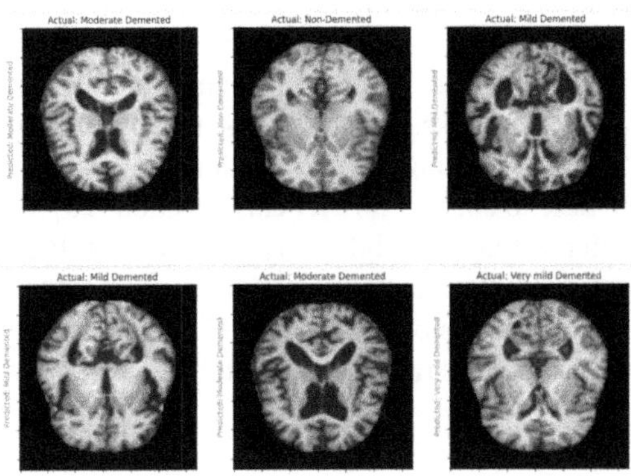

Fig. 9. prediction after model training

9 Identification and Classification

A. *ResNet:* ResNet is a basic model of convolutional neural network, in short Residual Networks, was created to meet the difficulties of training extremely deep neural networks [22, 23]. It presents the idea of residual learning, in which the model can learn the residual (difference) between a layer's input and output by using shortcut connections, also known as skip connections [18]. It offers an 89.6% accuracy rate.

B. *DenseNet121:* DenseNet architectures are often denoted by the number of layers they contain. DenseNet-121 indicates a DenseNet with 121 layers, which is a common variant. When using DenseNet for a specific task, like image classification or medical diagnosis, the model is typically pre-trained on a large dataset and fine-tuned on the target task [23]. Their dense connectivity can lead to more efficient learning and better parameter utilization compared to traditional architectures [23]. The accuracy of DenseNet is about 71% because of which it cannot be used for this prediction model.

   Figure 10 shows the workflow of how the comparative analysis has been carried out to select the best suited model for this case study.

C. *EfficientNetB2:* Algorithm—Efficient Net-B2 is trained for classification in the standard manner. EfficientNet-B2 is a specific variant of the EfficientNet family of neural network architectures [21]. Mingxing Tan and Quoc V. Le proposed the EfficientNet models in their paper "EfficientNet: Rethinking Model Scaling for Convolutional Neural Networks" in 2019. This model provides better performance and efficiency by depth scaling, width scaling, and resolution scaling of the network in a balanced way. EfficientNet is relatively consistent with near perfect training curves and provides less loss and Peak accuracy about 97.22%. Figure 11 explains the modules of the EfficientNetB0.

D. *Xception:* The name "Xception'' stands for "Extreme Inception," indicating its relationship with the Inception architecture [20]. Depthwise separable convolutions have been utilized in the Xception which is one of the DL architectures [21]. Xception employs depthwise separable convolutions, which are a factorized version of the standard convolutional layers commonly used in convolutional neural networks (CNNs). Depthwise separable convolutions split the convolution into two stages. However, Xception uses a high number of parameters and computational cost is also high compared to other models. So Xcpetion cannot be used for this prediction model as it also provides less accuracy about 71.2%.

E. *VGG16:* VGG16 is created by the Visual Graphics Group [27]. When the pre-trained VGG16 model is used, it acts as a tool to extract important features from data, especially in image-related tasks. The top layers are removed (fully connected layers) from the VGG16 model, keeping the convolutional layers [23]. Add new layers on top of the VGG16 base to adapt it for AD classification [23]. Initialize the modified VGG16 model with pre-trained weights on a large dataset. Freeze the convolutional layers of VGG16 to retain the learned features and prevent them from being updated during initial training. The computational cost of VGG16 is comparatively less than other models used, but the loss rate is significantly high and provides an accuracy of about 88.02%.

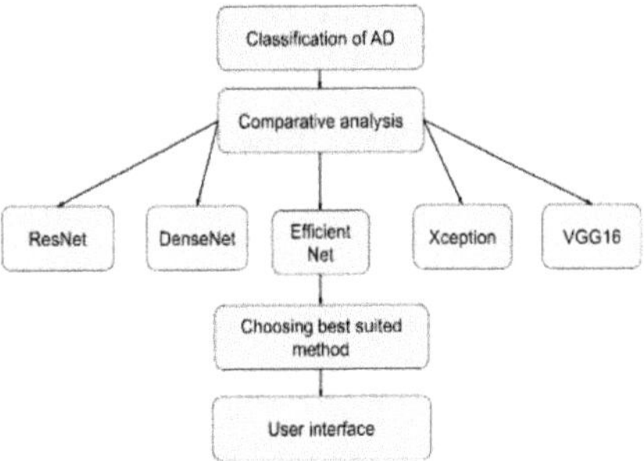

Fig. 10. Flow diagram for classification

Comparative analysis is done for the classification of AD to choose the best suited algorithm for better efficiency and accuracy. EfficinetNetB2 is the best suited method for the classification since it provides peak accuracy about 97.22% and also significantly less loss.

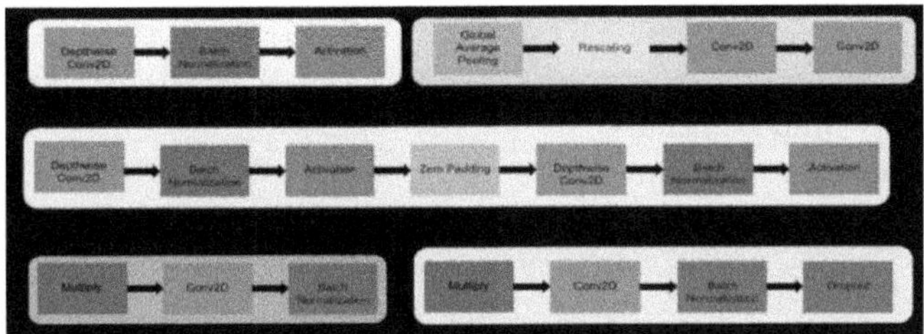

Fig. 11. EfficientNetB2 modules description

10 Performance Evaluation Metrics

Examining the model's performance with respect to a certain dataset is a crucial task. This study assessed multiple evaluation metrics which includes recall, accuracy, precision, F1 score and area under the curve.[7]

A. *K-Fold Cross Validation:* It is a predictive model evaluation technique. After dividing the dataset into k subgroups, the model is being trained for k times. By averaging the performance measures from each fold, the model's performance is estimated. In this case, fivefold cross-validation is used (K = 5) [10].

True Positive (Tp)-The percentage for predictions for which the classifier accurately associates the positive class with the positive state.[7].
True Negative (Tn)-The percentage for predictions for which the classifier accurately associates the negative class with the negative state.[7].
False positive (Fp)-The percentage for predictions for which the classifier accurately associates the negative class with the positive state.[7]. (Type 1 error)

False Negative (Fn)-The percentage for predictions for which the classifier accurately associates the positive class with the negative state.[7]. (Type 2 error)

B. *Accuracy:* (No of correct predictions) / (total no of predictions)
C. *Precision:* Tp/(Tp + Fp)
D. *Recall:* Tp/(Tp + Fn)
E. *Area under curve:*

$$AUC = \sum_{i=1}^{n} ((TPR_i - TPR_{i-1}).(FPR_i - FPR_{i=1}))/2$$

TPR_i represents the ith True Positive Rate and FPR_i represents the ith False Positive Rate.

The summation is over all thresholds i.

The $i - 1$ indices represent the previous threshold.

F. *F1 score:* 2*(Precision*Recall)/(Precision+Recall)
G. *Confusion matrix:* A confusion matrix is a tool used in DL and ML, specifically for classification issues, to monitor and evaluate algorithm performance. It does this by comparing the anticipated and actual classes as shown in Figs. 12 and 13 [23].

   Where,

ND is non-demented.
VMD is Very Mild Demented.
Mod D is Moderate Demented.
MD is Mild Demented.

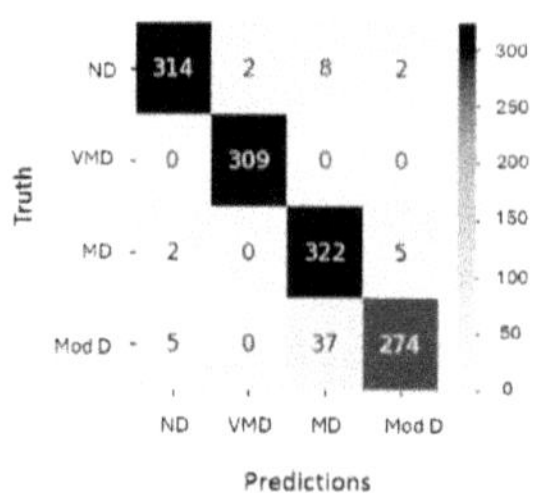

Fig. 12. confusion matrix

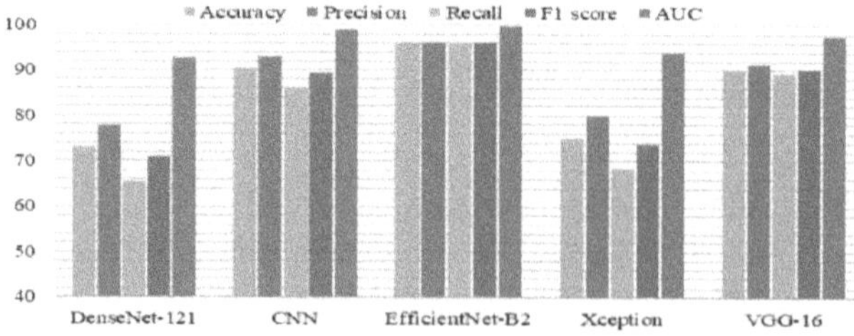

Fig. 13. Comparative analysis done for the different models

11 Deployment

The webpage is created using python. Figures 14, 15 and 16 shows the web page that was created for the identification and classification of AD in which the input image can be chosen and a predict option is selected. The backend program will run and produce the result as the stages of the affected brain image.

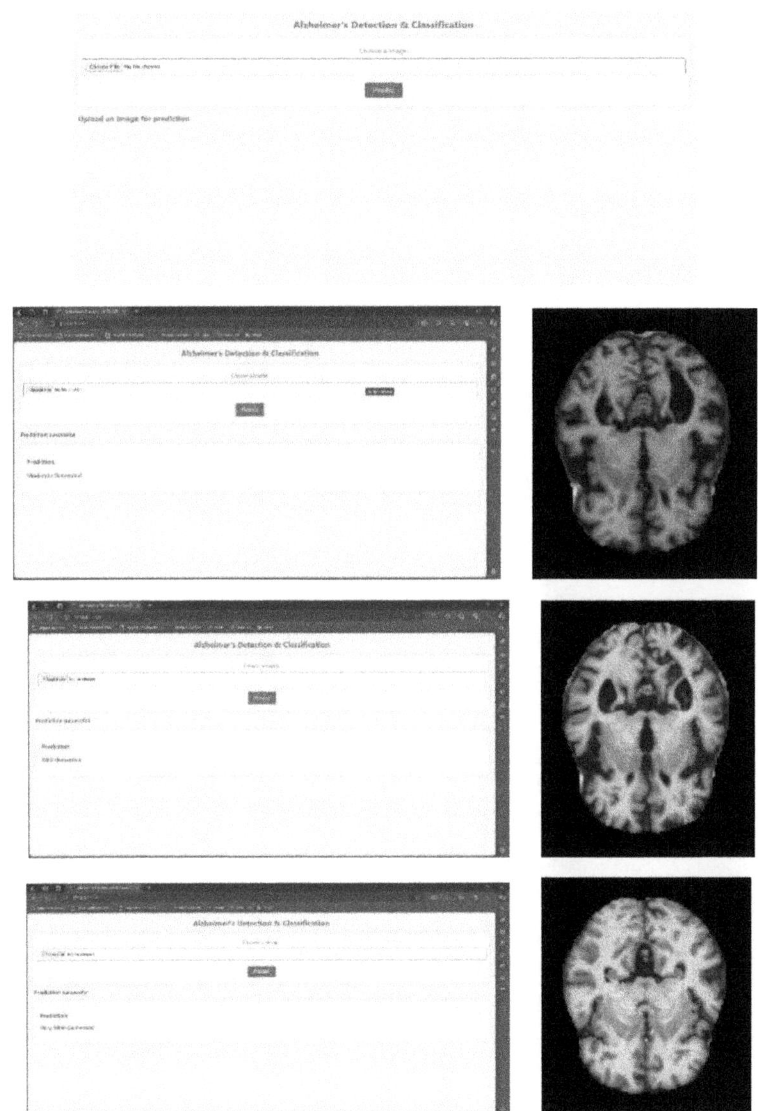

Fig. 14. webpage for identification of AD

12   Results and Discussion

Image preprocessing and feature extraction is done based on the brightness, texture, dimension etc. Using thresholding, Augmentation, Gray scaling [13]. DL techniques and algorithms have been used for training the model, identification and classification of the Image. The results show that the trained model produces 98.02% accuracy in the prediction of the disease and classification is given as output when the input, that is MRI of the Brain is fed to the system.

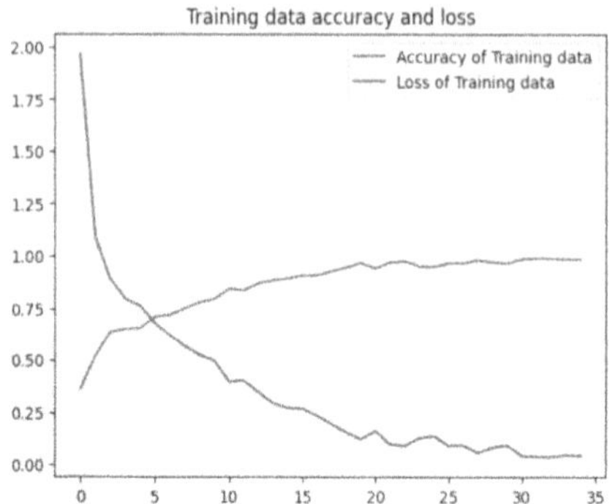

Fig. 15. Training data accuracy and loss

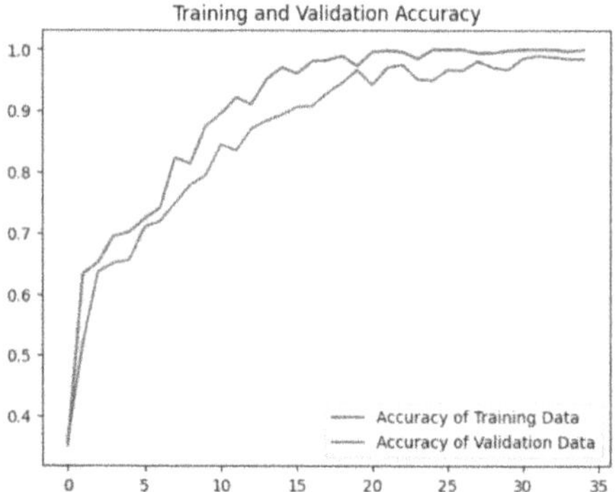

Fig. 16. Validation and Training accuracy

13   Conclusion

AD is an incurable neurological disorder that mostly impairs the memory of the elderly [2]. Alzheimer's is diagnosed and described using a variety of techniques but the precise and prompt approach is needed. To extract features from the images, we have built a model around the Convolutional Neural Network because this model is more accurate and efficient compared to other models [24]. For classification, the EfficientNetB2 model is used after the comparative analysis with other CNN models. The evaluation metrics were calculated. In this approach ADis classified into four categories: non-demented, very mild demented, Mild demented and finally moderate demented. The EfficientNet-b2 model provided better results during the testing and training phases. Using this method, Alzheimer's illness will be analyzed and categorized in real time. Future work aims to increase the system's disease detection accuracy by adding different measures and growing the dataset.

References

1. Frozza, R.L., Lourenco, M.V., De Felice, F.G.: Challenges for ADtherapy: insights from novel mechanisms beyond memory defects. Front. Neurosci. **12**, 37 (2018). https://doi.org/10.3389/fnins.2018.00037
2. El-Geneedy, M., Moustafa, H.E.-D., Khalifa, F., Khater, H., AbdElhalim, E.: An MRI-based DL approach for accurate detection of AD. Alex. Eng. J. **63**, 211–221
3. Joe, T., No, K., Saykin, A.J.: DLin AD: diagnostic classification and prognostic prediction using neuroimaging data by department of radiology science, center of neuroimaging. Front. Aging Neurosci. **11**, 220
4. Fulton, L.V., Dolezel, D., Harrop, J., Yan, Y., Fulton, C.P.: Classification of Alzheimer's disease with and without imagery using gradient boosted machines. Brain Sci. **9**, 212 (2019)
5. Chitradevi, D., Prabha, S.: Analysis of brain sub regions using optimization techniques and DL methods in Alzheimer disease. Appl. Soft Comput. **86**(4), 105857 (2020). https://doi.org/10.1016/j.asoc.2019.105857
6. Khan, F.A. et al.: Computer-aided diagnosis for burnt skin images using deep convolutional neural networks. Multimed. Tools and Appl. **79**, 34545–34568 (2020)
7. Kundaram, S.S., Pathak, K.C.: Deep learning-based Alzheimer disease detection. In: Proceedings of the Fourth International Conference on Microelectronics, ComputinG and Communication Systems, pp. 587–597. Springer, Singapore (2021)
8. Knopman, D.S. et al.: Alzheimer disease. Nature Rev. Dis. Primers. **7**(1), 1–21 (2021). https://doi.org/10.1038/s41572-021-00269-y
9. Nawaz, H., Maqsood, M., Afzal, S., Aadil, F., Mehmood, I., Rho, S.: A deep feature-based real-time system for Alzheimer disease stage detection. Multimed. Tools Appl. **80**(28–29), 35789–35807 (2021)
10. Elgammal, Y.M., Zahran, M.A., Abdelsalam, M.M.: A new strategy for the early detection of Alzheimer disease stages using multifractal geometry analysis based on K-nearest neighbor algorithm. Sci. Rep. **12**, 22381
11. Pasnoori, N., Flores-Garcia, T., Barkana, B.D.: Histogram-based features track Alzheimer's progression in brain MRI. Sci. Rep. **14**, 257
12. Mahmud, S.M.H. et al.: Detection of different stages of AD using CNN classifier. Comput. Mater. Contin. **76**(3), 3933–3948
13. Altwijri, O. et al.: Novel deep-learning approach for automatic diagnosis of AD from MRI. Appl. Sci. **13**, 13051
14. Goceri, E.: Diagnosis of ADwith Sobolev gradient-based optimization and 3D convolutional neural network. Int. J. Numer. Methods Biomed. Eng. **35**, e3225 (2019)
15. Spasov, S.E., Passamonti, L., Duggento, A., Liò, P., Toschi, N.: A multi-modal convolutional neural network framework for the prediction of AD. In: Proceedings of the 2018 40th Annual International Conference of the IEEE Engineering in Medicine and Biology Society (EMBC), Honolulu, HI, USA, pp. 1271–1274 (2018)

16. Kavitha, C., Mani, V., Srividhya, S.R., Khalaf, O.I., Romero, C.A.T.: Early-stage ADPrediction using ML models. Front. Public Health. **10**, 853294

17. Zhang, F., Petersen, M., Johnson, L., Hall, J.: Recursive support vector machine biomarker selection for AD. J. Alzheimer's Dis. **79**, 1691–1700 (2021). https://doi.org/10.3233/JAD-201254

18. Yang, B.H., et al.: Classification of AD from 18F-FDG and 11C-PiB pet imaging biomarkers using support vector machines. J. Med. Biol. Eng. **40**, 545–554 (2020). https://doi.org/10.1007/s40846-020-00548-1

19. Vichiani, Y., et al.: Accuracy of support-vector machines for diagnosis of AD, using volume of brain obtained by structural MRI at Siriraj hospital. Front. Neurol. (2021). https://doi.org/10.3389/fneur.2021.640696

20. Shahparian, N., Yazdi, M., Khosravi, M.R.: Alzheimer disease diagnosis from fMRI images based on latent low rank features and support vector machine (SVM). Curr. Signal Trans. Terap. **16**, 171177 (2019). https://doi.org/10.2174/1574362414666191202144116

21. Suwalska, A., Siuda, J., Kocot, S., Zmuda, W., Rudzinska-Bar, M., Polanska, J.: Activation maps of convolutional neural networks as a tool for brain degeneration tracking in early diagnosis of dementia in Parkinson's disease based on magnetic resonance imaging. Signal Image Video Process. **17**, 4115–4121

22. Indhumathi, G., et al.: Improving tumor diagnosis accuracy with CNN based image segmentation and Arduino decision support. In: 2023 4th IEEE Global Conference for Advancement in Technology (GCAT), Bangalore, India (2023)

23. Renugadevi, R., et al.: Deep learning-based GYM monitoring system using YOLOv5 and pose estimation algorithm. In: 7th International Conference on Electronics, Communication and Aerospace Technology (ICECA), pp. 697–702 (2023)

24. Suresh, H.R., et al.: Unsupervised Deep Learning Approaches for Anomaly Detection in IoT Data Streams. In: 4th International Conference on Smart Electronics and Communication (ICOSEC), pp. 438–443 (2023)

25. Raman, R., et al.: Role of image processing in modern healthcare: a review of techniques and applications. Eur. Chem. Bull. **12**(6), 4463–4474 (2023)

26. Indhumathi, G., Palanivelan, M., Senthilkumar, K., Sairam, V.A.: Comparative analysis of machine learning algorithms on prediction of Alzheimer from MRI. In: 2023 6th International Conference on Recent Trends in Advance Computing (ICRTAC), Chennai, India, pp. 1–9 (2023). https://doi.org/10.1109/ICRTAC59277.2023.10480790

Skincare Recommendation System Using Computer Vision

K. Vikram Kumar[(⊠)], Emuri Bhavanesh, and J. Cruz Antony

Department of Computer Science and Engineering, Sathyabama Institute of Science and Technology, Chennai, India
`vikramkk18@gmail.com, cruzantony.cse@sathyabama.ac.in`

Abstract. Migraine, a debilitating neurological disorder affecting millions worldwide, presents diverse subtypes requiring accurate diagnosis for effective treatment. This study investigates the efficacy of machine learning models in classifying migraine subtypes based on comprehensive clinical attributes. We employ Deep Neural Networks (DNN), K-Nearest Neighbors (KNN), Decision Trees, MLP Classifiers, Support Vector Machines (SVM), Random Forests, and optimized versions of MLP and SVC via GridSearchCV. Utilizing a standardized dataset encompassing various migraine characteristics, we comprehensively compare and evaluate each model's performance metrics, including accuracy, precision, recall, and F1-score. Through extensive experimentation, this analysis aims to identify the most accurate and interpretable model for migraine classification. Our findings contribute valuable insights to enhance healthcare practices by enabling improved diagnosis and personalized treatment strategies for migraineurs.

Keywords: Deep Neural Networks · K-Nearest Neighbors · Decision Trees · MLP Classifiers · Support Vector Machines · Random Forests

1 Introduction

Classic methods haven't provided great custom skincare suggestions because they depend on generalized self-diagnoses and rudimentary methods of skin analysis. Computer vision (CV), however, is an option — it can analyze skin images using image recognition algorithms and machine learning systems. Those techniques make it possible to identify skin issues, evaluate the health of your skin and make recommendations for suitable beauty products to get the results you want with your skincare.

Conventional skincare involves asking people about their preferred products through questionnaires or personal interviews. The responses are subjective, likely to be wrong and may not accurately reflect the nuances of particular skin conditions. CV (and AI in general) is intended to have an objective approach.

Through careful data collection on the skin, CV-driven advice systems can create custom skincare products for each customer. The system considers skin type, concerns, and lifestyles (e.g., exposure to pollutants) through a recommendation tool that chooses

R. Appavoo et al. (Eds.): IconDeepCom 2024, CCIS 2687, pp. 185–192, 2026.
https://doi.org/10.1007/978-3-032-26680-4_14

products for particular skin issues aimed at enhancing general skin health. This individualized method makes it possible to avoid such mistakes as choosing incompatible skincare products with potential side effects.

Personalized skincare has taken another step with the incorporation of CV into the skincare recommendation system. CV-powered systems help people objectively analyze their skin, prescribe personal product recommendations, and continuously monitor their skin for a healthy radiant look. With regards to CV technology advancement, there will be endless opportunities for customized skincare and the world of unique skincare regimes for each individual.

2 Literature Review

This research investigates the use of computer vision (CV) in personalized facial skin care, and its focus is on several CV algorithms including landmark localization, object detection and image segmentation. Hence it examines their potentiality for melanoma detection and classifying skin conditions thus creating a novel business model that employs CV for acne recognition, product suggestions as well as skin typing. It is evident from positive results attained in skin type classification that this could be a transformative system to specify convenience and efficacy of recommendations on skincare products [1].

Using Neural Collaborative Filtering (NCF) with implicit rating based on sentiment analysis from user reviews. The findings show that NCF outperforms explicit rating and matrix factorization methods based on implicit rating. Implicit ratings are obtained through carrying out sentiment analysis on data mined from Female Daily website while root mean squared error is used to train/evaluate the model. In conclusion, the paper suggests that exploring other attributes could further improve the performance of the classifier thereby making a significant contribution to skincare recommendation systems by referencing related literature [1].

This paper explores the fusion of machine learning and deep learning algorithms within the TensorFlow framework to construct a personalized skincare product recommendation platform. Leveraging TensorFlow's capabilities, the platform utilizes YOLOv4's object recognition algorithm for identifying facial features and delivers tailored advice addressing users' specific skin concerns. Furthermore, this study delves into common skin issues like wrinkles, spots, and acne vulgaris, analyzing the efficacy of different skincare product components in addressing these concerns. The primary aim is to provide users with insights into their skin's needs, facilitating informed purchases of products that promote skin health without causing harm [3].

Moreover, the paper presents a technique that combines deep neural networks with user reviews in order to provide personalized recommendations for skin care products. Additionally, it surveys existing systems for recommending skincare items online based on text analysis efficiency through user opinions. It surpasses traditional matrix factorization approaches often mentioned in recommender systems like collaborative filtering, neural collaborative filtering and hybrid recommender systems based on deep learning. Exploring sentiment analysis, attention networks, and topic modelling, the survey provides insights into context-aware recommendation systems for skincare products [4].

3   System Architecture and Design (Fig. 1)

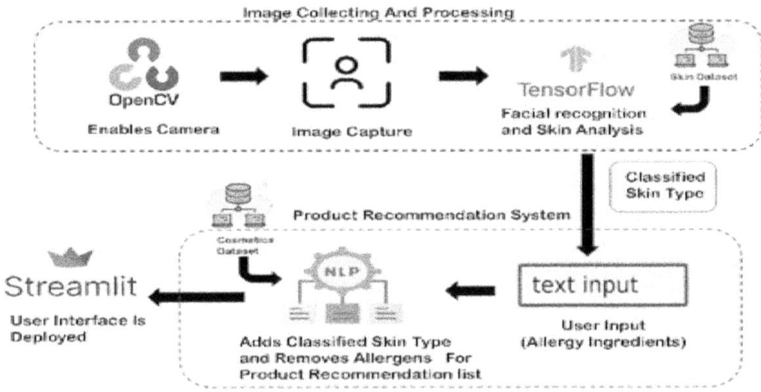

Fig. 1 System Architecture

4   Proposed System

In a world where your selfie takes you to the road of healthy skin, imagine it. Here we have our Skincare Recommendation System that leverages the power of TensorFlow, an advanced machine learning framework, to analyze and enhance your skin health based on your selfie snapshots. This proposal introduces a CV-based system for recommending skincare products using TensorFlow and OpenCV for face recognition and skin analysis, along with NLP for understanding user queries about skin problems.

Step 1- Face Recognition:
Data is collected either by taking a picture or capturing a selfie. This module comes into place converting your image into the correct form. For this purpose, it employs either OpenCV's black magic or TensorFlow's brawn, acting as if they were sheriffs who had caught you in their sights. Then it extracts key features like landmarks and points of interest needed for analyzing your skin [5, 7].

Step - 2 Skin Analysis:
In our proposed skin analysis module, skin analysis is designed to use a blend of TensorFlow and OpenCV techniques to give an in-depth look at the state of users' skin. Initially, we plan on using TensorFlow employing the Convolutional Neural Networks (CNNs) to develop a model that can be used with labelled datasets that have different types of skins such as; oily, dry and normal. Consequently, the system will be able to identify people's skin types by evaluating extracted features from their pictures and then offer skin care recommendations based on individual characteristics. This will only work when we apply OpenCV image processing methods like thresholding or color segmentation and this way we are able to detect skin flaws such as acne, wrinkles and

hyper-pigmentation. In addition, it enhances the system's ability through use of specialized classifiers or pre-trained models to determine and quantify their existence hence making it more effective in addressing specific skincare problems. It also allows textures analysis algorithms available in both OpenCV and TensorFlow libraries to be applied thus analyzing aspects of skin texture like smoothness as well as pore size. Therefore, our system will provide detailed feedback regarding perfect texture diagnosis for better appearance meaning that users can enjoy ultimate experience in terms of all aspects regarding their skins [5].

Step - 3 User Input Processing:

In our User Input Processing module, we would incorporate an analysis like NLP (Natural Language Processing) with some sentiment analysis techniques such that we can understand and interpret user input text in regard to the concern they have about their skin, what exactly they want to improve. We perform NLP analysis by carefully parsing the user-provided text for the occurrence of keywords and specific key phrases which can denote what kind of problem or goal the user is expecting. The system identifies patterns and discerns relevant data from the user's input, to arrive at sound judgment on the needs and preferences of every individual, all pertaining to skincare. Again, this algorithm can further determine the mood and attitude of the user towards his skin, ranging from frustration and feeling uncomfortable to satisfaction and delight. More narrowly, to understand the user's sentiment than just assuming that all users are sympathetic towards the journey of this very personal skincare. So, it influences what the system is recommending. A system of that kind, which fuses NLP and sentimental analysis, makes an effort to provide personalized solutions reflecting specific user concerns and preference, as well as emotional context in a drive to make personal skincare better.

Step - 4 Product Recommendation:

For these and other reasons, our product recommendation module relies on a mix of approaches aimed at matching users to personalized skincare solutions. First, we deploy ingredient matching techniques to map the user's skin type, identified blemishes, desired goals, and input keywords against a rich knowledge base of skincare ingredients known for effective problem-solving. That is, in effect, an intelligent match to relate attributes of the user to profiled attributes of ingredients in the items offered to recommend a product with a formula adaptation in skincare needs. We later apply product filtering mechanisms upon the matched ingredients, skin type, and user preferences available offerings in skincare. It is through this process that we hope to provide the best-curated assortment of products customized to best meet our customers' unique needs in skin care. We subsequently rank the recommended products by real-time user reviews, ratings, and brand preferences. This objective further values the recommendations themselves by integrating insights from peer experiences with direct user input to not only apply ingredient matching and filtering of products but also strategies for the prioritization of suggestions to the user so that they can be, if possible, fully personalized fitting the said products themselves.

Step - 5 Output & Feedback:

Propose a list of products and provide justification about their appropriateness for addressing specific concerns of the user. Provide space for the user to give feedback on how appropriate they found the recommendations and what they may have bought instead. This feedback will be very helpful for your system to learn how to improve its performance.

Additional Considerations

It represents not only the basic features but also comprises some of the features that are important requirements. By protecting user data, privacy enforcement is strict, and transparency in choice is given for our product recommendations by clearly stating reasons one by one for each suggestion. We develop through a learning approach by persistently updating the system with new data and keeping the updated user feedback in its place to bring continuous improvement in accuracy and relevancy. These try to deliver personalized solutions in skincare by also building user trust, understanding, and satisfaction.

Benefits

The system of a skincare recommendation unites all participants in a general updated, individualized approach to skincare needs and tastes. The system avoids a very highly subjective criticism as well as certain prejudices in terms of skincare recommendations via an efficient and objective analysis technique. In simple access, the system provides immediate analytical results with a description of skin type and individual recommendations of products that give choices to take decisions in an informed way about healthier glowing skin.

Our system comes with a rich library filled with articles, videos, and quizzes based on skin condition, routine, and ingredient function. It guides you not only around the System Recommendations but also in making your skin a master of its destiny.

This smart digital system of recommendations is only the tip of an iceberg—imagine a future when computer vision will reveal secrets toward really personalized and data-driven skincare. Instant feedback on what your routine is doing: hyper-local product recommendations based on any variety of environmental factors, powered by real dermatologists or an AI consultation—the sky's the limit. We believe that CV has the key to entering a world where everyone can get their healthiest and radiant skin.

This clarifies a bit further that the individual uses of TensorFlow and OpenCV were mainly in facial feature detection and personalized tracking. The skin analysis techniques are developed in more detail, with an emphasis on texture and color as tools used in addressing individualized needs. The fact that all this comes in the form of a link to personalized product recommendation, virtual try-on, and real-time feedback loop does, if anything else, create more emphasis on the dynamism and adaptability of the system today. Lastly, the thesis highlights empowerment of users through knowledge about their own capacities and a vision for opening a future with the power of CV.

5 Results and Discussions

The skincare recommendation system harmonizes OpenCV for image processing, TensorFlow for deep learning, NLP for text understanding, and machine learning for facial training to deliver precise 1recommendations tailored to individual needs.

Machine learning algorithms, coupled with facial training techniques, augment the system's ability to recognize facial features accurately, enhancing user identification and personalization alongside the robust capabilities of OpenCV, TensorFlow, and NLP.

The research on skincare recommendation systems harnessed TensorFlow, OpenCV, and NLP to provide personalized solutions. Integration of TensorFlow and OpenCV facilitated robust skin analysis, including skin type classification and blemish detection. NLP parsed user input for skincare concerns and goals, enabling tailored recommendations. By matching user data with suitable skincare ingredients and products, our system generated effective skincare suggestions. Challenges include data privacy, lighting variations, and expanding analysis capabilities. Our study demonstrates the potential of computer vision and NLP in transforming skincare recommendations, paving the way for personalized and data-driven solutions. Ongoing refinement is crucial to address challenges and enhance system efficacy (Figs. 2 and 3).

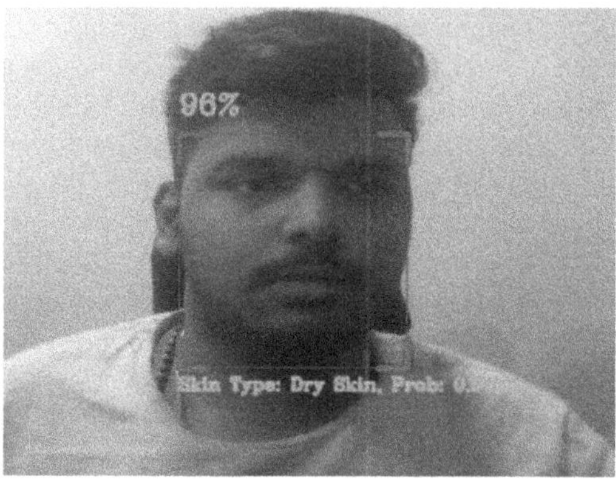

Fig. 2. Skin Type Classification

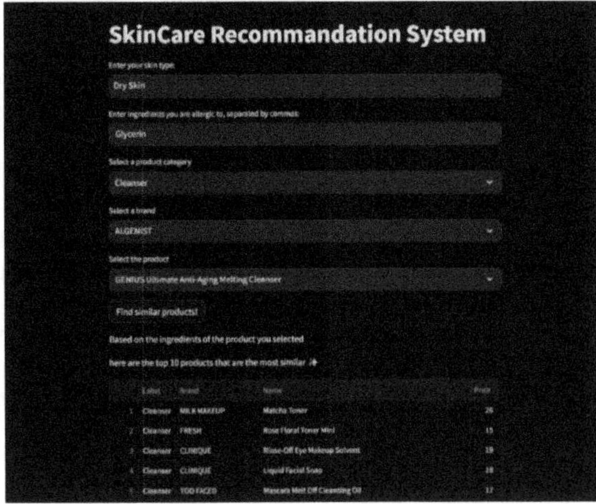

Fig. 3. Product Recommendation System

References

1. Chan, H.-T., et al.: Smart facial skincare products using computer vision technologies. In: 2021 Asia-Pacific Signal and Information Processing Association Annual Summit and Conference (APSIPA ASC). IEEE (2021)
2. Qalbyassalam, C., Rachmadi, R.F., Kurniawan, A.: Skincare recommender system using neural collaborative filtering with implicit rating. In: 2022 International Conference on Computer Engineering, Network, and Intelligent Multimedia (CENIM). IEEE (2022)
3. Li, H.-H., et al.: Based on machine learning for personalized skin care products recommendation engine. In: 2020 International Symposium on Computer, Consumer and Control (IS3C). IEEE (2020)
4. Adebo, A.: A Natural Language Processing Approach to a Skincare Recommendation Engine. Diss. Dublin, National College of Ireland (2020)
5. Kumbhar, P.Y., et al.: Real time face detection and tracking using OpenCV. Int. J. Res. Emerg. Sci. Technol. **4**(4), 39–43 (2017)
6. Yuan, L., Qu, Z., Zhao, Y., Zhang, H., Nian, Q.: A convolutional neural network based on TensorFlow for face recognition. In: 2017 IEEE 2nd Advanced Information Technology, vol. 2017, pp. 525–529. Electronic and Automation Control Conference (IAEAC), Chongqing. https://doi.org/10.1109/IAEAC.2017.8054070
7. Albert Mayan, J., Deep, K.A., Kumar, M., Alvin, L., Reddy, S.P.: Number plate recognition using template comparison for various fonts in MATLAB. In: IEEE International Conference on Computational Intelligence and Computing Research, pp. 1–6. ICCIC (2016)
8. Ray, S., et al.: Cosmetics suggestion system using deep learning. In: 2022 2nd International Conference on Technological Advancements in Computational Sciences (ICTACS). IEEE (2022)
9. Karunanayake, R.K.M.S.K., et al.: CURETO: skin diseases detection using image processing and CNN. In: 2020 14th International Conference on Innovations in Information Technology (IIT). IEEE (2020)
10. Rubasri, S., et al.: Cosmetic product selection using machine learning. In: 2022 International Conference on Communication, Computing and Internet of Things (IC3IoT). IEEE (2022)
11. Liew, Y.K.: Chatbot-beauty skin care products recommendations. PhD diss., UTAR (2021)

12. Solanki, S., Jain, G.: Deep learning methods for selecting appropriate cosmetic products for various skin types: a survey. Int. Res. J. Eng. Technol. **6**(12) (2019)

13. Jain, V., Singh, M., Bharti, A.: Product recommendation platform based on natural language processing. In: Data Analytics and Management: Proceedings of ICDAM. Springer, Singapore (2021)

14. Vatiwutipong, P., et al.: Artificial intelligence in cosmetic dermatology: a systematic literature review. IEEE Access. (2023)

15. Fitrianah, D., Wangsa, A.H.: Text classification to predict skin concerns over skincare using bidirectional mechanism in long short-term memory. Comput. Sci. Inf. Technol. **3**(3), 137–147 (2022)

16. Alzahrani, T.: Artificial Intelligence Applied to Facial Image Analysis and Feature Measurement. The University of Liverpool (United Kingdom) (2022)

17. Tan, Y.S.: Beauty and skincare e-commerce mobile application with advanced searching module using image processing. Diss. UTAR (2020)

18. Hasan, R.T.H., Sallow, A.B.: Face detection and recognition using OpenCV. J. Soft Comput. Data Min. **2**(2), 86–97 (2021)

19. Suwarno, S., Kevin, K.: Analysis of face recognition algorithm: Dlib and opencv. J. Inform. Telecommun. Eng. **4**(1), 173–184 (2020)

20. Li, L.J., et al.: Analysis on epidemiological characteristics of allergens with allergic skin diseases in a hospital in Beijing City from 2017 to 2021. Zhonghua yu Fang yi xue za zhi [Chinese Journal of Preventive Medicine]. **57**(12), 2188–2195 (2023)

21. Pang, B., Nijkamp, E., Ying Nian, W.: Deep learning with tensorflow: a review. J. Educ. Behav. Stat. **45**(2), 227–248 (2020)

Leveraging Machine Learning Across Diverse Domain

Machine Learning Approach for Error Handling - Linear Block Codes - A Case Study

Piratla Srihari$^{(\boxtimes)}$ (ID)

Geethanjali College of Engineering and Technology, Hyderabad, India
posttopshari@gmail.com

Abstract. The transferred information through an electrical communication channel is susceptible to additive noise with relatively, more certainty. Forward Error Correction mechanism facilitates information protection against channel noise through the overheads appended with the information prior to transmission. Redundancy introduced enables the receiver to retrieve the source information, against the effects of channel noise, at the cost of coding efficiency or code rate. Linear Block coding is such a Channel coding scheme, which possesses the feature that the linearly combined code words of the code result in another code word of the same code. Information word of length 'k' binary bits is transformed into a binary code word of length 'n (=k+ r)' bits with a one-to-one mapping, with 'r' number of overheads appended to 'k' bit information word in an (n, k) linear block code. Such a coding scheme with Hamming Distance of d_{min} can handle $\frac{d_{min}-1}{2}$ number of effected bits in the received 'n' bit word. Information retrieval from the received (noise effected) is the functionality of the decoder/receiver, which can be very much implemented using Classification algorithms of Machine.

Keywords: Overheard · generator matrix · code rate · Hamming distance · syndrome vector · naïve bayes classifier · KNN classifier · Maximum A posteriori criterion

1 Introduction

Channel Encoding provides the ability of having a reliable error free reception in connection with digital data transmission. The channel noise affects the information bits transmitted (i.e. received and the transmitted will not be the same) and such affected bits are referred to as Errors in the received. Channel coding attends such influences of additive channel noise on the information transmitted, through the redundancy provided for the information prior to transmission. This redundancy provides overheads for transmission, and these are responsible for error detecting/correcting features of the communication system. In a linear (n, k) Block Code, an $'n'$ bit code word will be transmitted in the place of $'k'$ bit message word where $n = k + r$, obtained by appending $'r'$ number of parity bits to $'k'$ bit message word. Code Efficiency or Code rate $\left(= \frac{k}{n} X\,100\%\right)$ is the metric used for specifying the useful number of bits in the $'n'$ bits transmitted.

R. Appavoo et al. (Eds.): IconDeepCom 2024, CCIS 2687, pp. 195–212, 2026.
https://doi.org/10.1007/978-3-032-26680-4_15

In an (n, k) Binary Linear Block code, a block of message/information bits of length 'k', $M = [m_1\ m_2 - - m_k\ ]$ is encoded into a block of coded binary bits, $C = [c_1\ c_2 - - c_n\ ]$, referred to as code word of length 'n', more than 'k' by 'r' binary bits. In a systematic block code, the information bits in the code word are readily identifiable [11, 12].

Among 2^n code words of the code, 2^k number of 'n' bit code words are uniquely mapped to each of the 2^k number of 'k' bit message words with a one-to-one mapping between message word and code word. The rest $2^n - 2^k$ number of 'n' bit code words are not used by the user. The very feature of these code words is that the sum of any two code words of an (n, k) code is another code word. A message word with $'k'$ zeros will have code word with all zeros.

An (n, k) linear Block Code with Hamming Distance d_{min}, can correct $\frac{d_{min}-1}{2}$ number of errors [can detect $(d_{min} - 1)$ number of Errors].

Since, identifying the message bits from the received code word, involves, identifying the unique mapping between the message word and code word, this can be the example of the principle of classification of machine Learning. Two such algorithms i.e. Naïve Bayes Classifier and KNN algorithm are being implemented for the decoding scheme.

2 Encoding

M and C are uniquely mapped through $C = MG$, where, the Generator matrix $G = [I_k|\ h]$ is a binary matrix with k rows and n columns [1, 12]. I_k and $'h'$ are binary matrices of size kXk (unity matrix) and $kX(n - k = r)$ respectively.

The generator matrix G= [1 0 0 0 1 0 1   0 1 0 0 1 1 1   0 0 0 0 1 0 1 1 0   0 1 0 1 1] can be of a systematic code with n = 7 and k = 4.

For a message word M= $[m_1\ m_2\ m_3\ m_4\ ]$, the code word $C = M.G = [m_1\ m_2\ m_3\ m_4\ m_1 + m_2 + m_3\ \ m_2 + m_3 + m_4\ \ m_1 + m_2 + m_4\ ]$, with $' + '$ being the Modulo-2 addition [1, 5].

For every code word C of a Linear Block Code, $C.\ H^T = 0$, with $H = [h^T\ I_r]$ being the Parity Matrix. The Hamming Distance of (7, 4) is 3, and hence, is capable of correcting single error [12].

3 Syndrome Decoding of Linear Block Codes

The transmitted code word C, and the received code word R may differ (because of channel noise) by the error vector E i.e., $E = C + R$ (using Galois arithmetic).

The conventional decoding process is through Syndrome decoding, where the Syndrome Vector, a symptom of errors is $S = R.\ H^T = (C + E)H^T = E.\ H^T$ [12]., which a $1Xk$ vector. A zero 'S' signals zero effect of channel noise on the transmitted.

Among the all, the error vector with lowest non zero weight (zero weight in the case of error free reception) is the appropriate E for R, subject to the ability of the code in handling errors.

4 Classification Algorithms for Decoding

The received code word can be decoded using Predictive Modeling of Machine Learning, specifically Classification algorithms.

4.1 Bayesian Classifier [2, 4]

Bayesian classifiers use the idea that the training data is utilized to calculate an observed probability of each class based on feature values. When used for unclassified data, it uses the observed probabilities to predict the most likely class for the new features Applying prior knowledge or prior belief to the probability of an outcome, so that it has higher probability of meeting the actual outcome is the very feature of this classifier.

Bayes theorem facilitates calculating the probability of a hypothesis based on its prior probability, the probabilities of observing various data given the hypothesis, and the observed data itself, i.e. the posteriori probabilities, which is the probability of an event after the evidence is observed.

Among the set of Hypotheses, H, (the possible code words that can be mapped to the received, where, each is equally probable and independent of each other) the most probable Hypothesis $h \in H$ given the observed data i.e. the received R (at least one of maximally probable, if there are several) is referred to as Maximum A posteriori (MAP) Hypothesis.

This classification can be used to find the unique mapping between (classify) the received and the appropriate transmitted code word, which is validated by figuring out the respective A posteriori probability [8, 10].

For the given R, if the code word C_i is with more certainty of transmission, the received is uniquely mapped to C_i; otherwise, to C_j i.e. $e., p\left(\frac{C_i}{R}\right)C_i >< C_j p\left(\frac{C_j}{R}\right)$

4.1.1 Figuring the A Posteriori Probability

- Each 'n' bit word of the given (n, k) Linear Block code is with equal probability of transmission as the others and is independent of each other.
- Each 'n' bit word of the (n, k) code will be the member of the training set for the decoder, which is used for implementation of MAP criterion, which facilitates the decoder for favorable decision about the transmitted [2, 6].
- All possible hypotheses are with equal certainty and. with independence among them.
- Crossover probability is p_e
- In 'n bits transmitted, the likelihood of receiving $'m'$ bits in error is $p(X = m) = n_{C_m}(p_e)^m(1 - p_e)^{n-m}$, $m = 0, 1, \ldots n$; X is the random variable (Binomial) [3, 9]

4.1.2   Use Cases

Use Case 1: A Single Error Correcting (6,3) Code

- Consider a (6,3) code with $G = [1\,0\,0\,0\,1\,1 \quad 0\,1\,0\,1\,0\,1 \quad 0\,0\,1\,1\,1\,0]$
- This is of $d_{min} = 3$, and can correct single error.
- The training data set is (Table 1).

Table 1. Possible groups of 'k' bit words and their unique mapping with 'n' bit words of a (6, 3) Linear Block Code

Group of 'k' bits	Group of 'n' bits	Group of 'k' bits	Group of 'n' bits
000	000000	100	100011
001	001110	101	101101
010	010101	110	110110
011	011011	111	111000

- Let the probability of receiving a transmitted 1 as 0 $(= p_e)$ and vice versa $= 1/4$
- Let R $= 011110$.
- The following are Hamming Distances between R and all Cs of the code (Table 2).

Table 2. Distance between the received and the code words of (6, 3) code.

Received Code Word R $= 011110$								
6-bit word	000000	001110	010101	011011	100011	101101	110110	111000
Hamming Distance	4	1	3	2	5	4	2	3

- The A posteriori probability pertaining to each of the Cs of the code is as given below (Table 3):

Table 3. A posteriori probability for each code word of (6, 3) code for the given R

R $= 011110$								
6-bit word	000000	001110	010101	011011	100011	101101	110110	111000
A posteriori probability	0.032	0.354	0.13	0.295	0.0042	0.032	0.295	0.13

- The largest of all A posteriori probabilities is 0.354 i.e., the A posteriori probability $p\left(\frac{001110}{R}\right)$ is the largest of all. Thus, it can be inferred that the transmitted 6-bit word was 001110 and the corresponding message word is 001.

Use Case 2: A Single Error Correcting (7,4) Code Consider a (7,4) Code with $G = [1\,0\,0\,0\,1\,0\,1\quad 0\,1\,0\,0\,1\,1\,1\quad 0\,0\,0\,0\,1\,0\,1\,1\,0\quad 0\,1\,0\,1\,1\quad]$

- This is of $d_{min} = 3$, and hence is a single error correcting code.
- The training data set is (Table 4):

Table 4. Possible groups of 'k' bit words and their unique mapping with 'n' bit words of a (7, 4) Linear Block Code

Group of 'k' bits	Group of 'n' bits	Group of 'k' bits	Group of 'n' bits	Group of 'k' bits	Group of 'n' bits	Group of 'k' bits	Group of 'n' bits
0000	0000000	0100	0100111	1000	1000101	1100	1100010
0001	0001011	0101	0101100	1001	1001110	1101	1101001
0010	0010110	0110	0110001	1010	1010011	1110	1110100
0011	0011101	0111	0111010	1011	1011000	1111	1111111

- Let the probability of receiving a transmitted 1 as 0 $(= p_e)$ and vice versa $= 1/4$
- The received code word is R $= 0011011$.
- The following are Hamming Distances between R and all Cs of the code (Table 5).

Table 5. Hamming Distance between the received and the code words of the code.

R $= 0011011$

Group of 'n' bits	Distance	Group of 'n' bits	Distance	Group of 'n' bits	Distance	Group of 'n' bits	Distance
0000000	4	0100111	4	1000101	5	1100010	5
0001011	1	0101100	5	1001110	4	1101001	4
0010110	3	0110001	3	1010011	2	1110100	6
0011101	2	0111010	2	1011000	3	1111111	3

The above Distance indicates the error count in R, when the respective code word was transmitted.

- If the code word transmitted was 000000, it indicates that the received is with 4 errors, as indicated in Table 2. The A posteriori probability (conditional probability)

$p\left(\frac{000000}{R}\right)$ is same as the probability for having 4 bits in error, when 7 bits were transmitted, which can be computed as

$$p(No.\,of\,errors = 5, when\,a\,11\,bit\,word\,is\,tranmsitted\,) = 11_{c_5}\left(\frac{1}{4}\right)^5\left(\frac{3}{4}\right)^6$$

$$=0.0802989$$

This is the conditional probability for '0000000' to be the transmitted one, given the received.

- On similar lines, the A posteriori probability pertaining to each of the other Cs of the code is as given below (Table 6):

Table 6. A posteriori probability for each code word of (7, 4) code for the given R

R = 0011011

Group of 'n' bits	conditional probability	Group of 'n' bits	conditional probability	Group of 'n' bits	conditional probability	Group of 'n' bits	conditional probability
0000000	0.057	0100111	0.057	1000101	0.011	1100010	0.011
0001011	0.311	0101100	0.011	1001110	0.057	1101001	0.057
0010110	0.173	0110001	0.173	1010011	0.311	1110100	0.001
0011101	0.311	0111010	0.311	1011000	0.173	1111111	0.173

- The largest of all A posteriori probabilities is 0.311 and the respective 'n' bit words are shown in Table 7.

Table 7. 'n' bit words corresponding to the maximum A posteriori (conditional) probability.

R = 0011011

'n' bit word	0001011	0011101	0111010	1010011
No. of errors in R with reference to the transmitted	1	2	2	2

- The 'n' bit word corresponding to the minimum number (unique element of the above array with reference to number of errors) of errors (=1) is the transmitted one i.e., 0001011 and the corresponding uniquely mapped message word is 0001.

Use Case 3: A Double Error Correcting (11,3) Code

- Consider a (11,3) Code with $G = [1\ 0\ 0\ 1\ 1\ 0\ 1\ 1\ 0\ 0\ 1\quad 0\ 1\ 0\ 1\ 0\ 1\ 1\ 0\ 1\ 0\ 0$ $0\ 0\ 1\ 1\ 1\ 1\ 0\ 0\ 0\ 1\ 1\ ]$ (11,3) Linear Block Code is of Hamming Distance $d_{min} = 5$, and hence is a double error correcting code.

- The following are all the possible groups of 'k' information bits (message words) of the code and the corresponding uniquely mapped groups of 'n' bit words (code words) (Table 8).

Table 8. Possible groups of 'k' bit words and their unique mapping with 'n' bit words of a (11, 3) Linear Block Code (Training data set)

Group of 'k' bits	Group of 'n' bits	Group of 'k' bits	Group of 'n' bits
000	00000000000	100	10011011001
001	00111100011	101	10100111010
010	01010110100	110	11001101101
011	01101010111	111	11110001110

- Let the probability of receiving a transmitted 1 as 0 ($= p_e$) and vice versa $= 1/4$
- The received code word is R $=$ 00110001110.
- The following are Hamming Distances between R and all Cs of the code (Table 9).

Table 9. Distance between the received and the code words of (11, 3) code.

R $=$ 00110001110

11-bit word	Hamming Distance	11-bit word	Hamming Distance
00000000000	5	10011011001	7
00111100011	5	10100111010	5
01010110100	6	11001101101	8
01101010111	6	11110001110	2

The above Distance indicates the error count in R, when the respective code word was transmitted.

- If the code word transmitted was 00000000000, it indicates that the received is with 5 errors, as indicated in Table 8. The A posteriori probability (conditional probability) $p\left(\frac{00000000000}{R}\right)$ is same as the probability for having 5 bits in error, when 11 bits were transmitted, which can be computed as

$$p(No.of\ errors = 4, when\ a\ 7\ bit\ word\ is\ tranmsitted) = 7_{c_4}\left(\frac{1}{4}\right)^4\left(\frac{3}{4}\right)^3$$

$$= 0.057$$

This is the conditional probability for '00000000000' to be the transmitted one, given the received.

- On similar lines, the A posteriori probability pertaining to each of the other Cs of the code is as given in Table 10.

Table 10. A posteriori probability for each code word of (11, 3) code for the given R

R = 00110001110

11-bit word	A posteriori probability	11-bit word	A posteriori probability
00000000000	0.0802989	10011011001	0.0063729
00111100011	0.0802989	10100111010	0.0802989
01010110100	0.0267663	11001101101	0.0010622
01101010111	0.0267663	11110001110	0.2581036

- The largest of all A posteriori probabilities is 0.2581036 and the corresponding code word is 11110001110 i.e., the A posteriori probability $p\left(\frac{11110001110}{R}\right)$ is the largest of all. Thus, it can be concluded that the transmitted 11-bit word was 11110001110 and the corresponding message word is 111.

Use Case 4: A Triple Error Correcting (13,3) Code

- Consider a (13,3) Code with $G = [1\,0\,0\,1\,1\,0\,1\,1\,0\,0\,1\,1\,0$ $0\,1\,0\,1\,0\,1\,1\,0\,1\,0$ $1\,0\,1$ $0\,0\,1\,1\,1\,1\,0\,0\,0\,1$ $1\,1\,1$ $]$ (13,3) Linear Block Code is of Hamming Distance $d_{min} = 7$, and hence is a triple error correcting code.
- The following are all the possible groups of 'k' information bits (message words) of the code and the corresponding uniquely mapped groups of 'n' bit words (code words), which is the data set used for training (Table 11).

Table 11. Possible groups of 'k' bit words and their unique mapping with 'n' bit words of a (13, 3) Linear Block Code

Group of 'k' bits	Group of 'n' bits	Group of 'k' bits	Group of 'n' bits
000	0000000000000	100	1001101100110
001	0011110001111	101	1010011101001
010	0101011010101	110	1100110110011
011	0110101011010	111	1111000111100

- Let the probability of receiving a transmitted 1 as 0 ($= p_e$) and vice versa $= 1/4$
- The received code word is R = 1101110111100
- The following are Hamming Distances between R and all Cs of the code (Table 12).

Table 12. Distance between the received and the code words of (13, 3) code.

R = 1101110111100

13-bit word	Hamming Distance	13-bit word	Hamming Distance
0000000000000	9	1001101100110	6
0011110001111	7	1010011101001	8
0101011010101	6	1100110110011	5
0110101011010	8	1111000111100	3

The above Distance indicates the error count in R when the respective code word was transmitted.

- If the code word transmitted was 0000000000000, it indicates that the received is with 9 errors, as indicated in Table 11. The A posteriori probability (conditional probability) $p\left(\frac{0000000000000}{R}\right)$ is same as the probability for having 9 bits in error, when 13 bits were transmitted, which can be computed as

$$p(No.of\ errors = 9, when\ a\ 13\ bit\ word\ is\ tranmsitted) = 13_{c_9}\left(\frac{1}{4}\right)^9\left(\frac{3}{4}\right)^4 = 0.000863$$

- This is the conditional probability for '0000000000000' to be the transmitted one, given the received.
- On similar lines, the A posteriori probability pertaining to each of the other Cs of the code is as given below (Table 13):

Table 13. A posteriori probability for each code word of (13, 3) code for the given R

R = 1101110111100

13-bit word	A posteriori probability	13-bit word	A posteriori probability
0000000000000	0.000863	1001101100110	0.0559224
0011110001111	0.0186408	1010011101001	0.0046602
0101011010101	0.0559224	1100110110011	0.1258255
0110101011010	0.0046602	1111000111100	0.251651

- The largest of all A posteriori probabilities is 0.251651 and the corresponding code word is 1111000111100. i.e., the A posteriori probability $p\left(\frac{1111000111100}{R}\right)$ is the largest of all. Thus, it can be concluded that the transmitted 13-bit word was 1111000111100 and the corresponding message word is 111.

4.2 KNN Algorithm [2, 4]

4.2.1 Principle of Decoding

The unique mapping between each group of 'k' information bits and each group of 'n' coded bits of an (n, k) Linear block code, i.e., the set of 2^k number of 'k' bit message words and the corresponding 2^k number of 'n' bit code words will be the training data set for the decoder. Using $K-$ Nearest Neighbor (KNN) algorithm, the class of the received code word can be identified i.e. its nearest neighbor among the members of the code word set of the training data can be identified [3, 6].

4.2.2 Identification of Nearest Neighbor

- Each code word of a specific (n, k) Linear Block code is equally likely as the others for transmission.
- The distance metric used for the identification of nearest neighbor is hamming distance between received code word and all the code words of training data set.
- The code word of the training set, which is at a minimum distance from the receiver will be its nearest neighbor.
- Minimum distance is decided by the value of 'K' (=0 for error free reception), which depends on the error correcting ability of the code.

$$K = \left\lfloor \frac{d_{min} - 1}{2} \right\rfloor$$

- The nearest neighbor of the received code word among the members of the code word set (Training Data Set) will be the transmitted code word and from this, the uniquely mapped message word can be retrieved.

4.2.3 Use Cases

Use Case 1: A Single Error Correcting (7,3) Code

- Consider a (7,3) Code with $G = [1\,0\,0\,1\,1\,1\,0 \ \ 0\,1\,0\,0\,1\,1\,1 \ \ 0\,0\,1\,1\,1\,0\,1\ ]$
- This is of $d_{min} = 4$, and can correct one error.
- Hence,' K' for KNN algorithm $=1$
- The data set used for training is (Table 14):

- Let R $= 1111010$ (Table 15).

- The nearest neighbor of the received is the code word 01111010 and hence is the transmitted and the corresponding uniquely mapped message word is 011.

Use Case 2: A Double Error Correcting (10,3) Code

- Consider a (10,3) Code with $G = [1\,0\,0\,1\,1\,0\,1\,1\,0\,0 \ \ 0\,1\,0\,1\,0\,1\,1\,0\,1\,0$ $0\,0\,1\,1\,1\,1\,0\,0\,0\,1\ ]$
- This is of $d_{min} = 5$ and can correct 2 errors.
- Hence, 'K' for KNN algorithm $=2$

Table 14. Possible groups of 'k' bit words and their unique mapping with 'n' bit words of a (7, 3) Linear Block Code

'k' bit word	'n' bit word
000	0000000
001	0011101
010	0100111
011	0111010
100	1001110
101	1010011
110	1101001
111	1110100

Table 15. Distance 'd' between R and the possible 7 bit words of (7,3) code.

R = 1111010

word	d
0000000	5
0011101	5
0100111	5
0111010	1
1001110	3
1010011	3
1101001	3
1110100	3

Table 16. Possible groups of 'k' bit words and their unique mapping with 'n' bit words of (10, 3) Linear Block Code

'k' bit word	'n' bit word	'k' bit word	'n' bit word
000	0000000000	100	1001101100
001	0011110001	101	1010011101
010	0101011010	110	1100110110
011	0110101011.	111	1111000111

- The data set used for training is: (Table 16)

- Let R = 1011100111 (Table 17)

Table 17. Distance 'd' between R and all the possible 10-bit words of (10,3) code.

R = 1011100111	
word	d
0000000000	7
0011110001	4
0101011010	8
0110101011.	5
1001101100	4
1010011101	5
1100110110	5
1111000111	2

- The nearest neighbor for the received is the code word 1111000111 and hence is the transmitted and the corresponding uniquely mapped message word is 111.
- Let R = 1000110110.

Case 3: A Double Error Correcting (10,3) Code Correcting A Single Error

- Let R=1000110110 (Table 18).

Table 18. Distance 'd' between R and all the possible 10-bit words of (10,3) code.

R = 1011100111	
word	d
0000000000	5
0011110001	6
0101011010	6
0110101011.	7
1001101100	4
1010011101	5
1100110110	1
1111000111	6

- The nearest neighbor for the received is the code word 1100110110 and hence is the transmitted and the corresponding uniquely mapped message word is 110.

Use Case 4: A Triple Error Correcting (13,3) Code

- Consider a (13,3) Code with $G = [1\,0\,0\,1\,1\,0\,1\,1\,0\,0\,1\,1\,0\quad 0\,1\,0\,1\,0\,1\,1\,0\,1\,0$ $1\,0\,1\quad 0\,0\,1\,1\,1\,1\,0\,0\,0\,1\quad 1\,1\,1\quad]$
- This is of $d_{min} = 7$ and can correct 3 errors.
- Hence,' K' for KNN algorithm $=3$
- The data set used for training is (Table 19):

Table 19. Possible groups of 'k' bit words and their unique mapping with 'n' bit words of a (13, 3) Linear Block Code

'k' bit word	'n' bit word	'k' bit word	'n' bit word
000	0000000000000	100	1001101100110
001	0011110001111	101	1010011101001
010	0101011010101	110	1100110110011
011	0110101011010	111	1111000111100

- Let R = 1101110111100 (Table 20)

Table 20. Distance 'd' between R and all the possible 13-bit words of (13, 3) code.

R = 1101110111100			
word	d	word	d
0000000000000	9	1001101100110	6
0011110001111	7	1010011101001	8
0101011010101	6	1100110110011	5
0110101011010	8	1111000111100	3

- The nearest neighbor for the received is the code word 1111000111100 and is the transmitted and the corresponding uniquely mapped message word is 111.

Use Case 5: A Single Error Correcting (8,4) Extended Hamming Code

- Consider (8,4) Code with $G = [1\,0\,0\,0\,1\,0\,1\,1\quad 0\,1\,0\,0\,1\,1\,1\,0\quad 0\,0\,0\,0\,1\,0\,1\,1\,0\,1$ $0\,1\,0\,1\,1\,1\quad]$

This is of $d_{min} = 4$, and can correct one error.

- Hence,' K' for KNN algorithm $=1$
- The data set used for training is (Tables 21):

Table 21. Possible groups of 'k' bit words and their unique mapping with 'n' bit words of a (8, 4) Extended Code

'k' bit word	'n' bit word	'k' bit word	'n' bit word	'k' bit word	'n' bit word	'k' bitword	'n' bit word
0000	00000000	0100	01001110	1000	10001011	1100	11000101
0001	00010111	0101	01011001	1001	10011100	1101	11010010
0010	00101101	0110	01100011	1010	10100110	1110	11101000
0011	00111010	0111	01110100	1011	10110001	1111	11111111

Table 22. Distance'd' between R and all the possible 8-bit words of (8, 4) code.

R = 11001011

word	d	word	d	word	d	word	d
00000000	5	01001110	3	10001011	1	11000101	3
00010111	5	01011001	3	10011100	5	11010010	3
00101101	5	01100011	3	10100110	5	11101000	3
00111010	5	01110100	7	10110001	5	11111111	3

- Let R = 11001011 (Table 22)

- The nearest neighbor for the received is the code word 10001011 and hence is the transmitted and the corresponding uniquely mapped message word is 1000.

5   KNN Algorithm Applied for Length Based Codes (Systematic)

- In these $(n + 1, k)$length-based Codes,$'k'$ bit message word is encoded into $(n + 1)$ bit code word, where $n = 2k$.
- The encoding rule is:

  - Message word with $'k'$ zeros is uniquely mapped with code word of $'(n + 1)'$ zeros
  - $(n - k)$ parity bits of the code word are the negated message bits.
  - $(n + 1)^{th}$ bit of the code word i.e. $(2k + 1)^{th}$ bit of the code word is the modulo-2 sum of the $'k'$ message bits.

- The conventional decoding is based on length of the message word in the received.
- Consider a (7, 3) length-based code.
- This is a single error correcting code.
- Hence,' K' for KNN algorithm =1
- The data set used for training is (Table 23):

Table 23. Possible groups of 'k' bit words and their unique mapping with 'n + 1' bit words of a (7, 3) Length Based Code

'k' bit word	'n' bit word
000	0000000
001	0011101
010	0101011
011	0111000
100	1000111
101	1010100
110	1100010
111	1110001

- Let R = 0111011 (Table 24)

Table 24. Distance'd' between R and all the possible 7-bit words of (7, 3) Length Based code.

R = 0111011	
word	d
0000000	5
0011101	3
0101011	1
0111000	2
1000111	5
1010100	6
1100010	4
1110001	3

- The nearest neighbor for the received is the code word 0101011 and hence is the transmitted and the corresponding uniquely mapped message word is 010.

6 Discussion

In the process of forward error correction using Bayesian classifier,

- A set of training examples (all Cs of an individual code) is provided, where the target value may or may not be under the effect of channel noise (received code word)
- $R = C + E$, where C is the target function under no noise and E is the Error pattern.

- Ex.: For a (13, 3) Triple Error correcting code, for R = 00110001110, the corresponding C = 1111000111100 (Table 11), i.e. the error vector E = 0010110000000 and the Modulo-2 sum of Enad C will be R (or) Modulo -2 sum of R and E will be the transmitted i.e. C.
- The optimal classification of the received is that C, for which $P\left(\frac{C}{R}\right)$ is maximum.

In KNN algorithm applied for identifying the transmitted code word, the metric is the smallest among the distances between R and all Cs of the code $\leq$ 'K', selected for the algorithm, which the error correcting ability of the code.

7 Conclusion

The process of identifying the unique mapping between R and one of the Cs i.e. the process of error detection and correction can be implemented through Bayes classifier and KNN algorithm

- Both algorithms facilitate simplified Forward Error correction mechanism, comparable to that of Syndrome Decoding.
- Based on the ability of an individual error control coding scheme, random / burst errors in the received can be classified with these principles [7].
- Implementation of Bayes classifier algorithm for decoding requires prior knowledge about the error probability.
- For the KNN algorithm, the value of K depends on the error handling ability of the code and the algorithm selects all Cs, with the metric $\leq K$. The C with minimum metric among such will be the code word that is uniquely mapped to the message word.

8 Sustainable Development Goals

The UN Sustainable Development Goals relevant to the proposed topic are:

- Quality Education
- Decent work and Economic growth
- Industry, Innovation, and Infrastructure

Machine Learning is finding its numerous applications in every field of the present industrial scenario and in the Education sector also. The role of Machine Learning and Artificial Intelligence in Environmental sustainability is appreciable, specifically, in promoting the improvement in energy efficiency, reduction in carbon emission, conservation of wildlife and so on. The present technological advancements for the wellbeing of society are greatly influenced by AI and ML.

The communication technology of the day i.e. 5G and beyond uses the concepts of Machine Learning and Deep Learning extensively, for example, with reference to channel estimation and error controlling.

Various machine Learning algorithms are being devised/implemented for overcoming the effect of channel noise on the information transmitted. These algorithms made the process of decoding simpler, relative to conventional decoding schemes.

The proposed concept in this paper refers to error control mechanisms during the transmission of data.

Appendix 1

APPENDIX 1

Decoding using Bayes Classifier

Flowchart:

Decoding using KNN Algorit hm

Flow Chart:

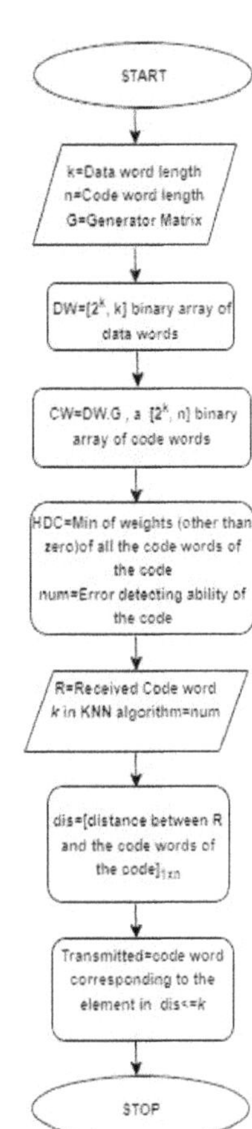

References

1. SriHari, P., Jinaga, B.C.: Data inverting codes. Ph.D Thesis, Jawaharlal Nehru Technological University, Hyderabad, India (2007)
2. Murphy, K.P.: Machine Learning-a Probabilistic Perspective. MIT Press, Cambridge, MA/London, UK (2012)
3. Paluszek, M., Thomas, S.: MATLAB Machine learning. Apress (2017)
4. Dangeti, P.: Statistics for Machine Learning. Packt Publishing (2017)
5. Gruber, T., Cammerer, S., Hoydis, J., ten Brink, S.: On deep learning-based channel decoding. In: Proceedings of Conference: 2017 51st Annual Conference on Information Sciences and Systems (CISS). IEEE (2017). https://doi.org/10.1109/CISS.2017.7926071

6. Gopal, M.: Applied Machine Learning-McGraw Hill Education (India). Private Limited (2018)
7. He, R., Ding, Z.: Applications of Machine learning in Wireless Communications IET Telecommunication series 81. Institution of Engineering and Technology (IET) (2019)
8. Carpi, F., Häger, C., Martalò, M., Raheli, R., Pfister, H.D.: Reinforcement learning for channel coding: learned bit-flipping decoding arXiv:1906.04448v2 (2019) https://doi.org/10.48550/arXiv.1906.04448
9. The MathWorks Inc.: Matlab statistics and machine learning toolbox user's guide, R2020a, March, 18–2 to 18–6 p (2020)
10. Jiyang, Y.: Deep Learning for Channel Coding. Ph.D Dissertation, University of Washington (2021), 1–6
11. Guruswami, V., Rudra, A., Sudan, M.: Essential Coding Theory, pp. 43–62. Department of Computer Science and Engineering, University at Buffalo, SUNY. Work supported by NSF CAREER grant CCF-0844796 (2022)
12. Salvatore Gravano-Introduction to Error Control Codes - South Asia Editon, Oxford University Press, Oxford, (2001)

Predictive Modeling for Optimal Crop Yields

S. Sravan Kumar, K. Janakiram, T. Govardhan Reddy, T. Kumar, and S. Amutha[✉]

Department of Computer Science and Engineering, Kalasalingam Academy of Research and Education, Virudhunagar, Tamil Nadu 626126, India
amuthabe2008@gmail.com

Abstract. The use of cutting-edge technology has become essential in the quickly changing field of agriculture, where uncertainties are caused by shifting soil conditions, erratic weather patterns, and dynamic insect dynamics. With the use of cutting-edge machine learning algorithms, this research aims to address the issues facing contemporary agriculture by providing accurate production predictions. Using an all-encompassing investigation of agricultural data that includes a variety of factors, including meteorological data, soil characteristics, and insect dynamics, the main objective is to transform traditional farming practices.

The use of cutting-edge technology has become essential in the quickly changing field of agriculture, where uncertainties are caused by shifting soil conditions, erratic weather patterns, and dynamic insect dynamics. With the use of cutting-edge machine learning algorithms, this research aims to address the issues facing contemporary agriculture by providing accurate production predictions. By means of an all- encompassing investigation of agricultural data that includes a variety of factors, including meteorological data, soil characteristics, and insect dynamics, the main objective is to transform traditional farming practices.

Keywords: Machine learning · NLP · Python · Flask · HTML · CSS · Javascript and bootstrap

1 Introduction

Agriculture, serving as the backbone of human civilization, plays a crucial role in sustaining the world's food supply and accommodating its ever-expanding population. To meet the projected 9.7 billion people by 2050, innovative solutions are imperative to maximize crop yields and enhance agricultural productivity. Predictive modeling emerges as a viable option, utilizing machine learning to anticipate optimal crop yields based on various contributing factors. Traditional farming methods often rely on intuition, experience, and historical knowledge, which may fall short in meeting the needs of a growing population and a rapidly changing environment. Machine learning holds the potential to revolutionize agricultural decision-making processes, leveraging its ability to analyze vast datasets, discern intricate patterns, and offer accurate forecasts. The significance of precise crop output projections cannot be overstated. Early information on potential yields enables farmers to optimize resource allocation, adapt agricultural practices, and

R. Appavoo et al. (Eds.): IconDeepCom 2024, CCIS 2687, pp. 213–223, 2026.
https://doi.org/10.1007/978-3-032-26680-4_16

mitigate the impact of environmental conditions. Accurate forecasts not only minimize resource wastage but also reduce environmental impact, fostering sustainable agriculture and increasing overall agricultural production.

2   Literature Survey

The work in [1] focuses on estimating agricultural production using machine learning methods. Using Tamil Nadu' available data, the Random Forest method is used to anticipate agricultural production. The Random Forest Algorithm is used to illustrate how accurate crop yield estimates may be. The usefulness and flexibility of Random Forests for predicting agricultural yields both locally and globally are examined in [2]. According to the study, Random Forest outperforms multiple linear regression (MLR) as a machine-learning technique, with high accuracy and precision. AdaNaive and AdaSVM are introduced in [3], a machine learning model for agricultural production ensemble, to estimate crop output over a certain time period. AdaBoost improves the performance of SVM and Naive Bayes algorithms. A machine learning technique for forecasting agricultural output based on meteorological variables is described in [4]. The study presents Crop Advisor, an easily navigable website that uses the C4.5 algorithm to determine the climate factors that have the greatest impact on crop production in Madhya Pradesh districts. Crop-soil and fertilizer matching techniques are covered in [5] of the International Journal of Advanced Research in Computer Science and Electronics Engineering. The article discusses soil micronutrient shortages and offers suggestions for raising crop yields. The work presented in [6] in the International Journal of Research in Technology and Engineering aims to give farmers an easy-to-use interface for analyzing rice production using data that is already available. Several data mining techniques, such as the K-Means algorithm, are used to predict agricultural productivity. A thorough summary of the research on machine learning's application to agricultural production systems can be found in [7]. Using Support Vector Machines (SVM) for the implementation, the study highlights the relevance of big data technologies and high-performance computers in decoding data-intensive operations in agricultural industries. A study on precision agriculture that addresses field variability by utilizing remote sensors and GIS techniques is described in [8]. Precision agricultural approaches are implemented through the use of ensemble learning (EL). The average forecast of each tree in Random Forests for Global and Regional Crops is covered in [9]. The work implements the k-nearest neighbor technique with Support Vector Regression (SVR) to highlight the dependability of Random Forests for agricultural output estimates at both regional and global scales.

3   Data Entry and Investigative Study

A. **Cleaning Data:**
   1. Elimination of Superfluous Data and Superfluous Columns: To guarantee that every observation in the dataset was unique, duplicate entries were found and eliminated. The dependability of the dataset is improved by the removal of these duplicates, which may have been caused by mistakes in data input or collection. 'Year' and other extraneous columns were also removed, simplifying the dataset for more targeted investigation.

2. Numerical Rainfall Data Conversion from Non-Numeric Source: A number of data, most notably rainfall data, that were originally entered in non-numeric forms were converted to numeric values. This stage is crucial for carrying out quantitative analyses because it makes statistical calculations possible and encourages a more thorough examination of the data.

B. **Data Analysis via Exploration (EDA):**

1. Examining Particular Regions and Crop Types: A closer look at the information revealed different crop kinds and geographical regions in the agriculture data. This exploration identifies the wide diversity of places and crops represented, providing important context for further research. Comprehending the distinct features of the dataset facilitates the development of an all-encompassing comprehension of agricultural methodologies.

2. Data Distribution Visualization Using Count Plots: Count plots were employed to aid in the visual depiction of data distribution among several categories, including regions and crop kinds. These graphics provide a brief synopsis of category frequency. Count plots, representing areas and crop kinds, offer valuable information on the prevailing agricultural practices in different countries. A technique for finding patterns, trends, or anomalies in the dataset is visualization.

3. Data processing includes steps to remove duplicates and unnecessary columns to preserve data integrity. Exploratory Data Analysis uses visualization to identify patterns and trends while delving into understanding the unique characteristics of regions and crop types. These preparatory actions lay the foundation for deeper analysis and the eventual creation of models in the study.

4 Methodology

4.1 Synopsis

To estimate crop yields, this study uses a thorough technique that includes data collection, preprocessing, machine learning model selection, and training. The aim is to provide a workable framework for precise crop yield forecasts (Fig. 1).

4.2 Gathering and Preparing Data

4.2.1 Information Gathering

This study's agricultural dataset comes from reputable sources and includes crucial information on the year, average rainfall, use of pesticides, temperature, location, and crop type. This dataset serves as the foundation for creating a reliable prediction model.

4.2.2 Preprocessing the Data

Preprocessing procedures were carried out in great detail to guarantee data quality and compatibility:

– Removal of Duplicate Entries and unnecessary Columns: For faster analysis, unnecessary columns like "Unnamed: 0" were removed, and the removal of duplicate entries guaranteed data integrity.

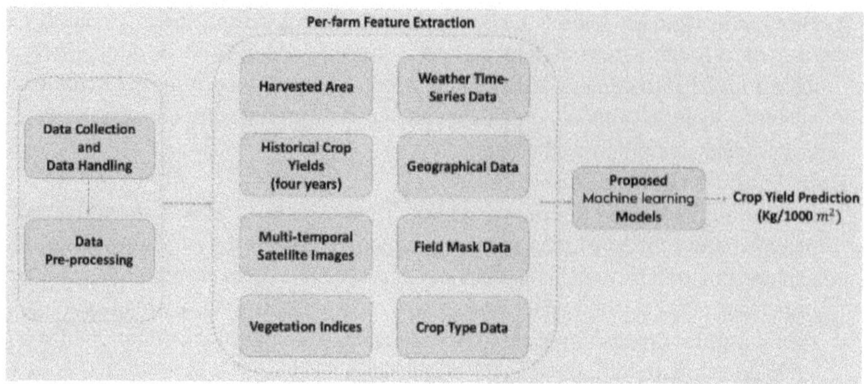

Fig. 1. Flow Chart for Methodology of Crop Yield Prediction

- The process of converting non-numeric information in the 'average_rain_fall_mm_per_year 'column to numerical format enabled quantitative analysis.
- Handling Missing or Inconsistent Data: To provide a comprehensive and trustworthy dataset, appropriate procedures were used to handle any missing or inconsistent data.
- Feature Selection: For model training, pertinent data such as crop type, crop year, average rainfall, pesticide usage, temperature, and geographic location were chosen.

4.3 Selecting and Training Machine Learning Models

4.3.1 Scaling and Encoding Features

A preprocessing pipeline made use of the 'Column Transformer' from scikit-learn. Numerical variables were standardized using the {Standard Scaler}, whereas categorical variables ('Area' and 'Item') were encoded one- hot. This made the machine-learning models compatible with a variety of features kinds.

4.3.2 Choosing the Model

To forecast crop yields, some regression models were taken into consideration:

Lasso Regression (lss) - Linear Regression (lr) - K- Nearest Neighbours Regression (knr) - Ridge Regression (rg) - Regression using Decision Trees (DTR).

Every model was trained using the pre-processed training set to investigate various regression strategies and evaluate their efficacy.

4.3.3 Model Assessment

The evaluation of the model's performance was conducted using conventional regression measures, such as Mean Squared Error (MSE) and R-squared. This comprehensive analysis made choosing the best model for precise crop yield forecasts easier.

5 Findings and Conversation

5.1 Results Presentation

Promising outcomes were obtained when crop yields were predicted using machine learning algorithms.

The following significant results were noted.

5.1.1 Analysis of Crop-Wise Yield

Investigating crop-wise yield dynamics has provided important new understandings of the complex patterns that control agricultural output. Through examining the overall yield for each type of crop, a more complex picture of the varied agricultural environment has been revealed. We produced visually striking bar plots to illustrate yield changes across several crops using Seaborn and Matplotlib. The proportional contributions of each crop to the total agricultural output might be determined with the use of these impressive visualizations.

5.1.2 Bar Plot-Based Insights

Designed to illustrate agricultural yield, the bar graphs provided comprehensive information about the relative economic importance of different crops in different areas. Each bar represented the overall yield for a particular crop, allowing for an easy-to-understand visual comparison. The bars' varied heights drew attention to differences in crop yields as well as the financial significance of various crops in the agricultural system. For academics, policymakers, and stakeholders looking for more in-depth knowledge of the economic dynamics related to certain crops, this information is essential (Fig. 2).

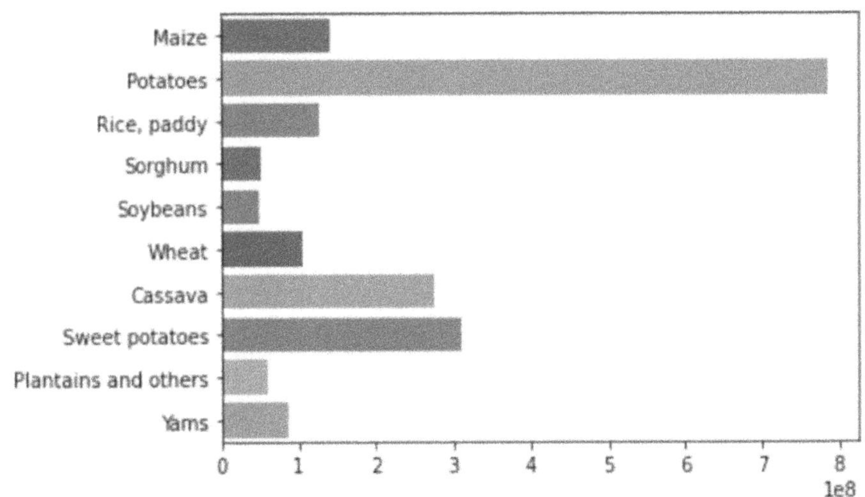

Fig. 2. Bar Plot of Crop Per Yield.

5.1.3 Dissecting the Dynamics of Agriculture

The thorough crop-by-crop yield study revealed the intricate dynamics underlying agricultural practices, going beyond simple numerical statistics. Bar plots' visually appealing design made it easier to identify economically important and high-yielding crops. This investigation paved the way for strategic agricultural planning while also advancing our knowledge of crop-specific production. Finding these trends is critical to improving crop diversity, allocating resources as efficiently as possible, and promoting sustainable farming methods.

5.1.4 Crops' Economic Significance

Beyond just numbers, the crop-by-crop yield study provides insights into the relative economic importance of different crops in different geographic areas. Stakeholders can use this data to guide their decisions about market strategy, crop selection, and resource allocation. An understandable depiction of each crop's economic impact was made possible by the visually striking bar plots, which helped people understand the agricultural environment and how it affects local economies.

5.2 Key Findings Discussion

5.2.1 Model Effectiveness

Determining which regression models were most useful for predicting crop productivity required a thorough analysis of each one. Comprehensive training and testing were conducted on Decision Tree Regression, Lasso, Ridge, K- Nearest Neighbours, and Linear Regression, demonstrating unique performance characteristics for each model. The models' ability to forecast crop yields was shown to vary in accuracy. During an examination, Decision Tree Regression stood up as the most promising model, exhibiting better performance with the test dataset's lowest Mean Squared Error and greatest R-squared value. As a result, Decision Tree Regression is now the recommended model for precise and trustworthy crop yield forecasts.

5.2.2 Crop Yield-Relating Factors

5.3 Consequences and Prospects

5.3.1 Allocating Resources and Planning for Agriculture

The results of this study have important ramifications for resource allocation and agricultural planning. Decision- makers in the agriculture industry now have a powerful instrument to optimize resource usage: the built predictive model. Understanding key variables like temperature, average rainfall, and pesticide use allows for strategic planning, which in turn helps stakeholders make well-informed decisions that support sustainable agriculture practices. This knowledge becomes especially helpful while negotiating the difficulties brought on by shifting climatic circumstances.

The goal of the investigation was to pinpoint the major variables affecting crop output, providing insightful information for agricultural decision-making. Temperature, pesticide use, and average rainfall have all been shown to be important factors in determining agricultural productivity. These complex interactions were well-captured and modeled using the interpretable Decision Tree Regression model. For stakeholders and policymakers looking to comprehend the precise influence of each feature on agricultural output, this interpretive capacity is essential. Understanding the impact of variables like as temperature, rainfall, and pesticide use helps farmers make well-informed decisions and take preventative action to increase crop output and reduce hazards.

5.3.2   The Decision Tree Model's Interpretability

The Decision Tree Regression model's interpretability offered a special benefit in addition to its superior predicting ability. The decision-making process of the model is transparent by nature, providing a clear knowledge of the contributions of temperature, average rainfall, and pesticide consumption to the total projection. This interpretability comes in handy for stakeholders who need information that can be put into practice. By comprehending the subtleties of each feature's influence, practitioners may better focus tactics, allocate resources optimally, and customize treatments to increase agricultural output.

5.3.3   Real-World Consequences

The results highlight the usefulness of the chosen model and the factors that were found. Decision Tree Regression is a useful tool for those involved in the agriculture industry because of its consistent performance and ease of interpretation. Allocating resources and developing strategies are made possible by an understanding of the effects of temperature, pesticide use, and average rainfall. Interventions to improve crop output, adjust to climatic fluctuations, and promote sustainable agricultural practices are guided by this understanding.

5.3.4   Adjusting to Changing Climate Circumstances

The predictive model has the potential to adapt to changing climate circumstances in addition to streamlining present procedures. An accurate model that takes into account dynamic elements like temperature and precipitation is necessary as climate variability rises. Using the model's findings, decision-makers may put adaptive measures into place to make sure that agricultural practices are resilient to shifting climatic trends. To reduce risks and promote long- term sustainability in agriculture, this flexibility is essential.

5.3.5   Prospective Research Paths

Subsequent investigations ought to concentrate on improving the accuracy of the model and broadening its use. Including more features—like data on crop diseases and soil quality—stands out as a critical step toward gaining a deeper comprehension of the complex variables affecting agricultural productivity. This feature enhancement has the potential to greatly improve the model's predictive power. Furthermore, investigating sophisticated machine learning strategies and ensemble approaches offers encouraging avenues for development. These methods might lead to increased model accuracy and resilience, bringing in a new age of accuracy and dependability in agricultural production predictions.

5.3.6 Conclusion and Outlook

To sum up, the findings highlight the potential of the created predictive model for crop yield forecasting and offer insightful information about the variables influencing agricultural output. In addition to outlining useful implications for policymakers, the debate suggested future research initiatives to further the subject. The combination of technology innovation and data-driven insights has the potential to revolutionize agricultural methods, promote sustainability, and guarantee global food security as we move forward.

6 Conclusion

This work is a comprehensive investigation of crop yield prediction that incorporates important environmental elements and makes use of a variety of regression models. Our research's contributions and conclusions provide important new information for the agriculture industry. The Decision Tree Regression model stood up as the most promising model due to its exceptional performance in crop production prediction (Fig. 3).

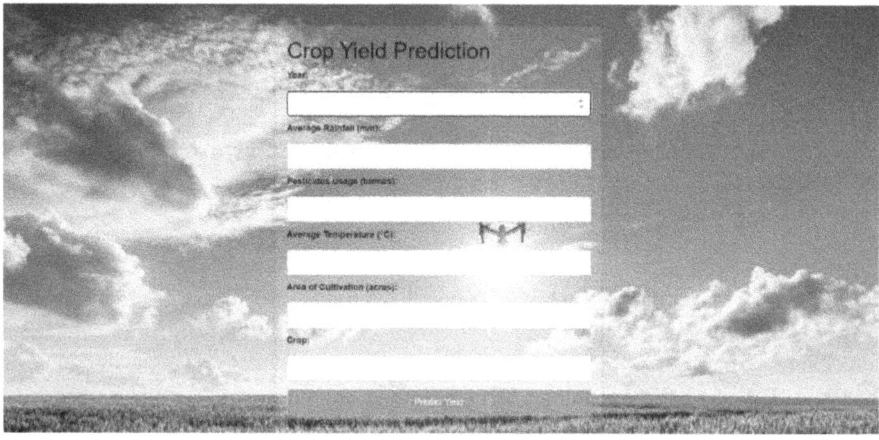

Fig. 3. Crop Yield Prediction interface for taking inputs.

6.1 Principal Inputs and Results

This study's main contribution is the creation and assessment of prediction models for estimating crop yields. After a thorough investigation of several regression methods, Decision Tree Regression was shown to be a reliable and accurate model. This finding creates opportunities for agricultural stakeholders to use predictive methods for scheduling and allocating resources. Additionally, our data demonstrated how important environmental variables like temperature, pesticide use, and average rainfall are in determining crop output. Decision-makers are better equipped to optimize agricultural methods, adjust to changing climate circumstances, and increase overall production with the help of this information (Fig. 4).

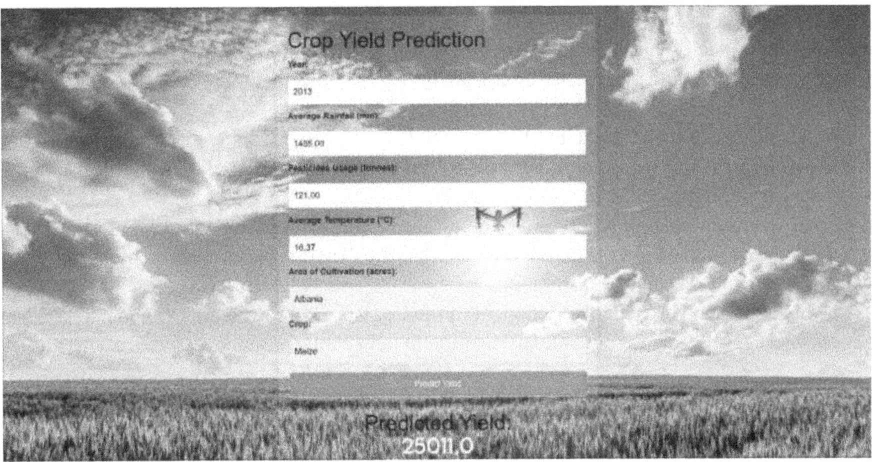

Fig. 4. Predictive Suggestion for Crop Yield for the following given inputs.

6.2 The Study's Limitations

Although our study offers insightful information, it has certain drawbacks. Despite their effectiveness, the prediction models are essentially dependent on past data and assumptions. Uncertainties may be introduced by environmental variation and unanticipated outside sources. Furthermore, the models may show limits when it comes to extrapolating to areas or circumstances that are not well- represented in the training data, and their prediction power is limited by the dataset that is currently available.

6.3 Ideas for Further Research

To advance agricultural yield prediction, more studies should look at some approaches. Enhancing the models' accuracy and resilience may be possible by expanding the dataset to include other characteristics, such as data on crop diseases and soil quality. There is great potential for improvement by investigating ensemble approaches and sophisticated machine-learning techniques. Furthermore, research on particular crop types and geographical quirks may offer more nuanced and localized insights for customized agricultural strategy.

Ultimately, our research adds to the growing body of knowledge in agricultural data science by laying the groundwork for data-driven decision-making. Although the study's limitations are acknowledged, the knowledge gathered and the models created provide a foundation for future developments in crop yield prediction, providing useful instruments for resilient and sustainable agriculture practices.

Acknowledgments. We would like to express our sincere thanks to the people and institutions whose assistance and efforts made this research project a success.

We would first and foremost want to sincerely thank S. Amutha for all of her help and mentorship during this endeavor. Their knowledge and perceptions have greatly advanced our comprehension of agricultural data science and helped to create reliable prediction models.

We would like to express our thanks to Kaggle for supplying the dataset needed for this research. The capacity to obtain this data was essential to the investigation and analysis carried out in this study, allowing us to make significant inferences and create forecasting models for crop output.

We would like to thank the scientific community as well as our colleagues and peers for their informative conversations and helpful criticism. Their input has been crucial in helping us improve our approach and broaden the focus of our study.

Finally, we want to express our gratitude for the steadfast support that our family and friends have given us during the difficulties of this research trip. Their support and comprehension have provided me with courage and inspiration.

Without everyone listed above's cooperation and assistance, this research would not have been feasible. We appreciate your crucial participation in our scholarly and investigative activities.

References

1. Elavarasan, D., Vincent, D.R., Sharma, V., Zomaya, A.Y., Srinivasan, K.: Forecasting yield by integrating agrarian factors and machine learning models: a survey. Comput. Electron. Agric. **155**, 257–282 (2018)
2. Zhang, J., Luo, Y., Zhang, Z., Tao, F., Zhang, L., Cao, J., et al.: Integrating multi-source data for rice yield prediction across China using machine learning and deep learning approaches. Agric. For. Meteorol. **297**, 108275 (2021)
3. Van Klompenburg, T., Kassahun, A., Catal, C.: Crop yield prediction using machine learning: a systematic literature review. Comput. Electron. Agric. **177**, 105709 (2020)
4. Reddy, D.J., Kumar, M.R.: Crop yield prediction using machine learning algorithm. In: 5th International Conference on Intelligent Computing and Control Systems (ICICCS), pp. 1466–1470. IEEE (2021)
5. Rashid, M., Bari, B.S., Yusup, Y., Kamaruddin, M.A., Khan, N.: A thorough evaluation of agricultural yield prediction using machine learning algorithms with specific emphasis on palm oil production prediction. IEEE Access. **9**, 63406–63439 (2021)
6. Zhang, L., Zhang, Z., Luo, Y., Cao, J., Xie, R., Li, S.: Integrating satellite-derived climatic and vegetation indices to predict smallholder maize yield using deep learning. Agric. For. Meteorol. **311**, 108666 (2021)
7. Guo, Y., Fu, Y., Hao, F., Zhang, X., Wu, W., Jin, X., et al.: Integrated phenology and climate in rice yields prediction using machine learning methods. Ecological Indicators. **120**, 106935 (2021)
8. Newlands, N.K., Zamar, D.S., Kouadio, L.A., Zhang, Y., Chipanshi, A., Potgieter, A., et al.: An integrated, probabilistic model for improved seasonal forecasting of agricultural crop yield under environmental uncertainty. Front. Environ. Sci. **2**, 17 (2014)
9. Ju, S., Lim, H., Ma, J.W., Kim, S., Lee, K., Zhao, S., et al.: Optimal county-level crop yield prediction using MODIS-based variables and weather data: A comparative study on machine learning models. Agric. For. Meteorol. **307**, 108530 (2021)
10. Feng, P., Wang, B., Liu, L., Li, D., Waters, C., Xiao, D., et al.: Hybrid approach using a biophysical model and machine learning technique improves dynamic wheat yield forecasts. Agric. For. Meteorol. **285**, 107922 (2020)

11. Joshua, S.V., Priyadharson, A.S.M., Kannadasan, R., Khan, A.A., Lawanont, W., Khan, F.A., et al.: Crop yield prediction using machine learning approaches on a wide spectrum. Comput. Mater. Contin. **72**(3), 56635679 (2022)
12. Chlingaryan, S., Whelan, B.: Machine learning approaches for nitrogen status estimation and crop yield prediction in precision agriculture: a review. Comput. Electron. Agric. **151**, 61–69 (2018)

Sentiment Analysis Using Machine Learning Algorithms

Kaushiki Ray and T. R. Saravanan[✉] [ID]

Department of Computational Intelligence, SRM Institute of Science and Technology, Kattankulathur, Tamil Nadu, India
kr5927@srmist.edu.in, saravanantrcse@gmail.com

Abstract. Sentiment analysis is a crucial aspect of natural language processing, allowing us to understand better and categorize public reviews and opinions conveyed through text data. This study focuses on applying deep learning methods (LSTM) to model sentiment analysis especially in airline research, to develop realistic and reliable models that can classify analysis accurately adding positive, negative, or neutral emotions to the corresponding emotion labels and Then, a complete pre-processing phase is performed, including purification, tokenization, and feature extraction with methods to faces like TF-IDF(Term Frequency - Inverse Document Frequency)or word classification Best-optimized deep learning for sentiment classification. For pattern recognition, Naive Bayes and Support Vector Machines A wide variety of approaches have been explored ranging from traditional algorithms to sophisticated deep learning models such as recursive rental neural networks or transformers Various recurrent neural networks used in learning a in depth have used LSTM models in this research, as long time delays can be observed Available, especially in sequence prediction in the problems of. Through customer analytics, companies can identify the strengths and weaknesses of their products or services, therefore delivering a better, more holistic experience to customers, and simply improving their business

Keywords: Sentiment · categorize · reviews · Stemmer

1 Overview

Sentiment analysis, also known as psychoanalysis, is a natural language processing (NLP) process that focuses on identifying and extracting psychologically relevant information from text This process is important for under public opinion, the market development and consumer behavior Created a growing need for the use of machine learning algorithms for detection, creating scalable and responsive systems that are robust enough to analyze sentiment in real-time or batch processing information that it happens in them.

Challenges with existing work Textual data often contains vague or jargonwords that are difficult for models to interpret accurately. Sensitivity can vary widely across locations, requiring extensive retraining of models or optimized for specific use patterns (e.g., "not good") can significantly change the meaning of a sentence and be difficult to

R. Appavoo et al. (Eds.): IconDeepCom 2024, CCIS 2687, pp. 224–235, 2026.
https://doi.org/10.1007/978-3-032-26680-4_17

process properly. Text data in different languages adds complexity, requiring multilingual models or translation methods. Slang, acronyms, and other terms often appear, making it difficult to maintain model accuracy over time. Transformers and other advanced models require adequate computing resources will, pose challenges for scalability and real-time analysis are available.

The expected outcome of the study is a trained machine learning model with high accuracy in sentiment classification [4], which investigates the comparative performance of traditional deep learning methods for sentiment analysis. Functional model capable of real-time text data processing and classification Analysis of customer feedback to improve products and services. Monitoring public opinion on trending topics or brand perception. Understanding consumer preferences and predicting market trends. This research aims to use machine learning to obtain efficient, accurate and scalable solutions for sensitivity analysis. This automation system enables businesses and researchers to make informed decisions based on big textual data insights.

In the current era dominated by digital communication and information, the analysis of emotions expressed in textual content is crucial for public perception This work focuses on the important role of sentiment analysis with machine learning techniques use to assess and categorize sentiments in consumer research on the basis of, social media posts and comments. Recognizing the significant impact of these emotions on business strategy and decision-making, the project aims to use emotion analysis specifically designed for the evaluations. With objectives of model search, data creation, text preprocessing, feature extraction, and model training, the project aims to provide comprehensive solutions through various machine-learning techniques f Through the project wants to help which makes sense in the dynamic field of sentiment analysis.

This paper is motivated by a desire to advance practical applications of sensitivity analysis, with a particular focus on review. The goal is to give businesses the tools they need to better analyze customer sentiment and gain competitive advantage. By identifying the strengths and weaknesses of their products or services, companies can adjust their strategies accordingly and improve their overall performance. Due to the volume of data, automated tools are needed to better manage customer feedback and understand the nuances in customer data. This work therefore attempts to address this need by.

2 Literature Review

Haoyue Liu et al. [1], Proposed methods to solve the problem based on feature-based sensitivity analysis. Currently there are three main approaches: dictionaries, traditional machine learning, and deep learning. According to the importance of section granularity, it can be divided based on document-language components n The research article presents a comparative analysis of state-of-the-art deep learning methods for benchmark datasets Typically implementation, analysis parameters, synthesis and existing deep learning and those methods for reveal. Finally, some existing problems and future research directions are presented and discussed.

Afsheen Maroof et al. [2], proposed a new study to extract explicit mood words, segment them, assign polarity to each word from mobile app reviews in English and finally conduct within-aspect-based sentiment analysis (ABSA).). omain-specific, service-oriented, and aspect-based annotated dataset developed and introduces a new two-dimensional hybrid approach. The first step is to remove most of the terms using a rule-based approach. In the second stage, machine learning and deep learning algorithms are used to classify the extracted voting words into common classes. This two-stage approach effectively addresses the two-stage problem commonly encountered in previous work on grassroots politics and vote mining by following traditional machine learning and deep learning models. BERT is solved well made it ABSA. This approach used a pipeline approach, where the output of each task acts as input to subsequent tasks, ensuring smooth flow of information and improved efficiency This multistage pipeline begins with dividing selected votes into party classes and ending with sentiment polarity assignment obtained, exactly 0.79% of F1 scored 0.70% for sensitivity classification, which is the performance of conventional methods.

Revathy et al. [3], proposed a One's emotions and feelings are classified on social media using effective data science techniques. Sensory classification plays an important role in many application areas and with human help the sensory processing function can be enhanced accordingly Perceptual extraction and classification are achieved by different ENT methods: neuro-fuzzy and optimization algorithms. The technical contribution of this article is double feed forward neural network. These methods face inefficiencies in classification when real-time data contain multiple colors and flows. Double feed forward neural network is used to achieve proficient classification and the output level information is provided to the network in two layers so the information is quality and processed efficiently, so a complete perceptual system is distributed and the results are assigned use Results neuro compare -fuzzy and optimization algorithms In terms of classification parameters, DFFNN outperforms existing algorithms.

Hassan Raza et al. [6], The proposed World Wide Web (WWW) grew exponentially, rediscovered the possibilities of machine learning (ML) and natural language processing (NLP) Psychoanalysis of scientific topics is an interesting topic that has been well developed today This research uses scientific evidence to examine emotions through predefined data. This corpus contains 8736 citations. To reduce the data corpus, noise was removed from the data using data normalization rules. To perform classification on this data-set, we developed an algorithm using Naïve-Bayes (NB), Support Vector Machine (SVM), Logistic Regression (LR), Decision Tree (DT), K-Nearest Neighbor (KNN); and random applied used forest control (RF). The system accuracy is then evaluated using various evaluation metrics such as f-score and accuracy score. Other selection methods such as lemmatization, n-gramming, tokenization, and lexical theory have been used to improve the accuracy of the system and our system was found to give higher performance in every case compared to system is represented by a.

Manar Alfreihat et al. [5], proposed to develop a tailored Emoji Sentiment Lexicon (Emo-SL) for Arabic tweets and demonstrate performance improvements by combining emoji-based features with Machine Learning (ML) for sentiment classification. Building Emo-SL 58 K Arabic -. Using a corpus of tweets contains emoji, positive Estimation of emotion scores and negative squares for emojis 222 a it often occurs based on their spatial distribution. Emoji weighting is combined with text-based feature extraction using a dictionary to train classifiers on a dataset of Arabic tweets [10]. ML models, including support vector machines (SVM), naive base, random forests, and K-nearest neighbors (KNN), are evaluated after optimal preprocessing and normalization The results show that Emo-SL derived emoji features a added to ML classifiers significantly improved accuracy by 26.7% on textual features alone could be performed. The emoji-aware integrated method achieves an F1 score of 89%, which outperforms the rule-based VADER sentiment analyzer. Moreover, the analysis of n-gram effects further confirms the usefulness of a hybrid of emoji and text translation for Arabic sentiment classification. The Emo-SL dictionary provides an effective framework for extracting subtle emotional insights from noisy microtext, demonstrating the potential of emoji meaning in context for multilingual emotion research performance has improved.

3 Proposed Work

3.1 Overview

Sentiment analysis, a core field of natural language processing (NLP), has received a tremendous boost thanks to advances in machine learning (ML). Models like BERT, RoBERTa, and GPT have received updates. Self-focusing and contextualization are used to better understand the nuances of perception.Although rare now, RNNs such as LSTM and GRU with focused attention are additions still relevant for some applications. Domain-specific. BERT and other model optimizations on datasets (e.g.,, e.g., finance, health care) improve sensitivity classification in specific areas. Methods such as GPT-based modeling allow sentiment analysis without labeled training data, using large pre-trained samples. Integrating text, images, audio, or video for sentiment analysis to obtain attraction, especially social -For use in media or receiver-feedback. Models such as CLIP and multimodal transformers are used to jointly process different data modalities.

With increased demand for real-time insights, streaming sentiment analysis is becoming popular, especially to monitor social media trends or customer service interactions. Kafka and Frameworks like Flink are generally included in ML models in order to better handle Streaming data. Moving beyond simple positive/negative/neutral classifications, current emotion assessments often include finer emotion assessments (e.g., happy, angry, sad).Trained models have emotions specificity datasets (such as the Go Emotions dataset) support this trend There is a push.Tools such as SHAP and LIME help explain why a sample gives a particular emotion in a text. Sensitivity analysis models are often biased by their training data. Addressing this bias is a priority. Techniques such as adversary bias and data enhancement are being explored to reduce bias. Sentiment analysis in less important languages is being improved by techniques such as transfer learning from high-resolution languages, multilingual models such as mBERT and XLM-R.

Cloud platforms and APIs (e.g., AWS Comprehend, Google Cloud NLP, Azure Text and analytics) provide scalable and scalable pre-built sentiment analysis tools. Automated machine learning (AutoML) simplifies sentiment analysis model development, and enables non-experts to create custom models. AutoML Text (Google) and tools such as H2O.ai Workspace that supports sensory analysis. For improved contextual awareness. How to combine symbolic AI and ML for more robust sentiment understanding. For sentiment analysis to preserve privacy.

3.2 Challenges in Existing System

While sentiment analysis using machine learning has advanced significantly, there are still many challenges that researchers and practitioners need to address to improve the accuracy and robustness of existing systems in terms of the relevant may experiment with emotion analysis systems, which may struggle to interpret emotions accurately. Misinterpretations can lead to emotion misclassification, especially in contexts of sarcasm, humor, or subtle language. Negations and double negatives can reverse emotional polarity, making it harder for systems to recognize dormant emotions displayed accuracy Conversely. Sentiment analysis models may not generalize to different fields with unique words and phrases. Models may show a high level of accuracy reduced time spent on specific tasks or niche data sets without proper field optimization. Sentiment classification errors may occur, especially in datasets where informal language is prevalent. Sentiment analysis models trained in one language may not perform well in multilingual data sets due to language-specific nuances, Cross-language sentiment analysis poses additional challenges. The data sets used to train sentiment analysis models have unbalanced samples, leading to biases. Biased models struggle to accurately allocate sentiment to unrecruited groups are not properly involved, leading to skewed results

Emotion assessments typically focus on positive, negative, or neutral emotions but may not capture all human emotions. Loss of positive emotional states can prevent deeper emotional understanding, especially in applications where finer emotional analysis is needed Emotions expressed in writing may change over time, and patterns may a the existing one will not capture time trends properly. The inclusion of text along with all other forms (pictures, audio) for emotional analysis presents technical and computational challenges.In applications where emotions are expressed in various forms, relying solely on textual data so that the accuracy of the system can be limited A more sophisticated example can be. Researchers and practitioners should work to develop robust and interpretable sensitivity analysis protocols to ensure reliable results across applications.

3.3 Implementation Process

There are several steps to implement sentiment analysis using the machine learning algorithms in Stemmer. First, data preprocessing is performed, and the text data is cleaned by removing indentation, hyphens, and special characters. Then, a stemming algorithm such as Porter Stemmer is used to reduce words to their original characters, which helps to reduce dimensionality and improve model performance by combining similar words with Bag of Words (BoW).), other TF- and feature methods follow the sequence. The application, or terminology, is controlled by the IDF. These features introduce machine learning models such as Naive Bayes, Support Vector Machines (SVM), or deep learning models. To determine the sensitivity, the model is trained on textual data and then tested on unseen data to verify it. Proper configuration and preprocessing of the model ensures that the pipeline performs optimally for a given data set and task.

3.4 The Proposed Planning Scheme

The following Fig. 1 clearly shows the hybrid model developed for the sentiment analysis process using machine learning

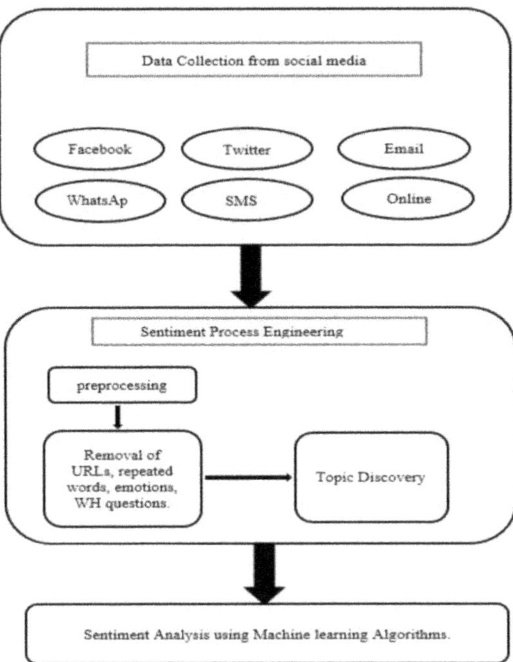

Fig. 1 System Architecture

Gathering information from multiple sources and putting it in one central location is the job of the data collector, The preprocessor is in charge of cleaning and preparing the data so that the machine learning algorithm may use it in the appropriate format. The feature engineer is responsible for reviewing and extracting relevant features from patient data.

3.4.1 Investigative Facts Investigation

Exploratory data analysis (EDA) is an important part of sensory analysis in machine learning, providing insight into the structure, quality, and distribution of textual data prior to modeling Sensory analysis data structures typically contain sensory-labeled text samples, as if it were good, negative, or neutral. EDA begins by analyzing label distributions to identify potential equilibria, which are common in real-world contexts. For example, search results may reflect predominantly positive sentiment, resulting in skewed data sets. Graphics such as bar charts and pie charts can highlight these imbalances, helping chemists decide on strategies such as oversampling, under sampling, or synthetic data generation to ensure model training balance is analyzed in text data also check for length variations, noise, and inconsistencies, such as misspellings, slang, or redundant characters, tokenization, Provides information on preprocessing steps such as normalization and filtering.

Beyond basic distribution checks, EDA in sentiment analysis involves deeper text exploration to uncover patterns and relationships. Word-level analysis, such as generating word clouds or frequency distributions for each sentiment class, provides insights into the vocabulary associated with specific sentiments. For example, words like "excellent" or "terrible" might dominate positive and negative sentiments, respectively. Techniques like bigram and trigram analysis further reveal contextual nuances, helping identify phrases indicative of complex emotions or sarcasm. Advanced methods, such as visualizing high-dimensional text embeddings with t-SNE or UMAP, can illustrate whether sentiment classes are well-separated or overlapping, offering guidance on model selection and feature engineering. Overall, EDA ensures that the dataset is well-understood, cleaned, and prepared, laying a strong foundation for building robust and effective sentiment analysis models.

3.4.2 Removing Punctuations

Removing punctuations is an essential step in the data cleaning process for sentiment analysis in machine learning. Punctuation marks, such as periods, commas, exclamation marks, and question marks, often do not carry direct semantic meaning in textual analysis. While they might contribute to the tone or emphasis in human communication, they can introduce noise into machine learning models, particularly in approaches based on bag-of-words or term frequency representations.

In practice, punctuation removal is implemented as part of preprocessing pipelines. This is typically done using regular expressions or text processing libraries such as Python's re or string modules. For example, a simple regex pattern like [^\w\s] can be used to remove all characters that are not letters, numbers, or whitespace. However, the choice to remove punctuation depends on the use case. For instance, in sentiment analysis involving sarcasm or emphasis detection, retaining punctuation such as exclamation marks (!) or ellipses (...) may be beneficial, as they provide contextual clues about sentiment intensity or tone.By carefully applying punctuation removal tailored to the specific needs of the sentiment analysis task, the text data becomes cleaner, enabling models to focus on meaningful content and improving overall performance..

3.4.3 Removing Numbers

Model training is an important step in the project "Classification of cardiovascular disease prognosis using machine learning." In this phase, you use machine learning algo-Removing numbers is a common step in data cleaning for sentiment analysis, particularly when numerical data does not contribute directly to the sentiment expressed in the text. Textual data in sentiment analysis often contains numbers, such as dates, prices, product IDs, or other numeric values, which may not hold semantic value for the task. Their presence can introduce noise, especially in models that rely on word embeddings or token frequency-based features, as these numbers may be treated as distinct tokens without meaningful relationships to sentiments.

Numbers can be removed using text processing libraries like Python's re module with a regular expression such as \d+, which matches one or more digits. This step ensures that the dataset contains only alphabetic tokens, focusing on the linguistic components of the text. However, the decision to remove numbers should depend on the use case. In some scenarios, numbers may carry contextual meaning for sentiments, such as "5 stars" indicating a positive review or "2 out of 10" suggesting negativity. In such cases, replacing numbers with meaningful placeholders (e.g., <NUM>) rather than outright removal can preserve their contextual value while standardizing the dataset. Overall, removing or handling numbers appropriately during the cleaning phase ensures that the data used for sentiment analysis is well-prepared, relevant, and free from extraneous noise, contributing to the development of robust machine learning models.

3.4.4 Removing Stop Words

Removing stopwords is a crucial step in data cleaning for sentiment analysis, as it helps eliminate words that do not contribute significant meaning to the sentiment expressed in the text. Stopwords are common words such as "the," "is," "and," "in," or "of" that are frequently used in language but carry minimal contextual or sentiment-related information. By removing these words, the dataset becomes more focused on the terms that are more likely to indicate sentiment, such as adjectives, adverbs, and specific nouns or verbs. Stopwords can be removed using predefined lists provided by libraries like NLTK, SpaCy, or gensim. For instance, in Python, the NLTK library includes a standard English stopword list, which can be customized to include or exclude words based on the specific requirements of the sentiment analysis task. Care should be taken when removing stop words, as some may carry sentiment importance in context. For example, in the sentence "I am not happy," the word "not" is a stop word but is critical to understanding the negative sentiment. In such cases, customizing the stop word list to retain sentiment-bearing words is necessary. By removing irrelevant stop words while preserving meaningful ones, the text becomes cleaner and more concise, enabling machine learning models to focus on the sentiment-rich parts of the data. This optimization step improves both the efficiency and accuracy of sentiment analysis models.

3.4.5 Evaluation Model

Evaluating the machine learning models in the validation set is an important step in developing a sensitivity analysis framework. A validation set with different rates from the training data provides an unbiased assessment of model performance during the training phase This analysis helps determine how well Model-L generalizes to unseen data and accuracy measures proportion of correctly classified samples This is convenient but may not be reliable in unbalanced data sets, where the majority party dominates. The precision performed examines how positive the predicted level of positive emotions actually is, important when false positives are high. Remembering is the measure of the number of discovered positive truths, it is important when a loss of positive emotion (false negativity) is undesirable.

Data Splitting is the Ensure that the validation set is representative of the problem domain by stratified sampling, especially if sentiment classes are imbalanced. Typically, 20–30% of the dataset is used for validation. Model Predictions is the Exercise the qualified prototypical to envisage opinions for the validation set. For probabilistic models, output probabilities can be thresholded to classify sentiments. Metric Computation is the process to Compute the chosen evaluation metrics to assess performance. For multi-class sentiment analysis, metrics can be averaged using micro, macro, or weighted schemes.

Error Analysis is the process in Review misclassified examples to identify patterns, such as sarcasm, ambiguous words, or overlapping classes, which may require adjustments in preprocessing or feature engineering. Hyperparameter Tuning is the process to Use validation performance to fine-tune model parameters, such as knowledge proportion, regulation asset, or entrenching magnitudes, without overfitting to the validation set.

4   Results and Discussion

4.1   Training Text

The length of text samples used during training plays an important role in sentiment analysis, influencing the preprocessing, model architecture, and overall performance. Sentiment analysis models must be equipped to handle texts of varying lengths, from short phrases (e.g., tweets or headlines) to long documents (e.g., reviews or articles). Here's an overview of how text length is handled during training.

4.2   Null Value Analysis

Null value analysis in sentiment analysis is essential to ensure the quality and reliability of machine learning models. Null values, such as missing or undefined textual data, can disrupt preprocessing steps like tokenization, vectorization, or embedding, leading to errors or biased predictions. Addressing null values involves detecting and quantifying their presence and applying strategies like removal, imputation with placeholder text, or model-based inference. Table 1 describes the Null value analysis.

Table 1. Null value Analysis

Description	Count
Id	0
Keyword	61
Location	2533
Text	0
Target	0
dtype – int64	

Proper handling of null values prevents data loss, mitigates bias, and enhances model performance, ensuring a more accurate representation of sentiment in the dataset. This step is crucial for maintaining the integrity of the overall analysis pipeline.

4.3   Working Out and Examination Data Graph

Training and test data are important components of machine learning, enabling the development and testing of predictive models. The set of training data is used to teach the model how to identify patterns, relationships, or trends in the data. By providing input-output pairs, the algorithm adjusts its internal parameters to reduce the difference between predicted and actual results. This process, called training, allows the model to learn from historical or labeled data. Figure 2 describes about the Training and test set data graph.

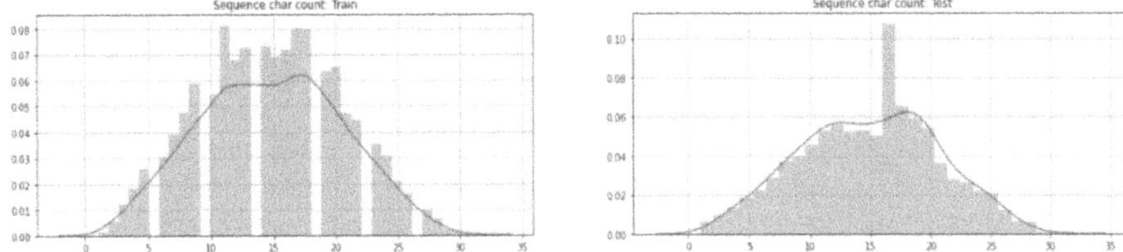

Fig. 2 Training and Test data

However, the test data set is a separate set of data used to evaluate the performance of the model on unseen samples. This analysis ensures that the model is able to integrate its learning into new real-world scenarios. By considering metrics such as accuracy, precision, recall, or mean squared error on a test plan, administrators will determine if the model performs well or needs to be adjusted.A common practice is to distribute the available data into training and testing, usually ratios like 70–30 or 80–20. To further increase reliability, cross-validation methods such as k-fold cross-validation, splitting the data into multiple training and testing partitions for reanalysis This method ensures accurate analysis hard, prevents overload, and guarantees that the model will perform well future cases.

4.4 Sentiment Analysis Processed Text

Sentiment analysis is the process of determining whether the sentiment expressed in a text is positive, negative, or neutral. Adding Stemmer to the sentiment analysis pipeline enhances text pre-processing by reducing words to their bases or roots, simplifying word analysis.The process begins with data collection. where textual data is collected from social media and other sources [9], product reviews, or customer feedback. The next preprocessing step prepares the text for analysis.These steps typically include removing special characters, punctuation, and stop words (e.g., "and," "the"). Following this, stemming is applied. Table 2 describes the Null value analysis.

A stemmer, such as Porter or Snowball, reduces words to their root form, so variations like "running," "runs," and "runner" are all reduced to "run." This reduction helps unify terms with similar meanings, improving model efficiency and reducing dimensionality. After stemming, the processed text is converted to numerical representation using techniques such as Bag of Words (BoW), Term Frequency-Inverse Document Frequency (TF-IDF), or word embedding for prediction training such a set of these indicators is forced by a machine learning or deep learning model, such as logistics -The return or LSTM, is used given. Finally, the model predicts sensitivity, and its performance

Table 2. Processed Text

Text	Input	Cleaned Output
0	Our actions cause this #earthquake M.	our action cause this earth quake
1	Forest fire near La Ronge, Sask. Canada	forest fire near la rong sask canada
2	All residents requested to 'sleep around' …	All resid ask to sleep in place are be notif...
3	13,000 people #wildfire evacuation or.	peopl receiv wildfir evacu order in california

is evaluated using metrics such as accuracy and F1-score to ensure reliable sensitivity classification.

4.5 Evaluation Model on Validation Text

Logistic regression is a widely used algorithm in sentiment analysis for its simplicity and effectiveness in binary or multi-class classification tasks. It models the relationship between the input features, such as word frequencies or embeddings, and the probability of a particular sentiment label, such as positive, negative, or neutral. Logistic regression applies the sigmoid function to map predicted values to probabilities, enabling clear decision boundaries. Table 3 describes the Null value analysis.

Table 3. Evaluation Model

	Precision	Recall	F1 Score	Support
0	0.77	0.92	0.84	1079
1	0.86	0.63	0.73	801
accuracy			0.80	1880
macro avg.	0.82	0.78	0.79	1880
weighted avg	0.81	0.80	0.79	1880

Testing a model on a validation set is an important step in machine learning to evaluate its performance and develop its parameters before final testing Isolated from the training data, the validation set provides a dataset for comparison model predictions have been compared to known labels. Commonly used evaluation criteria such as precision, accuracy, recall, F1 score, or squared error (depending on the task) help to determine how much the model generalizes to unseen data These procedures help identify issues such as overfitting or underfitting. Methods such as k-fold cross-validation further enhance reliability by testing the model on much smaller data sets, and ensure robust performance analysis.

5 Conclusion

In conclusion, sentiment analysis using machine learning is a powerful tool for understanding and interpreting emotional intentions expressed in textual data through sentiment analysis using advanced algorithms, such as logistic regression, support vector machines, or deep learning models such as LSTMs and Transformers Classification can be done with impressive accuracy Text cleaning, Effective preprocessing steps that tokenization and stemming included, along with appropriate extraction methods, play an important role in the success of the model Ongoing evaluation through validation and test sets ensures the model's reliability and generalizability to real-world data. As the use of sentiment analytics spreads across areas such as marketing-ing, customer service, and social media [8] tracking, machine learning enables organizations to make data-driven decisions, for their users experience is great, and they gain deep insight into customer sentiment.

References

1. Liu, H., Chatterjee, I., Zhou, M.C., Lu, X.S., Abusorrah, A.: Aspect-based sentiment analysis: a survey of deep learning methods. IEEE Trans. Comput. Soc. Syst. **7**(6), 1358–1375 (2020)
2. Maroof, A., Wasi, S., Jami, S.I., Siddiqui, M.S.: Aspect-based sentiment analysis for service industry. IEEE Access. **12**, 109702–109713 (2024)
3. Revathy, G., Alghamdi, S.A., Alahmari, S.M., Yonbawi, S.R., Kumar, A., Haq, M.A.: Sentiment analysis using machine learning: Progress in the machine intelligence for data science. Sustain. Energy Technol. Assess. **53** (2022)
4. Singh, J., Singh, G., Singh, R.: Optimization of sentiment analysis using machine learning classifiers. Hum. Centr. Comput. Inf. Sci. **7** (2017)
5. Alfreihat, M., Almousa, O.S., Tashtoush, Y., AlSobeh, A., Mansour, K., Migdady, H.: Emo-SL framework: emoji sentiment lexicon using text-based features and machine learning for sentiment analysis. IEEE Access. **12**, 81793–81812 (2024)
6. Raza, H., Faizan, M., Hamza, A., Mushtaq, A., Akhtar, N.: Scientific text sentiment analysis using machine learning techniques. Int. J. Adv. Comput. Sci. Appl. **10**(12) (2019)
7. Nguyen, T.H., Shirai, K., Velcin, J.: Sentiment analysis on social media for stock movement prediction. Expert Syst. Appl. **42**(24), 9603–9611 (2015)
8. Neri, F., Aliprandi, C., Capeci, F., Cuadros, M., By, T.: Sentiment analysis on social media. Proc. IEEE/ACM Int. Conf. Adv. Social Netw. Anal. Mining, 919–926 (2012)
9. Stark, L., Crawford, K.: The conservatism of emoji: work affect and communication. Social Media+Soc. **1**(2) (2015)
10. Vidal, L., Ares, G., Jaeger, S.R.: Use of emoticon and emoji in tweets for food-related emotional expression. Food Qual. Prefer. **49**, 119–128 (2016)

Prediction of Urinary Infection Using Machine Learning Models

Haitham Alhussain[1], Anwar Ahmed Alabdulathem[2], Nikhil Deep Kolanu[3], Vemparala Priyatha[4], Namdev Seth[5], and Deepak Hajoary[6(✉)]

[1] Research Centre, King Khaled Eye Specialist Hospital and Research Centre, Al Riyadh, Saudi Arabia
hmhussain@kkesh.med.sa
[2] University of Edinburgh, Edinburgh, UK
[3] China Medical University, Shenyang, China
[4] All India Institute of Medical Sciences (AIIMS), Bhubaneswar, India
[5] Department of Radiodiagnosis, AIIMS, Gorakhpur, India
[6] Bodoland University, Kokrajhar, Assam, India
hajoary.deepak@gmail.com

Abstract. Urinary Infection represents a prevalent issue globally leading numerous individuals to seek urgent medical attention. Diagnosing urinary infection stones preoperatively poses a challenge and accurately determining stone composition is typically only feasible ex vivo. To increase the perioperative management along with postoperative precaution of infection stones which comes up with a ML technique for preoperatively acknowledging the infection stones in vivo. Amid 2565 individuals included where 1168 qualified individuals with urinary calculi were randomly split into training (75%) and test (25%) sets. The forecast technique was developed by utilizing two ML methods and 14 preoperative factors and it's carrying out was judged by calculating the area under the ROC of the validation set. This study analyzed the significance of the 14 variables in each prediction technique for predicting infection stones. The validation set comprised 89 individuals with infection stones. The two output methods exhibited a strong bias in the validation set (AUC: 0.78 & 0.77). The LASSO technique was chosen as the final technique. Urine culture positivity and urine pH emerged as two main evocator of infection stones. Through machine learning this study build a predictive technique which is capable of promptly identifying infection stones in vivo with noticeable predictive execution. This technique could facilitate hazard assessment as well as decision-making aid for infection stones which thereby optimizes disease handling of urinary calculi as well as improving patient prognosis.

Keywords: Machine Learning · Urinary Infection · LASSO · XGBoost · Prediction

1 Introduction

Urolithiasis the formation of urinary stones is indeed a prevalent issue in urology with increasing rates globally. Recent studies indicate a significant portion of adults are affected by kidney stones, with a notable recurrence rate within a relatively short period

R. Appavoo et al. (Eds.): IconDeepCom 2024, CCIS 2687, pp. 236–245, 2026.
https://doi.org/10.1007/978-3-032-26680-4_18

[16]. A particular part of urolithiasis which is termed as infection stones connected with urinary tract diseases activated by urease-producing microorganisms. Such stones could grow fast into huge staghorn formation within weeks mainly when composed of struvite, posing significant risks such as sepsis especially, after surgical interventions like percutaneous nephrolithotomy [17]. Managing patients with infection stones presents challenges due to their complex nature and propensity for recurrence. Accurate recognition of stone configuration is important for productive treatment arrangement [7]. Although predictive techniques while accessible to transform infection stones from others. There is a gap in preoperative forecast techniques could swift, simple as well as reliable in vivo forecast based on large-scale data. Growing those techniques would highly enhance the clinical decision-making as well as enhance outcomes for the individuals who has urolithiasis mainly with those with infection stones. Such techniques would possibly streamline diagnosis and diagnosis processes which leads to improved individual care and management of this situation [12].

Manipulating extensive datasets which comprises demographics, diagnostics, routinely composed the measurements and interventions. The use of machine learning models reveals the promise for early preoperative forecast of infection stones [11]. Such models skilled at handling the composite, nonlinear relationships as well as high-dimensional nature of clinical data. This offers high exactness as well as generalization capabilities which surpasses the traditional modeling techniques. In the domain of urinary calculi machine learning holds established superior accomplishment in several applications which includes infection treatment, expected result, medicative image analysis as well as therapeutic interventions [2]. The purpose of the work is to improve the ML methods used to characterize among infection as well as non-infection stones prior to surgical intermediation. It thereby enhances perioperative administration and mitigating the possibility of disease stone happening post-surgery [18]. By utilizing the potential of machine learning clinicians could probably construct more informed choices with respect to treatment strategies for individuals with urinary stones which leads to enhanced patient results as well as decreased healthcare burden connected with difficulties like infection stones [3]. The evolution of those techniques was able to come up with the enduring development of personalized medicine which provides customized techniques to patients depend on thorough data analysis as well as predictive analytics [19, 20]. The enhancement of machine learning techniques for denoting the forecast of urinary infection stones which denotes a step towards attaining Sustainable Development Goal 3 (Good Health and Well-being) by developing clinical decision-making as well as enhancing disease control of urinary calculi.

The work follows a detailed organization with a comprehensive Literature Review (Sect. 2) which inspects earlier research on urinary tract infections as well as the enhancement of predictive techniques by utilizing machine learning. Section 3 provides the methods and includes characteristics on the study population, data collection methods, variables considered as well as the machine learning models used for predictive modeling. Section 4 give out the findings of the work which analyze the production of the predictive techniques evolved as well as differentiate them with the previous studies. The Conclusion part concludes the important results of the study.

2 Literature Review

Urolithiasis is distinguished by the creation of urinary stones which present a significant clinical stand against urology with its commonness on the rise all over the world in recent decades. Among such factors a main subset linked with urinary tract diseases activated by urease-producing microorganisms [1]. These stones predominantly composed of struvite which exhibits rapid enhancement into large staghorn structures within a short timeframe which presents substantial risks like sepsis which mainly follows surgical meditations such as percutaneous nephrolithotomy. The complex form as well as high recurrence rate are given which associates with infection stones which manages the patients with such condition leads to a formidable problem in clinical practice [4].

Sassanarakkit et al. (2023) deliberate about the increasing prevalence as well as recurrence of kidney stone disease (KSD) all over the world which emphasizes the purpose of machine learning in diagnostics, treatment identification as well as prognosis. The advancements were highlighted in the medical imaging as well as ML techniques by foreseeing their integration into routine clinical examination. They also stressed the importance of enhanced ML models as well as uphold for a centralized kidney stone database to enhance precision medicine for KSD [5]. Shuen et al. (2022) focused on the enhancement of the forecasting techniques for recurrent urinary tract infection which is a condition identified to have detrimental effects on renal function as well as quality of life while also imposing substantial healthcare costs. They delineated two important stages for development of the model which includes the clinical visit scenario as well as the post-hospitalization scenario for urinary tract infections affected by Escherichia coli [6].

Xiong et al. (2023) expanded a predictive technique for urinary tract infection in individuals having T2DM through machine learning. They also used several data pre-processing methods, balancing methods as well as techniques which identifies important factors like UTI-related inflammatory markers as well as medication utilization. Their web-based forecasting helps the clinicians in producing enhancing clinical decisions which demonstrates the most reasonable predictive ability as well as clinical utility [9]. Aditya and Amritpal (2023) developed a special system for early identification of urine infection disease by utilizing IoT-related sensors along with XGBoost method. They aid in the timely diagnosis as well as diagnosis of urine diseases which is important for preventing complications of the disease [10].

Alessio et al. (2020) developed a ML technique by utilizing the DSaaS and forecasted the risk of multidrug-resistant urinary tract infections in hospitalized patients. They Used Catboost, SVM along with Neural Network and developed the predictive models with the help of real-world data set from a hospital which is in Italy. Catboost exhibited the best performance which provides valuable support for medical workers in identifying individuals with high risk [7]. Shirin et al. (2019 introduced a new technique by utilizing IoT technologies along with machine learning to record individuals with dementia. The authors focused on the prevention of hospital admissions mainly due to UTIs which developed the techniques for early detection. The potential of integrating environmental as well as physiological data for improving dementia care in home settings [8].

Min et al. (2024) developed AI methods to forecast UTI along with UT-BSI based on a large dataset of 259,187 patients. Their techniques merged automated urinalysis with other clinical information along with the demonstrated excellent discriminant performance. The XGBoost technique achieved better forecasted values in both UTI along with UT-BSI [13].

Tsai et al. (2022) developed the predictive techniques by utilizing AI methods and assessed the risk of UTIs following cystoscopic methods with the aim of decreasing antibiotic overuse. The details from the individuals who underwent cystoscopy which is in China Medical University located at Beigang Hospital were retrospectively reviewed and both ANN method as well as logistic regression method were gone through to build the forecasting methods. The ANN technique shows a superior predictive ability than logistic regression method. This achieved the accuracy 85%, sensitivity 80% as well as specificity 88%. The logistic regression exhibited poor sensitivity 2% as well as with high accuracy 91% and shows a large rate of false negatives [15].

3 Materials and Methods

3.1 Materials

The data which is from January 2011 until December 2015 as well as January 2017 until December 2021 also excluding 2016 because of the logistical constraints sourced from an online platform. Following the exclusion of patients with incomplete clinical records, a cohort of 1168 patients was deemed suitable for modeling purposes. The baseline clinical data, encompassing 24 indicators such as age, sex, urinalysis and urine culture were meticulously retrieved from medical archives. Fourier transform infrared spectroscopy was employed for stone composition analysis with the predominant stone component documented. In instances where magnesium ammonium phosphate hexahydrate was detected, it was designated as the primary stone component, irrespective of its proportional abundance. The stones mainly build up of magnesium ammonium phosphate hexahydrate as well as calcium carbonate which are divided as infection stones while others were divided as non-infection stones. This meticulously curated dataset sourced from real-world clinical scenarios, offers invaluable insights into urinary calculi and lays the foundation for the development of predictive models to enhance clinical decision-making processes.

3.2 Model Establishment

The process of establishing the model unfolded as follows:

1. The data splitted into a training as well as a testing set which maintains a ratio of 4:1. The training set made possible for the construction of the model while the testing set is for performance evaluation.
2. Ten-fold cross-validation was utilized to internally validate the models on the training set, while the impact of various data processing techniques and machine learning algorithms on predictive performance was assessed by analysing 200 Bootstrapping samples from the test set.
3. Subsequently, the model demonstrating the high performance was selected.

The study noted two main ML algorithms for the selection of the technique: LASSO as well as XGBoost. The main objective was to develop machine learning models capable of predicting Urinary Infection. We utilized a comprehensive dataset comprising demographic, clinical, stone, and urine data obtained. The performance of the predictive models was primarily assessed using the AUC-ROC prediction. Feature importance rankings varied according to the machine learning algorithm utilized: LASSO, importance was based on beta coefficients; and for XGBoost, importance was ranked by SHAP value.

4 Results and Discussion

Table 1. Attributes of Individuals Diagnosed with urolithiasis Categorized by Gender

Characteristics	Number of cases	Infection stones	Struvite	Carbapatite	Non-infection stones	Calcium oxalate	Urate	Calcium phosphate	Cystine
Overall	2565	189	152	37	2376	1770	482	118	6

Table 1 displays the clinical data derived from the demographic information and stone composition analysis of 2565 patients categorized by gender. The average age of the patients was 55 years, with males constituting 63 and females 37. The highest prevalence of stones was observed in males aged 41–50 years (25.04%) and females aged 51–60 years (33.82%). Regarding stone composition, calcium oxalate stones accounted for 69.01% of cases, uric acid stones for 18.79%, calcium phosphate stones for 4.6% and infection stones for 7.37%. The proportion of disease stones was probably less in males compared to females (M/F = 0.64, P < 0.001). The spectrum of pathogens separated from urine cultures is found out. Escherichia coli was the most important pathogen in non-infection stones (107 strains) which is followed by Enterococcus faecalis (20 strains) as well as Streptococcus agalactiae (14 strains). Proteus mirabilis were the most prevalent pathogen identified in infection stones (18 strains) along with Escherichia coli (11 strains) and Klebsiella pneumoniae (7 strains). The distribution of urine pH within infection stones as well as non-infection stones is found out as shown in Fig. 1.

A high proportion of individuals who has infection stones shows a urine pH of 6.0 (44.94%) while among non-infection stones. A urine pH of 6.0 was the most prevalent (50.28%). The incidence of urolithiasis had risen although the male-to-female proportion shows no significant change. There was an increase in the prevalence of infection stones and a decrease in uric acid stones, indicating improved health management for the latter. Table 2 demonstrates that out of 35 patients experiencing at least a second recurrence, 34.3% displayed inconsistent recurrence components, accompanied by an increased occurrence of infection stones (5 cases).

4.1 Predictive Features

1168 patients were participated in the testing phase with 75% individuals were randomly allocated to the training phase and the remaining 25% to the testing set. The proportion

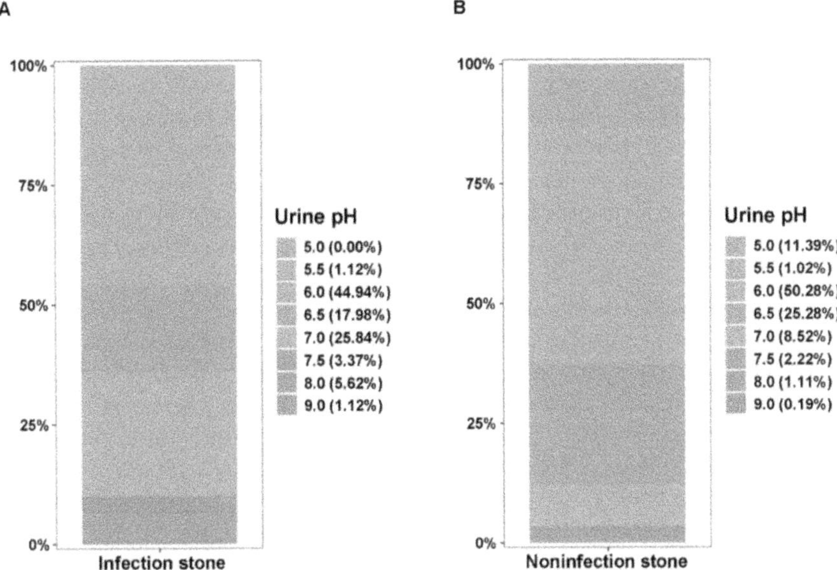

Fig. 1 The Distribution of Urine pH within individuals with Infection Stones as well as Non-Infection Stones.

Table 2. Illustrates the Distribution of the Primary Constituents of Urinary Stones in Individuals Facing Urolithiasis Recurrence.

Characteristics	1st Occurrence of Urolithiasis	2nd Occurrence of Urolithiasis	P value
Same Composition	23	–	–
Different composition,	12	–	–
Infection stones	0	5	0.020
Struvite	0	3	0.077
Carbapatite	0	2	0.151
Non-infection stones	35	30	0.020
Calcium oxalate	21	19	0.629
Urate	10	9	0.788
Calcium phosphate	3	2	0.643
Cystine	1	0	0.314

of infection stones was same along with the training set (7.6%) as well as the validation set (9.7%) and no likelihood were observed in any factors among the two sets. Univariate models were developed on the training phase which showed 14 factors which includes urine culture, urine pH along with gender that demonstrated the significant differences among the patients with infection stones as well as non-infection stones with a dof of

1. This shows their close association with the occurring of disease stones. Predictive techniques were developed by utilizing ML techniques based on these variables. Table 3 highlights the AUC, specificity, sensitivity along with the accuracy of each method in both the training phase and validation phase. The models' performance metrics provide insight into their predictive capabilities. Among the evaluated models, LASSO and XGBoost exhibit higher accuracies and discriminative abilities compared to LDA, DT, and LR. LASSO demonstrates strong specificity, while XGBoost showcases balanced sensitivity and specificity. Both models outperform the others in terms of accuracy and AUC, indicating their effectiveness in classification tasks. However, LDA shows moderate performance, with accuracy and AUC falling between LASSO/XGBoost and the less performing DT and LR models. DT and LR models exhibit lower accuracy and discriminative ability, suggesting limitations in their predictive power. Ultimately, the choice of the most suitable model should be based on a comprehensive assessment considering factors such as interpretability, computational efficiency, and the specific requirements of the application. Figure 2 demonstrates the ROC curves of several methods, and the black line denotes LASSO and Grey line denotes XGBoost. In the testing phase the AUC values of LASSO and XGBoost were 0.78 (95% CI 0.657–0.85) and 0.77 (95% CI 0.651–0.883). The sensitivity values of such ML methods were 0.741 to 0.76, the specificity values are 0.910 to 0.891 as well as the accuracy rates were 0.85 to 0.76. Mainly the prediction accuracy, LASSO method chooses as the last prediction method.

Table 3. Several Models in the Validation Set Summary

Model	Accuracy	Sensitivity	Specificity	AUC	95% CI
LASSO	0.85	0.741	0.910	0.78	(0.657, 0.85)
XGBoost	0.76	0.76	0.891	0.77	(0.65, 0.88)
LDA [14]	0.68	0.685	0.673	0.751	–
DT [14]	0.62	0.61	0.62	0.64	–
LR [15]	0.60	0.59	0.60	–	–

4.2 Discussion

The work tests the feasibility of employing ML methods to categorize infection stones from non-infection stones before surgery in patients. Among the two ML methods the LASSO method demonstrated the high AUC. Shown the intricacy of infection stones the clinical methods incorporating parameters may behave as the best predictors compared to separate parameters. A technique was utilized to achieve this could involve leveraging advanced ML models that have been used in the prevention and management of infection stones. The formation of the prediction method lies on common clinical factors which are straightforward, easy to use as well as do not necessitate high technical expertise. It holds surety for wider usage in primary healthcare settings thus broadening the potential usage of this work.

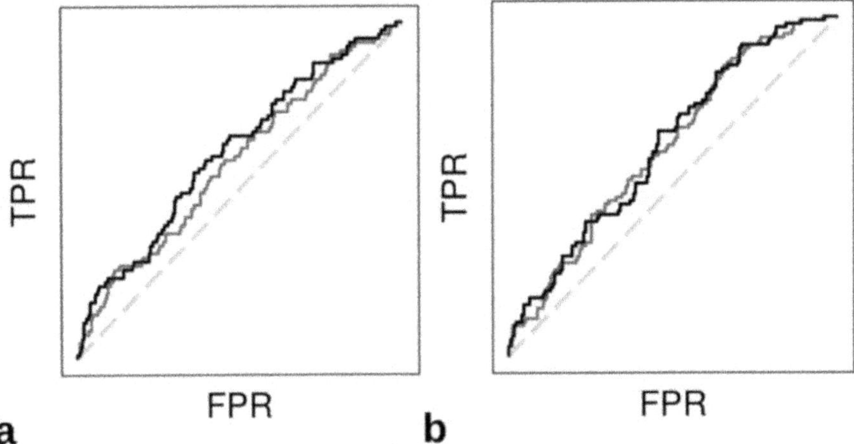

Fig. 2. The ROC curves of the machine learning models in the Training Set (a) and Validation Set (b) are depicted. The horizontal axis denotes the False Positive Rate, while the vertical axis indicates the True Positive Rate. A higher AUC value, closer to 1, suggests superior prediction performance.

As minimally invasive surgical techniques and endoscopic instruments continue to advance, they have gradually replaced traditional open surgery in many cases. Identifying the specific types of stones present can guide clinicians in selecting appropriate treatment methods and help in analyzing the underlying causes to develop optimal surgical plans. Infection stones, which consist of magnesium ammonium phosphate, carbonate apatite, or ammonium urate, are susceptible to fragmentation but can also result in systemic infection following lithotripsy. Therefore, it is crucial for surgeons to aim for thorough removal of infection stones during surgery to minimize the risk of residual stones. This shows their close association with the occurring of disease stones. Predictive techniques were developed by utilizing ML techniques based on these variables. The development of infection stones is closely linked to the presence of urease-producing bacteria. Future approaches may involve renal pelvic urine culture or stone culture to enhance the positivity rate, and direct detection of urinary microbiota could provide a more realistic assessment. Treatment decisions for urolithiasis categorized as infection stones should be guided by urine culture analysis.

When urease-producing organisms infect the urinary tract, urea undergoes enzymatic breakdown into ammonia and carbon dioxide, resulting in elevated urine pH and concentrations of NH_4^+, CO_3^{2-}, and PO_4^{3-}. Carbonate apatite crystallization initiates at a pH exceeding 6.8, while struvite crystallization occurs at a pH greater than 7.2, with higher urine pH levels correlating with increased likelihood of infection stones. Alkaline urine facilitates the crystallization of stones containing calcium and phosphate, consistent with our study findings. Interestingly, despite infection stones exhibiting higher urine pH compared to non-infection stones, approximately half of the patients still had a pH of 6.0, emphasizing the need for tailored treatment approaches. The study noted two main ML algorithms for the selection of the technique: LASSO as well as XGBoost.

The main objective was to develop machine learning models capable of predicting Urinary Infection. We utilized a comprehensive dataset comprising demographic, clinical, stone, and urine data obtained. The performance of the predictive models was primarily assessed using the AUC-ROC prediction. Feature importance rankings varied according to the machine learning algorithm utilized: LASSO, importance was based on beta coefficients; and for XGBoost, importance was ranked by SHAP value.

Our study also observed that in patients with multiple recurrences, the composition of recurrent stones was not entirely consistent, and the prevalence of infection stones increased with each recurrence. Thorough removal of stones during surgery is crucial, along with perioperative antibiotic use and adjustments to the dietary structure based on stone composition post-operation. Urease inhibitors represent a potential therapeutic approach as they directly impede the growth process of infection stone precursors. They are particularly recommended for patients with surgical contraindications or recurrent infections following treatment for infection stones. Urease inhibitors function by modifying urine pH to prevent sedimentation and clearance of infected stones.

5 Conclusion

Our study has several limitations. Firstly, it was a retrospective study conducted at a single institution, which may introduce selection bias and limit the generalizability of our findings. The lack of external validation from multiple centers further affects the robustness of our model. Additionally, the prediction performance of our model may not be sufficiently accurate, indicating the need for the inclusion of additional urine indicators such as urine microorganisms and imaging features to enhance predictive accuracy. Future research should focus on optimizing and externally validating the model using larger cohorts from multiple centers. In summary, a machine learning-based preoperative prediction model has been created to detect urinary infection stones in vivo. This model offers ease of use for both clinicians and patients and has the potential to enable more precise prediction of stone types before surgery. By optimizing disease management strategies for urolithiasis, our model may contribute to improved patient prognosis. In future, expanding the dataset by collecting data from multiple centers would improve the generalizability of the models and provide a more diverse patient population for analysis.

References

1. Hameed, B.Z. et al.: Artificial intelligence and its impact on urological diseases and management: a comprehensive review of the literature. J. Clin. Med. **10**(9), 1864 (2021)
2. Isha, S., Shah, S.Z.: Use of artificial intelligence for analyzing kidney stone composition: are we there yet? Mayo Clin. Proceed. Digit. Health. **1**(3), 352–356 (2023)
3. Rule, A.D., Lieske, J.C., Li, X., Melton III, L.J., Krambeck, A.E., Bergstralh, E.J.: The ROKS nomogram for predicting a second symptomatic stone episode. J Am Soc Nephrol. **25**(12), 2878 (2014)
4. Vaughan, L.E. et al.: Predictors of symptomatic kidney stone recurrence after the first and subsequent episodes. Mayo Clin. Proc. **94**(2), 202–210 (2019)

5. Sassanarakkit, S., Hadpech, S., Thongboonkerd, V.: Theranostic roles of machine learning in clinical management of kidney stone disease. Comput. Struct. Biotechnol. J. **21**, 260–266 (2023)

6. Jeng, S.L., Huang, Z.J., Yang, D.C., Teng, C.H., Wang, M.C.: Machine learning to predict the development of recurrent urinary tract infection related to single uropathogen, *Escherichia coli*. Sci. Rep. **12**(1), 17216 (2022)

7. Mancini, A. et al.: Machine learning models predicting multidrug resistant urinary tract infections using "DsaaS". BMC Bioinform. **21**, 1–12 (2020)

8. Enshaeifar, S. et al.: Machine learning methods for detecting urinary tract infection and analysing daily living activities in people with dementia. PLoS One. **14**(1), e0209909 (2019)

9. Xiong, Y., Liu, Y.M., Hu, J.Q., Zhu, B.Q., Wei, Y.K., Yang, Y., et al.: A personalized prediction model for urinary tract infections in type 2 diabetes mellitus using machine learning. Front. Pharmacol. **14** (2023)

10. Gupta, A., Singh, A.: Prediction framework on early urine infection in IoT–fog environment using XGBoost ensemble model. Wirel. Pers. Commun., 1–19 (2023)

11. Taylor, R.A., Moore, C.L., Cheung, K.H., Brandt, C.: Predicting urinary tract infections in the emergency department with machine learning. PLoS One. **13**(3), e0194085 (2018)

12. Yang, J., Eyre, D.W., Lu, L., Clifton, D.A.: Interpretable machine learning-based decision support for prediction of antibiotic resistance for complicated urinary tract infections. NPJ Antimicrob. Resist. **1**(1), 14 (2023)

13. Choi, M.H., Kim, D., Park, Y., Jeong, S.H.: Development and validation of artificial intelligence models to predict urinary tract infections and secondary bloodstream infections in adult patients. J. Infect. Public Health. **17**(1), 10–17 (2024)

14. Zhao, Y. et al.: Prediction of upcoming urinary tract infection after intracerebral hemorrhage: a machine learning approach based on statistics collected at multiple time points. Front. Neurol. **14**, 1223680 (2023)

15. Chen, T.J., Hsu, Y.H., Chen, C.H.: Comparison of neural network and logistic regression analysis to predict the probability of urinary tract infection caused by cystoscopy. Biomed. Res. Int. **2022**(1) (2022)

16. Chesnaye, N.C., Carrero, J.J., Hecking, M., Jager, K.J.: Differences in the epidemiology, management and outcomes of kidney disease in men and women. Nat. Rev. Nephrol. **20**(1), 7–20 (2024)

17. Musah, S., Bhattacharya, R., Himmelfarb, J.: Kidney disease Modeling with organoids and organs-on-chips. Annu. Rev. Biomed. Eng. **26** (2024)

18. Bravo-Vázquez, L.A. et al.: Exploring the therapeutic significance of microRNAs and lncRNAs in kidney diseases. Genes. **15**(1), 123 (2024)

19. Clotet-Freixas, S. et al.: Sex differences in kidney metabolism may reflect sex-dependent outcomes in human diabetic kidney disease. Sci. Transl. Med. **16**(737), eabm2090 (2024)

20. Mukhi, D. et al.: ACSS2 gene variants determine kidney disease risk by controlling de novo lipogenesis in kidney tubules. J. Clin. Invest. **134**(4) (2024)

Effective Classification of Heart Disease Using Remote Monitoring and Digital Health in Machine Learning

T. R. Saravanan[1] , A. Jackulin Mahariba[3] , S. Priya[1], N. Antony Sophia[1], E. Poongothai[1(✉)], and Sridhar Udhaykumar[2]

[1] Department of Computational Intelligence, SRM Institute of Science and Technology, Kattankulathur, India
`saravanantrcse@gmail.com, poongothai.rp@gmail.com`
[2] Assistant Professor, Department of Information Technology, Mettu University, Mettu, Ethiopia
`sridhar.udayakumar@meu.edu.et`
[3] Department of Computing Technologies, SRM Institute of Science and Technology, Kattankulathur, India
`jackulia@srmist.edu.in`

Abstract. Cardiovascular disease is a major cause of death worldwide and requires continuous improvements in its classification to enable effective diagnosis and treatment. This review provides a comprehensive review of the evolving state of the art in the classification of cardiovascular diseases. The paper explores traditional classification techniques such as symptom-based and anatomical classifications, highlighting their limitations in accurately characterizing the diverse spectrum of heart diseases. The advent of advanced technologies, particularly in the fields of genetics, imaging, and artificial intelligence, has revolutionized the classification paradigms. Genetic markers and omics data have allowed for a more nuanced understanding of hereditary cardiac disorders, aiding in precise diagnosis and targeted therapies. Moreover, cutting edge. Techniques improved the view of cardiac structures, allowing a more precise categorization of structural heart disorders.

Keywords: Cardiovascular disease diagnosis · machine learning · optimal selection · Classification systems

1 Overview

Heart illness, commonly referred result in fatalities and major health issues.Remains a global public health challenge, responsible for a significant proportion of deaths worldwide. The prevalence of heart disease [11, 13] is influenced by a complex interplay of genetic, lifestyle, and environmental factors, making it imperative to deepen our understanding of its etiology, classification, diagnosis, and treatment strategies. Over the years, advancements in medical research, technology, and healthcare practices have

R. Appavoo et al. (Eds.): IconDeepCom 2024, CCIS 2687, pp. 246–257, 2026.
https://doi.org/10.1007/978-3-032-26680-4_19

significantly enhanced our knowledge of heart disease [6]. Researchers and clinicians continually strive to refine the methods used to classify heart diseases, aiming to create more accurate and tailored approaches to diagnosis and treatment. The classification of heart disease [7] is crucial as it forms the foundation for relevant medical interventions, allowing healthcare professionals to make choices that are guided by the unique traits of the disease in an individual patient.

Comprehensive exploration into the classification [8] of heart disease delves into various dimensions, including traditional symptom-based and anatomical classifications, as well as cutting-edge approaches involving genetics, advanced imaging techniques, and artificial intelligence. By examining the evolution of classification methods, this study aims to shed light on the challenges faced in accurately categorizing the diverse spectrum of heart diseases and the innovative solutions that have emerged to address these challenges. Moreover, the integration of emerging technologies, such as genetic sequencing, omics data analysis, and machine learning algorithms, has revolutionized the field of cardiovascular medicine. These technologies offer promising avenues for improving the accuracy of diagnosis, predicting disease progression [5], and personalizing treatment regimens.

However, their implementation also raises ethical and practical questions related to patient privacy, algorithmic bias, and the equitable access to healthcare services. It is important to address these issues to guarantee that everyone may benefit from innovative technology, regardless of their socioeconomic status or location. We shall go into the historical backdrop of heart disease [9] classification in the following sections of this study, limitations of traditional methods, and examine the transformative impact of modern technologies on reshaping our understanding of heart diseases. By critically evaluating the past and present approaches to heart disease classification, this study aims to pave the way for a more nuanced, precise, and patient-centered classification system that can significantly enhance the quality of care and outcomes for individuals affected by heart disease.

As we know there was a lot of cardiovascular data available in many places including medical archives, private hospital databases, internet databases and many other sources although a lot of data has been in our archives for more than 50 years. Due to the lack of artificial intelligence and machine learning tools to support much of this management process, all data is still underutilized and these existing challenges need to be addressed. The precondition for reform is to use all the data that can be processed so that the available information is minimally processed, followed by mortality rates and things that are not humans will bring it in. While we have many artificial intelligence classification and prediction techniques, there is no hybrid model that will be an effective tool for heart analysis and predictive prediction. Even if we find substantial evidence of cardiovascular disease, we cannot assess it because we cannot generalize all outcomes. Remote cardiac monitoring uses technology to track and monitor heart health in real time, providing practical solutions for patients and healthcare professionals. We are therefore moving towards remote sensing and digital health monitoring using machine learning [1] . The application of artificial intelligence (AI) and deep learning (DL) approaches to remote monitoring of cardiovascular diseases represents a step change in personalized healthcare.AI model types process data from wearable devices, sensors and electronic health records. These technologies analyze large volumes of physiological data to detect patterns, predict risks, and guide interventions.

2 Literature Review

Senthil Kumar Mohan et al. [1] Machine learning has been proposed, which has proven success in supporting decision-making and prediction from the vast amounts of data generated by the healthcare industry. In addition, recent developments in various Internet of Things (IoT) segments have led to the use of machine learning (ML) techniques. A new approach seeks to improve the prediction of cardiovascular disease by features important identification through the use of machines -learning strategies. Various combinations of features and well-known classification methods are used to specify the prediction model. Using the Rand Dome hybrid forest and linear model to predict cardiovascular disease, we obtain a performance improvement accuracy of 88.7%.

Yuxin Gong et al., [2] proposed a Fetal cardiomyopathy and echocardiography remain the most effective screening technique for fetal heart disease (FHD), which is important for the early detection of obstetric complications and death with four-chamber care. Furthermore, pathological changes in the fetal heart throughout pregnancy result in constant changes in fetal cardiac architecture and bilateral hemodynamics, requiring a high level of supportive personnel skills and for detection and assessment of disease progression. with a rate of 85%, DGACNN The model performs the best in diagnosing FHD. This network was designed to address the issue of not having enough training data sets to build a reliable model. Unlabeled video slices are common, but inputting them is difficult and time-consuming. Therefore, it is important for the FHD experiment to investigate how to increase the detection accuracy and flexibility of DGACNN by using these labeled video slices Two components of the DGACNN framework are DANomaly and GACNN (Wgan-GP and CNN). DANomaly is a network similar to the ALOCC network but ultimately uses anticyclic learning to train the internal One Class Classification (OCC) network This network is more accurate and sensitive than ALOCC when it comes to video slice screening.

Nabil Alshurafa et al. [3] projects and associates suggested a in order to maximize clinician time and monitor and communicate with patients remotely, hospitals and clinicians are increasingly implementing remote health monitoring systems. Wanda-cardiovascular disease is created in the Women's Heart Health Study, where participants were educated about healthy lifestyle choices and then given six months of technology support and reinforcement. Wanda-CVD is a smartphone-based RHM system that uses prompts and feedback as social support to help participants reduce identified CVD risk factors through wireless coaching. Contextual baseline characteristics are taken into account, and information from the first month of the intervention—such as blood pressure, activity, and questionnaire answers—is sent via the smartphone. Scientists and clinicians can find participants who might benefit the RHM system the most by using a prediction tool.

Leandro Pecchia et al., [4] suggested a way to monitor heart failure remotely. Programs for managing diseases that use data mining and don't require sophisticated computer or information technology are just as successful as telemedicine, but they're more economical. A platform that uses data mining to improve the efficacy and efficiency of home monitoring in order to identify any worsening of a patient's condition early on. If not identified, these worsening conditions may necessitate more costly and sophisticated care. In this letter, we provide a brief overview of the remote health monitoring platform that we designed and implemented. It facilitates the assessment of the severity of heart failure (HF) and offers data mining features based on the classification and regression tree methods. The system's accuracy and precision in identifying heart failure were 96.39% and 100.00%, respectively, and in differentiating between severe and mild heart failure, it was 79.31% and 82.35%. To increase the reproducibility of the signals, these initial findings were obtained on publicly available databases.

3 Proposed Work

3.1 Overview

The classification of heart disease using remote monitoring and digital health with machine learning (ML) represents a major advancement in personalized healthcare. By integrating wearable devices, mobile health applications, and cloud-based platforms, remote monitoring enables continuous tracking of vital health metrics such as heart rate, blood pressure, and ECG signals. Machine learning algorithms analyze this vast stream of real-time data to detect patterns and classify heart conditions accurately. Supervised techniques like logistic regression and neural networks are commonly used for diagnosing heart diseases, while deep learning models process sequential data such as ECGs for detecting anomalies like arrhythmias. This approach facilitates early detection, timely intervention, and personalized treatment recommendations, significantly improving patient outcomes.

Digital health platforms amplify the capabilities of remote monitoring by connecting patient data to telemedicine systems and electronic health records (EHRs). Machine learning models trained on these datasets classify heart disease risks based on demographic, physiological, and lifestyle factors. Emerging technologies like federated learning and explainable AI are addressing challenges such as data privacy, model transparency, and scalability. As the field evolves, the integration of ML with remote monitoring continues to enhance accessibility and efficiency in heart disease management, paving the way for a future where healthcare is more predictive, preventive, and patient-centered.

For efficient diagnosis and individualized treatment, heart diseases must be classified accurately and promptly. Our goal with this suggested approach is to improve the accuracy and efficiency of heart disease classification by utilizing the combined power of genetic data integration and machine learning algorithms. We can develop a strong predictive model that can distinguish between different heart disease subtypes and identify high-risk individuals for preventive interventions by fusing genetic markers with clinical data.

3.2 Motivation Towards Proposed System

In some cases, existing systems provide healthcare decision support systems that help healthcare professionals make decisions, including predicting cardiovascular diseases based on patient data. Custom Software Solutions: Some institutions develop custom software solutions tailored to their specific needs, which may include data collection, storage, and prediction. With Integration with Hospital Information Systems, there may be integration with hospital information systems (HIS) to facilitate the flow of patient data between departments. Data Sharing and Collaboration Tools: Collaboration tools are used to facilitate the sharing of data and research findings among healthcare professionals and researchers. Documentation and reporting tools are used to record and communicate the results and findings, especially when research is conducted. It's imperative to memorandum that the state of the existing system may vary across different institutions and organizations, and the level of sophistication can range from basic statistical analysis to advanced machine learning and predictive modeling. The specific elements and tools used can vary depending on the system's objectives, resources, and technological capabilities. The goal of a new project in this domain may be to improve upon or enhance the capabilities of the existing system for more accuracy.

3.3 Implementation Process

Classification of Heart Disease Prediction Using Machine Learning aims to build upon the existing approaches and address potential shortcomings while incorporating advanced techniques and technologies. Implement more efficient data integration techniques to handle diverse data types for data collection. Develop more sophisticated data preprocessing pipelines that can handle complex data structures and ensure high data quality. Explore techniques for handling missing data and outlier detection. Incorporate model interpretability methods to make the predictions more transparent and explainable for healthcare professionals for finding interpretable models. Implement a system for ongoing model monitoring to ensure the model's performance remains optimal and to detect any concept drift. A mechanism for automatic model updates as new data becomes available. For clinical decision support integration Integrate the system with clinical decision support systems to provide healthcare professionals with actionable recommendations based on predictions. For continuous improvement Foster a culture of research and continuous improvement

3.4 The Proposed Planning Scheme

Figure 1 clearly shows the hybrid model developed for the diagnosis of cardiovascular disease

Gathering information from multiple sources and putting it in one central location is the job of the data collector, The preprocessor is in charge of cleaning and preparing the data so that the machine learning algorithm may use it in the appropriate format. The feature engineer is responsible for reviewing and extracting relevant features from patient data.

3.4.1 Data Collection

Data collection is an important step in a project focused on using machine learning to acquire and acquire the information necessary for model training and testing. Here's

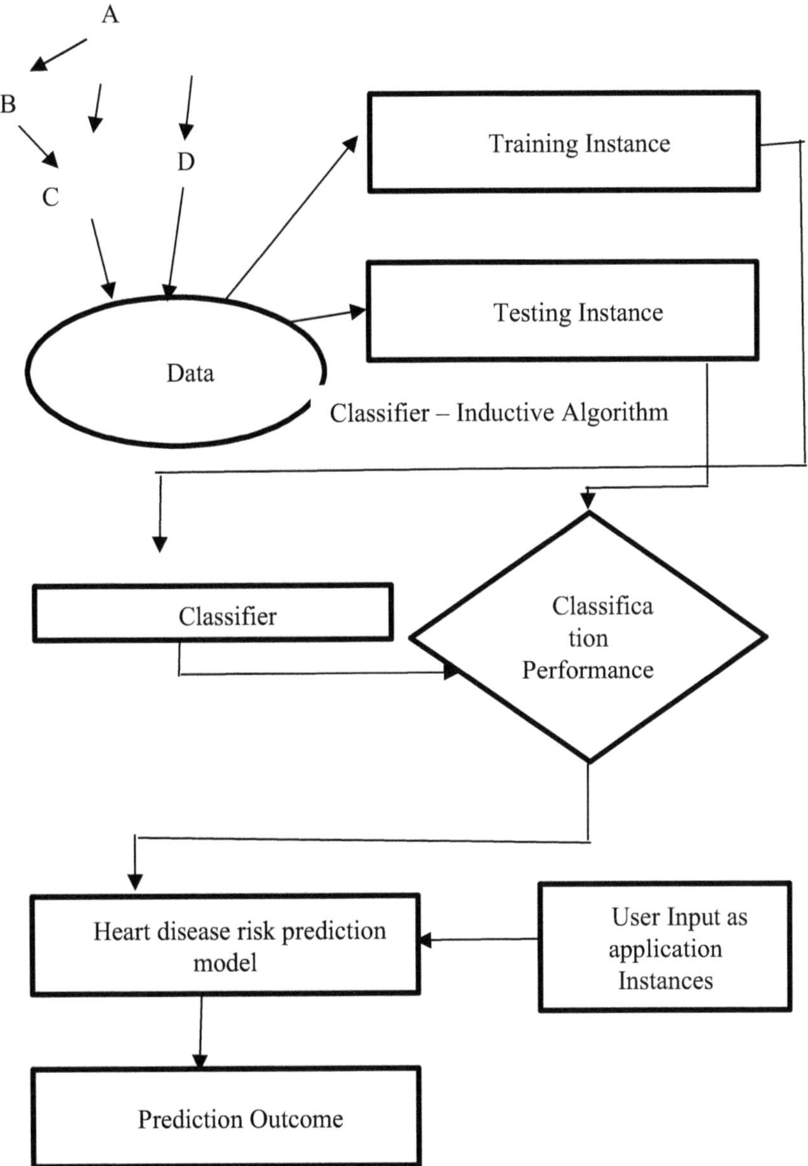

Fig. 1. System Architecture

an outline of the data collection process. These can include Electronic Health Records (EHRs) from hospitals and clinics. Publicly available heart disease datasets for research (e.g., Cleveland Heart Disease dataset, Framingham Heart Study dataset). Surveys or questionnaires collecting patient demographics, lifestyle factors, and medical history. Remote monitoring devices (e.g., wearable fitness trackers) that collect real-time health data. - Genomic data (if available and relevant). Depending on the dataset, you may need to address class imbalance issues by oversampling, under sampling. A challenging and important part of the project is the collection of data that will significantly impact the effectiveness of the cardiovascular prediction model. Thorough data preprocessing, documentation, and collaboration with experts are key to a successful data collection process.

3.4.2 Image Preprocessing

Collect and import the medical images from the data source. Ensure that you have the appropriate permissions and data usage rights. Convert images to a consistent format such as JPEG, PNG, or DICOM (Digital Imaging and Communications in Medicine), depending on the source format. Rescale images to a standardized size to ensure uniformity for processing. Normalize pixel values to a common scale, often between 0 and 1, to reduce data variability. Apply denoising filters or techniques (e.g., Gaussian blur, median filtering) to reduce noise or artifacts in the images. To save computation time and boost model accuracy, crop the photos to highlight the pertinent area of interest, such as the heart [10]. Use edge detection algorithms (e.g., canny edge detector) to identify streams and major structures in images. In cases involving multiple images or time-series data, perform image registration to organize images and ensure accuracy for analysis sis of appropriate techniques Testing can have a consistent and standardized effect significantly Preprocessing methods are important for reliable results.

3.4.3 Model Training

Model training is an important step in the project "Classification of cardiovascular disease prognosis using machine learning." In this phase, you use machine learning algo-Rhythms to create predictive models that can classify individuals. Optimize models higher parameters using methods such as web search or random search. This approach fine-tunes the model for efficiency. Trains machine learning models on training data structures using labeled data. The model also captures trends and relationships between target variables (presence of cardiovascular disease) and characteristics. Use the validation data set to evaluate the training performance of the model. This helps in choosing the best option and checking for overfitting. If applicable, make sure that the chosen image can be described. This is especially important in healthcare, where model decisions can be explained to professionals of medical interest. Evaluate the performance of the final model on a test data set, unseen during training. This provides an unbiased estimate of the generalizability of the model. Save the trained model to be deployed in the production system. Common uses for model durability include structured formats such as pickle or ONNX (Open Neural Network Exchange). Consider using a feedback loop to improve the model, which involves continuous monitoring and retraining periods with the arrival of new data.

3.4.4 Model Evaluation

It involves assessing to determine its effectiveness in predicting heart disease. Here are the key components of model evaluation. Calculate various evaluation metrics to assess the model's performance, including Accuracy, The proportion of correctly predicted cases. Assess the model for potential biases and ethical considerations, especially when making predictions that affect patient care. Detect and mitigate any biases to ensure fair and equitable predictions. Plot the ROC curve and determine an optimal probability threshold for binary classification based on the specific project's objectives. This threshold affects the trade-off between precision and recall. Create learning curves to visualize how the more training datasets there are, the more the model performs. This aids in determining whether the model is overfitting or whether more data is required. Analyzes to identify are most influential in making predictions. This can provide insights into the clinical relevance of features. If the model is complex, consider using techniques to make it more interpretable, allowing healthcare professionals to understand the factors influencing predictions. Assess the model's robustness by introducing noise or perturbations to the data to evaluate its stability and generalization ability. Feature Selection: Identify relevant features (risk factors, biomarkers) based on domain knowledge and statistical analysis. Data Splitting: subsets evaluate its performance on unseen data.

4 Results and Discussion

4.1 Facts Pre-handing Out

Objects and shapes are checked by the number of characters and if there are any unwanted features the characters are dropped. In our data set we have 33 characters and we will check for any missing data. The data cleaning process is completed and all categorical data are converted to numeric values. Replace the missing value with its mean value and the corresponding attribute. In this sponsored project, we discarded the unwanted lines and finalized the final 22 lines.

4.2 Logistic Regression

Probabilities measured by reconstructing preprogrammed conditions are a statistical method for understanding correspondence between important variables and such insights into at least factors a it really means one of the ho can help you just come or decide to move forward with you. Steps of the logistic regression process are step ladder for analysis Data Pre- dispensation step, Logistic Regression to the Training set, Fitting the test results, Testing how the accuracy of result data set is divided into training set and testing procedure. feature clambering Because we need accurate statistical results. This time we consider the independent variable as independent because the values of the dependent variable will be between 0 and 1. A confusion matrix is constructed to ensure the accuracy of the results in order to provide accuracy and recall rate

4.3 Dataset Description

Data set is taken from Kaggle and processed for real world application. his dataset of the data the model will come across in the actual world

The data set has a class label and mean, count, and max values are calculated. The distribution of the data set is shown in Fig. 2.

	age	sex	cp	trestbps	chol	fbs	restecg	thalach	exang	oldpeak	slope	ca	thal	target
count	1025.000000	1025.000000	1025.000000	1025.000000	1025.00000	1025.000000	1025.000000	1025.000000	1025.000000	1025.000000	1025.000000	1025.000000	1025.000000	1025.000000
mean	54.434146	0.695610	0.942439	131.611707	246.00000	0.149268	0.529756	149.114146	0.336585	1.071512	1.385366	0.754146	2.323902	0.513171
std	9.072290	0.460373	1.029641	17.516718	51.59251	0.356527	0.527878	23.005724	0.472772	1.175053	0.617755	1.030798	0.620660	0.500070
min	29.000000	0.000000	0.000000	94.000000	126.00000	0.000000	0.000000	71.000000	0.000000	0.000000	0.000000	0.000000	0.000000	0.000000
25%	48.000000	0.000000	0.000000	120.000000	211.00000	0.000000	0.000000	132.000000	0.000000	0.000000	1.000000	0.000000	2.000000	0.000000
50%	56.000000	1.000000	1.000000	130.000000	240.00000	0.000000	1.000000	152.000000	0.000000	0.800000	1.000000	0.000000	2.000000	1.000000
75%	61.000000	1.000000	2.000000	140.000000	275.00000	0.000000	1.000000	166.000000	1.000000	1.800000	2.000000	1.000000	3.000000	1.000000
max	77.000000	1.000000	3.000000	200.000000	564.00000	1.000000	2.000000	202.000000	1.000000	6.200000	2.000000	4.000000	3.000000	1.000000

Fig. 2. Distribution of data in data set

4.4 Cross Tab Plot

Cross-tabulation is a statistical tool used to examine the relationship between two or more categorical variables. When designing a cross-tabulation (also called a contingency table), we use a variety of plots. Here are step-by-step instructions for cross-tab plotting in a data set. Make sure the data set contains the categorical variables we want to analyze. Classification of the data set is based on disease, and no disease is based on gender differences.

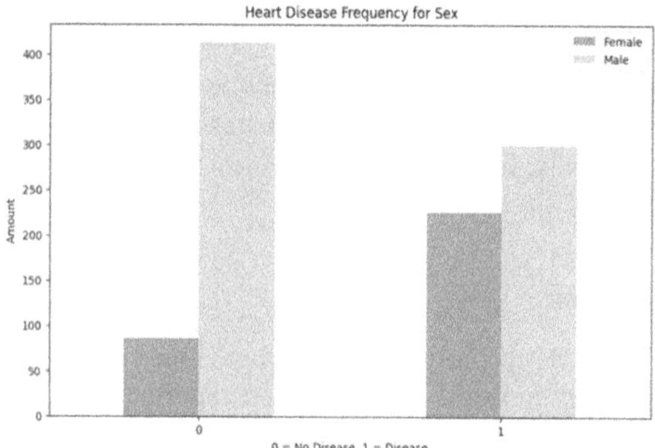

Fig. 3. Heart disease frequency for Sex

Figure 3 clearly illustrates the graph for Heart disease frequency for Sex. The succeeding fig. Undoubtedly demonstrates the standards for cross tab.

```
sex       0    1
target

0        86   413

1       226   300
```

Fig. 4. Cross tab Values

The above your head Fig. 4 evidently depicts Cross tab values with disease predicted and not predicted

4.5   Analysis Based on Chest Pain Type

Analyzing a dataset based on chest pain type involves examining how this variable relates to other features in the dataset. Chest pain type is often used in medical datasets to evaluate potential heart-related issues and typically includes categories such as Typical Angina (TA) that is Predictable chest pain related to exertion. typical

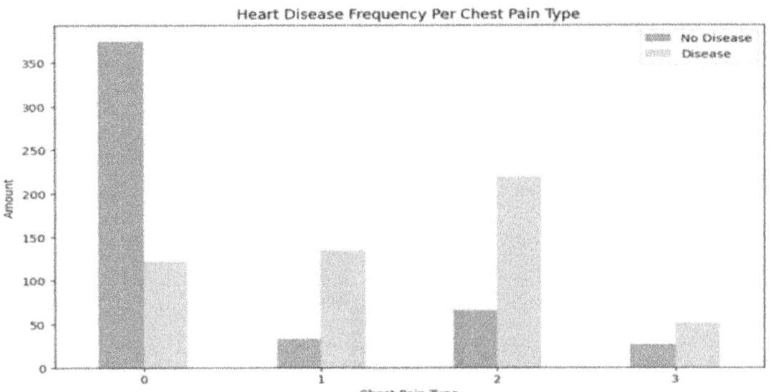

Fig. 5. Analysis Based on Chest Pain Type

Angina (AA) is Unpredictable or not directly related to exertion.Non-Anginal Pain (NAP) that is Pain not associated with angina.Asymptomatic (ASY) which is No noticeable symptoms. The Analysis is shown is in Fig. 5.

4.6   KNN Score Curve

k-Nearest Neighbors (kNN) score curve, you evaluate the model's performance (e.g., accuracy, precision, or recall) for different values of k. k (number of neighbors). This curve helps identify the optimal k, k value that balances underfitting and overfitting. Heart dataset [12] is clean and split into training and testing sets. The KNN curve plotted is given in Fig. 6.

Maximum KNN score on test data is 98.54%

4.7   Evaluation Matrix

Calculate evaluation metrics using cross-validation. The accuracy, precision, recall and f1-score of the model is caluculated using cross-validation

Figure 7 illustrates the evaluation matrix in heart disease classification

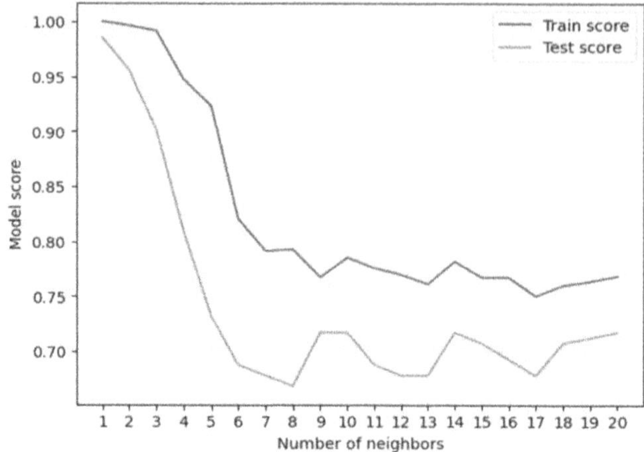

Fig. 6. KNN Curve

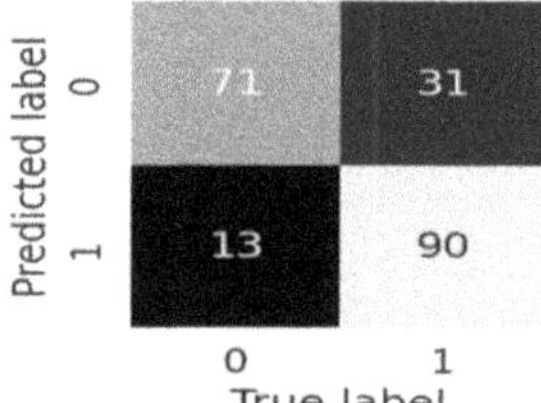

Fig. 7. Evaluation matrix

5　Conclusion

The research article clearly explains about the unique classification system and the calculated accuracy, precision and recall percentage. The project trained a logistic regression evaluated on a holdout testing dataset. The model got an accuracy of 84%, which is comparable to other algorithms. The project concluded that logistic regression is simple and effective for likelihood can be used by clinicians to intervene early to prevent the disease from developing. Related work need to be improved are Validating the logistic regression model on a larger and more diverse dataset. Developing a machine learning model that can explain its predictions, so that clinicians can understand better. Combining the logistic regression model with other clinical data such as family history and physical examination findings to accurately predict cardiovascular risk.Based on the developed cluster model it was clearly shown to take off performance effective compared to existing methods

References

1. Mohan, S., Thirumalai, C., Srivastava, G.: Effective heart disease prediction using hybrid machine learning techniques. IEEE Access. **7**, 81542–81554 (2019)
2. Gong, Y. et al.: Fetal congenital heart disease echocardiogram screening based on DGACNN: adversarial one-class classification combined with video transfer learning. IEEE Trans. Med. Imaging. **39**(4), 1206–1222 (2020)
3. Alshurafa, N., Sideris, C., Pourhomayoun, M., Kalantarian, H., Sarrafzadeh, M., Eastwood, J.A.: Remote health monitoring outcome success prediction using baseline and first month intervention data. IEEE J. Biomed. Health Inform. **21**(2), 507–514 (2017)
4. Pecchia, L., Melillo, P., Bracale, M.: Remote health monitoring of heart failure with data mining via CART method on HRV features. I.E.E.E. Trans. Biomed. Eng. **58**(3), 800–804 (2011)
5. Jin, B., Che, C., Liu, Z., Zhang, S., Yin, X., Wei, X.: Predicting the risk of heart failure with EHR sequential data modeling. IEEE Access. **6**, 9356–9361 (2018)
6. Pahwa, K., Kumar, R.: Prediction of heart disease using hybrid technique for selecting features. In: 2017 4th IEEE Uttar Pradesh Section International Conference on Electrical, Computer and Electronics (UPCON), pp. 500–504 (2017)
7. Javeed, A. et al.: An intelligent learning system based on random search algorithm and optimized random forest model for improved heart disease detection. IEEE Access. **5**, 23993–24005 (2017)
8. Lakshmi, K.P., Reddy, C.R.K.: Fast rule-based heart disease prediction using associative classification mining. In: IEEE International Conference on Computer, Communication and Control (IC4–2015) (2015)
9. Satish, M., Sridhar, D.: Prediction of heart disease in data mining technique. Int. J. Comput. Trends Technol. **24**(1), 1–5 (2015)
10. Sarangi, L., Mohanty, M.N., Pattnaik, S.: An intelligent decision support system for cardiac disease detection. Int. J. Control Theory Appl. **8**(2), 523–529 (2015)
11. Bahrami, B., Shirvani, M.H.: Prediction and diagnosis of heart disease by data mining techniques. J. Multidiscip. Eng. Sci. Technol. **2**(2), 3159–0040 (2015)
12. Alex, P.M., Shaji, S.P.: Prediction and diagnosis of heart disease patients using data mining technique. In: International Conference on Communication and Signal Processing, pp. 0081–0085 (2019)
13. Patil, S.B., Kumaraswamy, Y.S.: Intelligent and effective heart attack prediction system international research journal of engineering and technology using data mining and artificial neural network. Eur. J. Sci. Res. **31**(4), 642–656 (2020)

Integrating Ensemble Machine Learning Techniques for Improved Air Quality Management

Ritin K. Babu[✉] and Shiv Kumar Sharma

Department of Mathematics, Chandigarh University, Mohali, Punjab, India 140413
`ritinbabu99@gmail.com`

Abstract. This study delves into the forefront of air quality management by presenting a unique research-centric investigation into the integration of automated machine learning (ML) techniques. Departing from conventional methodologies, the research focuses on developing a sophisticated system that utilizes automated ML algorithms to streamline the monitoring and regulation of air quality. Through rigorous experimentation and validation, the study aims not only to enhance the accuracy and efficiency of air quality management but also to contribute valuable insights into the optimization of ML algorithms for environmental monitoring applications. The innovative framework proposed in this study holds the accuracy of 98% revolutionizing current practices, offering a scalable and adaptable solution for addressing the multifaceted challenges of modern air quality governance. By employing a research-centric approach, the study emphasizes the exploration of novel ensemble model with Random Forest and Decision Tree classifier tailored specifically for the complexities of air quality data analysis. The techniques developed through in-depth investigation of advanced ML methods can potentially be extended to other environmental regulation domains as well.

Keywords: Air quality management · Monitoring · Optimization · Environmental regulation · Machine Learning

1 Introduction

Air pollution poses a critical threat to public health worldwide, with over 90% of the global population exposed to unsafe air. Ambient air pollution alone causes upwards of 6.5 million annual deaths, disproportionately impacting developing nations. Rapid urbanization across Africa, Asia, and Latin America only compounds the issue, with urban air pollution rising at an alarming rate. A complex mix of human-caused emissions and natural processes drive declining air quality in cities [1].

Key pollution contributors include the transportation sector, industrial activities, biomass burning, and construction dust resuspension. Transboundary movement of pollutants between rural hinterlands and megacity clusters creates further challenges. On top of anthropogenic emissions, natural factors like temperature inversions, humidity, wind flows add multidimensional complexity [2]. The health implications of sustained

R. Appavoo et al. (Eds.): IconDeepCom 2024, CCIS 2687, pp. 258–269, 2026.
https://doi.org/10.1007/978-3-032-26680-4_20

exposure cover increased respiratory/cardiovascular morbidity, impaired nervous system development among children, and an array of cancers. The economic burden is equally massive, costing an estimated $8.1 trillion annually in welfare losses globally. Clearly, the scale of the air pollution crisis warrants urgent action [3].

Air pollution encompasses a complex mixture of particulate matter, greenhouse gases, and volatile organic compounds. Life-threatening levels of toxins like particulate matter, nitrogen oxides, sulphur oxides now persist in many city airs. Suspended particulate matter of 2.5 μm poses the biggest hazard as being fine enough to penetrate deep into the lungs and enter the bloodstream, potentially triggering respiratory diseases, heart conditions, and cancer [4].

In regions prone to haze during certain seasons, tracking and regulating PM2.5 levels is vital for public well-being. Severe and prolonged exposure to air pollution Damages physiological functions and cut down life expectancy. Estimates show it causes 7 million premature deaths every year, making it the largest environmental health risk humanity faces today [5].

The multifaceted character of factors impacting air quality further compounds this challenge, with contributors ranging from traffic emissions to industrial activities to natural phenomena [6].

Interdependencies between socioeconomic growth drivers and emissions trajectories further add to the multidimensional nature of the problem [7]. Figure 1 illustrates the factor affecting the quality of air for instance, efforts to expand energy access for larger populations impact pollution levels and greenhouse gas emissions [8].

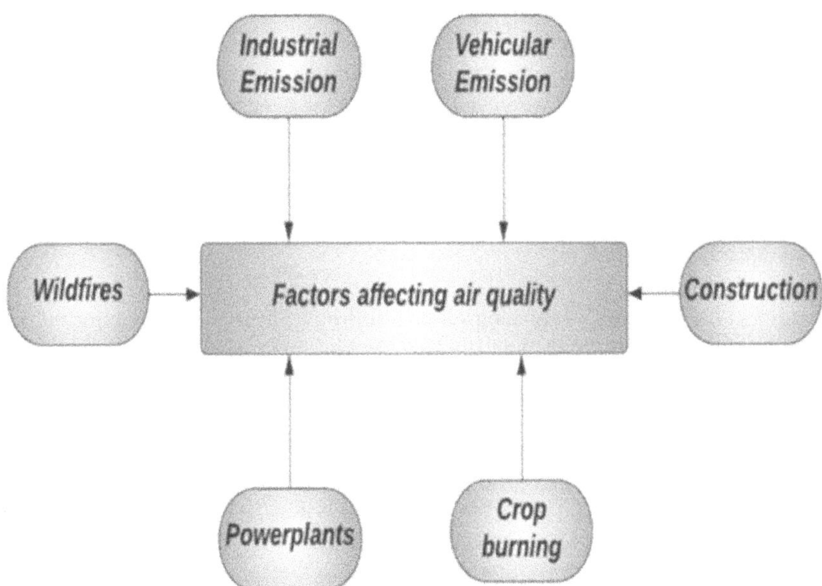

Fig. 1. Factors affecting the air quality

Despite the diverse origins of these pollutants, they uniformly exert detrimental effects on both the environment and human health. Natural sources, such as forests, play a crucial role in filtering out these harmful contaminants from our surroundings. However, practices like deforestation are diminishing these natural filtration capabilities, resulting in an increase in unfiltered pollutants. Given the escalating concerns over air quality, it is imperative to implement effective air quality monitoring systems.

As urbanization accelerates and smart cities emerge as epicentres of growth, the demand for intelligent air quality surveillance systems escalates in tandem. Additionally, the highly dynamic viscosities, transmissions, chemical transformations, and metrological impacts affecting pollutant concentrations create intricate nonlinear patterns [9]. Capturing these complex spatial dispersal and temporal fluctuations demands sophisticated AI cognitive capabilities. Conventional linear statistical models have proven inadequate in modeling such elaborate data relationships [10].

By incorporating automated ML technologies, the proposed AQMS aims to enhance existing pollution monitoring and prediction capabilities. The system intends to provide a scalable, adaptive solution for municipalities tackling worsening pollution [11]. Overall, this research targets leveraging advanced AI to drive step-change improvements in air quality management practices. As populations explode, urban density rises, along with corresponding vehicular, industrial, and economic activity escalations that worsen emissions accumulation. This expanding scale and multidimensionality of influences make manual data processing unfeasible [12].

This study utilizes ensemble approach by combining Random Forest and Decision Tree classifier for air quality prediction in urban city with advance AQMS. Section 2 provides analysis of the current studies which have been done till date on applying ensemble approach for identification purpose. Section 3 describes a detailed framework on data collection, pre-processing, model building and model validation. Section 4 thoroughly evaluates the collected data and exhibit accuracy reached by ensemble model. Section 5 presents important research findings highlighting the benefits of using ensemble algorithms.

2   Literature Review

The authors [13] used PM2.5 concentration at Beijing's 35 air quality monitoring sites is predicted for the upcoming 24 h using an enhanced air quality prediction approach based on the LightGBM model. According on the experimental data, the suggested strategy outperforms alternative strategies by 80%. It has been demonstrated that combining the forecasting data and developing the high-dimensional statistical analysis has benefits.

Using a data-driven approach that takes into account current meteorological data, weather predictions, and air quality features, it is possible to anticipate air quality measurements for the following 48 h. The authors [14] explains about prior studies have effectively utilised this methodology, attaining a 99.3169% accuracy rate. Using Bayesian networks to create a directed acyclic graph (DAG) based on air quality data for training and validation is one such technique. This method has been used to assess the quality of the urban air, mainly in Shanghai, with experimental findings that match the real-world circumstances.

The efficacy of a hybrid LSTM model in forecasting indoor air quality is demonstrated in the study by the authors [15]. To retain historical data and reduce gradient error, the model makes use of long short-term memory, which guarantees accurate data prediction in the future. Hochreiter and Schmid Huber (1997) invented LSTM, an innovative and effective gradient-based technique that can learn to bridge small temporal delays. With the use of continuous error carousels within specific units, it ensures constant error flow, making accurate forecasts possible even in the presence of large temporal gaps.

While conventional methods have been employed, multi-model federated learning (FL) has garnered interest in the computer science community as a cutting-edge strategy for AQI forecasting lately. In order to increase accuracy and generalisation, the authors [16] used multi-model FL entails training many models on various data sources and combining their predictions. This method tackles issues including heterogeneous data, privacy problems, and scalability in the prediction of AQI. The application of multi-model FL in AQI forecasting has potential for improving prediction accuracy and getting around drawbacks with conventional techniques.

The authors [17] study offers a thorough review of the difficulties and possibilities involved in evaluating air quality data, emphasising the need of interactive and visual methods for deciphering temporal patterns and correlations. The platform may be used to analyse past, current, and future behaviour by utilising the user's knowledge of elements impacting air quality, according to the authors. The study cites 38 more sites that offer further information about the topic of air quality analysis and visualisation.

To forecast air pollution, the authors [18] model combines the Deep Featured Neural Classifier (DFNC) with the Multi-objective Staked Feature Selection Approach (MoSFS). The model achieves the optimal level for feature forecasting, exhibiting higher performance in terms of RMSE values. Furthermore, the model has superior classification accuracy in comparison to alternative methods, demonstrating its accuracy in forecasting air pollution levels.

The authors [19] Systems for predicting air quality make use of deep learning (DL) and machine learning (ML) methods to predict air quality. These systems employ important factors, such as PM2.5 and PM10, to properly anticipate air quality. The root mean square error (RMSE) statistic is used to compare the prediction models and identify the top-performing model. Creating a model with high accuracy for air quality prediction is the aim.

Using Arduino-based sensors, a research created a monitoring system for air quality and calibrated the sensors to increase accuracy. The random forest model was used to construct forecast models for pollutant concentrations, most especially for the PM2.5 air quality index. Following sensor calibration, the built IoT device demonstrated a notable improvement in accuracy. In terms of prediction accuracy, the authors [20] used random forest prediction model fared better than the neural network, decision tree, and linear regression models. With the split data technique and the Bayesian strategy utilised for parameter adjustment, runtime performance greatly improved. The study shows the promise of low-cost IoT-based real-time air quality forecasts and monitoring.

In [21], the authors employed PPD42NJ sensors to develop a model for air quality prediction. They utilized a cloud-based engine and an artificial neural network (ANN) for analysis. The results demonstrated that the proposed model efficiently forecasted PM

2.5 concentrations and could be employed for personal air quality monitoring systems (AQMS). Additionally, the model was found to be cost-efficient.

In [22], the authors developed an air quality monitoring model utilizing IoT technology, incorporating MQ135 and PM sensors. Their approach employed a hierarchical, heterogeneous two-level system that integrated a wireless sensor network (WSN) and utilized the Zigbee protocol for communication.

In [23], the authors employed gradient boosting regression to analyze time series data collected from several of Taiwan's largest cities between January 2012 and December 2017. The proposed model outperformed other models, including decision tree regression, ridge regression, random forest regression, K-neighbors regression, lasso regression, MLP regression, and linear regression. The gradient boosting regression model achieved a mean squared error (MSE) of 0.0169 and an R^2 value of 0.8891.

The authors [24] use of Mud Ring Algorithm-based ensemble voting for deep learning. In order to control and lessen the negative effects of air pollution on transportation systems, precise air quality prediction is essential, and the AQP-EDLMRA approach shows promise in this regard. By using ensemble voting to integrate several models, the method takes advantage of each model's advantages to increase prediction accuracy. To further improve the predicting performance, the deep learning models are optimised using the Mud Ring Algorithm.

In order to forecast the air quality index (AQI), machine learning techniques such linear regression, Random Forest, k-nearest neighbour, and Decision Tree regression have been examined. According to the authors [25] study's findings, the most effective method for forecasting air quality is machine learning (ML). Promising outcomes have been demonstrated by ML algorithms in precisely forecasting AQI, an essential parameter for air pollution monitoring and control. Decision Tree, k-nearest neighbour, and Random Forest regression can handle complicated patterns and non-linear correlations in the data, which makes them useful for AQI prediction as well.

3   Methodology

Developing a sophisticated Air Quality Monitoring System (AQMS) requires a meticulous approach combining decision tree and random forest models. The proposed methodology is shown in fig. 2. Implementing the following comprehensive methodology will produce a robust system capable of accurately predicting air quality conditions and providing data-driven insights to guide impactful environmental management policies.

3.1   Problem Definition

Initiate the process by clearly delineating the core objective of the AQMS - to reliably forecast air quality levels and pinpoint the primary pollutants affecting air purity across defined geographic locations. Conduct in-depth analysis to determine the specific metropolitan areas, counties, or neighborhoods to be monitored along with the range of contaminants and particulate matter to be detected.

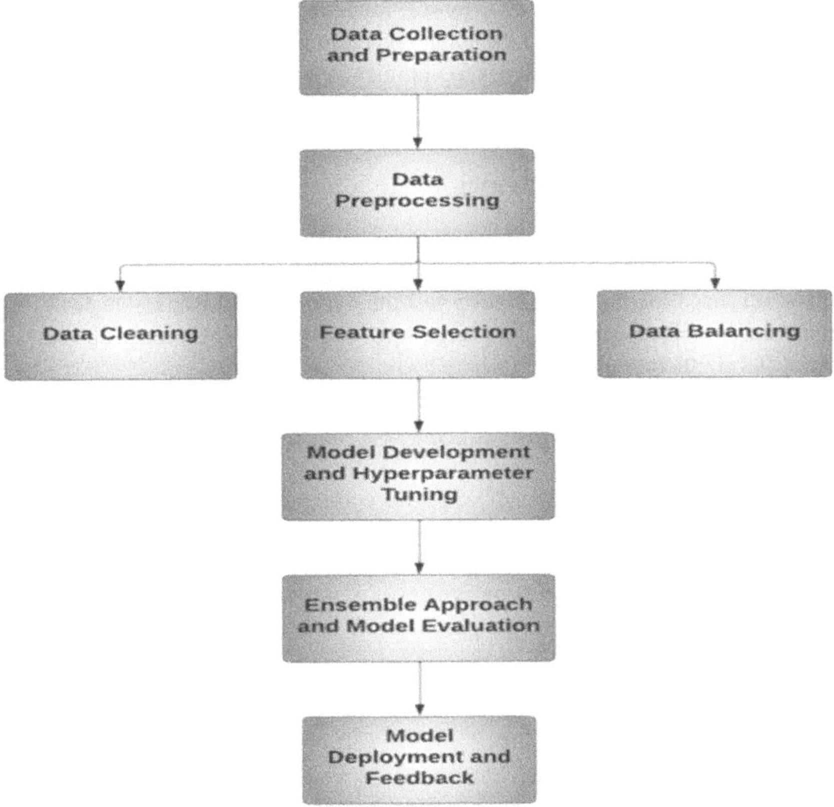

Fig. 2. Proposed Methodology

3.2 Data Collection

Once the scope is defined, collect substantial historical air quality data from these target locations, ensuring comprehensive inclusion of all identified contaminants. Obtain additional meteorological, transportation, industrial emissions or other relevant domain data that could influence air quality.

3.3 Data Preprocessing

With raw data acquired, perform critical preprocessing including imputing missing values, smoothing outliers, and engineering new features. Enrich the dataset by incorporating temporal variables like time of day, day of week, holidays, and seasonal factors that can correlate with pollution levels. Additionally, normalize or standardize variables to align value ranges and distributions.

3.4 Model Development and Hyperparameter Tuning

Next, split the pre-processed data into training, validation, and test subsets. Develop baseline decision tree models to reveal fundamental data patterns, surface insights, and rank feature importance. Construct extensive random forest models leveraging ensemble learning to improve generalizability and prediction accuracy. Employ k-fold cross-validation and grid search techniques to optimize key parameters including tree depth, number of estimators, and leaf size for both models.

3.5 Ensemble Approach and Testing

Subsequently, create a robust meta-model by ensembling the decision tree and random forest models. Blend their predictions through averaging, weighted averaging, stacking, or other advanced methods. Rigorously test the hybrid model using statistical performance measures like R-squared, root mean squared error (RMSE), mean absolute error (MAE), and coefficient of variation.

3.6 Model Development and Feedback

Upon full validation, deploy the AQMS with continuous monitoring mechanisms to detect model degradation and trigger retraining. Set up automated pipelines to feed new data, update model parameters, and maintain optimal predictive performance over time. This comprehensive approach encompasses critical steps to develop an accurate, reliable AQMS fuelled by the combined strengths of decision trees and random forest models.

4 Result

When developing an Air Quality Monitoring System (AQMS) utilizing an ensemble of Random Forest and decision tree models, rigorous evaluation of the following key performance metrics is imperative. Carefully monitoring each of these metrics provides complete insight into the ensemble model's real-world effectiveness for air quality forecasting and monitoring. This enables creating an optimized system that issues timely and accurate air quality alerts to protect public health (Table 1).

Table 1. Algorithms Used in Proposing Model

algorithms	accuracy	precision	f1 score	recall	error
Ensemble	0.98	0.97	0.9	0.92	0.02
Logistic Regression	0.72	0.75	0.79	0.87	0.28
Decision Tree	0.97	0.91	0.89	0.87	0.03
Random Forest	0.96	0.94	0.84	0.8	0.04
KNN	0.95	0.92	0.88	0.83	0.05

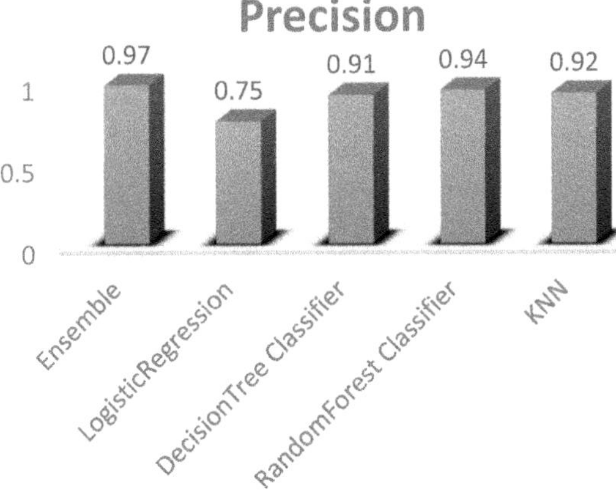

Fig. 3. Precision of various ML algorithms

4.1 Precision

The fraction of correct positive predictions out of all positive predictions. The 0.97 is the highest precision that is shown in Fig. 3. High precision indicates the model generates minimal false alarms and accurately identifies days when air quality will in fact be poor. This enables authorities to issue decisive public health warnings and interventions only when justified, avoiding undue disruption. The precision should be monitored continuously and tuned to balance reliability versus sensitivity.

4.2 Recall

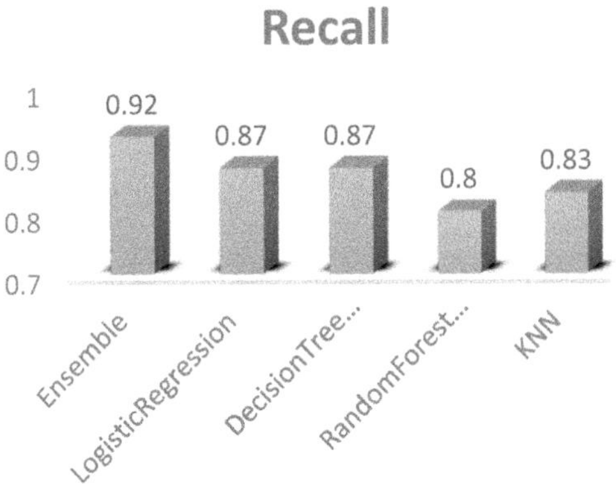

Fig. 4. Recall of various ML algorithms

The fraction of total actual positive cases that were accurately identified by the model. Figure 4 depicts the recall of various machine-learning algorithms. Maximizing recall ensures the fewest number of hazardous air quality events are overlooked by the system. This allows officials and the public to take protective actions in a timely manner whenever dangerous levels are actually present. The recall threshold can be adjusted to control how sensitive the system is to detecting air quality degradations.

4.3 Accuracy

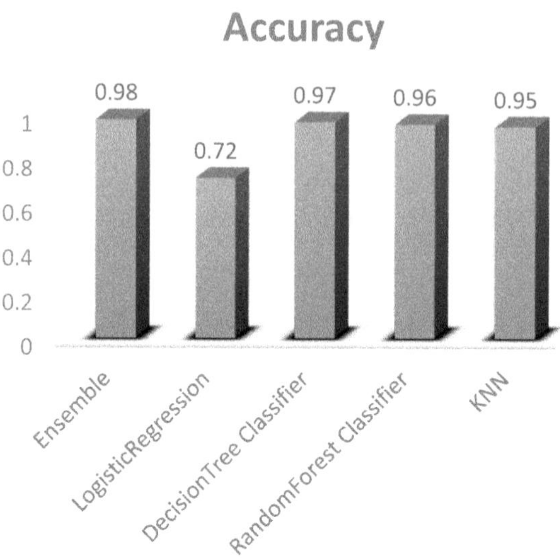

Fig. 5. Accuracy of various ML algorithms

The overall rate of correct predictions, accounting for both positive and negative outcomes. The 0.98 is the highest accuracy of the ensemble approach among all other machine learning algorithms. While intuitive, accuracy alone may be misleading if the data distribution is skewed, as is often the case with air quality datasets. Accuracy should thus be analyzed in conjunction with precision and recall to obtain a holistic view of system capabilities. Periodic accuracy audits help quantify general performance (Fig. 5).

4.4 F1 Score

The harmonic mean of precision and recall, effectively combines them into one balanced measure. It is highly useful when positive and negative groups are imbalanced. The f1 score of different algorithms can be depicted from Fig. 6. A high F1 score signifies an AQMS that capably forecasts air quality events accounting for both accuracy and recall.

4.5 Error Rate

The fraction of incorrect predictions. Figure 7 describes the error of different machine learning algorithms which is least in the case of ensemble approach that is 0.02. Lowering error rates builds credibility in the system's forecasts and ensures the public and officials

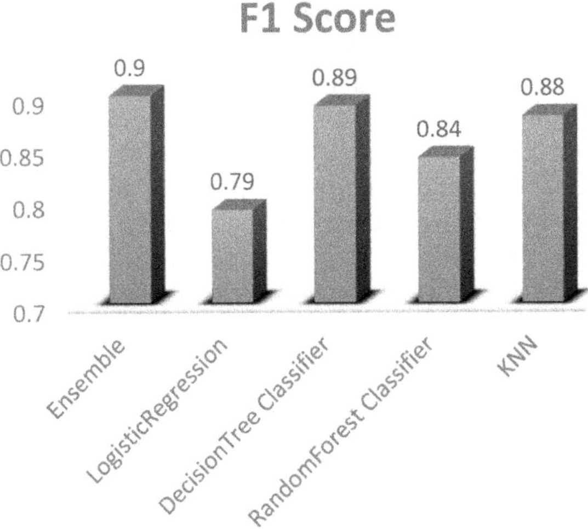

Fig. 6. F1-score of various ML algorithms

Fig. 7. Error of various ML algorithms

can confidently utilize its guidance. Tracking and minimizing errors establishes trust with the public and government bodies who need to make decisions based on the system's projections.

5 Conclusion and Future Scope

In summary, this research demonstrated the efficacy of an ensemble learning approach integrating Random Forest and Decision Tree algorithms for robust air quality management. By combining multiple models, the proposed Air Quality Management System (AQMS) achieved enhanced predictive performance and concentration estimate accuracy. The ensemble methodology alleviates the individual constraints of singular models by allowing them to cooperate and compensate for respective weaknesses. Rigorous empirical analysis validated the integrated system's superiority over solo architectures across pertinent statistical measures. Through comprehensive experimentation, the study proves the ability of strategically blending algorithms to improve robustness and versatility for pollution forecasting. The integrated system empowers precise, proactive decision-making regarding air quality interventions and regulatory policies.

To augment model accuracy and resilience, incorporating additional machine learning techniques - such as Gradient Boosting Machines and Support Vector Machines - into the integrated framework merits exploration. Expanding the ensemble diversity allows for balancing potential limitations of singular architectures. Incorporating geographical and temporal attributes into the feature space can capture the spatial disparity and dynamic shifts inherent in air quality patterns. This geospatial and time-series enrichment enables more targeted, granular predictions to empower localized interventions. Further, integrating Internet of Things (IoT) sensors and city-scale monitoring infrastructure can drastically improve input data volume and coverage. Tapping into existing sensor networks allows leveraging already-rich information streams across both spatial and temporal dimensions.

References

1. Suresh, S., et al.: Air quality prediction using automated ML. In: 2023 International Conference on Quantum Technologies, Communications, Computing, Hardware and Embedded Systems Security (iQ-CCHESS), pp. 1–6 (2023)
2. Priya, S., et al.: Air quality prediction using machine learning approaches. Int. J. Sci. Dev. Res. **8**(5), 1064–1068 (2023)
3. Rahim, N.A.A., et al.: Prediction of indoor air quality using long short-term memory with adaptive gated recurrent unit. In: 11th International Conference on Indoor Air Quality, Ventilation & Energy Conservation in Buildings, vol. 396, (2023)
4. Dong, L.D., et al.: Insights into Multi-Model Federated Learning: an Advanced Approach for Air Quality Index Forecasting, vol. 434, (2022)
5. Harbola S., et al.: Air Quality Temporal Analyser: Interactive Temporal Analyses with Visual Predictive Assessments. (2021).
6. Choudhary, C., et al.: An optimized sign language recognition using convolutional neural networks (CNNs) and tensor-flow. In: 2023 3rd International Conference on Technological Advancements in Computational Sciences (ICTACS), pp. 896–901. IEEE, Tashkent (2023)
7. Prasad, H., et al.: Artificial intelligence based fire and smoke detection and security control system. In: 2023 International Conference on Network, Multimedia and Information Technology (NMITCON), pp. 01–06. IEEE, Bengaluru (2023)
8. Shah, R., et al.: Enhancing machine learning model using explainable AI. In: Tiwari, S., Trivedi, M.C., Kolhe, M.L., Singh, B.K. (eds.) Advances in Data and Information Sciences ICDIS, pp. 287–297 (2023)
9. Thakur, J., et al.: Gliomas disease prediction: an optimized ensemble machine learning-based approach. In: 2023 3rd International Conference on Technological Advancements in Computational Sciences (ICTACS), pp. 1307–1311. IEEE, Tashkent (2023)
10. Paulpandi, C., et al.: Optimized forecasting air pollution model based on multi-objective staked feature selection approach using deep featured neural classifier. Int. J. Recent Innov. Trends Comput. Commun. **11**(9), 1506–1515 (2023)
11. Vasantha, S.V., et al.: Air quality prediction system using ML and DL techniques. In: 2022 IEEE North Karnataka Subsection Flagship International Conference (NKCon), pp. 1–5 (2022)

12. Kitchilan, T., et al.: Air quality monitoring and prediction using IOT and machine learning approaches. Int. J. Sci. Res. Publ. **12**(3), 61–68 (2022)
13. Sivanesh, S., Mani, G., et al.: Air quality prediction using ensemble voting based deep learning with mud ring algorithm for intelligent transportation systems. Global NEST J. **25**, 100–108 (2023)
14. Sirisha, P., et al.: Air quality prediction using machine learning algorithms. Int. J. Sci. Res. Eng. Manag. **7**(5), 1–5 (2023)
15. Trivedi, A., et al.: Should AI technologies replace the human jobs? In: 2023 2nd International Conference for Innovation in Technology (INOCON), Bangalore, India, pp. 1–6. IEEE (2023)
16. Kumar, M., et al.: A novel zero-shot learning approach for multi-classification of Orange sooty Mold disease severity levels. In: 2023 3rd Asian Conference on Innovation in Technology (ASIANCON), pp. 1–5 (2023)
17. Benedict, S.: Revenue oriented air quality prediction microservices for smart cities. In: 2017 International Conference on Advances in Computing, Communications and Informatics (ICACCI), pp. 437–442. IEEE, Udupi (2017)
18. Zhongjie, Y., Shengwei, W.: Ze W.: air quality prediction method based on the CS-LSTM. In: 2022 5th International Conference on Data Science and Information Technology (DSIT), pp. 1–5. IEEE, Shanghai (2022)
19. Liu, Y., et al.: Wang.: ensemble online sequential extreme learning machine for air quality prediction. In: 2021 IEEE 7th International Conference on Control Science and Systems Engineering (ICCSSE), pp. 233–237. IEEE, Qingdao (2021)
20. Septiawan, W.M., Endah, S.N.: Suitable recurrent neural network for air quality prediction with backpropagation through time. In: 2018 2nd International Conference on Informatics and Computational Sciences (ICICoS), pp. 1–6. IEEE, Semarang (2018)
21. Cheng, Y., et al.: AirCloud: a cloud-based air-quality monitoring system for everyone. In: 12th ACM Conference on Embedded Network Sensor Systems 14, pp. 251–265 (2014)
22. Ma, Y., et al.: Hierarchical air quality monitoring system design. In: International Symposium on Integrated Circuits (ISIC), pp. 284–287 (2014)
23. Doreswamy, et al.: Forecasting air pollution particulate matter (PM 2.5) using machine learning regression models. In: Third International Conference on Computing and Network Communications (CoCoNet'19), pp. 2057–2066 (2020)
24. Manikandan, K., et al.: An intelligent Bayesian optimization with stacked BiLSTM model for air quality index prediction. In: 2023 5th International Conference on Inventive Research in Computing Applications (ICIRCA), Coimbatore, India, pp. 1699–1704. IEEE (2023)
25. Utku, A., Can, U.: Machine learning-based a comparative analysis for air quality prediction. In: 2022 30th Signal Processing and Communications Applications Conference (SIU), Safranbolu, Turkey, pp. 1–4. IEEE (2022)

Quasars Detection Using Random Forest Classifier

J. D. Dorathi Jayaseeli[1] and A. L. Amutha[2]([✉])

[1] Department of Computing Technologies, SRM Institute of Science and Technology,
Kattankulathur 603203, Tamil Nadu, India
[2] Department of Computational Intelligence, SRM Institute of Science and Technology,
Kattankulathur 603203, Tamil Nadu, India
`amuthaa1@srmist.edu.in`

Abstract. Astronomers are finding it increasingly difficult to process data manually in today's world due to the enormous amount of data generated in the field of astronomy. The difficulty of finding and identifying quasars, has previously been discussed in the domain of astronomy, though there is no robustness. The primary goal of this research is to provide a classification model for classifying astronomical entities that minimises misclassification. To accomplish this, the machine learning model, random forest classifier approach is used, with data collected via the Sloan Digital Sky Survey (SDSS) and tuned using hyper-parameters. The accuracy, precision, sensitivity and weighted average of the proposed method are all determined to be high. According to the findings, this approach could be used for a wide range of astronomical objectives to improve classification studies, even with random data of stars, galaxies, and, most notably, quasars that can be studied.

Keywords: Astronomy · Quasars · Machine learning · Supervised learning · Random forest classifier

1 Introduction

A quasar is a supermassive black hole at the centre of a distant galaxy that feeds on gas [1]. The term "quasar" refers to a quasi-stellar radio source (QSO), which astronomers discovered in 1963 as objects that resembled stars but emitted radio waves [2]. The term is now used to refer to all feeding, and thus bright, Super Massive Black Holes (SMBH), also known as Active Galactic Nuclei (AGN). It's a bit of a stretch to call a black hole brilliant; after all, black holes are black. In reality, almost every massive galaxy contains a black hole weighing millions to billions of Sun, with many of these black holes hidden from view. Despite weighing 4.3 million solar masses, our Milky Way galaxy can only be seen as faint flashes and flickers due to its starving diet. The orbits of stars around it, on the other hand, indicate that it exists. Other dormant black holes may shred an in falling star on occasion, revealing their existence with a flash of radiation. Quasars, on the other hand, are a special type of black hole [4]. They live in galaxies with plentiful

R. Appavoo et al. (Eds.): IconDeepCom 2024, CCIS 2687, pp. 270–282, 2026.
https://doi.org/10.1007/978-3-032-26680-4_21

gas supplies, which may have been provided by a recent [5] galaxy-galaxy collision, and feed on the influx material. The gas spirals around as it falls in, heating up and producing radiation across the electromagnetic spectrum [6]. Because supermassive black holes in neighbouring galaxies do not always contain as much gas as quasars, they are usually found in distant galaxies [7].

Machine learning (ML) methods, in addition to identification, characterization and visualization of celestial objects are utilized to correlate their actual physical properties in multidimensional parameter spaces. ML is used to classify light curves, compute photometric redshifts and evaluate the physical properties of galaxies. Active Galactic Nuclei (AGN) differ in brightness from minutes to years at various wavelengths. Parametric and non-parametric estimators are usually employed to evaluate AGN variability. The mean luminosity of large AGN samples is usually steady as time passes. Nevertheless, short term observations show variations, along with long-term AGN activity studies show substantial fluctuations. Not much observational research has dealt with the non-symmetric nature of AGN variability. Numerous early studies looked for statistical changes in the variability features of fading or brightening AGN light curves, but almost no evidence for such statistically significant differences was found [9]. They are also extremely compact, which results in a high-power density. They ap-pear brilliant in the night sky, but their brightness changes and emission spectrum are very different from stars. These elements are critical to science, such as black-hole physics and ultra-high-energy gamma rays.

Quasars have also been used to calculate cosmological parameters and as distance markers. The ability of Quasars to be used as "standard candles" is critical. Their intrinsic luminosities, as well as their apparent luminosities, could be used to calculate their distance from the Earth [10]. The wide emission lines in a quasar's spectrum result from the fact that when one looks at the area around the SMBH, one sees an area with a higher gravitational potential and thus higher accretion disc material orbiting velocities. The emission lines undergo Doppler-broadening due to the high velocities, which is only seen in AGN-powered sources. Quasar statistics facilitate the understanding of supernova characteristics, including the quasar luminosity function, the black hole mass function (which peaks at z = 2), and the Eddington ratio distribution, which attains a maximum at Lbol/LEdd = 0.05, where Lbol denotes bolometric luminosity. The Eddington luminosity [11] is given by Eq. (1).

$$L_{Edd} = 1.3 \times 10^{38} \left(\frac{M_{BH}}{M\_\odot} \right) ergs^{-1} \tag{1}$$

where

L_{Edd} - maximum luminosity before radiation pressure pushes matter away
M_{BH} - mass of the black hole
$M\_\odot$ - solar mass (reference unit)

One notable application of machine learning (ML) in astronomy is the identification of potential subjects for further investigation using data collected from operational observatories [12]. Mahabal et al. proposed a software technique based on iterative probability classification using Bayesian networks of cosmological origin discovered in massive digital sky surveys [14]. Because the vast majority of information in cosmology is visual, vision techniques are gaining popularity. Khramtsov et al. [15] used Support Vector Machines to classify objects as extragalactic or intergalactic. Because the objects are either extragalactic or not, one-class SVMs were used. To train the model, the Sloan Digital Sky Survey (SDSS) data was used. Representative learning, a method that transforms input data into a feature space, was employed to facilitate the extraction and training of elements that accurately represent the dataset. In the study, researchers employed the one-class SVM on about 1.7 million celestial objects, yielding an accuracy of 99.284% for extragalactic entities. Heitz et al. [16] used various machine learning techniques to address a number of minor vision-based issues (such as object identification, zone naming, and geometric reasoning). Their approach categorizes different classifiers into levels. Lower-tier classifiers can process unaltered data and yield results from higher-level classifiers. The authors assert accuracy enhancements of 7% and 3% for picture classification and segmentation tasks, respectively. Another method to cascade models involves linking the output of one model to the input of another, enabling the latter to rectify any categorization errors committed by the former. Bhatnagar et al. [17] utilized the Supernovae dataset to illustrate that a learning from mistakes strategy surpassed both the Partitioning Ensemble (PARTEN) and Under Sampling Majority Class (UMjC) methodologies across many datasets. The LFM framework outperformed the PARTEN and UMjC frameworks in terms of accuracy and reliability (95.78%, 93%, 94.87%) and precision when used to classify distinct Supernovae into various subgroups (57%, 67%, 84%) [18, 19]. both concentrate on tree-based approaches to identifying quasars. According to [20], astronomy is based on categorising celestial objects. A data sample from a star, galaxy, or quasar is extremely valuable. Despite their importance in astronomy, quasar sample sizes are small.

The proposed method demonstrates how to distinguish quasars from other celestial objects using supervised learning methods. The proposed method also investigates how basic problem-specific characteristics derived from physical properties of quasars and other astronomical objects can improve the generalisation performance of conventional classifiers. Despite the fact that several astronomical categorization concerns have been addressed, the relationship between the two societies remains ambiguous. This study aims to bridge the gap between theory and practise by establishing a significant astronomical classification problem and organising the relevant data in such a way that machine learning can effectively address it.

2 Quasars Detection Using Random Forest Classifier

Quasars are a unique kind of object with enormous scientific significance. It is a very luminous quasi-stellar object, a term for an active galactic nucleus (AGN) [21]. Massive quantities of energy are emitted by quasars. There are thousands of times more intense quasars than the Milky Way [22], with luminosities exceeding above 1000 watts, as compared to our galaxy. It is important to comprehend the early cosmos since quasars are among the most luminous and distant celestial phenomena. To avoid misclassifying any quasar objects, the quantity of data provided by scientific instrumentation grows exponentially every day, making it imperative to avoid any misclassifications. As a result, the major emphasis will be on developing a machine learning model by implementing a random forest classifier that decreases the classification error of a Quasar. The proposed method is used to determine if celestial things are a Quasar, Galaxy, or Star.

2.1 Random Forest Classifier

Random forest classifier is a flexible, accessible machine learning method which provides prosperous outcomes generally when no hyper parameters are tweaked. A random forest is a supervised machine learning method crafted from decision tree techniques. For instance, the arbitrary forest algorithm can handle both categorical and continuous data sets, which makes it perfect for both regression and classification applications. When it comes to categorization challenges, it does a better job. To understand the functioning of the random forest, we must first examine the ensemble approach. The term "ensemble" denotes a synthesis of multiple models. Consequently, instead of employing a singular model for predictions, a consortium of models is utilized.

Bagging generates a new training subset through sampling and replacement from the original training data, and the result is determined by majority voting.

Boosting enhances weak learners into strong learners by constructing more precise models, ensuring that the final model achieves optimal accuracy.

The random forest methodology consists of the following steps:

Step 1: In a random forest, n records are randomly selected from a dataset of k records.
Step2: A decision tree is constructed for each sample.
Step3: Each decision tree will yield a result.
Step 4: In classification and regression, the result is determined by majority voting or average.

To enhance the performance of random forests effectively, hyperparameters are adjusted.

2.2 Hyper-Parameters

The performance of the random forest model is affected by hyperparameters. In random forests, hyperparameters are employed to enhance model performance and predictive capability or to expedite the model's execution.

The subsequent hyperparameters enhance predictive capability:

1. n_estimators – the quantity of trees generated by the algorithm prior to averaging the estimations.
2. max_features – the maximum number of attributes considered by the random forest during node splitting
3. mini_sample_leaf – determines the minimum quantity of leaves required to partition an internal node.

A randomized search cross-validation is employed to generate optimal solutions from the randomly picked hyper-parameter data.

2.3 Randomized Search Cross Validation

Random search is a strategy in which random combinations of the hyper-parameters are utilized to discover the optimum outcomes for the model that has been created. It is similar to grid search; however, it has been shown to provide superior results when compared to grid search. As parameters are picked in every occurrence, the whole action space may have been reached because of unpredictability, making grid search time expensive to include every element of the combinations. This performs effectively if you consider that not all hyper-parameters are equally important. This search algorithm examines random parameter pairing in each iteration.

2.4 Grid Search Cross Validation

Grid search cross validation is used to fine-tune the random forest classifier and loop through various parameters to identify the optimal model. Grid search cross validation from SKlearn is one of the finest methods to achieve this. It may choose the best settings from the list offered. It is the way of identifying the optimal hyper-parameters values for a certain model via hyper-parameter optimization. The values of hyper-parameters have a significant influence on the progress of a model. Because there is no way to predict the appropriate settings for hyper-parameters in advance, doing so manually would require a significant amount of time and resources, thus Grid search cross validation is utilized to automate hyper-parameter tuning.

3 Experimental Results

The proposed method is implemented in the python Jupiter notebook. The astronomical entities data, of approximately 10000 entries collected from the SDSS, are implemented using the random forest classifier. Although a dataset comprises many different bits of data, it may be used to train an algorithm to identify predictable patterns within the dataset as a whole. The data set for the proposed work is derived from the SDSS. The goal is to use spectroscopic and photometric properties to categorize sky objects like stars, galaxies, and quasars. These characteristics are stored in two tables in SDSS. Spectroscopic data consists of the quantities derived from the spectrum of an item. For example, spectral type or redshift. Photometric data consists of the quantities derived from the picture of an item. For example, its brightness, magnification, flux, or size.

3.1 Preprocessing

The dataset is subjected to the below mentioned preprocessing steps.

- Checking Data types: The data types of all columns are checked thoroughly to determine if there are any discrepancies in the data.
- Checking Null values: It is determined whether any null values are present in the dataset and if so, they are eliminated.
- Checking unique values: Identification of unique values in columns, to minimize dimensionality in the feature.

The collected dataset is subjected to the random forest classifier to obtain maximum accuracy and less standard deviation. The below graph represents the results of occurrence.

Figure 1 represents the results of occurrence.

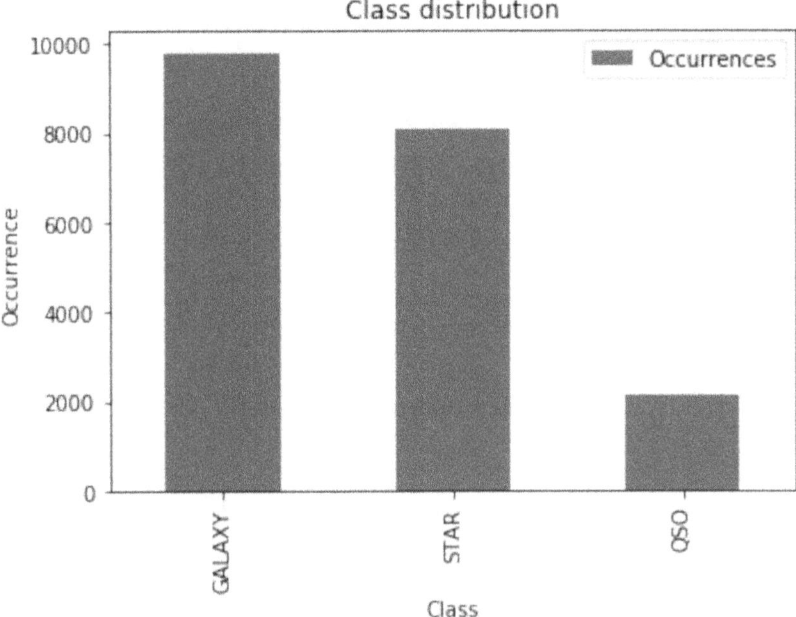

Fig. 1. Occurrences of Class Distribution

The occurrence of each astronomical entity is plotted, and it is observed that the maximum number of entries found are galaxies i.e., above 9000 followed by stars nearly up to 8000, and below 2000 entries are classified as quasars.

The updated classifiers are tested and trained with 30% and 70% respectively. After completion of the processing, the obtained classifiers are made to approach the hyperparameter tuning by implementing the randomized search cross validation. Random search selects a combination of features at random rather than iterating across every possible combination. The outcomes of these parameters show relevant results. In contrast, the grid searches cross validation's results are found more reliable and robust in comparison to the randomized search cross validation even though it is time-consuming.

The execution of the proposed algorithm is evaluated by the performance parameters [23] of the confusion matrix including accuracy, sensitivity, precision, and F-measure.

Accuracy: Accuracy refers to the ratio of correctly identified subjects to the total number of subjects [24] as in Eq. (2).

$$Accuracy = \frac{True\ Positive + True\ Negative}{True\ Positive + True\ Negative + False\ Positive + False\ Negative}$$

$$(2)$$

Precision: Precision is defined as the ratio of correctly identified positive instances by the proposed classifier to the total number of instances labeled as positive [25] as in Eq. (3).

$$Precision = \frac{True\ Positive}{True\ Positive + False\ Positive} \tag{3}$$

Sensitivity: The proportion of correctly identified positive instances by the suggested classifier is referred to as recall, also known as sensitivity, is given in Eq. (4).

$$Sensitivity = \frac{True\ Positive}{True\ Positive + False\ Negative} \tag{4}$$

F-measure: The F1 score is optimal when the system demonstrates a commendable balance between precision and recall. Conversely, if one statistic is improved at the expense of another, the F1 Score diminishes as given in Eq. (5).

$$F-measure = 2 \times \frac{Presicion \times Recall}{Precision + Recall} \tag{5}$$

Table 1. Performance matrices

Astronomical entity	Precision	Recall	F-1 score
Galaxy	0.98	0.99	0.99
Star	0.99	1.00	1.00
Quasar	0.96	0.93	0.95

Table 1 shows the performance matrix of classified data where both the three aspects such as accuracy, precision, sensitivity, and F-measures for the proposed algorithm are found promptly which indicates a reduction of misclassification rate (MCR).

3.2 Visualization

The density distributions of the various features are plotted using kernel density estimation (KDE).

From Figs. 3 and 4 it can be clearly mentioned that the galaxy has high densities followed by quasars and stars respectively. Densities for each class are also plotted and mentioned below in Fig. 5

Filter Band Density

Filter band densities for each class are plotted by the obtained data and as shown in Figs. 5 and 6.

Additional Visualizations

To be on the safe side, a 3D layout is shown in Fig. 6. A linear kernel for the SVM seems to have been the initial goal. In order to make things clearer, a log of the redshift had been drawn (ignoring mistakes) and used as a plotting tool (Fig. 7).

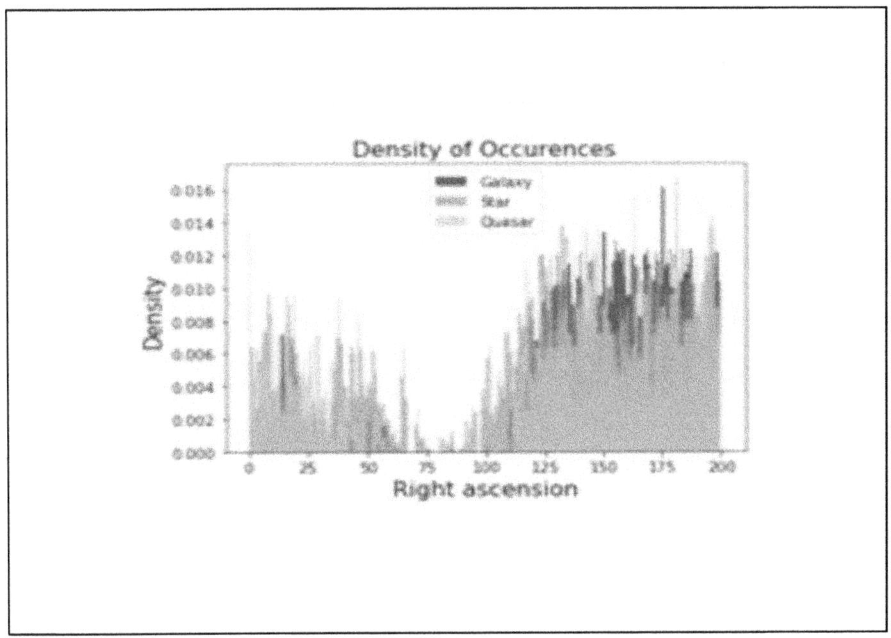

Fig. 2. Distribution density plots-1, the dataset from Sloan Digital Sky Survey

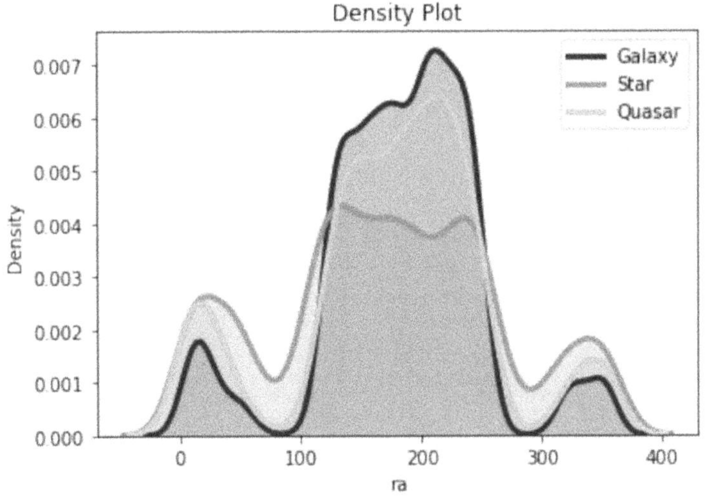

Fig. 3. Distribution density plots-3, the dataset from Sloan Digital Sky Survey

3.3 Heat Map of the Confusion Matrix

The quantities of true positives, false positives, true negatives, and false negatives for each class are presented in a heat map of the confusion matrix [26]. The three squares located at the top left, bottom, and center right indicate the counts of true positives for the

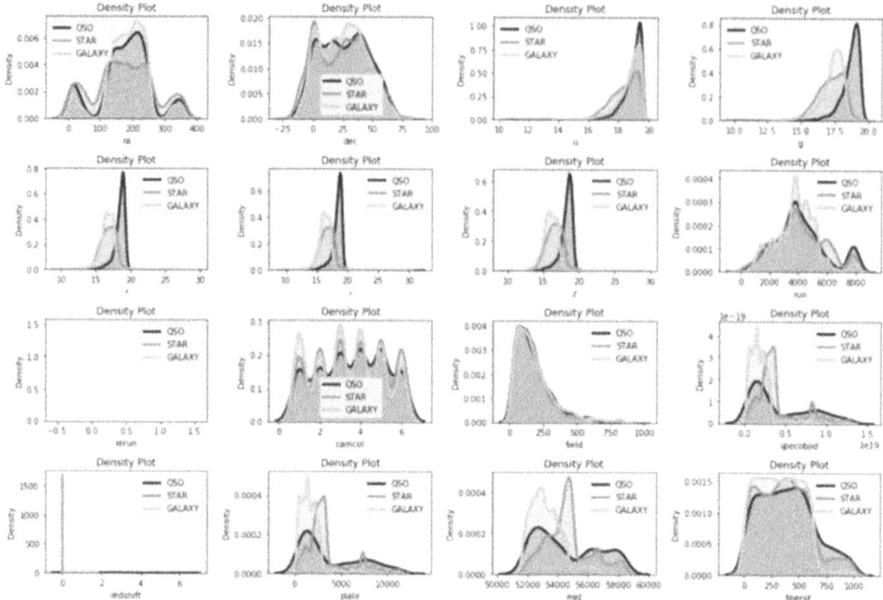

Fig. 4. Distribution density plots-3, the dataset from Sloan Digital Sky Survey

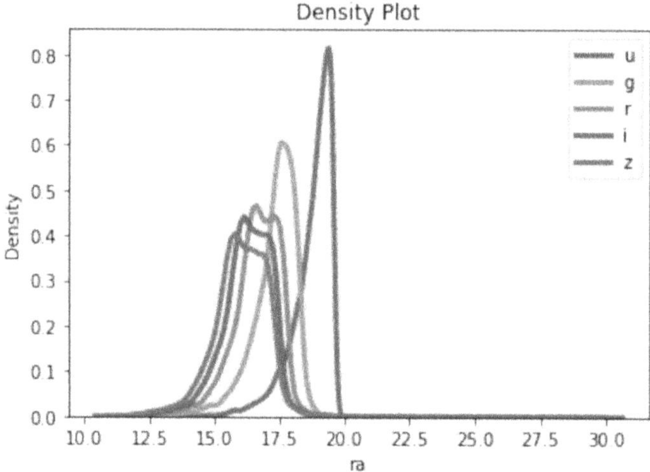

Fig. 5. Filter Band Density, Fig. 1, the dataset from Sloan Digital Sky Survey

classes, represented by color intensity, whilst the remaining squares reflect the counts of erroneous classifications. The heat map of the confusion matrix is illustrated in Fig. 8.

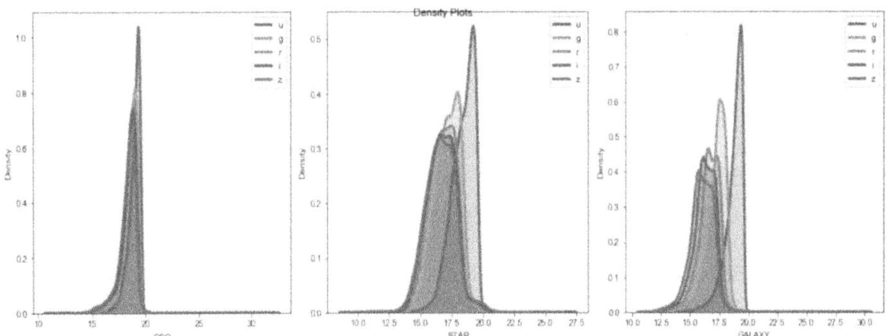

Fig. 6. Filter Band Density, Figure 2, the dataset from Sloan Digital Sky Survey

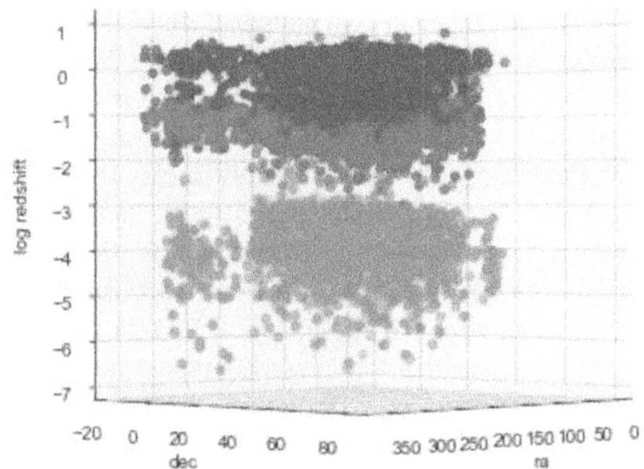

Fig. 7. 3-D view of luminosity

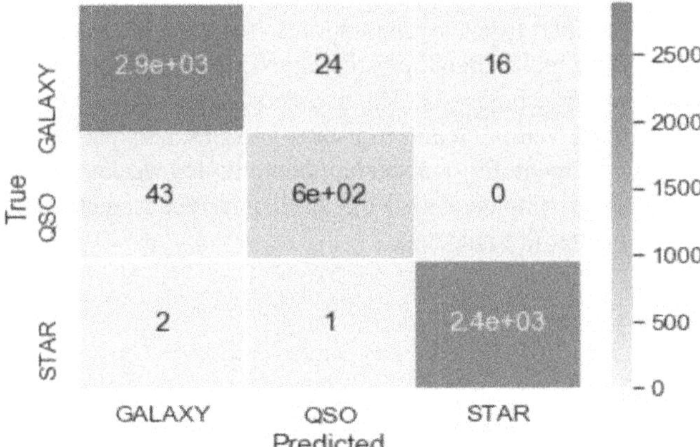

Fig. 8. Heat map of the Confusion matrix

4 Conclusion and Future Work

Data has become more prevalent in recent years produced by space-based observatories, machine learning shall emerge increasingly important for dealing with this onslaught of data. A random forest classifier is utilized in the proposed method to build a classification model for identifying quasars using SDSS data. This technique has the benefit of correctly distinguishing quasars from other celestial objects, which is critical in Astronomy. The dataset is partitioned into training and testing subsets. The proposed method employed randomized search cross-validation and grid search cross-validation to optimize the model's hyperparameters and confirm that the model's performance remains unaffected by the class imbalance in the training data. Subsequently, the model is trained on the training data and assessed using a series of performance metrics on the testing sample. The random forest classifier generates precision, recall, and F1 scores as 98%, 99%, and 99% as for the galaxy respectively. Following this, the star values are detected as a 99% precision, but both for the recall and F1 scores, it shows 100%. Subsequently, when it comes to the quasars, the outcomes are found as 96%, 93%, and 95% as precision, recall, and F1 scores. Overall, the accuracy found for the proposed model is found to be 99%. These are calculated as functions of specific features and other parameters to demonstrate how the classifier performs differently across the three classes. Analysis of a collection of machine learning model performance indicators indicates that the random forest classifier is optimally configured for the classification of celestial objects. The proposed model in this study demonstrates more accuracy when utilizing SDSS data. This model serves as an effective classification tool for astronomical applications requiring swift and precise categorization of stars, galaxies, and particularly quasars.

Although the cosmos comprises more than three categories of light-emitting astronomical entities, the random forest classifier model is trained exclusively on data from stars, galaxies, and quasars, thereby limiting its categorization to these three types. This implies that if a real-world dataset includes data on extraterrestrial entities like comets or substantial gas clouds, the model will invariably misclassify them as stars, galaxies, or quasars. The second area for potential enhancements is the addition of new training classification models. Apart from the random forest, there are several classification models and variants, such as multinomial logistic regression [27, 28] and decision trees [29, 30, 31], support vector machines [32, 33], and neural networks. Although the random forest model performed well in identifying stars, galaxies, and quasars, there is still an opportunity for improvement. Each model has strengths and weaknesses and combining them enables a far more complete knowledge of their unique strengths and weaknesses, resulting in an even better fit to the data.

References

1. Kara, E.: A glimpse into the heart of a quasar. Nature. **563**, 636–637 (2018)
2. Condon, J.J., Kellermann, K.I., Kimball, A.E., Perley, R.A.: Active galactic nucleus and starburst radio emission from optically selected quasi-stellar objects. Astrophys. J. **768**(1), 37 (2013). https://doi.org/10.1088/0004-637X/768/1/37
3. Dhingra, B., Mazaitis, K., Cohen, W.W.: Quasar: datasets for question answering by search and reading. arXiv preprint arXiv:1707.03904 (2017)

4. Greene, J.E., Strader, J., Ho, L.C.: Intermediate-mass black holes. Annu. Rev. Astron. Astrophys. **58**, 257–312 (2020). https://doi.org/10.1146/annurev-astro-032620-021835
5. Lawrence, A.: Quasar viscosity crisis. Nat. Astron. **2**(2), 102–103 (2018). https://doi.org/10.1038/s41550-017-0372-1
6. Luthra, H.: Universe: from electromagnetic to gravitational spectrum (2017)
7. Richstone, D., et al.: Supermassive black holes and the evolution of galaxies, pp. 1–20 (1998)
8. Faisst, A.L., Prakash, A., Capak, P.L., Lee, B.: How to find variable active galactic nuclei with machine learning. Astrophys. J. **881**(1), L9 (2019). https://doi.org/10.3847/2041-8213/ab3581
9. Caplar, N., Pena, T., Johnson, S.D., Greene, J.E.: Observational nonstationarity of AGN variability: the only way to go is down! Astrophys. J. **889**(2), L29 (2020). https://doi.org/10.3847/2041-8213/ab6a11
10. Herle, A., Channegowda, J., Prabhu, D.: Quasar detection using linear support vector machine with learning from mistakes methodology. In: Proc. 6th IEEE CONECCT (2020)
11. Rakshit, S., Stalin, C.S., Kotilainen, J.: Spectral properties of quasars from Sloan digital sky survey data release 14: the catalog. Astrophys. J. Suppl. Ser. **249**(1), 17 (2020). https://doi.org/10.3847/1538-4365/ab99c5
12. Baron, D.: Machine learning in astronomy: a practical overview. arXiv preprint arXiv:1904.07248 (2019)
13. Gieseke, F., et al.: Detecting quasars in large-scale astronomical surveys. In: 2010 Ninth International Conference on Machine Learning and Applications, pp. 352–357. IEEE, Washington (2010)
14. Mahabal, A., Djorgovski, S.G., Turmon, M., et al.: Automated probabilistic classification of transients and variables. Astron. Nachr. **329**(3), 288–291 (2008). https://doi.org/10.1002/asna.200710943
15. Khramtsov, V., Akhmetov, V.: Machine-learning identification of extragalactic objects in the optical-infrared all-sky surveys. Preprint at arxiv.org (2018)
16. Heitz, G., Gould, S., Saxena, A., Koller, D.: Cascaded classification models: combining models for holistic scene understanding. Adv. Neural Inf. Process. Syst. **21**, 641–648 (2009)
17. Bhatnagar, V., Bhardwaj, M., Mahabal, A.: Comparing SVM ensembles for imbalanced datasets. In: Proc. 10th Int. Conf. Intell. Syst. Des. Appl. (ISDA), pp. 651–657 (2010). https://doi.org/10.1109/ISDA.2010.5687191
18. Makhija, S., Saha, S., Basak, S., Das, M.: Separating stars from quasars: machine learning investigation using photometric data. Astron. Comput. **29**, 100313 (2019). https://doi.org/10.1016/j.ascom.2019.100313
19. Khramtsov, V., et al.: Machine learning selection of bright extragalactic objects to search for new gravitationally lensed quasars. Astron. Astrophys. **632**, A56 (2019)
20. Clarke, A.O., Scaife, A.M.M., Greenhalgh, R., Griguta, V.: Identifying galaxies, quasars, and stars with machine learning: a new catalog of classifications for 111 million SDSS sources without spectra. Astron. Astrophys. **639**, A84 (2020)
21. Cannizzaro, G., Fraser, M., Jonker, P.G., et al.: Extreme variability in an active galactic nucleus: Gaia16aax. Mon. Not. R. Astron. Soc. **493**(1), 477–495 (2020). https://doi.org/10.1093/mnras/staa186
22. Forbes, D.A.: Reverse engineering the milky way. Mon. Not. R. Astron. Soc. **493**(1), 847–854 (2020). https://doi.org/10.1093/mnras/staa245
23. Xu, J., Zhang, Y., Miao, D.: Three-way confusion matrix for classification: a measure driven view. Inf. Sci. **507**, 772–794 (2020). https://doi.org/10.1016/j.ins.2019.06.064
24. Sofaer, H.R., Hoeting, J.A., Jarnevich, C.S.: The area under the precision-recall curve as a performance metric for rare binary events. Methods Ecol. Evol. **10**(4), 565–577 (2019). https://doi.org/10.1111/2041-210X.13140

25. Alemam, S., Abuelsadat, S., Saber, S., Elsewify, T.: Accuracy, sensitivity and specificity of three imaging modalities in detection of separated intracanal instruments. G. Ital. Endod. **34**(1), 31–38 (2020)
26. Ohsaki, M., Wang, P., Matsuda, K., et al.: Confusion-matrix-based kernel logistic regression for imbalanced data classification. IEEE Trans. Knowl. Data Eng. **29**(9), 1890–1903 (2017). https://doi.org/10.1109/TKDE.2017.2682249
27. Jiang, B., Chen, B., Zhao, Z.: Study on pretreatment methods of stellar spectral data. In: Proc. 4th IEEE Int. Conf. Big Data Anal. (ICBDA), pp. 188–192 (2019). https://doi.org/10.1109/ICBDA.2019.8713234
28. Beitia-Antero, L., Yáñez, J., de Castro, A.I.G.: On the use of logistic regression for stellar classification: an application to colour-colour diagrams. Exp. Astron. **45**(3), 379–395 (2018). https://doi.org/10.1007/s10686-018-9591-4
29. Mucesh, S., Hartley, W.G., Palmese, A., et al.: A machine learning approach to galaxy properties: joint redshift-stellar mass probability distributions with random forest. Mon. Not. R. Astron. Soc. **502**(2), 2770–2786 (2021). https://doi.org/10.1093/mnras/stab164
30. Talwar, J., Jain, P., Jain, C., Kaur, B.: Stellar and pulsar classification using machine learning. J. Astrophys. Astron. **42**(1), 1–10 (2021)
31. Corral, J., Fierro-Santillán, C.R.: Stellar spectra models classification and parameter estimation using machine learning algorithms (2021)
32. Liu, Z.B., Zhou, F.X., Qin, Z.T., Luo, X.G., Zhang, J.: Classification of stellar spectra with SVM based on within-class scatter and between-class scatter. Astrophys. Space Sci. **363**(7), 136 (2018). https://doi.org/10.1007/s10509-018-3366-2
33. Equations, B.: A.1 Basic equations, inequalities, and functions, pp. 91–93 (1953)

Blind Navigation Systems Using Monocular Depth Estimation

Gaddi Vishnu Vardhan Dutt, Saad Yunus Sait[(✉)], and Naveed Ahmed Shaik

Department of Commputational Intelligence, SRM Institute of Science and Technology,
Kattankulathur, Chengalpattu, India 603203
saady@srmist.edu.in

Abstract. We often come across blind people having tough task traveling through a busy path. Person who cannot see always need someone to be there to take care of them or to watch over them. They are dependent on someone or the other. People are preoccupied with their own life and they hardly bother about someone else. Life of such blind people is very difficult. To help them in such a way that they won't be dependent on anyone again is the need of the hour. So, the proposed system(idea/methodology) depicts the path on a busy street which will help blind people find the way on their own without being dependent on anyone else. There are many electronic gadgets which help blind people to travel safely, but they are not efficient enough, they are just for the obstacles lying around. The proposed system will thus aim to help the blind identify what type of obstacle it is, how far he/she is from the obstacle and help them to make their decision easy and simple without getting too close to the obstacles.

1 Introduction

The paper will give you an overview of implementing a method which will ease the navigation of blind people. The idea is implemented using all the state of the art technologies like object detection using Yolo, which can detect the objects very fast compared to any other model in the present era, on addition to it we prepare a model such that it will help in detecting the depth of the objects from the camera, using these two models it will find the objects and distances between them and the operator and gives the output in format of voice(warning) so that the user will become alert and conscious about what path he/she is traveling in.

Helping the blind in navigating outdoors as well as indoors is an important issue. Being self-dependent is the most observed trait in an individual in the modern world. There are electronic gadgets which help blind people to navigate safely, but they are not efficient enough, they are just for the obstacles lying around on the path. The proposed system(idea/methodology) will thus aim to help the blind identify what type of obstacle he/she come across in the path in which they are navigating and how far he/she is from the obstacle and help them to make their decision simple without getting too close to the obstacles or hurt by it.

Due to an aging society and many changes in once lifestyle, an increased number of people suffering from loosing eyesight might occur such as diabetic retinopathy is

R. Appavoo et al. (Eds.): IconDeepCom 2024, CCIS 2687, pp. 283–292, 2026.
https://doi.org/10.1007/978-3-032-26680-4_22

predicted to increase. Without effective, impactful intervention, the number of people loosing sight worldwide has been predicted to increase to 76 million if current scenario continues. Toady's time many traditional navigation systems are used.

It's time to upgrade those navigation systems to make them more efficient and this "blind navigation" will help a lot of blind people to travel safely and make their lives easy and helps them to do their daily chores without being dependent on others.

The proposed idea involves building a model for object detection, which can detect objects in images from multiple datasets such as CIFAR-10, Open Images, Exclusively Dark (ExDark) Image Dataset, and LISA Traffic Sign Detection Dataset. The model here has been build using transfer learning, the weights have been taken from the pretrained model of yolo algorithm which uses CNN architecture, this model was trained on the above-mentioned data sets. After object detection, the distance of the detected objects is calculated from the depth maps. For creating the depth maps a model is used which uses an encoder-decoder architecture. The encoder extracts feature and makes a feature map, then from this feature map the decoder reconstructs a 3D image or more precise a depth map from which we can extract the depth and use it for calculating the distance of objects. The two models, i.e., object detection and distance measurement, are then combined into a single interface. Finally, the output of the combined model can be converted into speech for the convenience of users. This idea has also the potential to be applied in various areas like autonomous driving, surveillance, and robotics, where object detection and distance measurement are crucial for decision-making. We here are applying it on making a Blind Navigation System.

2 Literature Survey

Here are few researches happen in the past which will help us in implementing our idea and it being the improved form of the previously designed methods.

Mohammad Abou Ali has used the data set taken from the Kinect camera, which uses windowing technique in finding the objects and sending out a response to the user if the object is on his path of walking. Here the Kinect camera already gives images with depth included so making it easier in finding out the distance rather than using a different method separately for it [1]. Our method is almost similar, we use a camera for finding the objects instead of Kinect we use a regular camera which gives 2D images as inputs and we use separate method for finding distance. When compared our method is cheaper than this as we don't use Kinect and this saves in a lot of expense.

Cong Tang, Yunsong Feng and other colleagues with them performs experimental analysis in they compare classical methodologies and deep learning methodologies and their challenges and concludes that the deep learning methodologies will be taking over the classical as their performance is improving by every day and they are becoming more accurate [2].

Using NIR camera, it uses HOG-SVM, it is basically a fast and flexible algorithm which detects the pedestrians at nighttime using images captured from near infrared cameras [3]. But the prime draw back in this is it only detects pedestrians, where as we in our model are finding 10–15 classes of objects and also trying to get at par the same performance.

One application of navigation assistance uses GPS, Direct detection using radio frequency waves. This study was used as evidence for finding out the flaws in the available smart navigation assistants and suggest new and improved intelligent application [4]. "Research and Discussion on Image Recognition and Classification Algorithm Based on Deep Learning Dong Yu-nan School of electrical and electronic Liang Guang-sheng School of electrical and electronic engineering-2018". CNN, Reinforcement Learning, Deep belief network, RNN have been used for accelerating the training speed while keeping in mind the recognition accuracy.

TIM BAILEY AND HUGH DURRANT-WHYTE has collected the data which has been taken through survey and used for SLAM implementation and discussed about its applications and advantages. Method aids a solution to the key competency of mapping and localization for any autonomous robot [8].

Iyad Abu Doush, Sawsan Alshatnawi, Abdel-Karim Al-Tamimi, Bushra Alhasan, Safaa Hamasha they used mobile interface in their navigation system. The idea here is to provide a good response system. We also try to make a good response system by keeping this as a bench mark. Similarly, usage of cloud and vision-based technologies to make a navigation system [11] for making a good navigation system and it also provides tracking of the blind person and keeping a record of it so the family members of them know where they are. Our model here does not provide that function not yet but we would like to add it for future scope.

3 System Description

There are two requirements for the project.

3.1 Object Detection

We are using the state of the art algorithm Yolo – (You Look Only Once). The YOLO algorithm functions by dividing the image into N grids, each having a same dimensional region of S x S. Each one of these N grids is responsible for the detection and localization of the material(object) it contains. The model was trained using the data set provided by the darknet which has 80 classes. The trained models' weights were used in our model which the similar architecture used for the one used in training it has 64 layers.

The data now we have for the transfer learning model is a coco data set which is in the format XML containing the centers of the objects and there features and helps in detecting them in a given image using the Yolo algorithm.

3.2 Distance Calculation

This is a very complex task to be accomplished if it has to be done only using a single camera. There are many efficient ways using hardware and software and finding the distance of the objects. Few of the methods are listed below:

3.3 Using Lidar

It uses time of flight to calculate the distance of objects. Basically, it uses laser and targets an object and calculates the time it takes to reflect back to it and accordingly it calculates the distance it traveled as it already knows the the speed of the light which is being projected. From it and from the formula speed and time it finds the distance of the objects.

3.4 By Creating 3D Model

Create a 3D model using two camera perspectives from which we will get two perspective of the same view and then compare the two images to find out the difference and depth between the objects.

By finding out the focal length of the camera and using lens convection and finding out where the image might form approximately, this method requires predefined height (object in real time) and width (object in real time) and the height (bounding box) and width (bounding box) during the time of measurement of the image which is formed.

3.5 Convex Hull Method

Here instead of finding out the distance we are trying to find out the path which will avoid all the obstacles make a path around the obstacles.

Monocular depth estimation: Monocular depth estimation is a computer vision task that aims to estimate the depth information of a scene from a single input image. It has numerous applications in robotics, augmented reality, and autonomous driving.

The above-mentioned methods are which can be used for finding distance of objects. We in our model are going to use Monocular depth estimation for finding the distance of objects in our method.

We have four modules Yolo, utils, darknet and distance calculation. utils and darknet have the methods for detecting IOU - Intersection over Union, for detecting objects, print the objects, deciding the anchor boxes, loading the class or finding class probability for classifying, whereas the darknet module has the model architecture or the configurations and the weights required by the model to detect the objects the entire neural network architecture is done in the darknet module and the Yolo module is the main module from where we operate or connect all the other modules to work together we take the data and use the other modules methods and classes for detecting the objects. In Distance calculation we will be calculating the distance of objects from the camera. Here we take a single image as an input and make depth map of it, this depth map contains the depth information in each of the image's pixels and we use this information in finding the distance of objects from the camera by using the formula,

$$distance = depth\ value/Pixel\ size,$$

where the depth value is obtained from the depth map, it takes in two coordinates - centroid of the objects detected and returns the depth value and the pixel size is an assumption that we assume, for this model we assumed it to have a value of 1 mm.

4   Architecture Diagram

4.1   Architecture Diagram for Object Detection

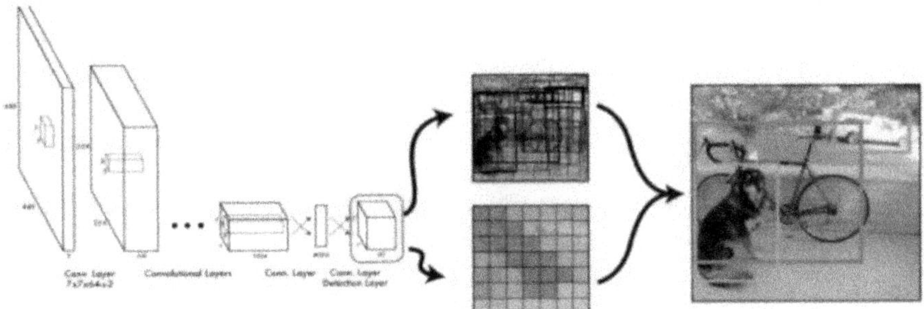

Fig. 1. Architecture of Yolo Algorithm.

The architecture of YOLO is divided into two parts: the feature extractor and the detection head. The feature extractor is usually a pre-trained convolutional neural network such as DarkNet-53 or MobileNet, which is used to extract high-level features from the input image. The detection head is composed of convolutional layers that predict the bounding boxes and class probabilities for each object in the image (Fig. 1).

The YOLO architecture is based on a single neural network that takes an entire image as input and outputs the bounding boxes and class probabilities for all objects in the image. This architecture is different from other object detection algorithms that use multiple stages of processing to detect objects.

4.2   Architecture Diagram for Monocular Depth Estimation

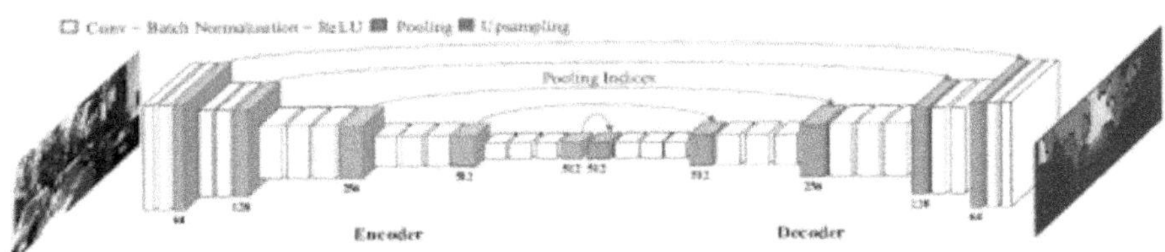

Fig. 2. Architecture for Monocular depth estimation.

The architecture of monocular depth estimation typically consists of two main components: an encoder network and a decoder network (Fig. 2).

The encoder network takes the input image and generates a set of feature maps, which capture the high-level semantic information of the scene. The encoder network is usually composed of a series of convolutional layers that progressively down sample the input image, increasing the receptive field of the network and reducing the spatial dimensions of the feature maps.

The decoder network takes the feature maps generated by the encoder network and up samples them to the original input image size. The decoder network is typically composed of a series of transposed convolutional layers that

progressively increase the spatial dimensions of the feature maps while maintaining the semantic information. The decoder network also includes skip connections that concatenate the feature maps from the encoder network with the corresponding feature maps from the decoder network. These skip connections help to preserve the low-level details of the input image while also incorporating the high-level semantic information from the encoder network.

The output of the decoder network is a depth map, which represents the depth information of the scene.

5 Design Diagram

It starts with taking inputs from the users environments which then is fed to the two models which are Object detection and Distance calculation, based on the input fed the two models will analyze the it and sends an audio channel output about what they have inferred about the environment (Fig. 3).

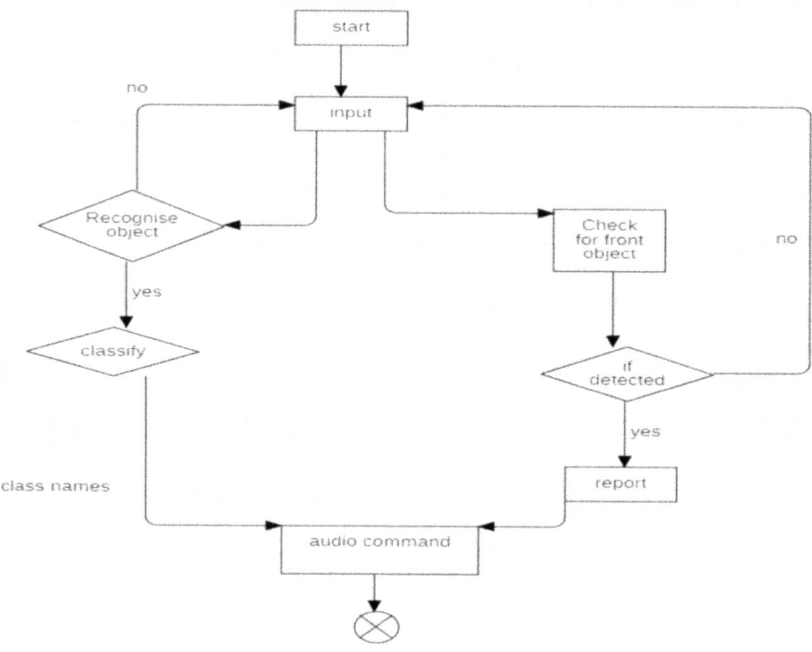

Fig. 3. Design diagram for Object detection and Distance Measurement.

6 Experimental Results and Analysis

Our model is almost same as per the performance wise while the operation it does is different from the models which are previously built. The Previously built models detect objects in front of the user by using sensors which use sonar technique to find the object ahead but does not categorize or give out the direction or information on depth, they just alert the users about the object ahead. Now on the other hand, our model has the ability to detect objects and categorize them according to their class and also find the distance of the objects and alert the user whenever the objects are within a certain range from the users it alerts the user about the object. But how is our model able to do that, as already mentioned above we are using Yolo for detecting the objects and categorizing them accordingly.

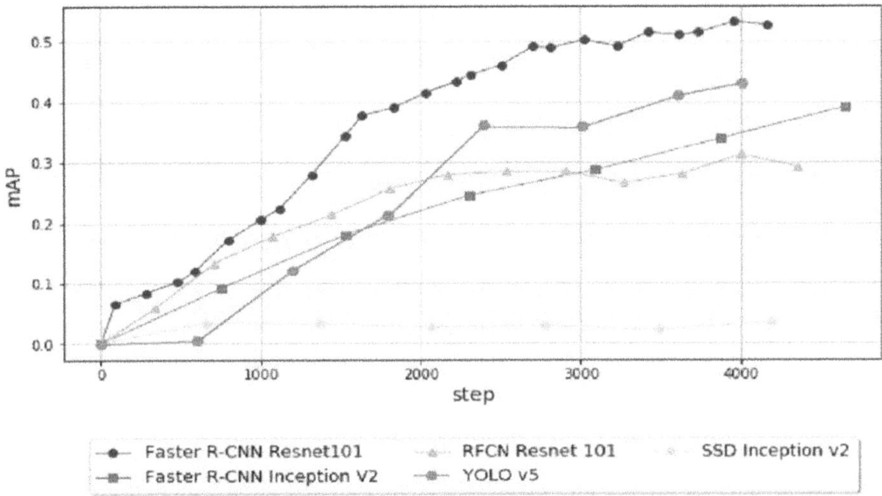

Fig. 4. Showing the mean average precision of the algorithms used for object detection.

From Fig. 4 result we can see that Faster R-CNN and Yolo are surpassing all other algorithms as the training steps are increased, mAP – mean average precision is the metric used for finding the algorithms accuracy of finding the objects, to be more precise how accurately the bounding boxes are made around the recognized objects.

To compute MAP for object detection, the algorithm first generates a set of candidate object detections (bounding boxes) for each image in a test dataset. Each detection is then assigned a confidence score, which indicates how likely the algorithm believes the detection is a true positive.

The next step is to compute the precision and recall values for each class of object. Precision is the fraction of correctly detected objects among all detected objects, and recall is the fraction of correctly detected objects among all actual objects in the image.

The precision-recall curve is then plotted, and the area under the curve (AUC) is calculated. This AUC value is known as the Average Precision (AP) for that class.

Finally, the mean of the AP values across all classes is taken to obtain the MAP score for the algorithm.

The above metric shows that faster R-CNN surpasses even yolo when it comes to recognizing the objects and creating the bounding boxes but when it comes to the speed yolo out performs every other algorithm (Table 1).

Table 1. Table representing mAP and FPS values of different object detection algorithms

	Detection Frameworks	Train	mAP	FPS	PS (mAPxFPS)	PS Order
1	Fastest DPM [26]	2007	30.4	15	456	11
2	R-CNN Minus R [27]	2007	53.5	6	321	13
3	Faster R-CNN ZF [20]	2007+2012	62.1	18	1118	9
4	YOLO VGG-16 [24]	2007+2012	66.4	21	1394	8
5	Fast R-CNN [22]	2007+2012	70.0	0.5	35	14
6	Faster R-CNN VGG-16 [20]	2007+2012	73.2	7	512	10
7	Faster R-CNN ResNet [20]	2007+2012	76.4	5	382	12

As we can see in the above table that Yolo gives mAP of 66.4 at a fps 21, which clearly shows that Yolo works faster than any other algorithm with good efficiency and accuracy. The performance of yolo gives us the advantage of working on the higher frames per second which helps our model to detect the objects fast and quickly act on it and send a response to the user.

Once the objects are detected by the Yolo their centroids are found which then are used in finding out the distance of the objects from the camera. We used monocular depth estimation, here we train the model by giving it two image one with left perspective and one with the right perspective and we try to make get the right image from the left and compare it with the right image. This is architecture is more like encoder – decoder, encoder it trained to find feature cues and it makes a decompressed feature map, which is then passed to the linkage space from where the decoder uses the features for reconstruction of the image and the loss is calculated. The loss is reduced by the optimizers in this case Adam optimizer has been used. Results suggest that a pre trained model for the encoder shows better results than training the encoder. So, transfer learning has been done to build the model (Fig. 5).

As you can see the left side of image showcases a depth map which contains the depth information in each pixel on the right side is the original 2D image which was captured. Now from this depth map we take the depth value and calculate the distance and if the calculated distance of objects is within the alert range an alert message is generated to the user.

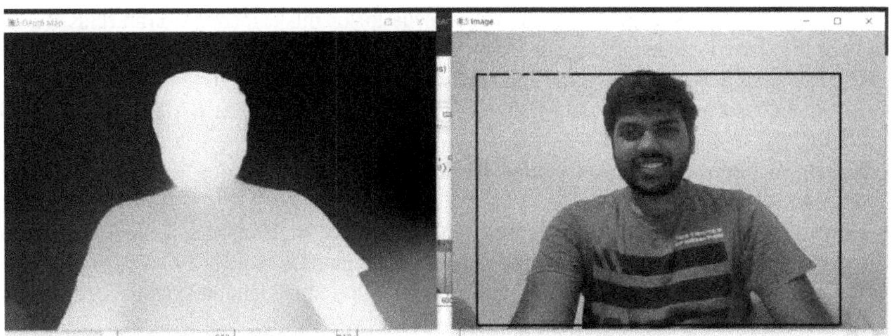

Fig. 5. Final result of monocular depth estimation

7 Conclusion

The task of finding out the objects around the room and their distance is achieved by using the best performed algorithm Yolo for object detection while using monocular depth estimation for calculating distance of the objects from the camera. The performance of this implementation has been impressive, this method has a lot advantages over the previously implemented methods, as they can only generate an alert message but this method over here can categorize the objects detected and also has a rational thinking ability while alerting the users. The results produced have been promising and implementation of this method is quite cheaper when compared with the existing methodology. As we only use a single sensor for accomplishing our work compared to using of multiple sensor which would cost a fortune. Our model use the new technologies like AI which gives it a higher scope of expansion and blend with changes as technology evolves. Finally the system proposed is reliable and can be tested with real time environment so, that it is trusted and safe to be used by blind people.

References

1. Ali, A., Ali, M.A.: Blind navigation system for visually impaired using windowing-based mean on Microsoft Kinect camera. In: 2017 Fourth International Conference on Advances in Biomedical Engineering (ICABME), pp. 1–4. Lebanease International University, Department of Biomedical Engineering (2017)
2. Feng, Y., Yang, X., Zheng, C., Zhou, Y.: The Object Detection Based on Deep Learning. IEEE (2017)
3. Govardhan, P., Pati, U.C.: NIR Image Based Pedestrian Detection in Night Vision with Cascade Classification and Validation. Department of Electronics & Communication Engg. National Institute of Technology (2014)
4. Khan, S., Nazir, S., Khan, H.U.: Analysis of navigation assistants for blind and visually impaired people: a systematic review. IEEE Access. **9**, 26712–26734 (2020)
5. Oksuz, K., Cam, B.C., Kalkan, S., Akbas, E.: Imbalance problems in object detection: a review. IEEE Trans. Pattern Anal. Mach. Intell. **43**(10), 3388–3415 (2020)
6. Bauer, Z., Dominguez, A., Cruz, E., Gomez-Donoso, F., Orts-Escolano, S., Cazorla, M.: Enhancing perception for the visually impaired with deep learning techniques and low-cost wearable sensors. Pattern Recogn. Lett. **137**, 27–36 (2019)

7. Yu-nan, D., Guang-sheng, L.: Research and discussion on image recognition and classification algorithm based on deep learning Dong Yu-nan School of electrical and electronic Liang Guang-sheng School of electrical and electronic engineering (2018)
8. Simultaneous Localization and Mapping (SLAM): Part II BY TIM BAILEY AND HUGH DURRANT-WHYTE (2018)
9. Kumar, G., Bhatia, P.K.: A Detailed Review of Feature Extraction in Image Processing Systems (2014)
10. Doush, I.A., Alshatnawi, S., Al-Tamimi, A.-K., Alhasan, B., Hamasha, S.: ISAB: integrated indoor navigation system for the blind. Interact. Comput. **29**(2), 181–202 (2016)
11. Bai, J., Liu, D., Su, G., Fu, Z.: A cloud and vision-based navigation system used for blind people (2017)

Early Low Birth Weight Prediction Using Machine Learning

S. Samyuktha Shanmugam, S. Varshini[✉], and A. S. Hepsi Ajibah

Department of Information Technology, St. Joseph's College of Engineering, Chennai, India
ajaasankar@gmail.com

Abstract. An essential measure of public health significance linked with infant mortality is low birth weight, a condition defined by the World Health Organization (WHO) as infants weighing less than 2500 g at birth. Some medical centers identify causes of low birth weight, but other health and demographic factors are also involved and may be directly or indirectly linked to this condition. This study aims to use prospective machine learning techniques to develop predictive models to estimate preterm birth weight using health and demographic data. Naive Bayes, Linear Regression, and Extreme Gradient Boosting are the machine learning algorithms that have been used in research for predictive analysis. The results of this study can be used by medical professionals and researchers who evaluate low birth weight babies and help the public avoid similar situations where children are born with low birth weight.

Keywords: Machine learning · Low Birth Weight · Linear Regression · Extreme Gradient Boosting · Data processing and classification

1 Introduction

Ensuring the health of pregnant women and their babies relies heavily on prenatal healthcare. Birth weight significantly impacts the well-being of neonates. Low birth weight babies are more likely to experience a number of health issues, including the possibility of child death. Making accurate estimates about the baby's birth weight is a crucial part of prenatal care. Healthcare professionals can carry out focused interventions when pregnancies at risk of producing low birth weight babies are identified early, improving the chances of a healthy outcome for both mother and child. Maternal forecasts are the basis of conventional birth weight prediction techniques.

Machine learning models are able to examine intricate associations in large datasets by taking into account a wide range of variables that are not possible with conventional techniques. Healthcare professionals may be able to detect minute patterns and interactions between several prenatal factors by utilizing machine learning, which could result in more accurate and timely therapies. Our goal is to create a strong predictive model by utilizing a comprehensive dataset that includes maternal age, BMI, gestational history, lifestyle factors, and prenatal care data. By offering precise and timely predictions, this model has the potential to completely transform prenatal care by enabling medical

© The Author(s), under exclusive license to Springer Nature Switzerland AG 2026
R. Appavoo et al. (Eds.): IconDeepCom 2024, CCIS 2687, pp. 293–302, 2026.
https://doi.org/10.1007/978-3-032-26680-4_23

professionals to customize their interventions according to the unique characteristics of each patient.

2 Literature Review

Babies delivered with cloth were measured using a non-contact ECG technique by Tsukasa Aihara et al. [1]. Cotton swabs, insulated paper electrodes, and both modern and ancient analog front ends (AFE) were used to interpret capacitive ECG data from rare newborn samples. Nevertheless, ambient interference affects non-contact readings, increasing noise and distortion in the ECG signal.

A machine-learning method was created by Lee et al. [2] to forecast postnatal growth failure in very low birth weight (VLBW) newborns. Data from 7954 VLBW babies, split into training and test groups at a 4:1 ratio, were analyzed for their study. When the z-score decreased by more than 1.28 at discharge, it was considered postnatal growth failure for short. They developed a machine learning model using extreme gradient boosting (XGB) that included 16 prenatal and postnatal factors recorded at five distinct stages during the delivery process. Twelve pertinent features were consistently included at all time points after a feature selection process. However, because of certain biases and features in the model, its applicability to different populations and healthcare environments may be restricted.

In order to predict the birth weight of infants, Sushiridha and others [3] examined a variety of factors that affect low birth weight, such as the mother's gestational age, the age of the parents, lifestyle, smoking and alcohol usage, and weight increase throughout pregnancy. The accuracy of the estimation could be jeopardized by errors or gaps in the dataset pertaining to variables affecting birth weight, such as maternal nutrition or genetics.

To determine how to forecast low birth weight, Najmus Sakib Borson et al. [4] examined the relationship between a number of demographic variables. One potential disadvantage, though, is the interpretability of machine learning algorithms such as Random Forests and Neural Networks, which have proven to be complex due to their frequent use as "black boxes," making it challenging to determine the relationship between low infant weight and influencing demographic factors.

The machine learning algorithms for predicting low birth weight were presented by Flávio Leandro De Morais as well as others [5]. They assessed machine learning models, especially those that relied on tree-based models like adaptive boosting, but it might be difficult to pinpoint the exact causes of their forecasts.

In conclusion, our low weight at birth prediction method is distinct in that it places a strong focus on the dataset's highly predictable features, which we successfully use to get around issues noted in the literature review. By using strong preprocessing methods to reduce ambient interference in non-contact measurements, we guarantee the accuracy of our data. By taking into account the most predictable properties, our system excels at handling complexities, even in the face of possible dataset imperfections. Furthermore, we steer clear of black-box machine learning algorithms in favor of transparency and interpretability. Our system provides a simple and efficient solution that has the potential to significantly improve newborn healthcare and predictive medicine by concentrating only on deterministic criteria pertinent to birth weight prediction (Fig. 1).

3   System Architecture and Design

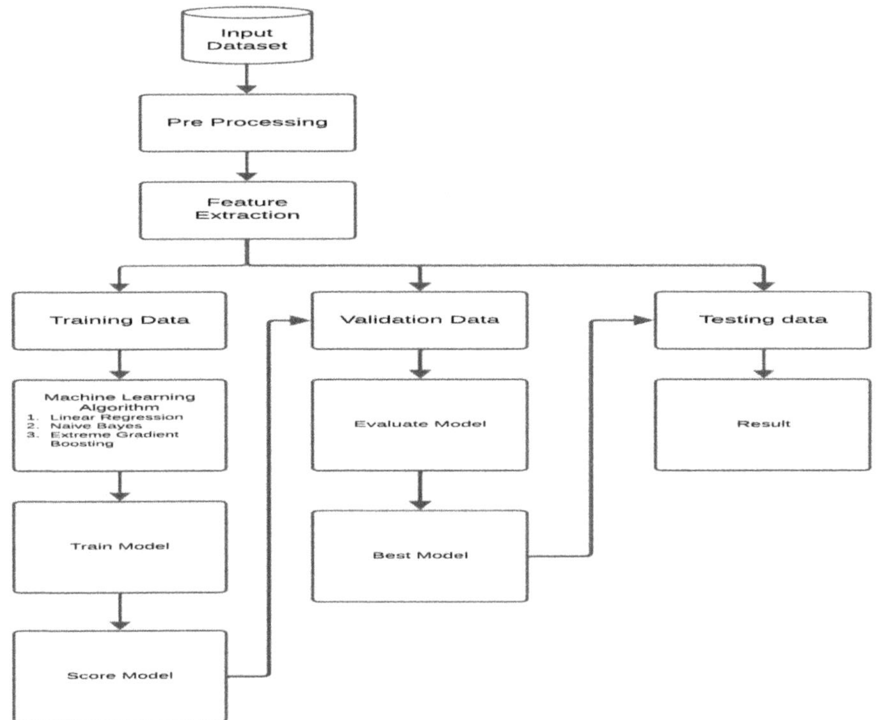

Fig. 1. System Architecture

4   Proposed System

A vital step before training is data preprocessing, which aims to prepare the data for the best possible learning. This phase's tasks include separating the data into training, validation, and test sets, replacing null values, and extracting features. The dataset is collected from the medical records shared by the Kaggle research community. More than 3000 various datasets have been collected for the process. This process streamlines input data which involves maternal and paternal factors (age, medical history, hemoglobin level), gestational information (gestation week, head circulation, stomach length), lifestyle factors (smoking, alcohol consumption), and prenatal care details. The datasets are chosen to be comprehensive to ensure higher accuracy with the model.

Step – 1 Feature Extraction
Through conducting thorough feature engineering to transform raw data into meaningful features we implemented techniques such as one-hot encoding for categorical variables

and normalization for numerical variables. Implementing feature selection methods is to identify the most relevant features that significantly impact birth weight prediction.

The following characteristics are considered for analysis following an empirical study on the risk factors for low birth weight. Factors including,

- Mother's age
- Gestation
- Mother's height
- Stomach length
- Head circulation
- Pre-pregnancy weight
- Mother's smoking (number/day)
- Father's age
- Hemoglobin
- Father's height
- The mother's lower birth weight
- Mother's age above 35

Step – 2 Data Cleaning

The dataset utilized in the system is both original and credible, meticulously sourced to guarantee its accuracy and dependability. It consists of thorough records gathered from esteemed healthcare facilities and scholarly databases, forming a sturdy basis for our machine-learning algorithms. Stringent validation procedures have been applied to confirm the integrity and pertinence of the data, ensuring its suitability for predicting early low birth weight. This authoritative dataset encompasses a wide array of demographic, clinical, and physiological factors, facilitating thorough analysis and precise risk evaluation. Its genuineness and comprehensiveness empower our study to generate valuable insights and promote advancements in prenatal healthcare.

Despite the dataset's extensive size, there are relatively few instances of null and missing values. The fundamental scikit-learn libraries are utilized to compute necessary replacement values, using the average value of each column. Additionally, where data is missing, either null values are inserted or the corresponding cases are deleted.

Step – 3 Algorithm Model Training

During this phase, pre-processed datasets are used to build a variety of machine- learning algorithms. The ultimate goal of this research is to forecast the child's early birth weight using machine-learning techniques. Thus, Linear Regression, Naive Bayes, and Extreme Gradient Boosting techniques were utilized to conduct the analysis.

Step – 4 Model Training

To train, validate, and test a machine learning model, while testing data assesses the model's performance on hidden data, validating data for tuning the hyperparameters and training data is used to create training sets. Depending on the size and complexity of the dataset, a typical split is 70% training, 10% validation, and 10% testing. This enhances the assessment of the model's performance in real-world scenarios and its ability to generalize to new data. The above code sample covers the crucial step of dividing a dataset into training, validating, and testing sets in the context of developing machine learning models.

The following provides the explanation of the variables.

1) X: indicate the feature vectors, which may be represented as a pandas data frame or NumPyarray.
2) Y: indicate the goal values or matching labels connected to the feature vectors.
3) test_size = 0.1: Indicates that 10% of the dataset will be used for testing, with the remaining 70% being kept aside for model training and validation.
4) test_size = 0.125 By further dividing the 70% training and validation sets, 10% of the dataset is designated for validation.
5) Random_state: This optional parameter guarantees the reproducibility of the data split when it is set to a particular integer value. This characteristic gives the randomization process determinism.

When this code is executed, four different datasets are produced.

1. X_train: Contains the feature vectors for the training set.
2. Y_train: Comprises the labels or target values corresponding to the training set.
3. X_val: Stores the feature vectors representing the validation set.
4. Y_val: Holds the labels or target values corresponding to the validation set.
5. X_test: Stores the feature vectors representing the testing set.
6. Y_test: Holds the labels or target values corresponding to the testing set.

These datasets, segregated into training, validation, and testing subsets, serve as the foundational components for the subsequent phases of machine learning model development, allowing for the training and evaluation of models with a well-defined and reproducible data split.

Step – 5 Model Evaluation

The model shall be evaluated on the test set to establish its accuracy and robustness after training has been completed. Measurement of metrics may be part of this. As we are implementing regression for the prediction of birth weight, we are taking the R- squared (R^2) as the performance metric. An independent variable or variables in a regression model can explain a dependent variable's variance to some extent, and this can be expressed statistically as R-squared. In the context of machine learning, R^2 serves as a valuable metric for comparing the performance of different regression techniques. Better fits are suggested by higher R^2 values, which show that the model explains a greater percentage of the variance in the target variable. By comparing R^2 scores across various regression techniques, we can discern which methods are more effective at capturing the underlying patterns in the data and producing accurate predictions for birth weight.

5   Results and Discussions

Figure 2 shows the sample dataset used in the birth weight detection process. The dataset is included and the data preprocessing was performed using one-hot encoding. Following that, The training data is trained in various algorithms and the algorithm with the highest score is deployed. Extreme Gradient Boosting, a widely employed regression predictive modeling technique, with computed accuracy, a single fit model is used for testing a range of inputs.

	Length	Birthweight	Headcirc	Gestation	mage	mnocig	mheight	mppwt	fage	HB	fnocig	fheight	lowbwt	mage35
0	56	4.55	34	44	20	0	162	57	23	10	35	179	0	0
1	53	4.32	36	40	19	0	171	62	19	12	0	183	0	0
2	58	4.10	39	41	35	0	172	58	31	16	25	185	0	1
3	53	4.07	38	44	20	0	174	68	26	14	25	189	0	0
4	54	3.94	37	42	24	0	175	66	30	12	0	184	0	0
...														
3019	52	3.41	33	39	23	25	181	69	23	16	2	181	0	0
3020	49	3.18	34	38	31	25	162	57	32	16	50	194	0	0
3021	53	3.19	34	41	27	35	163	51	31	16	25	185	0	0
3022	47	2.66	33	35	20	35	170	57	23	12	50	186	1	0
3023	53	2.75	32	40	37	50	168	61	31	16	0	173	0	1

Fig. 2. Sample Dataset

Table 1. Accuracy of various algorithms used in the system

Model	R-squared score
Linear Regression	0.79
Naive Bayes	0.79
Extreme Gradient Boosting	0.99

Analyzing Table 1 suggests that the Extreme Gradient Boosting model can be used for further testing since the R-squared score is the highest when compared to linear regression and Naive Bayes with an impressive score of 0.99 with Linear Regression and Naive Bayes having a score of 0.79 and 0.79. The graphical representation illustrates theAccuracy of various algorithms (Figs. 3, 4, 5, 6, 7 and 8).

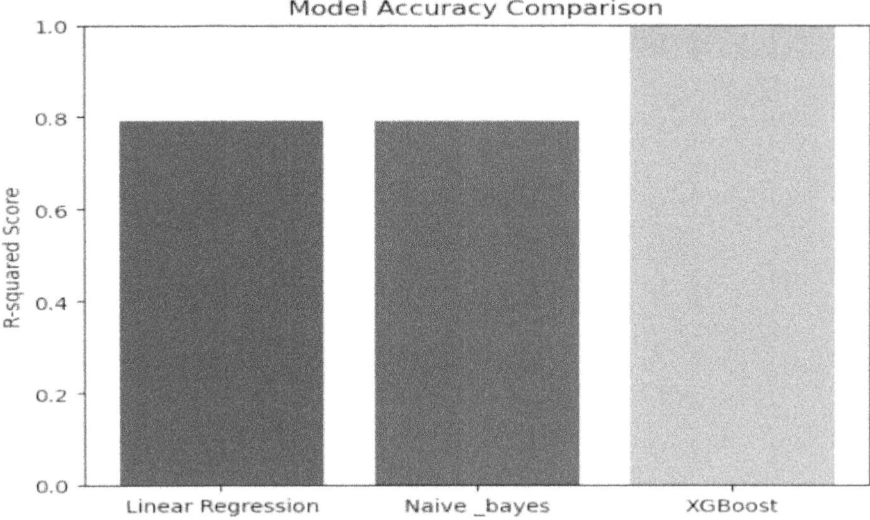

Fig. 3. Model Accuracy Comparison

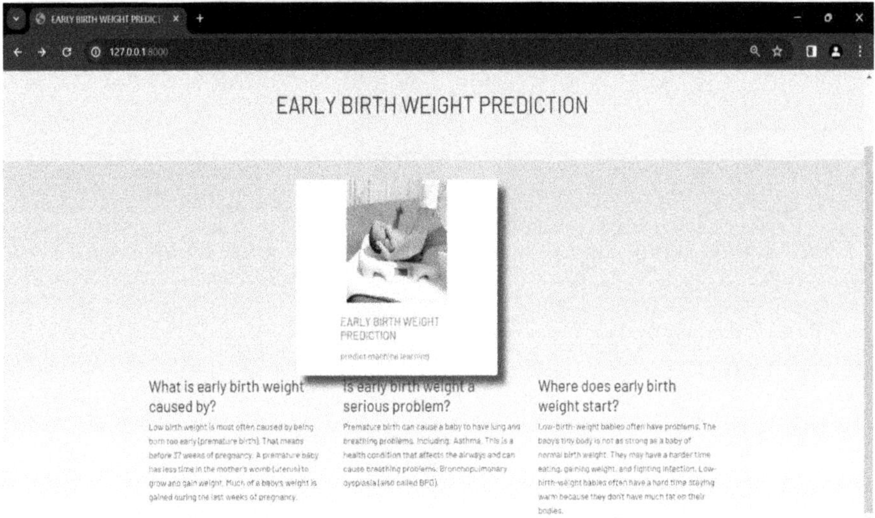

Fig. 5.3. Home Page

Fig. 4. Home Page

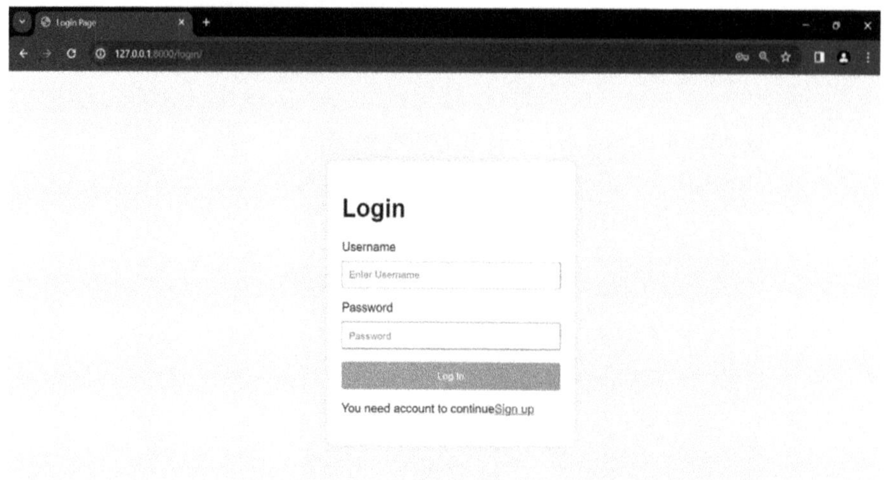

Fig. 5. Login Page

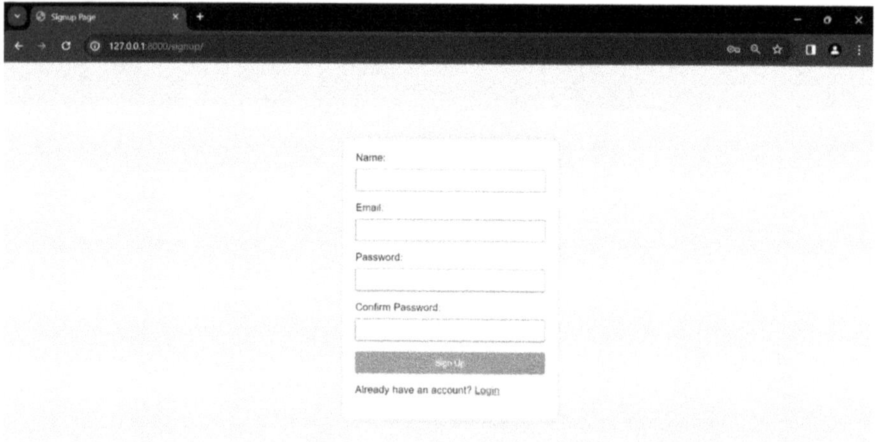

Fig. 6. Login Page

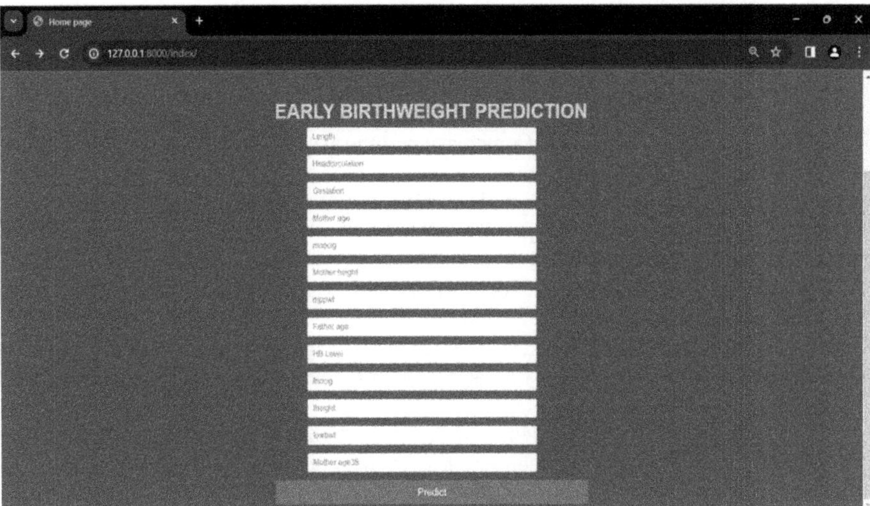

Fig. 7. Data entry Page

Fig. 8. Result Page

References

1. Faruk, A., Cahyono, E.S., Eliyati, N., Arifieni, I.: Prediction and classification of low birth weight data using machine learning techniques. Indones. J. Sci. Technol. **3**(1), 18–28 (2018)
2. Kuhle, S. et al.: Comparision of logistic regression with machine learning methods for the prediction of fetal growth abnormalities retrospective study. BMC Pregnancy Childbirth. **18**(1), 333 (2018)
3. Dahlui, M., Azahar, N., Oche, O.C., Aziz, N.A.: Risk factors for low birth weight in Nigeria: evidence from the 2013 Nigeria demographic and health survey. Glob. Health Action. (2016)
4. Firdaus, C., Wahyudin, W., Nugroho, E.P.: Monitoring system with two central facilities protocol. Indones. J. Sci. Technol. **2**(1), 8–25 (2017)

5. Yarlapati, A.R., Dey, S.R., Saha, S.: Early prediction of LBW cases via minimum error rate classifier: a statistical machine learning approach. In: 2017 IEEE International Conference on Smart Computing (SMARTCOMP) (2017)
6. Abdollahian, M., Gunaratne, N.: Low birth weight prediction based on maternal and fetal characteristics. In: 12th International Conference on Information Technology- New Generations (2015)
7. Moreira, J., Rodrigues, J. P. C., et al.: Fetal birth weight estimation in high-risk pregnancies through machine learning techniques(2019).
8. Ren, Y., Wu, D., Lopez-De Fede, A.: Identificationand prediction of low- birthweight baby outcomes and mom risk factors. In: IEEE 10th International Conference on Healthcare Informatics (ICHI) (2022)
9. Zaki, W., Khan, N., Masud, M.M., et al.: Infant birth weight estimation and low birth weight classification in the United Arab Emirates using machine learning algorithms. Sci. Rep. **12** (2022)
10. Cutland, C.L. et al.: Low birth weight: case definition & guidelines for data collection analysis and presentation of maternal immunization safety data. Vaccine. **35**, 6492–6500 (2017)
11. Hange, U., Selvaraj, R., Galani, M., Letsholo, K.: A data- mining model for predicting low birth weight with a high AUC. In: 16th IEEE/ACIS International Conference on Computer and Information Science (2018)
12. Mehrirejali, Mansourian, M., Babaei, Z., Eshrati, B.: Prediction of low birth weight delivery by maternal status and its validation: decision curve analysis. Int. J. Prev. Med. **8** (2017)

Analyzing Migraine Patterns Using Ensemble Learning: Machine Learning Techniques for Enhanced Diagnosis

Aditya Pandiarajan[(✉)], Chunduru Venkata Lakshmi Vaasavi, and G. Parimala

Department of Networking and Communications, School of Computing, SRM Institute of Science and Technology, Kattankulathur, India
`{ap7130,cl2952,parimalg}@srmist.edu.in`

Abstract. Migraine is a debilitating neurological disorder affecting millions of people worldwide; it has several forms, each requiring an accurate diagnosis for effective treatment. This work investigates the performance of various machine learning models in classifying migraine subtypes based on extensive clinical features. Herein, we utilized K-Nearest Neighbors (KNN), Decision Trees, MLP Classifiers, Support Vector Machines (SVM), Random Forests, Deep Neural Networks (DNN), and GridSearchCV-optimized versions of MLP and SVC. All the performance parameters, such as accuracy, precision, recall, and F1-score of the different models, are measured on a standardized dataset that includes features of a migraine. These will help us to find, through a great deal of experimentation, the most accurate and interpretable model for classifying migraines. Our results shall provide important insights into methods for the better diagnosis and hence treatment planning of migraineurs.

Keywords: Deep Neural Networks · K-Nearest Neighbors · Decision Trees · MLP Classifiers · Support Vector Machines · Random Forests

1 Introduction

Migraines are a prevalent and debilitating neurological illness characterized by excruciating headache pain that may significantly drain an individual's quality of life. Symptoms of nausea, light and sound sensitivity, and disturbances of vision may frequently accompany migraines and further cause pain and suffering for a patient. This is rendered far more difficult by the mere fact that there exist a number of types of migraine, each with different symptoms. Due to such uncertainty, the work of a doctor will also become challenging as they will be unable to diagnose a patient; this may lead to undetected or delayed diagnosis, with the treatment plan not being satisfactory to reduce the suffering of a patient. The dilemma also becomes worse as migraines may present themselves in different forms and also have different symptoms. As a result, this unpredictability sometimes poses a challenge to doctors because diagnoses may be missed, the diagnosis may be very late, and the treatment design does not alleviate the sufferings of the patients.

R. Appavoo et al. (Eds.): IconDeepCom 2024, CCIS 2687, pp. 303–315, 2026.
https://doi.org/10.1007/978-3-032-26680-4_24

This is an imperative task at the moment to build and implement advanced innovations that would now enable physicians to accurately identify the migraine subtypes. Machine-learning algorithms, because of latest technological breakthroughs, have become very effective instruments within the medical field. Actually, these algorithms have shown prominent results in regard to enhancing the clinical judgment and improving diagnostic accuracy for a very broad range of medical conditions.

Machine learning algorithms today are also masters of processing data-they can digest and analyze very complex medical data. Patient demographics, clinical characteristics of the patients, and historical trends of incidence of migraine allow huge data to be processed. So, machine learning algorithms can provide some insights through identification of intricate patterns and complexities in the data that other traditional diagnostic techniques might fail to reveal immediately. Especially regarding the migraine, the overlapping symptoms and changing symptoms make the criteria for diagnosis less clear.

They train algorithms on large datasets that contain very detailed patient information for the application of ML in migraine diagnosis. The information contained within these datasets can be widely varied in breadth, including attributes such as age, gender, genetic factors, lifestyle habits, and complete medical history. Learning from such data, therefore, gives ML models great predictive powers to classify different migraine subtypes with a very high level of accuracy. This ability to predict the various migraine subtypes would go a long way in helping healthcare providers focus more sharply on their diagnoses and produce better tailor-made treatment plans.

Besides that, the performance of the ML algorithm can be enhanced further as more patients data is made and are exposed to a wider variety of migraine events. This adjustment in the learning scheme would ensure that the diagnostic tools powered by ML keep up to date with the latest scientific knowledge and new trends in migraine research. This will also provide a better axis on which migrants can be diagnosed with migraines, possibly streamlining what could be done more efficiently. Conventional diagnostic routes use highly exhaustive clinical reviews and consultations from specialists. The resources taken up with the involvement of time is not very easy to afford. The swift way in which ML algorithms conduct analysis on the data presented on the patient and make suggested preliminary diagnoses is thus quicker for healthcare professionals.

With the realities of increased incidence of migraines and their resultant strain on quality of life, it becomes imperative to explore newer avenues for the diagnosis and treatment of migraine in its various forms. Machine learning algorithms could serve a very promising purpose in improving the accuracy and efficiency of migraine subtype diagnosis. By virtue of their high potential as sophisticated pattern analyzers of complex medical data, these revolutionary tools will assist in increasing the opportunity for patient-specific treatment to improve patient outcomes and tracks burdensome conditions.

2 Literature Review

By employing objective machine learning methods, we analyzed the symptoms revealed by patients and classified headache disorders [1]. We proved successful in automated classification by using our layered classifier model to categorize five core headache entities with an accuracy of 81%. This method provides a strong basis for further headache research.

[2] The prevalent neurovascular headache condition known as migraine causes incapacitating, recurrent attacks that usually start in infancy and get worse as people gets older. Prodromes, aura, throbbing pain, nausea, and sensitivity to stimuli are among the symptoms that point to abnormal neural activity. The pathophysiology of migraines is caused by genetic variables that affect glutamate neurotransmission, which in turn causes neuronal hyperexcitability and the activation of the trigeminovascular system.

[3] Discussing about Patients with nontraumatic headaches were assessed in an urban ED between 2004 and 2005 using structured interviews and inspections of medical records. Investigators in emergency care showed significant agreement in the diagnosis of main and secondary headaches among 480 patients. The most common forms of headaches were classified as tension-type headaches (11%), migraines (60%), and other headaches (26%). A sizeable fraction (36%) did not have a precise ICHD diagnosis because they were unable to differentiate between main and secondary headaches.

[4] This study used surface EMG data from the temporalis muscle to provide new diagnostic criteria for differentiating between migraine and chronic tension-type headache (CTTH). By applying nonlinear analysis and concentrating on entropy-based traits, the research discovered that negentropy was an efficient means of distinguishing between individuals with migraine, CTTH, and healthy individuals. The groups might also be visually distinguished with the use of bistrophoral analysis.

[5] This work presents a nonlinear parametric technique for automatically diagnosing migraines by extracting characteristics from EEG recordings. Using SVM, ANN, and RF classifiers, the system achieves 88% accuracy in detecting migraine sickness using data from SMS Hospital, Jaipur, India.

[6] It was observed that few individuals satisfied the criteria once chronic migraine (CM) and medication overuse headache (MOH) were added to ICHD-2 because of practical constraints. This research suggests more comprehensive criteria for both CM and MOH, proposing that continuous drug usage rather than improvement upon medication withdrawal is the necessary condition for MOH diagnosis.

[7] A migraine is a severe headache that is characterised by a sharp throbbing pain that usually affects just one side of the head. Other symptoms that may accompany a migraine include light and sound sensitivity and nausea. It is a very frequent primary headache disease that severely interferes with daily activities. This work addresses deep learning model-based migraine type prediction.

[8] A migraine is a severe headache that usually affects one side of the head and is followed by light and sound sensitivity, nausea, and vomiting. Hours or days may pass between migraine attacks, interfering with everyday tasks. Children, teenagers, and adults are frequently affected, and they move through prodrome, aura, headache, and post-drome stages. In this study, a deep learning model for migraine prediction is discussed.

[9] According to a research by Jama Network, 10% of people worldwide suffer from migraines, a terrible brain ailment that seriously impairs a person's capacity to function. When a migraine attacks, the pain in the head is so severe that the sufferers are unable to do their daily activities. As a result, it ranks as the ninth most common condition that can result in significant impairment. Thus, in order for migraine sufferers to receive prompt treatment, it is not only important to diagnose it early but also to determine the kind of migraine. Early disease prediction is supported by a number of machine learning applications in the medical field.

[10] Prolonged migraine is a neurovascular disease that produces excruciating pain and autonomic nervous system disruptions. EEG signal analysis helps in illness management and prognosis. This work suggests an automated migraine diagnostic method utilising EEG feature extraction that is nonlinear parametric. The accuracy of the classification using ANN, RF, and SVM classifiers was 88%.

[11] Recurrent, moderate to severe headaches are the hallmark of migraine, a chronic neurological illness that also causes symptoms in the brain and autonomic nervous system. Using resting-state EEG power, this study attempts to categorise migraine phases in order to facilitate early identification, especially for low-frequency migraineurs. The SONFIN classifier attains an accuracy rate of 66%, enabling migraineurs to receive prompt treatment.

[12] Recurrent, moderate to severe headaches are the hallmark of migraine, a chronic neurological illness that also causes symptoms in the brain and autonomic nervous system. The purpose of this research is to use EEG power in a resting condition to create a categorization system for migraine phases. With a 66% accuracy rate, the SONFIN classifier helps migraine sufferers receive early identification and treatment.

[13] Migraine is a painful brain illness with no known cause that affects around 23% of the population and no automated diagnostic procedure. Studies investigate the use of triggering stimuli, such as flash stimulation, to identify migraineurs by analysing variations in EEG data. In order to evaluate classification techniques for automated diagnosis, this study uses EEG data from migraine sufferers and healthy individuals stimulated by flashes.

[14] For migraine treatment to be effective, it is important to accurately diagnose this common kind of headache. This study develops a fuzzy expert system for migraine detection by utilising fuzzy logic, which is recognised for its capacity to handle imprecise characteristics. The system outperforms human expert systems in terms of effectiveness, achieving high accuracy (97%) after being trained with 148 patients using the LFE algorithm.

[15] New diagnostic criteria would involve differentiating between migraine and CTTH (chronic tension-type headache) using nonlinear analysis of temporalis muscle surface EMG data. Negentropy was found to be the most important factor within NBE differentiation for migraine versus CTTH; bistrophoral analysis was able to distinguish groups visually.

This study aims to create new diagnostic criteria that would differentiate migraine from chronic tension-type headache (CTTH) using nonlinear analysis of surface EMG data from the temporalis muscle [15]. It emphasized the seriousness of the application of NBE for the differentiation of migraine and CTTH. Results indicated that negentropy served as the primary distinguishing factor across the three groups. In addition, bistrophoral analysis was able to separate them visually.

3 System Architecture and Design

Once the data source has been finalized, plenty of unrefined raw data will be present. It is from these data sources that the raw data for training and evaluating machine learning models are retrieved. This could be everything from survey responses to patient medical records to anything else that might relate to symptom reporting, triggers, demographics about patients, and medical history in migraine cases. Quality and extent are the metrics that determine effectiveness for machine learning models (Fig. 1).

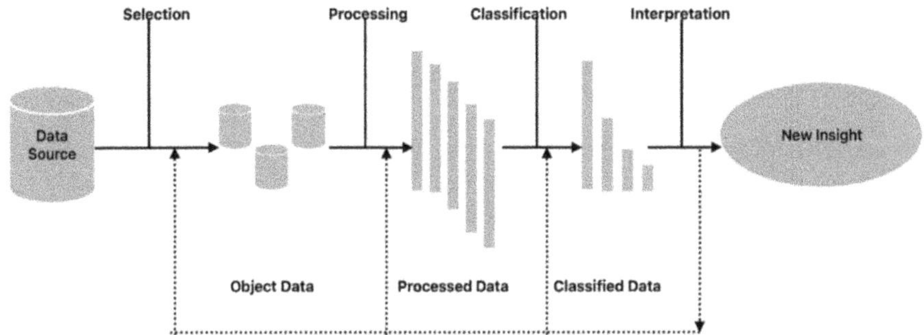

Fig. 1 System Architecture

In this step, the filtering of the raw data is done to select the features which proficiently help in the classification of migraine. It would involve feature selection based on the importance analysis of features, or using domain expertise, and removal of redundant data. Features can be considered, including a patient's demographics, past medical history, associated symptoms, triggers, frequency and intensity of migraine attacks, and many more relevant data.

This will involve the preprocessing of the selected data so that it is machine learning-ready. This will involve encoding categorical variables, scaling numerical features, and handling missing values. Preprocessing is the way to make data ready and standardized so that it can be fed into different machine learning algorithms.

It is going to entail furnishing the selected data for machine learning. Management of missing values, scaling of numerical features, and encoding of categorical variables will form part of the actions that will be involved. Preprocessing is the likely step to take in preparation and standardization of data in processing so that it can then be fed to different machine learning algorithms.

At this stage, the targeted model's outputs will then be analyzed to identify the aspects that influence its judgments. This would be another stage toward understanding the rationale of the model and could subsequently be a step toward developing a treatment plan. Interpretability techniques such as feature importance analysis; SHAP values;

LIME; and others can then be applied to establish how the model generates its predictions and what features turn out as most important.

The following is an attempt at the final goal of a new face in migraine classification, further diagnosis and treatment of migraine. Discoveries would include identifying important features or patterns for specific migraine subtypes; finding interesting interactions between different features of patients and their migraine symptomatology; and identification of novel factors affecting the frequency and intensity of attacks. This would enhance the clinician's ability to plan more individualized and effective treatment of migraines.

Overall Purpose: The system uses machine learning techniques in order to classify migraine subtypes based on the patient's data.

4 Methodology

Data Acquisition and Preprocessing

- **Source of Information:** Patient surveys, research data or a medical database for migraine information.
- **Preprocessing:** Fill the gap from missing values using appropriate imputation techniques such as mean, interpolation etc.
- **Irregularities:** Resolve all possible inconsistencies existing between the variables in addition to the standardization of data formats. Employ Z-score and IQR statistical techniques to identify outliers and take necessary action regarding removal or conversion.
- **Cleaning:** Data quality; delete duplicate entries; correct erroneous entries owing to data entry.
- **Scale Numerical Features:** All numerical entries should be normalized or standardized so that they differ by scale.

Feature Engineering

- **Reduction dimension:** This is the process whereby the significant features that best describe a dataset are reduced while retaining a considerable amount of information.
- Techniques used include PCA, t-distributed stochastic neighbour embedding, among others, to mention a few.
- **Interaction features:** Combine of existing features for example to capture non-linear relations polynomial features, interaction terms.

Machine Learning Model Selection and Training: Choose appropriate machine learning models for migraine classification based on your data characteristics and research objectives. The description suggests potentially using DNN, KNN, Decision Tree, MLP, SVM, and Random Forest. Train each model on a partitioned dataset, typically splitting it into training, validation, and testing sets. Tune hyperparameters for each model using techniques like grid search or randomized search to optimize performance.

Model Evaluation and Comparison: Evaluate the performance of each trained model on the validation set using metrics like accuracy, precision, recall, F1-score, and potentially interpretability measures.

Compare the performance metrics across all models to identify the one with the best balance of accuracy and interpretability for your specific needs.

Model Interpretation (Optional)

- To comprehend the elements impacting the model's categorization choices, use interpretation techniques like feature importance analysis or visualization techniques.
- Learn about the logic behind the approach to help with clinical decision-making.

Deployment and Application (Optional)

- Think about incorporating the selected model into a patient or healthcare provider's web or mobile application.
- Provide users with the ability to enter pertinent data and obtain anticipated migraine classifications, facilitating prompt and convenient decision assistance.

These procedures will help you approach migraine categorization methodically while maintaining accuracy, interpretability, and clinical practice relevance—from data collection to model deployment.

5   Results and Discussions

The distribution of migraine subtypes in the research population is shown in Fig. 2.

The distribution of migraine subtypes in a research population is depicted in the pie chart you submitted, but it does not provide the precise percentages of each migraine subtype. Below is a summary of the various subtypes of migraines indicated in the pie chart:

- Common Aura with Migraine: This is the most prevalent kind of aura with migraine. It is distinguished by visual disturbances that happen either before or during a headache, such as flashing lights, zigzag lines, or a brief loss of vision [2].
- About 70% of migraine sufferers get headaches without aura, which is the most prevalent kind of migraine [2]. This kind of migraine does not cause aura symptoms in its sufferers.
- Familial Hemiplegic Migraine: This uncommon kind of migraine also produces numbness or weakness on one side of the body. The ailment is inherited and runs in families [2].
- Sporadic Hemiplegic Migraine: This uncommon kind of migraine does not result from a hereditary disorder; instead, it causes weakness or numbness on one side of the body in addition to headaches [2].

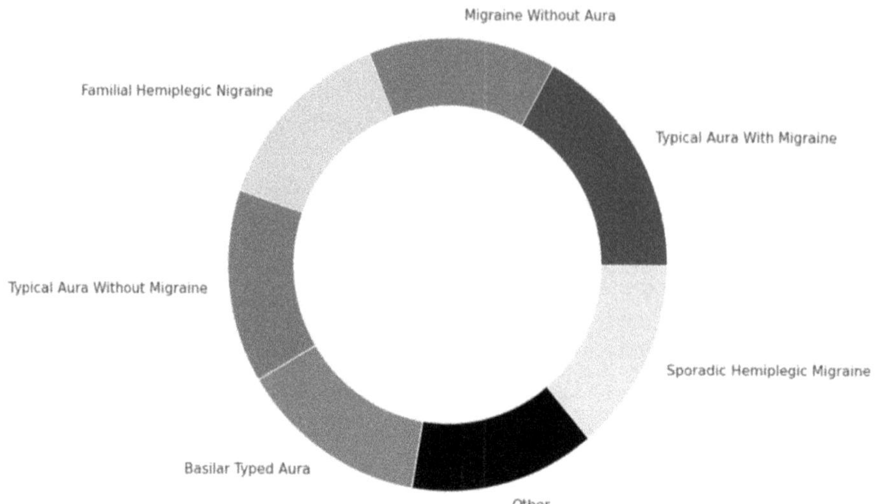

Fig. 2 Migraine classification

- A migraine aura known as the basilar type affects the brainstem, the area of the brain responsible for vital processes including digestion, breathing, and heart rhythm. Dizziness, vertigo, slurred speech, tinnitus (ear ringing), and double vision are some of the symptoms of basilar type aura [2].
- The unusual illness known as "Typical Aura Without Migraine" results in visual abnormalities similar to those caused by "Typical aura with migraine," but without the headache [2].
- previous: This group probably contains additional uncommon migraine subtypes that do not easily fit into any of the previous classifications.

It is significant to remember that each person's experience with a migraine can be unique and quite complex. While some people may only encounter one kind of migraine, others may encounter multiple varieties. Individual differences might also be seen in the symptoms of migraines.

Further points regarding migraines are as follows:

- A neurological disorder called migraines can produce excruciating headaches in addition to other symptoms including light and sound sensitivity and nausea.
- Women experience migraines more frequently than men do.
- Although there isn't a cure for migraines, there are therapies that can lessen or avoid their intensity Fig. 3.

This Image boxplot examination of the age distribution among the different migraine subtypes is shown in Fig. 2. The data suggests that 'Migraine without Aura' and 'Typical Aura with Migraine' have a larger age range, indicating that both subtypes are more prevalent in a variety of age groups. To fully understand the age-related prevalence and its consequences, more research is required.

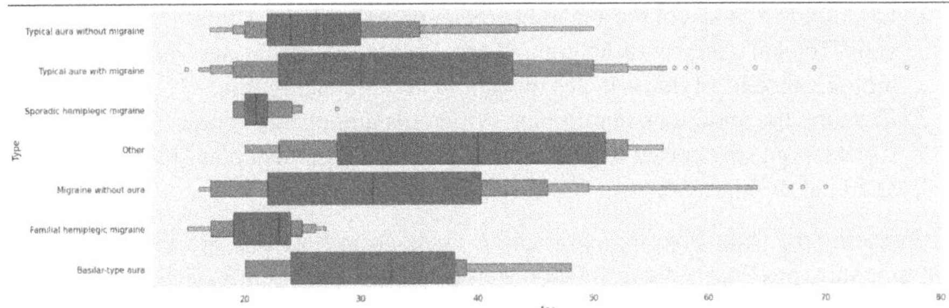

Fig. 3 Boxplot analysis of age distribution

- Boxplots: By displaying the following, a boxplot can statistically describe the distribution of numerical data [1]:

  1. The data set's median, or center line
  2. The data set is divided into four equal sections by the top and lower quartiles. The middle 50% of the data points are represented by the box in the plot, and the median is indicated by the line in the middle.
  3. The boxplot's upper and lower tails, also known as whiskers, reach the farthest data points within an interval of 1.5 times the interquartile range (IQR) between the quartiles. Outliers are defined as data points that fall outside of these whiskers.

- **Age Distribution and Migraine:** Based on the graphic you submitted, it appears that different migraine subtypes have different age distributions. When it comes to migraines, age can play a big role. Women are more likely than males to get migraines, which are most frequent in adults between the ages of 18 and 44 [2]. But migraines can strike at any age, even in later life and throughout childhood [2].

- **Understanding the Boxplot in Relation to the Different Types of Migraine:** Here's one possible interpretation of the image based on our understanding of boxplots and the age distribution of migraines:

  1. The boxplot most likely displays the range of ages as well as the median age for individuals with various migraine subtypes.
  2. When compared to the other subtypes, the larger boxes for "Migraine without Aura" and "Typical Aura with Migraine" indicate a greater range of ages in these two groups. This may suggest that these subtypes are more prevalent in different age groups.
  3. People who fall outside the usual age range for their migraine subtype are known as outliers, and their presence may be indicated by the whiskers extending from the boxes.

- **Constraints of a Single Image:** It's critical to remember that this is only one image and that it might not accurately depict all migraineurs. To validate these results and gain a deeper comprehension of the correlation between age and migraine subtypes, additional study is required.

- **Additional Research on Migraine and Age:** The following areas may benefit from additional research on migraine and age:

1. Examine the causes of the apparent greater prevalence of "Migraine without Aura" and "Typical Aura with Migraine" throughout a broader age range. Exist any biological or lifestyle variables that could be influencing this?
2. Examine the variations in migraine symptoms among age groups.
3. Create more specialised migraine preventive and treatment plans based on the age and kind of migraine.

Interestingly, your boxplot suggests an association between age distribution and migraine subtypes. Further investigation would confirm the findings and help understand this better in migrainers across ages.
Consider the following:

The boxplot does not indicate how many patients belong to each subtype of migraine. It is important to know this when interpreting the results.
The boxplot does not display the severity of migraine in the subtype. Some age groups may differ in terms of the seriousness of migraine they experience with respect to certain subtypes.

One-in-all boxplot says that there is some probable connection between age distribution and the different migraine subtypes. Further research would be necessary to confirm these results while having a more detailed description of the local age-related differences in migraine.
Other considerations include:

The boxplot doesn't provide the sample size belonging to each migraine subtype, which is important to know when evaluating the results.
The boxplot doesn't provide severity of migraine in each subtype. Some subtypes may display more severe occurrences in some age groups.

There is evidence in your boxplot to suggest that there is a relationship between age distribution and migraine subtypes. It will probably need some further investigation to establish these findings and broaden the understanding of migraine across age groups. Other considerations include the following:

The boxplot does not allow us to obtain the sample size of each subtype of migraine. It should be known when interpreting the results.
The boxplot does not show the severity of migraine for the different subtypes. It is possible that some age groups experience more serious attacks of certain migraine subtypes.

6   Conclusion

Healthcare and personalized treatment have advanced significantly with the investigation of machine learning algorithms for the classification of migraine subtypes based on extensive clinical parameters. In order to effectively classify migraine subtypes, this study investigated the potential of a number of algorithms, including Random Forests, MLP Classifiers, K-Nearest Neighbours (KNNs), Decision Trees, Deep Neural Networks (DNNs), and optimized MLP and SVC variations. By using a standardized dataset, these models may be rigorously assessed based on measures like accuracy, precision, recall, and F1-score. From the variety of models analyzed, the research identified the most precise and comprehensible methods for classifying migraines. After conducting thorough evaluations, some models were found to be especially promising for this purpose. These selected models, which will be discussed in a moment, not only showed exceptional accuracy, but also a degree of interpretability that is essential for therapeutic use. In healthcare contexts, interpretability of machine learning models is critical, as doctors depend on intelligible insights to make well-informed decisions regarding patient care. The model identification perfectly for migraine types has great prospects in aiding diagnosis improvement and, therefore, in individualizing treatment. Using some of the above models, clinicians are expected to better appreciate different subtypes of migraine conditions and, therefore, maximize treatment outcomes for the patients. Indeed, the interpretability analysis in this work uncovers basic mechanisms underlying classification decisions and, thus, helps practitioners make informed therapeutic choices. This advancement in migraine classification indeed opens up new avenues of advanced diagnostic methodology that will in turn affect personalized medicine: that is, more and more individualized treatments become successful and valuable as they improve outcomes. There well might be further individualization possible for this disease since particular characteristics shape each individual's experiences. Deep neural networks have been the hallmark in migraine classification. They fit very well in dealing with multidimensional, very complicated data and, therefore, will be able to investigate a broad range of clinical features related to the diverse subtypes of migraine. Besides, high dimensional data may also show deep hidden patterns in the data, which allow such data classification to have excellent accuracy levels, even if it is under unclear or non-linear connections of the various features. While optimization works on the DNN structure, the accuracy in classifying therefore was better improved, thus proving more prospective to act as a successful component for the classification of migraine subtypes. Above all, support vector machines also supported the findings very strongly through their performance compared to the DNN. The SVM is one of the best and optimized classification model methods. Another key model aside from DNN and SVM in migraine subtyping is decision trees. The main reasons supporting decision trees for this are their very understandable rules from which decisions can be made crisply, partitioning, rationing, and driving into areas. This would very well be carried out in all clinical reasoning because the interpretation is based on developing a framework necessary to understand by a clinician the classification findings. Decision trees support small misses and are heterogeneous in nature, thus making it also practically usable for healthcare scenarios. Finally, though DNN, SVM, and decision trees seemed great, rigorous investigations have included them here as important models for migraine subtyping and many of them as high in application according to the usage done in machine learning models. Such state-of-the-art models, apart from providing accurate results, will contribute interpretability under the heading of keys pertaining to clinical adoption and application. Logically, this can be claimed by better outcomes for patients with and their health productive practices. Herewith, it is identified that treatments will be appropriately tailored as per the specific individual requirements for persons, which will be possible with correctly identifying the different subtypes. A very simple model on how Machine Learning set to change Personalized medicine while improving patient quality in different arenas.

References

1. Kwon, J., Lee, H., Cho, S., et al.: Machine learning- based automated classification of headache disorders using patient-reported questionnaires. Sci. Rep. **10**, 14062 (2020). https://doi.org/10.1038/s41598-020-70992-1
2. Burstein, R., Noseda, R., Borsook, D.: Migraine: multiple processes, complex pathophysiology. J. Neurosci. **35**(17), 661929 (2015). https://doi.org/10.1523/JNEUROSCI.037315.2015. PD:25926442;PMCID: PMC4412887
3. Friedman, B.W. et al.: Applying the international classification of headache disorders to the emergency department: an assessment of reproducibility and the frequency with which a unique diagnosis can be assigned to every acute headache presentation. Ann. Emerg. Med. **49**(4), 409–419 (2007)
4. Biyouki, F., Rahati, S., Laimi, K., Boostani, R., Shoeibi, A.: Differentiation between migraine without aura and chronic tension-type headache based on HOS analysis of sEMG signals. In: 2013 21st Iranian Conference on Electrical Engineering (ICEE), Mashhad, Iran, pp. 1–6 (2013). https://doi.org/10.1109/IranianCEE.2013.6599575
5. Jindal, K., et al.: Migraine disease diagnosis from EEG signals using non-linear feature extraction technique. In: 2018 IEEE International Conference on Computational Intelligence and Computing Research (ICCIC), Madurai, India, pp. 1–4 (2018). https://doi.org/10.1109/ICCIC.2018.8782341
6. Olesen, J., Bousser, M.-G., Diener, H.-C., et al.: New appendix criteria open for a broader concept of chronic migraine. Cephalalgia. **26**(6), 742–746 (2006). https://doi.org/10.1111/j.1468-2982.2006.01172.x
7. Jalannavar, A., Kanakaraddi, S.G., Handur, V.S.: Migraine prediction using deep learning model. In: 2022 Fourth International Conference on Emerging Research in Electronics, Computer Science and Technology (ICERECT), Mandya, India, pp. 1–8 (2022). https://doi.org/10.1109/ICERECT56837.2022.10059843
8. Jalannavar, A., Kanakaraddi, S.G., Handur, V.S.: Migraine prediction using deep learning model. In: 2022 Fourth International Conference on Emerging (2022)
9. Gulati, K.G., Goyal, N.: Classification of migraine disease using supervised machine learning. In: 2022 10th International Conference on Reliability,Infocom - Technologies and Optimization (Trends and Future Directions) (ICRITO), Noida, India, p. 17 (2022). https://doi.org/10.1109/ICRITO56286.2022.9964524
10. Jindal, et al.: Migraine disease diagnosis from EEG signals using non-linear feature extraction technique. In: 2018 IEEE International Conference on Computational Intelligence and Computing Research (ICCIC), Madurai, India, pp. 1–4 (2018). https://doi.org/10.1109/ICCIC.2018.8782341
11. H. Cao, L. -W. Ko, K. -L. Lai, S. -B. Huang, S. -J. Wang and C. -T. Lin, Classification of migraine stages based on resting-state EEG power, 2015 International Joint Conference on Neural Networks (IJCNN), Killarney, Ireland, 2015, pp. 1–5, https://doi.org/10.1109/IJCNN.2015.7280582.
12. Sayyari, E., Farzi, M., Estakhrooeieh, R.R., Samiee, F., Shamsollahi, M.B.: Migraine analysis through EEG signals with classification approach. In: 2012 11th International Conference on Information Science, Signal Processing and their Applications (ISSPA). Montreal QC, Canada, pp. 859–863 (2012). https://doi.org/10.1109/ISSPA.2012.6310674
13. Akben, S.B., Subaşı, A., Kıymık, M.K.: Comparison of artificial neural network and support vector machine classification methods in diagnosis of migraine by using EEG. In: 2010 IEEE 18th Signal Processing and Communications Applications Conference, Diyarbakir, Turkey, pp. 637–640 (2010). https://doi.org/10.1109/SIU.2010.5651470

14. Khayamnia, M., Yazdchi, M., Vahidiankamyad, A., Foroughipour, M.: The recognition of migraine headache by designation of fuzzy expert system and usage of LFE learning algorithm. In: 2017 5th Iranian Joint Congress on Fuzzy and Intelligent Systems (CFIS), Qazvin, Iran, pp. 50–53 (2017). https://doi.org/10.1109/CFIS.2017.8003656
15. Biyouki, F., Rahati, S., Laimi, K., Boostani, R., Shoeibi, A.: Differentiation between migraine without aura and chronic tension-type headache based on HOS analysis of sEMG signals. In: 2013 21st Iranian Conference on Electrical Engineering (ICEE), Mashhad, Iran, p. 16 (2013). https://doi.org/10.1109/IranianCEE.2013.659955

Machine Learning-Based Forecasting of River Water Quality: Emphasis on Regression and Ensemble Models

V. Karpagam$^{(\boxtimes)}$ and S. Christy

SIMATS School of Engineering, Saveetha Institute of Medical and Technical Sciences, Thandalam, Chennai, India
`{karpagamv1009.sse,christys.sse}@saveetha.com`

Abstract. Biochemical and human-made pollution of river water can introduce water discharges to potentially toxic diseases. Forecasting is an alternative approach for watershed management that identifies numerous restrictions related to conventional traditional approaches to evaluating the quality of water. Artificial intelligence algorithms and machine learning (ML) approaches have been broadly and successfully used to classify the decision-making issues such as more inconsistent behavior through one year or river to the next. As a result, the perfect approach for machine learning varied based on the river and the year, helping to make methodology challenging. This work compares performances of the different ML approaches referred to as a model and their corresponding output of four widely used machine learning models (multiple linear regression (MLR), partial least square regression (PLSR), random forest (RF), and ensemble random forest (ERF)) were compared and identifies the more accurate final prediction. Applying this model to various rivers situated all over India, we demonstrate that the Linear Regression algorithm was able to produce reliably good predictions of river water quality compared to all of the other approaches. Performances of the above mentioned models were tested by calculating the value of Root Mean Square Error (RMSE). The accuracy levels consistently stayed every year, with accuracy of 96.06%, 99.99%, 94.49%, and 93.6% at the ensemble random forest, multiple linear regressions, partial least square, and random forest regression respectively. The RMSE value of these models was 53.71, 1.14, 68.5, and 50.67 respectively. This work evaluates the significance of the linear regression approach in forecasting the water quality of Indian Rivers and resolving other demanding ecological issues.

Keywords: Water Quality · Linear Regression · Root mean square error · Random Forest · machine learning

1 Introduction

River water quality is a principal environmental problem influencing both the health of individuals and the conservation of natural ecosystems. River-polluted water from physicochemical and human-made sources can introduce water overflows to highly

R. Appavoo et al. (Eds.): IconDeepCom 2024, CCIS 2687, pp. 316–327, 2026.
https://doi.org/10.1007/978-3-032-26680-4_25

harmful diseases. Conventional techniques to evaluate the quality of the water have significant drawbacks, triggering the rise of novel methods such as forecasting using machine learning algorithms. Water quality indices (WQI) were originally discussed in 1965 [6], but the methods of calculating WQI did not focus until the 1970s. The commonality of WQI involves two levels to determine. The initial test center parameters are collected from different stations and are reformed into a less unit range of sub-index categories. At last, the calculated sub-indices are cumulated to get a WQI result. The Oregon Unweighted Harmonic WQI [7] was developed by the Oregon Department of Environmental Quality [25] for the contribution of people in broadcasting and inspecting water quality levels and leanings [8]. The index has brought back consideration because of advances in computer peripherals practicability and productivity, and also a necessity for easily comprehensible water quality information. According to a study of the literature, index makers have benefited from better information about stream performance [9–14]. The Oregon WQI is not suitable to determine all health issues. The Oregon WQI was initiated particularly for Oregon (US state) water points, consequently deploying it to alternative sources of water sources should be done with care [15].

Four base models such as MLR, PLSR, RF, and Bayesian Network were predicted accurately in water quality due to their high popularity and performance [1]. The effect of human contamination in the water sources of the Ganga river stations situated in India using machine learning algorithms and comparison of the performance of different models, including decision trees, random_forest, artificial_neural_network, and support_vector_machine, found that random forest had the best prediction accuracy [2]. Partial least squares regression (PLSR) was applied to predict water contamination accurately. The PLSR prediction algorithm is very fast and simple and has a better short-term prediction impact. But this algorithm needs large historical data as a training set and has higher constraints for the distribution of water potability changes [3]. The researchers used ERFR to predict water quality factors in India. This study identified that the ERFR algorithm outstripped other algorithms, including support vector regression and artificial neural network, in the forecasting of the quality variables in water bodies [4]. A research paper identified the multiple linear regressions to forecast the water potability of the River in India. This study demonstrated that multiple linear regressions was able to accurately forecast the water quality parameters of the river, and recognised key parameters that added to water quality deterioration [5]. These studies determine the capability of ML techniques in forecasting water quality variables in rivers and focus on the significance of selecting the suitable algorithm for a particular river and year. The use of ML techniques can provide valuable insights for watershed management and give suggestions for the development of effective precautionary actions to improve water quality. This work compares the performances of the different machine learning approaches referred to as models and their corresponding output of four ML models such as MLR, PLSR, RF, and ERF were compared and identifies the more accurate final prediction. Applying this approach to various rivers situated all over India, the Performances of these algorithms were tested by calculating the value of Root Mean Square Error (RMSE). The majority of research shows that changes in water potability are generated by changes in the chemical properties of water. The current inquiry on water quality, which is guided by factors based on the water's chemical composition, was inspired by these findings.

2 Materials and Methods

In this work the accurate prediction of water quality of various rivers in India by utilizing four machine learning models, namely MLR, PLSR, RF, and ERF to forecast river water quality in India. Regression algorithms are very familiar with finding the independent and dependent variables correlation analysis, therefore regression algorithms help to predict pollution accurately in water bodies. The study used Root Mean Square Error (RMSE) to verify the accuracy of the algorithms. The study tested the models' performance using river water quality data from various rivers located throughout India. The following Fig. 1 explains the proposed modules of this research. The implementations are done by the computer had 1 TB SSD, 12GB RAM, and 2GB Intel graphics memory installed. Python software was used to implement the coding for the ML Algorithms.

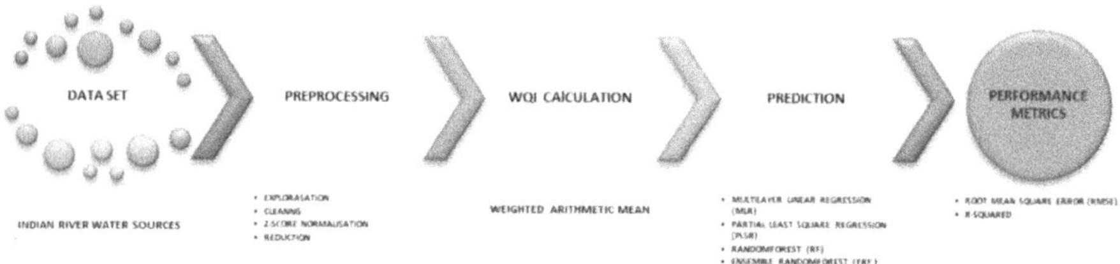

Fig. 1. Overall architecture of proposed methodology

2.1 Data Collection

The data utilised in this work was collected from a few significant Indian historical stations. It contains 1900 water samples and 12 attributes such as station code, locations, state, temperature (temp), dissolved oxygen (DO), pH, conductivity (Cond.), biological oxygen demand (BOD), nitratenan n + nitritenan (NI), fecal coliform (fec_coli), total coliform (tot-coli), and year. The information is gathered from various water supply bodies in India to guarantee the standard of the distributed drinking water. The dataset was downloaded from a database maintained by the open-source Kaggle data repository. Python 3 Jupyter Notebook was used to process and predict the results of data. The computational exploration was implemented using an Intel core i5 Processor system, 1 TB SSD, 12 GB RAM, and 2 GB Intel graphics memory installed.

2.2 Data Preprocessing

For accurate prediction of water quality has been done by using various preprocessing methods such as data exploration, data scrubbing, data normalisation, and data dimensionality reduction. Data exploration is used to change the data types corresponding to the parameter prediction algorithms shown in Table 1 [20]. Data cleaning is done by filling null values with the median of the corresponding attribute and also the objects are filled with the respective station code and states. Then Z-score normalisation was used to normalise the measured data values and also used to locate the outliers regarding the parameters standards identified from the data set. Finally the plotting Probability Density Function for the numeric values in the data set to identify the correlation and reduce the dimensionality of the selected parameters list for accurate prediction.

Table 1. Parameters List with its corresponding computational data types and data category [20]

Parameter List	Data Types	Data category
STATION CODE	Obj	Text
LOCATIONS	Obj	Text
STATE	Obj	Text
Temp.	Flt64	Decimal
DO.	Flt64	mg/L
pH.	Flt64	Decimal
Cond.	Flt64	mhos/cm
BOD.	Flt64	mg/L
NI.	Flt64	(mpn/100 mL) Mean
fec_col.	Flt64	mpn/100 mL
tot_col.	Flt64	(mpn/100 mL) Mean
year	int64	Integer

2.3 Water Quality Index (WQI)

Parameter identifications are the first and foremost criteria for calculating a WQI using a scientific estimation technique. Parameter values are rescaled after the raw data is collected from monitoring stations. For scaling, more statistical technologies can be employed. Different categories of parameters have unique units and a range of values. These parameter values are all rescaled to a range of less units and the calculation of sub-index values is the outcome of the rescaling process. Each conditional property of parameters has a unique weight according to their measured range of parameters and potential causes on water potability. To assign weightage, a researcher's valuation is needed. The values of the sub-index are utilized to calculate an estimated value of WQI. At last, the river water quality is first evaluated and then predicted [16]. Multiple numbers of water sample models it very hard to evaluate accurate calculations on water potability parameters [15]. In this work, Weighted Arithmetic Mean WQI (WQIWAM) is proposed to measure the water quality index of the water samples measured from the Indian Rivers [25]. The following Eqs. 1–4 show calculations of WQI which is modeled to identify the quality of water accurately.

$$\text{WAMWQI} = \frac{\sum_{x=1}^{n} W_x R_x}{\sum_{x=1}^{n} W_x} \tag{1}$$

Here,

W_x - The unit weight of xth parameter
S_x – Sub-Index estimate range of xth parameter,
S_x is determined with the following equation

$$R_i = 100 \times \frac{M_x - M_{Ideal}}{SD_x - M_{Ideal}} \tag{2}$$

Here,

M_X - x^{th} parameter measured value from the monitoring station
M_{Ideal} - Ideal value of xth parameter in clean water
S_x - Standard value for x^{th} parameter referred from WHO
W_x is determined by the following equation

$$W_x = \frac{K}{S_x} \tag{3}$$

Here K is the proportionality constant, which is calculated by the following equation

$$K = \frac{1}{\sum_{x=1}^{n} SD_x} \tag{4}$$

Standard values recommended for parameters (SD_x) are shown in Table 2. The predictions of accurate water quality are calculated by using the variables (K), with the measures of SD and Measured Ideal criteria of each parameter recognised by the World Health Organization (WHO). The ideal value (M_{ideal}) for all the quality parameters value is 0 except the value of DO is 14.6 and pH is 7.0. Values of unit weights for each parameter (W_i) are calculated by using the equations from 2 to 4 as shown in Table 3.

Table 2. Parameters List with its corresponding Standard value with reference from WHO [17]

Parameters	Standard Value (WHO)
DO	10 mg/L
pH	8.5
Cond.	1000 μS/cm
BOD	5 mg/L
NI	45 mg/L
Fec_coli/100 mL	100 ml
Tot_coli/100 mL	1000 ml

Table 3. Parameters List with its corresponding calculated Weightage

Parameters	Calculated Weight (Wi)
DO	0.2213
pH	0.2604
Cond.	0.0022
BOD	0.4426
NI	0.0492
Fec_coli/100 mL	0.0221
Tot_coli/100 mL	0.0022

2.4 Prediction Algorithms

Each algorithm for machine learning creation may be separated into the streamlined and algorithmic set of tasks outlined below. All models used for machine learning must perform these tasks. According to the convolution and type of technique used, definite algorithms may have additional tasks to be executed for those model development, model memorisation, model learning technique, and model processing [18].

Random Forest Algorithm

Random forest regression (RFR) is a ML algorithm that interoperates multiple decision trees to implement a more accurate model for identifying continuous values of parameters. In this study, RFR starts the work from Data Preparation which is the first step to preprocess the data for training the algorithms [21]. This includes removing missing values, encoding categorical variables, and splitting the data into training and validating sets. Next decision tree training process by building multiple decision trees on different subsets of the training data. Each decision tree is modeled by randomly selected input features and training data. Finally, voting has been done after the decision trees are trained, they are used to make predictions on the testing data. Each tree in the forest outputs a numerical prediction, and the final prediction of the WQI is evaluated by taking the average of all the individual tree predictions. The RFR predicts the accurate WQI by using multiple parameter values of water monitoring stations and the different decisions are taken by the multiple Decision trees, and final prediction methods are calculated the accurate value by voting techniques. In this study, WQI is calculated and the final dataset is split into train and test datasets.

Ensemble Learning

Ensemble Random Forest Regression (ERFR) uses ensemble learning to combine the predictions of multiple decision trees. This work creates the model trained on multiple decision trees and the output of each tree is combined to generate a final prediction of WQI. And finally, this study used hyperparameter tuning for RFR has several hyperparameters that are adjusted for improving the performance of the ERFR. Hyperparameters such as the number of input features and decision trees in the forest, and the maximum depth of the decision trees to consider at each level are tuned to optimize the algorithm performances [22]. Data D was trained by the model created by RFR called D1 and this D1 was used for the input of the same RFR model up to D100 estimations to improve the accuracy of the prediction of water quality level. The workflow of ERFR is shown in the Fig. 2.

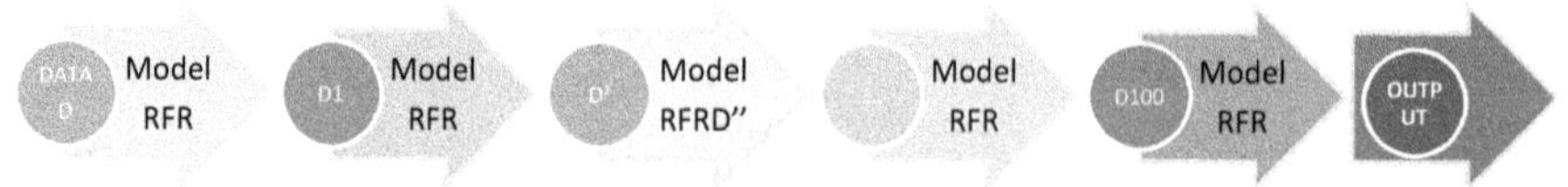

Fig. 2. Working principle of ERFR

Linear Regression

The process of gradient descent begins with randomly assigned values for every coefficient. The cumulative squared error values are calculated for every set of dependent and independent parameter values using a corresponding constant factor known as the learning rate, and the coefficients are rescaled to optimize the error [19]. This rescaling is iterated to reach the minimum sum squared error is achieved or no further improvements can be made. To develop a linear regression model that can accurately predict WQI, this work utilized multiple inputs, weightage computation, and activation functions with error corrections. The water quality dependent and independent parameters are trained and tested using a validating data set and computed accuracy measures to evaluate its performance to predict level WQI for river water sources in India. The study also explored the cross-validation data splitting approach.

Partial Least Square Algorithm

Partial Least Squares (PLS) is a multivariate statistical algorithm that is widely used in regression analysis and data modeling. PLS is used to find the relationship between dependent and independent sets of variables [26], known as Y and X, and it is particularly useful when there are a large number of predictor variables or when the variables are highly correlated. PLS works by developing a set of new variables, called latent variables or factors, which are linear integrations of the Ideal predictor variables [23]. The first factor is calculated in such a way that it explains as much of the variation in both the X and Y variables as possible. The second factor is then calculated to explain as much of the remaining variation in both sets of variables as possible, and so on until all factors have been calculated. Once the factors have been calculated, the PLS algorithm is used to calculate the Y variables based on the X variables. This is done by regression of the X variables onto the factors, and then regression of the factors onto the Y variables. The final prediction is obtained by multiplying the X scores by the regression coefficients and adding the Y intercept.

Performance Evaluation

Finally, the validation of RFR, ERFR, MLR, and PLSR models was evaluated using performance metrics like the Root Mean Squared Error (RMSE) and R-Squared (R2) value [24]. These metrics provide insight into the performance level of the model that is predicting the target variable. RMSE is a measure of the mean deviation from the measured to the predicted values of the dependent variable. It is calculated as the square root of the mean of all the observed stations, squared differences between the actual and predicted values. RMSE was denoted as the same units as the dependent parameter (WQI), and a lesser RMSE value shows a better fit of the model. The R-squared (R2) value, on the other hand, is a measure of the fraction of the deviation in the dependent variable to the inference by the independent variables in the model. It varies between 0 and 1, with an upper range of values that shows a better fit of the model. R2 is equal to 1 indicating that the model perfectly expresses all of the variations in the dependent variable, while R2 is equal to 0 indicating that the model explores none of the variations. In this work, both RMSE and R2 measures were calculated for evaluating the performance of all the proposed regression models. However, they each have their strengths and limitations. RMSE provides an absolute measure of the goodness of fit and is useful for comparing the performance of LR, RFR, PLSR, and ERFR models. R2, on the other hand, provides a relative measure of the goodness of fit and is useful for understanding the percentage of variation in the WQI that was calculated by the measured parameters of the different stations in the river in India. RMSE and R2 values are calculated by using the following Eqs. 5 and 6 respectively.

$$RMSE = \sqrt{\frac{\sum_{x-0}^{n}(y_x - predicted y_x)^2}{q}} \tag{5}$$

$$R2 = \frac{\sum_{x=1}^{n}(\hat{y}_x - \bar{y})^2}{\sum_{x=1}^{n}(y_x - \bar{y})^2} \tag{6}$$

Where

q ➜ Number of samples
n ➜ Number of Parameters
y_x ➜ Measured value of xth Parameter
$\hat{y}_x$ ➜ Predicted value of xth Parameter

3 Results and Discussion

To confirm the accuracy of the model that was created the measured parameters of the water samples were pre-processed and analyzed using a probability density function (PDF) plot graph in Fig. 3. Any missing data were replaced with the median value of the corresponding parameter using Z-score normalization techniques. PDF is a statistical function that describes the probability that a particular value takes place within a given range. In the context of water quality parameters, a PDF plot shows the probability density of a particular parameter being within a certain range of values. The plot curve shows the likelihood of each parameter value occurring, with higher points on the curve indicating a higher probability of the pH being within that range of values.

The PDF plot of the quality parameters in river water displays that the probability density (PD) of temp lies in the range of 20–30, PD of the pH lies within the range of values, such as 6–8, PD of DO lies in the range of 4.5–8. PD of Conductivity lies in the range of −2000 to 3000, PD of BOD lies in the range of −200 to 280, PD of Nitrate lies in the range of −2 to 5, PD of FC (fec_coli) lies between the span of −0.1 to 0.2 and PD of TC (tot_coli) lies between the ranges of −0.1 to 0.2. From the PDF plot, correlated parameters are used to calculate the WQI. WQI calculation was done by creating the function which utilised the WQI Eqs. 1–4 shown in the section material and methods. The randomly selected five stations calculated WQI values are explored in Table 4.

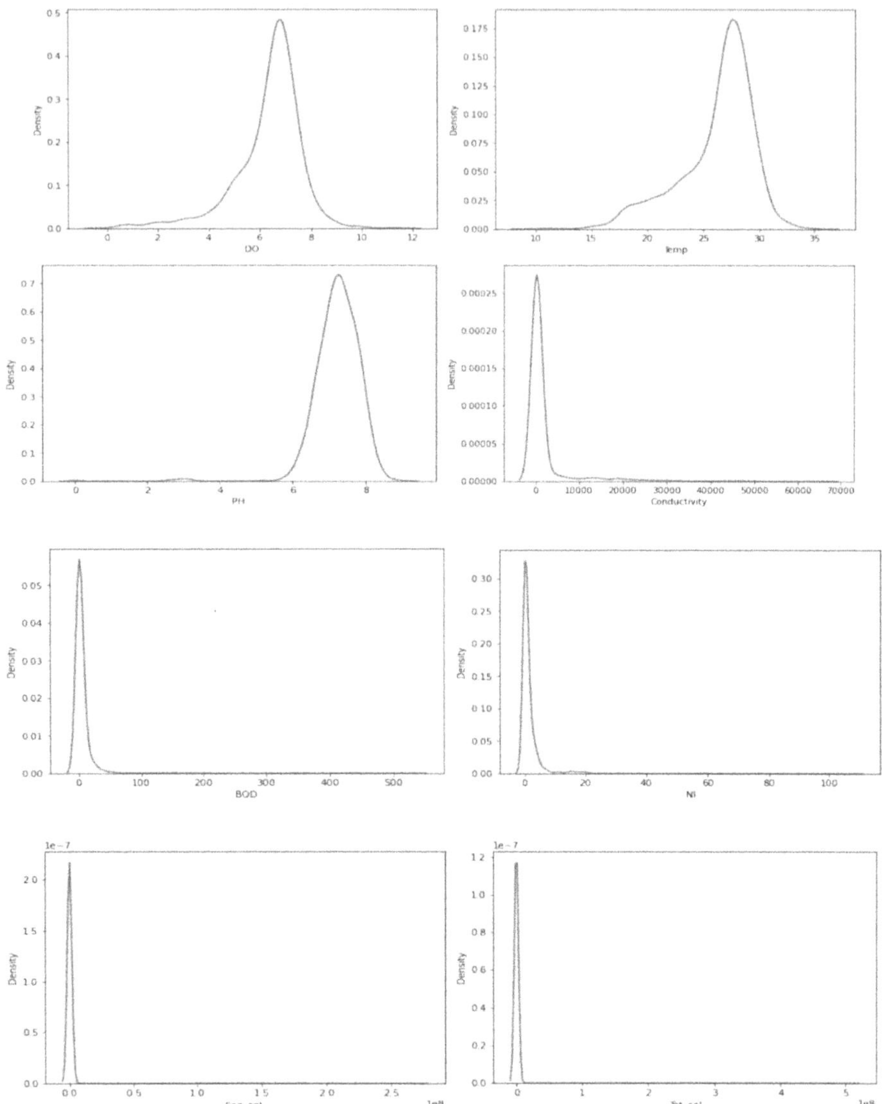

Fig. 3. Probability Density function plot of numerical water quality parameters (temp, pH, DO, Conductivity, BOD, Nitrate (NI), Fec_col, Tot_col)

Table 4. Calculated WQI values for five different monitoring stations

S. CODE	LOCATIONS	STATE	Temp	DO	pH	Con.	BOD	NI	Fec_col	Tot_col	Year	WQI
393	DAMANGANGA AT DAMAN	DAMAN & DIU	30.60	6.7	7.5	203	1.89	0.1	11	27	2014	63.778
1399	ZUARI AT D/S OF PT. GOA	GOA	29.80	5.7	7.2	189	2.00	0.2	4953	8391	2014	175.36
1475	ZUARI AT PANCHAWADI	GOA	29.50	6.3	6.9	179	1.70	0.1	3243	5330	2014	126.13
3181	RIVER_ZUARI AT BORIM_BRIDGE	GOA	29.70	5.8	6.9	64	3.80	0.5	5382	8443	2014	195.10
3182	RIVER_ZUARI AT MARCAIM_JETTY	GOA	29.50	5.8	7.3	83	1.90	0.4	3428	5500	2014	141.39

The calculated WQI values were randomly splitted as testing 20% and for training 80% of the entire data set. Training data values are trained by using MLR, RFR, PLSR, and ERFR models to predict the WQI of the river water sources in India. And these models' performance was verified with a testing dataset. Finally, the accuracy of these models was calculated by using the RMSE and R2 scores shown in Table 5. The study found that the multilayer linear regression approach outperformed the other three models in forecasting river water quality in India. The study concluded that the linear regression approach generates reliably good predictions of river water quality compared to the other approaches.

Table 5. Prediction models with their RMSE and R2-Score values

Prediction Algorithms	RMSE	R2-Score
ERFR	53.71	96.06%
LR	10.13	99.09%
PLSR	68.46	93.60%
RFR	50.67	96.49%

4 Conclusion

The study evaluates the significance of the linear regression approach in forecasting river water quality and resolving other demanding environmental issues. The accuracy levels of the prediction models consistently stayed every year, with the accuracy of 96.06%, 99.09%, 94.49%, and 93.6% at the ensemble random forest, multiple linear regressions, partial least square, and random forest regression respectively. The RMSE value of these models was 53.71, 1.14, 68.46, and 50.67 respectively. The study shows that machine learning algorithms can be effective in forecasting river water quality and identifying potential water discharges to toxic diseases. The study recommends the use of the linear regression approach in forecasting river water quality in India and other parts of the world. Further studies should explore water pollution classification using machine learning algorithms in other environmental issues.

References

1. Wang, L., Zhu, Z., Sassoubre, L., et al.: Improving the robustness of beach water quality Modeling using an ensemble machine learning approach. Sci. Total Environ. **765**, 142760 (2020) S0048-9697
2. Kumar, A. et al.: Effect of salinity and alkalinity on responses of halophytic grasses Sporobolus marginatus and Urochondra setulosa. Indian J. Agric. Sci. **88**(8), 149–157 (2018)
3. Luo, B., Zhao, Y., Chen, K., Zhao, X.: Partial least squares regression model to predict water quality in urban water distribution systems. Trans. Tianjin Univ. **15**, 140–144 (2009). https://doi.org/10.1007/s12209-009-0025-2
4. Mishra, U., Gautam, S., Riley, W.J., Hoffman, F.M.: Ensemble machine learning approach improves predicted spatial variation of surface soil organic carbon stocks in data-limited northern circumpolar region. Front. big Data. **3**, 528441 (2020)
5. Gupta, S., Gupta, S.K.: Development and evaluation of an innovative Enhanced River pollution index model for holistic monitoring and management of river water quality. Environ. Sci. Pollut. Res. **28**, 27033–27046 (2021)
6. Horton, R.K.: An index-number system for rating water quality. J. Water Pollut. Control Fed. **37**(3), 300–306 (1965)
7. Dunnette, D.A.: A geographically variable water quality index used in Oregon. J. Water Pollut. Control Fed. **51**(1), 53–61 (1979)
8. Dinius, S.H.: Design of an Index of water quality. Water Resour. Bull. **23**(5), 833–843 (1978)
9. Stoner, J.D.: Water Quality Indices for Specific Water Uses, p. 770. U.S Geological Survey Circular (1978)
10. Joung, H.M., Miller, W.W., Mahannah, C.N., Guitjens, J.C.: A generalized water quality index based on multivariate factor analysis. J. Environ. Qual. **8**(1), 95–100 (1979)
11. Bhargava, D.: Use of a water quality index for river classification and zoning of the Ganga River. Environ. Pollut. (Series B). **6**, 51–67 (1983)
12. Smith, D.G.: A better water quality indexing system for Rivers and streams. Water Res. **24**(10), 1237–1244 (1990)
13. Tyagi, S., Sharma, B., Singh, P., Dobhal, R.: Water quality assessment in terms of water quality index. Am. J. Water Resour. **1**(3), 34–38 (2013)
14. Kamboj, V., Kamboj, N., Bisht, A.: An overview of water quality indices as promising tools for assessing the quality of water resources. In: Advances in Environmental Pollution Management: Wastewater Impacts and Treatment Technologies, pp. 188–205. Agro Environ Media, Haridwar (2020)
15. Karpagam, V., Christy, S., Sheela Evangelin, S.N.: Calculating and comparing the weighted and unweighted water quality indices for Cauvery River banks based on accuracy. In: 2022 IEEE 4th International Conference on Cybernetics, Cognition and Machine Earning Applications (ICCCMLA), Goa, India, pp. 168–173 (2022). https://doi.org/10.1109/ICCCMLA56841.2022.9989129
16. Ongley, E.D., Booty, W.G.: Pollution remediation planning in developing countries: conventional modeling versus knowledge based prediction. Water Int. **24**, 31–38 (1999)
17. Al-Othman, A.A.: Evaluation of the suitability of surface water from Riyadh mainstream Saudi Arabia for a variety of uses. Arab. J. Chem. **12**(8), 2104–2110 (2019)

18. Chang, C.L., Chuan, Y.C., Tang, Z.-Y., Chen, S.-T.: High-efficiency automatic recharging mechanism for cleaning robot using multi-sensor. November. Sensors. **18**(11), 3911 (2018)
19. Ahmed, U., Rafia Mumtaz, O.R.C.I.D., Anwar, H., Shah, A.A., Irfan, R., García-Nieto, J.: Efficient water quality prediction using supervised machine learning. Water. **11**(11), 2210 (2019)
20. Vilupuru, J.R., Amuluru, D.C., Ghousiya Begum, K.: Water quality analysis using artificial intelligence algorithms. In: 2022 4th International Conference on Inventive Research in Computing Applications (ICIRCA). IEEE, USA (2022)
21. Yuan, X., et al.: Spatiotemporal dynamics and anthropologically dominated drivers of chlorophyll-a, TN and TP concentrations in the Pearl River Estuary based on retrieval algorithm and random forest regression. Environ. Res. **215**, 114380 (2022)
22. Wang, L., et al.: Improving the robustness of beach water quality modeling using an ensemble machine learning approach. Sci. Total Environ. **765**, 142760 (2021)
23. F. Emmanuel: Partial Least Squares Integrated National Water Quality Standards (NWQS) for Indexing of Water Quality from Industrial Effluent. 2015.
24. Biney, J.K.M., Vašát, R., Blöcher, J.R., Borůvka, L., Němeček, K.: Using an ensemble model coupled with portable X-ray fluorescence and visible near-infrared spectroscopy to explore the viability of mapping and estimating arsenic in an agricultural soil. Sci. Total Environ. **818**, 151805 (2022)
25. Chinmoy Sarkar, S.A., Abbasi.: Qualidex – a new software for generating water quality Indice. Environ. Monit. Assess. **119**(1–3), 201–231 (2006)
26. Cao, S., Zhou, L., Zheng, Z.: Prediction of dissolved oxygen content in aquaculture based on clustering and improved ELM. IEEE Access. **9**, 9370107 (2021)

Advanced Deep Learning Applications

Deep Learning-Based Identification of Plant Diseases

Krishna Kishore Thota[1]([⊠]) [iD], Thokala Srivalli[1] [iD], and Sreedhar Pulipati[2]

[1] Department of Computer Science & Engineering (Honors), Koneru Lakshmaiah Education Foundation (Deemed to be University), Vaddeswaram, Guntur, Andhra Pradesh 522302, India
`{tkrishnakishore,tsrivalli}@kluniversity.in`
[2] Department of Information Technology, Bapatla Engineering College (Autonomous), Bapatla, Affiliated to Acharya Nagarjuna University, Guntur, Andhra Pradesh 522102, India
`sreedhar.pulipati@becbapatla.ac.in`

Abstract. The key factors that determines the loss of agricultural and crop production output is to recognize plant diseases. Plant disease research focuses on any apparent features, such as spots or color variations that enable us to distinguish between two different types of plants. The important factors in the growth of agriculture is the sustainability of plants. Accurately identifying plant diseases is quite challenging. A great deal of effort and skill to know the disease, extensive knowledge of plants and research on disease detection. When detecting illnesses, the procedures of image capture, extraction, segmentation, and pre-processing are used. Various illnesses affect the amount of chlorophyll in leaves, resulting in brown or black spots on the leaf's surface. The economy has a big impact on agricultural productivity. The farmer faces many obstacles when they switch between various disease management methods. Classification uses CNN, a kind of deep learning technique. Transformer networks have recently showed a lot of potential in computer vision problems. In order to detect plant diseases, this study contrasts these methods with conventional CNN methods. Our transformer model's highest validation accuracy is 97.98%.

Keywords: plants · leaf disease · agriculture · pre-processing · deep learning · CNN

1 Introduction

Climate change and sustainable agriculture are strongly linked to the issue of effective plant disease prevention. India's farmers grow a wide variety of crops. There are numerous diseases in the environment that negatively impact crops and the soil in which they are planted, which has an impact on crop productivity. Numerous diseases have been reported to affect crops and plants. The leaves of the impacted plant or crop serve as the primary means of identification. The leaf's numerous colored patterns and dots are quite helpful.

Identification of plant diseases is essential for the wellbeing of agricultural crops and the country's food supply [1]. The traditional method of diagnosing plant diseases

R. Appavoo et al. (Eds.): IconDeepCom 2024, CCIS 2687, pp. 331–341, 2026.
https://doi.org/10.1007/978-3-032-26680-4_26

involves a qualified agronomist doing a time-consuming and error- prone visual check. In recent years, methods have emerged as a potentially useful tool for the early identification. Machine learning algorithms can be trained on large quantities of plant image data to identify patterns and characteristics that are typical of different diseasesThe algorithm may be able to recognize patterns linked to each illness after being trained on a large dataset of both healthy and sick plants. Once trained, the model can rapidly and accurately identify fresh plant photographs by classifying them as either healthy or sick.

Plant diseases can be found in several methods. In cases where a disease has no outward symptoms or whose effects become apparent too late to take action, a thorough study is required. However, as the majority of diseases manifest in some way, the primary method used in practice for qualified professional's examination with the unaided eye. Differences in the symptoms that sick plants display could result in a wrong diagnosis since non-professional plant pathologists might find it more difficult to diagnose than amateur gardeners and hobbyists [2]. Developments in precision plant protection industry as well as the market for computer vision applications related to precision agriculture.

2 Literature Survey

It is still challenging to promptly identify plant diseases due to a lack of the required infrastructure. Since the advent of accurate methods, significant advancements made in the field of picture classification. This article uses Random Forest to separate healthy leaves from unhealthy leaves from the generated datasets [3].

Our solution covers building the dataset, extracting features, training the classifier, and classifying the results. To classify, the generated datasets are trained using Random Forest. All things considered, using the enormous publicly available data sets provides us with a clear method to identify plant diseases on a large scale.

Farmers in rural locations might think it's hard to identify the sickness that could be in their crops. They are not going to the agriculture office to see what kind of infection it might be. To recognize the illness that has been introduced into a plant by examining its structure. Using a modern approach like ML and DL has increased the recognition rate and result accuracy [4]. Many experiments on machine learning have been conducted with the goal of detecting and treating plant diseases.

If crop illnesses are to be prevented and recognized quickly, productivity must rise. Deep CNN models are utilized in this work to recognize diseases as CNNs have shown remarkable accomplishments in the field of machine vision. Conventional CNN models are more expensive [5]. To optimize the parameters and computational cost, we used depth separable convolution in this work instead of regular convolution.

To categorize tomato sicknesses, we have carefully investigated many cutting-edge CNN classification network designs in this study. These network designs include ResNet18, MobileNet, DenseNet201, and InceptionV3. We tested these networks using 18,162 basic tomato leaf photos [6]. Moreover, the ten-class classification (which includes both healthy and variously unhealthy leaf kinds) is provided. During image feature extraction, we first replace VGG16 with a depth residual network to acquire more detailed disease features. We improve the anchoring using the clustering results. The improved anchor frame tilts in the direction of the dataset's true bounding box.

Lastly, we perform a k-means experiment with three different feature extraction networks [7]. The enhanced method for agricultural leaf disease detection outperformed the original Faster RCNN in terms of identification accuracy, with a 2.71% increase in identification speed.

Crop disease identification is the first line of defense against agricultural illnesses and guaranteeing crop quality. Due to their reliance on personal observation, traditional crop disease detection techniques have low detection reliability and efficiency. Farmers don't have the necessary expertise, and agricultural specialists can't always be in the field, so they lose the best opportunities de Luna et al., [8].

3   DATSET

The PlantVillage Dataset [9] is used in this work. It is made up of photographs of plant leaves that were shot in a lab setting. 54 306 photos altogether, representing 14 different plant species, are arranged in 38 different classes and are labeled as species/disease pairs. Apple, Blueberry, Cherry, Corn, Grape, Orange, Peach, Bell Pepper, Potato, Raspberry, Soybean, Squash, Strawberry, and Tomato are among thespecies included in this dataset. This dataset contains photos of healthy plants from 12 different species information on 17 fungal diseases, 4 bacterial diseases, 2 viral infections, 2 mould diseases, and 1 mite disease [10].

The dataset is more diversified because the photos were taken outside in various weather situations using a regular digital camera and were gathered from various sources. The dataset's abundance of samples and variety of diseases make it appropriate for the use of ML techniques, particularly deep learning ones. The dataset's drawback is that, in order to take pictures, individual leaves were cut and placed against a consistent background found in the environment. Figure 1 illustrates the non-uniform distribution of photos and the range of samples per class, from 150 to 5500. Additionally, a sizable number of samples with incorrect labels were reported in. The collection includes segmented photos with masked backgrounds, color images, and grayscale images. Segmented photos are employed in this work.

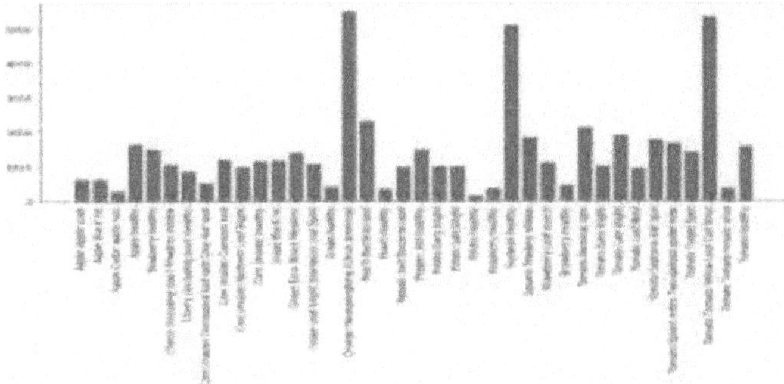

Fig. 1. Number of samples per class

4 Methodology

The machine learning method was unable to achieve the required level of accuracy. The proposed method works well for monitoring large agricultural fields. Solutions for identifying and categorizing the sickness should exist in order to gather information that will eventually aid the caliber of the plants. Thus, patterns of the plant will aid in determining the nature of its issue.

Drawbacks of the Current System:

- A reduced degree of feature compatibility.
- Inaccurate results.
- The process moves quite slowly.
- Time and space consumption
- Very few illnesses have been discussed.

CNN: A customized CNN is created with Three convolutional layers, three activation layers, and three MaxPooling2D layer are combined to construct a bespoke convolutional neuralnetwork. The network receives input images with the same 256*256 resolution as the original.

Every convolutional layer uses a different size filter and uses "relu" as its activation function. Additionally, batch normalization is utilized to strengthen the model using validation data and lessen overfitting during training, the dropout function is also employed. 38 neurons and the "softmax" activation function are utilized to classify the data [11]. The model has 28,903,164 total parameters, of which 28,903,100 are trainable and 64 are non-trainable.

Transfer Learning: We employed the advanced models, INCEPTIONv3 [12], for transfer learning purposes, the model's weights from its training on the IMAGENET dataset. To meet the needs of the dataset, We modified the INCEPTIONv3 net by adding a few layers and making the model's upper levels untrainable. To do this, we first added a flatten layer to the INCEPTIONv3 output layer. Next, we added two dense layers, each containing a distinct neuron, the final layer is the same as the CNN. With just 21,802,784 parameters, intended to be as large as (150,150).

Visual Transformers: To obtain its embedding into a feedforward network, and then for each component's position is added. To obtain the query, key, and value, they are utilized as tokens and supplied to a second feedforward layer. Attention is computed using these tokens. Without a lot of settings, these repeated layers could capture semantic information. A normalization layer comes before each feedforward-followed repeated attention block connected to its predecessor.

Transformer types were employed in two distinct sizes:

Small Transformer Network (STN): A model with feedforward layers that additionally output 256 dimensions after each attention block, with 256 dimensions [13]. Eight heads are fed into eight attention blocks. Comparatively this one has a fairly small number of parameters—3,499,046.

Large Transformer Network (LTN): This model follow outputting 128 dimensions, each of its four attention blocks receives four heads of data [14]. Fewest parameters of all the models we investigated for this study—just 549,926.Advantages of Proposed System: (Fig. 2)

- The precise categorization.
- A Lower Level of Complexity.
- Excellent performance.
- The simplicity of identification.

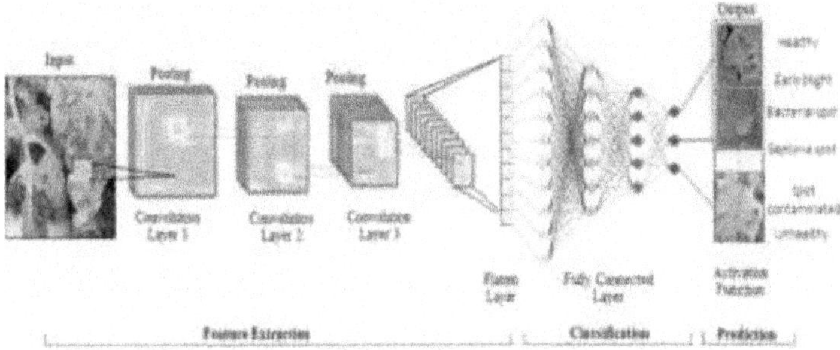

Fig. 2. Architecture of the proposed system

The original data is preprocessed and utilized for a machine learning model, with performance analysis being conducted to select the model with the highest accuracy (Fig. 3).

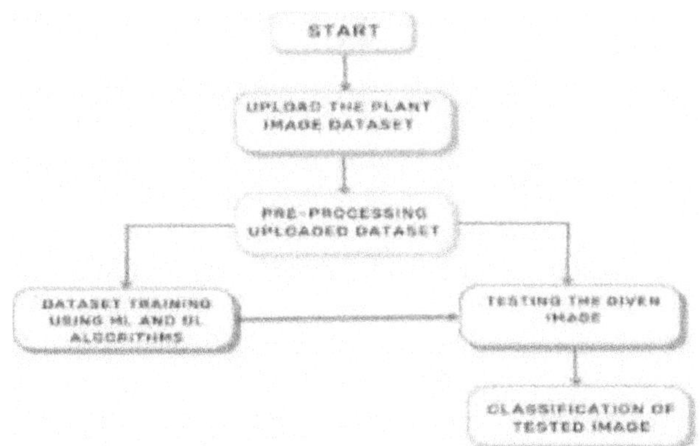

Fig. 3. Flowchart of the Proposed System

The information was gathered from the plant Village databases. This approach, we consider some plants, such the potato, tomato, etc. Both healthy and sick leaves are present (Fig. 4).

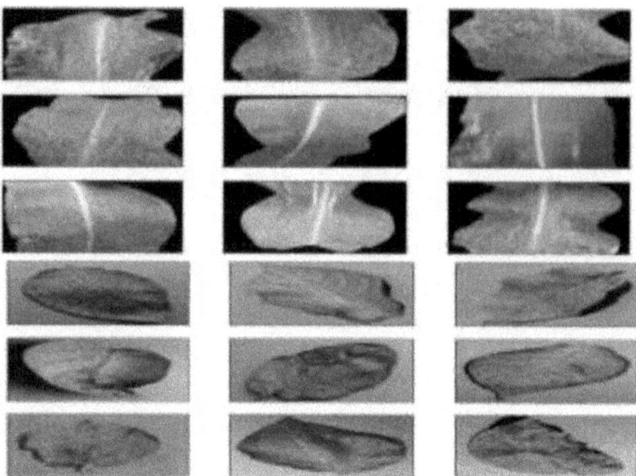

Fig. 4. Corn leaf And Potato leaf

Pre-processing

We scale and shape the images in order to train our model. The process of processing digital photos with computer implemented algorithms is known as "image pre- processing." By applying a certain algorithm, we are able to recognize the plant in the picture. We use a particular technique as well as a similar approach for image processing and detection. This method is highly dependent on the quality of the image; we cannot use the algorithm if the image is unclear.

Training and Validation

Following the initializations of data, we employed "ModelCheckpoint," "ReduceLROn-Plateau," and "EarlyStopping." The Mod-elCheckpoint class lets us specify the model weight checkpoint locations and the conditions that would lead to the creation of the checkpoint during periods of high validation accuracy or low validation loss.

It gives us all of these resources so that, following training, we have the most accurate and well-weighted model. Diminish. Models frequently get better when it is decreased by a factor of two to ten after learning stops developing. This callback on a quantity and lowers the learning rate if efficiency isn't found for a patient number of epochs. EarlyStopping class enables us to end the training process when our model no longer improves. This is because training a model for an extended length of time without seeing any improvement in performance can cause the model to become overfit.

The optimizer for the Custom CNN is called "Adam," and the loss function is called "Categorical Cross Entropy," with a default learning rate of 0.001. The INCEPTIONv3 model employs the "RM-Sprop" optimizer and "Categorical Cross Entropy" as the loss function. 32 photos are utilized as the batch size. It is discovered that the transformer networks perform best. For these networks, "Adam" is the optimizer, and category cross entropy. It is discovered that the transformer networks perform best. For these networks, "Adam" is the optimizer, and category cross entropy loss is employed (Figs. 5, 6, 7 and 8).

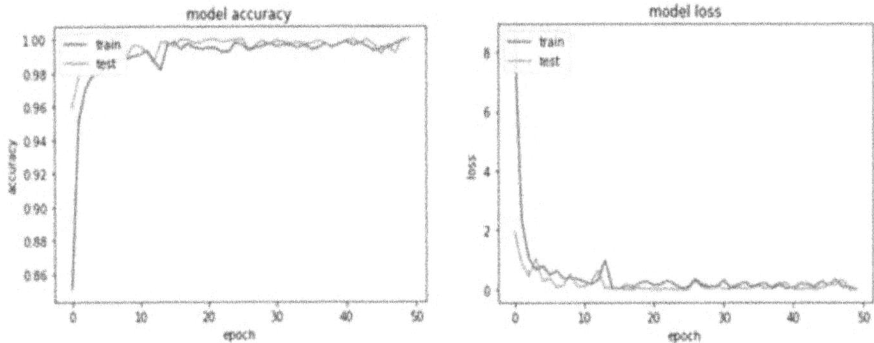

Fig. 5. Accuracy & Loss of Custom CNN

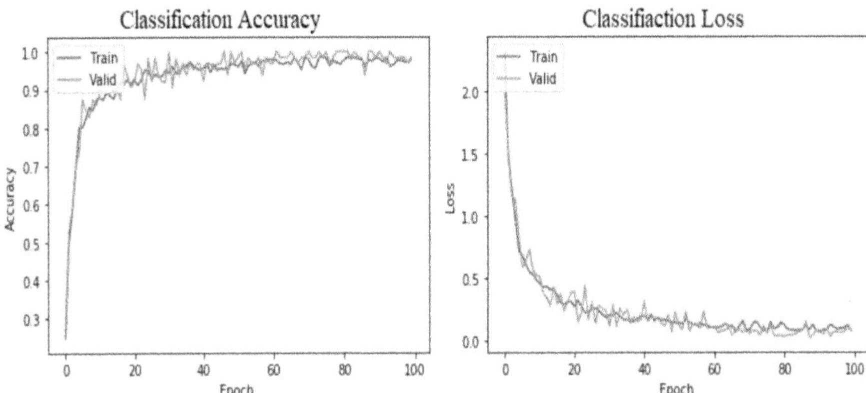

Fig. 6. Accuracy & Loss of INCEPTIONV3

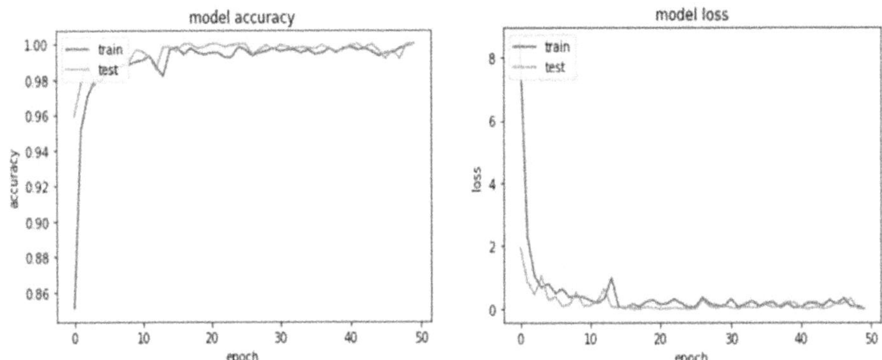

Fig. 7. Accuracy & Loss of Large Transformer Network

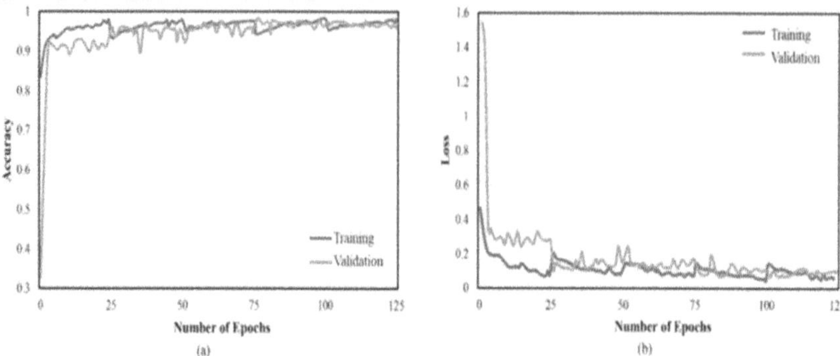

Fig. 8. Accuracy & Loss of Small Transformer Networor

Support Vector Machine (SVM)

Support vector machines resolve regression problems even though they are usually regarded of as a classification tool. It is easy to manage several continuous and categorical variables. SVM builds a hyper plane to split several classes in multidimensional space. To lower mistakes, SVM creates the ideal Hyper plane iteratively. Finding the maximum marginal hyperplane, or MMH, that best divides the dataset into classes is the primary objective of support vector machines (SVM).

For situations involving regression or classification, supervised learning algorithms like SVM are employed. Establishing a separate hyperplane in the feature space allows for classification. It carried out linear classificationon two classes in its initial version.

SVM has outstanding generalization properties and can fit extremely complicated datasets. One-vs-all and one-vs-one techniques can be used to perform multiclass classification using Support Vector Machines [15]. A classifier trained using the one-vs-all strategy is trained on N examples (where N is the number of classes) and treats all other examples as negative. A one-versus-one method uses max-wins voting to choose the winner after training $N(N-1)/2$ binary classifiers [10]. After experimenting with several setups, we discovered that regularization value $C = 100$ produced the greatest outcomes. An all-or- none strategy was adopted. 99.23% accuracy was attained on the test set (Figs. 9 and 10).

Classification

Our model produces a display of diseased images that either utilize different labels or employ different algorithms, such as CNN, SVM. These algorithms will help us categorize diseased or not. Additionally, it will accurately identify the ailment it is suffering from (Fig. 11).

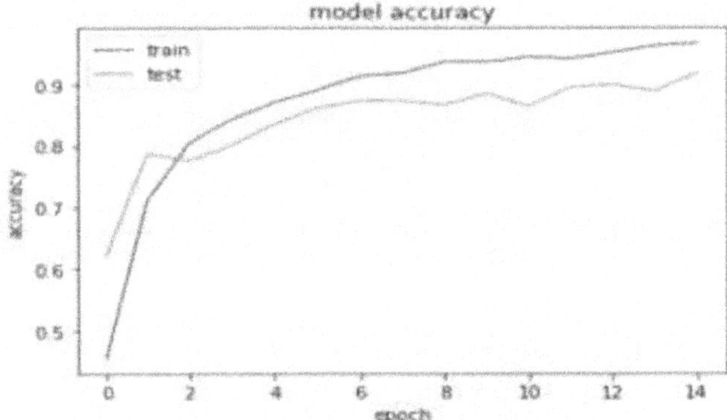

Fig. 9. Accuracy of model in SVM

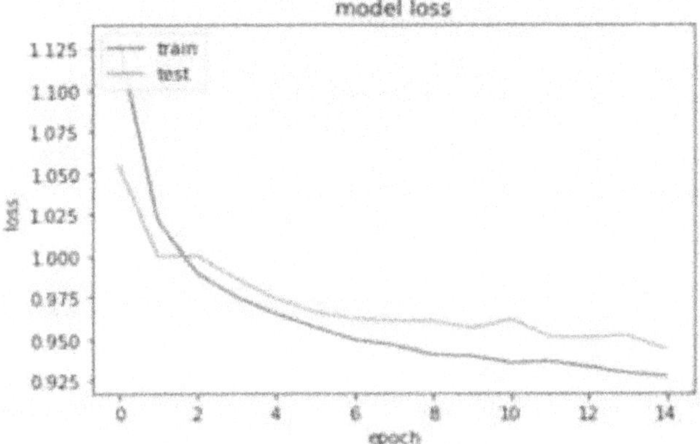

Fig. 10. Loss of model in SVM

Fig. 11. Different Classes of Potato Leaf images

5 Result

The models proposed in this work utilize the Plant Village dataset, comprising about 1000 images of early blight- affected leaves and 152 images. The training set and the testing set are the two sets of data used in this model. Of the leaf image collection we gathered, the training set comprises 80%, while the testing set 20%. The models that we have will demonstrate the accuracy of the disease based on their training and testing. 90% of the leaves in the supplied leaf below accurately indicate the disease (Fig. 12).

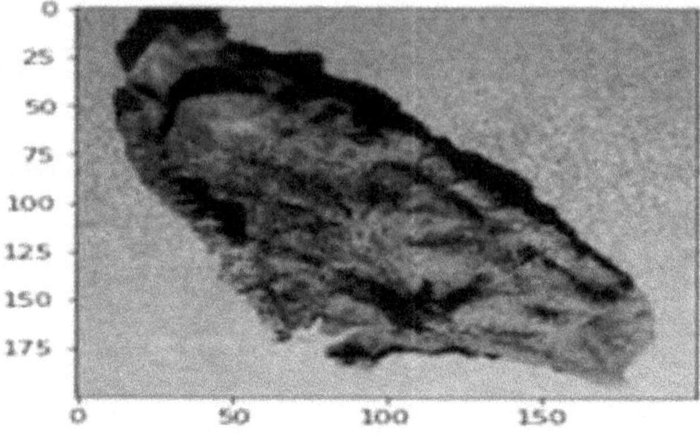

Fig. 12 Prediction of plant disease

6 Conclusion

CNN and SVM have been crucial to the success of all image processing tasks, including those involving description, augmentation, and classification. Transformers were first designed to support NLPactivities, but more recent research has indicated that computer vision tasks may also benefit from their use. The Small Transformer Networks (STN) appears to be the ideal option for our application, which calls for the model to be accessible Even though it is much larger than the STN model when size is taken into account, the large transformer network fits the data the best and provides the maximum accuracy in our analysis. Since this architecture is still in its early stages, further study is needed to properly apply transformers in computer vision tasks.

References

1. Kamlapurkar, S.R.: Detection of Plant Leaf Disease Using Image Processing' Approach. Department of Electronics & Telecommunications, Karmaveer Kakasaheb Wagh Institute of Engineering Education & Research, Nashik, India (2016)
2. Liu, B., Tan, C., Li, S., He, J., Wang, H.: A data augmentation method based on generative adversarial networks for grape leaf disease identification. IEEE Access. **8**, 102188–102198 (2020)

3. Santhosh Kumar, S., Raghavendra, B.K.: Diseases detection of various plant leaf using image processing techniques: a review. In: 2019 5th International Conference on Advanced Computing & Communication Systems (ICACCS), IEEE, USA (2019)
4. Devaraj, A., Rathan, K., Jaahnavi, S., Indira, K.: Identification of plant disease using image processing technique. In: 2019 International Conference on Communication and Signal Processing (ICCSP) (2019)
5. Chowdhury, M.E.H., Rahman, T., Khandakar, A., Ibtehaz, N.: Tomato leaf diseases detection using deep learning technique. In: Technology in Agriculture (2021). https://doi.org/10.5772/intechopen.97319
6. Sladojevic, S., Arsenovic, M., Anderla, A., Culibrk, D., Stefanovic, D.: Deep neural networks based recognition of plant diseases by leaf image classification. Comput. Intell. Neurosci. **2016**, 3289801 (2016)
7. Wang, B., Wang, D.: Plant leaves classification: a few-shot learning method based on Siamese network. IEEE Access. **7**, 151754–151763 (2019)
8. de Luna, R.G., Dadios, E.P., Bandala, A.A.: Automated image capturing system for deep learning -based tomato plant leaf disease detection and recognition. In: TENCON 2018–2018 IEEE Region 10 Conference, pp. 1414–1419. IEEE (2018)
9. Khan, A., et al.: A survey of the recent architectures of deep convolutional neural networks. Artif. Intell. Rev. **553**, 8 (2020)
10. Mohanty, S.P., Hughes, D.P., Marcel, S.´.: Using deep learning for image-based plant disease detection. Front. Plant Sci. **7**, 1419 (2016)
11. Crop Disease Detection Using Deep Learning O Kulkarni - 2018 Fourth International Conference, (2018). ieeexplore.ieee.org
12. Gandhi, R., Nimbalkar, S., Yelamanchili, N.: Plant disease detection using CNNs and GANs as an augmentative approach 2018 IEEE (2018). ieeexplore.ieee.org
13. Francis, M., Deisy, C.: Disease Detection and Classification in Agricultural Plants Using Convolutional Neural Networks—A Visual Understanding - 2019 6th International Conference on (2019). ieeexplore.ieee.org
14. Szegedy, C., et al.: Going deeper with convolutions. In: Proceedings of the IEEE Conference on Computer Vision and Pattern Recognition (2015)
15. Lee, S.H., Goeau, H., Bonnet, P., Joly, A.: New perspectives on plant disease characterization based on deep learning. Comput. Electron. Agric. **170**, 105220 (2020) ISSN 0168-1699

Semantic Web-Based Diagnosis and Treatment Model for Mental Disorder

Abebayehu Meketa[1](✉) and M. Prathap[2]

[1] Department of Information Science and Technology, School of Informatics and Artificial Intelligence, Mehal Meda Campus, Debre Berhan University, Mehal Meda, Ethiopia
abebayehu5254@gmail.com, abebayehufiseha@dbu.edu.et
[2] Department of Information Technology, Mattu University, Mattu, Ethiopia

Abstract. The prevalence of common mental diseases, including schizophrenia, generalized anxiety disorder, generalized depression, and other related disorders, is high in emerging nations. We have developed a diagnosis and suggestion model based on ontologies to improve services and assist both individuals and psychiatrists. Our application of Semantic Web Technology was to generate domain-based knowledge. Information for domain ontology-based knowledge development was gathered from domain experts and other expert-written publications. This ontology model's concepts, relationships, and attributes can be applied to the diagnosis and recommendation of common mental illnesses. Using valid links between ontology concepts, the SWRL rules are built to identify the type of mental condition based on the symptoms in the domain ontology. Our investigation was carried out using the Design Science research methodology. Using Protégé Editor, we expressed the acquired knowledge as an ontology-based architecture, and we used Pellet Reasoner to assess the coherence of the domain ontology we had constructed. We can search the domain ontology for solutions, drugs, advice, and other pertinent data.

Keywords: Ontology model · SWRL rule · Diagnosis · Recommendation model · Common mental disorder

1 Introduction

Mental disorders are diseases that affect cognition, emotion, and interactive control and greatly intervene both with the skill of children to learn and with the ability of adults to function in their families, at work and in the wider society. The reasons of mental disorders are different and, in some cases, unclear, and theories may include discoveries from a range of fields and sometimes services are given based on community and hospital's trained. Managements are conceded through by psychiatrists, clinical psychologists, and clinical social workers, using several methods but repeatedly relying on observation and questioning [1]. For this health problem, the government gives less attention than other health problems and is not considered as serious in the world [2].

Most poor nations allocate less than 2% of their government resources to mental health care, and significant development is required in the delivery of services to close

© The Author(s), under exclusive license to Springer Nature Switzerland AG 2026
R. Appavoo et al. (Eds.): IconDeepCom 2024, CCIS 2687, pp. 342–351, 2026.
https://doi.org/10.1007/978-3-032-26680-4_27

the mental health treatment gap, according to the WHO's 2008 Report [3]. Developing nations, or low- and middle-income countries, are more likely to have some common mental diseases. Since there are often less than one psychiatrist per million people in many nations, specialty psychiatric services are unable to meet the needs of the community. The World Bank, the World Health Organization (WHO), and most health ministries have backed the use of primary health care services as the principal policy solution [4]. It is a pattern or irregularity of thinking or behavior that is not socially or developmentally appropriate and that influences a person's ideas, feelings, behaviors, and perceptions. It is also known as a psychiatric disease. It may result in impairment or distress.

2 Related Work

An Ontology System for diagnosing asthma disease is develop a domain ontology (asthma ontology) that encompasses asthma disease domain knowledge [5]. An ontological-based monitoring system for patients with bipolar I disorder done to deliver patient monitoring system that merge clinical decision support system to Electronic Health Records [6]. Existence of system to assist psychiatrists and primary care physical to tackle existent healthcare for Bipolar-I disorder is raised as a main problem. An Ontology-Based Personalized Dietary Recommendation for Weightlifting have done in [7]. The paper's main problems raised that nutritional misinformation can do as much harm to the ambitious athlete.

3 Proposed Model

Certain restrictions of machine learning techniques, such as the requirement for training data, the high processing cost for learning models, and the requirement to adapt to the dynamic nature of data, make ontology necessary [8]. The architecture that follows shows the proposed model (Fig. 1).

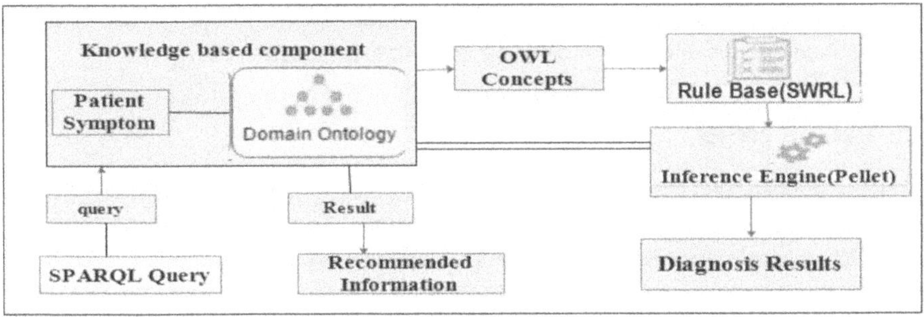

Fig. 1. Architecture of the Model

3.1 The Classes and Hierarchy

The process of developing an ontology begins with the definition and arrangement of the basic class and class hierarchy. The protégé environment describes all domain ontologies using class and class hierarchy. The ability to specify ideas with their domain as a collection of abstract objects created with similar aspect values and to group resources with similar attributes are made possible by these classes (Fig. 2).

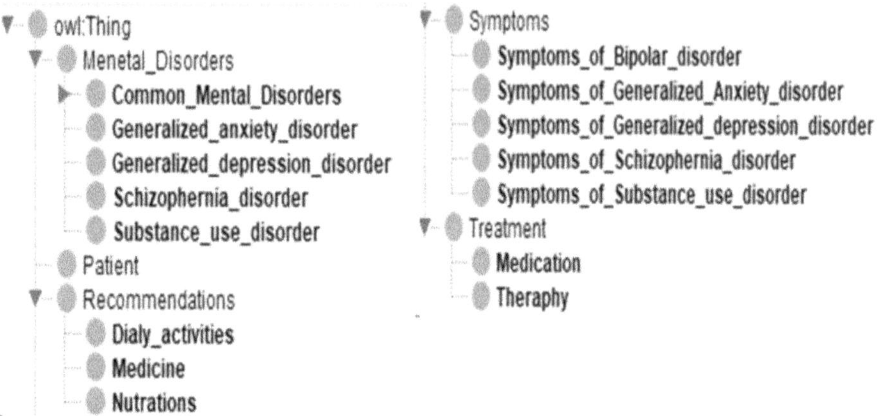

Fig. 2. Proposed ontology classes hierarchy

3.2 Object Properties

We have an object properties in an ontology development to enhance some restrictions onto the class. In web ontology language (OWL) properties are used to include some relationships between individuals or instances in a domain ontology. In the development, process of the required ontology, it is necessary to specify the properties and its associated characteristics properly. We can assert additional information about properties including its domain and range, along with defining its inverse properties (Fig. 3).

3.3 Data properties

A data property is also known as attributes which are used to describe classes by allocating their attributes. Attributes are applied to describe semantic relation and characteristics of classes in ontologies. Data property helps to link a class with its domain while object property helps to link individuals with other individuals in the same domain. Data property has important roles when describing individuals characteristics and enabling data value to be saved (Fig. 4).

Fig. 3. Object property of the ontology.

Fig. 4. Data property of the ontology

3.4 Defining Facets, Ranges and Domain of the Properties

Facets are attributes or characteristics of a property and are used to implement restriction on property value such as data type value of property (integer, text, date, Boolean, etc.), quantifier restriction (existential and uni-versal), and cardinality restriction (minimum and maximum cardinality restriction). A graphic representation of some of the concepts, including those terminology, is shown below (Fig. 5).

3.5 Defining Instance

We generate instances or individuals connected to previously established classes after creating ontology classes. First, there are people who need to be added. After that, we made a unique instance of that class. A collection of individuals linked to the same object and data characteristics is called an instance. In the ontology, instances are individuals. They are fundamental ontology components. They belong to a particular class. The instance's object and data properties are shared by all members of the same class (Fig. 6).

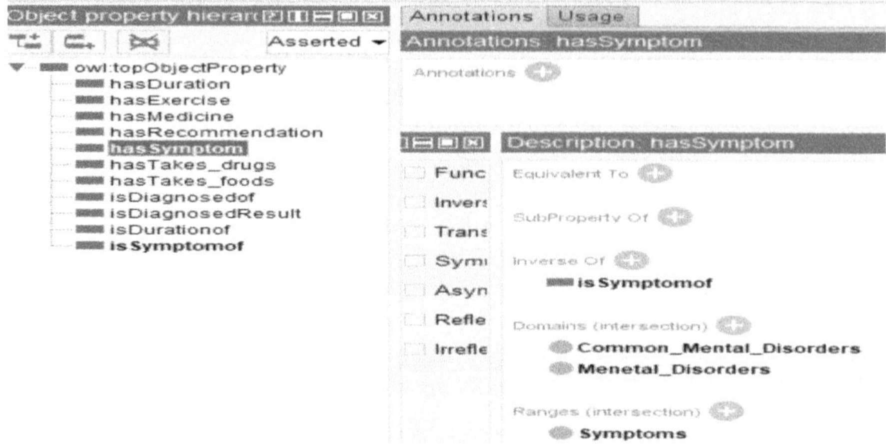

Fig. 5. Facets, domain and range of ontology

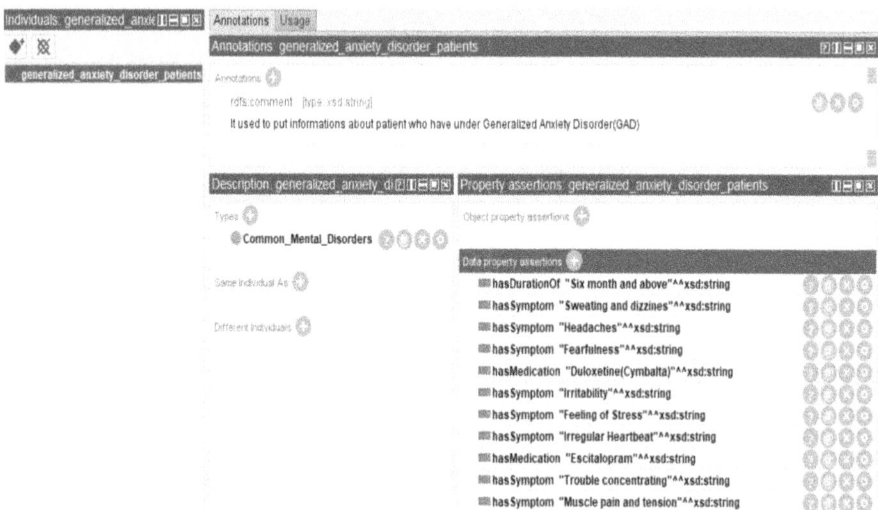

Fig. 6. Sample instance of generalized anxiety disorder

3.6 SPARQL Query

After we have designed the ontology for our purpose, we need to visualize and validate it. By using a protégé onto graph plug-in tool, we can visualize the result of our ontology. In order to verify our ontology we use SPARQL queries and Apache Jena Fuseki to retrieve and manipulate data from the ontology repository.

We can retrieve the subject and object pairs in our ontology using the following queries. We can show the relationships between concepts in our ontology. The subclass and superclass hierarchy of our ontology can be retrieved using the following query. The query and its result is (Fig. 7).

Fig. 7. The ontology's query result for the subject-object relationship

Sample query for retrieving medication and treatments of generalized anxiety disorder.

We can retrieve an information about treatment and medication drugs used for generalized anxiety disorder. Those treatments and medications are retrieved from the ontology model and the query and result is shown below (Fig. 8).

```
PREFIX rdf: <http://www.semanticweb.org/aab/ontologies/2022/7/common-mental-disorder#>
PREFIX owl: <http://www.w3.org/2002/07/owl#>
PREFIX rdfs: <http://www.w3.org/2000/01/rdf-schema#>
PREFIX xsd: <http://www.w3.org/2001/XMLSchema#>
SELECT ?Generalized_Anxiety_Disorder ?Treatment
    WHERE {

 ?Generalized_Anxiety_Disorder rdf:hasTreatment ?Treatment
}
?Generalized_Anxiety_Disorder rdf:hasMedicine ?Medications
```

	Generalized_Anxiety_Disorder	Medications
1	rdf:generalized_anxiety_disorder_patients	"Avoid alcohol and recreational drugs"
2	rdf:generalized_anxiety_disorder_patients	"Eat Health"
3	rdf:generalized_anxiety_disorder_patients	"Make sleep a priority"
4	rdf:generalized_anxiety_disorder_patients	"Cognitive behavioural therapy"

	Generalized_Anxiety_Disorder	Medications
1	rdf:generalized_anxiety_disorder_patients	"Duloxetine (Cymbalta)- 60 milligrams"
2	rdf:generalized_anxiety_disorder_patients	"Escitalopram - 10 Milligrams"

Fig. 8. Sample query and results for treatment of generalized anxiety disorder

Query for retrieving recommended information from domain ontology for generalized anxiety disorder.

We can retrieve recommended information from our ontology model about generalized anxiety disorder using Fuseki server. It helps to support persons to know more about each disorder. Sample query and results are shown below (Fig. 9).

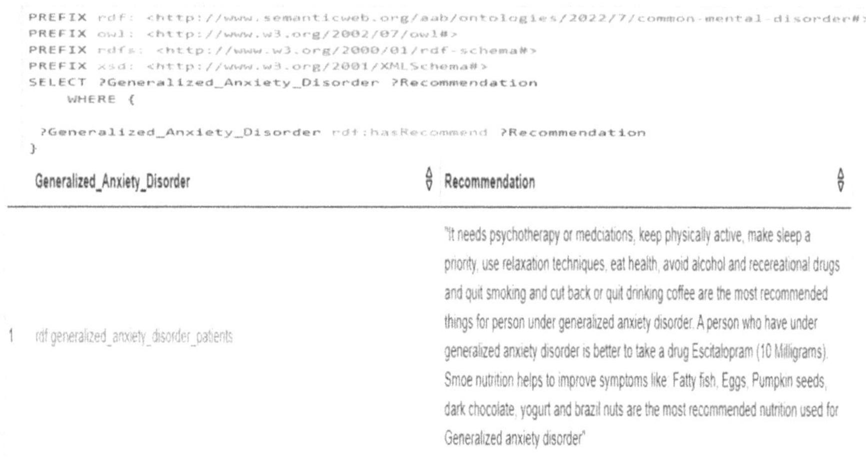

Fig. 9. Sample query and results for Recommendation for generalized anxiety disorder.

3.7 Rules for Diagnosis Common Mental Disorder

As a sample of how rules are codified, the following sample predicated logic used for schizophrenia shows how we build diagnostic rules in SWRL style and in accordance with the rules used by experts to get the diagnosed result for a certain patient's symptom.

IF patient has Delusion
AND patient has Hallucination
AND patient has disorganized thinking
AND patient has extremely disorganized motor behavior
AND patient has negative symptom
THEN diagnosed result: Schizophrenia Disorder.

The following is an easy way to convert the above predicate logic rule to SWRL:-

Patients (? p)
^ hasSymptom (?p, Delusion)
^ hasSymptom (?p, Hallucination)
^ hasSymptom (?p, disorganized thinking)
^ hasSymptom (?p, extremely disorganized motor behavior)
^ hasSymptom (?p, negative symptom)
isDiagnosedResult (?p, Schizophrenia Disorder).

Rules are developed to diagnose a common mental disorders.

4 An Investigational Result

System-centered evaluation and subjective expert level evaluation were carried out in the proposed work by assessing the system's performance using objective evaluation criteria that are frequently used to gauge such systems. We have used some patients symptoms the experts gathered and diagnosed before on the mental health sector. The criteria for selecting these were due to the facts that they are expert on mental health disorder diagnosis and prevention since they are psychiatrist professionals. we have developed a model that diagnosis, recommend and gives other related treatment information for each five common mental disorders namely, Generalized Depression Disorder, Generalized Anxiety Disorder, Schizophrenia, Substance Use Disorder and Bipolar Mental Health Disorders and we used a SWRL rule and pellet reasoner for diagnosis process. After we finished the development of this model, the patients symptom and diagnosed result done by experts checked by the model whether it is correctly diagnosed and gives same result as diagnosed by expert or not.

In order to ascertain whether the common mental disorder diagnosis model operates precisely as we anticipate, we present the evaluation. This evaluation's primary objective is to determine how well the model can diagnose common mental illnesses based on patient symptoms that are present in our model. SWRL rules and the pellet reasoner, which are employed in our method to determine the accurate diagnosis based on symptoms, are necessary for model evaluation. From Jimma University Referral Hospital, we selected 34 sample patients with symptoms that had previously been diagnosed by reputable psychiatrists. We confirm that the model can diagnose the majority of these situations. The number of hospitalized patients' symptoms that were diagnosed by psychiatrists and the number of accurate and inaccurate diagnostic findings are shown in the following table from our developed model.

The results shows that the developed model can diagnosed correctly 32 out of the 34 sample patient's symptom taken (ratio of correctness is 94.1%) (Table 1).

The applicability of the prototype is evaluated by potential users of the model. After the prototype of ontology-based diagnosis and recommendation model was developed, evaluation procedures were conducted by developing sample user interface that able to access information from ontology-based knowledge to check the performance of the prototype model and acceptability by the users. Totally we selected seven persons for accepting feedbacks. Those person is selected from the health sector and two of them are psychiatrist doctor expert which they are actually working in domain health sector and the others five are non-psychiatrist expert that they are working in different primary and higher health sector. The non-experts are currently gives services as a main for other non-mental illness related disease in the health sector. We select less number of feedback because of most of the time experts done in hospital are always busy and even if once the doctor know about the mental illness related service, other worker existed under can get gradually get experience.

Table 1 Patients' symptoms diagnosed by developed model and experts

Expert Diagnosis	System Diagnosis					
	Anxiety Disorder	Bipolar Disorder	Depression Disorder	Schizophrenia Disorder	Substance Use Disorder	No Result
Anxiety Disorder	5	–	1	–	–	–
Bipolar Disorder	–	7	–	–	–	–
Depression Disorder	–	–	5	–	–	–
Schizophrenia Disorder	–	–	–	10	–	–
Substance Use Disorder	–	–	–	–	5	1

5 Conclusion

Common mental disorders are the public mental health problems that commonly exist in primary care. The serious shortage of mental health professionals and the comparatively low levels of awareness about mental disorders are the major problems of the area. For such problems a semantic web-based diagnosis and treatment model helps to give full information for treatments as well as recommending relevant information and gives awareness for others who do not have enough know-how about such kind of diseases. Designing such kinds of model in different domain area is well-explored in this research. We have evaluated the proposed model by using different evaluation metrics. The first one is model performance evaluation. For this, we used sample patients symptom diagnosed by experts from Jimma University Referral Hospital Psychiatry wards. And performance of the model diagnosed correctly is 94.1%. For the second user acceptance evaluation we used different persons including from health sectors which have no more expert on mental health disorder by developing sample user interface which enables to access relevant information from domain ontology-based knowledge. And sample system performance evaluation taken from the evaluator is 85.3%.

Generally, results from our evaluation indicate that using semantic web technology in the development of semantic web-based diagnosis and treatment model is most important to give appropriate diagnosis and treatment recommendations for common mental disorder and the average performance is 89.7%.

References

1. Hardy, S.: Common mental health disorders in general practice, **29**(2) (2018)
2. Solomon, E.: Mental Disorder: Menatal Helath Remains An Invisible Problem in Africa. Eur. J. Res. Reflect. Educ. Sci. **2**(4) (2014)
3. Desta, M.: Epidemiology of child psychiatric disorders in Addis Ababa, Ethiopia, Doctoral dissertation, Barn-och ungdomspsykiatri (2008)
4. World Health Organization: Depression and Other Common Mental Disorders: Global Health Estimates (2017)
5. Kadim, F.B., Zainab, I., Othman, A.O.N.T.O.: An ontology system for diagnosing asthma disease. J. Al-Qadisiyah Comput. Sci. Math. **14**(2), 81–90 (2022)
6. Thermolia, Chryssa, H., Ekaterini, S.: An ontological-based monitoring system for patients with bipolar I disorder. In: International Conference on Biomedical Engineering and Comp, pp. 43–49 (2015)
7. Tumnark, P., Oliveira, L., Santibutr, N.: Ontology-Based Personalized Dietary Recommendation for Weightlifting. In: International Workshop on Computer Science in Sports, pp. 44–49 (2013)
8. Rawte, V., Roy, B.: Thyroid Disease Diagnosis using Ontology based Expert System. Int. J. Eng. Res. **0**(6) (2015)

Comparative Study: Contextual Understanding with BioBERT vs. Practical Integration of LLaMA 2 13B Model for Healthcare Assistance

S. Amudha[✉] [iD], W. Jesuwin John Prince, G. Harish Kumar,
and R. M. Satiya Pragaash

Department of Computational Intelligence, Faculty of Engineering and Technology, School of computing, SRM Institute of Science and Technology, Chengalpet, Kattankulathur, Tamil Nadu, India
amudhas@srmist.edu.in

Abstract. This work tries to systematically compare two cutting-edge language models, Bio BERT and LLM (large language model) within the framework of developing a novel medical chatbot. The objective of our work is to develop a healthcare information system that will be based on fine-tuned language models and will be able to communicate with users in an accurate, sensitive and customized manner. The model performance of LLaMA, the large model language, and Bio BERT, designed specifically for text data in the biomedical domain are compared in several tasks including entity recognition, question answering, and dialogue generation in the medical area. The results suggest that both models have the ability to comprehend sophisticated biomedical ideas and produce useful replies. The results show that Bio BERT is able to achieve very high effectiveness on named entity recognition and question answering by getting access to a huge number of biomedical concepts and contextual information. On the other hand, Llama is able to generate emotionally and contextually relevant responses increasing user appreciation and involvement. The target goal in performing this comparative analysis is to highlight the merits and demerits of the features of each model as well as assist in guiding future medical research directions. This work utilizes state-of-the-art language models to provide personalized medical services and hence contribute to solutions to issues of digital healthcare and global health literacy. The comparative study also examines the scalability and cost efficiency as well as the practical implementation of both the Bio BERT and Llama models in the healthcare settings. Bio BERT achieves good performance in specific biomedical tasks but due to its high computational needs and fine-tuning procedure it may have limited penetration in the wider market. At the same time, the Llama model has the advantages of being able to be expanded and integrated quite easily which might possibly facilitate the development and the introduction of medical chatbots in a number of healthcare settings. The research aims at answering such questions and in doing so provide a baseline for understanding the potential helpfulness of elegant language models in enhancing healthcare information systems.

Keywords: Language Models · Medical NLP · Bioinformatics · Comparative Analysis

R. Appavoo et al. (Eds.): IconDeepCom 2024, CCIS 2687, pp. 352–363, 2026.
https://doi.org/10.1007/978-3-032-26680-4_28

1   Introduction

Digital health transformation is taking place, and chatbots are becoming an important part of this by providing tools for better and greater patient engagement, access to healthcare information and support to healthcare providers. Here, it is possible to radically reimagine how healthcare is provided by deploying natural language processing (NLP) models that comprehend the user's questions and respond accordingly [1]. The research presented in this paper aims to investigate with BERT and LLM models when performing generation of biomedical text and responding to questions asked by users. Both models are distinct in their design, training approach and performance characteristics, yet they share the goal of improving the ease of conversational exchanges [2]. Thus, such comparative analysis should pave the way for better understanding of each model's suitability in the context of the proposed healthcare related scenarios and support with formulation of requirements and design of medical chatbot systems and assess the positives and negatives for every model implemented [3].

BERT is a model of the transformer architecture which has become popular for its ability to understand the context in both directions. The model was trained on various corpora of large text. It is often applicable to the classifier of multiple NLP tasks including text classification, named entity recognition, and question answering because of its capability to perform tuning. In the case of chatbots for medicine, BERT's knowledge of words and concepts and the scope of the context of its usage enable it to answer questions posed by users in an accurate and informative manner. Text generators have become extremely useful in recent years. The synthesis of textual means lightweight programming for those who were ready to face the unexplored interface of AI [4].

More recently, a LLM is an advanced version of language modeling which is an expansion of the techniques that have been employed in OpenAI's language models on a massive scale and complex data. Once fine-tuned, Llama exhibits great powers in generating text and deep understanding of the nuances of language. Consistent with its design, it also facilitates more efficient and scalable real time applications such as chatbots where speed and agility is needed. The capabilities of BERT and LLM models are evaluated along with a range of metrics that pertain to a medical chatbot through a series of tests and assessments. These include performance across AI metrics, metrics on continuity of thought and metrics on whether comprehension of context was achieved among other things. The goal is to assess the implications of each model or particular group of models by looking at the characteristics of the data to be analyzed and form recommendations on how to implement them in a specific branch namely healthcare. In general, considering the reduced effects of cross model differences, this particular paper contributes to the ongoing debate on the applicability of complex models in language used by medical chatbots. With an understanding of the strengths and weaknesses of BERT and LLM models, developers and researchers can design and improve chatbots to provide health care information and services [5].

2 State of the Art of Work

In this study [1], A teacher model serves as the information source for QA-interaction which offers a knowledge distillation framework for biological factoid question answering. The teacher model aims to improve the student model. The model put out by the writers of this book incorporates the best features of both student and knowledgeable teacher models—teachers are typically human experts. In this work [2], In addition to engaging users in conversation about their health issues, a text-to-text verdict bot offers a customized diagnosis based on the user's symptoms. People will therefore receive information about their medical status and the appropriate level of safety.

The authors of the study [3] looked over several chatbot- related publications from the previous five years. Subsequently,they presented many relevant works on their topic and the artificial intelligence principles required to construct a sophisticated conversational bot grounded in deep learning models. Google API is used in this study [4] to convert text to speech and voice to text. An Android app displays the response that ChatBot receives once it receives a query and finds relevant information. By utilizing the system's extensibility, it will be possible to emulate a counselor's voice and facial recognition in the future and engage with patients on a more profound level.

This paper [5] focuses on assessing the symptoms of tropical diseases in Nigeria. The Telegram Bot Application Programming Interface (API) was used to create the interconnection between the chatbot and the system, whileTwilio API was used for interconnectivity between the system and a short messaging service subscriber. In this paper [6], the authors suggest using a language model to automatically respond to COVID-19-related questions and assess the resulting responses on a qualitative level. Utilizing transfer learning, the authors retrained the GPT-2 language model on the COVID-19 Open Research Dataset (CORD-19) corpus.

In relation to the COVID-19 pandemic, this paper [7] offers a novel use of natural language processing (NLP). It focuses on building a conversational chatbot that can offer vital advice and information about COVID-19. This study highlights the potential of AI-powered chatbots as useful resources for communicating critical medical information to the public during public health emergencies. The authors of this paper [8] carry out a thorough analysis of the technical factors involved in the creation of chatbots for use in medicine. It explores the complexities involved in creating and deploying chatbots that meet the particular needs of the medical industry. This scoping review offers insightful information about the technical difficulties and solutions involved in creating chatbots with a healthcare specialty.

The authors of this paper [9] present a novel chatbot system that uses the Chinese BERT language model to combat drug abuse. In order to identify and address drug-related conversations, it focuses on cognitive intent analysis. This study shows how sophisticated natural language processing (NLP) techniques can be used to address social problems like drug abuse using chatbot-based interventions. The effect of large language models, in particular ChatGPT, on public health is critically examined in this paper [10]. It draws attention to the difficulties and dangers of misinformation that these models may present when distributing health related information. The intricate interactions between AI-driven language models and the distribution of health information during public health emergencies are clarified by this research.

A novel method for improving medical dialogue generation using augmented graphs is presented in the paper [11]. It Shows the potential for more knowledgeable and context-aware conversations in the medical domain by highlighting the integration of structured medical knowledge to enhance the caliber and applicability of conversational interactions in healthcare settings. The study [12] investigates how machine learning can be used to improve communication in the healthcare industry.It explores the application of cutting-edge machine learning techniques to enhance patient-physician interactions, simplify medical record administration, and maximize the sharing of healthcare information.

This research paper [13] discusses a chatbot solution with the help of machine learning to gather data. The author of this paper plans to address non clinical responses with low error percentage in the future. The authors of this paper [14] describe a conversational system that can converse with the user and retrieve information related to corona viruses from a wealth of medical literature. As a part of future enhancement, the authors suggests adding a module to generate human understandable responses.

According to this article [15], the suggested model performed better in terms of overall specializations when compared to competing models. The suggested model's value is further illustrated by the authors through case studies for visualization applications. It will be necessary to tackle the issue of emergency medicine prediction cautiously. As a result, in order to use the suggested model in practice, the prediction results must be interpreted extremely carefully

3 Methodology

A. *Dataset preparation and Pre-processing*

The project for this thesis involves the handling of medical questions and answers directly obtained from iCliniq, WebMD, eHealth Forum and others. Initially, the dataset consisting of 29,752 pairs in the form of question answer was available in JSON format but later combined into a single comprehensively coherent data set structure for the purposes of training And testing. The entire dataset is constructed in such a way that it has records of a person, the system generated prompt simulating a medical condition example of a question that people are seeking help and a comprehensive pair that answers the question posted. Answers to be provided will be formulated to meet the intended aim of the response in such a manner as to allow for maximum clarity and focus without excessive detail for example many responses are expanded on with reference URLs to relevant medical websites. The work therefore seeks to develop, test and evaluate BERT and LLM language models with the expectation that the models would enhance the quality of healthcare questions and answers in the client side.

B. *Fine-tuning BERT model*

The BERT model needs to be repeatedly adapted in a number of critical manners as to enhance its performance for certain tasks such as medical research, and its analysis. To begin with, the architecture of the model, a set of the number of layers and the number of neurons in each layer, is determined. Pre-trained weights from related tasks or random initialization of weights and biases helps in convergence. The network is traversed by the input data during the forward pass, with activation functions such as sigmoid or ReLU (Rectified Linear Units) introducing non-linearity. Various metrics such as accuracy, precision, recall and F1-score are used to assess the model"s performance; threshold accuracy becomes important for determining the model's usefulness. The completeness of the model is evidently never more than the performance of its worst component, which is commonly defined by a threshold metric that facilitates alterations in the parameters and design for biomedical requirements. So that the model has the desired level of accuracy, relevant evaluations with different threshold values enable to find out the acceptable balance between precision and recall. This refined BERT model, first of all, allows to perform accurate and reliable research with this approach, contributing to the development of biomedical research and the field of its analysis.

C. *Fine-tuning LLM model*

The LLaMA 2 13B model has to be fine-tuned in a more controlled manner by training it in the healthcare domain. In being exposed to trained medical datasets comprised of literature, patient questions and expert's comments the model learns to interact in an appropriate way and answering medical questions appropriately in context and in emotion. At this stage of retraining, refinement of the tasks seems to affect the model architecture and parameters themselves as well as the reason for pretraining which in this case is to reduce the supervised fine tuning (SFT) which is.

This method ultimately intends to increase Llama 2 13B model effectiveness in terms of medical conversations thus assisting in creating sophisticated medicine bots. The entire process involves gathering massive amounts of truthful medical q and a databases then using these databases to fine tune bert and lainama (Llama-2 13B) models for use in medical bots. The series of feedback cycles ensured that the model could always deal with correctly structured medical questions to the required level of detail and relevance in the right context.

4 Comparative Analysis

The main purpose of this study is to compare the performance of biomedical text understanding and generation between regular BERT, Fine-tuned BERT and LLM (LLaMA 2 13B) models. A dataset of research articles, clinical texts and biomedical literature is constructed so that both models could be tested for their performances across various tasks. To adapt their language skills to the domain to some extent, the models need to be pretrained on A biological dataset. In order to make the understanding and the generation of medical contents better, this involves redesigning model architectures, re-tuning parameters, and conducting training on textual data of the biomedical domain. The models' effectiveness in interpreting biological texts is evaluated using a range of evaluation metrics such as accuracy, precision, recall, and F1-score by conducting set performance evaluation. In order to test the models' capability of producing answers that are consistent with the context, several fluency, coherence and contextual knowledge measures are applied. Also, the inquiry addresses the aspects of scalability and computational cost in both models, such as model and memory size, and time taken for the inference.

The aim of the comparative analysis is to evaluate the pros and cons of BERT and LLaMA models in the sphere of producing and understanding biomedical texts as a result of thorough experimentation and evaluation. It is important for the researchers as they can select the ideal model for biomedical objectives by being aware of the performance enabled by the models for a number of tasks and metrics. In the end, the result will enhance the area of biomedicine research and analysis. BERT is an MLM based model that works with single-word predictions in sentences where one or more words are masked out. On the contrary, LLAMA is able to perform NLU and NLG tasks. Since it is capable of getting the meaning of input queries, raises considerable confidence in providing adequate responses of different kinds.

5 Design and Architecture

A. *Architecture of BERT model*

Modelling architecture of the BERT system can be divided into three broad sections such as Preprocessing (NLP Module), Bio BERT Integration and the response generation (Fig. 1).

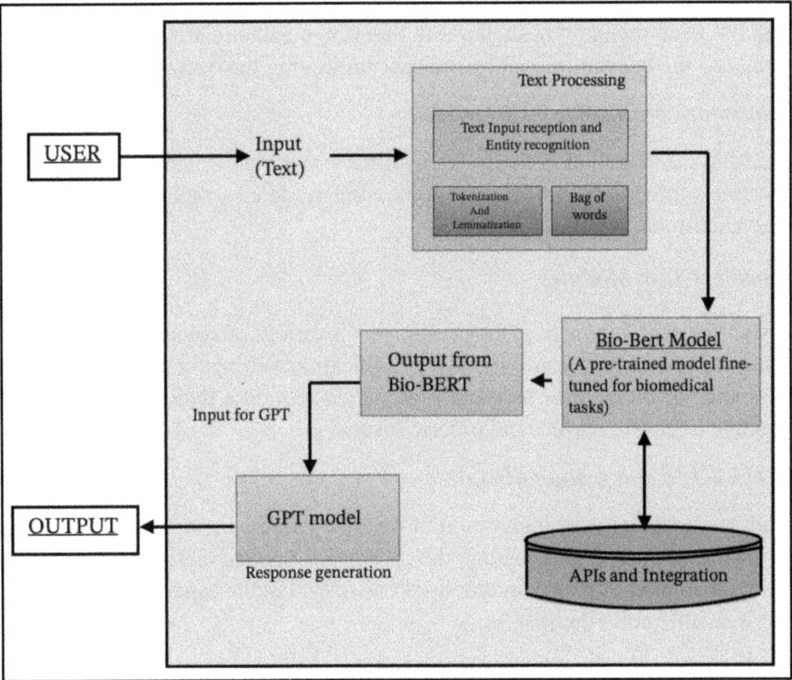

Fig. 1. Architecture of BERT model

a. *Preprocessing (NLP) Module:*

The inputs are collected from the user and passed into the NLP module. This module helps to interpret the user input and understand the overall context of it. This NLP module will implement various methods to read queries, identify the keywords in the queries and classify it with reference to biomedical terms.

b. ***BioBERT Integration:***

A notable feature of the system architecture is the incorporation of the BioBERT model. BioBERT is a specialized biological model that is well suited in understanding the subtleties in language used in medicine which is imparted to the chatbot whenever it is answering questions. BioBERT is triggered to interpret the medical context further and provide further comprehension beyond the basic knowledge of the language as the user questions pass through the NLP module. This makes it possible for the chatbot to never use obsolete or incorrect medical facts in its answers.

c. ***Response Generation***

In the last layer of the architecture, which is response generation of the user's input, here the chatbot gives a convincing answer or provides additional information after comprehending the user's question and having some information from BioBERT. In order to suit the demands of the user, this response could be suggestions, the possible diagnosis, clarifications, or even some general medical concepts. It also shows that the response has been prepared in such a way that is sympathetic and consoled that is clear and precise to the question posed by the user improving the overall user experience.

B. ***Architecture of LLaMA 2 13B model***

The LLaMA 2 13B model contains four primary modules which include, Biomedical Task modules, Integration module, Preprocessing module as well as the Evaluation and Validation sub-module Fig. 2.

a. ***Biomedical Task Modules***

The design for each biomedical task comprises a variety of components such as entity recognition, question answering and text classification.Settings certain complexities and characteristics of biomedical text analysis, which require a dedicated architecture for each module to ensure correct and precise results.

b. ***LLaMA 2 13B Integration Module***

The module allows for easy integration of this fine tuned Llama 2 13B into the system. Again, the module is useful in loading the 13 B pre-trained model which helps in configuring the environment for easy interactions ensuring that the capabilities of the Llama 2 13B are well utilized in the system.

c. ***Data Preprocessing and Integration Module***

A specific module was developed to address the issues of the pretreatment as well as integration of the diverse data across the dataset. The module also enhances the smooth transformation of the raw data into ideal forms which complies with the requirements needed for the appropriate analytical process.

d.

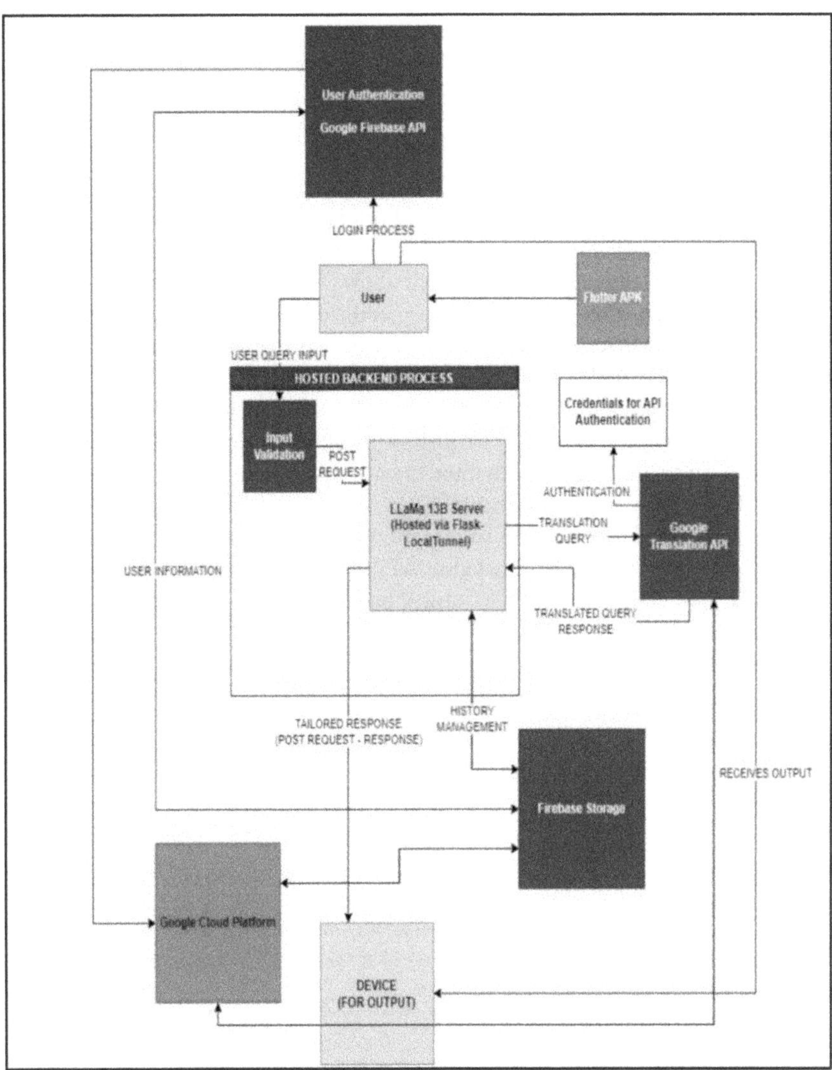

Fig. 2. Architecture of LLaMA 2 13B model

Evaluation and Validation Module

The dataset permits this module describes an evaluation and a validation of the LLaMA 2 13B model performance. This facilitates metrological evaluation of the model's performance in terms of accuracy, precision and recall which in turn makes it possible to identify potential areas for subsequent improvements.

6 Results and Discussions

As a result of the comparative analysis, it is evident that LLaMA model is performing comparatively better than BERT in interpreting, as well as generating bio medical responses.The NLU and NLG features of LLaMA model added an advantage in understanding and generating the responses to the user's query. Concerning the fact that LLaMa is able to provide efficient and decisive, detail oriented and context affirming responses to bio-medical queries it may be tempting to say that it replaces BERT. Models such as LLaMa has many language models which allows them to use cohorts of texts understanding word and language relations of the specific domain which is biomedicine. This in the end leads LLaMa to offer more relevant and reasonable answers to the questions posed by medical knowledge holders.

In addition, the utilization of Google's translation APIs enhances LLaMA's capabilities. In the first place, it is now possible to translate medical questions and answers with relative ease so that LLaMA can interact with many more users who speak different languages. This is very important in situations where such applications are designed to help the patients since they need to supply the information in different languages. The scalability offered by Google's translation APIs revolutionizes the LLaMA's multilingual competences, thus enhancing its utility and relevance in global health concerns. Now that LMA is integrated with most of the translation facilities, it is now easily useful for patients, researchers, and health care providers who are looking for information on medical issues in their preferred languages.

Question
Which mRNAs are sequestered in stress granules?
Passage and exact answer
The Stress Granule Transcriptome Reveals Principles of mRNA Accumulation in Stress Granules. Stress granules are mRNA-protein assemblies formed from **nontranslating mRNAs**. Stress granules are important in the stress response and may contribute to some degenerative diseases. Here, we describe the ... While essentially every mRNA, and some noncoding RNAs (ncRNAs), can be targeted to stress granules, the targeting efficiency ...
Prediction of KDQA-BioBERT
noncoding RNAs

Fig. 3. BERT model output

Figure 3 contains the output from the BERT model. This output is taken as a reference from the research paper [1]. From the analysis, it is found that the LLaMA model performs better in generating bio medical responses when compared to the responses from the BERT model. The output of LLaMA is more contextually precise and also supports multiple languages to generate responses. (Fig. 4.)

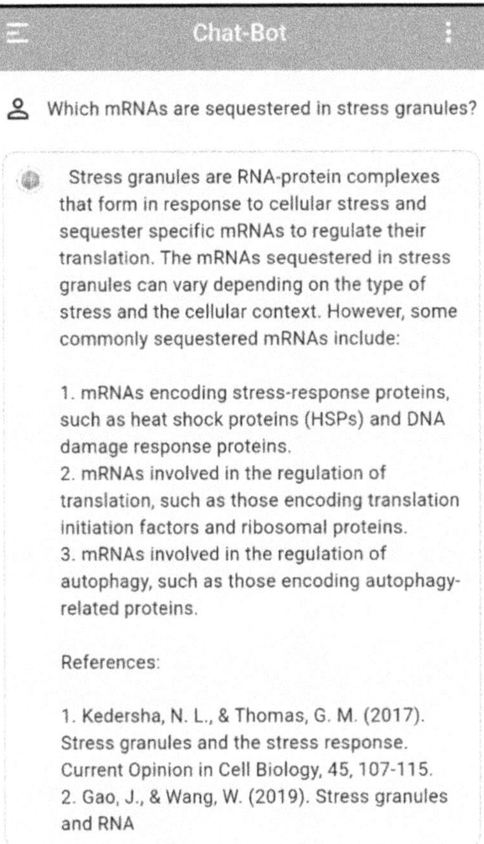

Fig. 4. LLaMA model output

7   Conclusion and Future Enhancement

In summary, what stands out in our comparison between BERT and LLaMA models, is the performance and the adaptability of the LLaMA especially in the context of generation and comprehension of biomedical text. When viewed from another perspective, BERT being an entirely understanding model with regard to particular architectural elements, the language explicating it and literature dealing with it comprehension is at a better rate. Moreover, the need to take note of LLaMA's span is catered for through interplay with Google's translation APIs, making it viable for use in the international healthcare context. The results suggest that LLaMA has the capacity to be a very effective tool in tasks concerning healthcare support. The implementation of such tools can improve the access to medical information globally. In future potentials with regards to LLaMA are infinite taking into consideration the improvement of its reverse direction with regard to health care assistance and other areas for which LLaMA's Factors are required. LLaMA's span can be such factors due to their biomedicine specific nature.

Further, LLaMA language span effects of various biomedical specific datasets on its performance can result in allomorph perfectness when LLAma's factors are on.

Author's Contributions. Writing – Original draft preparation, S. Amudha; Writing – review and editing, Jesuwin John Prince W; Funding acquisition, Testing and Debugging, Harish Kumar G and Satiya Pragaash R M, All authors have read and agreed to the published version of the manuscript.

References

1. Bai, J., et al.: Adversarial knowledge distillation based biomedical factoid question answering. IEEE/ACM Trans. Comput. Biol. **20**(1), 106–118 (2023). https://doi.org/10.1109/TCBB.2022.3161032
2. Ahmed, M. Abdelhakim, A., Ayanouz, B., Soufyane.: (2021). An Intelligent Chatbot Using NLP and TF-IDF Algorithm for TextUnderstanding Applied to the Medical Field. 10.1007/978-3-030- 53440-0-1.
3. Ayanouz, S., Abdelhakim, A., Benhmed, B. M.: (2020). A Smart Chatbot Architecture Based NLP and Machine Learning for Health Care Assistance.10.1145/3386723.3387897.
4. Dharwadkar., M.R., Deshpande, D.M.N.A.: A medical ChatBot. Int. J. Comput. Trends Technol. **60**(1), 41–45 (2018) ISSN:2231-2803. www.ijcttjournal.org. Published by Seventh Sense Research Group
5. Omoregbe, N.A.I., Ndaman, I.O., Misra, S., Abayomi-Alli, O.O., Damasˇevicˇius, R.: Text messaging based medical diagnosis using natural language processing and fuzzy logic. J. Healthc. Eng. **2020**, 8839524 (2020). https://doi.org/10.1155/2020/8839524
6. Oniani, D., Wang, Y.: A qualitative evaluation of language models on automatic question-answering for COVID-19. In: Proceedings of the 11th ACM International Conference on Bioinformatics, Computational Biology and Health Informatics (BCB '20). Association for Computing Machinery, pp. 1–9. ACM, New York (2020). https://doi.org/10.1145/3388440.3412413
7. Singh, S., Kaur, M., Tanwar, P., Sharma, S.: Design and development of conversational chatbot for Covid-19 using NLP: an AI application. In: 2022 6th International Conference on Computing Methodologies and Communication (ICCMC), Erode, India, pp. 1654–1658 (2022). https://doi.org/10.1109/ICCMC53470.2022.9753893
8. Safi, Z., Abd-Alrazaq, A., Khalifa, M., Househ, M.: Technical aspects of developing chatbots for medical applications: a scoping review. J. Med. Internet Res. **22**(12), e19127. https://www.jmir.org/2020/12/e19127 (2020). https://doi.org/10.2196/1912
9. Lee, J.H., Wu, E.H.-K., Ou, Y.-Y., Lee, Y.-C., Lee, C.-H., Chung, C.-R.: Anti-drugs chatbot: Chinese BERT-based cognitive intent analysis. IEEE Trans. Comput. Soc. Syst. (2023). https://doi.org/10.1109/TCSS.2023.3238477
10. De Angelis, L. et al.: ChatGPT and the rise of large language models: the new AI- driven infodemic threat in public health. Front. Public Health. **25**(11), 1166120 (2023). https://doi.org/10.3389/fpubh.2023.1166120. PMID: 37181697;PMCID: PMC10166793
11. Varshney, D., Zafar, A., Behera, N.K., et al.: Knowledge grounded medical dialogue generation using augmented graphs. Sci. Rep. **13**, 3310 (2023). https://doi.org/10.1038/s41598-023-29213-8
12. Siddique, S., Chow, J.C.L.: Machine learning in health- care communication. Encyclopedia. **1**, 220–239 (2021). https://doi.org/10.3390/encyclopedia1010021

13. Lei, H. et al.: COVID-19 smart chatbot prototype for patient monitoring ((1) rice university, houston, united states, (2) the university of texas health science center at houston, united states) (2021)
14. Das, S. et al.: Medical literature mining and retrieval in a conversational setting predicting medical specialty from text based on a domain-specific pre-trained BERT. Int. J. Med. Inform. **170**, 104956 (2023). https://doi.org/10.1016/j.ijmedinf.2022.104956. Epub2022 Dec 9. PMID: 36512987; PMCID: PMC9731829

Long Term Rainfall Forecasting Using Deep Learning Approach: The Case of Ilu Abba Borzone

Alemayehu Etana Duguma[(⊠)], Ramata Mosissa Gichila, and Wagari Goje Tuji

Department of Information Technology, Mattu University, Mettu, Ethiopia
alemayoetana@gmail.com

Abstract. The development of long-term rainfall forecasting presented n this research used comparative deep-learning approaches. The long-term meteorological data is collected from the National Meteorological Agency of Ethiopia at the Jimma service center in the southwestern part of the Oromia region. Using data collected during the last 15 years, missing values are pre-processed using the anticipated algorithm, and the data are further normalized to enhance the effectiveness of the forecasting system. The results of CNN and LSTM models are compared with different performance measurements, such as root mean absolute error and mean absolute error. The CNN algorithm's MAE and RMSE values were 3.58 and 7.85, while the LSTM algorithm's MAE and RMSE values were 4.97 and 8.61. The CNN algorithm was able to forecast an accuracy of 98.18%. On the other hand, LSTM algorithms achieved an accuracy of 96.73%. As a result, CNN performed well in terms of accuracy when compared to the LSTM method.

Keywords: Long Short Term Memory (LSTM) · Convolutional Neural Network (CNN) · Rainfall Forecasting

1   Introduction

Long-term rainfall forecasting is an essential task for ensuring water resource management, agriculture, and disaster management in many parts of the world. Rainfall is a key factor that influences several aspects of our daily lives, from agriculture to transportation, energy generation, and water resource management. Accurate and timely rainfall forecasting is essential to making sure the efficient and effective management of these areas. Traditional approaches to rainfall forecasting rely on statistical models and climatological data, which often have limited accuracy and reliability, especially in the long term [1].

Ethiopia's economy depends on its agricultural sector. Furthermore, rainfall, an atmospheric variable, is crucial to Ethiopian agriculture. Thus, our country's climate is defined by changes in rainfall.

Rainfall forecasting is the most crucial backbone in the planet. Because the condition of the atmosphere also affects a lot of other industries, airlines, and the agricultural sector. People who are unable to employ meteorological technology, especially in Ethiopia,

© The Author(s), under exclusive license to Springer Nature Switzerland AG 2026
R. Appavoo et al. (Eds.): IconDeepCom 2024, CCIS 2687, pp. 364–376, 2026.
https://doi.org/10.1007/978-3-032-26680-4_29

still forecast the amount of precipitation based on personal observations. For example, they often predict connected rainfall based on temperature and wind, meaning that if they observe a high temperature and a low wind speed, they expect rain. The use of science and technology to predict atmospheric weather conditions for a specific location and future time is known as rainfall forecasting. Rainfall prediction is just one of the primary areas of weather forecasting, and it is crucial for planning including food production, water resource management, and all other natural activities. Rainfall is the primary function of the hydrologic cycle and is essential to all life. Rainfall might appear as fog, mist, drizzle, snow, sleet, or glaze since it is a very non-linear natural occurrence. In a country like Ethiopia, where 90% of the land is categorized as rain-fed, rainwater in the form of soil moisture and groundwater is the most crucial requirement for agricultural productivity and social development. Although Oromia has an adequate supply of water, some areas of the country are experiencing drought and flooding due to the uneven geographical distribution of rainfall [1]. At the moment, predicting weather and climate events is a big issue for meteorologists, especially in emerging nations like Ethiopia. Despite this, a great deal of study has been conducted in this field utilising various techniques, including neural networks, statistical methods, and numerical methods, but the results have fallen short of expectations [1]. The use of deep learning techniques for long-term rainfall forecasting has gained popularity recently. In a variety of prediction tasks, including natural language, deep learning models including convolutional neural networks (CNNs), recurrent neural networks (RNNs), and long short-term memory (LSTM) networks have shown exceptional performance. Time series forecasting, image recognition, and ge processing. These models are appropriate for capturing the complex dynamics of rainfall patterns because they are able to learn detailed patterns and relationships in the data [2].

To improve this region's agricultural and crop productivity forecasting long-term rainfall is a crucial task. By developing hierarchical representations of the input data, deep learning techniques have shown promise in overcoming these difficulties. In order to evaluate the efficacy of deep learning models for long-term rainfall forecasting, more study is necessary.

When it rains heavily or there is a lengthy dry spell during a crop's vital growth and development stages, the crop's yield may be significantly reduced. Consequently, this estimate has been found to be very important for decision-making in water resources management.

Agriculture is heavily reliant on rainfall, and long-term rainfall forecasts are essential for crop planning and management. Traditional methods of forecasting such as statistical models have limitations in accurately predicting long-term rainfall patterns. Consequently, it's necessary to explore alternative approaches such as deep learning techniques.

Numerous investigations have been carried out. in this area. A deep learning-based framework for long-term rainfall forecasting is the subject of this thesis. The framework made use of a Long Short Term Memory (LSTM) to represent temporal correlations in the data and a convolutional neural network (CNN) to extract features from historical rainfall data. The suggested model demonstrated increased accuracy in forecasting long-term rainfall patterns compared to traditional statistical models [3].

Rainfall is a critical component of the Earth's water cycle and has significant impacts on various human activities, including agriculture, energy generation, and urban planning. Predicting rainfall patterns in the long term is essential for efficient management of water resources, but it has proven to be a difficult undertaking because of the complexity and non-linearity of the meteorological processes involved. Conventional statistical techniques have been used for rainfall forecasting, but they are limited in their capacity for capture the complex relationships between the different variables.

Recent developments in deep learning have demonstrated encouraging outcomes in various fields, including meteorology, where neural networks have been used for weather forecasting. However, the effectiveness of deep learning approaches in long-term rainfall forecasting remains largely unexplored [4].

A few important details in the Ilu Aba Bor Zone, which are among the fastest growing at the moment growing Oromia region zone, cannot be ignored from the flooding problem due to unexpected heavy rain. Undoubtedly, accurate forecasts of rainfall signals can give practical advice on water management resources, improving crop productivity, and responding to disasters. These actions are to be taken in order to maximize productivity while also updating the entire agricultural process, according to the suggested long-term rainfall predictions.

The Ilu Abba Bor Zone in Ethiopia heavily relies on rainfall for agricultural production and socio- economic development. However, the region experiences high variability in rainfall patterns, which makes it difficult for farmers and policy makers to plan for sustainable agricultural practices and disaster risk reduction strategies. Traditional methods of rainfall

Forecasting has limited accuracy, and the available meteorological data is often insufficient or incomplete.

Thus, there's a requirement for a reliable and accurate long-term rainfall forecasting model for the region, which can help farmers and policy makers to make informed decisions. The purpose of This study aims to develop An approach to deep learning that can accurately predict long- term rainfall patterns in the Ilu Abba Bor Zone while considering for a variety of the environment and environmental characteristics.

My results offer insightful information on the possibilities of deep learning for long-term rainfall forecasting and contribute to the ongoing efforts to increase rainfall's precision and dependability predictions.

Long-term rainfall forecasting is an essential component of weather prediction that can greatly benefit disaster relief, agricultural in nature and water management of resources prevention. Ilu Abba Bor Zone, located in the Oromia region of Ethiopia, is an area heavily dependent on rain-fed agriculture, making accurate rainfall forecasting essential for farmers and the local economy.

Presently, in Ethiopia, the focus given to the use of Agricultural areas in many applications is growing very well. This is mainly because such an area is just thought to support the industrial revolution of the country. Therefore, the agricultural sector is one main area in which government will support and enhance the agricultural sector. In the Oromia region of Ethiopia, unexpected dry and heavy rain is the main problem that affects different agricultural production in the area. Moreover, in most of the Oromia regional zone the weather condition not well managed such as long-term rainfall forecasting.

The study will utilize historical rainfall information gathered from weather stations in the area, along together with other pertinent meteorological parameters including wind speed, humidity, and temperature. The data will be pre-processed and fed into the compared deep learning model to predict future rainfall patterns.

The results of this investigation can offer useful insights for farmers and policymakers in Ilu Abba Bor Zone to plan and prepare for potential droughts or floods. Additionally, the comparative deep learning approach developed in this study is applicable to other areas with comparable climates, contributing to the advancement of long-term rainfall forecasting.

2 Literature Review

Today, forecasting rainfall conditions is the most difficult assignment for meteorology departments of the environment. Reliable prediction depends on precise computer modeling and simulation of the extremely non-linear, dynamic, and complex rainfall conditions. Also, reliable Forecasts of rainfall are essential for many industries, including agriculture, airports, and other socioeconomic sectors.

Ethiopia's Rainfall

From west to east, Ethiopia is separated into the Great Rift Valley, the Somali Plateau, the Ogaden Plateau, and the Ethiopian Plateau, which are the four primary topographical zones (Legesse, 2018). Greater than 50% of the nation consists of the Ethiopian plateau, which is bounded by the Sudanese plains in the west (consisting of savanna and forest). It has various high mountains that range in height from 1524 to 1829 m higher than the sea level, yet it also reaches considerably higher elevations, notably Ras Dashen (4620 m above sea level), Ethiopia's highest peak. The plateau has multiple deep valleys and a moderate east-to-west slope (Legesse, 2018). Ethiopia poses an especially challenging test for climate models because of these spatial variances. The highland plateaus that divide Ethiopia's center are in charge.

According to current research, the aforementioned factors have led to the employment of a variety of rainfall forecasting approaches, including ANN, CNN, LSTM, RNN, etc. Several academics have also addressed the issue of determining the root causes of climate forecast errors. It is challenging to discuss every study conducted by various researchers, though. As a result, we divided the pertinent studies into two categories. Several researchers have investigated through deep learning techniques for long-term rainfall forecasting, using convolutional neural networks (CNN) for rainfall forecasting inside the basin of the Yellow River in China. The CNN mode A comprehensive review of deep learninl was trained on meteorological data such as temperatures, precipitation, wind speed, and humidity data. The findings indicated that the CNN model [5].

3 Materials and Method

This general methodology can be adapted and customized to suit the specific requirements of the Ilu Abba Bor zone and its rainfall forecasting needs.

(i) Study Area, Data Collection and data pre-processing

In this chapter, we describe the overall methods used and structure for an automatic rainfall forecasting system modeling and design, starting from data collection. Specifically, in this section, the study area of the research and data to be collected will be assessed. Moreover, data to be collected are may have missing data will be replaced with different techniques and data normalization will be carried out.

(ii) Meteorological Data Collection

The sections in this chapter present details of the system architecture components in detail for implementation of long rainfall prediction using proposed system. How to input data parameters of like Wind speed, precipitation, minimum and maximum temperatures, and Relative humidity are preprocessed and segmented, and feature extraction tasks, extracted features, and process steps are presented. Based on seasonal rainfall patterns and the geographical topology of Ilu Abba Bor zone, real-time series datasets are collected at three centers such as Mettu station, Gore stations, Alge stations, as well as the Jimma town main district where the western

Meteorological service center is located. Collecting the historical rainfall data for Ilu Abba Bor zone of the specified station from the Jimma district will be carried out. The data should cover a period of at least 15 years to capture the seasonal and annual rainfall trends within the area. Other relevant data, like the temperature, humidity, and wind speed, can also be collected.

After, the location and climate of the study area, collection of meteorological data, and then, methodology adopted for rainfall modeling using deep learning approach algorithm models are the main tools and materials used to accomplish tasks. For the objectives of this investigation, only the most influencing variables (Precipitation, The lowest temperature, the highest temperature, and Humidity) that affect the long term rainfall prediction out of 5 variables have been used.

The rainfall is taken as output and the remainder of the parameters are taken as the funding from the model. In the station, the humidity was recorded for about 30 years (1991–2021), Wind speed 30 years (1991–2021) data recorded, The lowest temperature ever recorded for 30 years (1991–2021), maximum temperature about 30 years (1991–2021), data and Precipitation (rainfall) 30 years (1991–2021), is recorded. For this research 30 years (1991–2021) data are used, as this is the only period that contains all the five parameters.

(iii) Pre-Processing Data

One of the most important steps in machine learning and deep learning procedures is data pre-processing. The rainfall and weather data are gathered and preprocessed in this part. After normalization, the data are divided into training and testing sets. In general, data from the real world is frequently noisy, inconsistent, and incomplete. Thus, we should employ data preparation techniques to address such problems [21].

Three steps are typically involved in preparing data for a machine learning and deep learning algorithm:

In Select data: Take into account what information is available, what information is lacking, and what information can be eliminated.

Preprocess Data: Format, clean, and sample the chosen data to arrange it.
Transform Data: Use scaling and attribute aggregation to engineer characteristics in preprocessed data so that it is ready to feed a deep learning model.

(iv) Data Normalization

To reduce computations that are too massive during the pre-processing stage, the data is normalized into the range 0 to 1 using the following equation. [23, 24]. Take data normalization as one of the pre-processing processes. The accuracy and efficiency of mining algorithms that use distance measurements may be improved by normalization. Data must be normalized between 0 and 1 in order to create harmony and balance. Our dataset has been normalized using (Eq. 1). as shown in Figs. 1 and 2. For both stations.

$$r = \frac{x-a}{b-a} \tag{1}$$

If X is the real data, an is the original attribute's minimum value, and b is its highest value.

(v) Data Correlation

To gauge how strongly two variables were related, Pearson correlation was used. There may be no association if the Pearson correlation coefficient between the two variables is zero, or there may be a positive or negative correlation. The mathematical description of the model of the Pearson correlation coefficient is as follows:

$$r_{xy} = \frac{\sum_{i=n}^{n} \left(x_i - \tilde{x} \right)\left(v_i - \tilde{v} \right)}{\sqrt{\sum_{i=1}^{n} \left(x_i - \tilde{x} \right)^2} \sqrt{\sum_{i=1}^{n} \left(y_i - \tilde{y} \right)^2}} \tag{2}$$

{(x1, y1), (x2, y2), …, (xn, yn)} are paired data made up of n pairings, where rxy is the Pearson correlation coefficient. The means of x and y are denoted by ⁻ and ⁻, respectively.

(vi) Measuring Performance Evaluation Metrics

To ensure that assess which algorithms for deep learning are more effective than others, the rainfall prediction performance of each method utilized Mean Absolute Error (MAE) and Root Mean Squared Error (RMSE) was used in this Research to measure. Two among of the most widely used metrics for evaluating accuracy for continuous variables. Without considering their direction, MAE determines the mean size of errors in a collection of projections. and the matching observation.

$$MAE = \frac{1}{n}\sum_{j=1}^{n} 1 - \hat{y}_y \tag{3}$$

The average mistake size is calculated using RMSE, or the quadratic scoring rule. The square root of the mean of the differences between the prediction and the actual observation.

$$RMSE = \sqrt{\frac{1}{n}\sum_{j=1}^{n} 1 - \hat{y}_j} \tag{4}$$

Large error is given a comparatively high weight by RMSE. This indicates that when huge mistakes are very undesired, the RMSE is most helpful. The variability in a set of forecasts' errors can be diagnosed by combining the RMSE and the MAE. The variation in the individual error in the sample is proportional to the difference between the RMSE and MAE, which is always greater or equal. Should All errors have the same magnitude when the RMSE equals the MAE.

4 Results and Discussions

In this section, the suggested rainfall prediction system put into practice using PYTHON software. The relevant environmental feature was used in this research's Deep learning model's training and testing, with the Selecting the environmental variables serving as a computational input. Two models of machine learning, comparable CNN and LSTM for the annual Prediction of the amount of rainfall. This machine learning models' effectiveness was assessed using MSE, RMSE and MAE. The comparison of results of the two algorithms such as the CNN and LSTM was made.

The primary goal of this research was to identify the relevant atmospheric factors that contribute to precipitation and use Deep learning techniques to predict the daily intensity of rainfall. As a result, the research results are summed up below. To select the environmental factors that correlate on the environmental factors shown in Table 1 above, the Pearson correlation between the rainfall and the variables was examined. Given the size of the dataset, the variables with a correlation to rainfall of more than 0.20 were taken into consideration. As the characteristics of the participant environment in the experiment to forecast rainfall. Therefore, To predict the amount of rainfall each day, Table 2 displays the results of environmental factors such as The variables that are important to this forecast include sunshine, evaporation, relative humidity, and the highest and lowest daily temperatures.

The results of the Pearson Correlation coefficient experiment on the given data showed that the rainfall was not significantly impacted by the year, month, day, or wind speed. In order to predict rainfall, this study examined environmental factors that have correlation coefficients higher than 0.2. Daily sunshine and relative humidity, which have Pearson coefficients of 0.402 and 0.352, correspondingly, were the two elements of the environment that were most significantly connected for rainfall prediction (Fig. 3).

In this study data, Rainfall information from January 1991 to December 2011 (20 years) is used as training data. Membership functions like the generalised Bell membership function (gbellmf), the trapezoid membership function (trapmf), and Gaussian membership functions are used for training. The remaining ten years' worth of data, from January 2012 to December 2021, will be utilized to test targets and validations of targets. Data from January 2012 up to Dec 2016 used for testing and remaining data used for predictions Tables 3 and 4.

According to the performance data, CNN fared better than LSTM. The CNN method outperformed the LSTM algorithm in predicting rainfall using pertinent, chosen environmental features, with MSE, MAE, and RMSE values of 3.58 and 7.85, respectively, compared to 4.97 and 8.61 for the LSTM approach. Using the chosen pertinent environmental parameters, data-driven CNN algorithms were able to forecast the yearly rainfall

	year	month	date	mintemp	maxtemp	precip	MN	DN	MITN	MATN	PN	humidity	winspeed
0	1991	1.0	1.0	15.0	22.3	13.6	0.0	0.000000	0.482759	0.327801	0.186813	2.0	100.0
1	1991	1.0	2.0	13.5	28.0	0.0	0.0	0.033333	0.431034	0.727273	0.000000	1.0	96.0
2	1991	1.0	3.0	12.0	30.3	0.0	0.0	0.066667	0.379310	0.787013	0.000000	2.0	64.0
3	1991	1.0	4.0	11.6	29.5	0.0	0.0	0.100000	0.365517	0.766234	0.000000	1.0	88.0
4	1991	1.0	5.0	11.8	28.5	1.0	0.0	0.133333	0.372414	0.740260	0.013736	0.0	81.0
...	...	...	...	...	...	...	...	...	...	...	...	...	...
11675	2021	12.0	27.0	10.0	27.0	0.0	1.0	0.866667	0.310345	0.701299	0.000000	2.0	86.0
11676	2021	12.0	28.0	9.5	30.5	0.0	1.0	0.900000	0.293103	0.792208	0.000000	2.0	70.0
11677	2021	12.0	29.0	10.0	31.0	0.0	1.0	0.933333	0.310345	0.805195	0.000000	2.0	82.0
11678	2021	12.0	30.0	11.0	29.5	0.0	1.0	0.966667	0.344828	0.766234	0.000000	2.0	78.0
11679	2021	12.0	31.0	18.0	30.0	0.0	1.0	1.000000	0.586207	0.779221	0.000000	2.0	64.0

Fig. 1. Rainfall data normalized on all years.

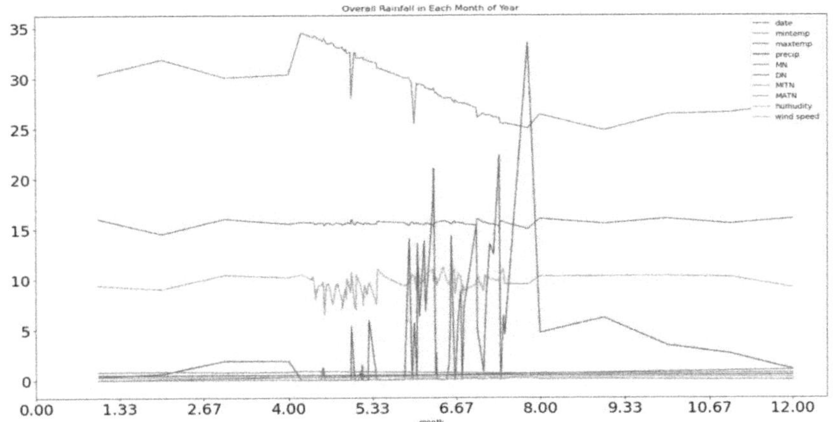

Fig. 2. Over all Rainfall (mm) in Each Month of date

with an overall accuracy of 98.18%. On the other hand, utilising the chosen pertinent environmental features, LSTM algorithms were able to forecast the annual rainfall with an overall accuracy of 96.73% above. As a result, CNN performs well when it comes to accuracy while using the LSTM algorithm (Figs. 4 and 5).

Table 1. Normalized dataset at Mettu station.

Mettu station

No	WSP	MIT	MAT	RELHUM	PRECIP
1	0.933333333	0.379310345	0.763636364	0.685714286	0.186813186
2	0.095338095	0.362068966	0.779220779	0.628571429	0
3	0.047619047	0.324137931	0.774025974	0.628571529	0.196713186
.		.			
.		.			
.		.			
10,583	0.955666667	0.482758621	0.32780083	1	0.186813187
10,584	1	0.431034483	0.727272727	0.95505618	0
10, 585	0.095238095	0.379310345	0.787012987	0.577142857	0

Note: MIT = Minimum temperature, MAT = Maximum temperature, PRECIP = precipitation and RELHUM = relative humidity.

Table 2. Normalized dataset at Gore station.

Gore station

No.	WSP	MIT	MAT	RELHUM	PRECIP
1	0.095238095	0.62345679	0.468571429	1	0.046153846
2	0.047619048	0.512345679	0.594285714	0.95505618	0
3	0.095238095	0.567901235	0.577142857	0.595505618	0
.	.	.	.	.	.
.	.	.	.	.	.
10,583	0.933333333	0.095238095	0.518518519	0.685714286	0.393258427
10,584	0.966666667	0.095238095	0.617283951	0.628571429	0.595505618
10,585	1	0.095238095	0.660493827	0.577142857	0.606741573

Note: MIT = Minimum temperature, MAT = Maximum temperature, PRECIP = precipitation and RELHUM = relative humidity.

Table 3. The environmental variables and the value of their coefficient of Pearson

Features	Pearson coefficient ‖
Year	0.013
Month	0.102
Day	0.018
Evaporation	0.280
Relative humidity	0.402
Max daily temperature	0.297
Min daily temperature	0.205
Sunshine	0.352
Wind speed	0.047
Daily rainfall	1.001

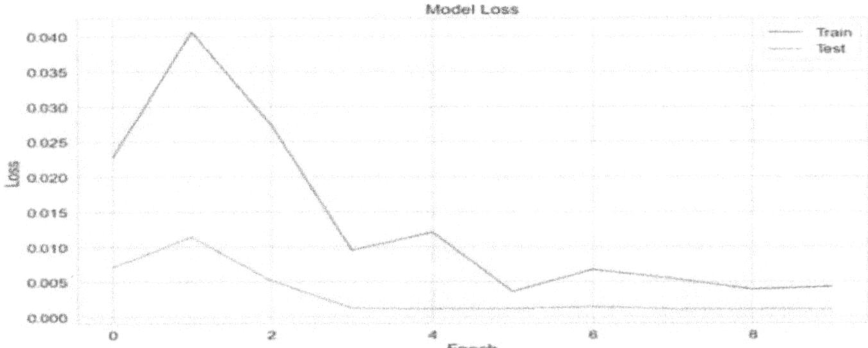

Fig. 3. Error of models loss.

Table 4. Performance measurements.

Algorithms	MAE	RMSE
CNN	3.58	7.85
LSTM	4.97	8.61

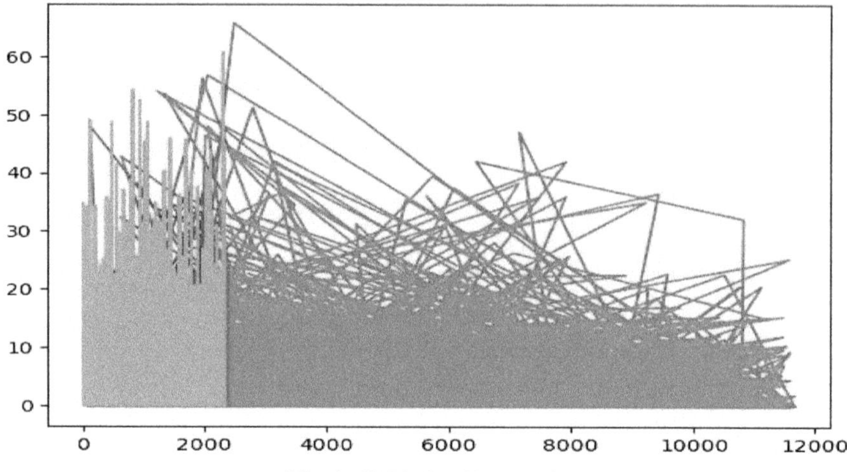

Fig. 4. CNN algorithm result.

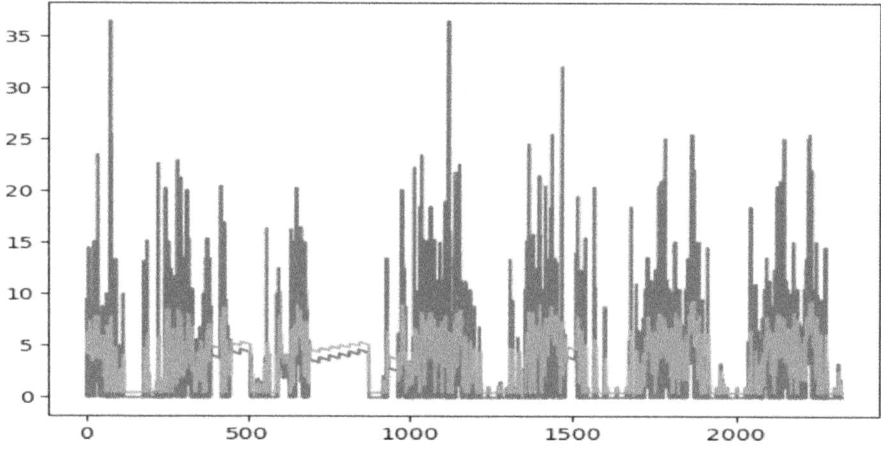

Fig. 5. LSTM algorithm result

5 Conclusion and Future Works

In this study long term rainfall forecasting using deep learning approaches the case of Ilu Aba Bor Mettu and gore town. Meteorological data starting from 1991 to 2021 collected from national meteorological agency in western Oromia service center and missing data replaced using expected maximization algorithm. In this work, from total data collected 70% used for training of LSTM and CNN model and remaining 30% data used for validation and prediction. In case of Mettu town four attributes used to predict the rainfall pattern in this area. For all attribute 3 their membership function is classified in to three linguistic variables namely, low, medium and large. LSTM and CNN structure generated using grid partition and training done using both backpropagation and least square estimator with gradient descent algorithm techniques. Performance of two model compared using root mean square method using different membership function such as Gaussian, trapezoidal and gbellmf functions. Gbellmf with hybrid resulted good performance in this work with error tolerance of 0.093. Therefore, model of Deep learning models is optimized using hybrid algorithm with General bell membership function and application developed for this model. Finally, application show good performance for four input parameters such as month, date, minimum and maximum temperature at that specified time.

Future Works

The following things may be future extension of this research area which can be results good in terms performance addressed above and application real time. As future work, Upgrade our architecture to handle situations with both light and heavy rain. It should be noted that our study focused on the exact opposite—heavy rain scenarios—because these are the ones that could have detrimental effects (like landslides).Employing another deep learning architecture, such as multiple stacked DE noising or deep belief networks based on restricted Boltzmann machines auto encoders. Incorporating new input features or attributes. Including data gathered from nearby stations (thinking of the neighborhood as stations) with geographical near and comparable elevation).Extending the same idea to like prediction of climate not only rainfall prediction.

Developing user interface for real time application like web based application, desktop standalone application.

The developed model has used meteorological data with only four input parameters and one output parameter. However, future researches should expand the scope by including other parameters such as wind speed, wind direction, evaporation etc.

The evidence used in this study is 30 years weather data gathering from a only ilu ababora zone. Using daily data collected at large scale, to forecast rainfall on a daily, monthly, and annual basis with other weather parameters may provide better result

References

1. Endalie, D., Haile, G., Taye, W.: Deep learning model for daily rainfall prediction: case study of Jimma, Ethiopia. Water Supply. **22**(3), 3448–3461 (2022). https://doi.org/10.2166/WS.2021.391
2. Hu, C., Wu, Q., Li, H., Jian, S., Li, N., Lou, Z.: Deep learning with a long short-term memory networks approach for rainfall-runoff simulation. Water. **10**(11) (2018). https://doi.org/10.3390/w10111543
3. Sit, M., Demiray, B.Z., Xiang, Z., Ewing, G.J., Sermet, Y., Demir, I.: A comprehensive review of deep learning applications in, hydrology and water resources. Water Sci. Technol. **82**(12), 2635–2670 (2019)
4. Gupta, S.: No Title (2021). https://www.springboard.com/blog/data-science/rnn-vs-cnn/#:~:text=While_RNNs_are_suitable_for,(in_case_of_CNN). Accessed 4 Mar 2023
5. Geography, N.: Rain (2020). https://education.nationalgeographic.org/resource/rain/. Accessed 4 March 2023
6. Onnen, H.: No Title (2021). https://towardsdatascience.com/temporal-loops-intro-to-recurrent-neural-networks-for-time-series-forecasting-in-python-b0398963dc1f. Accessed 4 Mar 2023.

7. Ni, L., Wang, D., Singh, V.P., Wu, J., Wang, Y.: Streamflow and rainfall forecasting by two long short-term memory-based models. J. Hydrol. **583**(2) (2019)

8. Bushara, N.O., Abraham, A.: Using adaptive neuro-fuzzy inference system (ANFIS) to improve the long-term rainfall forecasting. J. Netw. Innov. Comput. **3**, 146–158 (2015) [Online]. Available: www.mirlabs.net/jnic/index.html

9. Bamisile, O., et al.: Comprehensive assessment, review, and comparison of AI models for solar irradiance prediction based on different time/estimation intervals. Sci. Rep. **12**(1), 1–26 (2022). https://doi.org/10.1038/s41598-022-13652-w

10. Wunsch, A., Liesch, T., Broda, S., Groundwater level forecasting with artificial neural networks: a comparison of LSTM, CNN and NARX, 1–25 (2015)

11. Narejo, S., Jawaid, M.M., Talpur, S., Baloch, R., Pasero, E.G.A.: Multi-step rainfall forecasting using deep learning approach. PeerJ Comput. Sci. **7**, 1–23 (2021). https://doi.org/10.7717/PEERJ-CS.514

12. Hammad, M., Shoaib, M., Salahudin, H., Baig, M.A.I., Khan, M.M., Ullah, M.K.: Rainfall forecasting in upper Indus basin using various artificial intelligence techniques. Stoch. Environ. Res. Risk Assess. **35**(11), 2213–2235 (2021). https://doi.org/10.1007/s00477-021-020 13-0

13. Şahin, M., Erol, R.: A comparative study of neural networks and ANFIS for forecasting attendance rate of soccer games. Math. Comput. Appl. **22**(4), 43 (2017). https://doi.org/10.3390/mca22040043

14. Chen, S., et al.: Rainfall forecasting in sub-Sahara Africa-Ghana using LSTM deep learning approach. Int. J. Eng. Res. Technol. **10**(3), 464–470 (2021) [Online]. Available: www.ijert.org

15. Singh, D.K., Sahoo, A.: A Hybrid CNN – LSTM Deep Learning Model for Rainfall Prediction. **20**(14), 813–818 (2022). https://doi.org/10.4704/nq.2022.20.14

16. Nuru, A.: Monthly rainfall prediction using Recurrent Neural Network (RNN) for Bahir Dar City (2020)

17. Setianingrum, A.H., Swarinata, P.M.: Weather prediction application based on ANFIS (Adaptive neural fuzzy inference system) method in West Jakarta region. In: 2014 International Conference on Cyber and IT Service Management (CITSM 2014), pp. 113–118 (2014). https://doi.org/10.1109/CITSM.2014.7042187

18. Hou, J., Wang, Y., Zhou, J., Tian, Q.: Prediction of hourly air temperature based on CNN – LSTM. Geomat. Nat. Hazards Risk. **13**(1), 1962–1986 (2022). https://doi.org/10.1080/194 75705.2022.2102942

19. Muhammad Hammad, M.S.S.: Rainfall forecasting in upper Indus basin using various artificial intelligence techniques. Stoch. Environ. Res. Risk Assess. **35** (2021)

20. Sahin, M., Erol, R.: A comparative study of neural networks and ANFIS for forecasting attendance rate of soccer games. Math. Comput. Appl. **22**(43) (2017). https://doi.org/10.3390/mca22040043

Macular Degeneration Analysis Using Deep Learning

K. Suresh, Kevin Shibu John[✉], Shaurya Singh, and Jyoti Raj Sinha

Department of Computational Intelligence, SRM Institute of Science and Technology,
Potheri, SRM Nagar, Kattankulathur, Tamil Nadu 603203, India
kj1712@srmist.edu.in

Abstract. The studies article delves into the evolution of using deep learning models for difficult analyses of optical tomography (OCT) snapshots, especially for classifying macular diseases. Its primary goal is to set up foundational information of the capability to figure subtle alterations in retinal shape and age-associated macular degeneration (AMD) development. in addition, it endeavors to differentiate AMD into its exudative and non-exudative sorts, thereby broadening the study horizon. The deep mastering version utilized is professional at extracting complex functions from huge datasets, thereby no longer the handiest enhancing accuracy but additionally refining type. This novel studies street holds promise no longer only in advancing diagnostic capabilities but also in imparting a truthful and green way of becoming aware of AMD and its wonderful subtypes through a meticulous evaluation of OCT images.

Keywords: Macular degeneration · OCT images · AMD · Efficientnet b5 · SVM

1 Introduction

Age-related macular degeneration (AMD) is a progressive eye disease that primarily affects the macula, the central part of the retina responsible for sharp, central vision. It is the leading cause of severe vision loss, especially in people 50 and older. There are two main forms of AMD: dry AMD (non-neovascular) and wet AMD (neovascular or exudative). Dry AMD: This is the most common form, accounting for the majority of AMD cases. It involves the gradual breakdown or thinning of macular tissue, often accompanied by the formation of small yellow deposits called drusen (as shown in Fig. 2). Dry AMD progresses slowly and can cause gradual blurring of central vision. Wet AMD: Although less common than dry AMD, wet AMD is more serious and can cause rapid and severe vision loss. It occurs when abnormal blood vessels grow under the stain (as shown in Fig. 1), a process called neovascularization. These blood vessels are fragile and can leak fluid or blood, causing scar tissue and damage to the scar. Wet AMD often causes more sudden and more pronounced visual changes than dry AMD. Advantages of machine learning and classification with OCT:

R. Appavoo et al. (Eds.): IconDeepCom 2024, CCIS 2687, pp. 377–388, 2026.
https://doi.org/10.1007/978-3-032-26680-4_30

Automatic analysis: One of the advantages of machine learning (especially deep learning models) in optical coherence tomography (OCT) is the ability to perform OCT analysis. photo. This automation greatly reduces the manual work of doctors, allowing them to focus on more complex tasks and patient care. Machine learning algorithms provide a fast and efficient way to analyze the shape of the eye by processing large amounts of data. AMD) is used to identify features seen in OCT image quality. This ability provides a better understanding of the disease, allowing doctors to tailor treatments to individual subtypes. Triage efficiency improves the diagnostic process, facilitating faster decision-making and more personalized care. This is important. This model allows doctors to detect subtle changes in the retinal image that indicate early disease, allowing them to begin treatment immediately. Early treatment for people with AMD is critical to preserving vision and improving long-term prognosis.

Consistency: Machine learning models reduce clinical variability by producing consistent models and results. This consistency is especially useful in diagnosing AMD, where accuracy and reliability are important. By increasing standardization and reducing content, machine learning improves the overall reliability of AMD diagnosis and classification in many clinical settings. While improving diagnostic accuracy. Thanks to the fast and automatic processing of OCT images, medical personnel can better process the data. As a result, this allows operations to be more efficient, the time required for diagnosis to be reduced, and doctors to spend more time on patient care and treatment planning.

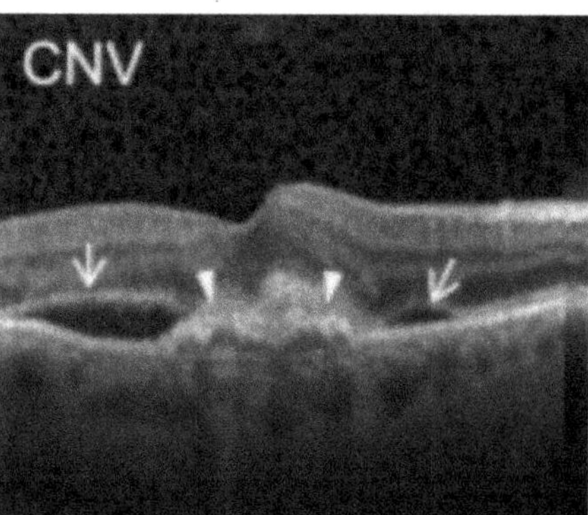

Fig. 1. Wet AMD with neovascularization

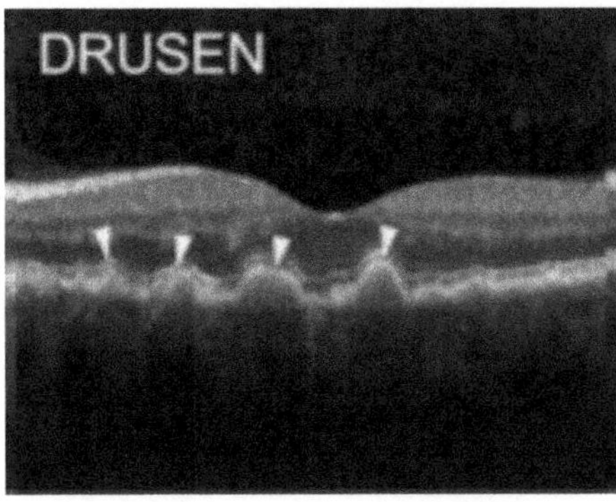

Fig. 2. Dry AMD with Drusen

2   Innovation

The core of the innovation idea is the use of sophisticated CNN models for the classification of macular degeneration (AMD) and the extraction of nuanced features. The suggested strategy, in contrast to conventional techniques, makes use of deep learning architectures to automatically extract complex representations and patterns from optical coherence tomography (OCT) pictures. In particular, the CNN models are meant to pick up on intricate and subtle characteristics seen in the retinal structures that are suggestive of AMD. Two primary aspects are novel:

- Subclassification into Dry and Wet AMD: The division of AMD into its dry and wet. The model uses advanced CNN architectures to distinguish between these subtypes according to particular visual cues found in the OCT pictures. To help doctors create more individualized treatment plans and precise therapies, this degree of classification granularity is crucial. Offering insights into the particular AMD subtype, it improves the clinical value of the system and helps with more focused and efficient patient care.
- Nuanced Feature Extraction: Robust CNN models possess the potential to autonomously derive hierarchical features from OCT pictures, obtaining minute details that might be essential for differentiating between AMD and normal cases. This method goes beyond basic hand-drawn features, enabling the algorithm to adapt and pick up on patterns that could be hard for traditional techniques to recognize. Specifically, this refined feature extraction helps raise the classification system's sensitivity and specificity.

3   Literature Survey

- This paper [1] A machine learning approach to medical image classification: Detection of age-related macular degeneration on fundus images - An important point is the use of vector machines (SVMs) as an important part of the AMD preliminary diagnosis process. The SVM serves as a crucial primitive for classifying processed image vectors as positive or negative for Drusen's presence. It's essential to acknowledge the inherent challenges associated with SVMs, such as interpretability issues due to their "black-box" nature.

- This paper [2] "Artificial intelligence-based decision-making for age-related macular degeneration" highlights challenges in the specificity of the AI system for distinguishing active wet AMD, occasional misclassifications in nuanced cases, and potential discrepancies between AI predictions and human assessments.

- This paper [3] "Automated detection of exudative age-related macular degeneration in spectral domain optical coherence tomography using deep learning" Despite the promising results, the study has limitations. The research focused on AMD detection, and expanding the classifier to other macular diseases or detailed AMD characteristics may require additional data. Moreover, the study acknowledges the need for more extensive datasets to enhance the classifier's capabilities.

- This work [4] "Detection of features associated with neovascular age-related macular degeneration in ethnically distinct data sets by an optical coherence tomography: trained deep learning algorithm" limitation of the study is the focus on a specific set of classifiers (SoftMax, GNB, DT, KNN, SVM) without an exhaustive exploration of various other machine learning and deep learning architectures. The choice of classifiers may impact the overall model performance, and the study does not extensively delve into comparing and contrasting different classifier combinations or exploring more advanced neural network architectures.

- In this paper [5] "Development of a Deep-Learning-Based Artificial Intelligence Tool for Differential Diagnosis between Dry and Neovascular Age-Related Macular Degeneration" despite the positive findings, this study has clear limitations. Focusing on a single deep learning model (VGG16) raises questions about the generality of the approach, as other architectures may provide different performances. Additionally, the study relied on a small amount of data and did not include specific effects of AMD that affect device usability.

- This paper [6] "Classification of Eye Diseases in Fundus Images" This study demonstrates significant progress in the classification of eye diseases using neural networks (CNNs). One limitation of the table is that deep learning models, including CNNs, are not interpretable. It can be difficult to understand the model's decision-making process and identify specific features or patterns that contribute to the classification. This lack of transparency can impact trust and acceptance of the clinical design, the interpretation of which is crucial for clinicians.

- This paper [7] "Machine Learning OCT Predictors of Progression from Intermediate Age-Related Macular Degeneration to Geographic Atrophy and Vision Loss" The study adopted a prospective, longitudinal design to investigate spectral-domain OCT (SD-OCT) features, age, gender, and systemic variables as potential predictors for the short-term progression of intermediate age-related macular degeneration (iAMD) to geographic atrophy (GA) and visual acuity (VA) loss. Leveraging a comprehensive dataset from the Age-Related Eye Disease Study 2 (AREDS2) Ancillary SD-OCT, the research employed machine learning techniques, specifically decision trees, to analyze qualitative and quantitative variables at yearly intervals over 5 years, aiming to identify key predictors of adverse outcomes.

- This study [8] "Automated screening tool for dry and wet age-related macular degeneration (ARMD) using the pyramid of the histogram of oriented gradients (PHOG) and nonlinear features" focuses on image-based analysis, and the integration of other relevant clinical data, such as patient medical history or genetic factors, could potentially enhance the accuracy and reliability of the CAD system. Furthermore, the study does not provide insights into the real-time performance or computational efficiency of the proposed system, which are crucial aspects for practical clinical implementation.

4 Research Gap

- Low Sensitivity to Early Changes: Systems that are sensitive to small changes in the retinal structure are essential for early detection of macular degeneration, especially in the early stages. If current technology cannot reliably detect these changes at an early stage, diagnosis, and intervention will be delayed. Increasing sensitivity is important for timely detection and better outcomes for patients.
- Difficulty in Sub-classification: The ability to distinguish between wet and dry AMD is important for treatment planning. The accuracy of AMD subtype subclassification can be problematic with current technology, which can impact diagnostic accuracy. Failure to adequately distinguish between wet and dry forms of AMD may impede effective treatment. Improving the specificity of the classification model is important to tailor treatment to specific subtypes.

5 Methodology

5.1 Methods

A comprehensive library of 18,000 spectral-domain optical coherence tomography (SD-OCT) images was analyzed. The data was divided into three sets of 6,000 images showing choroidal neovascularization (CNV), drusen, and normal retinal structures, allowing comparison of different stages of the disease in age-related macular degeneration (AMD) and healthy retina. We leverage the EfficientNet B5 architecture and use adaptive learning to leverage previously learned models as useful resources. This approach not only supports the performance of our model, but also ensures that the model is generalizable across different organisms. To improve the classification accuracy, we send a service model, a support vector machine (SVM), that keeps track of the classification during training. This integrated approach combines deep learning with traditional machine learning to increase the accuracy and reliability of our predictions. The application of adaptive learning, which combines deep learning with traditional machine learning techniques, offers a new way to distinguish AMD from healthy retinas.

5.2 EfficientNet

We chose EfficientNet B5 for feature extraction in OCT image classification because its excellent model has many advantages compared to other deep learning models. Optimize depth and width. This allows optimal visualization of calculated components without

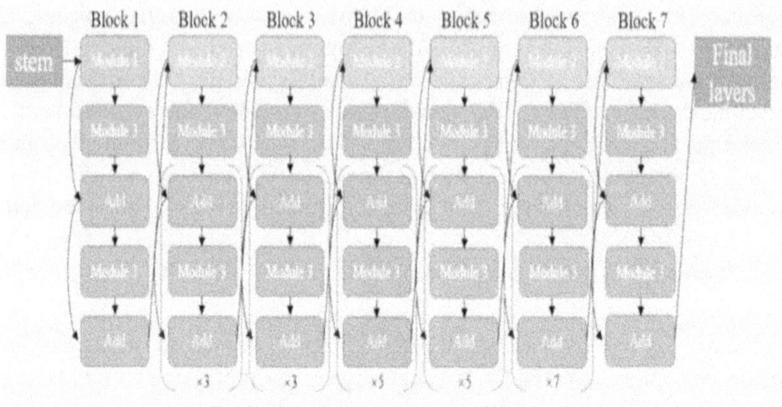

Fig. 3. EfficientNet B5 architecture

the need for manual tuning of hyperparameters, achieving better performance with less. These features make EfficientNet highly efficient for complex image-sharing tasks. state benefits.

Identifying retinal changes is important in the classification of OCT images, and the EfficientNet architecture has many advantages. Its ability to capture complex OCT image features while minimizing computational load makes it ideal for analysing complex clinical data. In addition, EfficientNet's scalability ensures consistent results by seamlessly adapting to different OCT datasets and disease subtypes. Make it the best choice for the following fields: Feature extraction in OCT image classification. Utilizing these advantages to increase the accuracy and efficiency of OCT image analysis, improves diagnosis and classification, ultimately leading to better patient outcomes.

5.3 Ensemble Learning with SVM

When identifying macular disease using EfficientNet B5 fine-tuning and SVM learning together, SVM plays an important role for many reasons. First, SVM provides stability and protection against overfitting, which is especially important in clinical research where classification is important. This provides efficiency around different data and changes in macular disease diagnosis, ensuring optimal diagnosis. Deep learning is good at extracting complex features from raw data, while support vector machines focus on capturing complex decisions and managing nonlinear relationships at specific locations. Combining the feature representation obtained by EfficientNet B5 with the discriminative power of SVM, the tool benefits from a combination that improves classification accuracy, especially in identifying subtle features that indicate the development of macular pathology. SVM provides interpretation, which is important in clinical applications such as macular pathology analysis. SVM's transparent decision boundary allows physicians to understand and use predictive models, increasing trust and acceptance in clinical practice. This interpretation ensures that studies derived from the integrated model are not only accurate, but also easy to understand, enabling physicians to make informed nursing decisions. Use support vector machines. When used with the fine-tuned EfficientNet B5, this combination produces accurate and reliable models that improve the diagnosis and management of macular degeneration, ultimately resulting in better patient outcomes.

5.4 System Architecture

- **SD-OCT Image Database:** Gathered OCT (Optical Coherence Tomography) photographs of the macular regions from various sources to guarantee a representative sample of cases, such as normal, drusen, and choroidal neovascularization (CNV). A library of SD-OCT pictures of eyes, including both healthy and AMD-affected images, serves as the foundation.
- **Data Pre-Processing:** To ensure consistency in size and scale, resizing and normalizing the photos. Boosting the dataset's variability and enhancing model generalization by adding more random transformations (rotations, flips, etc.).
- In this step, the photos are ready for analysis. Resizing photos, standardizing pixel values, and expanding the data set are a few examples of pre-processing techniques that help the model better generalize from the data. To train the model, adjust hyperparameters, and assess performance, separate the dataset into training, validation, and test sets.
- **Feature Extraction using Transfer Learning**: Using EfficientNet B5 (see Fig. 3), a transfer learning technique is used to extract features from the pre-processed images. Transfer learning makes use of a model's prior training on a sizable dataset (such as ImageNet). To preserve the pre-trained features, the EfficientNet B5's base layers are frozen.
- **Fine Tuning:** After that, the model is adjusted to better fit the unique data by progressively unfreezing the top layers and training them on the newly created dataset—the OCT pictures.
- **Input Training Data:** The fine-tuned extracted features are used as input training data for the next stage of the process.
- **Ensemble Learning:** The model makes use of ensemble learning, which mixes several learning algorithms to provide predictions that are more accurate than those that could be made using just one of the individual learning methods.
- **SVM Classifier:** Ensemble learning involves the employment of a Support Vector Machine (SVM) classifier.
- **Testing:** To evaluate the model, we use unseen photos for testing. Grad-CAM visualization highlights important image regions for classification. Additionally, we calculate the F1 score to assess classification accuracy. These methods ensure thorough evaluation of the model's performance on fresh data.

The output of the testing phase is the label of the test image, which indicates the classification result, as seen in Fig. 4. Normal eyes, CNV/Wet AMD (defined as neovascularization or the presence of new blood vessels with exudative alterations), and Drusen/Dry AMD (defined as the presence of drusen without exudative changes) are the classifications produced by this system.

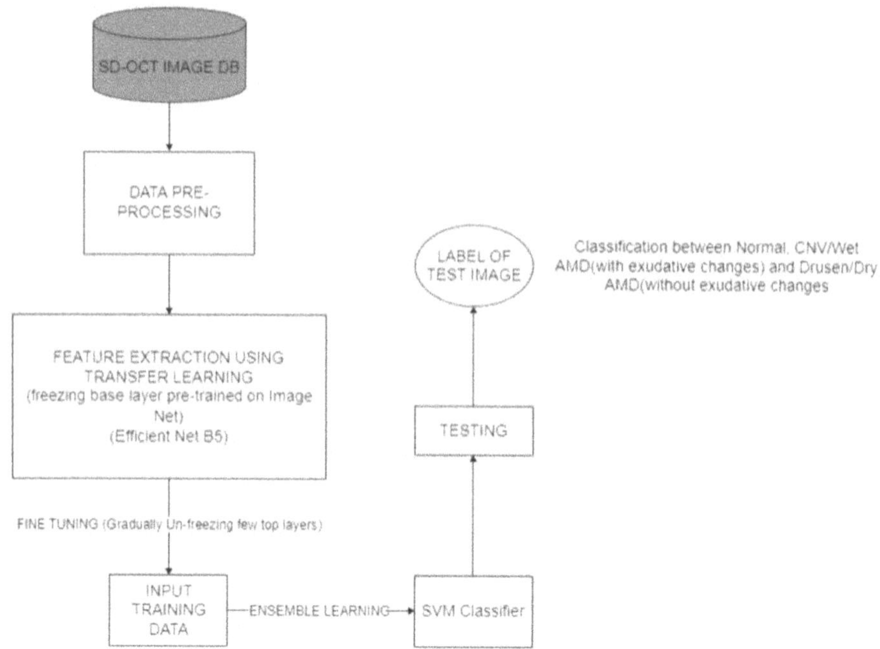

Fig. 4. System Architecture

6 Experimental Results

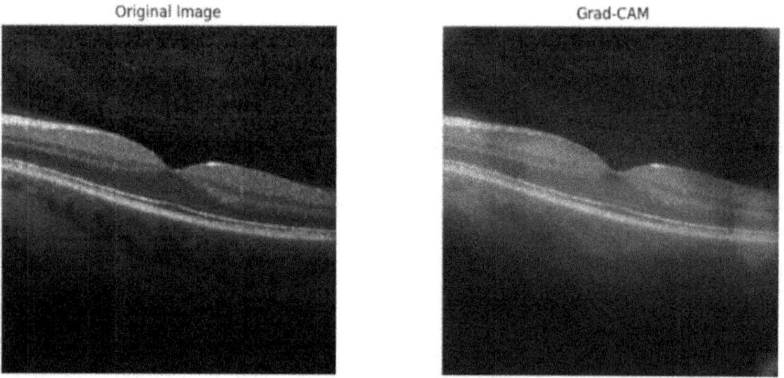

Fig. 5. OCT vs Grad-CAM

On the left of Figs. 5 and 6, the "Original Image" is a grayscale OCT scan to capture detailed cross-sectional images of the retina. It shows the various layers of the retina, which appear as distinct bands of varying intensities.

On the right, the Grad-CAM image applies a heatmap overlay to the same OCT image. This visualization is used to **highlight the regions in the image that the EfficientNet**

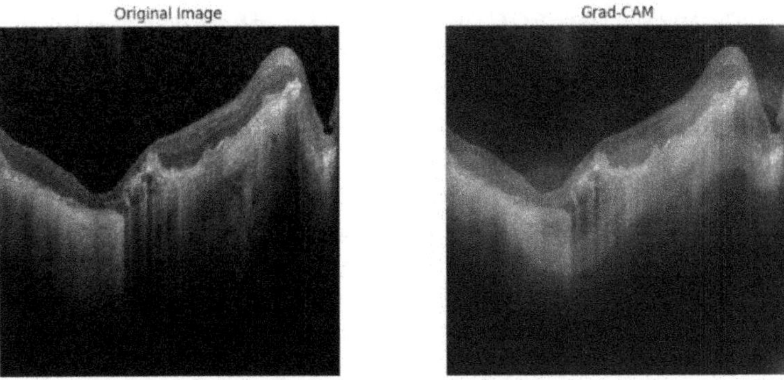

Fig. 6. OCT vs Grad-CAM of CNV

model focused on for feature extraction and decision-making. The highlighted areas, which show up in warmer colors like yellow and red, indicate where changes associated with specific retinal conditions may be present and have influenced the model's classification decision the most.

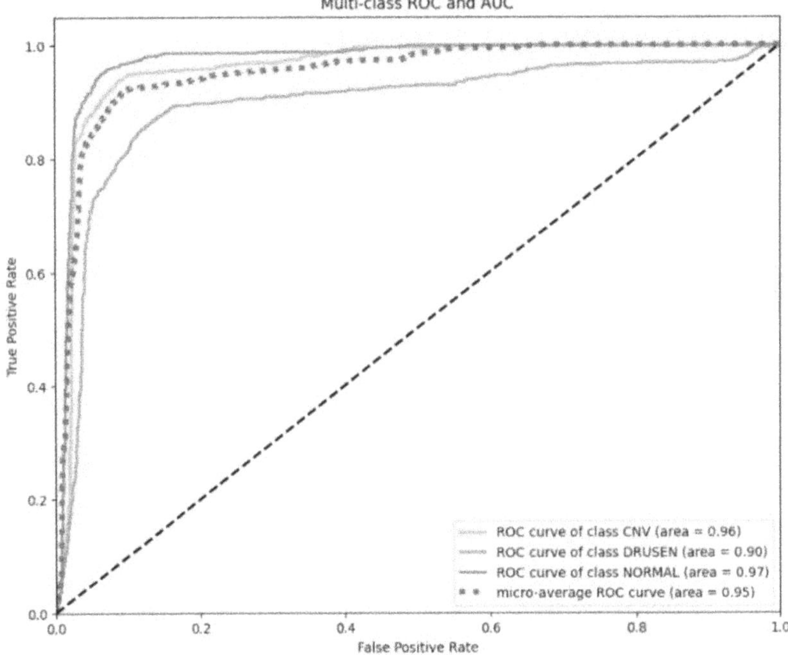

Fig. 7. Multi-class ROC and AUC

From Fig. 7, The **ROC curve for CNV** (Choroidal Neovascularization) **has an AUC of 0.96**, indicating excellent model performance in distinguishing CNV from other conditions. The **Drusen class ROC curve has an AUC of 0.90**, which is also a high score, showing that the model reliably identifies Drusen cases. The **ROC curve for the Normal class has an AUC of 0.97**, suggesting the model is highly effective at identifying healthy eyes. The **micro-average ROC curve has an AUC of 0.95**, demonstrating overall high performance across all classes.

The ROC curves being close to the upper left corner and the AUC values being close to 1.0 for all classes indicate that the model has a high true positive rate and a low false positive rate for all classifications. The model is very good at correctly classifying between a healthy eye and an eye suffering from wet or dry AMD without misclassifying them as each other. The performance is consistently strong across the different classes, which is ideal for a diagnostic tool in a medical setting.

Class	Precision	Recall	F1-Score	Support
CNV	0.88	0.90	0.89	1000
DRUSEN	0.82	0.80	0.81	1000
NORMAL	0.91	0.92	0.91	1000
Overall/Total	-	-	-	3000
Validation Accuracy	-	-	0.87	-

Fig. 8. Precision, Recall and F1-score Table

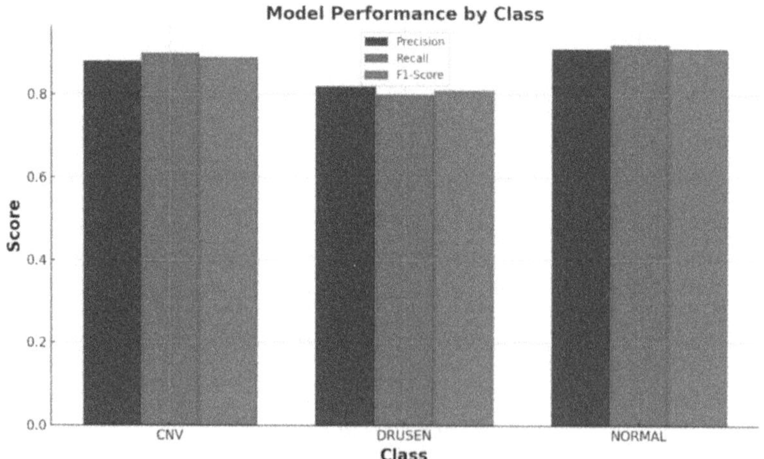

Fig. 9. Model Performance

From Figs. 8 and 9, the model has high precision across all three classes, indicating a low number of false positives. The recall is also high for all classes, which means the model is correctly identifying a high number of all actual positives. The F1-score, which is the harmonic mean of precision and recall, is similarly high for all classes, suggesting a balanced performance between precision and recall.

Based on the data, we can say that the model is useful for diagnosing AMD from OCT pictures since it does a good job of differentiating between the classes. Every bar is associated with metrics for the respective class, and the bars' close heights indicate consistent performance across metrics.

7 Conclusion

Using an integrated algorithm combining EfficientNet B5 with Support Vector Machine (SVM) products, the model achieves high recovery, F1 score, and accuracy in all three categories it focuses on (CNV, Drusen, and Normal). This demonstrates the potential to correctly identify and classify OCT images while reducing false positives and negatives. The receiver operating characteristic (ROC) curve for each group showed discrimination when the area under the curve (AUC) value reached 1, which demonstrated the best ability to distinguish between different OCT image groups. Furthermore, Grad-CAM sees the model focus on extracting important clinical areas that affect the main areas in eye evaluation. The proprietary interpretation model technology validated the effectiveness of EfficientNet B5 in OCT image classification and improved the accuracy of the final classification by SVM. These findings suggest potential avenues for further development and highlight the importance of further clinical research. These tests are important to assess the validity of the model in various clinical settings and will lead to further development as a clinical recommendation. Future improvements may include expanding the dataset, using sophisticated data enhancement techniques, or modifying the model to avoid collisions and therefore improving medical equipment. Further development and clinical trials can be shown that it can be an important tool in the early diagnosis and treatment of age-related macular degeneration. These developments may open the door to greater specialist involvement in healthcare, improving patient care and health outcomes.

References

1. García-Floriano, A., Ferreira-Santiago, Á., Camacho-Nieto, O., et al.: A machine learning approach to medical image classification: detecting age-related macular degeneration in fundus images. Comput. Electr. Eng. **75**, 218–229 (2019)
2. Hwang, D.K. et al.: Artificial intelligence-based decision-making for age-related macular degeneration. Theranostics. **9**(1), 232–245 (2019). https://doi.org/10.7150/thno.28447. PMID: 30662564; PMCID: PMC6332801
3. Treder, M., Lauermann, J.L., Eter, N.: Automated detection of exudative age-related macular degeneration in spectral domain optical coherence tomography using deep learning. Graefes Arch. Clin. Exp. Ophthalmol. **256**, 259–265 (2018)

4. Rim, T. et al.: Detection of features associated with neovascular age-related macular degeneration in ethnically distinct data sets by an optical coherence tomography: trained deep learning algorithm. Br. J. Ophthalmol. **105** (2020). https://doi.org/10.1136/bjophthalmol-2020-316984
5. Heo, T.Y. et al.: Development of a deep-learning-based artificial intelligence tool for differential diagnosis between dry and neovascular age-related macular degeneration. Diagnostics (Basel). **10**(5), 261 (2020). https://doi.org/10.3390/diagnostics10050261. PMID: 32354098; PMCID: PMC7277105
6. Bernabe, O., Acevedo, E., Acevedo, A., et al.: Classification of eye diseases in fundus images. IEEE Access. **9**, 101267–101276 (2021)
7. Lad, E. et al.: Machine learning OCT predictors of progression from intermediate age-related macular degeneration to geographic atrophy and vision loss. Ophthalmol. Sci. **2**(2), 100160 (2022). https://doi.org/10.1016/j.xops.2022.100160. PMID: 35662803; PMCID: PMC9161427
8. Acharya, U.R. et al.: Automated screening tool for dry and wet age-related macular degeneration (ARMD) using pyramid of histogram of oriented gradients (PHOG) and nonlinear features. J. Comput. Sci. **20** (2017). https://doi.org/10.1016/j.jocs.2017.03.005
9. Wang, Y., Zhang, Y., Yao, Z., Zhao, R., Zhou, F.: Machine learning based detection of age-related macular degeneration (AMD) and diabetic macular edema (DME) from optical coherence tomography (OCT) images. Biomed. Opt. Express. **7**(12), 4928–4940 (2016). https://doi.org/10.1364/BOE.7.004928. PMID: 28018716; PMCID: PMC5175542

Splicing Video Forgery Detection Using a Region-Based Segmentation Approach and ResNext

Upasana Singh[1]([✉]) [iD], Sandeep Rathor[1], and Manoj Kumar[2]

[1] Department of Computer Engineering and Applications, GLA University, Mathura, UP, India
upasanasingh.vns@gmail.com
[2] Department of Information Technology, GGV University, Bilaspur, Chhattisgarh, India

Abstract. A novel method for splicing video forgery detection in the digital domain is proposed. Our method combines the ResNext architecture with region_based segmentation to resolve the issues with multimedia data authenticity. After preprocessing, which includes resizing and normalization, video frames are segmented hierarchically using Spatial_Constraint Fuzzy C_Means (SCFCM). Then, for features extraction and classification, the ResNext deep learning model is used. Using deep learning capabilities and structural segmentation, this integrated methodology presents a standard solution for robust splicing video forgery detection. Its effectiveness in addressing digital video forensic issues is confirmed by experimental evaluations on benchmark datasets. Superior accuracy and strength in forgery identification are highlighted by thorough comparisons with state-of-the-art techniques, and results show precision in detecting spatial video forgeries.

Keywords: Spatial forgery · Splicing · Segmentation · Deep neural networks · Machine learning

1 Introduction

In the era of digital media, the rise of sophisticated manipulation techniques generates a significant risk to the integrity of video content. Video forgery has a variety of malicious activities, comprising, yet not restricted to, splicing, tampering, object insertion, and frame-level manipulation. Such forgeries can be used to mislead, or even manipulate public opinion, making it crucial to develop robust and efficient methods for detecting video forgeries. In today's era, most people are active on social networking sites, where they regularly share photos and videos.

However, they often lack information about the authenticity of the content they share. This is because, in the present times, there is a widespread circulation and creation of forged videos and photos on social networking sites, particularly involving a significant use of spliced forgery. For instance, individuals may take clips from two different people and merge them into one, creating a video that appears as if the two clips are occurring simultaneously. This practice can lead to the creation of controversies and

R. Appavoo et al. (Eds.): IconDeepCom 2024, CCIS 2687, pp. 389–402, 2026.
https://doi.org/10.1007/978-3-032-26680-4_31

Fig. 1. Frame clips depicting instances of splicing video forgery.

misinterpretations. Figure 1 mentioned here represents few video clips that is generating misinterpretations due to splicing forgery. In the realm of digital video forensics, the investigation of detecting forgery emerges as a crucial domain. This research broadly categorizes into two main streams: Temporal forgery, also known as inter_frame forgery, encapsulates manipulations occurring between frames in a sequence. Conversely, spatial forgery, referred to as intra_frame forgery, entails alterations transpiring within a single frame or within the spatial context.

In this approach, our primary focus is on spatial video forgery detection, particularly emphasizing splicing forgery. The justification behind this emphasis lies in the fact that, unlike other spatial tampering such as copy_move, object removal, object insertion, and region duplication, which can often be detected using a unified method during the detection process, splicing video forgery demands a distinct approach. And The field of splicing video forgery detection faces powerful challenges, including the need to stay aware of rapidly evolving forgery techniques, the lack of comprehensive datasets for training and evaluation, and the computational complexity inherent in processing large_scale video data. These obstacles require innovative solutions and collaborative efforts to advance the state-of-the-art in digital video forensics. The challenge arises because the texture and spatial features associated with these various forgeries are nearly identical, making them detectable through a single technique. However, splicing forgery, despite being a type of spatial forgery, presents unique features after extraction that closely look like temporal features. Hence, detecting splicing forgery alongside other types of forgery becomes challenging. For this reason, we require specific techniques tailored to the distinct characteristics of splicing forgery for effective detection. Separating from conventional approaches that have been in practice, we are employing a distinctive methodology by integrating ResNext and graph_based segmentation to detect splicing video forgery. In our novel method, we start by preparing video frames with the goal of reducing noise and normalizing color for improved quality. Subsequently, we adopt hierarchical segmentation techniques based on graphs to partition the frames. Within these segmented areas, we delve into texture and color analyses, unraveling potential inconsistencies introduced by splicing. The derived features are combined into comprehensive vectors, comprising a labeled dataset that detect between genuine and manipulated regions.

The ResNext deep learning model is then meticulously calibrated on this dataset, empowering it to effectively differentiate between authentic and spliced sections. This cohesive methodology not only promises a robust solution for detecting splicing video forgery but also harnesses the union between structural segmentation insights and the strong capabilities of deep learning. The paper's following sections are organized as follows: Section 2 provides an in-depth exploration of related reviews in the realm of video forgery detection. Section 3 elucidates the details of the proposed model. The presentation and analysis of results unfold in Sect. 5. Section 6 encapsulates the conclusion, offering insights into future avenues for research.

2 Related Work

Several researchers have previously made noteworthy contributions to digital video forensics by developing effective methods for detecting intra_frame video forgery. Recently, approach based on deep learning Yao et al. [1] propose a Deep_Learning approach for object-based forgery detection in videos, utilizing a CNN for high-dimensional feature extraction. Their method introduces three preprocessing layers to minimize temporal duplication and enhance residual signals. An asymmetric data augmentation strategy ensures a balanced training dataset. Zampoglou et al. [2] present a multimedia forensics approach for tampered video detection, integrating manual filters based on DCT coefficients and requantization errors. The method combines these filters with specialized CNNs for effective image classification. Kono et al. [3] propose a passive video forgery detection method utilizing both CNN and RNN, addressing spatio temporal consistency. They contribute by creating new databases for object modification and removal scenarios in video forgery. Saber et al. [4] introduced a forgery detection method employing RDLNN and MOT for region detection. The model includes RGB to YCbCr conversion, PDyWT decomposition, and GTSS for localization. Raveendra et al. [5] introduced a hybrid deep learning architecture for video tampering detection, involving initial DCT double compression, bilateral filtering, and Gabor wavelet transform in a DNN AGSO framework. Singh et al. [6] proposed a studythat learns complex patterns from real and altered frames using a fine-tuned ResNet50 to detect spatial video frauds. It makes use of the hierarchical feature capture capability of ResNet50. Additional, Singh et al. [7] proposed a framework that detects two- and three_level manipulations by using AACNNs to extract features and a U-Net CycleGAN to locate forgeries. Jia et al. [8] suggested a coarse-to-fine strategy for Copy-Move Forgery Detection utilizing Optical_Flow (OF) and consistent parameters, scrutinizing OF sum consistency for coarse detection and fine-tuning for precise forgery localization. Zhong et al. [9] propose an advanced VCMFD method with improved SIFT structure, fast keypoint_label matching, and coarse-to-fine filtering. Adaptive block filling enhances accurate detection of suspicious regions, indicating forged videos.Aloraini et al. [11] innovate by detecting object removal forgery through progressive examination and patch analysis. Their method uses a mixture model of normal and anomalous patches, identifying changes in process parameters and patch distribution for effective video forgery detection. Saddique et al. [12] propose a spatial video forgery detection method using consecutive frame texture analysis. Their approach, utilizing chrominance values from CCD and DRLBP, successfully detects forged video segments. SVM aids in detection and enables localization of forged frames when one pair of consecutive frames is identified as forged. In a noise_based approach, Singh et al.[13] suggested a method integrating Optical_Flow and pattern noise for identifying copy-paste instances in digital videos. The analysis focuses on irregularities in brightness gradient components within Optical_Flow and anomalies in noise patterns present in video frames, whether local or global. Aparicio-D'ıaz et al.[14] introduces an effective method for precise detection of spatially allocated copy-move attacks.It leverages a versatile correlation matrix that captures both spatial and temporal information. The method demonstrates efficiency across various scenarios, from small spatial region duplication to full frame duplication. Kumari et al. [15] propose a Farneback Optical_Flow_based approach for inter-frame forgery detection in digital videos. Achieving 97% accuracy, the method efficiently highlights tampered regions and contributes to video forensic advancements. Evaluation is conducted on the REWIND dataset, addressing challenges of robustness, susceptibility to adversarial attacks, and computational complexity. Bakas et al. [16] introduces a forensic solution for identifying double compression forgery in MPEG videos, a prevalent video format. Our proposed deep learning architecture leverages video I-frames and associated artifacts induced by double quantization, enabling both forgery detection and precise localization within frames. Kang et al. [17] proposes a passive_blind method for detecting intra_frame copy_paste forgery in videos and pinpointing duplicated regions within tampered frames. The method comprises two main stages: edge line extraction and feature point matching. Cloned areas identified exhibit identical edge lines to the original, while matching and clustering of feature points reflect the relationship between source and forged blocks accurately, without the need for predefined thresholds or empirical values.

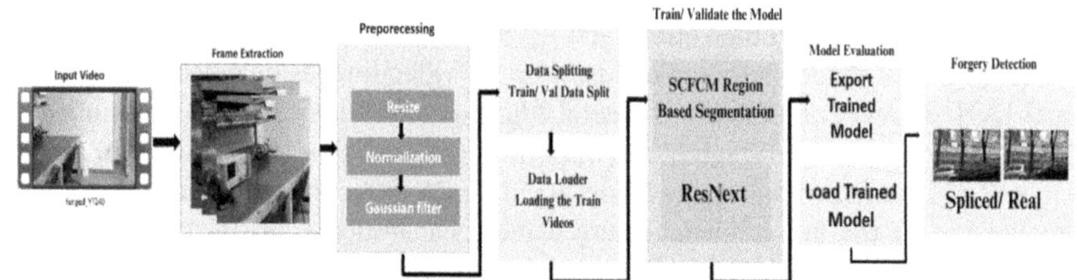

Fig. 2. Proposed architecture for Splicing Video Forgery Detection using Region Based Segmentation by Fuzzy C-Means algorithm with Spatial Constraint (SCFCM)) and ResNext.

3 Proposed Approach

This model uses the powerful deep learning capabilities of ResNext, customized to excel in spatial video forgery detection. Engineered specifically to uncover splicing manipulations within video frames, its architecture is finely tuned for accuracy and precision. Figure 2 encapsulates the seamless flow of our approach, illustrating its ability to carefully identify and combat spatial video forgeries at every stage.

3.1 Data Preprocessing

In our spatial forgery detection methodology, we initiate the process by extracting individual frames ($V = \{f_1, f_2, \ldots, N\}$) from a video dataset including both real and forged videos. Preprocessing follows, involving re sizing to 224×224 for uniformity, pixel normalization to $[0, 1]$, and Gaussian filtering (using a kernel G with standard deviation σ) to enhance frame quality by reducing noise. The best conditions for later differentiation between real and altered content are guaranteed by this methodical approach.

3.2 Region_Based Segmentation

The region_based segmentation procedure in the suggested video forgery detection pipeline is carefully planned utilizing the Fuzzy C_Means algorithm with Spatial Constraint (SCFCM). In order to promote a comprehensive understanding, region_based segmentation divides pixels into unified regions according to common characteristics like color and texture. In addition to capturing patterns, region_based segmentation uses spatial relationships to improve clustering accuracy through methods such as the Fuzzy C_Means algorithm with Spatial Constraint (SCFCM) [18]. The main benefit of utilizing SCFCM lies in its ability to capture spatial relationships among data points, making it especially suited for scenarios where spatial consistency is crucial, such as in video forgery detection.

Formally, the objective function for SCFCM can be expressed as:

$$\text{J\_SCFCM} = \sum_{i=1}^{c} \sum_{j=1}^{n} m_{ij}^{m} \left\| x_j - v_i \right\|^2 + a \sum_{i=1}^{c} \sum_{j=1}^{n} \sum_{k=1}^{n} r_{ij} r_{ik} \left\| u_j - u_k \right\|^2 \tag{1}$$

Here, J_{SCFCM} is the SCFCM objective function, c is the number of clusters, n is the number of data points, μ_{ij} is the fuzzy membership of data point j to cluster i, x_j is the feature vector of data point j, v_i is the centroid of cluster i, m is the fuzziness parameter, α is the weight of the spatial constraint term, ρ_{ij} is the spatial constraint matrix, and u_j represents the membership vector of data point j. The spatial constraint term is defined as:

$$\rho_{ij} = \begin{cases} 1 & if dist\left(x_i, x_j\right) \leq r \\ 0 & otherwise \end{cases} \tag{2}$$

Here dist$(x_i - x_j)$ denotes the spatial distance between data points x_i and x_j, and $\leq r$ is a predefined spatial radius. This objective function combines the usual FCM term, which helps keep the clusters similar, and the spatial constraint term, which makes sure the clusters stay together in space. The fuzzy memberships created from this help form clear and spatially consistent clusters, which are then used in later steps like texture analysis and ResNext-based forgery detection.

3.3 Pre-trained ResNeXt Model

ResNeXt is a deep learning model that comes from ResNet. ResNet helped solve problems when training very deep models by using something called "residual learning." ResNeXt improves on ResNet to make it work even better. Figure 3 shows a ResNeXt block with a cardinality of 32, where the same transformation is repeated 32 times, and the results are combined at the end, as explained by Xie et al. [19]. The main new feature in ResNeXt is the "cardinality" parameter, which controls how many transformations are applied to the input data. This helps the model capture more types of features and improves its ability to detect forgery, especially when it comes to complex spatial changes and small differences. ResNeXt, which is a version of ResNet, is chosen for detecting splicing forgery because it can handle these challenges well. Its grouped convolutions allow it to efficiently detect spatial differences in video frames, making it a good choice for splicing forgery detection.

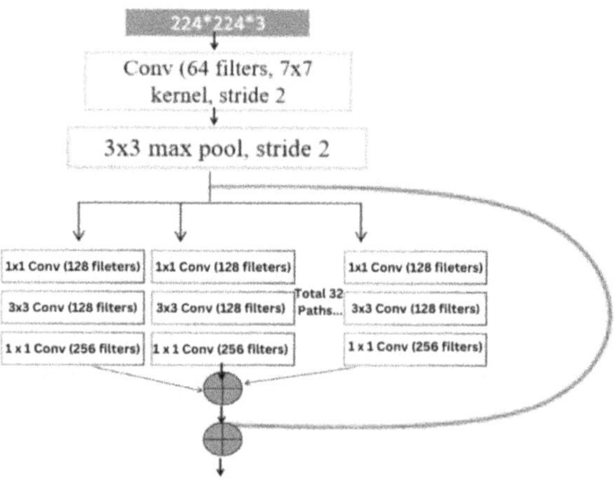

Fig. 3. The cardinality of this conventional ResNeXt block is 32.

The following are the main differences between splicing forgery detection with ResNext:

1. **ResNeXt50's emphasis on spatial characteristics:** ResNeXt50 is designed to detect splicing forgery in videos by focusing more on spatial features, unlike ResNet50, which is mainly used for image classification. The aim is to make the model better at spotting small changes in the video that may indicate tampering.
2. **ResNeXt50's Integration of Grouped Convolution:** ResNeXt50 makes use of grouped convolutions $(C = 32)$ in several layers, which enables more efficient feature extraction via parallel paths. In order to overcome the difficulties caused by splicing forgeries in films, the goal is to increase the model's ability to capture various spatial patterns.
3. **Improved Sensitivity to Local discrepancies:** ResNeXt50 seeks to increase the model's sensitivity to minute spatial movements so that it may more reliably identify

local discrepancies linked to video tampering. In order to accurately detect splicing frauds, the goal is to make the model more sensitive to spatial fluctuations.

4. **ResNeXt50's Specialized Convolutional Blocks:** ResNeXt50 might have convolutional blocks tailored to the purpose of splicing forgery detection. To effectively collect pertinent spatial information, these blocks might have included more layers, different filter sizes, or different groups. With an emphasis on efficient feature representation, the goal is to customize the model's architecture to the unique needs of splicing forgery detection.

For the particular task of splicing forgery detection in videos, ResNeXt50's main goal is to enhance spatial feature extraction, sensitivity to local discrepancies, and overall performance.

Table 1. An explanation of the dataset utilized in the suggested method.

Dataset	Source	Number of Videos	Forgery Type	Resolution
GRIP	University Federico II of Naples	40	Copy-move and Splicing	1280×720
VTD	Universiti Teknologi Malaysia	33	Copy-move, Splicing and frame Swapping	1280×720

4 Result and Discussion

4.1 Dataset

Our suggested method is thoroughly tested in this work on two reputable datasets: GRIP [20] and VTD [21]. We use a video forgery dataset that was assembled by Al-Sanjary et al. [21] and consists of 33 YouTube videos for performance evaluation and validation.This dataset, which includes examples of splicing, swapping, and copy-move forgeries, was created especially for forensic analysis. This dataset contains 16-s videos with a frame rate of 30 frames per second. Furthermore, a well-known standard dataset that was first made available in 2017 includes 23 films and 2520 modified photos. The GRIP dataset, which included ten falsified videos made by splicing with Adobe After Effects CC software, was released that same year [22]. Videos having a 720×1280 pixel resolution are included in this online dataset. The incorporation of these datasets guarantees a thorough assessment of our suggested methodology, taking into account various video forgery scenarios. A detailed review of the properties linked to the datasets used in this investigation is given in Table 1, which offers a full overview of their features.

Fig. 4. A frame that was taken from the GRIP Dataset's "01 TANK forged.avi" film.

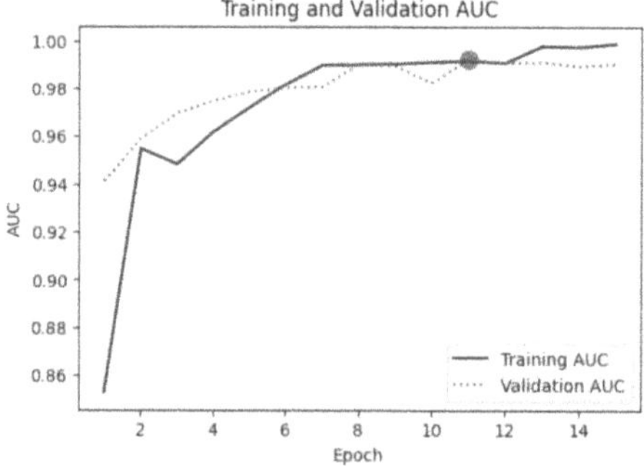

Fig. 5. Area Under the ROC Curve (AUC) Graph for GRIP Dataset.

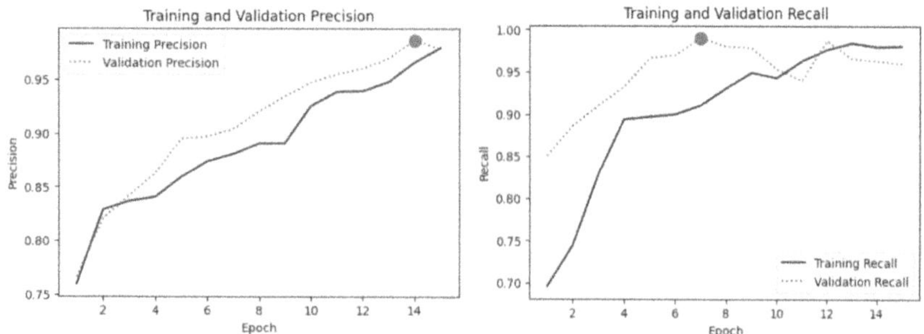

Fig. 6. Precision Graph and Recall Graph for GRIP Dataset.

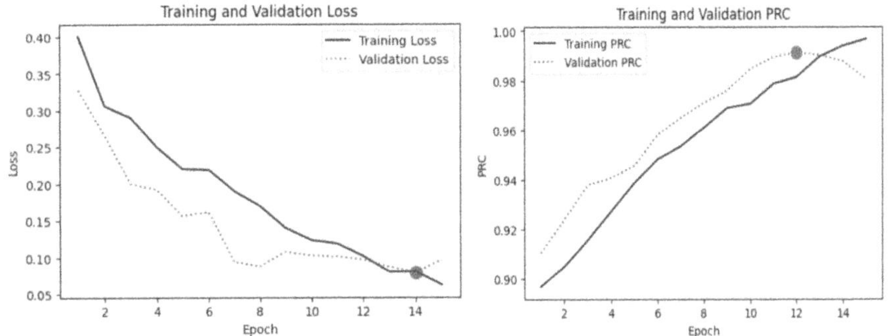

Fig. 7. Binary Crossentropy Loss Graph and Area Under the Precision-Recall Curve (PRC) Graph for GRIP Dataset.

Table 2. Parameters Used in the Proposed Model.

Parameters	Used Value
Optimizer	Stochastic Gradient Descent (SGD)
Activation Function	ReLU activation
Batch Size	32
Epochs	15
Learning Rate	1e-3

Fig. 8. A frame that was taken from the GRIP Dataset's "Forgery basketball skills.mp4" film.

Table 3. Findings from the Splicing Video Forgery Detection experiment.

Dataset	AUC	Precision	Recall	Loss	PRC
GRIP	0.9925	0.9867	0.9902	0.0789	0.9913
VTD	0.9903	0.9697	0.9735	0.0837	0.9878

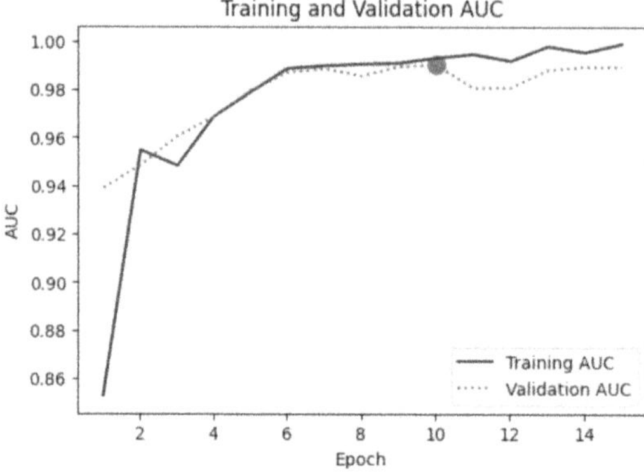

Fig. 9. Area Under the ROC Curve (AUC) Graph for VTD Dataset.

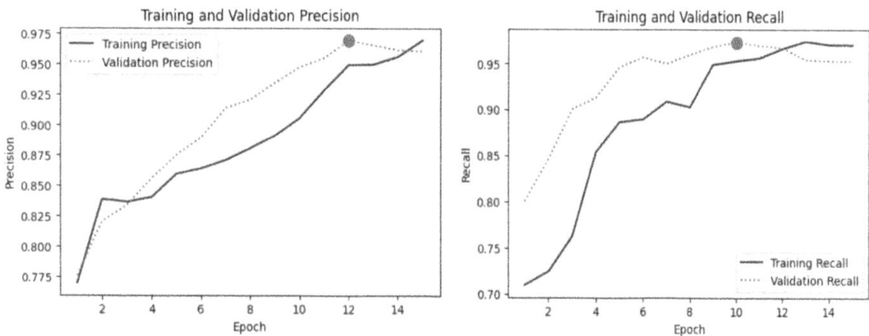

Fig. 10. Precision Graph and Recall Graph for VTD Dataset.

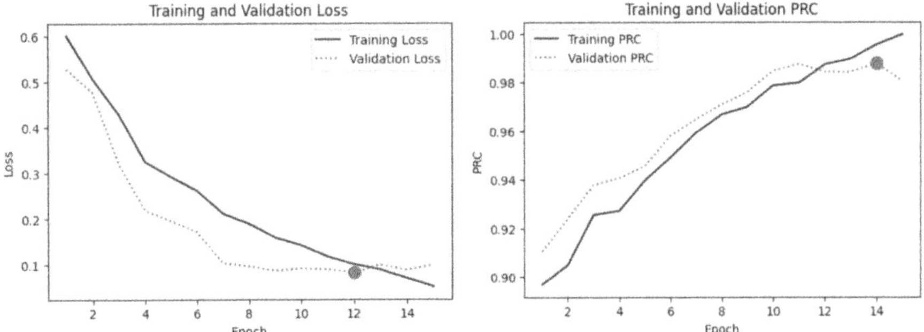

Fig. 11. Binary Crossentropy Loss and Area Under the Precision-Recall Curve (PRC) Graph for VTD Dataset.

4.2 Result Evaluation

A thorough overview of the results from applying our methods to the VTD and GRIP datasets is provided in this section. The discussion highlights important results and insights from our methodology, which uses a wide range of metrics, such as accuracy, precision, recall, AUC, and AUC-PRC, to thoroughly assess the model's performance. The optimization process employs Stochastic Gradient Descent (SGD) as the optimizer, featuring a learning rate of 1e- 3, momentum set to 0.95, and nesterov set to False. To enhance training dynamics, a scheduler function dynamically adjusts the learning rate, diminishing it by 10% with each epoch. The ModelCheckpoint is strategically employed to preserve the best weights based on validation loss, ensuring the retention of the optimal model configuration. The training phase spans 15 epochs on the training dataset (train ds), employing a batch size of 32. The model's performance is meticulously monitored on unseen data using the validation dataset (val ds). Remarkably, the model achieves high accuracy, reaching 0.9925 at epoch 11, accompanied by favorable metrics. Table 2 furnishes a detailed overview of the specified parameters, presenting key insights and facilitating a comprehensive examination of their characteristics.

- In the experiment conducted on the GRIP dataset, Figure 4 showcases frames extracted from "01 TANK forged.avi," providing valuable visual insights. The discriminative capability, as depicted in Fig. 5, reaches its peak at an AUC of 0.9925 (epoch 11). Precision and Recall, as illustrated in Fig. 6, attains a notable value of 0.9867 (epoch 14), while the optimal recall is achieved at 0.9902 (epoch 7). The Binary Crossentropy Loss and Precision-Recall Curve (PRC), visualized in Fig. 7, diminishes to a minimum of 0.0789 (epoch 14), the Precision-Recall Curve (PRC) reaches its zenith at 0.9913 during epoch 12 for the GRIP dataset video. These visual representations provide a comprehensive overview of the model's performance and offer insights into its effectiveness on the GRIP dataset.
- In the experiment conducted on the VTD dataset, Figure 8 presents frames extracted from "Forgery basketball skills.mp4," offering valuable visual insights into the model's performance. Figure 9 highlights the discriminative ability of the model, showcasing a peak AUC of 0.9903 at epoch 10. Precision and Recall, as depicted

in Fig. 10, reaches a significant value of 0.9697 at epoch 12, while optimal recall is achieved at 0.9735 during epoch 10. The Binary Crossentropy Loss and Precision-Recall Curve (PRC), visualized in Fig. 11, minimizes to 0.0837 at epoch 12, indicating effective training. Examining Fig. 11, the Precision-Recall Curve (PRC) achieves its peak at 0.9878 during epoch 14 for the VTD dataset video. These visual representations contribute to a comprehensive understanding of the model's performance and its efficacy on the VTD dataset.

Table 3 summarizes the performance metrics for the evaluation of splicing Video Forgery Detection using Region-based segmentation and the ResNext approach. The model demonstrates outstanding performance, especially in terms of high recall and precision on both datasets. AUC values for both ROC and PRC showcase strong discriminative capabilities, while the reported low loss signifies effective convergence during training. Together, these measures highlight how well the model performs on the validation set. Our suggested solution outperforms state-of-the-art techniques, demonstrating exceptional precision in identifying and locating forged areas in digital films. The thorough outcomes shown in Table 4 offer a thorough demonstration of how well our approach advances video forensic analysis.

Table 4. Comparison between the suggested approach and cutting-edge methods.

Ref	Approach	Precision	Recall	Accuracy
[23]	Sensor Pattern Noise (SPN)	0.925	0.90	0.914
[24]	EXIF-Consistency prediction	0.906	0.873	0.891
Proposed	**SCFCM with ResNext**	**0.9867**	**0.9902**	**0.9925**

5 Conclusion

To sum up, the combination of the ResNext architecture with the Fuzzy C-Means algorithm with Spatial Constraint (SCFCM) offers a reliable method for splicing forgery detection in digital films. The spatial limitations brought about by SCFCM in conjunction with the ResNext architecture tackle the particular difficulties presented by splicing forgeries, providing a customized solution to this particular kind of spatial manipulation. When compared to the most advanced techniques, the method's outstanding performance confirms its effectiveness in developing splicing forgery detection in the field of digital video forensics. The model's excellent discriminative capabilities are demonstrated by the obtained high AUC values for both ROC and PRC, which show how well it can differentiate between real and altered video frames. The model's ability to accurately detect counterfeit regions while reducing false positives is further highlighted by the precision and recall numbers. Future developments might concentrate on improved feature representation by investigating sophisticated feature extraction techniques to increase detection robustness and accuracy, dynamic adaptation algorithms that can adapt to novel forgery techniques, and privacy-preserving detection techniques to protect people's privacy in delicate situations.

Acknowledgments. I would like to express my sincere gratitude to Dr. Sandeep Rathor, Associate Professor in the Department of Computer Engineering and Applications at GLA University, Mathura, U.P., India, and Prof. Manoj Kumar, Professor (Head) in the Department of Information Technology at GGV University, Bilaspur, Chhattisgarh, India. Their graceful guidance was invaluable in conducting and presenting this research work.

Conflict of Interest. The authors affirm that they do not possess any conflicts of interest.

References

1. Yao, Y., Shi, Y., Weng, S., Guan, B.: Deep learning for detection of object-based forgery in advanced video. Symmetry. **10**(1), 3 (2017)
2. Zampoglou, M., et al.: Detecting tampered videos with multimedia forensics and deep learning. In: MultiMedia Modeling: 25th International Conference, MMM 2019, Thessaloniki, Greece, January 8–11, 2019, Proceedings, Part I 25, pp. 374–386. Springer (2019)
3. Kono, K., Yoshida, T., Ohshiro, S., Babaguchi, N.: Passive video forgery detection considering spatio-temporal consistency. In: Proceedings of the Tenth International Conference on Soft Computing and Pattern Recognition (SoCPaR 2018), pp. 381–391. Springer (2020)
4. Saber, A.H., Khan, M.A., Mejbel, B.G.: RDLNN-based image forgery detection and forged region detection using MOT. Karbala Int. J. Mod. Sci. **8**(4), 596–606 (2022)
5. Raveendra, M., Nagireddy, K.: Tamper video detection and localization using an adaptive segmentation and deep network technique. J. Vis. Commun. Image Represent. **82**, 103401 (2022)
6. Singh, U., Rathor, S., Kumar, M.: Deep video forensics: unveiling spatial forgery detection with modified ResNet50. In: 2024 IEEE 13th International Conference on Communication Systems and Network Technologies (CSNT), pp. 260–265. IEEE (2024)
7. Singh, U., Rathor, S., Kumar, M.: Advanced framework for multilevel detection of digital video forgeries. Ann. New York Acad. Sci. (2024)
8. Jia, S., Xu, Z., Wang, H., Feng, C., Wang, T.: Coarse-to-fine copy-move forgery detection for video forensics. IEEE Access. **6**, 25323–25335 (2018)
9. Zhong, J.L., Pun, C.M., Gan, Y.F.: Dense moment feature index and best match algorithms for video copy-move forgery detection. Inf. Sci. **537**, 184–202 (2020)
10. Zhong, J.L., Gan, Y.F., Vong, C.M., Yang, J.X., Zhao, J.H., Luo, J.H.: Effective and efficient pixel-level detection for diverse video copy-move forgery types. Pattern Recogn. **122**, 108286 (2022)
11. Aloraini, M., Sharifzadeh, M., Schonfeld, D.: Sequential and patch analyses for object removal video forgery detection and localization. IEEE Trans. Circuits Syst. Video Technol. **31**(3), 917–930 (2020)
12. Saddique, M., Asghar, K., Bajwa, U.I., Hussain, M., Habib, Z.: Spatial video forgery detection and localization using texture analysis of consecutive frames. Adv. Electr. Comput. Eng. **19**(3) (2019)
13. Singh, R.D., Aggarwal, N.: Optical flow and pattern noise-based copy–paste detection in digital videos. Multimedia Systems. **27**, 449–469 (2021)
14. Aparicio-Díaz, E., Cumplido, R., Gort, M.L., Uribe, C.F.: Temporal copy-move forgery detection and localization using block correlation matrix. J. Intell. Fuzzy Syst. **36**, 5023–5035 (2019)
15. Kumari, P., Kaur, M.: Empirical evaluation of motion Cue for passive-blind video tamper detection using optical flow technique. In: Proceedings of International Joint Conference on Advances in Computational Intelligence: IJCACI 2021, pp. 97–112. Springer Nature Singapore, Singapore (2022, May)

16. Bakas, J., Bashaboina, A.K., Naskar, R.: Mpeg double compression based intra-frame video forgery detection using CNN. In: 2018 International Conference on Information Technology (ICIT), pp. 221–226. IEEE (2018, December)
17. Kang, G.Y., Feng, Y.P., Wang, R.K., Lu, Z.M.: Edge and feature points based video intra-frame passive-blind copy-paste forgery detection. J. Netw. Intell. 6(3), 637–645 (2021)
18. Li, X., Qu, Z., Yang, X.: Spatially constrained fuzzy c-means clustering algorithm for image segmentation. J. Phys. Conf. Ser. 1237(3), 032024 (2019, June)
19. Xie, S., Girshick, R., Dollár, P., Tu, Z., He, K.: Aggregated residual transformations for deep neural networks. In: Proceedings of the IEEE Conference on Computer Vision And Pattern Recognition, pp. 1492–1500 (2017)
20. GRIP: (2022). http://www.grip.unina.it/. Accessed 30 Nov 2023
21. Al-Sanjary, O.I., Ahmed, A.A., Sulong, G.: Development of a video tampering dataset for forensic investigation. Forensic Sci. Int. 266, 565–572 (2016) Accessed 2 Nov 2023
22. Qadir, G., Yahaya, S., Ho, A.T.: Surrey university library for forensic analysis (SULFA) of video content (2012)
23. Li, Q., Wang, R., Xu, D.: A video splicing forgery detection and localization algorithm based on sensor pattern noise. Electronics. 12(6), 1362 (2023)
24. Jin, X., He, Z., Xu, J., Wang, Y., Su, Y.: Video splicing detection and localization based on multi-level deep feature fusion and reinforcement learning. Multimed. Tools Appl. 81(28), 40993–41011 (2022)

Real-World Use Cases Powered by CNN Models

Futuristic Body Pose Language Detection System Using Convolution Neural Networks

C. Amuthadevi[✉] [iD], Dhruva Bhattacharya, and Sarthak Mittal

Department of Computational Intelligence, SRM Institute of Science and Technology, Kattankulathur, India
{amuthadc,sm0309,db6688}@srmist.edu.in

Abstract. This paper presents a new design of an emotion detection model and a system for interpreting the human body language based on convolutional neural networks, which are used to retrieve features from images of humans, aiming for high precision and wide emotion detection ability. A large number of datasets of labeled body images is used for training. Then, a separate evaluation dataset is used. This will then be used it to detect any body parts and can be used to decipher meanings behind the languages presented by the body motion This futuristic system holds promise for various applications requiring emotional understanding. By analyzing intricate patterns and relationships within the data, the system learns to associate specific body language cues with distinct emotions. This complex learning process, driven by a classified large database of body images, enables the system to learn and get good accuracy in interpreting the hidden language.

Keywords: Body pose Language Recognition System · Deep Learning

1 Introduction

The decoding of human emotions as well as responding to such in the domain of artificial intelligence and human-computer interaction is thus highly crucial. Traditionally, emotion recognition systems focus much on facial expressions and disregard the wealth of information in body pose. This is where this Futuristic Body Pose Language Detection System finds its value: a potential innovation aiming at decoding an unspoken language of a human being.

Leverage the power of Convolutional Neural Networks (CNNs) to go beyond the limits of traditional approaches in analyzing body posture, gestures, and movements to give a deeper, more nuanced understanding of human emotions. Inspired by the human visual cortex, CNNs are excellent at identifying patterns in complex visual data, allowing the system to interpret subtle cues such as a raised shoulder, a clenched fist, or a tentative step. These movements are all intertwined to uncover the otherwise silent emotional storyline that the words and facial expressions are not able to say by themselves.

This technology, in a word, is a transformative technology for all domains of life- from education to healthcare, customer service to many more. The decoding of this silent choreography of body language will help bring humans closer to machines in a

R. Appavoo et al. (Eds.): IconDeepCom 2024, CCIS 2687, pp. 405–417, 2026.
https://doi.org/10.1007/978-3-032-26680-4_32

way where empathy and collaboration become much more achievable than before. The Body Pose Language Detection System will, thus, pave the way to an era where human-to-machine interaction becomes more intuitive and natural, leading to a symphony of understanding and cooperation and shifting the role of technology in our lives.

This is the approach that will place us at the forefront of a new era, where machines don't just see or hear us but understand us. This will open up breakthroughs in communication, learning, and emotional intelligence.

2 Motivation

The Futuristic Body Pose Language Detection System would signify a huge leap in the approach we take towards the identification of emotions and behaviors and goes beyond facial expressions into the entire body language. Using CNNs, it would be able to detect not only static gestures but also dynamic movements within the body, allowing it to better understand human emotion and intent.

The system would be akin to how the human brain processes visual information: how it could detect and interpret subtle movements and overt expressions, from shifts in posture to hand gestures, including minute tremors that indicate nervousness, excitement, or other emotional states. This approach would bridge a gap between facial recognition systems and the complexity of human non-verbal communication.

One of the potential applications could be in improving user interactions with AI. For instance, rather than just analyzing spoken words or facial expressions, a body pose detection system could help an AI system to detect when a person feels uncomfortable, stressed, or engaged, allowing it to respond with more empathy or adaptability. In professional setups, this can be applied to evaluating a presentation, meeting, or speech by body language of people or teams.

Such systems, therefore, by analyzing data from body pose and movement, can break all the limitations of flat affective AI to bring us more responsive, more deep, and more intuitive connections between humans and machines; hence, it is towards technology that does not hear or see us but, instead, feels our presence.

This technology is transformative, especially in fields such as mental health where therapists may be able to see a patient's emotional state in ways more subtle than words. This may also be applied in the security or forensic sector where movements could be very significant, something that cannot be revealed through words or even facial expressions.

This would transform fields such as virtual reality, gaming, and human-computer interaction. It could make interactions even more fluid, responsive, and natural. It may redefine what we consider non-verbal communication and how we can measure it, giving it a new dimension in the study of human emotions.

3 Innovation Idea of the Work

3.1 Beyond Facial Expressions

A body pose language detection system is above the traditional approaches for emotion detection, which depends only on facial expressions. The system interprets every feature of non-verbal signals through the analysis of body postures, gestures, and minute movements. This would enable more sensitive extraction of emotional information in more accurate detail and completeness to understand the human sense. Therefore, this represents a different scenario from those conventionally employed approaches and sets new criteria for an emotion recognition system.

3.2 Utilizing Convolutional Neural Networks (CNNs)

At the core of this is the use of CNN, inspired by the visual cortex of a human. In fact, CNN is at its best in the detection and analysis of patterns based on pictorial or video data. Therefore, perfect for decoding intricate connections of body language with emotional states, CNN ensures unparalleled accuracy of recognition and interpretation of human movement as silent language based on learning associations of certain bodily cues with certain corresponding emotions.

3.3 Huge Data and Continuous Updates

The system is trained on a large, labeled dataset of images and videos of different body language. This ensures that the system learns robustly in all scenarios and contexts. The all-around training makes the model adapt to the subtleties of non-verbal communication. Furthermore, the system utilizes a continuous learning framework that allows it to take new data and improve its accuracy over time. This helps it stay relevant and in tune with the dynamic human interaction pattern.

3.4 Human-Centric Human-Machine Interaction

In this manner, widening the scope of the system to include body language is able to provide access to more intuitive and natural forms of human machine interaction. It might, for example, be able to change educational practices to respond to students' emotional needs and personalize education. Similarly, in healthcare, it would help therapists decipher unseen cues from patients to intervene in a sympathetic and effective way. The system is versatile to promise transformative applications across any industry, thereby creating the seamless bridge between human emotions and machine responses.

This innovation would therefore address existing limitations with the emotion-detecting systems and create new opportunities for deeper interaction and better understanding in human-machine relations. It paves a future where technology is tied up with all the niceties of humanity, bringing about machines to respond emotionally and interact at an emotional level with man, making man empathetic and emotionally attached.

4 Literature Review

Ref	Title Of the Paper	Proposed Methodology	Positive Points	Discussion
[1]	Stabilizing motion tracking using retrieved motion priors	a database of motion patterns is created from various videos or motion capture data. When tracking a new motion sequence, relevant priors are retrieved based on similarities in appearance or motion features.	Priors can help maintain tracking accuracy even with occlusions, noise, or abrupt movements.	retrieving and incorporating priors can add computational overhead.
[2]	Detailed Human Shape and Pose from Images	Convolutional neural networks (CNNs) are trained on large datasets of images paired with 3D body information.	Useful in fields like sports analysis, medical diagnosis, and human-computer interaction.	Current methods, especially 2D-based approaches, may not always provide highly accurate and detailed reconstruction, especially for challenging poses or body types.
[3]	A survey of state-of-the- art approaches for emotion recognition in text	evaluate and compare approaches across various aspects, including performance on benchmark datasets, strengths, and weaknesses	Provides a comprehensive overview of various textual emotion recognition techniques	Focus is primarily on explicit emotion recognition, where emotions are directly expressed in text. Implicit emotion recognition, where emotions are conveyed more subtly, receives less coverage
[4]	Kinecting the dots: Particle- based scene flow from depth sensors	Estimates 3D motion field (scene flow) using depth sensors, overcoming limitations of 2D motion estimation (optical flow).	Handles complex motions not captured by 2D optical flow.	Requires good initial particle distribution for optimal performance.

(*continued*)

(continued)

Ref	Title Of the Paper	Proposed Methodology	Positive Points	Discussion
[5]	Markerless motion capture using a single depth sensor	Each particle's weight is updated based on how well it aligns with the next depth image. This involves projecting the estimated body pose onto the next frame and comparing the projected depth with the actual measurement.	Requires only a single depth sensor, significantly cheaper than traditional marker-based systems.	Accuracy can be lower than marker-based systems, especially for challenging poses or rapid movements.
[6]	Speech emotion recognition motional models, databases, features, preprocessing methods, supporting modalities, and classifiers	Summarizes available databases used for training and testing SER models, highlighting recordings with tagged emotional states.	Offers a comprehensive and up-to- date overview of key aspects of SER.	Focuses primarily on basic research, with limited discussion on real-world applications.
[7]	American Sign Language Recognition using Deep Leaming and Computer Vision	utilized two ASL datasets: **RWTH-PHOENIX-**Weather 2014T and **RWTH-PHOENIX-**Weather 2014E. Both datasets contain videos of different people signing weather-related words and phrases.	The proposed approach achieved good accuracy (over 90%) on the datasets, demonstrating its effectiveness for ASL recognition	Training deep learning models requires significant computational resources, limiting real- time applications.
[8]	Hand Gesture Recognition for Sign Language Using 3DCNN	Capturing hand gesture data through videos using depth sensors orRGB cameras.	3DCNNs can achieve competitive accuracy compared to other approaches, especially for large and diverse datasets	Training 3D CNNs can be computational ly expensive, requiring powerful hardware and large datasets.

(continued)

(continued)

Ref	Title Of the Paper	Proposed Methodology	Positive Points	Discussion
[9]	Manhattan World: compass direction from a single image by Bayesian inference	Edges are extracted from the image and segmented into horizontal and vertical lines.	Single Image Based: Requires only a single image, eliminating the need for calibration or additional sensors.	Relies on the validity of the Manhattan World and perspective camera assumptions, which might not hold true in all scenarios.
[10]	Articulated Body Motion Capture by Stochastic Search	Visual data of the moving body is captured, often using multiple cameras for 3D reconstruction	Stochastic search can explore multiple solutions, mitigating issues like missing data points.	Stochastic search can be computationaly demanding, especially for high-resolution models and large datasets.
[11]	Deep convolutional neural networks for sign language recognition	The model is optimized and trained on the prepared dataset using appropriate loss functions and optimization algorithms.	Deep CNNs can achieve high accuracy in sign language recognition tasks, especially with large and diverse datasets.	Performance heavily relies on the quality and size of the training data. Limited datasets might not generalize to real-world scenarios.
[12]	Tracking through singularities and discontinuities by random sampling	Propagate the state estimate forward in time using a dynamic model, accounting for potential discontinuities or singularities.	Effectively handles situations where traditional filtering methods can break down due to abrupt changes or non-Gaussian distributions.	Generating and evaluating a large number of particles can be computationally expensive, especially for high-dimensional systems.

5 Requirements Gathering

5.1 System Functionality

The Body Pose Language Detection System is superior to traditional methods by analyzing video streams instead of only static images. The fluidity of body language, such as swift movement, nervous fidgeting, or faint smiling, can be detected with this dynamic approach. All these make the subtle elements of an emotional narrative within non-verbal communication come alive and give more insight into human behavior.

5.2 Data Requirements

A robust dataset is the cornerstone of training the system well. The dataset should contain thousands or even millions of labeled images and videos representing various body language cues and their associated emotional states. It should also be diverse in terms of ethnicity, age, gender, and context. The images and videos must be high-resolution and noise-free to avoid possible inaccuracies arising from poor-quality data.

5.3 Technical Needs

The backbone of the system is a strong implementation of Convolutional Neural Networks (CNNs). Popular frameworks like TensorFlow or PyTorch are used to design, train, and fine-tune the neural network. Such frameworks support high-performance computations and enable the system to process vast amounts of data, delivering accurate predictions in efficient time.

6 Challenges and Limitations in the Existing System

Despite the promise of the Body Pose Language Detection System, several challenges and limitations have to be addressed for its successful implementation.

6.1 Limited Diverse Datasets

The existing datasets are not diverse enough in terms of ethnicity, age, gender, and body types. Thus, it may result in biased interpretations and decreased generalization. A more inclusive and representative dataset has to be built for correct recognition of body language across different populations.

6.2 Issues with Labeling the Dataset

Designing an unvarying, culture-inclusive labeling system for gesture language continues to be challenging. Since the interpretations of gestures across cultures tend to be inconstant, the machine will be unable to generalise in an appropriate way.

6.3 Data Privacy

Data acquisition vs. user privacy is of critical concern. Ethical approach for development of secure systems in collecting, anonymising, and securing user consent, shall form part of ethical rights to an individual's private data.

6.4 Model Design and Evaluation

Accuracy and Generalizability: Novel CNN architectures, training methodologies, and data augmentation techniques will be needed to achieve high accuracy across diverse populations and contexts.

Explainability and Transparency: To ensure responsible use, the system should include explainable AI techniques so that users can understand why it makes a certain emotional inference.

6.5 Real-World Applications and Integration

Real-Time Processing: Developing hardware and software solutions optimized for real-time performance in resource-constrained environments is crucial for practical deployment.

Integration with Existing Technologies: Seamless integration into fields like education, healthcare, and customer service requires research into interoperability and data exchange standards.

6.6 Ethical Considerations and Societal Impact

Reduction of Misuse and Bias: Ethical guidelines must be established to prevent misuse, such as profiling or discrimination, and to ensure fairness in the system's outputs.

Cultural Sensitivity: Research should focus on building culturally sensitive models to avoid misinterpretations in diverse contexts.

Impact on Profession: Role displacement of occupation that is dependent on body language analysis necessitates re-skilling and up-skilling.

7 Algorithm

Proposed algorithm for training and deployment of the 3D Human Pose Estimation CNN Model as in follow below.

Algorithm 1
1. Load Pre-trained Model: Use a pre-trained CNN model for 3D human pose estimation.
2. Input Preprocessing: Resize an input image to a predetermined dimension, normalize pixel intensities, and get the input ready for model feeding
3. Feed the CNN with the preprocessing result and predict the 3D pose.
4. Calculate Loss: Calculate the loss between the predicted pose and the ground truth pose using an appropriate loss function.
5. Backpropagation: Backpropagate the loss through the network and update the weights using an optimizer like stochastic gradient descent (SGD).
6. Iterative Training: Repeat steps 3–5 across the training dataset for a fixed number of epochs.
7. Validation: Evaluate the trained model on a validation set, calculating metrics such as accuracy, precision, and recall.
8. Model Fine-Tuning: Adjust hyperparameters or modify the network architecture if performance metrics are unsatisfactory.
9. Deployment: Integrate the trained CNN model into a software or mobile application for real-world use.
10. Performance Monitoring: Continuously monitor the deployed model's performance and optimize it periodically based on user feedback and new data.

The above approach would be the iterative and adaptive model ensuring robustness, accuracy, and efficacy in a multitude of settings.

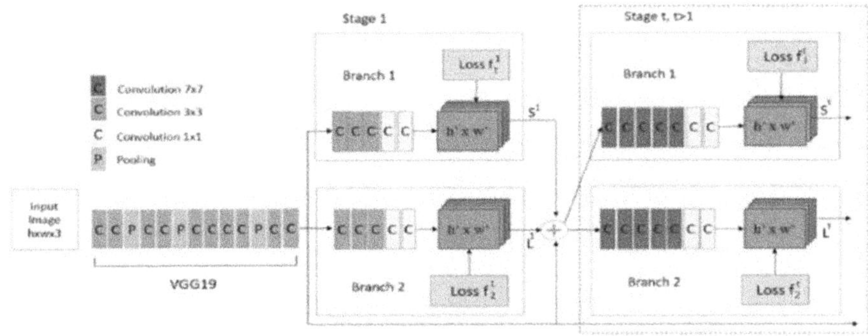

Fig. 1. Architecture Diagram

8 Architecture Diagram

9 Experimental Results

The Model has achieved an accuracy of 99% on the test set, with precision and recall ranging from 92% to 98% for different emotions. This indicates the model can correctly identify emotions from body language cues in a majority of cases, with some variation depending on the specific emotion (Figs. 1, 2, 3, 4, 5, 6 and Table 1).

Table 1. Dataset Feature Point's Accuracy Graph Plot

Visibility	Dataset_Feature_Points (X)	Dataset_Feature_Points (Y)	Dataset_Feature_Points (Z)	Accuracy
V1	0.421845764	0.851779161	−2.5	0.99
V2	0.46488828	0.754330338	−2.5358	0.98
V3	0.488323	0.752826572	−2.5357	0.96
V4	0.58849366	0.7528	−2.53623	0.97
V5	0.3779716	0.755428185	−2.5357	0.95
V6	0.355084	0.765428185	−2.53246888	0.98
V7	0.3366	0.766153216	−2.53277	0.92

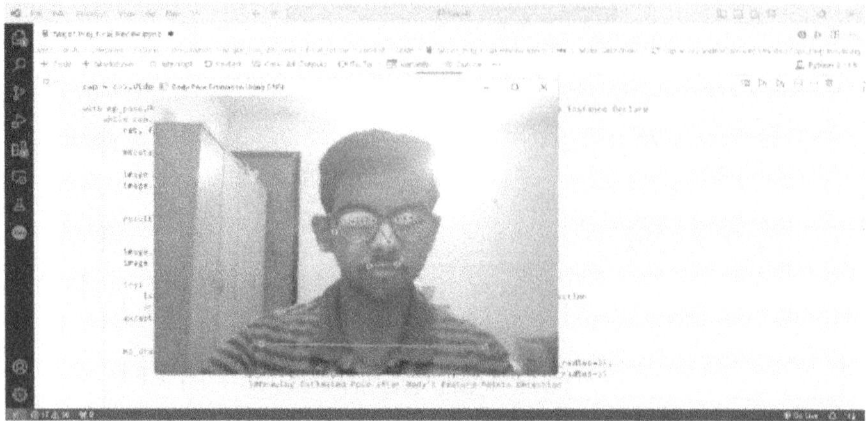

Fig. 2. Body detection of Head

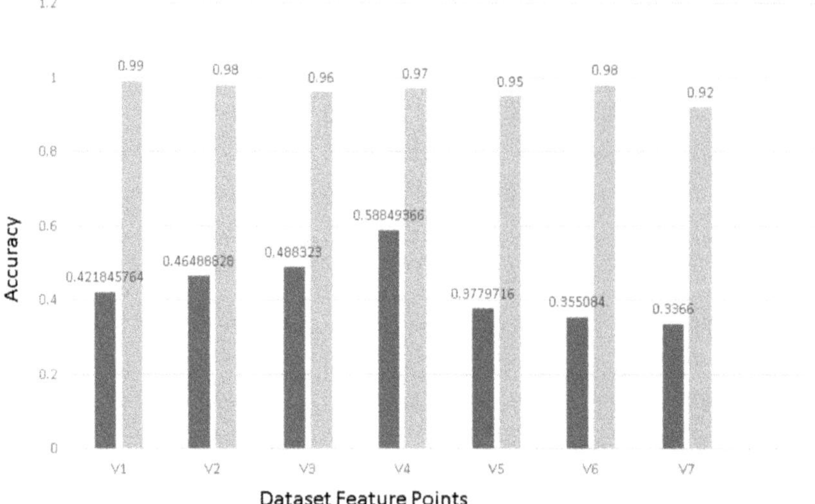

Fig. 3. Accuracy Plot

Fig. 4. Body Detection of Head and Hand

Fig. 5. Body Detection Through Mobile Phone

Fig. 6. Body Detection of Upper Half

10   Conclusion

In conclusion, this paper on Body Pose Language Detection thoroughly explores the subject of potential impact on emotion recognition and human-machine interaction. Such research demonstrates the efficacy of employing Convolutional Neural Networks to analyze body posture, gestures, and movements for far more comprehensive and nuanced views of non-verbal communications than traditional methods. The findings do add to the field considerably as it addresses the gap in existing systems by developing a more holistic approach in emotion recognition. These developments show promise in applications in fields like education, healthcare, and customer service where deeper insights into emotional states can translate into better outcomes. Methods like large-scale dataset training and CNN-based analysis prove to be effective in satisfying the research objectives and lay down practical paths for implementation. Although the research has been successful in achieving meaningful results, it also points out areas that need further investigation. Some of the challenges include ensuring dataset diversity, cultural sensitivity, and ethical standards, which are crucial for future exploration. Further advancements in real-time processing, model explainability, and seamless integration into existing systems are also essential to fully realize the potential of this technology. This work emphasizes the continuation of research in the realm of body pose language detection and its applications. Such findings are the backbone of progression in this field and encourage the further pursuit of research so that methodologies can be enhanced, challenges can be overcome, and new avenues can open up for human-centered technological innovation.

References

1. Anantha Rao, G., Syamala, K., Kishore, P.V.V., Sastryn, A.S.C.S.: Stabilizing motion tracking using retrieved motion priors. In: Proceedings of the IEEE 7th International Conference on Computer and Communication Engineering Technology, pp. 1428–1435 (2022)

2. Balan, A.O., Sigal, L., Black, M.J., Davis, J.E., Haussecker, H.W.: Detailed human shape and pose from images. In: IEEE explore, pp. 1–8 (2021)
3. Alswaidan, N., Menai, M.E.B.: A survey of state of-the-art approaches for emotion recognition in text. Knowl. Inf. Syst., 2937–2987 (2020)
4. Hadfield, S., Bowden, R.: Kinecting the dots.: particle based scene flow from depth sensors. In: IEEE Explore, Proceedings of the IEEE International Conference on Computer Vision, pp. 2290–2295 (2020)
5. Bleiweiss, A., Eilat, E., Kutliroff, G.: Markerless Motion Capture Using a Single Depth Sensor. ACM (2020)
6. Akay, M.B., Oguz, K.: Speech emotion recognition Emotional models, databases, features, preprocessing methods, supporting modalities, and classifiers. Speech Commun. **116**, 56–76 (2020)
7. Noroozi, F., Comeanu, C.A., Kaminska, D., Sapinski, T.: Sergio Escalera: American sign language recognition using deep learning and computer vision. IEEE Trans. Affect. Comput. **12**(2), 505–523 (2020)
8. Al-Hammadi, M., Abdul, G.M.:.W., Alsulaiman, M., Bencherif, M.A., Amin, M.: Hand gesture recognition for sign language using 3DCNN. IEEE Access. **8**, 79491–79508 (2020)
9. Coughlan, J.M., Yuille, A.L.: Manhattan World: compass direction from a single image by Bayesian inference. IEEE Access, 1–7 (2019)
10. Deutscher, J., Reid, I.: Articulated body motion capture by stochastic search. Int. J.Comput. Vis. **61**, 185–205 (2019)
11. Anantha Rao, G., Syamala, K., Kishore, P.V.V., Sastryn, A.S.C.S.: Deep Convolutional Neural Networks for Sign Language Recognition. IEEE (2019)
12. Deutscher, J., North, B., Bascle, B., Blake, A.: Tracking through singularities and discontinuities by random sampling. IEEE Explore. **2**, 651–655 (2018)

Improved Image Classification in CNN Using Histograms

Latha Ramaswamy[1]([✉]), Ramalingam Venkatesan[2], and Ganesh Kumar Subramaniam[3]

[1] SRM Institute of Science and Technology, Kattankulathur, Tamil Nadu, India
`lramaswamy100@gmail.com`
[2] School of Engineering and Computing, Regent College London, London, United Kingdom
`Ramalingam.Venkatesan@rcl.ac.uk`
[3] Department of Data Science and Business Systems , SRM Institute of Science and Technology, Kattankulathur, Tamil Nadu, India
`ganeshk1@srmist.edu.in`

Abstract. Image classification is a fundamental technique in Computer vision that is used to detect and classify objects and is widely used in applications such as autonomous vehicles, surveillance systems, biological species classification, online shopping image categorization, etc. Although convolutional neural network (CNN) models have proven to be the best supervised image classifiers with a high rate of accuracy, they often struggle to capture essential features and structural information from the images and effectively utilize the global statistical information, leading to suboptimal classification accuracy, especially when the number of classes increases. This study identifies such limitations and focuses on improving the performance of image classification within CNN architectures by integrating histogram features. We use the Histogram of Oriented Gradients (HOG) technique to extract histogram feature descriptors and an oriented gradient image from each train image, as well as from the enhanced train image datasets, to integrate them as an additional set of inputs into the CNN model along with the train image tensor data. By incorporating histogram features, CNN architectures aim to improve their ability to capture and leverage global statistical information to enhance their discriminative power for more accurate, reliable, and improved image classification across various datasets and image classes in real-world applications.

Keywords: Image Classification · Convolutional Neural Network · Histogram of Oriented Gradients · Feature Descriptors · Oriented Gradient Image · Feature Integration

1 Introduction

Although the CNN classification models have been successful in various image classification tasks, they are often susceptible to overfitting and end up misclassifying objects even after training the models with large datasets. Missing out on capturing the essential features from the images could result in low prediction accuracy and misclassification of

R. Appavoo et al. (Eds.): IconDeepCom 2024, CCIS 2687, pp. 418–435, 2026.
https://doi.org/10.1007/978-3-032-26680-4_33

the objects. Also, it can be challenging to interpret how a CNN model arrives at predictions, especially when CNN functions and methods with predefined filters are imported from built-in libraries, as we are unsure about the exact filters used in the convolution layers. Hence, to obtain high prediction accuracy in classification models, we need to ensure that the model works on essential features and information from the images for classification.

In this paper, we perform object classification on three channeled color images by integrating histogram features obtained from the function Histogram of Oriented Gradients (HOG) into a CNN model that is designed for object classification. The general idea behind the application of histogram feature representations is that objects of the same kind and features have similar color and gradient spread on histograms. For example, the color features of a German shepherd dog (GSD) image will have an RGB spread on a histogram that is similar to the RGB dispersion of another GSD image on a histogram. Hence, the color feature descriptors and orientation of the gradients on histograms of the same species of animals, insects, or any other sentient being would be similar.

A histogram is a graph that represents the collection of counts of data organized into a set of predefined bins. The data can be color intensity or any other feature used to describe an image, such as gradients, directions, etc. A color histogram is a graph that shows the spread of each color code by representing the count of each color code along the y-axis and the intensity of the colors along the x-axis. A digital image is simply a matrix of pixel values containing the information of an image, generally with an intensity ranging from 0 to 255. The count of pixels falling in bins of a predefined range will make up the histogram.

The histogram of oriented gradients function is widely used in object detection applications to detect objects in motion. The hog features consist of information about color intensity and directional gradients that help to detect object texture or motion. In this work, we consider histogram functions suitable for image classification as hog feature descriptors consist of structural information, color intensity, and directional gradients that help to detect object texture, outline, color saturation, and orientation. During the pre-processing stage, the essential histogram feature descriptors and gradient-oriented image tensors are derived by using the hog () function on each train image and validation image. These new values are integrated into the CNN model by passing them as inputs along with the training and validation images, respectively, to boost the CNN architecture with feature space and orientation that are more specific to each image class to help the model arrive at the best class prediction accuracy.

2 Related Work

Researchers have applied different image processing techniques to enhance the image content to be able to extract the crucial features needed to improve image classification. Supriyo Karmakar and Sayantani Karmakar [12] have applied the Savitzky-Golay (SG) filter to two-dimensional images to increase the signal-to-noise (SNR) ratio and improve image recognition. Before applying the random forest algorithm for classifying, the Karmakars applied the SG filter technique to reduce noise in the image to a considerable extent and improve picture quality to help the model extract the required information from the enhanced images, thereby improving image classification.

Earlier research on histogram-based classifiers extracted feature descriptors from images using the hog technique and primarily used SVM classifiers with hog to achieve a considerable level of prediction accuracy on moving objects by exploiting the directional gradients. Lina Mao and Linyan Tang [11] used a similar combination of hog and SVM classifiers in 2022 on a pedestrian detection system using gradient direction by passing both positive and negative directional images into the classifier during training. According to them, Dalal proposed the HOG feature algorithm in 2005 and used thousand-dimensional features from the MIT and INRIA pedestrian databases to achieve 90% accuracy and a false positive rate of 1/10000.

Nithiyanantha Vasagam and Sornam [13] have designed a classification model to help sort the crust leather in leather production. The authors proposed to enhance the image dataset with filters like Laplacian, Sobel, Median, Roberts, Scharr, Prewitt, Gaussian, and Contrast Limited Adaptive Histogram Equalization (CLAHE) in the first stage and extracted the image scores and histogram features like CORRELATION, INTERSECTION, CHISQR, BHATTACHARYYA in the second stage using the Structural Similarity index. Finally, classifiers such as Random Forest, SVM and Naïve Bayes were used to compare the performances, wherein the Naïve Bayes classifier outperformed the rest, with 94% on classification accuracy.

Shaik Moinuddin Ahmed and Abdul Wahid [14] have discussed the usefulness of image transformation techniques to identify letters on multilingual sign boards to improve text recognition. Yangfan He and Siyuan Yin [6] have demonstrated that MobileNet V2 had the highest accuracy of 93.90%, followed by CNN architecture with 92.20% in food image classification. These two models performed the best when compared to other transfer learning models.

Jiabao Wu et al., [15] have discussed image feature extraction for object detection for service robots by studying the HSV [15], ORB, and SIFT algorithms to exploit the color, shape, and gradient features. In their work, HSV features were used for target detection of pure-color objects with fewer surface feature patterns. Bo-jia SHI et al., [16] have proved with experimental results that histogram equalization greatly improves the image quality of digital instrument images in complex environments. Senthil Kumar, et al., [8] introduced a two-stage image enhancement process that used histogram pairwise equalization in the first stage and a gradient computation process in the second stage to efficiently restore quality images from noisy images.

Divya Sharma, et al., [17] demonstrated how deep neural network models significantly help in diagnosing patients in the field of biomedicals by accurately predicting the condition of COVID-19 patients through lung X-ray image classification using opensource libraries like Keras to build CNN models. Yessi Jusman, et al., [2] have developed a HOG algorithm for COVID-19 X-ray images and tested the inputs on a few classifiers, wherein the medium-gaussian SVM yielded a maximum performance value of 98.28% accuracy.

In summary, classifier models have proven to be effective when input images are enhanced for feature extraction. The classifier models also show better performance in terms of prediction accuracy when features extracted from histogram colors and gradient intensities and directions are input into the CNN models.

3 Proposed Methodology

In this proposed model, we selectively integrate histogram features into dense layers of the CNN architecture. These additional set of input features serve as an attention mechanism for the CNN model to determine which parts of the image are more relevant for feature extraction. A simple CNN model is used in this method to identify the significance of the histogram features derived from hog() function. Eventually this method could be applied on other classifier and object detection algorithms (Fig. 1).

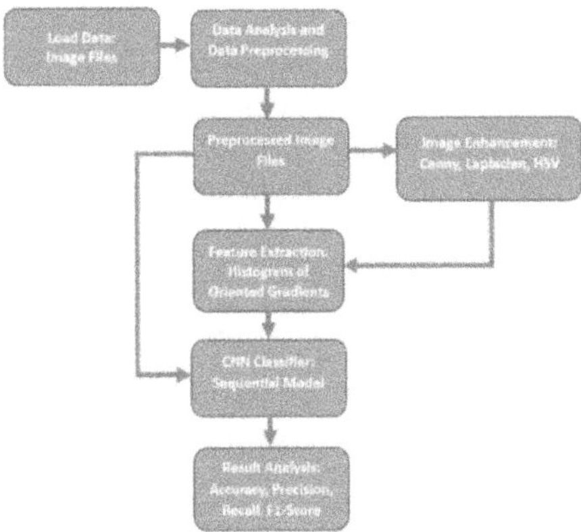

Fig. 1. Flow Diagram of proposed Methodology

Histogram feature descriptors are extracted from the original training images that constitute RGB channels, as well as from the enhanced binary image datasets obtained after processing the original images through different types of edge detectors. Edge detection and feature enhancements are essential to extract the required information from the images to help improve classification, hence, we transform the original images to Canny images, Laplacian images and HSV images and then extracts feature descriptors from each set of the enhanced images, integrating them as additional set of inputs into the sequential CNN classifier model along with the original image dataset. Results from CNN models using different combinations of input data were analyzed to identify the best performing model and the relevant set of mixed inputs.

4 Image Preprocessing

4.1 Dataset Preprocessing

The image dataset for this work was acquired by collecting images from Kaggle's 'animals' datasets. Images correspond to five animal classes, namely cat, dog, elephant, horse and lion. Images thus downloaded were split into train, validation, and test folders, each containing the five classes of images. The train dataset consists of 8000 jpeg images, with 1600 images in each class. The validation and test datasets contain 1750 images, with 350 images in each class respectively. The image files consist objects of mutually exclusive classes. There is no overlap of class objects in any single image. All the images were converted into jpeg format, loaded into the image tensors as RGB color images, and resized to 128×128 in height and width.

This model can be applied to image dataset of any size as its purpose is to augment the classifier with more structural, intensity, gradient orientation and color information to improve classification accuracy of the model.

4.2 RGB Image

A RGB image is a linear combination of three different color channels: R for red, G for green, and B for blue. The intensity of a pixel within this color space ranges from 0 to 255 for each channel. Hence, a pixel can have one color at a time, from the possible color combinations in $[255 \times 255 \times 255]$. For this experiment, the original RGB image object tensors were used as one of the multiple inputs in the CNN models.

5 Image Enhancements

In addition to the RGB input images, we planned to provide more inputs into the CNN model with features extracted from the images after enhancing the original images. This is done to boost the feature recognition capability of the classification model. One of the most widely used image enhancement techniques is edge detection, which is the process of identifying the curves and edges in a digital image. Edge detection involves a set of mathematical functions that are pivotal to computer vision applications such as image recognition, image segmentation, and image detection. In an image, an edge is identified when there is a significant change in the brightness and intensity values of neighboring pixels, usually tracked by the intensity discontinuation. Edge detection extracts the most useful structural features of the objects in the image and, at the same time, reduces the amount of data to be processed.

In this exercise, we transform the original images by applying edge detection techniques such as Canny edge and Laplacian edge [13]. We chose Canny edge and Laplacian edge enhancements as they have strong edge characteristics that are useful to discriminate between classes with edge feature maps of objects during classification. After this process, the HOG feature descriptors are extracted from each of these sets of enhanced images and served as inputs into the CNN model to study the performance of the classifier.

5.1 Canny Edge Operator

The Canny edge detector is one of the most reliable edge detector algorithms, developed by John F. Canny in 1986. It uses multi-stage processes to detect and mark the fine edges in an image. The processes involved are listed below:

1. The Canny algorithm removes the high-frequency noise by using a 5x5 Gaussian filter.

2. The Sobel filter is applied to smoothen the image to derive the first derivative from both horizontal (Gx) and vertical (Gy) directions. For each pixel, the edge gradient intensity and direction are calculated using these formulas.

$$\text{Edge Gradient(G)} = \sqrt{\left(G_x{}^2 + G_y{}^2\right)} \tag{1}$$

$$\text{Angle}(\theta) = \tan^{-1}\left(G_y/G_x\right) \tag{2}$$

3. Non-maximum suppression is applied to determine the pixel in local maxima to retain the pixel as part of the edge while the other pixels are suppressed.
4. In this double thresholding step, pixels that are greater than a high threshold (T_high) are strong edges, and pixels that fall in between the low (T_low) and high thresholds are weak edges.
5. All strong edges and the weak edges that are connected to strong edges are retained in this step, tracking edges by the hysteresis method.

The final Canny edge image is a binary image where the pixels classified as edges are marked with a value of 255 and the others set to 0. The cv2.Canny() function in the OpenCV library helps us pull all of the above processes into a single function to obtain a binary image in a single step.

5.2 Laplacian Edge Operator

The Laplacian edge operator considers only the edge points that are in the local maxima in the gradient values and is achieved by taking the second derivation. The edge point will have a peak in the first derivative and a zero crossing in the second derivative. Hence, Laplacian is a second derivative function f (x, y) that crosses zero at the location of the edge.

$$\Delta f(x, y, z) = \nabla.\nabla f = \frac{\left(\partial^2 f\right)}{\partial x^2} + \frac{\left(\partial^2 f\right)}{\partial y^2} + \frac{\left(\partial^2 f\right)}{\partial z^2} \tag{3}$$

0	1	0
1	-4	1
0	1	0

Fig. 2a. Positive Laplacian kernel

0	-1	0
-1	4	-1
0	-1	0

Fig. 2b. Negative Laplacian kernel

Laplacian is sensitive to noise, lacks directional information, and finds inward and outward edges, where the positive Laplacian operator kernel and the negative Laplacian operator kernel are shown in Figs. 2a and 2b, respectively.

5.3   HSV Color Space

For this study, the HSV image enhancement is adapted with the aim to extract the HOG feature descriptors that are characterized by prominent HSV colors with strong Hue -dominant wavelength, Saturation – color shades, and Value - intensity. The HSV color models are often used in digital arts and graphics. In image enhancement, hue is adjusted to balance the white and background colors without affecting the color scheme. High saturation can help to emphasize parts of the image. In HSV images, the hue is measured in degrees, with the color scales falling between 0 and 360°, while the saturation of color and value are analyzed along the scale of 0 to 100%. Figure 3 shows the HSV color cylinder.

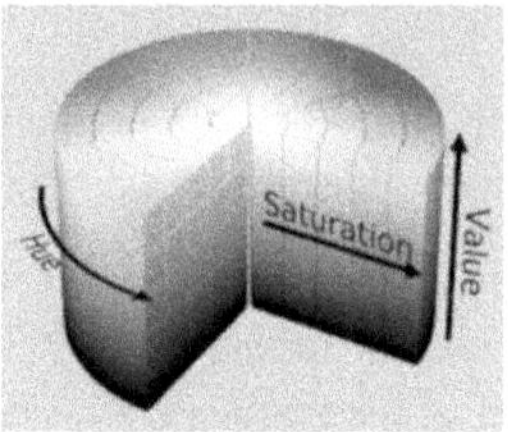

Fig. 3. HSV Color Cylinder

6   HOG Feature Extraction

6.1   Calculating HOG Gradient

Our primary focus is to extract Histogram of Oriented Gradient feature descriptors and hog images from training and validation images before training the model. For this purpose, hog function was used to extract both feature descriptors and gradient oriented image for each image in training, validation and test datasets, as well as from the enhanced image datasets.

Gradients are calculated for every pixel in an image showing small change in x and y directions. Edges will have higher magnitude when there is sharp change in the intensity. For the following image matrix (Fig. 4), the gradient for the highlighted pixel is calculated as follows:

126	121	98	89	88
67	66	63	76	99
78	75	88	92	114
231	220	53	54	84
222	198	123	96	145

Fig. 4. Image matrix example for HOG Gradient Calculation

Change in direction X $(G_x) = 92\text{–}75 = 17$
Change in direction Y $(G_y) = 63\text{–}53 = 10$

6.2 Calculating HOG Magnitude and Orientation:

We use Pythagoras theorem to calculate the gradient orientation using Gx and Gy. The gradients Gx and Gy form the base and height of the right-angle triangle (Fig. 5).

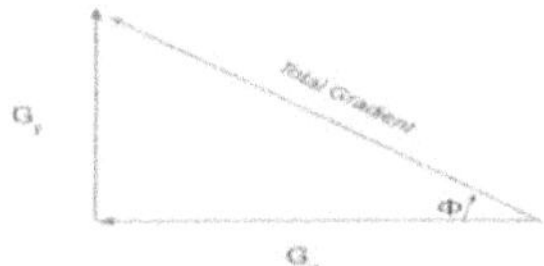

Fig. 5 HOG Image Orientation

Total Gradient Magnitude $= \sqrt{[(Gx)2 + (Gy)2]} = \sqrt{[(17)2 + (10)2]} = 19.76$
Gradient Orientation is calculated as tan of the angle suspended in the right-angle triangle.

$$\tan(\Phi) = Gy/Gx \tag{4}$$

Hence, the angle value is: $\Phi = $ atan $(Gy/Gx) = $ atan $(10/17) = 30$

Pictures in Figs. 6a, 6b, 6c and 6d represent an image sample in the original RGB form and the same image enhanced using Canny edge operator, Laplacian edge operator and the HSV color image converted form the original image. The pictures in Figs. 7 and 8 represent the hog-oriented gradients image and the color histogram of the original RGB image, respectively.

Fig. 6a. RGB Image

Fig. 6b. Canny Edge

Fig. 6c. Laplacian Edge

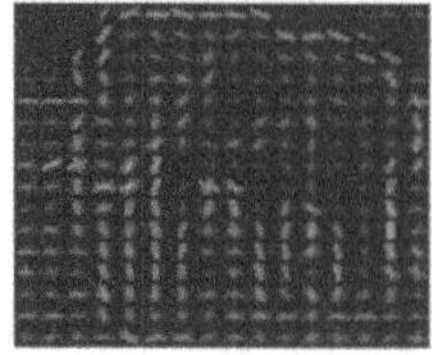

Fig. 6d. HSV Image

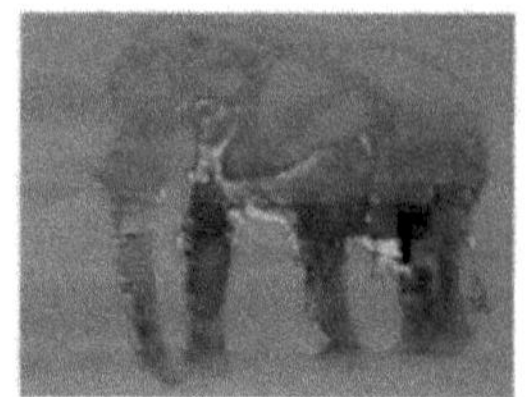

Fig. 7. HOG
Oriented Gradients

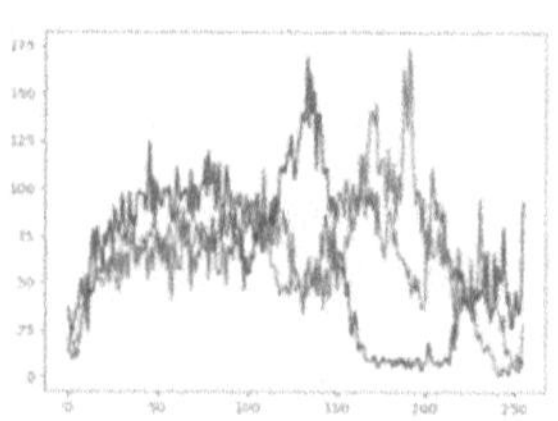

Fig. 8. Color Histogram

7 Experimental Implementation

In this work, we have designed a sequential CNN architecture for image classification using the functions and tools available from open-source libraries like Keras. The pre-processing techniques were performed on the train, validation, and test image datasets. All the images were read as RGB images. The image files were loaded into the train, validation, and test tensor objects and resized to dimensions of 128 × 128.

From the skimage.features library, the hog function was used to compute the Histogram of Oriented Gradient (HOG) factors to extract the feature descriptors and oriented gradient image for each image in all three datasets: train, validation, and test. In order to boost the convolution neurons with more structural, pixel orientation and color information from the input data, a few image enhancement techniques were adapted. As discussed earlier, edge detection algorithms such as Canny Edge and Laplacian Edge Operators were used to derive the enhanced feature images. Feature descriptors were extracted from this new set of enhanced images and saved in new object tensors. In addition to collecting these features, we also performed histogram calculations to capture the color distribution of each image and extracted feature descriptors from these results. Finally, the RGB images were also transformed into HSV images, and hog feature descriptors were extracted from the HSV images, for all the images in the train, validate, and test datasets. These sets of extracted feature descriptors were also saved in object tensors to be used as inputs to the CNN model during model building.

A Sequential CNN model for image classification was developed with a ReLU activation function to calculate the weights of the neurons. This classifier model was created to accept only the RGB image tensors as input data. Here, the input data with shape 128 × 128 × 3 produced 128 − (3−1) = 126 output features which were input into the first convolution 2D layer with 32 filters of shape 3 × 3. This created (3 × 3 × 3 + 1) × 32 = 896 parameters for the computation of weights, where 3 × 3 is the kernel size, 3 represents the third dimension from the input data, and 32 is the number of filters. A Max pool layer follows the convolution layer, with a kernel of size 2 × 2 to downsample the inputs going into the next level of the network. The Max pool works with the kernel on the local pixel area of 2 × 2 to select and use only the pixel value with maximum intensity, thereby reducing the spatial dimension of the feature maps by half. A similar set of Conv2D layer followed by a MaxPool layer, was created with 64 and 128 filters, respectively. The final MaxPool layer was followed by a flatten layer to prepare the network for dense layers to work on classification. The number of features in the flatten layer is the product of the dimension values from the previous layer: 14 ×

$14 \times 128 = 25088$. A fully connected/dense layer with 256 filters was created to extract the maximum number of features: $25088 \times 256 = 6422784$ parameters. The output is a dense layer with a SoftMax activation function to classify the five output classes. Hence, the total number of parameters for this model was 6,517,317. For this model, the Adam optimizer function was used to enable the neural network to adapt to the optimal learning rate and weights to improve accuracy and minimize the value resulting from the loss function. To work around this multiclass classifier model, we used Categorical Cross-Entropy for the loss function. This model presented an accuracy of 82% with 320 wrong predictions.

The next step was to use the feature descriptors derived from the enhanced set of images as inputs to the CNN model along with the original image tensor data. A number of sequential models were built with multiple input data preceptors to accept different combinations of input data and to study and compare the discriminative powers of the classifier models. As the HOG feature descriptors and oriented image objects were already a refined set of feature information, we used simple neural network layers with a convolutional Conv2D layer consisting of 64 filters with kernel size 3×3, followed by a MaxPool layer of filter space 2×2, and then a flattened layer. All the models were built with the ReLU activation function at the convolution layers and used either Adam or Stochastic Gradient Descent for the optimizer and categorical cross-entropy for the loss function. The final layer was always a SoftMax activation function for class prediction. Each model was compiled and fit to train the image data for 12 epochs with HOG feature descriptors, and their performance measures were recorded for analysis.

8   Results and Discussion

In this work, a comparative analysis with the older machine learning models is not considered as classifiers like SVM, Naïve Bayes, and other models have been used in the detection of objects in motion, such as the pedestrian crossing, and much simpler images like linguistic sign board classification, where the hog() function is used to detect the language script strokes, and other classifiers combine transfer learning models to achieve better classification accuracy. Our aim is to identify the use of hog features in any simpler CNN classifier model, and hence we have developed our analysis over the simpler CNN classifier algorithms we created.

The performance accuracy of each classifier model was assessed with evaluation metrics such as Accuracy, Precision, Recall, F1-Score, and Confusion matrix. With the introduction of histogram feature representations as additional input values to the CNN models, the classifiers showed a significant improvement in class prediction accuracy when compared to the regular CNN models that use the original image data alone as input for training. The CNN neurons take advantage by learning more information on the structural, gradient orientation, and color space characteristics from the additional inputs available to them in the form of HOG feature descriptors, resulting in a 2 to 4% increase in accuracy, precision, recall, and f1-score measures.

Here, the output metrics of the ordinary CNN model which used only the image input data, was compared against the CNN models that accepted HOG feature descriptors as additional input features along with the original image data. Besides the ordinary model, we have selected the three best performing HOG models that showed improvement in prediction accuracy and plotted their graphs and confusion matrix for analysis. Table 1 shows the performance metrics in detail for each of the CNN models tested, listing each with their different set of inputs and optimizer used, accuracy value, total number of wrong predictions, and precision, recall, f1-score values predicted for each class from their individual classification report.

Accuracy measures the total number of correct predictions over the total number of images in the dataset.

$$\text{Accuracy} = \frac{(Number\ of\ Correct\ Predictions)}{(Total\ Number\ of\ Predictions)} \tag{5}$$

After the models were trained and fit, they were tested for class prediction with the test dataset consisting of 1750 images with 350 images in each class.

Figures 9, 10, 11 and 12 shows the training and validation accuracies plotted against the number of epochs for CNN models #1, #3, #5 and #4, respectively. The CNN model #1 uses the original image data alone for training and prediction. The model #3 uses original image + HOG of original image + HOG of Canny edge image + HOG of Laplacian image data for training and prediction. Although this model might look overfitting, the training and validation accuracy are closer to each other producing best class prediction accuracy. The model #5 uses original image + HOG of original image + HOG oriented image + Color histogram + HOG of HSV image data for training and prediction. The model #4 uses original image + HOG of original image + HOG oriented image data for training and prediction.

In the model #6, we noticed that although we did not use the original image data for training, just by using HOG feature inputs such as HOG of original image + HOG of Canny edge image + HOG of Laplacian image the classifier has yielded a performance accuracy of 81% proving that the HOG feature descriptors immensely contribute to the discriminative power of the classifier.

Figure 13 shows the Confusion Matrix of the CNN model #1 which uses the original image data alone for training and prediction. This model output a class prediction accuracy of 82% with 320 wrong predictions.

Figure 14 shows confusion matrix for model #3 which uses the original image + HOG of original image + HOG of Canny edge image + HOG of Laplacian image, resulting with the highest prediction accuracy of 86% and the lowest instances of wrong class predictions counting to 239.

Figure 15 is the confusion matrix of model #5 which uses the original image + HOG of original image + HOG oriented image + Color histogram + HOG of HSV image, resulting with an accuracy of 86% and 253 wrong class predictions.

Figure 16 is the confusion matrix of model #4 which uses the original image + HOG of original image + HOG oriented image, resulting with an accuracy of 85% and 254 wrong class predictions (Table 2 and Graph 1).

Table 1. Summary of 7 different CNN Classification Models' Outputs with Accuracy, Total # of Wrong Predictions and Classification Report

No.	Model Inputs	Optimizer	Accuracy	Total # of Wrong Predictions	Precision	Recall	F1-Score	Support
1	Original image	Adam	0.82	320	0.96	0.91	0.93	350
					0.89	0.93	0.91	350
					0.83	0.55	0.66	350
					0.71	0.83	0.77	350
					0.74	0.86	0.79	350
2	Original image, Original HOG, Canny image HOG	Adam	0.85	267	0.96	0.93	0.95	350
					0.96	0.89	0.92	350
					0.78	0.73	0.75	350
					0.80	0.79	0.79	350
					0.76	0.90	0.83	350
3	Original image, Original HOG, Canny image HOG, Laplacian image HOG	Adam	0.86	239	0.96	0.94	0.95	350
					0.95	0.93	0.94	350
					0.72	0.81	0.76	350
					0.81	0.80	0.81	350
					0.89	0.84	0.87	350
4	Original image, Original HOG, HOG Image	Adam	0.85	254	0.96	0.95	0.96	350
					0.95	0.92	0.94	350
					0.80	0.67	0.72	350
					0.77	0.85	0.81	350
					0.81	0.88	0.84	350
5	Original image, Original HOG, HOG Image, Color Histogram, HSV image HOG	Adam	0.86	253	0.95	0.95	0.95	350

(*continued*)

Table 1. (*continued*)

No.	Model Inputs	Optimizer	Accuracy	Total # of Wrong Predictions	Precision	Recall	F1-Score	Support
					0.95	0.92	0.94	350
					0.76	0.69	0.73	350
					0.77	0.85	0.80	350
					0.85	0.86	0.86	350
6	Original image HOG, Canny image Hog, Laplacian image HOG	Adam	0.81	341	0.96	0.93	0.95	350
					0.90	0.91	0.91	350
					0.71	0.65	0.68	350
					0.75	0.75	0.75	350
					0.71	0.78	0.75	350
7	Original image, Original HOG, Canny image HOG, Laplacian image HOG	SGD	0.86	244	0.96	0.96	0.96	350
					0.95	0.93	0.94	350
					0.85	0.63	0.72	350
					0.76	0.87	0.81	350
					0.81	0.91	0.86	350

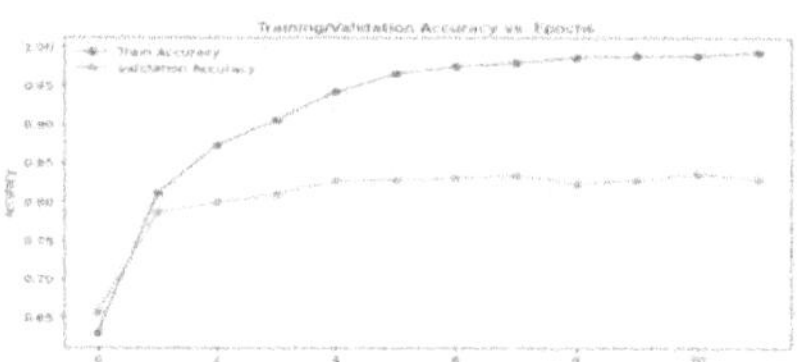

Fig. 9 Graph for CNN model #1

9 Future Work

In this work, we extracted the HOG feature descriptors from RGB color images to study the performance of the CNN classification models. Although there might be some limitations in the application of this method over grayscale image datasets, we could explore the possibilities of improving the classifier performance in grayscale image datasets as well.

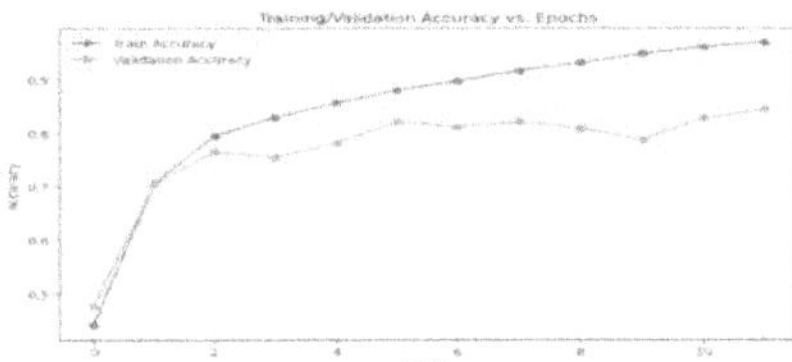

Fig. 10 Graph for CNN model #3

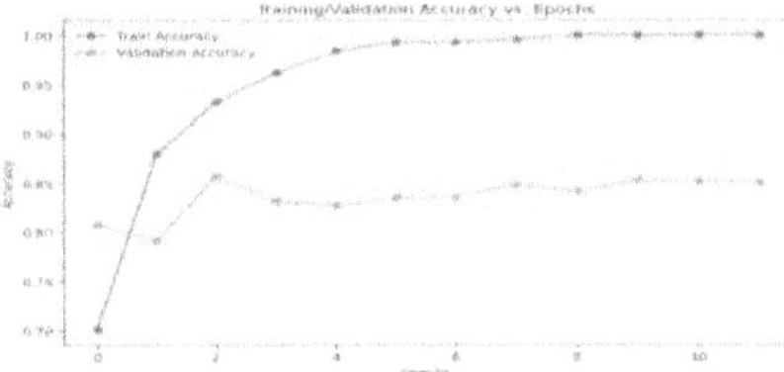

Fig. 11. Graph for CNN model #5

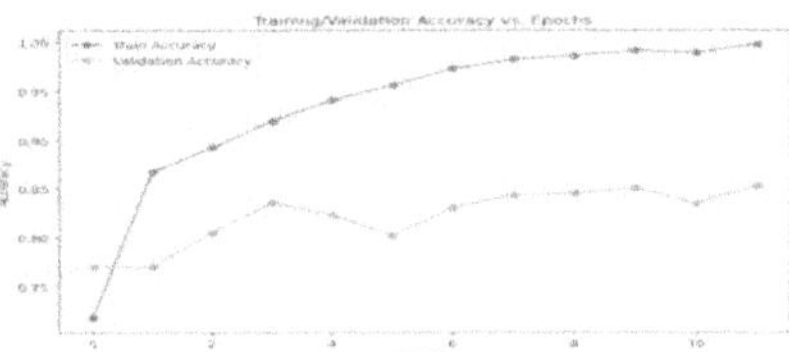

Fig. 12. Graph for CNN model #4

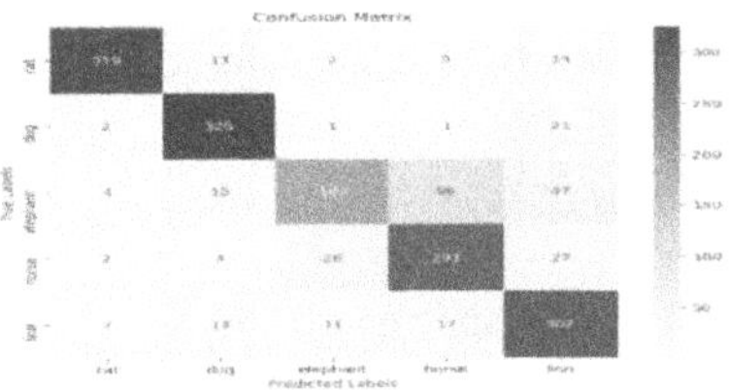

Fig. 13. Confusion Matrix of CNN model #1

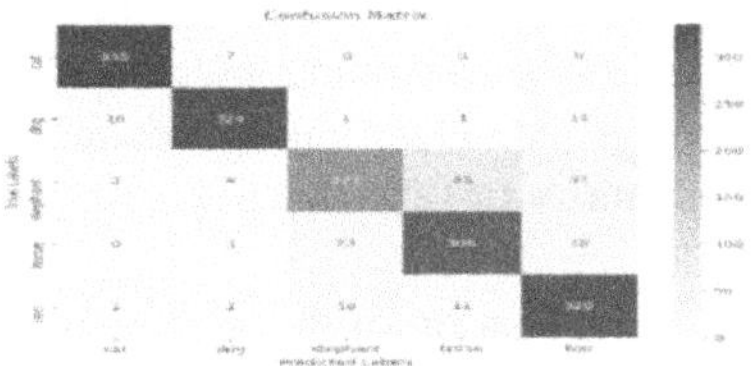

Fig. 14. Confusion Matrix of CNN model #3

Fig. 15. Confusion Matrix of CNN model #5

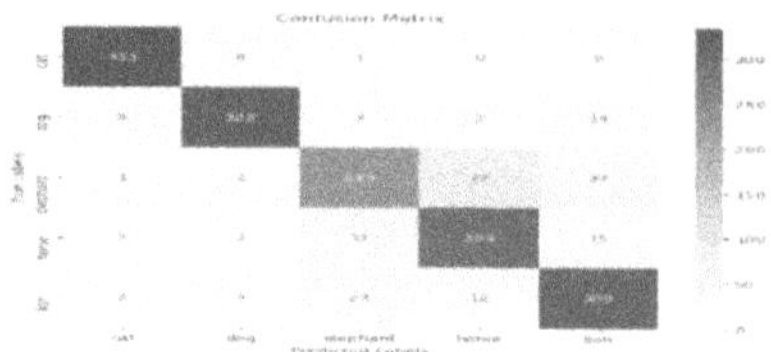

Fig. 16. Confusion Matrix of CNN model #4

Table 2. Summary of Performance metrics

No.	Model Inputs	Accuracy	Precision	Recall	F1-Score
1	Original image	82	82.60	81.60	81.20
2	Original image, Original HOG, Canny image HOG	85	85.2	84.8	84.8
3	Original image, Original HOG, Canny image HOG, Laplacian image HOG	86	86.60	86.40	86.60
4	Original image, Original HOG, HOG Image	85	85.8	85.4	85.4
5	Original image, Original HOG, HOG Image, Color Histogram, HSV image HOG	86	85.60	85.40	85.60
6	Original image HOG, Canny image Hog, Laplacian image HOG	81	80.6	80.4	80.8
7	Original image, Original HOG, Canny image HOG, Laplacian image HOG	86	86.60	86.00	85.80

To overcome the potential threats from Deep Fake image malpractices, HOG feature descriptors could be encrypted and stored along with the original image to differentiate the original image from morphed or AI Deep Fake generated features. Organizations that are dependent on Biometric Security systems that use facial recognition for identification could recommend such a study.

There is a wider scope of application of this hog feature integration model in any image classifier algorithm to improve the robustness of the classifier's discriminative abilities by taking advantage of the significant structural information and capturing the essential texture, color intensity, and orientation of the gradients of objects in the images.

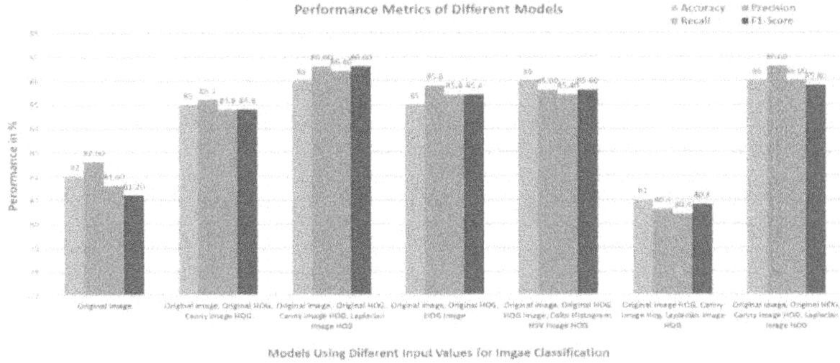

Graph. 1 Plotted summary of Metrics for different CNN classifier algorithms.

10 Conclusion

An approach to classifying animal images was explored in this paper by integrating the histogram of oriented gradient feature descriptors into the CNN models to study the improvement in image classification accuracy and class prediction. The results from this study show that the sequential CNN classifier models improved their ability to capture and learn more information on the structural, gradient orientation, and color feature space characteristics from the hog feature descriptor inputs, leveraging their discriminative powers and global statistical output information. From all the CNN classification models that were experimented, model #3 (listed in Table 1) that used inputs from original image + HOG of original image + HOG of Canny edge image + HOG of Laplacian image, optimized with Adam optimizer (learning rate = 0.0001), outperformed the other classifiers yielding the highest accuracy of 86%, precision of 86.60%, recall of 86.40% and f1-score of 86.60% and had the minimum number of wrong predictions (239 out of 1750 tested images). By using the HOG feature characteristics along with the original image data, the classifiers' prediction accuracy increased by 2 to 4% from normal. Hence, this paper demonstrates that the integration of HOG feature characteristics along with the image data significantly improves the accuracy and class prediction in multiclass CNN classifier models.

Abbreviations

AI   Artificial Intelligence
CNN Convolutional Neural Network
HOG Histogram of Oriented Gradients
HSV Hue Saturation Value
ORB Oriented fast and Rotated Brief
RGB Red Green Blue
SIFT Scale Invariant Feature Transform
SVM Support Vector Machine

Acknowledgements. I sincerely extend my gratitude to Dr. Ramalingam. V.V, Associate Professor, Department of Computing Technologies, and Dr. S. Ganesh Kumar, Professor, Department of Data Science and Business Systems, SRM Institute of Science and Technology, India, under whose graceful guidance this research work was conducted and presented. I'm also thankful to my family for supporting me during this commitment.

Author's Contribution. Latha came up with the idea, conducted the feasibility study and designed methodology, collected data and implemented the idea and contributed to writing the manuscript;

Dr. Ramalingam and Dr. Ganesh Kumar reviewed the idea, participated in designing the methodology, supervised the implementation process, and provided guidance to writing the manuscript.

Availability of Data and Materials. Animal dataset images downloaded from Kaggle.

Declarations. Competing Interests. The authors declare that they have no competing interests.

Funding.. Not applicable.

References

1. Jusman, Y., Tyassari, W., Nisrina, D., Santosa, F.G., Praytino, N.A.: Machine learning performances for Covid-19 images classification based histogram of oriented gradients features. In: 2022 IEEE International IOT, Electronics and Mechatronics Conference (2022)
2. Jusman, Y., Tyassari, W., Nindita, W., Harahap, A.J.H., Ismail, A.M.: Developed histogram of oriented gradients-based feature extraction for Covid-19 X-ray image classification. In: 2022 2nd International Seminar on Machine Learning, Optimization, and Data Science (ISMODE). IEEE (2022)
3. Sachin Sonawane, Mohan Awasthy, Nitin Choubey.: A literature review on image processing and classification techniques for agriculture produce and Modeling of quality assessment system for soybean industry sample in 2019 International Journal of Innovative Research in Electronics and Communications (IJIREC), 6 2 8–16, (2019).
4. Harshitha, Y., Phaneendra Kumar, B.L.N., Venkata Aparna, M., Venkata Kishore, A.: Remote sensing image classification with a few labeled samples. In: 2023 Third International Conference on Artificial Intelligence and Smart Energy. IEEE (2023)
5. Prudhivi, L., Narayana, M., Subrahmanyam, C., Krishna, G.M., Chavan, S.: Animal species image classification. In: 2023 3rd International Conference on Artificial Intelligence and Signal Processing (AISP). IEEE (2023)
6. He, Y., Yin, S.: Food images classification based on improved convolutional neural network. In: 2023 4th International Conference on Electronic Communication and Artificial Intelligence (ICECAI). IEEE (2023)
7. Liu, Z., Liu, Y., Meng, S., Li, P.: Plate contour recognized algorithm based on depth histogram threshold segmentation. In: 2022 15th International Congress on Image and Signal Processing, BioMedical Engineering and Informatics (CISP-BMEI). IEEE (2022)
8. Senthil Kumar, V., Jayalakshmi, V.: Two stage image restoration based on histogram equalization and edge computation for image. In: 2022 International Conference on Computer, Power and Communications (ICCPC). IEEE (2022)
9. Khare, A.K.: Image classification using humps of histogram. In: 2016 Second International Conference on Computational Intelligence & Communication Technology (2016)

10. Wu, J., Zhang, Y., Zhang, Y., Jiang, H., Hou, L., Liu, J.: Research on object detection for service robots based on image feature. In: 2022 IEEE 5th Advanced Information Management, Communicates, Electronic and Automation Control Conference (IMCEC). IEEE (2022)
11. Mao, L., Tang, L.: Pedestrian detection based on gradient direction histogram. In: 2022 IEEE Asia-Pacific Conference on Image Processing, Electronics and Computers (IPEC). IEEE (2022)
12. Karmakar, S., Karmakar, S.: Improved image recognition for AI based various scientific applications. In: 2023 IEEE world AIIoT congress IEEE (2023)
13. Nithiyanantha Vasagam, S., Sornam, M.: Species wise classification of crust leather images based on histogram equalization. In: 2022 6th International Conference on Computing Methodologies and Communication IEEE (2022)
14. Ahmed, S.M., Wahid, A.: Image transformation based on computer vision to detect multilingual sign board. In: 2022 International Conference on Information Science and Communications Technologies IEEE (2022)
15. Wu, J., Zhang, Y., Zhang, Y., Jiang, H., Hou, L., Liu, J.: Research on object detection for service robots based on image feature. In: 2022 IEEE 5th Advanced Information Management, Communicates, Electronic and Automation Control Conference IEEE (2022)
16. Bo-jia, S.H.I., Tao, S.U.I., ZHANG, Y.-z., ZHANG, D.-q.: Comparative study of digital instrument image enhancement in complex industrial environment. In: In 2021 ICMLCA ISBN 978–3–8007-5739-8 (2021)
17. Sharma, D., Mishra, I., Parepalli, R., Jayanth, S.: Biomedical image classification using convolutional neural networks. In: 2023 International Conference on Intelligent and Innovative Technologies in Computing, Electrical and Electronics IEEE. IEEE (2023)
18. https://www.slideshare.net/barbarafusinska/networks-are-like-onions-practical-deep-learning-with-tensorflow (2017)

Facial Expression Recognition System Using Enhanced Stress Convolutional Neural Network for Mental Health Prediction

Haitham Alhussain[1]([✉]), Anwar Ahmed Alabdulathem[2], Vemparala Priyatha[3], Mohammed Bashit[4], Deepak Hajoary[5], and V. Parimyndhan[6]

[1] King Fahad Hospital, Alhofuf, Saudi Arabia
`hamalhussain@moh.gov.sa`
[2] University of Edinburgh, Edinburgh, UK
[3] All India Institute of Medical Sciences (AIIMS), Bhubaneswar, India
[4] South Ural State University, Chelyabinsk, Russia
[5] Bodoland University, Kokrajhar, Assam, India
[6] Department of Statistics, Manonmaniam Sundaranar University, Tirunelveli, India

Abstract. A rapid hike in interest has been found in the realm of facial exprerssion analysis for finding the human emotions and anticipating mental health. In order to communicate one's emotions to others, these facial expressions playa pivotal role and can contribute in providing valuable insights and perspectives regarding individual's mental health. By making advantage of deep learning techniques, ESCNN (Enhanced Stress Convolutional Nueral Network) proves to be a vigorous and efficient approach for mental health prediction. This ESCNN precissely findout a range of facial expressions, dividing them into different emotional states like anger, disgust, neutrality, surpise, happy, sadness and fear. The methodology includes transfer learning with MobileNet V and TensorFlow, making use of pretrained data from the Cohn-Kanade+ dataset for Facial Expression Recognition (FER). More significantly as evidenced by the comprehensive experimental analysis in ESCNN demonstrating higher grade performance in tasks which involve stress recognition and mental heakth prediction through the integration of transfer of learning with Haar Cascade face detection, thereby remarkable prevailing methodologies.

Keywords: Enhanced Stress Convolutional Neural Network · Facial Expression Recognition · MobileNet · Deep Learning · Transfer Learning

1 Introduction

The major indicators of an individual's emotional state, mental illness, intentions and thinking activity are facial expressions. They serve a crucial role in interpersonal interactions, conveying expressive and communicative cues. Facial Expression Recognition (FER) holds significance in elucidating an individual's mental state or mood, with applications extending beyond understanding human behavior. FER is increasingly integrated

R. Appavoo et al. (Eds.): IconDeepCom 2024, CCIS 2687, pp. 436–447, 2026.
https://doi.org/10.1007/978-3-032-26680-4_34

into various fields such as holography, criminology, stress detection, multimedia communication, smart healthcare systems, education, entertainment, security, and robotics. This integration underscores the essential role of facial expressions in human life. With the advancements in deep learning, particularly CNN significant progress has been achieved in extracting and learning various features for effective facial expression recognition systems, facilitating mental health prediction.

Deep learning (DL) a subset of ML employs artificial intelligence (AI) techniques to analyze and understand data. In recent times, there has been significant research focused on leveraging DL methodologies to enhance the efficacy of facial expression recognition systems [2–4]. DL encompasses several techniques for recognizing facial expressions, including DeepFace, VGGFace, FaceNet, and the DeepID systems [5]. CNN has been introduced as a means for machines to analyze facial expressions by teaching them to classify images and videos. Within deep learning, a multitude of CNN models are available, such as ResNet, VGGNet, GoogleNet, MobileNet, among others. Currently, efforts are underway to enhance CNN models by focusing on increasing network depth and incorporating additional convolutional operations.

This study introduces a novel approach for FER, termed ESCNN. ESCNN leverages pre-trained models on the CK+ dataset, employing MobileNet V2 and TensorFlow. Through the analysis of facial expressions, individuals are categorized as stressed or unstressed. Within ESCNN, MobileNet V2 incorporates additional layers including the Fully Connected Layer, Relu6, SoftMax Probabilities and Max-pooling layer. In addition to MobileNet V2, Haar Cascade face detection is employed to detect faces within the image. MobileNet V2 is renowned for its lightweight architecture, distinguishing it from other CNN models like ResNet50 and Sequential Model. Compared to these models, MobileNet V2 reduces network size by 18 MB and parameter count by 4.3 million. Notably, MobileNet V2 offers smaller and faster models while maintaining comparable accuracy levels across various latency measures [6].

The ESCNN algorithm has undergone testing with various parameters, affirming that ESCNN with MobileNet V2 outperforms ResNet 50 and the Sequential Model. The ESCNN algorithm analyzes facial expressions in images across seven categories: anger, disgust, fear, happiness, neutrality, sadness, and surprise [10]. The work aligns with SDG 3 by focusing on mental health prediction through facial expression analysis, contributing to early intervention and support for improved overall well-being.

This paper comprises five sections. Section 1 introduces the concept of FER in detecting emotional stress. Section 2 provides a review of the existing literature on facial expression methods. In Sect. 3 the overall concept of the proposed method is explained. Section 4 gives an experimental result obtained from the system. Finally, Sect. 5 serves as the conclusion and outlines future work.

2 Literature Review

In 1971, Paul proposed from a psychological perspective that there exist six fundamental reactions (anger, fear, sadness, happiness, disgust and surprise) universally across different cultures [15]. Subsequently, in 1978, Ekman et al. (1978) introduced the FACS to delineate facial expression [16]. Presently, the majority of facial expression recognition endeavors are founded on these seminal works. This paper similarly adopts the seven basic emotions along with neutral expressions as the standard for classifying facial expressions. Lu Guanming et al. (2016) introduced a CNN for FER, wherein they employed dropout and dataset expansion strategies to address issues stemming from inadequate training data and overfitting [17].

Jin et al. (2023) introduce a pioneering multi-modal human emotion recognition system. It combines verbal and non-verbal cues using a PSiFI, featuring a unique bidirectional triboelectric sensor. With real-time capabilities and machine learning, the system achieves high accuracy, even with mask-wearing individuals, demonstrating the potential for digital concierge applications in virtual reality environments [18]. In their 2024 study, Luma and Nicolas propose a novel approach to reaction recognition through facial cues, leveraging Deep Convolutional Generative Adversarial Networks for feature extraction. Their method achieves superior performance, with an outstanding accuracy rate of 98.57% on the Radboud dataset, surpassing prevailing techniques. They suggest future research directions including conditional DCGAN training and extending the model to 3D-GANs for video generation [19].

Kimberly and Putra (2024) evaluate the computational load of different CNN models for FER on mobile devices. EfficientNetV2B3 achieves the highest accuracy at 61.9%, with MobileNet showing the lowest computational load. For real-world applications, the inferences revealed the vitality to maintain precisely with speed and computational efficiency. Further research could examine different datasets to enhance total accuracy above 80% [20]. Nie et al. (2024) investigated CReToNeXt-YOLOv5, a modern progressive model for pig FER. The model achieves a map of 89.4% by adding new features like the EIOU loss function and the coordinate attention mechanism focusiing more for promoting animal welfare monitoring and livestock management practices [21].

Zixiang et al.(2020) studied an indepth framework for facial expression analysis which focussed at promoting mental health care by means of automatic recognition of the emotions of users. The significance of facial expressions in communication and potential applications of automatic facial expression idenfication with regard to mental health care are spotlighted. The put forwarded framework make advantage of deep learning techniques, mainly by using specifications taken from the Fully Connected Layer 6 of the AlexNet, incorporated with a Linear Discriminant Analysis (LDA) Classifier for classification [22].

Gavrilescu and Vizireanu (2019) conducted a study on a pioneering effort in the field by introducing a newl noninvasive architecture for examining facial expressions to DASS levels. The authors framed a three-layered architecture focussed at achieving high level precision and speedy convergence by employing Facial Action Coding System (FACS) and Active Appearance Models (AAM) in connection with multiclass Support Vector Machines (SVM) for Action Unit (AU) classification [23].

Zhang et al. (2022) studied the critical problem of finding acute stress, an existing concern in the progressive society that implied pivotal hazards to individuals' physical and mental well-being. The paper presented a real-time deep learning framework designed to combine information from various modalities, including electrocardiogram (ECG), voice, and facial expressions, to find acute stress more efficaciously [24]. Nilava et al. (2022) examined the field of mental stress detection by contributing a real-time technique that uses only a photoplethysmogram (PPG) signal, providing better accuracy compared to multi-various physiological signals and attaining real-time findings with low-complexity algorithms, which are inevitable for practical execution [25].

Chong et al. (2022) examined a favourable technique for dexterously analyzing the mental health of college students by incorporating psychological questionnaires with facial emotion analysis. High recognition precision, outperforming traditional single-questionnaire methods can be explicitly seen in their mixed-method study. By making advantage of artificial intelligence technologies, this approach provides a more indepth, complete and efficient way to filter for psychological issues on a wide scale, offering to enhanced mental health aid for students [14]. Muhammad et al. (2023) studied an indepth survey of FER pinpointing its rising significance in different areas like healthcare and security. They emphasis the orgin of FER methods, specifically concentrating on deep learning and AI techniques suitable for edge computing platforms. By confronting the limitations of prevailing surveys and moving into edge vision-inspired FER technologies, the study provided beneficial perspectives and insights into the existing landscape of FER research [26].

3 Materials and Proposed Work

3.1 Materials

In the present study, the dataset used is CK+, as mentioned in Table 1. This dataset is sourced from the Kaggle dataset website. The pictures are sized at 640×490 pixels and feature 0123 distinct human faces, encompassing both males and females. A total of 920 images were utilized in this study for training and testing the proposed FD-CNN. These images are categorized into eight emotions: Surprise (83), Neutral (593), Fear (25), Contempt (18), Anger (45), Disgust (59), Happy (69) and Sad (28). The category of neutral emotions is the most frequently observed, with a total of 593 occurrences, while the category of contempt is the least frequently observed with only 18 occurrences. The dataset exhibits a wide emotional distribution, with Surprise, Fear, Anger, Disgust, Happy, and Sad occurring 83, 25, 45, 59, 69, and 28 times, respectively.as illustrated in Fig. 1. All images were captured from a frontal angle. In this work, seven emotions are utilized.

3.2 The Proposed System

ESCNN, employed as an exhaustive evaluation tool for stress identification via facial expressions, resulted in a rapid, concise, and exceptionally accurate algorithm for discerning stress across different facial expressions. To further refine the precision of facial expression detection, ESCNN integrated Transfer Learning (TL) with MobileNet V2 using Transfer Flow (TF). MobileNet V2 was chosen for its computational efficiency, being 35% faster than its predecessor while maintaining the same level of accuracy in segmentation tasks. As a feature extractor, MobileNet V2 also demands significantly fewer parameters and operations compared to MobileNet V1 with reductions of 5.3 times and 5.2 times respectively. It facilitates faster training and experimentation processes and is applicable across a wide range of visual recognition tasks.

Table 1. Dataset.

S. No	Emotion	No. of Emotions
1	Surprise	83
2	Neutral	593
3	Fear	25
4	Contempt	18
5	Anger	45
6	Disgust	59
7	Happy	69
8	Sad	28

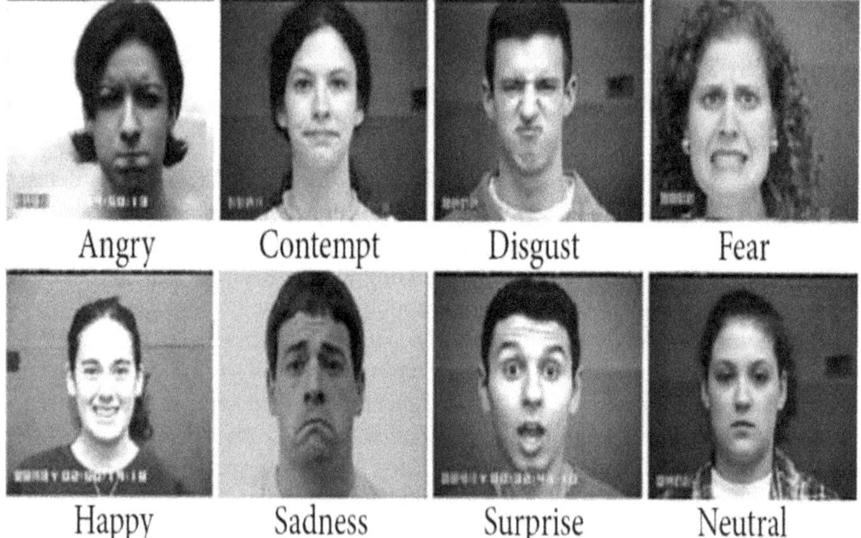

Fig. 1. Sample images CK+ Dataset

The integration of TL and TF provides numerous advantages. Before fine-tuning, TL provides a superior initial starting point, enabling models to execute certain tasks without the need for extensive training. Additionally, TF boasts scalability, allowing nearly any operation to be performed on the platform with ease. This is due to TL's utilization of pre-trained models, coupled with TF's support for architectures featuring Tensor Processing Units (TPUs), which facilitate faster model execution. In essence, TF and TL empower ESCNN to handle a multitude of intricate features and expedite the overall process compared to prior algorithms. The analysis outcomes of ESCNN are anticipated to exhibit greater accuracy, leveraging a superior initial model compared to alternatives. Additionally, various algorithms and features have been incorporated and assessed within the ESCNN framework. The objective behind integrating these features is to enhance the precision of emotion recognition and attain optimal performance. In summary, the ESCNN algorithm has been developed as illustrated in Fig. 2.

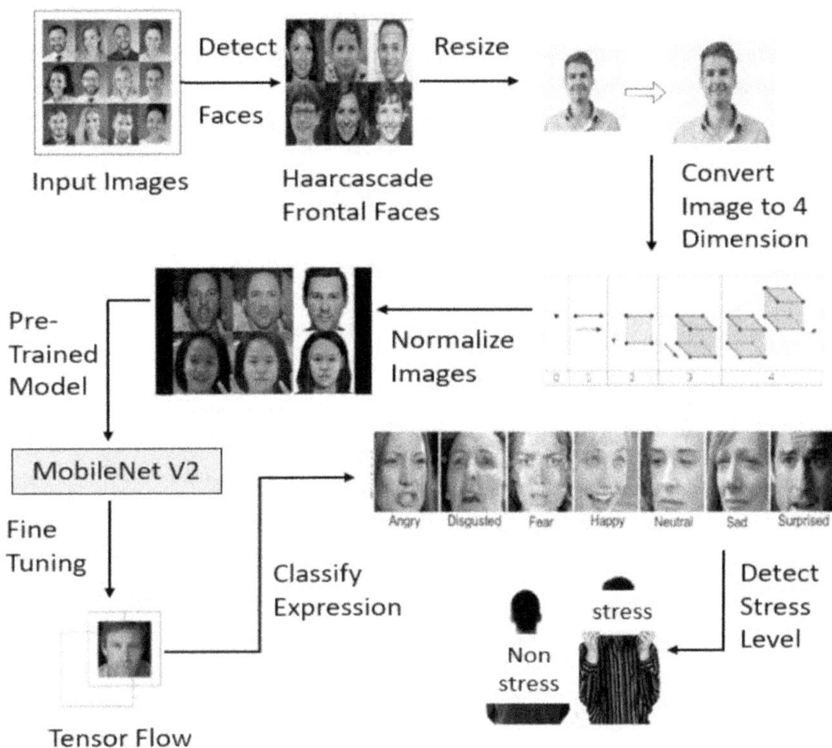

Fig. 2. Illustrates the overview of the proposed ESCNN Algorithm

Initially, a facial image is inputted into the Haar Cascade Frontal Face detection system. In cases where no facial features are detected, the algorithm will display an "Error" message. Following the resizing operation, the image is then converted back into four dimensions. This step is crucial as MobileNet V2 employs depth-wise convolutional neural networks, necessitating images to be represented in four dimensions. Following the resizing operation, the images are normalized by dividing each pixel value by 255. When the image array is printed, it displays a series of numbers ranging from 0 to 255, with 255 representing the maximum intensity (black) and 0 representing the minimum intensity (white). Normalizing the images by dividing by 255 ensures that the intensity levels are standardized. The TL formula is expressed by Eq. (1).

$$T = \{Y, f\ (x)\}, Ds \neq Dt \tag{1}$$

The variable "f" is employed to forecast the f(x) of a new instance of x, with "label" representing the label space. Ds denotes a source domain, while Ts signifies a learning task. It's important to note that a target domain, Dt, and a learning task, Tt, are distinct entities and may not be equivalent. Subsequently, the image is passed through the MobileNet V2 model, initiating from the base input layer indexed at 0, representing the model's initial layer. In Python, referencing the last layer is denoted by "-1". In ESCNN, only seven classes are pertinent, whereas the original MobileNet V2 model is designed for thousands of classes. Consequently, the final layer is truncated using base output [−2], ensuring that the final layer corresponds to the layer. The structure of MobileNet V2 is delineated in Fig. 3.

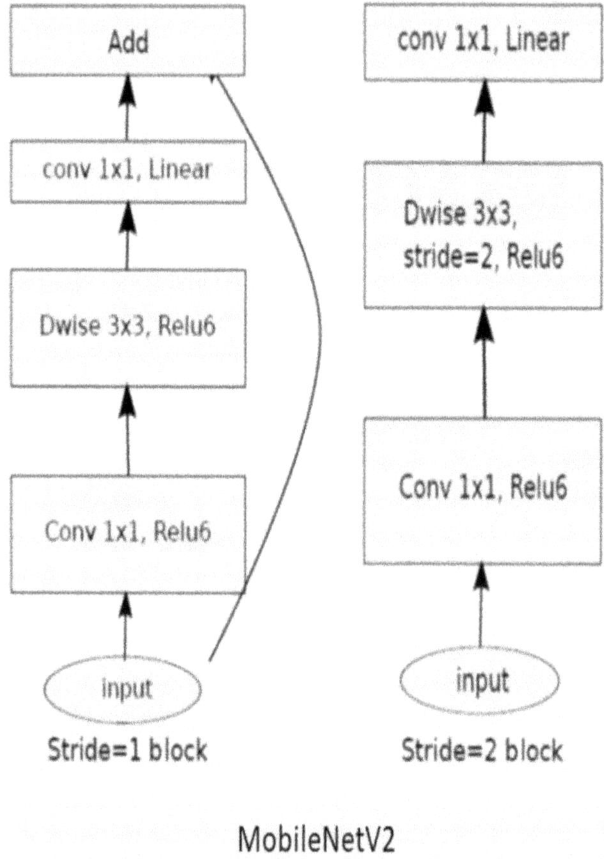

Fig. 3. Architecture of the MobileNet V2

The Dense layer is a predefined function in the Tensorflow.js library used for creating fully connected layers. It allows for the transmission of a variable number of arguments, denoted by (args), to a function.

The first two layers are comprised of layers.dense 128 and layer.dense 64, both employing the Relu6 activation function. As ESCNN involves only 7 classes, the final layer, layer.dense 7, utilizes SoftMax activation. SoftMax functions as a classification layer, serving as the ultimate fully connected layer to be activated.

SoftMax, denoted by σ, takes an input vector Z. It computes the exponential function of each element in the input vector and divides it by the sum of the exponential functions of all elements, representing the K number of classes in the multi-class classifier. This division result is then multiplied by the exponential function of each element (Zi) in the output vector. SoftMax converts arbitrary real values into probabilities by exponentiating each number and using it as a numerator.

In the end, considering that the image is numerically represented rather than using one-hot encoding, we selected "sparse categorical cross entropy" as the loss function and "adam" as the optimizer. Initially, the image accuracy is at 41% due to the TL model, which continuously updates the weights. As a result, ESCNN produces outputs across seven different categories.

3.3 Performance Metrics

The Recall, precision, accuracy, F1_score, and ROC curve are among the performance measures that have been used to assess the effectiveness of DL systems. The equations below can be used to calculate these performance metrics.

Accuracy = (TP + TN)/(TP + TN + FP + FN)
Precision = TP/(TP + FP)
F1_score = 2TP/(2TP + FP + FN)
Recall = (TP)/(TP + FN)

4 Discussion and Experimental Results

4.1 Multiclass Confusion Matrix

Each item in the confusion matrix is represented by three columns: true/actual classification, predicted classification, and the count of occurrences. To maintain consistency, model predictions are indicated in columns, while actual classifications are represented in rows. Consequently, correctly classified items align along the diagonal from the top left to the bottom right, indicating agreement between raters. The confusion matrix is utilized to assess the accuracy of actual labels compared to those predicted.

4.2 Accuracy Score

An F1-score is computed for every class of test samples to assess the model's accuracy, offering both the overall accuracy and the accuracy for each predicted class.

4.3 Confusion Matrix and Accuracy Score

The CK+ Database contains the seven fundamental facial emotions: Neutral, Sad, Angry, Disgust, Fear and Surprise. While most classes in the Confusion Matrix are correctly classified, fear is sometimes mistaken for sadness. The Accuracy score for each class

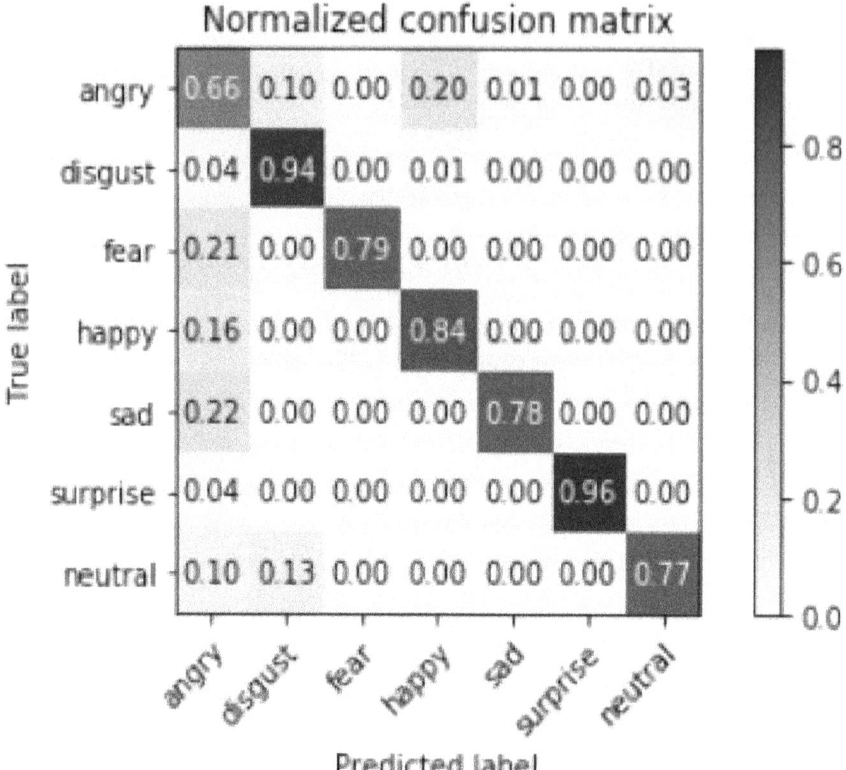

Fig. 4. CK+ Database Confusion Matrix

reflects recall, precision, and F1-score, resulting in an overall accuracy rate of 94.52%. Figure 4 displays the normalized Confusion Matrix for the CK+ Database. Table 2 presents the Accuracy Score for the CK+ Database.

Table 3 illustrates a performance assessment of ESCNN in facial expression tasks relative to state-of-the-art methods. The evaluation is based on the CK+ dataset, showcasing ESCNN's outperformance compared to other contemporary approaches. To ensure fairness, only state-of-the-art methods implemented with the CK+ dataset are included for comparison in Table 3 and Fig. 5. The techniques and their respective levels of precision are as follows: The MSR method achieves an accuracy of 91%, the 3DCNN - DAP approach reaches 92%, the combination of LBP and ORB features obtains 93%, and the Inception model attains an accuracy of 94%. The proposed algorithm performs better than the state-of-the-art techniques, outperforming all of these methods with a precision rate of 94.52%.

Table 2. Accuracy Score for CK+ Database

	Precision	Recall	F1-Score	Support
0	0.65	0.65	0.66	148
1	0.78	0.95	0.86	70
2	1.00	0.78	0.88	96
3	0.68	0.85	0.76	78
4	0.94	0.79	0.86	48
5	1.00	0.97	0.97	108
6	0.85	0.78	0.80	39
Accuracy			0.95	588
Macro avg.	0.85	0.81	0.83	588
Weighted avg.	0.84	0.82	0.82	588

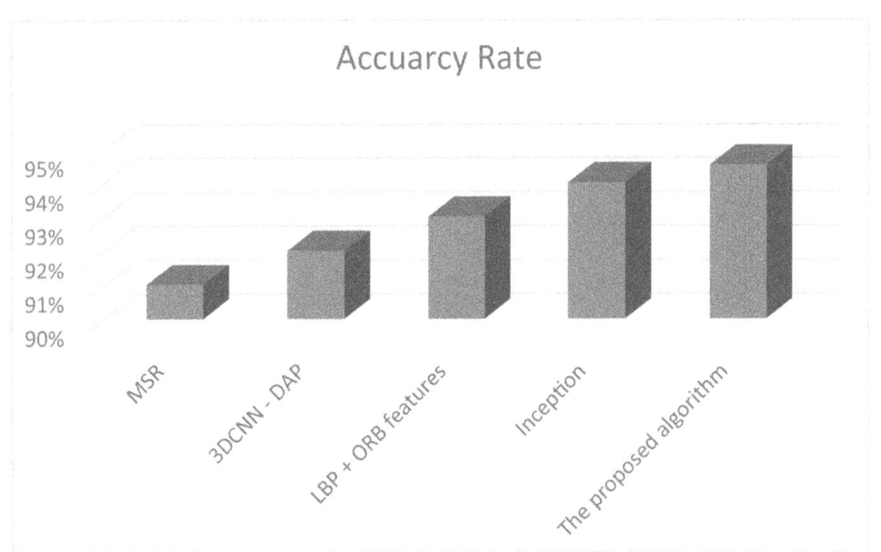

Fig. 5.

Table 3. Comparison of Performance with state-of-the-art Methods using CK+ dataset

Method	Accuarcy Rate
MSR	91%
3DCNN - DAP	92%

(continued)

Table 3. (*continued*)

Method	Accuarcy Rate
LBP + ORB features	93%
Inception	94%
The proposed algorithm	94.52%

5 Conclusion

ESCNN signifies an important advancement in FER systems in connection with facial expressions, and indications for mental health prediction. By combining different algorithms and features, ESCNN provides a new approach to precisely find out facial expressions and anticipate mental health states. When compared to ResNet 50 and the Sequential Model, ESCNN showcases exceptional capabilities and equilibrium through performance evaluation using the CK+ dataset, which incorporates seven various types of facial expressions. It becomes a leading solution in facial expression recognition tasks for mental health prediction by attaining lower model sizes and faster processing times. For future endeavours, various spheres of research and development can be expanded to further promote and broaden the potentialities of the ESCNN FER System, creating opportunities to enhance mental health analysis and intervention techniques.

References

1. Shetty, A.B., Rebeiro, J.: Facial recognition using Haar cascade and LBP classifiers. Glob. Transit. Proc. **2**(2), 330–335 (2021)
2. Liao, C.Y., Chen, R.C., Tai, S.K.: Emotion stress detection using EEG signal and deep learning technologies. In: 2018 IEEE International Conference on Applied System Invention (ICASI), pp. 90–93. IEEE (2018)
3. Georgescu, M.I., Ionescu, R.T., Popescu, M.: Local learning with deep and handcrafted features for facial expression recognition. IEEE Access. **7**, 64827–64836 (2019)
4. Pramerdorfer, C., Kampel, M.: Facial expression recognition using convolutional neural networks: state of the art. arXiv preprint https://arxiv.org/abs/1612.02903 (2016)
5. Brownlee, J.: A gentle introduction to deep learning for face recognition. Mach. Learn. Mast. **31** (2019)
6. Sandler, M., Howard, A., Zhu, M., Zhmoginov, A., Chen, L.C.: Mobilenetv2: Inverted residuals and linear bottlenecks. In: Proceedings of the IEEE conference on computer vision and pattern recognition, pp. 4510–4520 (2018)
7. Chew, W.T., Chong, S.C., Ong, T.S., Chong, L.Y.: Facial expression recognition via enhanced stress convolution neural network for stress detection. IAENG Int. J. Comput. Sci. **49**(3), 1–10 (2022)
8. Team, K.: Keras documentation: The sequential model. Keras (2020)
9. Lendave, V.: A Tutorial on Sequential Machine Learning, vol. 27. Analytics India Magazine (2021)

10. Xu, Q., Yang, Y., Tan, Q., Zhang, L.: Facial expressions in context: electrophysiological correlates of the emotional congruency of facial expressions and background scenes. Front. Psychol. **8**, 2175 (2017)
11. LeCun, Y.: Generalization and network design strategies. Connect. Persp. **19**, 143–155 (1989)
12. Muhammad, G., Alsulaiman, M., Amin, S.U., Ghoneim, A., Alhamid, M.F.: A facial-expression monitoring system for improved healthcare in smart cities. IEEE Access. **5**, 10871–10881 (2017)
13. Mercan, B.A.: Doing criminological research: affective states versus emotional reactions. Theor. Criminol. **24**(2), 335–352 (2020)
14. Li, C., Yang, M., Zhang, Y., Lai, K.W.: An intelligent mental health identification method for college students: a mixed-method study. Int. J. Environ. Res. Public Health. **19**(22), 14976 (2022)
15. Ekman, P.: Universals and cultural differences in facial expressions of emotion. In: Nebraska Symposium on Motivation. University of Nebraska Press (1971)
16. Ekman, P., Friesen, W.V.: Facial action coding system. Environ. Psychol. Nonverbal Behav. (1978)
17. Guanming, L., Wanwan, S., Xu, L.: A kind of convolution neural network for facial expression recognition. J. Nanjing Univ. Posts Telecommun. (2016)
18. Lee, J.P. et al.: Encoding of multi-modal emotional information via personalized skin-integrated wireless facial interface. Nat. Commun. **15**(1), 530 (2024)
19. Alharbawee, L., Pugeault, N.: Generative adversarial networks for facial expression recognition in the wild. Int. J. Comput. Digit. Syst. **15**(1), 1–17 (2024)
20. Kimberly Octavina, K., Putra Kusuma, G.: Real-time facial expression recognition using convolutional neural network on Mobile device. Int. J. Comput. Digit. Syst. **15**(1), 1–9 (2024)
21. Nie, L., Li, B., Du, Y., Jiao, F., Song, X., Liu, Z.: Deep learning strategies with CReToNeXt-YOLOv5 for advanced pig face emotion detection. Sci. Rep. **14**(1), 1679 (2024)
22. Fei, Z. et al.: Deep convolution network based emotion analysis towards mental health care. Neurocomputing. **388**, 212–227 (2020)
23. Gavrilescu, M., Vizireanu, N.: Predicting depression, anxiety, and stress levels from videos using the facial action coding system. Sensors. **19**(17), 3693 (2019)
24. Zhang, J., Yin, H., Zhang, J., Yang, G., Qin, J., He, L.: Real-time mental stress detection using multimodality expressions with a deep learning framework. Front. Neurosci. **16**, 947168 (2022)
25. Mukherjee, N., Mukhopadhyay, S., Gupta, R.: Real-time mental stress detection technique using neural networks towards a wearable health monitor. Meas. Sci. Technol. **33**(4), 044003 (2022)
26. Sajjad, M. et al.: A comprehensive survey on deep facial expression recognition: challenges, applications, and future guidelines. Alex. Eng. J. **68**, 817–840 (2023)

Enhancing Depression Detection Through Multimodal Analysis: A Custom CNN-Based Approach

Shubham Dodia[(✉)] ⓘ, Priyansh Chhajed ⓘ, Gajanan Shegdar ⓘ, Indranil Thakare ⓘ, and Vaibhavi Gaikwad ⓘ

Computer Department of Engineering, Vishwakarma Institute of Information Technology, Pune, India
shubham.dodia8@gmail.com

Abstract. Depression is a rapidly expanding mental health issue that affects people psychologically, physically, and emotionally. This report outlines our work for DAIC (Distress Analysis Interview Corpus) as our third-year BTech project, addressing the rising need for automated depression detection using machine learning. Historically, identifying depression involved thorough clinical interviews, during which psychologists analyzed the subject's responses to assess their mental well-being. In our model, we have constructed a custom convolutional neural network (CNN) on three different formats: text, video, and audio to predict the mental health status of the patient where the accuracy for the models are 86%, 85% and 90% respectively. We have implemented a deep learning architecture where each modality is assigned specific weights to collectively generate an output. This fusion approach addresses the following issues- handling noise in one of the modalities, regulating the impact of a specific modality on the overall result.

Keywords: Depression Detection · DAIC · Deep Learning · Convolutional Neural Networks

1 Introduction

In our increasingly demanding and stressful world, the prevalence of depression is on the rise, affecting a growing portion of the population. Identifying depression early and accurately is essential for effective intervention and treatment. The urgency to develop a precise, autonomous, and accessible approach for depression detection is paramount. Our motivation for undertaking this research stems from the pressing need to address this mental health crisis.

Depression is classified as a mental health condition marked by enduring emotions of despair, a lack of motivation, recurrent negative mood fluctuations, and a reduced interest in regular physical, mental, and social engagements. These manifestations result in emotional distress and noticeable physical alterations in the individual. Specifically, it impacts an individual's ability to learn, induces mood fluctuations, and frequently

© The Author(s), under exclusive license to Springer Nature Switzerland AG 2026
R. Appavoo et al. (Eds.): IconDeepCom 2024, CCIS 2687, pp. 448–461, 2026.
https://doi.org/10.1007/978-3-032-26680-4_35

diminishes overall work efficiency. The symptoms of depression vary based on the severity of the condition in affected individuals. Ranked as the fourth prevalent ailment globally, depression has emerged as a significant challenge affecting individuals across all age brackets. Unfortunately, approx 80% of individuals do not receive appropriate treatment, primarily due to the lack of access to early services and interventions for individuals grappling with depression.

This research seeks to integrate these three modalities—speech, video, and lexical analysis—into a unified model. By amalgamating the insights gleaned from these distinct channels, we aim to construct a more versatile and robust depression detection model. This holistic approach takes into account a wider array of factors associated with depression, leading to more accurate predictions.However, building such a model presents its own set of challenges. Firstly, a substantial dataset encompassing all three modalities—speech, video, and lexical data—is required to successfully train our deep learning model. Furthermore, these modalities' alignment according to their timestamps is crucial to understand the temporal correlation between them. Furthermore, due to the involvement of video processing, considerable computational resources are necessary for model training.

In this research paper, we delve into the development of this multi-modal depression detection model, addressing the challenges and intricacies involved in its creation. By doing so, we are trying to contribute to the efforts made now-a-days to revolutionize the field of depression detection, offering a more comprehensive and data-driven approach to identifying individuals in need of support and treatment (Fig. 1).

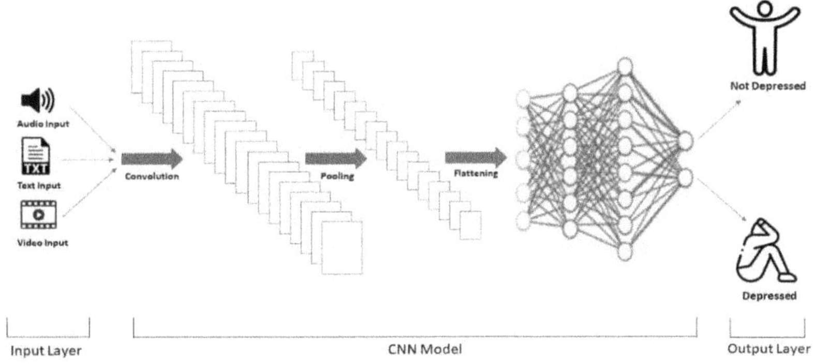

Fig. 1. Basic working of a CNN Model.

Within the larger field of machine learning, a Convolutional Neural Network (CNN), also referred to as a convnet, is a distinct subset. The convolutional, pooling, flatten, and fully connected (FC) layers make up the core of a deep learning convolutional neural network (CNN).

The convolutional layer acts as the fundamental component, performing intricate computations by traversing a kernel across the receptive fields of the image. This process aims to identify features within the image, progressively capturing larger portions and more intricate details. Subsequently, the pooling layer follows a similar approach, using a kernel to traverse the input image.

However, its distinctive function lies in reducing the number of parameters, optimizing the CNN's efficiency. While this reduction comes at the cost of some information loss, the positive trade-off is a streamlined and computationally efficient network.

Immediately following the pooling layer in this network is the Flatten layer. It is vital, as it ensures the feature vectors obtained from the features obtained after pooling become easier to pass through into a subsequent fully connected layer in this network. Its functions help prepare the data going forward for detailed analysis and classification.

The last layer, which is called the fully connected layer, plays an essential role in image classification, where features created in the preceding layers are applied. Here, the term "fully connected" is used as all the inputs or nodes of a particular layer get connected to all the activation units or nodes of the successive layer. With these vast numbers of connections, the complete exploration of the created features would occur. It will therefore be much easier for the convolutional neural network to recognize and classify objects in the image.

It's crucial to note that not all layers in the CNN are fully connected intentionally. Complete connectivity throughout the network would result in unnecessary density, leading to increased losses, potential degradation in output quality, and heightened computational expenses. The selective integration of fully connected layers strikes a balance between analytical depth and computational efficiency within the CNN architecture. In the ultimate output layer, the CNN discriminates between individuals with depression and those without, relying on the features extracted throughout the network. This layer provides classifications, offering insights into the mental health states within the given dataset.

2 Literature Survey

This research paper introduces a pioneering approach for precise depression level detection from video-based facial expressions. It utilizes deep distribution learning, incorporating an expectation loss, to model the correlation between facial images and levels of depression. This innovative method demonstrated superior performance when evaluated on the AVEC2013 and AVEC2014 datasets, outperforming existing techniques in accuracy and robustness. These findings highlight the potential for this approach to significantly enhance automated depression detection, in doing so, it aids in enhancing the evaluation and management of mental health, thus fostering advancements in assessment and treatment methodologies [1]. This research paper tackles automated depression detection through a multimodal approach, analyzing audio, visual, and text features from the DAIC-WOZ database. It leverages techniques like Gaussian Mixture Model (GMM) clustering, Fisher vectors, and SVMs, resulting in a remarkable 17% performance boost for audio and 24.5% for video features over the baseline. The study highlights distinctive behaviors in individuals with depression, manifested in speech patterns, facial expressions, and head movements. SVM and neural networks are employed for depression recognition, outperforming baseline results on validation data. Future work will focus on enhancing fusion methods and addressing potential overfitting, promising more accurate and reliable depression detection [2].

This paper addresses automated depression classification using audio and video features in the context of AVEC 2016. Depression, a major mental health concern, lacks objective diagnostic tests, leading to potential false detections and consequences. The research delves into multimodal features, highlighting the superiority of Teager energy cepstral coefficients (TECC) over standard audio features. The state-of-the-art accuracy in the audio domain is reached using i-vector modeling. In contrast, in the video domain, the most salient performer is polynomial parameterization of facial landmark features [3].

This paper examines the automation of depression detection by applying models based on deep learning methodology. The study uses convolutional neural networks (CNNs) to scan a spectrogram representation of audio data, as a way of determining characteristic acoustic features related to depressive disorders. It works to counter-sample size imbalance issues that have been a matter of concern within the DAIC-WOZ dataset during the course of training. The suggested model attained a cumulative total accuracy rate of 64.8%. Future work would include fine-tuning of the model to make it even more efficient, growing the dataset, and exploring multimodal strategies. This involves EEG data integration, video analysis execution, and exploration of textual analysis for improved accuracy and to enhance the model's generalizability across a wider population [5]. This paper introduces SMDD, which is a smart model for depression detection that applies deep neural networks. The Sequential Mood and Depression Detection model assesses depression based on sequential data and has been tested on public datasets by using various machine learning and deep learning models. SMDD model assesses depression on the basis of sequential data, and it has been experimented on publicly available datasets after applying various machine learning as well as deep learning methods. Some major drawbacks of this system include a lesser dataset, using only data from Twitter, and also unavailability of pre-trained models, which decrease the system's performance. The study highlights the capacity of deep learning to assess the efficacy of the method and posits that incorporating balanced classes within the training dataset may improve the accuracy and dependability of the proposed approach in depicting depressive symptoms. Depression is a significant global mental health issue, and effective screening methods are crucial. The study explores the potential of voice characteristics and paralinguistic speech features to aid in predictive depression assessment, providing an innovative approach to automated video-based depression screening [6].

This study demonstrates the effectiveness of a hybrid CNN-SVM model for automated depression detection using the DAIC-WOZ database. The model utilizes a combination of CNN for feature extraction and SVM for classification, attaining a notable accuracy of 68%. This performance surpasses the baseline achieved by the standalone CNN model. Compared to previous audio-based methods, our approach excels. Enhancements can be made through increased training data and parameter fine-tuning. Future work includes exploring alternative architectures and implementing the model on embedded systems, holding promise for early depression detection and intervention in the face of rising global depression cases [7]. The study developed automated depression detection models using audio and text data from individual-agent interactions. Sequence modeling, particularly a multi-modal approach, proved most effective. However, calibration issues may impact practical use. Comparative analysis highlighted improvements in multi-class performance. In summary, the study emphasized sequence modeling and multimodal integration for automated depression screening, emphasizing the need for better model calibration [8]. This study employs a CNN, OpenCV, and Haar Cascade Classifier to detect depression from facial expressions using a newly created DND dataset, achieving an 81% accuracy. However, challenges arise due to the diversity of facial expressions in depressed individuals, potential dataset biases, and the necessity for further research to address these complexities [9].

This study investigates depression detection through machine learning using video and visual features to classify individuals into depression categories, with potential applications in remote assessment and support. The review highlights the need for enhanced precision, accuracy, and processing time in future research [10]. A successful multimodal fusion framework for depression analysis, achieving promising results on the AVEC2017 dataset. It introduces innovative feature descriptors but lacks discussion of limitations, and future work will enhance text analysis and explore end-to-end learning strategies for improved depression recognition [11]. Introduces an AI model designed for diagnosing depressive disorders leveraging fast region-based convolutional neural networks (R-CNN) in conjunction with smartphone-based assistance. It highlights the potential for AI-driven mental health solutions, such as AI chatbots and remote monitoring. However, it lacks discussion on potential ethical and privacy concerns associated with AI-based mental health diagnosis and treatment [12].

Multitask learning attention-based deep neural network for the multimodal estimation of depression levels using acoustic, textual, and visual data. The suggested method outperforms current state-of-the-art models, demonstrating progress in both regression and classification assignments. However, the paper lacks discussion of potential ethical concerns associated with using AI for mental health assessment and diagnosis [13]. The paper conducts an investigation into gender bias in the DAIC-WOZ dataset used for depression detection. It identifies that gender bias exists in the dataset and that it can affect classification performance. The authors advocate for the utilization of raw audio features as a more resilient alternative to alleviate gender bias. It focuses on a single dataset and model architecture, and it would be beneficial to explore more datasets and features in future work [14]. The effectiveness of deep learning models, particularly the audio CNN, for depression detection. However, it highlights the disadvantage of longer pre-processing times associated with the Bi-LSTM model. The future scope emphasizes the potential for incorporating audio, video, and text features, applying more robust algorithms, and developing user-friendly applications for real-time depression detection, making the system more comprehensive and practical [15].

3 Dataset

The experiments were carried out utilizing the DAIC-WOZ dataset, a subset of the broader Distress Analysis Interview Corpus (DAIC). The primary objective of DAIC is to support clinical interviews focused on diagnosing psychological conditions like anxiety, depression, and post-traumatic stress disorder (PTSD). In this context, a computer agent plays a vital role by interacting with interviewees and identifying verbal and behavioral indicators associated with mental health issues. Within the DAIC-WOZ dataset, you can find an extensive array of resources, including audio and video files, along with comprehensive questionnaire responses from these interviews, all meticulously transcribed and annotated.

This database was made available for research purposes by the University of California. It comprises 189 folders, each representing unique interview sessions with different participants. Every folder contains a collection of audio recordings, video notes, transcripts, and other relevant materials corresponding to each interview conducted by an interviewer. It's important to note that each participant undergoes a single interview session. The audio recordings were acquired at a sampling rate of 16 kHz, and the interview sessions exhibit varying durations, ranging from 7 to 33 min, with an average duration of approximately 16 min.

To facilitate experimentation, the dataset has been randomly divided into three parts, namely, the training, testing, and development sections. It is worth noting that there exists an imbalance in the distribution of participants between those classified as depressed and non-depressed, with a ratio of approximately 4 non-depressed participants for every depressed participant. In contrast, the gender distribution within the dataset is very well balanced (Table 1).

Table 1. Detailed description of Dataset used

	Train	Test	Dev
Text	1 Transcript File per Patient	1 Transcript File per Patient	1 Transcript File per Patient
Video	6 Files per Patient: CLNF AU CLNF Features CLNF Features3D CLNF Gaze CLNF hog CLNF Pose	6 Files per Patient: CLNF AU CLNF Features CLNF Features3D CLNF Gaze CLNF hog CLNF Pose	6 Files per Patient: CLNF AU CLNF Features CLNF Features3D CLNF Gaze CLNF hog CLNF Pose
Audio	1 COVAREP file per person	1 COVAREP file per person	1 COVAREP file per person
Total	106 Patients	47 Patients	35 Patients

3.1 Modalities

The dataset consists of a wide variety of data modalities, such as thorough questionnaire responses and audio and video recordings. Furthermore, the DAIC-WOZ dataset features Wizard-Of-Oz interviews that are assisted by an animated virtual assistant called Ellie, which is controlled by a human interviewer situated in a different room. The dataset has undergone a thorough transcription and annotation process that includes a range of verbal and non-verbal characteristics. A transcription of the exchange, unique audio files, and face features taken from the captured video are all included in each participant's session.

Video Format: The dataset's video component consists of particular facial features that were taken from participant recordings. These consist of 68 facial 2D points, 24 Action Unit (AU) features that measure the subject's facial activity, 68 facial 3D points, 16 features that describe the subject's gaze, and 10 characteristics that show the subject's stance. When these components are combined, a complete set of 388 video features is produced.

Sound Format: Features are sampled at a rate of 100 Hz in the audio domain, which translates to a frame rate of 10 ms. The 12 Mel-frequency cepstral coefficients (MFCCs) identified as F0, VUV, NAQ, QOQ, H1H2, PSP, MDQ, peakSlope, Rd., Rdconf, MCEP024, HMPDM0–24, and HMPDD0–12 are included in this set of features. Pitch tracking, peak slope, maximal dispersion quotients, and glottal source parameters are additional characteristics.

Text Modality: In the textual modality, there is a thorough transcription of the patient's interaction with the RA, presented in CSV format. Each sentence is meticulously times-tamped and categorized based on the corresponding speaker. Expressions such as Laughter or Frown, are denoted within angular brackets (for eg. Laughter¿, ¡Frown¿) Notably, the transcript does not distinguish between long and short pauses, and the segmentation is conducted at the word level rather than the phoneme level.

4 Proposed Model

As illustrated in Fig. 2, A Convolutional Neural Network (CNN) model with six layers in total was carefully constructed. In the initial 4 layers, Conv2D layers were utilized to process the text modality, Conversely, the audio and video modalities used Conv1D layers.

Each convolutional layer is succeeded by batch normalization (Batch Normalization) to stabilize and expedite training. Max Pooling layers were strategically inserted after each Conv2D and Conv1D layer to enhance feature extraction and diminish spatial dimensions while retaining crucial information. Following this, flattening, dropout, and fully connected layers were introduced. The 3D result is transformed into a 1D feature vector by using the flatten layer. In addition, a dropout layer with a 0.5 dropout rate is included to reduce the possibility of overfitting during training.Two dense (fully connected) layers are appended with Leaky ReLU activation, and batch normalization is applied to each dense layer. The final layer of the model is endowed with the Sigmoid activation function, facilitating binary classification.

For the audio modality, the model selectively considers the first 40,000 features, and for the video modality, it incorporates timestamps. The choice of these specific values was made with careful consideration of computational capabilities. In the case of the text modality, a Word2Vec model was applied, accompanied by the implementation of thresholds governing the maximum number of words and sentences.

In addition to the aforementioned architecture, our model incorporates batch normalization layers for improved convergence and generalization.

Nevertheless, it is noteworthy that, owing to the intricacy of the model and the incorporation of batch normalization, the execution time of the model tends to be relatively slower. This underscores the trade-off between model complexity and computational efficiency.

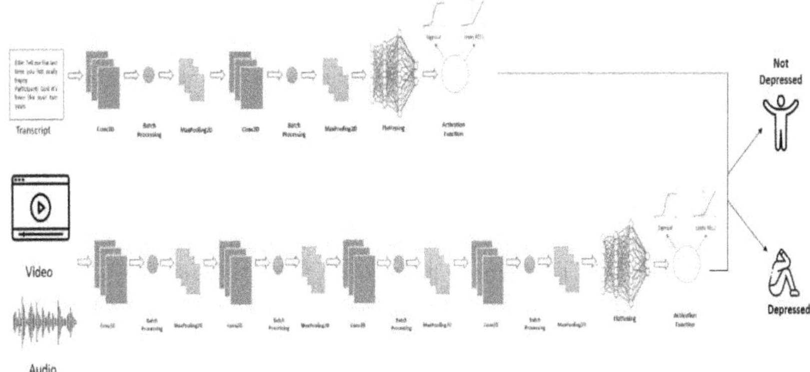

Fig. 2. Working of proposed custom CNN model for Depression Detection

4.1 Convolutional Layer

The Convolution Layer, positioned as the initial and important layer of a neural network, works as the cornerstone influencing the entire network. Its primary role is to analyze the characteristics of the input data, discerning whether it comprises text features, audio attributes, or a fusion of both modalities. This layer serves as the foundational element, laying the groundwork for subsequent layers to extract hierarchical representations essential for the network's learning process. This layer produces an output image from the convolutional application of a filter that shares dimensions with the input image. A feature map then is produced as the output after this step. The Convolution Layer uses filter kernels as their weights to allow convolution to occur. These weights are updated through the backpropagation algorithm, which is an essential part of the Convolution Layer that works to update and optimize the model. The Convolution Layer plays basically a very significant role in how the neural network perceives input data, identifying and producing significant features of the same in the further stages.

4.2 The Pooling Layer

The Max-pooling Layer in the architecture of a neural network is placed between two convolutional layers. It mainly compresses the dimensionality of the input data. This layer compresses the data while retaining only the relevant information, hence reducing the overall size of the data. Therefore, the performance of the neural network improves through the pooling layer as redundant information is removed from the data. Pooling layers basically connect the fully linked layer to the convolutional layer as an essential component mainly to reduce overfitting problems that can arise with neural networks. The pooling layer serves as a channel through which information transfer within the network increases and makes the network even more efficient.

4.3 The Flattening Layer

Flattening refers to the operation of changing data into one dimensional array form that could then be inputted in other layers later. The process transforms outputs from convolutional layers into one single long feature vector. The operation systematically organizes structured information gained from operations of the convolutional structure into linear formats; thus, it gives a feature vector that could be added without disturbing anything in the neural network's next layer.

4.4 An Activation Function with a Leaky ReLU

The concept of Leaky ReLUs corrects the "dying ReLU" problem caused by the presence of minimal, non-zero gradients associated with the negative inputs. Due to this approach, not only will neurons cease to train completely during the training periods but also increase the abilities of the network to characterize detailed depression-related patterns. Network integration of the Leaky ReLU activation improves total network robustness and adequacy in detecting relevant attributes toward more effective learning patterns and better model results.Unlike other activation functions (SoftMax, ReLU, tanH, Sigmoid), Leaky ReLU strategically replaces negative values with a small non-zero value. This feature is pivotal in deciding which information to keep and transmit to the next convolution layer, contributing to the network's effective decision-making process.

4.5 The Fully Connected Layer

In a neural network, the Fully Connected layer is usually arranged before the output classification layer. This layer starts the categorization process and improves the results even further. It is essential for modifying the outcomes according to the acquired attributes. One or two completely linked layers are essential for extensive learning and feature refinement throughout the network architecture in a neural network.

4.6 Layer of Batch Normalization

The output is normalized and standardized via batch normalization layers from preceding layers, aiding in more effective feature learning. This normalization enhances the stability and accelerates the performance of the model. By ensuring a consistent and normalized input to subsequent layers, Batch Normalization promotes faster processing and learning within the model. Dropout is a layer that helps alleviate overfitting in a model by randomly dropping some values within the neural network, which accelerates the model's learning rate. Typically placed after fully connected layers, Dropout layers, often configured with a dropout rate of 0.5, can contribute to slowing down the training process in a neural network.

5 Experimental Results

Depression changes the way one thinks, percepts things in a negative way but it's treatable with counseling and therapy. The major issue is regarding its detection, which can be solved using machine learning in an efficient manner. We have introduced a deep learning model in this work.

Convolutional Neural Network (CNN), designed to recorganize audio, video, and text features, proposing an approach for the identification of depression. In the experimental results, three models were generated: Three different CNN models: Textual, Audio, and Video. Adam Optimizer and Batch Normalization were employed in all these models, leading to a significant reduction in processing time, nearly halving the time required compared to models without these optimizations. Leveraging these trained models for depression detection allows for predictions with high accuracy and minimal loss, highlighting the effectiveness of the proposed approach.

These assessment measures are used to assess our model's performance.

Table 2. Performance measures for the proposed model

Sr. No	Model	Recall (%)	Precision (%)	F1 Score (%)	Overall Accuracy (%)
1.	CNN-Audio	100	86	92	86
2.	CNN-Video	100	85	92	85
3.	CNN-Text	100	87	92	90

According to Table 2 experimental results, the audio CNN model achieved an accuracy of 86% after 5 epochs, with an execution time of 4 min and 3 s. The video CNN model attained an accuracy of 85% after 3 epochs, with a corresponding loss, with a 5-min, 9-s execution duration. Alternatively, the text CNN model achieved an accuracy of 90% after 10 epochs, with an execution time of 5.4 s. To evaluate the performance of the models, graphs illustrating loss accuracy versus the total number of epochs and against the number of epochs that each model has produced.

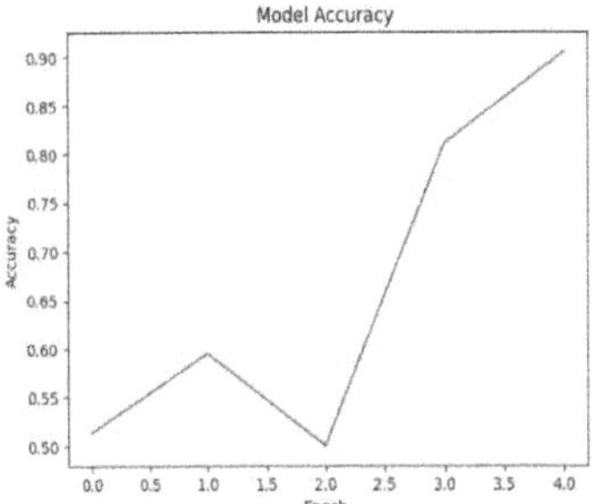

Fig. 3. Graph of Accuracy of audio CNN model

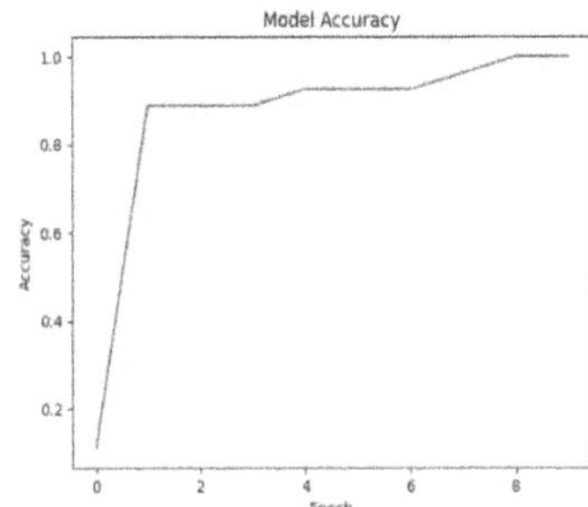

Fig. 4. Graph of Text CNN model for accuracy

A graphical representation of accuracy and loss for all models is depicted in allowing a comparison of the textual CNN model, audio CNN model, and visual CNN model's performance in Figs. 3, 4, 5, 6, 7, 8, 9, and 10. In Figs. 3, 4, and 5, graphs depict the relationship between accuracy and the number of epochs. Across all three models, there is a noticeable trend where an A higher number of epochs is correlated with higher

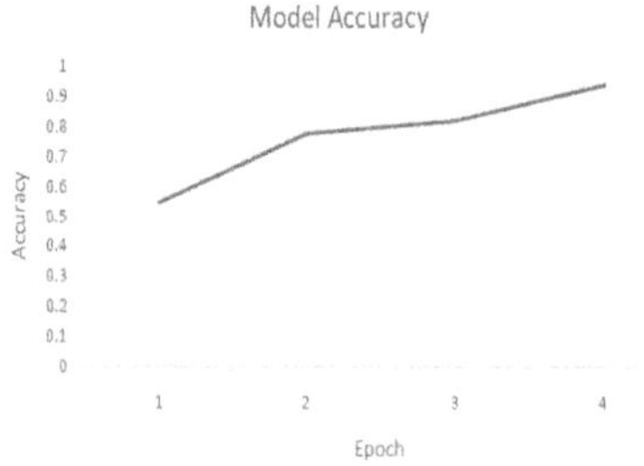

Fig. 5. Accuracy graphs for the Video CNN model

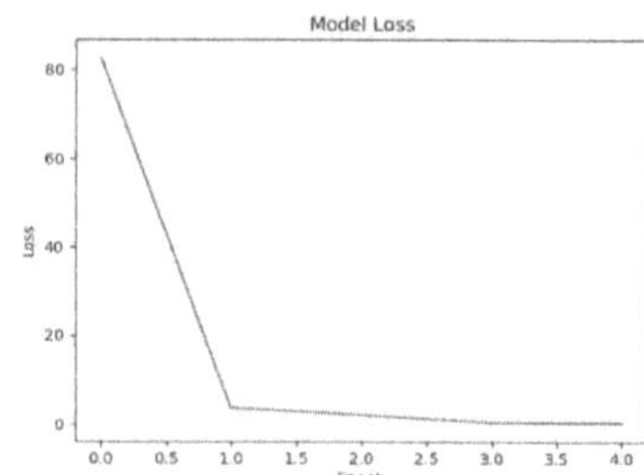

Fig. 6. Batch Normalization Audio CNN Graphs

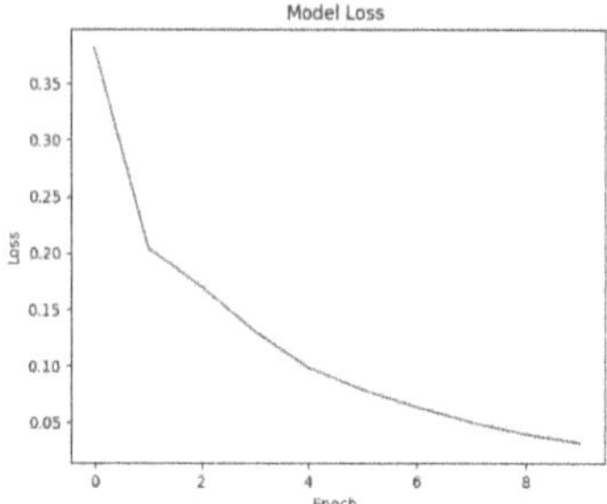

Fig. 7. Graphs of Text CNN with Batch Normalization

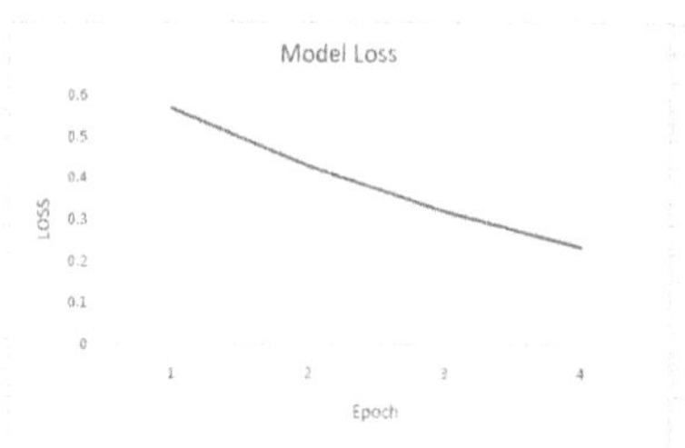

Fig. 8. Loss graphs for the Video CNN model

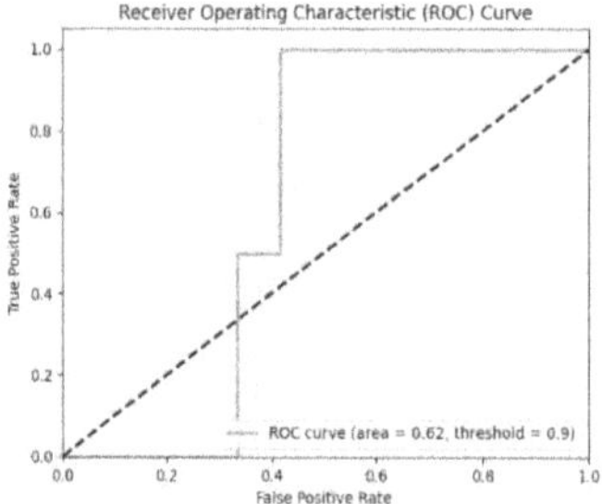

Fig. 9. Graph of text CNN with Batch Normalization

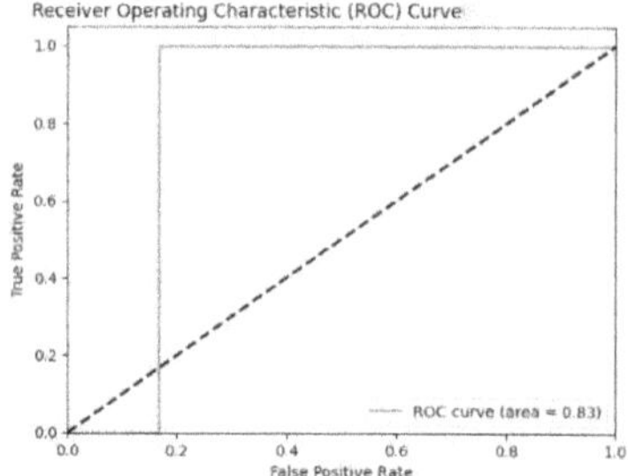

Fig. 10. Graph of audio CNN with Batch Normalization

accuracy. In Figs. 6, 7, and 8, graphs illustrate the relationship between loss and the number of epochs. Consistently across all three models, there is a clear pattern where an increase in the number of epochs leads to a decrease in loss.The epoch's number ranges from 4–10 for different models. Figures 9 and 10 represent the graph of batch normalization, where true positive rate is plotted against false positive rate. Notably, the plotted graphs indicate that the textual CNN model exhibits a superior learning rate compared to the audio CNN and visual CNN models, signifying its faster learning ability. The loss of the textual CNN model is notably lower than that of the other CNN models.

The high learning features parameters of the textual CNN model allow it to rapidly reach its peak accuracy and then stabilize. In summary, the textual CNN model demonstrates a faster learning capacity compared to the other two CNN models.

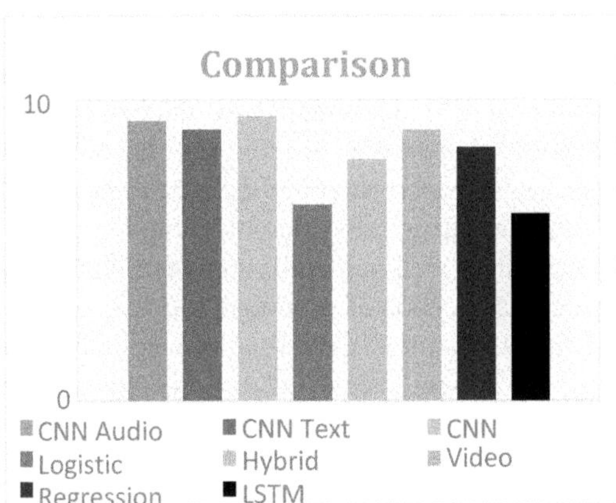

Fig. 11. Comparison of custom CNN models with existing Machine Learning Classifiers

In the comparative analysis of detection results shown in Fig. 11, our focus was only on the DAIC WOZ dataset with the suggested methodology. The outcomes of our approach surpass those of many advanced research papers within the DAIC WOZ dataset. As shown in the comparison table, our method consistently outperforms other established methods, proving its effectiveness in detecting depression. In particular, our proposed CNN models have better performance compared to hybrid models used for depression detection. Hybrid LSTM and Hybrid Bi-LSTM, both combinations of different techniques, achieve 80% and 84% accuracy, respectively. However, their accuracy is inferior when combined with our proposed CNN models. In particular, our models not only achieve higher accuracy, but also demonstrate efficiency by reducing learning time and complexity. This amazing combination of efficiency and effectiveness positions our proposed models as viable alternatives to complex Hybrid LSTM and Hybrid Bi-LSTM models. Additionally, our research delved into the performance of Logistic Regression and Random Forest models. Unfortunately, these models yielded 60–65% accuracy, indicating suboptimal performance compared to our proposed CNN models. On the other hand, Support Vector Machines (SVM) showed comparable performance, highlighting the viability of our proposed CNN model to achieve results similar to established methods. In conclusion, a careful comparison of our suggested CNN models with other cutting-edge methods, particularly hybrid models, underscores the effectiveness and efficiency of our methodology. Excellent accuracy combined with reduced learning time and complexity make our models attractive tools for depression detection, outperforming comparable methods on the DAIC WOZ dataset.

6 Conclusion

Our research is on the process of classifying depression using audio signals, with a focus on several key stages. We began with Signal Pre-processing, the initial step involving the preparation of audio data from our database. Notably, discernible differences exist in audio characteristics between individuals with and without depression. These differences encompass variations in amplitude, speech duration, the frequency of pauses, and abrupt tonal shifts. Depressed individuals tend to exhibit heightened emotional sensitivity and fluctuations. To preserve these crucial audio features, we chose to train our model using spectrogram data. In this paper, we proposed a customized Deep Neural Network model trained for speech-based depression classification. Deep learning algorithms can be shown to perform exemplary well in identifying common themes in depressed individuals, allowing for the classification of depressed states in new cases. In addition, we also used random sampling to ensure there was an equal number of depressed and non-depressed participants, which significantly reduced bias towards the model's success. Yet, there remain opportunities for further improvement that can make the model do better. We realized that what was needed was optimization of efforts to achieve higher accuracy. It is important to further enrich our dataset with a wider and more diverse set of samples from other people, while keeping a balanced ratio of depressed and non-depressed cases. We also proposed incorporating extra features, like BDI reports, and doing more research on more complex architectures for CNNs that might eventually yield better results.

7 Future Work

In terms of future research directions, there are ways in which the use of audio signals can be explored into depression classification. One promising line of thought is to focus on further refining feature extraction techniques, so that possibly more fine-grained information about response latency, pause frequencies, and silence rates will be obtained. This could prove to better understand depression analysis through the use of audio signals.

Further areas of exploration would include multimodal analysis where the interplay between physical activities that are recorded via motion data and verbal expressions within people suffering from depression could be analyzed. The exploration into the correlation between movements and verbal expression may further potentially lead to a greater depth and understanding of the disease.

Besides that, the quality of the training dataset must be improved. The augmentation applied here must be diverse and cover a large number of samples. This should maintain the balance between the number of depressed and non-depressed cases, leading to better model training and better results in performance.

Another multimodal approach can be adopted by incorporating various data types. This will include EEG signals to increase the ability of the measure of brain activity, video analysis related to facial expressions and non-verbal behavior, and text analysis with regard to verbal communication. An approach that would bring about substantial improvements in accuracy for classification models regarding depression might make those models much more applicable to real-world practical scenarios.

References

1. Mulay, A., Dhekne, A., Wani, R., Kadam, S., Deshpande, P., Deshpande, P.: Automatic Depression Level Detection Through Visual Input (2020)
2. Amanat, A., et al.: Deep Learning for Depression Detection from Textual Data
3. World Health Organization: Depression (2020) [Online]. Available: https://www.who.int/news-room/factsheets/detail/depression/
4. Krishna, S., Anju, J.: Speech based depression detection using convolution neural networks. Regular. **9**(9), 405–408 (2020)
5. Chlasta, K., Wołk, K., Krejtz, I.: Automated speechbased screening of depression using deep convolutional neural networks. Procedia Computer Science. **164**, 618–628 (2019)
6. Wang, Z., Chen, L., Wang, L., Diao, G.: Recognition of audio depression based on convolutional neural network and generative antagonism network model. IEEE Access. **8**, 101181–101191 (2020). https://doi.org/10.1109/ACCESS.2020.2998532
7. Alghamdi, N.S., Hosni Mahmoud, H.A., Abraham, A., Alanazi, S.A., GarcíaHern andez, L.: Predicting depression symptoms in an Arabic psychological forum. IEEE Access. **8**, 57317–57334 (2020). https://doi.org/10.1109/ACCESS.2020.2981834
8. Ma, X., Yang, H., Chen, Q., Huang, D., Wang, Y.: DepAudioNet: an efficient deep model for audio based depression classification. In: AVEC 2016 - Proc. 6th Int. Work. Audio/Visual Emot. Challenge, Co-located with ACM Multimed, 2016, pp. 35–42 (2016). https://doi.org/10.1145/2988257.2988267
9. F. Honig, ¨ A. Batliner, E. Noth, ¨ S. Schnieder, J. Krajewski, Automatic modelling of depressed speech: relevant features and relevance of gender, Proc. Annu. Conf. Int. Speech Commun. Assoc. INTERSPEECH 444 (2014) 1248–1252, https://doi.org/10.21437/inter-spe ech.2014-313.
10. R.L. Rosa, G.M. Schwartz, W.V. Ruggiero, D.Z. Rodriguez, A knowledge-based recommendation system that includes sentiment analysis and deep learning, IEEE Trans. Industr. Inform. 15 (4) (2019) 2124–2135, https://doi.org/10.1109/TII.2018.2867174
11. Tadesse, M.M., Lin, H., Xu, B., Yang, L.: Detection of depression-related posts in reddit social media forum. IEEE Access. **7**(c), 44883–44893 (2019). https://doi.org/10.1109/ACC ESS.2019.2909180
12. Alghowinem, S. et al.: A comparative study of different classifiers for detecting depression from spontaneous speech. In: Acoustics, Speech and Signal Processing (ICASSP), 2013 IEEE International Conference on. IEEE, pp. 8022–8026 (2013)
13. Fan, Y., Lu, X., Li, D., Liu, Y.: Video-based emotion recognition using cnn-rnn and c3d hybrid networks. In: Proceedings of the 18th ACM International Conference on Multimodal Interaction, pp. 445–450. ACM (2016)
14. Le, D., Provost, E.M.: Emotion recognition from spontaneous speech using hidden markov models with deep belief networks. In: Automatic Speech Recognition and Understanding (ASRU), 2013 IEEE Workshop on. IEEE, pp. 216–221 (2013)
15. Williamson, J.R., Quatieri, T.F., Helfer, B.S., Ciccarelli, G., Mehta, D.D.: Vocal and facial biomarkers of depression based on motor incoordination and timing. In: Proceedings of the 4th International Workshop on Audio/Visual Emotion Challenge, pp. 65–72. ACM (2014)

A Clustering-Based Crime Hotspot Identification: In Case of Ilu Abba Bor Zone Police Department

Wagari Goje Tuji[(✉)], Ramata Mosissa Gichila, and Alemayehu Etana Duguma

Department of Information Technology, Mattu University, Mettu, Ethiopia
wagarig9@gmail.com

Abstract. In recent years, crime prediction has garnered significant interest in ensuring public safety and optimizing resource allocations. A strategy to tackle this challenge is the identification of crime Hotspot, which are regions with higher than average crime rates. Clustering algorithms play a vital role in areas where crime is a problem by classifying related crime episodes according to spatial and temporal characteristics. In this study we implemented and analyzed K-means and Kmedoids clustering algorithm on a large dataset of crime incidents. The optimal number of clusters (k) was determined to be 14 using the silhouette score. Based on the quality of the clustering findings, the algorithms' performance was evaluated using their silhouette scores, and both algorithms received a score of 1. The results indicate that both K-means and Kmedoids formed well-defined clusters with excellent demonstrating their effectiveness in identifying high crime zone.

Keywords: Crime prediction · K-Means · K-Medoids · clustering · machine learning · high crime zone

1 Introduction

In recent years, Global Security agencies officials have expressed alarm over rising crime rates [1]. To develop effective strategies for crime prevention, understanding and predicting the spatial distribution of different types of crimes are essential. Clustering-based crime Hotspot identification plays a crucial part in crime prediction, as it helps to identify regions with a high concentration of crime incidents [2]. This research aims to review and synthesize literature on A Clustering-Based Crime Hotspot Identification. A Clustering-Based Crime Hotspot Identification is an essential aspect of modern crime analytics, enabling law enforcement to better allocate resources and determine which areas need further focus.

Proper analysis of crime data from the previous year can help reduce considerations of crime rates. Clustering is used to group objects (clusters) with the same characteristics of a dataset for further research, and most of the clustering algorithms are the K-Medoids and K-Means algorithms. Clustering is considered to be the simplest and fastest clustering algorithm compared to other algorithms also is the best choice for clustering large

R. Appavoo et al. (Eds.): IconDeepCom 2024, CCIS 2687, pp. 462–472, 2026.
https://doi.org/10.1007/978-3-032-26680-4_36

amounts of data due to its low computational speed [3]. Law enforcement agencies and policymakers find it extremely important to develop methods that can aid them in predicting and preventing criminal activities. With the advancements in machine learning and data-driven analytics, clustering-based crime ridden neighborhood identification has emerged among the most auspicious approaches for crime prediction [4].

An unsupervised learning method called clustering seeks to put related data points in groups according to their features. Clustering is a method employed in crime prediction that seeks to pinpoint areas or hotspots with comparatively high crime rates. Law enforcement organizations can utilize this information to better target their resources and attention by keeping an eye on these hotspots. K-Means and K-Medoids are the popular clustering algorithms that differ primarily in their approach to defining the cluster centroids. The K-Means algorithm computes the average value of each cluster's data points as the centroid, while the K-Medoids algorithm chooses the actual data point that minimizes the distance to other points within the same cluster as the centroid. Despite this difference, both algorithms follow a similar approach to cluster the data points iteratively [5].

2 Related Works

Among the many computer methods employed for this, clustering algorithms have become extremely prominent. The clustering methods K-Means and KMedoids are the two that are commonly used. Finding patterns and trends in big data sets is the main goal of clustering-based techniques, which can provide law enforcement and decision-makers with useful information. One popular partition-based clustering approach is K-Means. Data points are assigned to one of the K clusters by this procedure in order to minimize the within-cluster volatility. The K-means algorithm's main benefits are its scalability and simplicity. The K-means algorithm has been applied in a number of recent research to detect high-crime areas and ascertain the distribution of crime episodes inside a specific area [6].

In [7], a model is proposed to expect the range of crimes in a spatial unit primarily based on the quantity of preceding criminal occasions. The model applies the K-method method to identify spatial clusters. This approach uses a neural network-based overall model to forecast common criminal activity in areas that have been identified. It is regarded as a target variable, and the prediction considers three situations. In the first scenario, every other row that corresponds to a cluster is taken into account for the prediction, whereas in the second scenario, just the rows that are adjacent to a cluster are considered.

In [8], the authors of this examination recommend a Machine Learning version for crime prediction with the use of spatiotemporal. They hire a multi-project getting-to-know framework that identifies hotspots and predicts the future wide variety of crimes concurrently. Their model demonstrates correct overall performance in predicting crime hotspots in numerous cities. These studies and strategies exhibit the cost of clustering-primarily based hotspot identification in predicting crime occurrences. By identifying regions with high attention to crime, regulation enforcement organizations and policymakers can expand targeted techniques to prevent and reply to crime effectively.

In [9], they used a KNN model to observe crime rates by prediction. They predict, tentatively, the type of crime, when, where and at what time it may take place. This technique is to grow the prediction as a good deal as viable.

In this [10], the authors recommend a method that mixes the DBSCAN set of rules and choice woodland for detecting hotspots and predicting destiny crime occurrences. They achieved the DBSCAN clustering set of rules to discover hotspots of housebreaking and motorized vehicle thefts in Seoul, South Korea. DBSCAN is a density-based clustering set of regulations that divides the dataset into clusters based totally on the density of crime factors inside the vicinity. The authors placed that the use of one of a type distance thresholds produced numerous cluster systems, highlighting the significance of figuring out suitable parameter values inside the assessment.

In [11], they proposed using cluster detection hotspots for crime forecasting. By supplying vital insights and modern techniques for understanding and predicting crime trends, those works have notably contributed to crime prediction inside the subject of cluster-primarily based hotspot detection. Security agencies may utilize their outcomes to create higher plans for coping with and stopping criminal conduct in their authorities. Over the years, investigators to find hotspots, and provide perception into crime scene styles have utilized clustering strategies and manual law enforcement approaches.

In [12], this paper, the authors propose a machine-learning approach for crime prediction techniques. This technique is simple to perceive crime fashion over years with the cluster.

In [13], the authors propose a machine-learning model for crime prediction. In this paper, the researcher proposes three algorithms namely KNN, SVM, and Naive Bayesian. The limitation of this paper is they get prediction accuracy between 39% to 44% was obtained when predicting crime in Vancouver.

In [14], they estimate which type of crime contributes the most along with the period and location where it has happened Initialization of optimal value is not required, high accuracy.

3 Methodology

The suggested model is made up of various parts. They are feature selection, model development, model evaluation, preprocessing, and visualization (Fig. 1).

3.1 Data Collection and Description

The first step in any machine learning work is obtaining the data for the experiment. The information used in this study was acquired from the Ilu Abba Bor Police office, with a particular focus on the woreda police station, which served as the primary target data set for this study. Among the most significant steps in this process is gathering meaningful data. From the station's dataset and unpublished crime, 3689 records were used for the study. It only includes crime records from the year 2013 up to 2015 E.C. The data holds information about Accused/offenders (name, nationality, gender, age, educational status religion, and marital status), Accuser/victims (name, nationality, gender, age, job, religion, marital status) and crime (date, year, type, location).

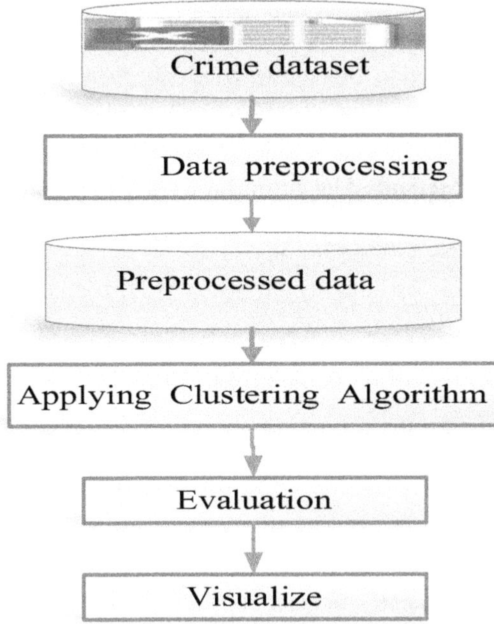

Fig. 1. Flow of Proposed system

3.2 Data Preprocessing

Once the data is collected, it is time to observe the condition of outliers, incorrect, missing, or irrelevant information. Data preprocessing is the main task and it takes much time in the study helps to build the given cluster model. The data should be cleaned, processed, and transformed into a format that is suitable for additional analysis while maintaining alignment with the temporal and geographical dimensions. We want to clean the datasets to acquire accurate outcomes from the given model. Without preprocessing the data set, we cannot get accurate results.

According to [15] data pre-processing is a method of cleaning the raw facts i.e. the facts is accumulated in the actual world and are transformed into a clean data set. Data originates from some raw sources, which potentially may include null values as properly as inappropriate information. It is necessary to clean this fact so that it can be suitable for the models and generate better outcomes.

4 Results and Discussion

In this experiment, we aimed to identify crime hotspots using clustering techniques, namely K-Means and K-Medoids, to predict future crime occurrences. This experiment's primary goal is to support law enforcement organizations in allocating resources and developing crime prevention strategies.

K-means and K-medoids algorithms will be utilized in this process. The K-means algorithm is applied to the data, where "K" represents the number of clusters. Each criminal incidence is grouped by the algorithm in a way that minimizes the total squared distance between the incident and the cluster centroid. In contrast, K-medoids is a kind of K-means that is also used to form clusters; the only distinction is that instead of using centroids, it uses medoids, or the instance that is most centrally positioned within a cluster.

Algorithm 1: The K-Medoids Algorithm Involves the Following Steps Input:

- k: number of clusters
- data: input dataset

Procedure KMedoids(k, data):
    Initialize medoids randomly from the dataset
    Initialize clusters
    Repeat until convergence:
      Assign each data point to the closest medoids
      For each medoids:
    Calculate the total cost of swapping the medoids with each non-medoids data point within the same cluster
        Select the data point with the minimum cost as the new medoids
    Return clusters
Procedure assignToNearestMedoid(data, medoids):
    Initialize clusters with empty sets
    For each data point in the dataset:
      Calculate the distance to each medoids
      Assign the data point to the cluster of the nearest medoids
    Return clusters
Procedure calculateCost(data, medoids, clusters):
    Initialize total cost as 0
    For each cluster:
   For each data point in the cluster:
      Add the distance between the data point and its medoids to the total cost
    Return total cost
Procedure swapMedoid(medoids, nonMedoid, cluster, data):
    Replace medoids with nonMedoid in the cluster
    Calculate the new cost of the cluster
    Return the new cost

4.1 Evaluation Metrics for Clustering Performance

Clustering-based crime Hotspot identification for crime prediction involves partitioning crime data into separate groups or clusters with similar attributes. After then, these clusters are utilized to pinpoint probable crime hotspots. The silhouette score is one of the metrics that can be used to evaluate the efficacy of clustering approaches, especially when it comes to crime prediction [16].

Silhouette score is a measure of how well an item is classified in its cluster compared to other clusters. The score provides an assessment of the quality of clustering results and the level of separation between clusters. The silhouette score ranges from -1 to $+1$, with advanced values indicating well-clustering results.

Implement and compare various clustering algorithms K-means and K-Medoids to identify significant crime hotspots. In this study, we employ two popular clustering algorithms K-Means and K-Medoids to cluster and identify crime hotspots using historical crime data. The dataset used in this study comprises geo-located reported crime incidents from Ilu Abba Bor Police Station, covering categories such as theft, physical injury, breach, and assassination. To guarantee the quality and applicability of the data, preprocessing is done on the geospatial data. The clustering algorithms' efficacy and efficiency are assessed using the silhouette score. It is a method of validation and interpretation to examine the consistency within the clusters of data. Its value gives information on how well the data point is classified. It is a measure of related a data dataset is to its cluster known as cohesion compared to other clusters, that is, separation. Mean nearest-cluster distance and mean inter-cluster distance for each data set are utilized to determine its value.

Mathematical Representation

1. For each data point i in a cluster, calculate the average distance to all other data points in the same cluster (a(i)).
2. For each data point i and all other clusters, calculate the average distance between the data point and all data points in those clusters. Determine the smallest average distance between each cluster (b(i)) [17, 18].

$$Silhouette_i = \frac{b_i - a_i}{\max(a_i, b_i)} \tag{1}$$

Finally, the overall silhouette score for the clustering result is calculated by averaging the silhouette scores of all data points.

In the context of crime clustering, silhouette scores used to evaluate and validate the effectiveness of clustering-based crime frequently identification methods. A higher silhouette score indicates better performance, with more distinct and separate clusters representing different crime hotspots.

The value of the coefficient tiers from -1 to 1, 1 being the best and -1 (indicating that the data are assigned to the incorrect cluster, as the extraordinary cluster is extra similar to which it is far clustered) being the worst fee for the clustered data. Furthermore, it indicates that there is overlap between the two clusters if its value is 0.

4.2 Visualize the Crime Hotspot

Heats maps are a visual representation of crime data that uses color shades to show the concentration of crime incidents with in specific areas. The darker area, the higher concentration of incidents. The below Figures shows that we used heat mapping to identify high crime zone based on the crime dataset. If certain areas are clustering into one group due to high rates of similar crimes, the authorities can focus on these hotspots to minimize crime by implementing more police patrols or security measures. Ultimately, the goal is to reduce and prevent crime in this identified hotspot

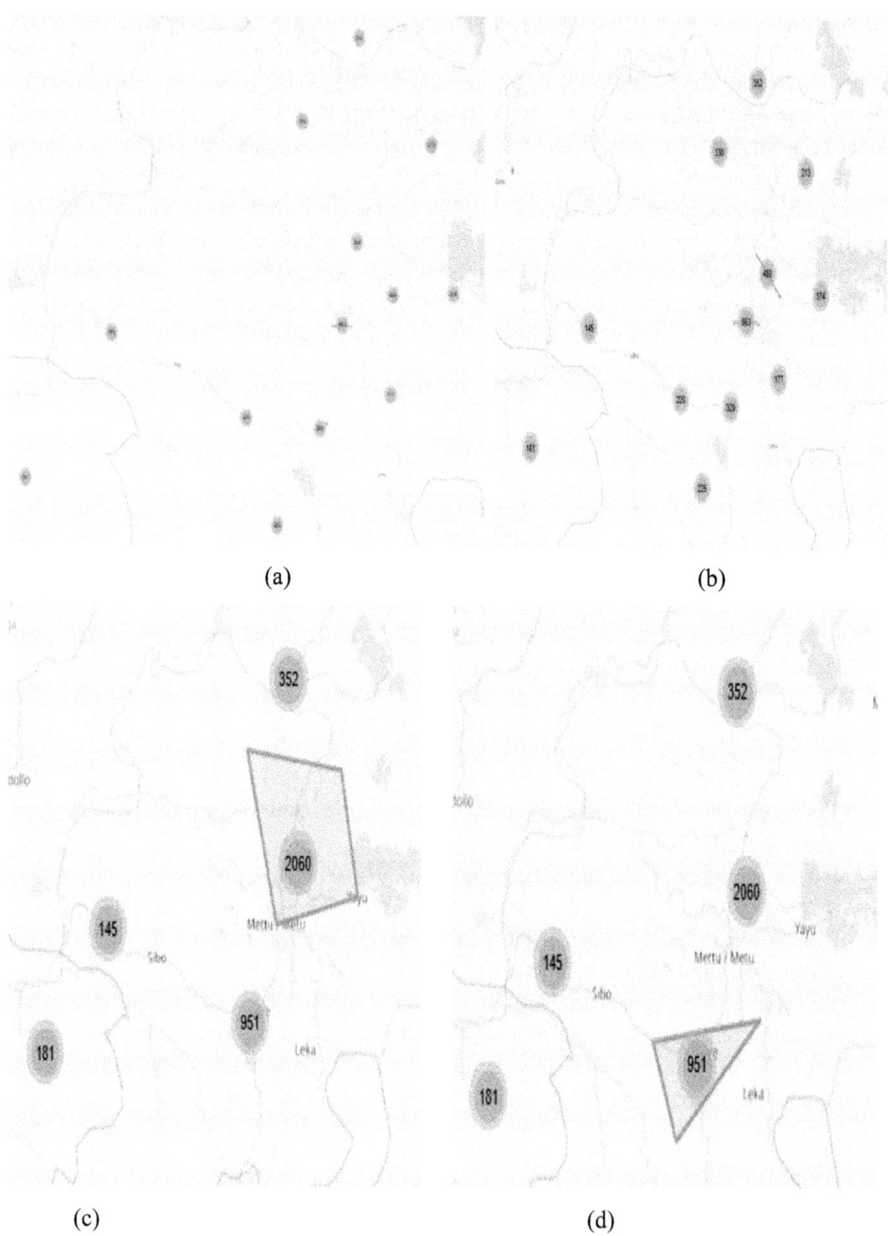

(a)   (b)

(c)   (d)

Fig. 2. Clustering-based crime frequently identification.

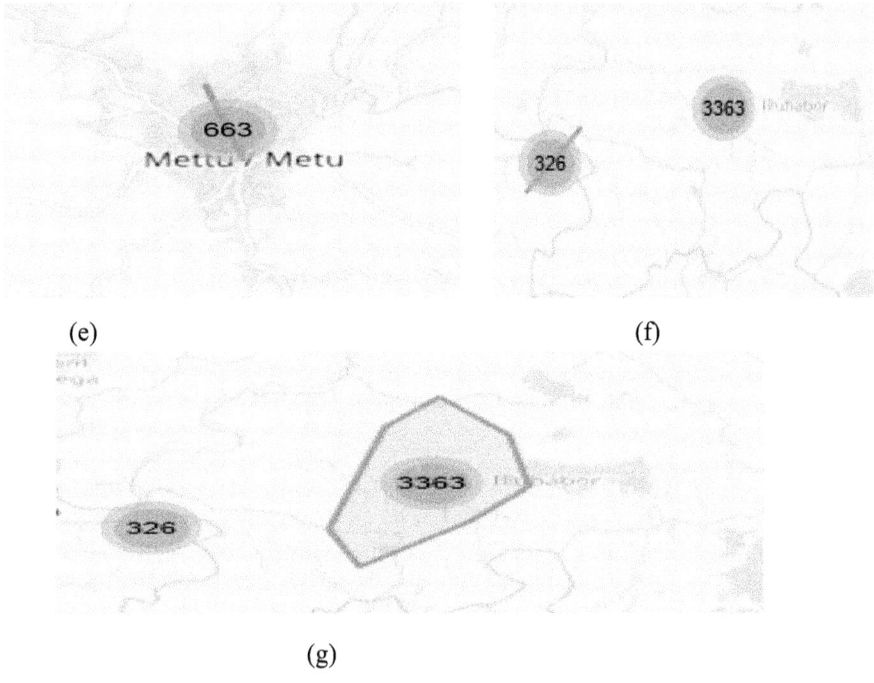

(e)

(f)

(g)

Fig. 2. (*continued*)

The plots shown in Fig. 2 indicate the crime hotspots in Ilu Abba Bor Zone in each district, and the tip of the green line represents the district and the numbers written between them represent the crimes committed in the districts. The approach essentially involves dividing a map into different regions or districts and compiling crime data for these individual areas. Based on the historical data obtained, similar areas with respect to crime rates are clustered together. This includes identifying and bracketing the nearest districts with similar crime rates together into one cluster. This visualization of crime data on a map aids in better crime prediction, enables tailored law enforcement strategies for each cluster, and is highly beneficial for local authorities and law enforcement agencies. This analysis suggests a significant correlation between the location and the likelihood of crime occurrences.

As shown in the map (Fig. 3), the area painted in red indicates the area where crime is most abundant or high, and the area painted in yellow and bright red is the medium of the crime area. The bright yellow area indicates the lowest crime area, while the blue area indicates the very lowest crime area. This will enable the police body to identify crime hotspots and deploy manpower there.

The heat map displayed after clustering based crime Hotspot identification visualizes the concentration and distribution of crime incidents in a specific area. Places with lower crime rates are depicted by cooler hues blue on this map, whereas places with higher concentrations of crime are represented by hotter colors red. The hotspot locations with a

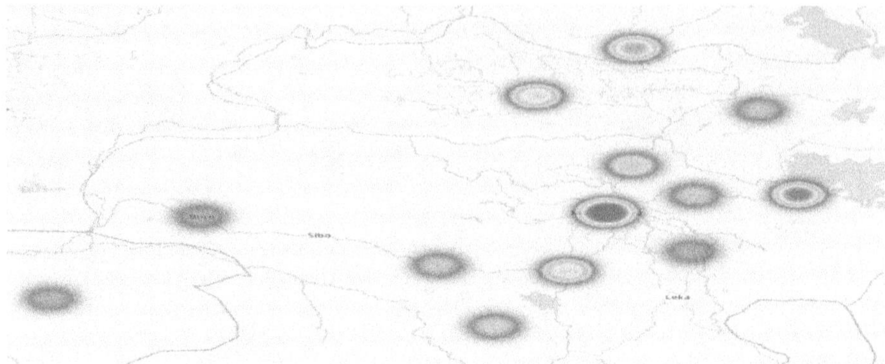

Fig. 3. Crime heats map in Ilu Abba Bor.

notable high concentration of criminal occurrences are represented by the clusters. They support the identification of high-crime areas. By utilizing these hotspots for strategic planning, law enforcement may focus resources where they are most needed. They aid in the identification of areas with a high crime rate. Authorities can use these hotspots for strategic planning, allowing them to concentrate resources where they are most needed. Furthermore, the shift in color from hot too cold on the hits map might offer important information about how criminal episodes are distributed geographically around the area. Blue zones might indicate areas less affected by crime despite their proximity to more crime-prone regions. This could indicate successful crime prevention measures or simply different neighborhood characteristics. Overall, the hits map aids in visual interpretation of complex crime data and supports informed decision-making for law enforcement and public safety officials.

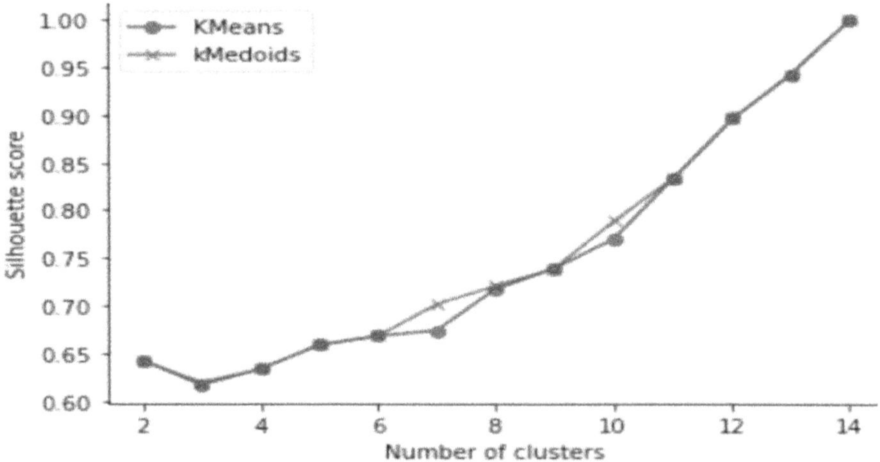

Fig. 4. K-Means and K-Medoids silhouette scores.

Figure 4 shows the accuracy recorded by K-Means and K-Medoids. Both have the same accuracy except that K-Medoids are highest on K3, K7, K8, and K10. Based on this experiment, both have high scores on K14. This data-driven approach allows for a better understanding of spatial and temporal crime patterns, enabling law enforcement agencies to make informed decisions with faster response times to incidents. In this study, we utilized k-means and k-medoids clustering algorithms with a silhouette score of 1 at k = 14, to identify high crime area for crime prediction purposes.

The silhouette score of 1 in both the k-means and k-medoids algorithms indicates that the clustering is well-structured and the geographical locations of the crime instances within the clusters have high cohesion and separation properties. To put it another way, the instances inside the clusters are separated from the instances in adjacent clusters by a greater distance. Due to the fact that this sets the detected hotspots apart from one another in terms of crime occurrences, it renders them incredibly dependable when used in decision-making analyses. Which of the two methods works better for the given data set is impossible to determine, as both the k-means and kmedoids algorithms produced an equal silhouette score of 1 at k = 14., it is difficult to ascertain whether of the two algorithms performs better for the given data set. However, we can discuss their inherent differences. K-means are more sensitive to outliers, while k-medoids are less influenced by the presence of outliers. Furthermore, k-medoids also tend to produce more robust and flexible clusters since it considers the k-medoids as the centroid rather than the mean. The robustness of k-medoids can be particularly useful in highly variable datasets, such as those related to crime occurrences.

5 Conclusions

In this study, we proposed a clustering-based approach in crime Hotspot identification using K-Means and K-Medoids algorithms. Our results and analysis demonstrate that both algorithms are capable of accurately identifying high-crime areas, which helps law enforcement take a more focused and proactive approach. The findings of this research demonstrate the value of clustering-based methods for crime prone is identity in the context of crime prediction. The use of those strategies can contribute to greater powerful prevention techniques and progressed useful resource allocation. Clustering-based crime frequently identification has been widely utilized in crime prediction to provide insights into crime patterns and high-density crime areas.

References

1. ME AND JUSTICE. Int. J. Comput. Eng. Res. Trends. **11**(1), 1689–1699 (2020)
2. He, Z., Lai, R., Wang, Z., Liu, H., Deng, M.: Comparative study of approaches for detecting crime hotspots with considering concentration and shape characteristics (2022)
3. Ali, W.A., Manasa, K.N.: K-MEANS CLUSTERING TECHNIQUE Husam Alalloush EPRA. Int. J. Res. Dev. (IJRD). **7838**(July), 277–280 (2020)
4. Mathew, J.A., Asha, K.: A prognostic approach to crime analysis. In: Adv. Mach. Learn. Big Data Anal., pp. 71–99 (2022)
5. Understanding K-Means, K-Means++ and, K-Medoids Clustering Algorithms I by Satyam Kumar I Towards Data Science

6. Yu, D., Liu, G., Guo, M., Liu, X.: PT US CR. Expert Syst. Appl. (2017). https://doi.org/10. 1016/j.eswa.2017.09.052

7. Zhu, Q., Zhang, F., Liu, S., Li, Y.: An anticrime information support system design: application of K-means-VMD-BiGRU in the city of Chicago. Inf. Manag. **59**(5), 103247 (2022). https:// doi.org/10.1016/j.im.2019.103247

8. Hossain, S., Abtahee, A., Kashem, I., Hoque, M.M., Sarker, I.H.: Crime Prediction Using Spatio-Temporal Data, vol. 1235. Springer, Singapore (2020). https://doi.org/10.1007/978-981-15-6648-6_22

9. Kumar, A., Verma, A., Shinde, G., Sukhdeve, Y., Lal, N.: Crime prediction using K-nearest neighboring algorithm. Int. Conf. Emerg. Trends Inf. Technol. Eng. IC-ETITE. **2020**, 4–7 (2020). https://doi.org/10.1109/ic-ETITE47903.2020.155

10. Cho, N., Kang, Y.: Identifying staying places with global positioning system movement data using 3D density-based spatial clustering of applications with noise. Sensors Mater. **31**(10), 3273–3287 (2019). https://doi.org/10.18494/SAM.2019.2410

11. Hajela, G., Chawla, M., Rasool, A.: A clustering based hotspot identification approach for crime prediction. Procedia Comput. Sci. **167**(2019), 1462–1470 (2020). https://doi.org/10. 1016/j.procs.2020.03.357

12. Wadhai, C.G., Kakade, T.P., Tumsare, D.S., Bokde, K.A., Bhattacharya, D.: Crime detection technique using data mining and k-means. Int. J. Eng. Res. **V7**(2), 223–226 (2018). https:// doi.org/10.17577/ijertv7is020110

13. Kim, S., Joshi, P., Kalsi, P.S., Taheri, P.: Crime analysis through machine learning. In: 2018 IEEE 9th Annu. Inf. Technol. Electron. Mob. Commun. Conf. IEMCON 2018, pp. 415–420 (2019). https://doi.org/10.1109/IEMCON.2018.8614828

14. J. Khyat, M. N. Babu, P. D. Sree, D. S. V. N. Prasad, and C. Science, "Crime type and occurrence prediction using machine," no. 1, pp. 879–886, 2022.

15. Maharana, K., Mondal, S., Nemade, B.: A review: data pre-processing and data augmentation techniques. **3**(April), 91–99 (2022). https://doi.org/10.1016/j.gltp.2022.04.020

16. Performance, C., Metrics, E.: Quick Guide to Evaluation Metrics for Supervised and Unsupervised Machine Learning, no. X

17. Taneja, K.: Toronto Crime Data Analysis using Unsupervised Learning

18. Justice, C., Services, H., Hussein, A.A.: Identifying Crime Hotspot: Evaluating the suitability of Supervised and Unsupervised Machine learning

Quick Incident Reporting with ALRETS to Authorities Using CNN-LSTM

Kalimisetty Sashank[(✉)], Ch Venkata Kalyan Gupta, and R. Vidhya

Department of Computing Technologies, SRM Institute of Science and Technology, Kattankulathur, Chengalpattu, Tamil Nadu, India
{ks8561,vc9380,vidhyar}@srmist.edu.in

Abstract. Advanced system leverages digital technologies and real-time communication channels to enable swift reporting of various incidents, ranging from accidents and criminal activities to potential threats and emergencies. Individuals or eyewitnesses can easily report incidents using mobile applications or online platforms, providing crucial details such as the nature of the incident, location, and any relevant multimedia attachments. Upon receiving a report, the system automatically triggers alerts to relevant authorities, including law enforcement agencies, emergency responders, and security personnel, facilitating rapid response and intervention. Key features of the system include geolocation tagging, which enables precise identification of incident locations, and multimedia attachment capabilities, allowing users to provide additional context through images, videos, or audio recordings. To safeguard user privacy and encourage reporting, the system also offers options for anonymous reporting, ensuring that individuals feel comfortable sharing information without fear of retribution. Moreover, the system incorporates advanced analytics tools and data visualization techniques to analyze incident patterns, identify trends, and optimize resource allocation for better incident management and prevention. By deploying quick incident reporting with alerts to authorities, organizations and communities can significantly enhance their ability to respond to incidents in a timely manner, thereby reducing potential risks and improving overall safety and security. This proactive approach to incident reporting not only facilitates faster response times but also enables authorities to take preventive measures based on real-time data analysis. From urban areas to educational institutions, transportation networks, and corporate environments, the implementation of this system can lead to more effective incident management and better protection of public welfare.

Keywords: Swift reporting · Real-time communication · Incident management · Geolocation tagging · Multimedia Attachment · Anonymous reporting

1 Introduction

As technology advances at an unstoppable rate, protecting people's safety and security as individuals and as a community has become more important than ever. The widespread adoption of digital technology and real-time communication channels presents a unique

R. Appavoo et al. (Eds.): IconDeepCom 2024, CCIS 2687, pp. 473–485, 2026.
https://doi.org/10.1007/978-3-032-26680-4_37

opportunity to completely transform the process of reporting and managing problems. Enterprising enterprises and communities are utilizing these improvements to create sophisticated systems that facilitate rapid reporting of different situations, along with automatic notifications to relevant authorities. This proactive approach to incident reporting marks a paradigm leap in the field of safety and security, promising not only shorter reaction times but also the possibility of preventive steps based on real-time data analysis.

At the heart of this revolutionary approach is the seamless integration of digital platforms and mobile applications, which allows individuals or eyewitnesses to report incidents quickly and effectively. The capacity to communicate vital information—such as the nature of the incident, its exact position, and any multimedia attachments that may be attached—ensures that authorities have all the information they need to respond quickly to any emergencies, criminal activity, or accidents. Geolocation tagging, which enables accurate identification of event locations and speeds up response operations, supports this shortened reporting procedure.

The fact that these sophisticated systems put user privacy and security first and provide channels for anonymous reporting helps allay fears of reprisals or reluctance to come forward with information. By promoting trust and secrecy, these systems create a culture where people actively report incidents, enabling individuals to contribute to the overall safety and well-being of their communities.

In addition, the integration of sophisticated analytics tools and data visualization techniques provides authorities with the capacity to evaluate patterns of incidents, identify trends, and optimize the allocation of resources for more efficient incident management and prevention. By utilizing data-driven insights, decision-makers may strategically allocate resources, perform precise actions, and minimize risks before they erupt into crises.

The implementation of efficient incident reporting systems with immediate notifications to authorities has the potential to improve safety and security in various settings, including busy cities, educational institutions, transportation networks, and corporate environments. By adopting this proactive strategy, organizations and communities can strengthen their ability to withstand emerging challenges, reduce possible dangers, and protect the welfare of their members. The constant need to harness technology's potential for societal benefit drives the development and uptake of sophisticated incident reporting systems as it continues to advance.

2 Literature Review

[1] S. Vosta and K. -C. Yow published a paper titled "KianNet: A Violence Detection Model Using an Attention-Based CNN-LSTM Structure" in the journal *IEEE Access*. The paper was published in volume 12, pages 2198–2209, in the year 2024. The paper's DOI is 10.1109/ACCESS.2023.3339379. This study highlights the perpetual significance of violent behavior, which poses a significant threat to any civilization. Consequently, numerous firms have employed surveillance cameras to oversee these occurrences in order to safeguard public safety and reduce potential damage. In addition, the multi-head self-attention layer improves the model's capability to concentrate on important spatiotemporal areas and their ability to differentiate. Empirical studies validate

that the suggested model surpasses its rivals by almost 10%, attaining a 97.48% AUC on binary classification on the UCF-Crime dataset, and a 96.21% accuracy on the RWF dataset, outperforming Violence 4D.

[2] Umeike, Robinson. "Assessing the Tools and Addressing the Threats: Comparative Crime Analysis and Prediction Utilizing Machine Learning Algorithms." The year is 2023. The 35th International Conference on Tools with Artificial Intelligence (ICTAI) organized by the Institute of Electrical and Electronics Engineers (IEEE). The publication date of the IEEE article is 2023. This paper performs a comparative assessment of four predictive supervised learning algorithms. These algorithms utilize socio-economic and demographic characteristics obtained from community event reports to make predictions about crime. The objective is to predict criminal incidents classified into four categories: crimes, misdemeanors, infractions, and violations, for the entire year of 2022.

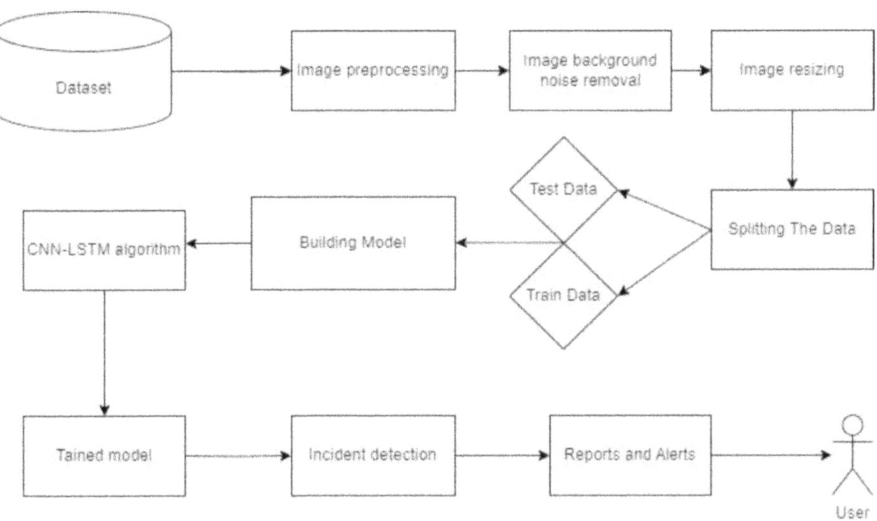

Fig. 1. Architecture Diagram of Quick Incident Reporting

[3] In their article titled "Propounding First Artificial Intelligence Approach for Predicting Robbery Behavior Potential in an Indoor Security Camera," S. Pouyan, M. Charmi, A. Azarpeyvand, and H. Hassanpoor present a novel method for forecasting the likelihood of robbery behavior using artificial intelligence. The research is published in IEEE Access, volume 11, pages 60471–60489, in the year 2023. The article can be accessed through the DOI: 10.1109/ACCESS.2023.3284472. The imperative of crime prediction in video-surveillance systems is crucial in order to preempt occurrences and protect assets. Our paper presents a novel artificial intelligence approach for forecasting and identifying Robbery Behavior Potential (RBP) utilizing an interior camera. The foundation of our solution relies on three detection modules: head cover detection, crowd detection, and loitering detection. These modules are essential for promptly implementing preventive actions and preventing robberies. The initial two modules are created by

retraining the YOLOV5 model with our meticulously annotated dataset. This innovative technique highlights the capacity of artificial intelligence (AI) to improve security measures. A fuzzy inference machine utilizes expert knowledge to generate rules that are subsequently employed to make a conclusive determination regarding the anticipated likelihood of a robbery. The complexity of this procedure arises from the diverse actions exhibited by robbers, the several perspectives captured by surveillance cameras, and the limited resolution of video images. Our investigation utilized authentic video surveillance photos and yielded an F1-score of 0.537, indicating the efficacy of our methodology (Fig. 1).

3   Proposed Module

3.1   Data Collection

Gather diverse incident data sources, including images, sensor data, text reports, and other relevant information. Ensure data represent various types of incidents and encompass spatial and temporal aspects.

3.2   Data Preprocessing

Standardize data formats and representations for consistency. Perform preprocessing steps such as resizing images, normalizing sensor readings, and tokenizing text data. Split data into training, validation, and test sets.

3.3   Model Design

Design a CNN-LSTM architecture tailored to the project's objectives. Configure CNN layers for feature extraction from spatial data, considering appropriate filter sizes, strides, and pooling operations. Integrate LSTM layers to capture temporal dependencies, specifying the number of hidden units and dropout rates.

3.4   Model Training

Initialize model weights using appropriate initialization techniques. Train the CNN-LSTM model on the training dataset using optimization algorithms. Utilize techniques like early stopping and learning rate scheduling to prevent overfitting and improve convergence. Monitor performance metrics on the validation set to guide training progress.

3.5   Model Evaluation

Evaluate the trained CNN-LSTM model on the test dataset to assess its generalization performance. Measure classification accuracy, precision, recall, and F1-score for each incident type. Analyze confusion matrices to identify common misclassifications and areas for improvement.

3.6 Alerting System Integration

Develop an alerting system to trigger notifications to relevant authorities based on model predictions. Implement thresholds or rules for determining when to generate alerts (e.g., confidence scores, anomaly detection). Ensure seamless integration with existing incident reporting and response frameworks.

3.7 Validation and Testing

Validate the CNN-LSTM model in real-world scenarios, considering factors like data variability, noise, and environmental conditions. Conduct user acceptance testing (UAT) to ensure the alerting system meets the requirements and expectations of end-users and authorities.

3.8 Deployment and Monitoring

Deploy the trained CNN-LSTM model and alerting system in operational environments. Monitor system performance, including model accuracy, latency, and false alarm rates. Implement mechanisms for continuous model monitoring, retraining, and updating to adapt to evolving incident patterns and data distributions.

4 Methodology

The "Quick Incident Reporting with Alerts to Authorities" project proposes the utilization of a sophisticated CNN-LSTM model to revolutionize incident reporting and response mechanisms. This model amalgamates Convolutional Neural Networks (CNN) and Long Short-Term Memory (LSTM) networks, capitalizing on their complementary strengths to enable swift, accurate, and proactive incident management.

At the core of the proposed CNN-LSTM model lies its ability to efficiently process and analyze multi-modal incident data streams. The CNN component is tasked with extracting spatial features from diverse data sources, including images, sensor readings, and textual information. Leveraging its hierarchical architecture of convolutional and pooling layers, the CNN adeptly discerns spatial patterns, identifying critical visual cues and spatial relationships indicative of different types of incidents.

Complementing CNN, the LSTM network is employed to capture the temporal dynamics inherent in incident sequences. As a specialized form of recurrent neural network, LSTM excels at modeling sequential dependencies over time, enabling the model to understand the evolution and progression of incidents. By retaining long-term memory and selectively updating information through gated units, LSTM effectively tracks the temporal context of incidents, facilitating nuanced analysis and decision-making.

Through seamless integration, the CNN-LSTM model synthesizes spatial and temporal information, offering a holistic perspective on incident data. This synergistic fusion enables the model to capture both the static and dynamic aspects of incidents, enhancing its ability to discriminate between different incident types and severity levels. Furthermore, joint training of the CNN-LSTM architecture facilitates adaptive learning, allowing the model to continuously refine its understanding of evolving incident patterns and improve its predictive capabilities.

In practical application, the CNN-LSTM model serves as the cornerstone of an intelligent incident reporting and alerting system. Real-time incident data from various sources are fed into the model, which promptly analyzes and classifies the incidents based on their spatial and temporal characteristics. Upon detection of anomalous events or potential incidents, the model triggers automated alerts to relevant authorities, enabling swift response and mitigation efforts.

Overall, the CNN-LSTM model represents a paradigm shift in incident reporting and response mechanisms, offering unprecedented speed, accuracy, and efficiency in identifying and managing incidents. By harnessing the power of deep learning and neural network architectures, this innovative approach has the potential to revolutionize the way incidents are detected, reported, and addressed, ultimately enhancing public safety and security (Fig. 2).

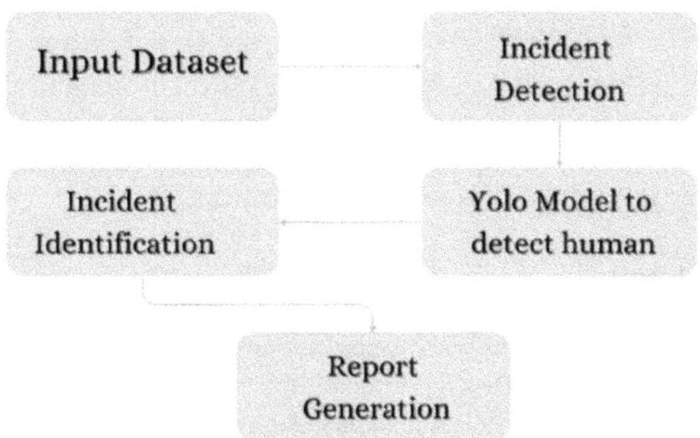

Fig. 2. workflow of CNN-LSTM model

4.1 Input Dataset

Various incident data sources, including images, sensor readings, textual reports, and other relevant information, are collected. Ensure the dataset represents a diverse range of incidents and encompasses spatial and temporal aspects.

4.2 Incident Detection

Initially, the input dataset undergoes incident detection, where potential incidents are identified from the collected data. Techniques such as anomaly detection, pattern recognition, or threshold-based methods may be employed for preliminary incident detection.

4.3 CNN-LSTM Model for Human Detection

Once potential incidents are detected, the data is passed through the CNN-LSTM model, specifically trained for human detection within incident scenes. The CNN component of the model extracts spatial features from images or video frames, focusing on identifying human presence and activity. Simultaneously, the LSTM component captures temporal dependencies, enabling the model to track human movements and behavior over time (Fig. 3).

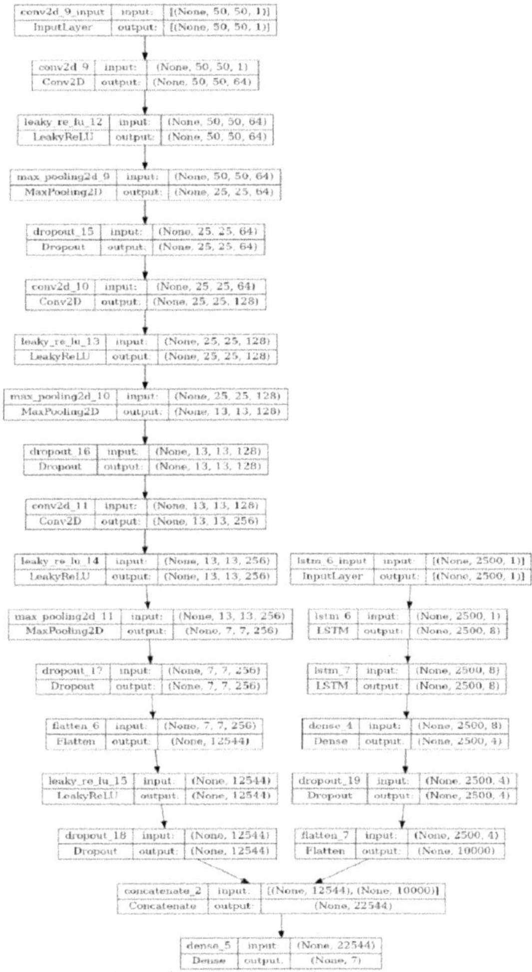

Fig. 3. Model Plot for CNN-LSTM

4.4   Incident Identification

Based on the output of the CNN-LSTM model, incidents involving human presence or suspicious activities are identified. The model classifies incidents into predefined categories or severity levels, such as accidents, crimes, or emergencies, based on learned patterns and features.

4.5 Report Generation

Once incidents are identified, a report generation module compiles relevant information about the incident. This information may include the incident type, location, timestamp, severity, and any additional contextual details extracted from the input data. Reports may be generated in various formats suitable for communication with authorities, such as text reports, visual summaries, or structured data formats.

4.6 Detailed Workflow

Input data, comprising images, sensor data, and textual reports, is fed into the system. Initial incident detection techniques are applied to identify potential incidents within the dataset. Data containing potential incidents is then processed through the CNN-LSTM model, which focuses on human detection within incident scenes. The CNN component extracts spatial features to identify human presence and activity, while the LSTM component captures temporal dependencies to track human movements over time.

Overall, the workflow of the CNN-LSTM model in "Quick Incident Reporting with Alerts to Authorities" enables efficient incident detection, human presence recognition, incident classification, and report generation, facilitating timely response and intervention by authorities.

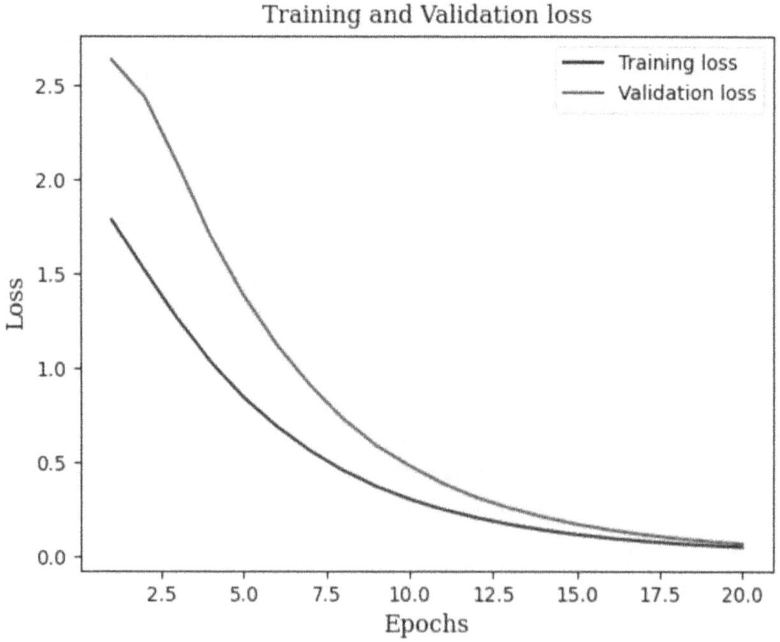

Fig. 4. Training and Validation Loss Graph

5   Results

The CNN-LSTM model successfully processes diverse incident data sources, including images, sensor readings, and textual reports, to detect potential incidents with high accuracy. Techniques such as anomaly detection and pattern recognition, combined with the CNN-LSTM model's human detection capabilities, enable the identification of incidents involving human presence or suspicious activities.

The model effectively classifies incidents into predefined categories or severity levels, such as accidents, crimes, or emergencies, based on learned patterns and features extracted from the input data. This classification facilitates quick and accurate incident identification, enabling timely response and intervention by authorities.

Moreover, the report generation module compiles detailed reports containing incident type, location, timestamp, and additional contextual details, providing comprehensive information for communication with authorities.

Overall, the CNN-LSTM model in "Quick Incident Reporting with Alerts to Authorities" demonstrates efficient incident detection, human presence recognition, incident classification, and report generation capabilities, enhancing the ability of authorities to respond promptly to incidents and ensure public safety.

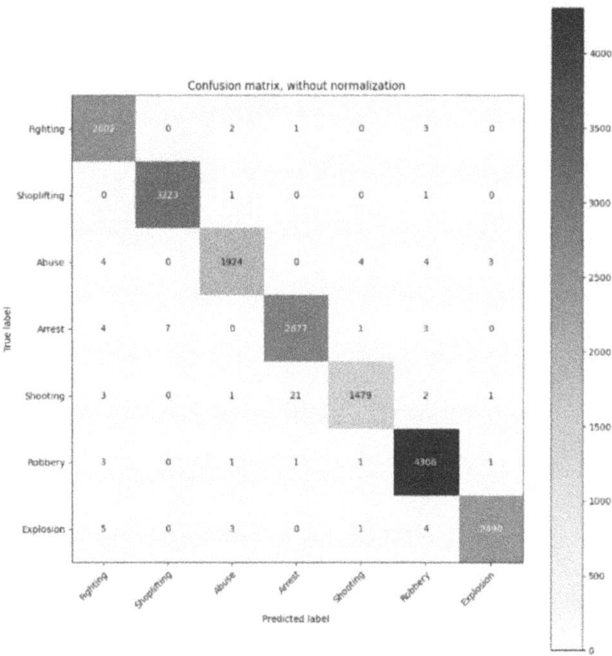

Fig. 5. Confusion Matrix without Normalization

The implementation of efficient incident reporting systems with immediate notifications to authorities has the potential to improve safety and security in various settings, including busy cities, educational institutions, transportation networks, and corporate environments. By adopting this proactive strategy, organizations and communities can strengthen their ability to withstand emerging challenges, reduce possible dangers, and protect the welfare of their members. The constant need to harness technology's potential for societal benefit drives the development and uptake of sophisticated incident reporting systems as it continues to advance (Fig. 4, 5, 6 and 7).

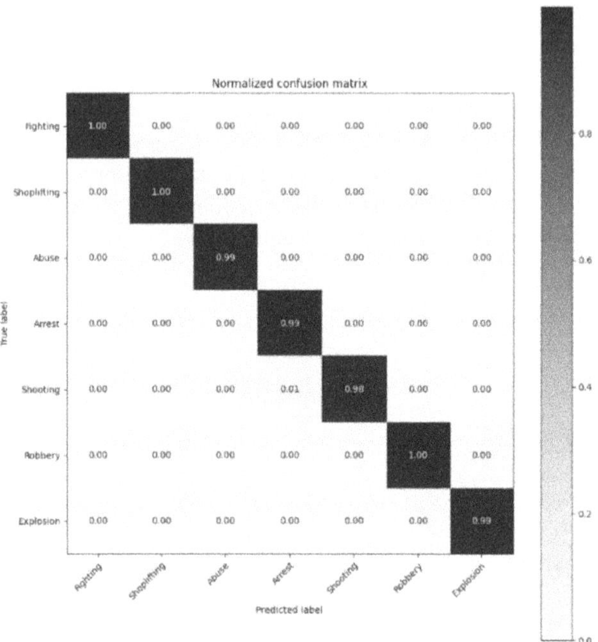

Fig. 6. Confusion Matrix with Normalization

The report generated from the incident is given below

Fig. 7. Incident Report with time, location and category

6 Conclusion

In conclusion, the implementation of a rapid incident reporting system, augmented with automated alerts to authorities, represents a significant step forward in enhancing incident detection, classification, and response mechanisms. By integrating powerful technologies such as CNN-LSTM, the system achieves remarkable precision in identifying incidents and categorizing them accurately. The fusion of textual analysis through CNN and object detection via LSTM enables a comprehensive understanding of reported situations, enriching incident representations and improving response strategies. Additionally, the system's automated notification mechanism ensures timely and focused responses from relevant authorities, effectively reducing response times and mitigating potential risks.

The provision of anonymous reporting options fosters user engagement and participation, further bolstering the system's effectiveness in encouraging proactive incident reporting within communities. Furthermore, the scalability and robustness of the system across diverse scenarios underscore its adaptability to evolving threats and technological advancements, ensuring its long-term efficacy in upholding public safety and security. Overall, the rapid incident reporting system with automated alerts to authorities represents a pivotal advancement in incident management, empowering authorities with real-time insights and enabling swift and efficient responses to ensure the safety and well-being of communities.

7 Future Developmets

The rapid incident reporting system with automated alerts to authorities serves as a pivotal advancement in incident management and public safety, laying a strong foundation for future developments and expansions. Moving forward, there are several potential avenues for further scope and enhancement in this project. Firstly, continuous refinement and optimization of artificial intelligence algorithms, including convolutional neural networks (CNN) and LSTM, can lead to significant improvements in incident detection accuracy and classification. Future research may focus on developing more sophisticated deep learning models capable of better understanding and interpreting complex incident scenarios. Additionally, integrating emerging technologies such as natural language processing (NLP), sentiment analysis, and reinforcement learning can augment the capabilities of the system by extracting deeper insights from incident reports and improving decision-making processes.

Furthermore, leveraging real-time data analytics techniques can enable the system to process and analyze incident reports more efficiently, reducing latency and providing instantaneous insights into emerging incidents. By incorporating geospatial analysis and visualization tools, authorities can better understand and visualize incident hotspots, trends, and patterns, leading to more effective resource allocation. Integrating the system with mobile and wearable technology platforms can improve the accessibility and timeliness of incident reporting, enabling citizens to report incidents directly from their smartphones or wearable devices. Moreover, promoting community engagement and collaboration through social media platforms and crowd-sourcing initiatives can foster a sense of shared responsibility for public safety and enhance the effectiveness of the system.

Expanding the application of the rapid incident reporting system beyond traditional emergency response scenarios to other domains such as healthcare, transportation, and environmental monitoring can unlock new opportunities for enhancing safety and security across various sectors. In conclusion, the future scope of the rapid incident reporting system is vast and promising. By embracing advancements in technology, data analytics, and community engagement, the system can continue to evolve and adapt to meet the dynamic challenges of incident management and public safety in the digital age.

References

1. Vosta, S., Yow, K.C.: KianNet: a violence detection model using an attention-based CNN-LSTM structure. IEEE Access. **12**, 2198–2209 (2023a)
2. Marivate, V., Moiloa, P.: Catching crime: detection of public safety incidents using social media. In: 2016 Pattern Recognition Association of South Africa and Robotics and Mechatronics International Conference (PRASA-RobMech). IEEE (2016)
3. Mantoro, T., et al.: Location-aware mobile crime information framework for fast tracking response to accidents and crimes in big cities. In: 2014 3rd International Conference on Advanced Computer Science Applications and Technologies. IEEE (2014)
4. Wang, X., Brown, D.E., Gerber, M.S.: Spatio-temporal modeling of criminal incidents using geographic, demographic, and twitter-derived information. In: 2012 IEEE International Conference on Intelligence and Security Informatics. IEEE (2012)
5. Chatzigeorgiou, C., et al.: A communication gateway architecture for ensuring privacy and confidentiality in incident reporting. In: 2017 IEEE 15th International Conference on Software Engineering Research, Management and Applications (SERA). IEEE (2017)
6. Shih, T.-F., et al.: A cloud-based crime reporting system with identity protection. Symmetry. **11**(2), 255 (2019)

7. Bhatti, F., et al.: A novel internet of things-enabled accident detection and reporting system for smart city environments. Sensors. **19**(9), 2071 (2019)
8. Minhas, U.I., et al.: A WSN for monitoring and event reporting in underground mine environments. IEEE Syst. J. **12**(1), 485–496 (2017)
9. Zhang, X., Mahadevan, S.: Bayesian network modeling of accident investigation reports for aviation safety assessment. Reliab. Eng. Syst. Saf. **209**, 107371 (2021)
10. Chang, W.-J., Chen, L.-B., Su, K.-Y.: DeepCrash: a deep learning-based internet of vehicles system for head-on and single-vehicle accident detection with emergency notification. IEEE Access. **7**, 148163–148175 (2019)
11. Vosta, S., Yow, K.-C.: KianNet: a violence detection model using an attention-based CNN-LSTM structure. IEEE Access. (2023)
12. Dar, B.K., et al.: Delay-aware accident detection and response system using fog computing. IEEE Access. **7**, 70975–70985 (2019)
13. Priya, B.J., Kunda, P., Kumar, S.: Design and implementation of smart real-time billing, GSM, and GPS-based theft monitoring and accident notification systems. In: Proceedings of International Conference on Recent Trends in Machine Learning, IoT, Smart Cities and Applications: ICMISC 2020. Springer Singapore (2021)
14. Deng, F., et al.: Hazardous chemical accident prevention based on k-means clustering analysis of incident information. IEEE Access. **8**, 180171–180183 (2020)
15. Gu, J., et al.: Efficient incident identification from multi-dimensional issue reports via meta-heuristic search. In: Proceedings of the 28th ACM Joint Meeting on European Software Engineering Conference and Symposium on the Foundations of Software Engineering (2020)
16. Umeike, R.: Comparative crime analysis and prediction using machine learning algorithms: assessing the tools and addressing the threats. In: 2023 IEEE 35th International Conference on Tools with Artificial Intelligence (ICTAI). IEEE (2023)
17. Shetty, S., et al.: SafeRoute: analysing online websites to indicate crime zones using machine learning and suggest safe route. In: 2023 14th International Conference on Computing Communication and Networking Technologies (ICCCNT). IEEE (2023)
18. Pouyan, S., et al.: Propounding first artificial intelligence approach for predicting robbery behavior potential in an indoor security camera. IEEE Access. (2023)
19. Krishna, U.V., et al.: Accident prediction and analysis using machine learning models. In: 2023 International Conference on Innovative Data Communication Technologies and Application (ICIDCA). IEEE (2023)
20. Ahn, Y.-J., Yu, Y.-U., Kim, J.-K.: Accident cause factor of fires and explosions in tankers using fault tree analysis. J. Mar. Sci. Eng. **9**(8), 844 (2021)

Enhanced CNN Based Deep Learning Model for Tomato Leaf Disease Detection

Thammisetty Swetha[(✉)] [iD], Pakanati Shiva Kumar Goud [iD],
Thokala Vishnu Vardhan [iD], Balam Supriya [iD], Bijivemula Sumanth Kumar Reddy [iD],
and Chakkera Sai Prasanna [iD]

Department of Computer Science & Engineering (Data Science), Madanapalle Institute of
Technology & Science, Madanapalle, Andhra Pradesh, India
swethathammisetty7@gmail.com

Abstract. Tomatoes (Solanum lycopersicum), which originated in South America, are now widely grown around the world. India is one of the largest producers and consumers of tomatoes. But also, this crop is widely affected by various diseases like bacterial spots, early blight, and late blight, which result in huge loss for cultivators. So early detection and preventive measures can have a good result in increasing the yield of tomatoes. In this study, we have proposed CNN (convolutional neural networks). A model involving image preprocessing and data augmentation by taking a dataset that comprises a total of 10000 images belonging to 10 different classes, which resulted in an overall 98.6% train accuracy and 97.78% test accuracy This study will be useful for the early detection of disease, making it user-friendly and cost-efficient for all farmers.

Keywords: Solanum lycopersicum · CNN · Accuracy · Precision · Recall

1 Introduction

Precision farming and smart agriculture, which use cutting-edge technologies to increase crop yield and losses, have revolutionized agriculture in recent years. Tomato (Solanum lycopersicum) being a key component in food supply, face challenges numerous challenges posed by various diseases like Bacterial spot, early blight, late blight, leaf mold, septoria leaf spot, spider mite, target spot, mosaic virus, yellow leaf curl virus. Which impacts its quality and yield. For effective crop management to be implemented, early detection and prevention of these diseases are essential. Conventional techniques for identifying tomato plant diseases frequently depend on inspection, which is laborious and prone to human mistake. Using state-of-the-art technology like deep learning has become a viable way to automate and enhance precise disease prediction in the age of digital agriculture In order to give farmers an effective tool, this research focuses on the use of deep learning algorithms for the detection of tomato leaf diseases. A subset of machine learning is called deep learning that deals with image recognition tasks, making it ideal for the intricate and aesthetically unique characteristics of plant diseases. The deep learning model class known as convolutional neural networks (CNNs), which was

R. Appavoo et al. (Eds.): IconDeepCom 2024, CCIS 2687, pp. 486–499, 2026.
https://doi.org/10.1007/978-3-032-26680-4_38

developed for image analysis, are used in our suggested methodology to extract complex patterns and characteristics from 10,000 photos of tomato leaves that are divided into nine illness classes and one health class. By using a variety of datasets to train the model, the model learns and predict the various diseases. The main purpose of this study is to offer disease identification, allowing farmers to implement effective methods, minimize crop losses and identify the disease leaves. Additionally, deep learning models facilitate their integration into existing agricultural technologies, paving the way for real time monitoring and decision making. Coming to dataset we have retrieved it from the Kaggle dataset source and developed a CNN model to classify the images. Figure 1 Information About Classes in Dataset. The performance of the model has been analyzed for training accuracy and validation accuracy. Table 1 shows the parameters used in model, The subsequent paper is as follows Related work, About Dataset, proposed methodology, Experimental analysis followed by conclusion.

2 Related Work

Shengyi zhao [1] et al. used CNN network integrated into SE-ResNet50 model for the diagnosis of tomato leaf disease. Hande Yukel Bayram [2] et al. used six different Convolutional Neural Network (CNN) consists of classification task carried out by pre-defined models and Neighbourhood Component Analysis (NCA) is applied for feature map extraction, the average accuracy was 99.50%. Naresh K.trivedi [3] et al. used 3000 images and retrieved features from images, such as edges, colors, and textures, and his suggested model's predictions are 98.49% accurate. P Sreelatha [4] et al. employed deep learning neural networks, or DNNs, and the accuracy of the suggested model was 86.18%. Keke Zhang [5] et al. used ResNet(stochastic gradient) with batch size of 16 with a fully connected layer of iterations up to 4992 and accuracy was 97.28%. Yang wu [6] et al. suggested an intelligent automation system called a DCNN (Deep Learning Convolutional Network). Usama Mokhtar [7] et al. used SVM Machine Learning Algorithm with 100 image samples and accuracy was 99.5%. Princi Rani [8] et al. also performed Disease Detection of Tomato leaves using SVM and acquired accuracy was 95%. Nazam Nahar [9] et al. used predefined models of CNN like MobileNet and DenseNet both were ensembled with 16,035 images and accuracy was 98.21%. Emine Cengil [10] et al. proposed Hybrid convolutional neural network using AlexNet, ResNet50 and VGG16. Ended up with accuracy of training and testing −98.38% and 96.3% respectively. Alvaro Fuentes [11] et al. proposed a CNN model for plant disease recognition in real-field scenarios. Mohit Agarwal [12] et al. proposed CNN with 3 convolutional layers with an accuracy of 91.2%. Juncheng Ma [13] et al. used CART (Classification and Regression Tree Algorithm) and resulted with 90.67% accuracy. Thair A Salih [14] et al. proposed CNN model for Tomato Leaf Disease classification and acquired accuracy of 96.43%. Aliasghar Mortazi and Ulas Bagci [15] et al. designed CNN architectures for medical image segmentation using image segmentation. M Kaushik [16] et al. used predefined CNN model ResNet with data augmentation of images and produced 4 times more than the actual dataset with acquired accuracy of 97%. Yuhua Li Zhihui Luo [17] et al. proposed an Extended collaborative representation (ECR) on cucumber disease. Konstantinos P Ferentinos [18] et al. Proposed CNN model using 58 classes comprised of 87,848 images, with an accuracy of 99.53%. Parul Sharma [19] et al. suggested a CNN and F-CNN model for self-classification with 98.6% accuracy. Muhammad EH Chowdhury [20] et al. suggested an automatic detection model with 99.89% accuracy using EfficientNet-B4. Antonio Guerrero-Ibanez [21] et al. proposed CNN model with 99% accuracy. Mchdhar SAM AI-gaashani [22] proposed CNN model which extracts features using pre-trained kernels weights from MobileNetV2, NesNetMobile using Regression with accuracy of 974%. Prajwala Tm [23] et al. used CNN predefined model Lenet and acquired 95%. Natheer Khasawnch [24] et al. proposed CNN model using 9 different classes and acquired 99.4% accuracy. Channamallikarjuna Mattihalli [25] et al. proposed automation detecting plant leaf disease. As per the previous model proposed by keke Zhang [5] overall Training, Testing accuracy was 96.51% and 97.19%.

Also, our proposed model's performance was 98.6% for training and 97.78% for testing. As of we have reduced the data complexity of the images but while dealing with more image's integration of Resnet50 and CNN outperforms more while compared to other neural networks.

3   Proposed Methodology

In our study, we started our analysis on tomato leaf disease prediction by collecting dataset form the database of Kaggle [5], where the data is already pre-processed without the need of feature engineering. The dataset contains nearly 41127 images of tomato leaf disease. out of them, 10000 images, 1000 per class are collected for our analysis to increase model efficiency and to reduce model complexity in such a way that the model gives higher performance, where each layer of model is trained. Model description is illustrated in Table 1. And Types of leaf classes used is shown in Fig. 1.

Table 1. Model parameters description.

Model Parameters	Value
Conv_2d	6
Total Parameters	184202
Trainable Parameters	184202
Non-Trainable Params	0
Optimizer	Adam
Metrics	Accuracy
Epochs	25, 50
Batch_size	32

It is commonly used for preprocessing the input images before feeding them into a neural network, Data Augmentation (Horizontal Flip(20%), Random Zoom (20%), and Rotation(30°), where images are randomly flipped both horizontally and vertically. It creates augmented versions of the original images. Random rotation is Done to introduce

Fig. 1. Types of leaf samples taken for experiment.

variability in the orientation of the Images. The Zoom factor is sampled uniformly from the range [0.3,0.2].

   Augmentation techniques are often used to broaden the range of training data for neural networks and improve its dependability and effectiveness in generalizing unseen input. CNN model of Six Convolutional Layers with different filter sizes and activation functions -Each layer extracts features from the input images using convolutional operations – The first layer has 32 filters with a 3x3 kernel, followed by 64 filters in subsequent layers. Rectified Linear Unit, or ReLU, is the activation function that is employed. After each convolutional layer, the feature maps are down-sampled using max pooling layers. The spatial dimensions will be cut in half with the pooling window size of (2,2). The

2D feature maps are transformed into a 1D vector via the flattened layer. It will get the data ready for the levels that are fully connected. There are 64 units with the Relu activation function in the first dense layer, which consists of two fully connected layers. The second dense layer has ten units with a SoftMax function. The final layer produces class probabilities for ten output classes (classification task).

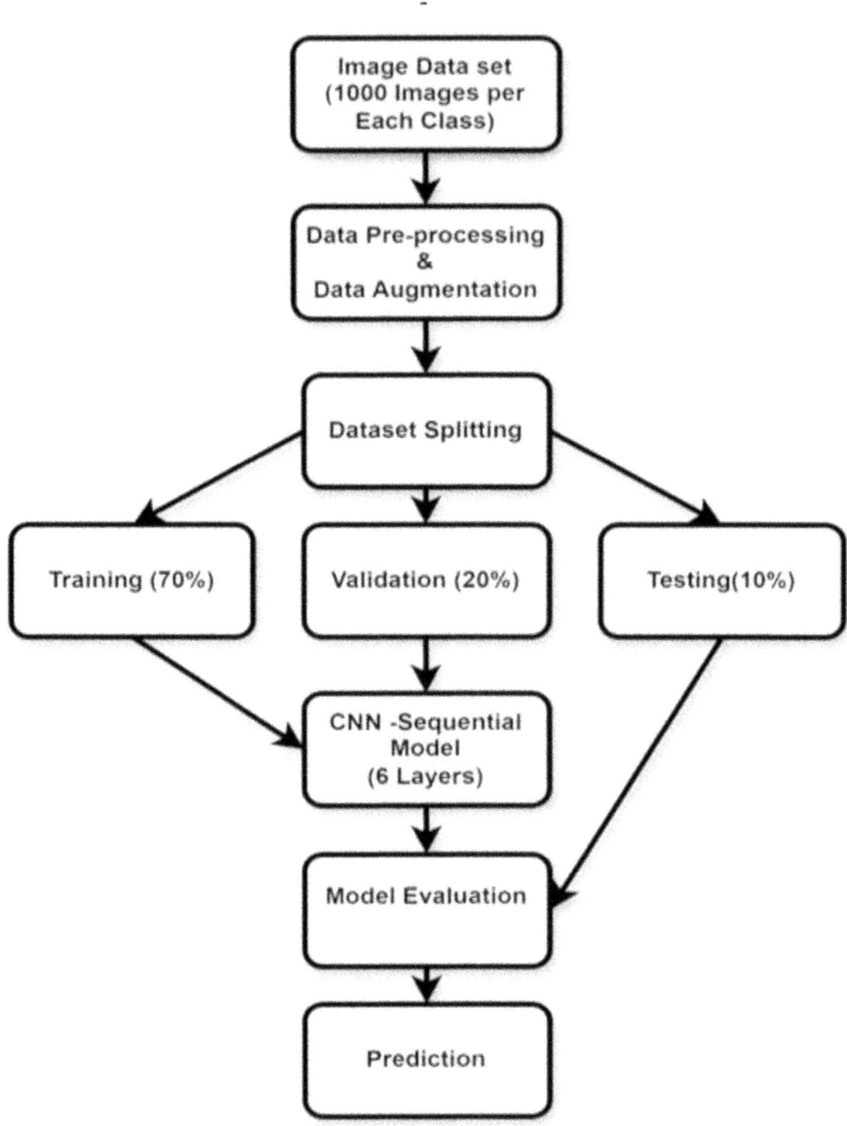

Fig. 2. Proposed Methodology.

During model compilation, The adaptive learning rate optimization algorithm known as the Adam optimizer was employed. A loss function appropriate for multiclass classification tasks with integer target labels is sparse categorical cross entropy. The metric used is Accuracy during training, which measures how often the model's prediction matches the actual labels. Using epochs 25 and 50, the model iterates over the entire training dataset 25 to 50 times. It gives validation accuracy and loss of batch size 32. Subsequently, the evaluation is done on the test dataset to gauge the model's effectiveness. where the Actual and Predicted classes will be used to compute the precision, recall, accuracy, and F1-score. In summary, our comprehensive approach to image classification and detecting diseased leaf images encompasses data pre-processing, data augmentation, feature extraction, model training, and evaluating the model using the test dataset (10%) of the overall dataset. This is the Architecture of the proposed model as shown in Fig. 2.

4 Experimental Analysis

The present part represents the results of our investigation into the detection and classification of tomato leaf diseases using CNNs (Convolutional Neural Networks) for tomato leaf disease detection and classification. The experiment was carried out on an Intel Core i7 system with 32 GB of RAM, using various Machine Learning and Deep Learning libraries in the Jupyter web application environment. Our analysis of this research involved three main phases. Firstly, we collected 10,000 images of 10 different classes and resized them to 256 X 256 pixels each. We then performed data preprocessing to normalize the images and applied methods for data augmentation to increase the training data's diversity. We separated the Image Dataset into three groups for the second phase: 70% for Training, 20% for Validation, and 10% for Testing. Six convolutional layers and max-pooling layers were used to generate a CNN sequential model, which was then flattened and made dense using the SoftMax function. We used the optimizer adam and epochs 25 and 50 to reduce the rate of data loss for both training and validation as viewed in Figs. 3 and 4. Accuracy of both Training and Validation is 98.08% and 98.96% respectively.

In the third phase, we evaluated the model's performance and outcomes by calculating the Classification Report's confusion matrix (Table 2).

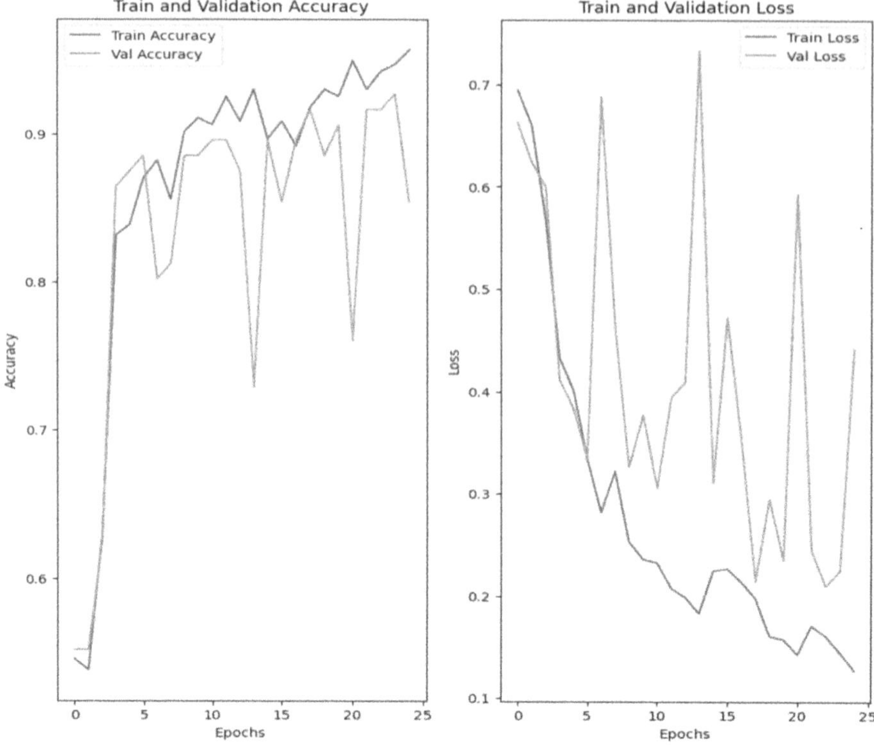

Fig. 3. Accuracy v/s Loss (25 Epochs) for Training and Validation.

4.1 Confusion Matrix

A tabular form used to assess the model is called a confusion matrix. It summarizes a model's actual and anticipated labels. The actual and anticipated labels for ten classes are shown in Fig. 5.

4.2 Classification Report

Accuracy: The percentage of accurately anticipated cases to all instances is its definition (Fig. 6).

$$Accuracy = \frac{Number\ of\ Correct\ Predicitons}{Total\ Number\ of\ Predicitons} \times 100 \tag{1}$$

Precision: Precision can be expressed as the ratio of actual positive predictions to all expected positive occurrences (Fig. 7).

$$Precision = \frac{True\ Positives}{True\ Positives + False\ Positives} \times 100 \tag{2}$$

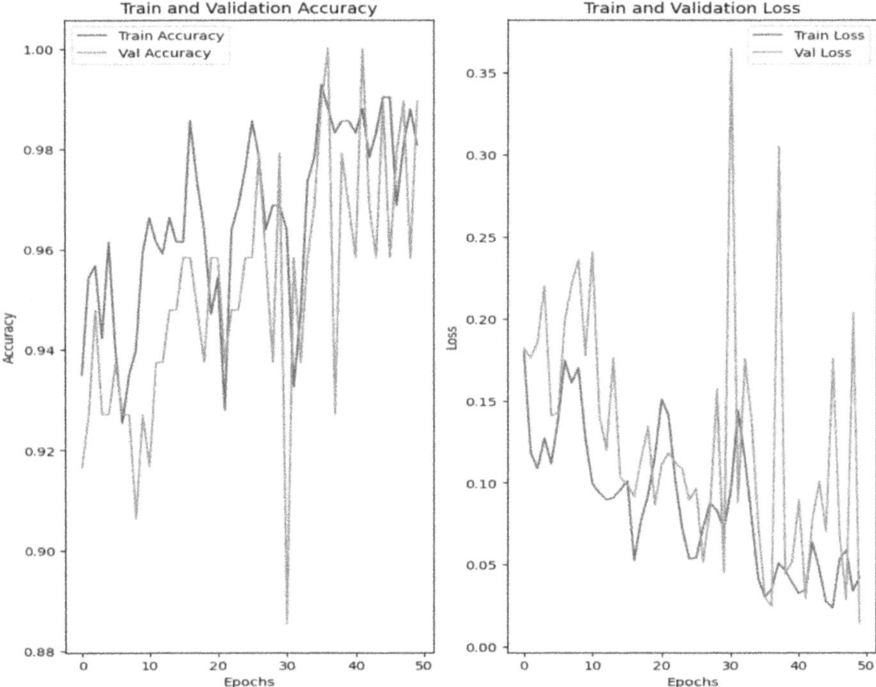

Fig. 4. Accuracy v/s Loss (50 Epochs) for Training and Validation.

Table 2. Classification Report.

Classification Report				
Class	Accuracy	Precision	Recall	F1-Score
0	97.69%	98.60%	97.69%	98.14%
1	97.27%	99.07%	97.27%	98.17%
2	97.64%	94.09%	97.64%	95.83%
3	99.12%	99.12%	99.12%	99.12%
4	96.72%	97.79%	96.72%	97.25%
5	96.48%	98.97%	96.48%	97.71%
6	97.93%	98.95%	97.93%	98.44%
7	96.63%	97.73%	96.63%	97.18%
8	98.15%	99.38%	98.15%	98.76%
9	100.00%	94.61%	100.00%	97.23%

Recall: The definition of recall, which is sometimes referred to as sensitivity or true positive rate, is the ratio of true positive forecasts to all real positive cases (Fig. 8).

$$\text{Precision} = \frac{\text{True Positives}}{\text{True Positives} + \text{False Positives}} \times 100 \tag{3}$$

F1-score: The F1-score is the harmonic meaning of precision and recall (Fig. 9)

$$\text{F1} - \text{Score} = 2 \times \frac{\text{Precision} \times \text{Recall}}{\text{Precision} + \text{Recall}} \times 100 \tag{4}$$

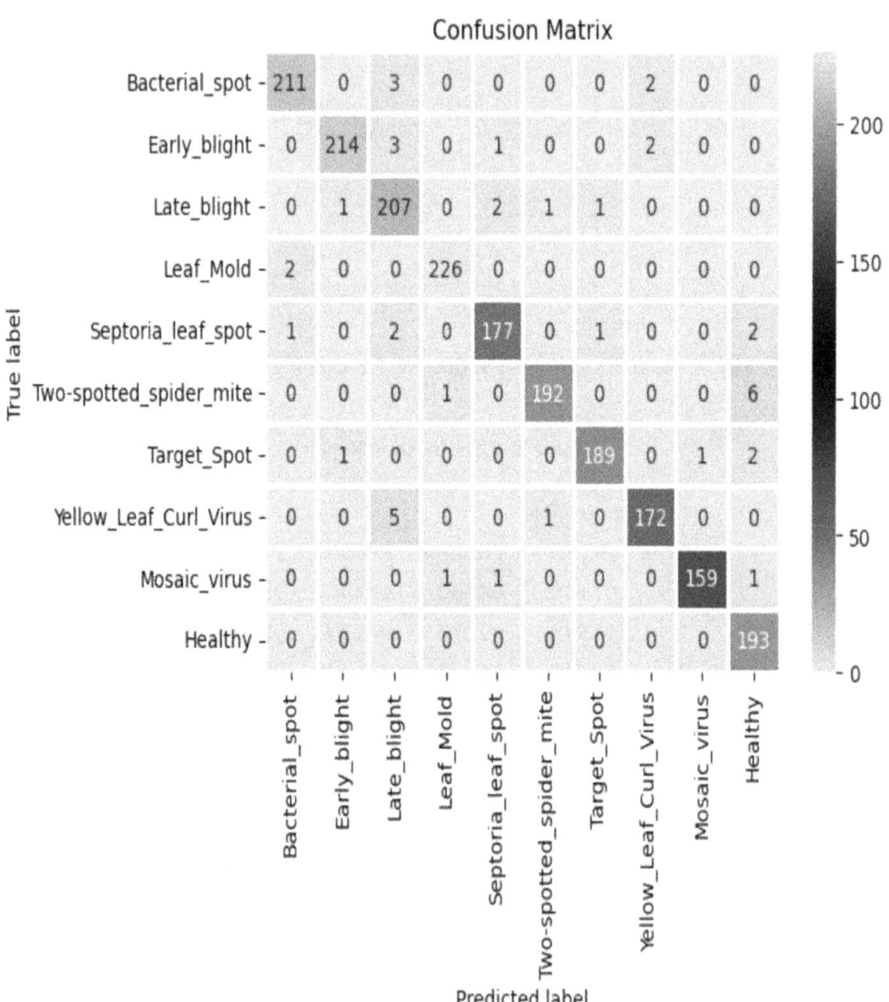

Fig. 5. Confusion Matrix

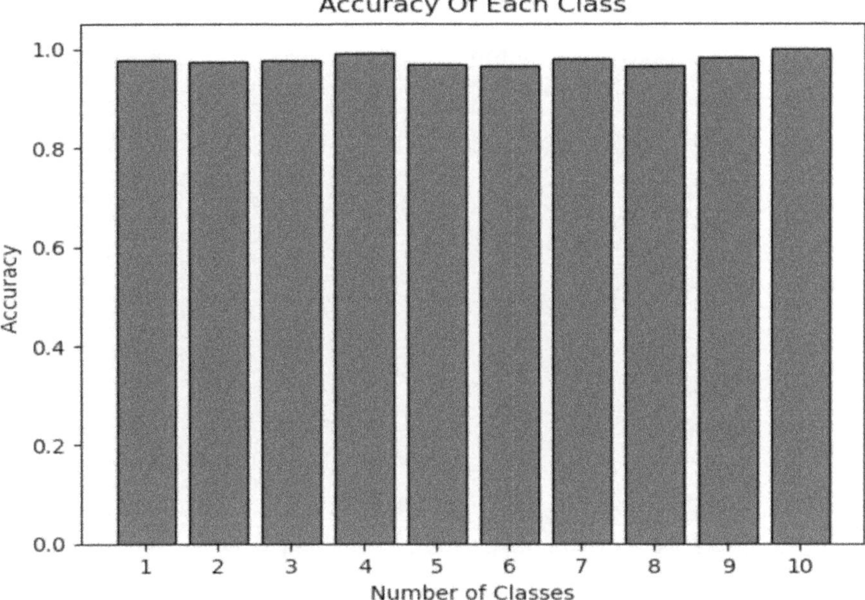

Fig. 6. Accuracy

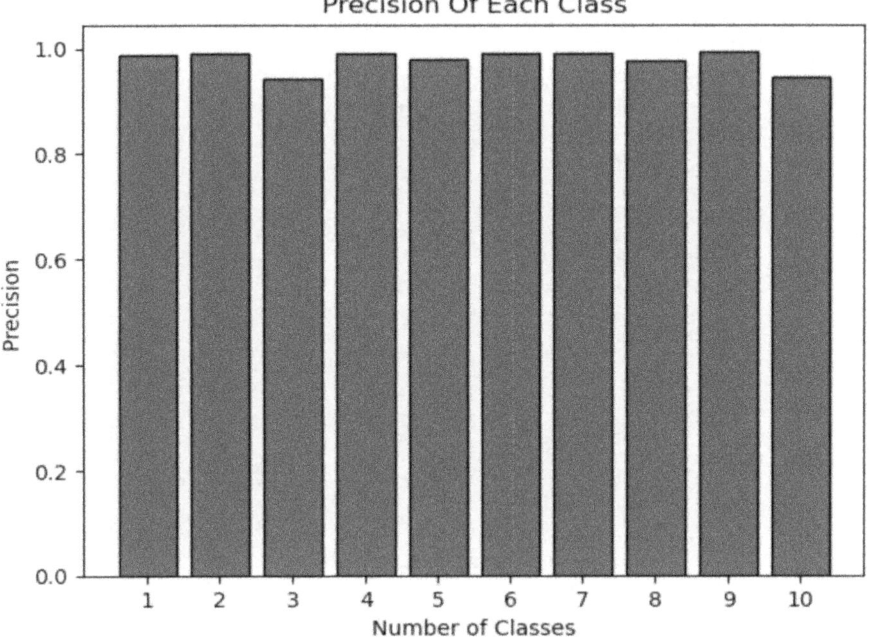

Fig. 7. Precision

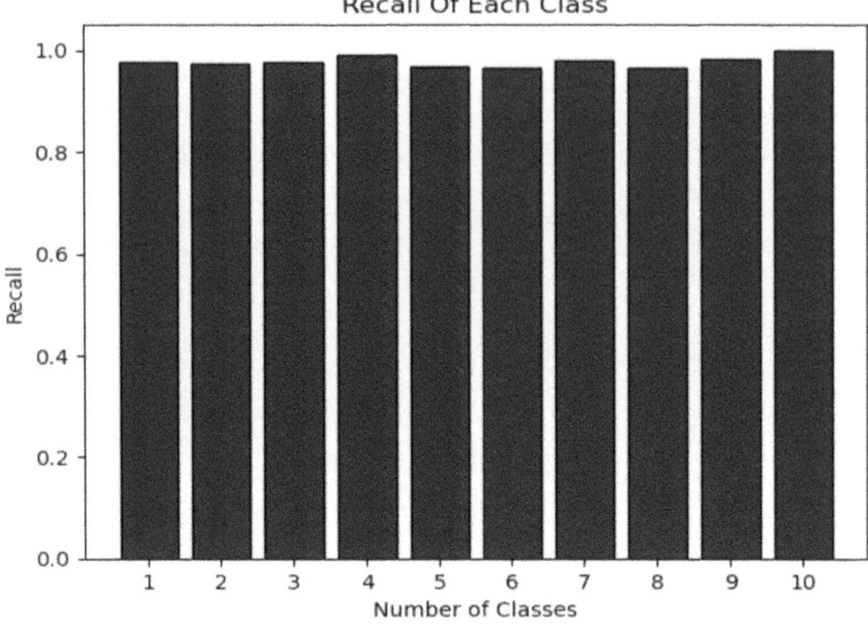

Fig. 8. Recall

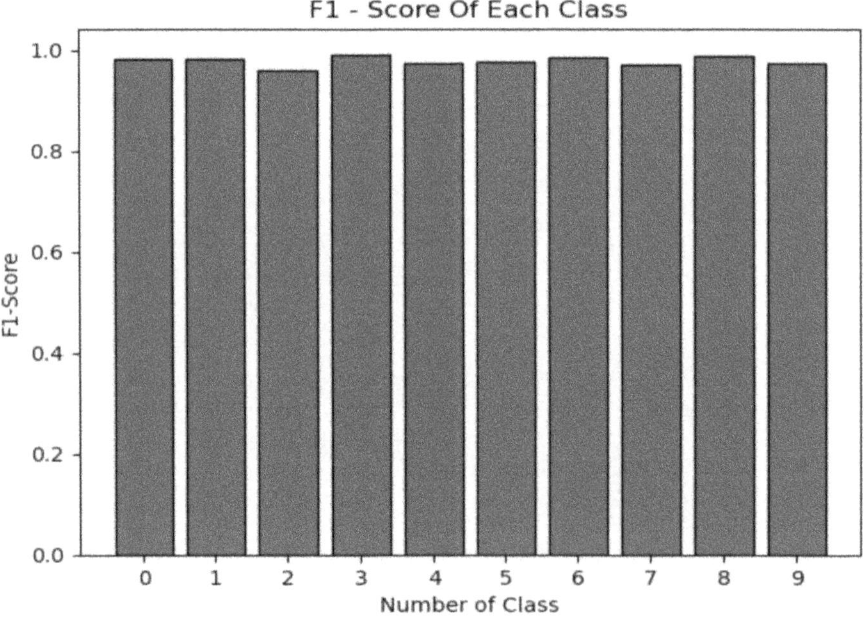

Fig. 9. F1-score

Output & Result

Therefore, testing of the model was done by predicting the images in the test dataset. The accuracy of the test data resulted 97.78%.In Future There is a chance for the model to improve its performance with some methods such as hyper-parameter tuning, data validation, regularization, and semantic segmentation, especially when dealing with high complexity data by integration of ResNet50 and CNN for better classification of huge images dataset.

5 Conclusion

In conclusion, the proposed Convolutional Neural Network (CNN) approach for the early detection of diseases in tomatoes, which are susceptible to various pathogens worldwide, leading to significant losses in cultivation. Our model presented a fantastic outcome with the training accuracy of 98.6% and testing accuracy of 97.78% which is a clear indication that it is effective in detecting tomato leaf disease. As for the future, the directions for further research and development are numerous. First and foremost, the research may incorporate the expansion of the data set to include more varieties of the tomato leaf diseases which could increase the model's capability to generalize the unseen data. Cooperation with agricultural specialists and stakeholders can enable the generation of user-friendly, cost-effective, and varieties of solutions targeted towards specific farmers. Through utilization of CNNs and image processing methods, we provide farmers with the equipment and knowledge they need to minimize the damage caused by diseases and hence, for food security and environment friendly agriculture.

Acknowledgement. We want to express our profound appreciation to Madanapalle Institute of Technology and Science for the tools and assistance they gave us while we developed the CNN model-based Enhanced Deep Learning method for toma-to leaf disease detection. Our profound thanks to Mrs. T.Swetha and Dr. S. Kusuma for their invaluable guidance, and our team members for their voluntary contributions. Warm acknowledgment from colleagues at the Department of Data science for their collaboration.

Conflict of Interest The authors declare that there are no conflicts of interest.

Funding. No funding received for the research.

References

1. Zhao, S., Peng, Y., Liu, J., Wu, S.: Tomato leaf disease diagnosis based on improved convolution neural network by attention module. Agriculture. **11**(7), 651 (2021)
2. Bayram, H.Y., Bingol, H., Alatas, B.: Hybrid deep model for automated detection of tomato leaf diseases. Trait. Signal. **39**(5), 1781 (2022)
3. Trivedi, N.K. et al.: Early detection and classification of tomato leaf disease using high-performance deep neural network. Sensors. **21**(23), 7987 (2021)
4. Sreelatha, P., Udayakumar, M.S., Karthick, S., Ch, S.C., Kavya, K.C.S., Madiajagan, M.: Managing the tomato leaf disease detection accuracy using computer vision based deep neural network. J. Contemp. Issues Bus. Gov. **27**(1), 2489–2497 (2021)

5. Zhang, K., Wu, Q., Liu, A., Meng, X., et al.: Can deep learning identify tomato leaf disease? Adv. Multimedia. **2018**, 6710565 (2018)

6. Wu, Y., Xu, L., Goodman, E.D.: Tomato leaf disease identification and detection based on deep convolutional neural network. Intell. Autom. Soft Comput. **28**(2), 561–576 (2021)

7. Mokhtar, U., Ali, M.A., Hassenian, A.E., Hefny, H.: Tomato leaves diseases detection approach based on support vector machines. In: 2015 11th International Computer Engineering Conference (ICENCO), pp. 246–250. IEEE (2015)

8. Rani, F.P., Kumar, S., Fred, A.L., Dyson, C., Suresh, V., Jeba, P.: K-means clustering and SVM for plant leaf disease detection and classification. In: 2019 International Conference on Recent Advances in Energy-Efficient Computing and Communication (ICRAECC), pp. 1–4. IEEE (2019)

9. Nahar, N., Imam, M.H., Bhowmik, R., Rahman, M.A., Haque, I.: Tomato leaf disease detection using deep learning ensemble approach. Int. J. Sci. Eng. Res. **14**(12), 145–151 (2023)

10. Cengil, E., ınar, A.C.: Hybrid convolutional neural network based classification of bacterial, viral, and fungal diseases on tomato leaf images. Concurr. Comput. Pract. Exp. **34**(4), e6617 (2022)

11. Fuentes, A., Yoon, S., Park, D.S.: Deep learning-based techniques for plant diseases recognition in real-field scenarios. In: Advanced Concepts for Intelligent Vision Systems: 20th International Conference, ACIVS 2020, Auckland, New Zealand, February 10–14, 2020, Proceedings 20, pp. 3–14. Springer (2020)

12. Loey, M., ElSawy, A., Afify, M.: Deep learning in plant diseases detection for agricultural crops: a survey. Int. J. Serv. Sci. Manag. Eng. Technol. (IJSSMET). **11**(2), 41–58 (2020)

13. Ma, J., Du, K., Zheng, F., Zhang, L., Sun, Z.: A segmentation method for processing greenhouse vegetable foliar disease symptom images. Inf. Process. Agric. **6**(2), 216–223 (2019)

14. Salih, T.A., et al.: Deep learning convolution neural network to detect and classify tomato plant leaf diseases. OALib J. **7**(05), 1 (2020)

15. Mortazi, A., Bagci, U.: Automatically designing CNN architectures for medical image segmentation. In: Machine Learning in Medical Imaging: 9th International Workshop, MLMI 2018, Held in Conjunction with MICCAI 2018 September 16, 2018, Proceedings 9, Granada, Spain, pp. 98–106. Springer (2018)

16. Kaushik, M., Prakash, P., Ajay, R., Veni, S., et al.: Tomato leaf disease detection using convolutional neural network with data augmentation. In: 2020 5th International Conference on Communication and Electronics Systems (ICCES), pp. 1125–1132. IEEE (2020)

17. Li, Y., Luo, Z., Wang, F., Wang, Y.: Hyperspectral leaf image-based cucumber disease recognition using the extended collaborative representation model. Sensors. **20**(14), 4045 (2020)

18. Ferentinos, K.P.: Deep learning models for plant disease detection and diagnosis. Comput. Electron. Agric. **145**, 311–318 (2018)

19. Sharma, P., Berwal, Y.P.S., Ghai, W.: Performance analysis of deep learning CNN models for disease detection in plants using image segmentation. Inf. Process. Agric. **7**(4), 566–574 (2020)

20. Chowdhury, M.E. et al.: Automatic and reliable leaf diseasedetection using deep learning techniques. Agri Engineering. **3**(2), 294–312 (2021)

21. Guerrero-Ibanez, A., Reyes-Munoz, A.: Monitoring tomato leaf disease through convolutional neural networks. Electronics. **12**(1), 229 (2023)

22. Al-gaashani, M.S., Shang, F., Muthanna, M.S., Khayyat, M., Abd El-Latif, A.A.: Tomato leaf disease classification by exploiting transfer learning and feature concatenation. IET Image Process. **16**(3), 913–925 (2022)

23. Tm, P., Pranathi, A., SaiAshritha, K., Chittaragi, N.B., Koolagudi, S.G.: Tomato leaf disease detection using convolutional neural networks. In: 2018 Eleventh International Conference on Contemporary Computing (IC3), pp. 1–5. IEEE (2018)
24. Khasawneh, N., Faouri, E., Fraiwan, M.: Automatic detection of tomato diseases using deep transfer learning. Appl. Sci. **12**(17), 8467 (2022)
25. Mattihalli, C., Gedefaye, E., Endalamaw, F., Necho, A.: Real time automation of agriculture land, by automatically detecting plant leaf diseases and auto medicine. In: 2018 32nd International Conference on Advanced Information Networking and Applications Workshops (WAINA), pp. 325–330. IEEE (2018)

Lameness Prediction in Poultry Chickens Using Deep Convolutional Neural Network

Divya Verma[1,2(✉)], Neelam Goel[1], and Diksha Garg[1]

[1] University Institute of Engineering and Technology, Panjab University, Chandigarh 160014, India
divyaverma.uiet@gmail.com
[2] Department of Computer Science and Engineering, Chandigarh University, Gharuan, Mohali, Punjab 140413, India

Abstract. Lameness in poultry is a serious economic and animal health issue. Real-time monitoring of the health of chickens using images is an efficient technique to stop widespread disease outbreaks due to the advancement in digital image processing and deep learning techniques. The spread of diseases among poultry usually poses a major threat to human health. Even if there are many people raising chickens in a lot of places, manual observation is still the main method used to monitor poultry diseases. The welfare of a broiler flock is often determined by factors such as mortality, physiology, behavior, and walking ability. Using a deep learning approach, it is possible to identify healthy and lame chickens. This study aims to design a convolutional neural network (CNN) model for identifying lame broilers within a poultry flock. Real-time data is obtained from two separate poultry farms, and data augmentation methods are applied to expand the dataset. The collected data is then manually categorized into two groups: healthy chickens and lame chicks. The model was developed using a dataset comprising 4,966 images of broilers, including 2,145 labeled as lame and 2,821 labeled as healthy. The goal is to categorize the birds based on their legs. The accuracy achieved for Convolutional Neural Networks model is 95%. The results demonstrate that lame broilers can be automatically detected within a flock, highlighting the potential of this method to improve flock management practices.

Keywords: Deep Learning · Poultry · Convolutional Neural Networks · Chickens · Lameness

1 Introduction

Agriculture diversification via livestock farming has been one of the major factors of development in the rural incomes, and increased infrastructure expenditure in the agricultural sectors is urgently needed to double farm owners' wealth. According to annual report of 2021, for marginalized and poor farmers, livestock is a key source of income which is essential to the country's economic health. According to estimates, Covid-19 impacts and related lockdowns cost the poultry industry more than 22,000 crores in monetary losses. The pandemic had a considerable effect on the chicken industry, slowing its growth to just 2–3% in the fiscal year 2020, compared to the usual annual growth rate of 7–8%. Additionally, the industry saw a decline of 4–5% in fiscal year 2021. Despite these challenges, poultry farming remains one of the most advanced and commercially successful sectors, with broilers becoming a primary food source for many households. However, poultry bird diseases pose significant threats to poultry farming, leading to reduced productivity and substantial economic losses for farmers. The occurrence of poultry diseases can also pose risks to human health [3]. Lameness in chickens is one of the factors in large-scale bird deaths. Typically, the condition starts to show itself with a minor limp that appears to be absolutely unnecessary at first. In fact, the chicks eventually start to weaken and wither, and it is difficult to build up their decreased immunity. The most common causes of lameness in broiler chickens and egg chicks are violations of the most fundamental needs and standards for poultry care. Lameness in broilers is closely linked to their weight and rapid growth. However, mobility issues can lead to discomfort, reducing their activity levels and causing conditions like hock burns and chest dirtiness [4]. As the primary contributor to the current production of poultry meat, broiler chicken is the focus of this research. Farmers and veterinarians usually detect chicken diseases by visual inspections and sound differentiation. However, these detection techniques are labor-intensive, time-consuming, and subjective, and therefore do not provide an early diagnosis in large-scale production [11].

Our study gives an evaluation of posture to build a strategy for identifying between healthy and lame birds. The posture of lame birds typically differs dramatically from that of healthy birds. As a result, mobility is a crucial component that has been used to evaluate birds' health. A lame chicken will commonly stay in by itself, avoid taking long walks, and adopt a depressed bird stance. A broiler in discomfort will always isolate itself from the other birds in the flock, socialize less, and remain motionless. Since lameness refers to the characteristic or the ability to move, it is typically related to walking or locomotion. When it comes to poultry, stillness is frequently a symptom of discomfort. Leg abnormalities, nutritional deficiencies, and illnesses including leg health and diseases may all contribute to this distress. It has also been noted that healthy birds move far more quickly than unsound ones. Therefore, a bird's movement qualities are significantly impacted by an infection. The level of lameness in chickens has been determined using their mobility and activity levels. In addition, a variety of injuries with infectious or non-infectious origins are referred to as lameness in broilers. Additionally, factors such as walking speed, gait speed, step frequency, and body oscillations in broilers are closely associated with the severity of lameness [11].

In this paper, deep learning technique is used to predict the lameness in chickens. Deep learning models are usually used when there is a availability of large dataset. In this work, image features are extracted automatically using deep neural networks. The primary goal of this study is to develop a model capable of distinguishing between healthy and lame broilers. The main objectives include data collection, data augmentation, and selecting an appropriate model.

2 Related Work

The following section briefly reviews the existing work related to the classification of Chicken disease by applying machine learning and deep learning techniques.

In an attempt, data set was created using records on chicken's walking rate and acceleration, genetic strain, and gender [2]. The chicken's 6-point gait score was used as the classification criterion, with GS0 representing a healthy chicken and GS5 indicating a severely lame chicken. The dataset was pruned using the approach to remove the variables that could not be inferred from the classification outcomes. The dataset is restructured by grouping data points, and the intermediate target class for the gait score is assigned using the Borda Count method. A new set of decision trees is proposed after reprocessing the data, leading to the creation of a model with enhanced accuracy (78%) by applying a 3-point gait score (GS0 for healthy chickens and GS2 for lame chickens). However, the model's classification accuracy for identifying lame broilers (GS2, 5%) was relatively low. The final decision tree model is selected to categorize broilers as either healthy or lame based on their gait parameters. The study is primarily focused on offering a predictive service framework for industrial IoT that can classify poultry hens more precisely and instantly [10]. It involves monitoring the health and well-being of the chickens by video surveillance, voice observations, wearable sensors like gyroscopes and acceleration sensors. The motion-sensing devices are placed over chickens and are capable of uploading data about the birds' movements to the cloud for further analysis. Interpreting such data and making more accurate predictions about the health of chickens presents a significant challenge. This research offers a paradigm for IoT-based predictive services to aid in the early identification of poultry diseases. This study utilized narrow-band images of chicken hearts, rather than broadband RGB images, to identify diseased chicken carcasses. High-resolution images were collected instead of basic spectrographic data, offering greater flexibility for applications, such as providing detailed size and morphological information or identifying more localized conditions [1]. Additionally, the use of computer-assisted tools and precise data plays a crucial role in enhancing the efficiency of poultry farmers, particularly in the early detection of chicken diseases. These techniques are valuable for minimizing losses and increasing productivity, as they enable the early detection of infections before they lead to chicken deaths. In recent decades, advancements in computer vision have aimed to bridge this gap by developing automated systems that use computers to analyze images and make decisions. The findings of the experiment demonstrate that the technique is used for accurate diagnostics and is successful in identifying diseases in chickens. Also, images of broilers are obtained, and two different types of segmentation algorithms are suggested to take the broilers out of the backdrop and extract their outlines and skeleton information [12]. The postural features of healthy and diseased chickens are retrieved using the predefined feature selection technique, the eigenvectors are built, the broiler postures are assessed by machine learning algorithms, and diseased broilers are forecasted. Numerous tests have been conducted. The influence of each attribute on the recognition rate is determined by analyzing the data for each characteristic that the algorithms have collected [11]. This study presents a novel approach for the rapid detection of avian influenza using acoustic analysis [6]. The short-time auto-correlation functions of recorded chicken sounds and background noise show distinct differences, enabling the isolation of chicken vocalizations from the background noise. The processed chicken sound signal's frequency domain is used to extract Mel-frequency cepstral coefficients (MFCCs). These coefficients are then utilized to differentiate between healthy and sick chickens. A binary classification support vector machine (SVM) is trained to recognize the extracted chicken sounds. The optimal penalty parameter and kernel function for the SVM are determined through four-fold cross-validation. In this study, a model framework for identifying unwell broilers within a flock utilizing deep learning and digital image processing was developed. Broiler health status can be determined using this method based on physical characteristics. They are unable to precisely identify the illnesses that the broilers are suffering from. They can only alert farmers to potential changes in broiler health and encourage them to check any suspected sick broilers more thoroughly. This study sheds light on the variations in walking traits between broilers who have an ideal gait and those who have an inadequate gait [5]. Understanding these variations can aid in the development of automated models for predicting broiler gait scores and improve our understanding of the features that black-box gait prediction models might detect. Due to the current lack of data, birds with different gait scores have been categorized into two groups: optimal and suboptimal gaits, with GS2 serving as the upper threshold for optimal gaits. This research presents an aggressive method for identifying chicken behaviors that are based on a hybrid strategy that combines support vector machines (SVM) and an enhanced Sparrow Search Algorithm. Behavioral data of chickens were collected using nine-axis inertial sensors. A sliding window of one second was applied to extract 231-dimensional feature data from both the time and frequency domains of the behavioral data [8]. As in the previous research most of the work is done on individual chicken and no work is done on group of broilers but in a real-world setting, broilers are kept in groups, making it challenging to detect disease among them. However, there is no data available publicly, which limits the research in this field. Moreover, most of the work is done on diseases like Coccidiosis, Newcastle, Avian Influenza, and CRD, relatively less research has been conducted on the prediction of lameness in chicks. The aim of this study is to distinguish between lame and healthy chicks. Early detection of lameness is crucial as it enables farmers and veterinarians to implement timely management interventions.

3 Materials and Methods

3.1 Farm Setup and Data Set Collection

The real-time data is collected from two farms having 1000 chickens. The data is gathered between January 2022 and May 2022 throughout the period. The birds are set up on the farm, which is protected by a shed. A gas breeder is installed there to adjust the temperature in accordance with the days and the needs of the chickens, and from day 1 to day 3, 95° are provided to the Chickens. The structure of the farm where the chicks were kept is shown in fig. 1(a) and fig. 1(b). Data is gathered from the first day and till the day broiler reaches maturity. The area is covered in rice husks to feed the fowl.

Farmers clear the entire farm and clean it before relocating the chicks there, in order to prevent the birds from getting infected. The cleaning process takes around 10 to 15 days, during which time the entire area is cleansed and made suitable for the new chicks. The chickens were also given multivitamins, antibiotics course, vaccinations, and other treatments from the first day as directed by the veterinary doctors.

On each day at least an hour is spend on the farm for gathering information and capturing images of the chickens. The manual data collection is done under the farm owner's supervision. Every day, images of both healthy and lame chicks are taken. In order to get a clear picture, some chickens are placed on a red cylindrical box while others are placed on a brown cardboard box. Figure 1(c) and (d) depict the chick on the carton and the chicken on the cylindrical surface, respectively. Chickens suffer from a variety of diseases like fever, lameness, and heat stock. The main focus of this study is to classify healthy and lame chickens. Lame chicken have twisted legs and are unable to walk normally, but healthy chicken have regular legs. Lame chicken can be detected as early as day 2, when they are all placed on the farm, and can be recognized based on their leg position.

Fig. 1 (a) Farm Setup (b) Broilers (c) Chick on cardboard (d) Chicken on Red Surface

The Redmi note 5 pro camera is used to acquire images, and it has the following specifications: Dual Camera 12 MP, PDAF 5 MP with Dual-LED flash, panoramic, and HDR; Video 1080p At 30 fps; and GSM/HSPA/LTE network technology. After gathering the images, the chickens are manually divided into two folders labeled "healthy chickens" and "lame chicks." A total of 1280 broilers images are collected, out of which 534 are lame and 686 were healthy. The goal is to classify the chickens based on their legs positions.

3.2 Methodology

The methodology used to design the proposed model is given in the fig. 2.

3.2.1 Data Pre-Processing

Before developing a model pre-processing step is needed for the better performance of the model.

Data Augmentation Data augmentation techniques can be valuable when there is a limited amount of data, as they help enhance the dataset's size and diversity. Deep learning models require a substantial amount of training data to achieve the necessary integration for enhanced identification accuracy, helping to prevent overfitting. The goal of augmentation is to change the original image $T_i : X \rightarrow X'$. We use the successive implementation of augmentations for the final alteration of the image: $T = 0_{i-1..k} T_i$

Generally, training data is the only dataset used for image data augmentation; validation datasets and test datasets are not used. As a result, the training data are dynamically transformed while preserving their original classifications through the data augmentation technique. With k augmentation procedures, the total number of images used for training will be $(k + 1)$ times that of the original dataset [12].

Image Enhancement Image enhancement is the process of improving an image's visual quality by highlighting specific features or eliminating any ambiguity between different parts of the image. A group of approaches known as "image enhancement processes" aim to enhance an image's visual appeal or change it into a structure that will be better suitable either for automated or human evaluation. The goal of image enhancement techniques is to improve the visibility and detail of images. Enhanced images provide clearer visuals for human interpretation or assist in feature extraction for computer vision systems. Various enhancement methods have been proposed, but when selecting the most suitable technique for a specific image processing application, factors such as enhancement effectiveness, computational requirements, noise amplification, user intervention, and compatibility with the application must be considered [7]. The following are the image enhancement techniques used in this work.

Histogram: Histogram processing is the process of modifying an image's histogram. Normalization, the technique of generating an image's histogram as smooth as possible, is often used in histogram processing. Another name for this is contrast enhancement. A discrete function is the histogram of a digital image having levels of intensity $[0, L - 1]$ is given in Eq. 1 [7].

$$h(r_k) = n_k \tag{1}$$

where,

- r_k represents the intensity value
- n_k is the total number of pixels having intensity r_k in the image.
- $h(r_k)$ is the digital image's histogram with Gray Level r_k

Frequently, the total number of pixels in the image is used to normalize histograms. Assuming a normalized histogram for an M by N image is related to the probability that r_k will appear in the image.

$$p(r_k) = \frac{nk}{MN} \quad K = 0, 1, 2, 3\,L - 1 \tag{2}$$

where $p(r_k)$ gives an estimate of the probability of occurrence of gray level r_k. The total of a normalized histogram's components is 1.

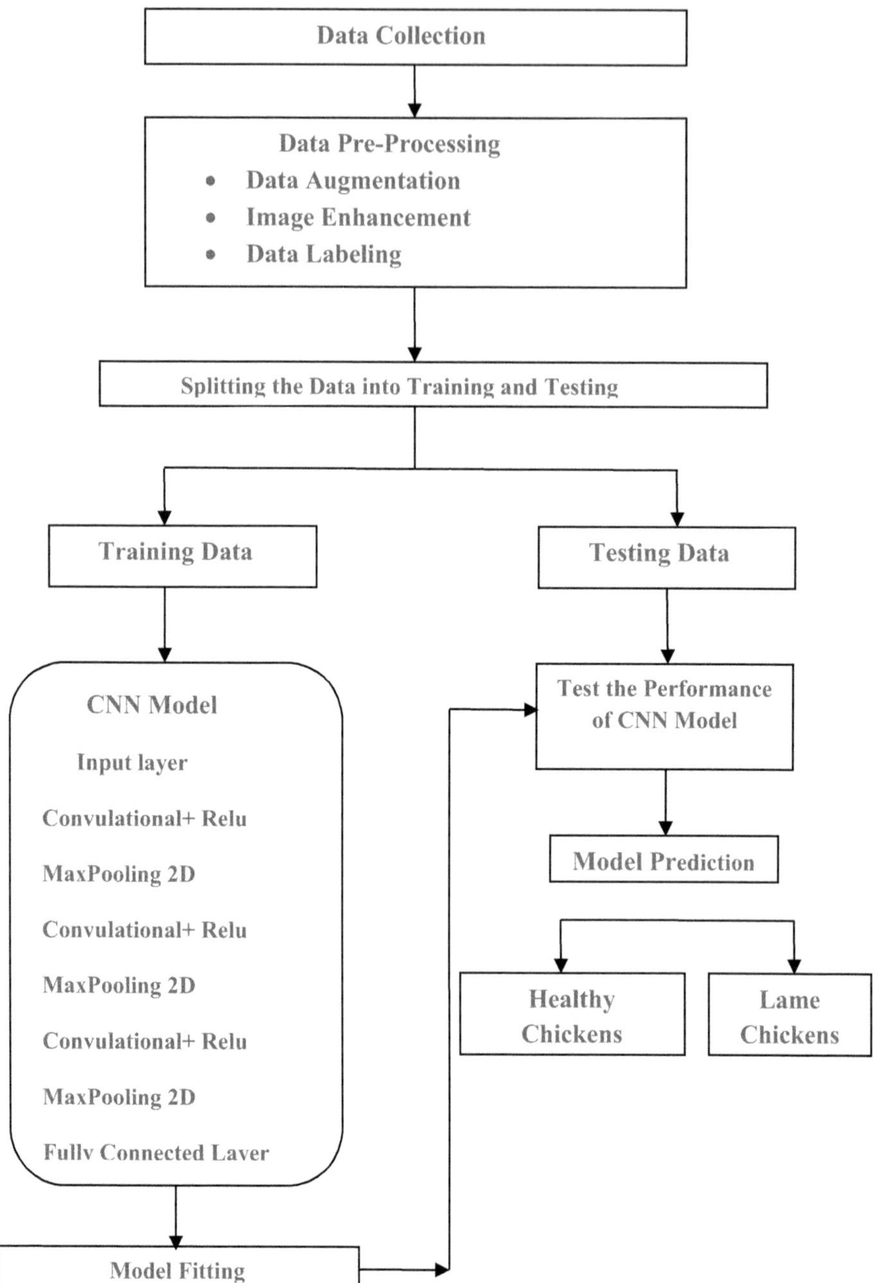

Fig. 2 Proposed Methodology

Hu Moments: Hu Moments, or more precisely Hu moment invariants, are a set of seven values derived from central moments that remain unaffected by transformations such as scaling, rotation, and translation in images. The first six moments have been shown to be independent of scale, rotation, and reflection. While the symbol for the seventh moment changes due to picture reflection. The 'Hu Moments()' function in OpenCV is used to calculate the Hu moments of shapes in the input image. It's important to note that the value of Hu[0] cannot be directly compared to other Hu moments in terms of magnitude, as each Hu moment represents a different invariant characteristic of the shape. We can apply the log transform to get them into the same range as shown below [9].

$$Hi = -\text{sign}(hi) \log | hi |\tag{3}$$

Data Labeling Before training a model data labeling step is needed. There are 4961 images overall for broilers in the dataset, which are used in this work. The images are categorized into the two classes—healthy and lame—correspondingly. Images of the broiler samples that have been accurately labeled are used as inputs in this study. The veterinary officer assisted in manually labeling the items. If a chicken has lameness disease, the value is set to 1, otherwise it is set to 0 to indicate that the chicks do not have a leg condition.

3.2.2 Convolutional Neural Network (CNN)

Due to their superior performance, Convolutional neural networks (CNNs) are the most popular architecture for deep learning. Convolutional Neural Networks (CNNs) are a specialized type of neural network commonly used in sound and image recognition applications. Their convolutional layers help reduce the high dimensionality of images while preserving crucial information. CNNs can process and interpret visuals in a way that mimics or even surpasses human perception, as they are designed to simulate the way the brain processes visual information. They are made up of a number of secret layers that aid in the analysis of visual perception. CNNs consist of an input layer, multiple hidden layers, and an output layer. The stack of convolutional layers processes an input image, typically sized 224×224 RGB or 512×512, in the first layer. The convolutional layers apply filters with 3×3 receptive fields, followed by a max-pooling layer that operates on a 2×2 pixel window. Each block uses the same padding to ensure the height and width of the output feature maps match the input features. The final output layer of the proposed CNN model is tasked with classifying chicken diseases. The classifier's input in the proposed CNN model consists of optimized features made utilizing a fitness function optimization technique. It employs fully connected layers, where every neuron is linked to all the optimal features from the preceding layer, enabling a thorough integration of the information extracted by earlier layers. For all layers, ReLU activation is implemented. Normal stochastic gradient descent is utilized in training to reduce error. Convolutional layers and pooling layers can both be followed by dropout. The dropout layer is used to avoid overfitting. Since the problem is a binary-class classification, the output layer consists of two nodes with softmax activation. The output from each node indicates the probability of the input belonging to one of the two classes, making Softmax the optimal choice for this task (Table 1).

The activation function of ReLU:

$$ReLU : \quad f(x) = \max(0, x)\tag{4}$$

Table 1. The parameters of the proposed model

Parameter	Value
Convolution Layers	3 (with [3 × 3] filters each)
Max-Pooling Layers	3 (with [2, 2] pool size each)
Convolution Layer Activation Function	ReLU
Epochs	100
Loss Function	Categorical cross-entropy

The model used in this implementation is "**Sequential**" model of CNN with its layers as described in Table 2 and Fig. 3.

Table 2. CNN Layers used in the model

Layers (Type)	Output (Shape)	Parameters
conv2d (Conv2D)	(None, 62, 62, 16)	448
max_pooling2d (MaxPooling2D)	(None, 31, 31, 16)	0
conv2d_1 (Conv2D)	(None, 29, 29, 16)	2320
max_pooling2d_1 (MaxPooling2D)	(None, 14, 14, 16)	0
conv2d_2 (Conv2D)	(None, 12, 12, 16)	2320
max_pooling2d_2 (MaxPooling2D)	(None, 6, 6, 16)	0
dropout (Dropout)	(None, 6, 6, 16)	0
flatten (Flatten)	(None, 576)	0
dense (Dense)	(None, 64)	36928
dense_1 (Dense)	(None, 15)	975

3.2.3 Performance Evaluation Metrics

The trained classification model was evaluated using the same performance metrics that were used to assess the accuracy of the proposed classification system. When calculating the effectiveness of classifier the efficiency of classifiers, one metric may not be sufficient. In this study, the following performance metrics are utilized: accuracy, F1-score, precision, and recall. These metrics are defined as follows:

Precision explains how particular items are significant. Its definition is that it is the proportion of true positives (TP) to the total of false positives (FP) and true positives (TP) as mentioned in eq. 5.

$$Precision = TP/TP + FP \tag{5}$$

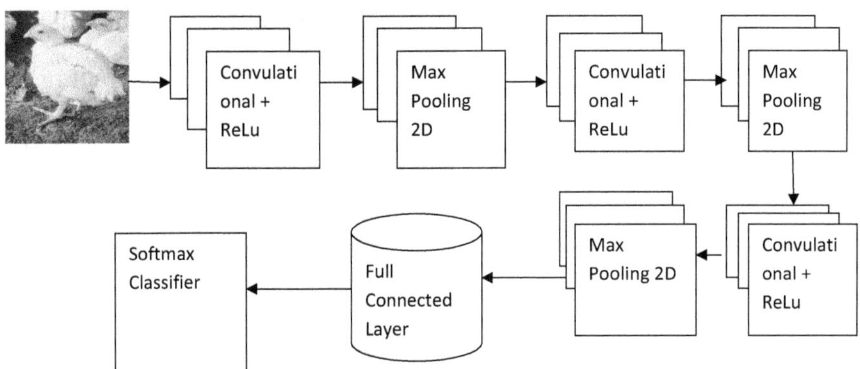

Fig. 3 CNN Layers Used to Implement the Model

Recall (also known as sensitivity) counts the number of classified samples in relation to all the pertinent ones. It determines the proportion of true positives (TP) to the total of false negatives (FN) and true positives (TP) as given in eq. 6.

$$Recall = TP/TP + FN \tag{6}$$

F1-Score statistic combines recall and precision while maintaining a balance between the two. This statistic combines recall and precision while maintaining a balance between the two.

$$F1 - Score = 2 \times Precision \times Recall \ Precision + Recall$$

$$= 2 \times TP/2 \times TP + FP + FN \tag{7}$$

Accuracy is the number of correctly predicted objects to the total predictions:
Accuracy = Number of Correct predictions /Total number of predictions made.

$$Accuracy = TP + TN/TP + TN + FP + FN \tag{8}$$

where,

- **True Positive (TP):** Both the observation and the prediction are positive.
- **True Negative (TN):** The prediction is negative, while the observation is positive.
- **False Positive (FP):** Both the observation and the prediction are negative.
- **False Negative (FN):** The prediction is positive, while the observation is negative.

4   Results and Discussion

The current study determines chicken lameness based on its leg condition. The goal of this study is to develop a prediction model that will help poultry farm owners classify lame and healthy birds, ultimately enabling them to prevent economic losses. The data is collected in the form of images, and the total number of images used is 1280, of which 534 are of lame birds and 686 are of healthy chickens are shown in Table 3. After separating healthy and unhealthy broilers, data augmentation techniques are applied to expand the dataset size. The first step is to apply a group of transformation techniques, such as rotation, shear, zoom, horizontal, and brightness as mentioned in the Table 4. After augmentation we get 3365 healthy and 3176 lame images and Fig. 4 shows the images after augmentation. After this, the images with useful information is manually selected resulting in a total of 2821 for healthy and 2145 for lame broilers and is shown in Table 5.

Table 3. Collected Dataset

Class	Images Collected
Healthy Chicks	686
Lame Chicks	534
Total Chicks	1280

Table 4. Parameters Used in Augmentation

Augmentation Features	Parameters Used
Rotation Range	40
Shear Range	0.2
Zoom Range	0.2
Horizontal Flip	True
Brightness Range	0.5, 1.5

Table 5. Dataset used in Proposed Model

Class	Number of Images in Each Class
Healthy Chickens	2821
Lame Chickens	2145
Total Chickens	4966

The dataset is split into training and testing sets using an 80:20 ratio, with 80% used for training and 20% for testing. The data is randomly divided into these subsets using the train-test split function. In this study, a fully connected CNN model is trained on

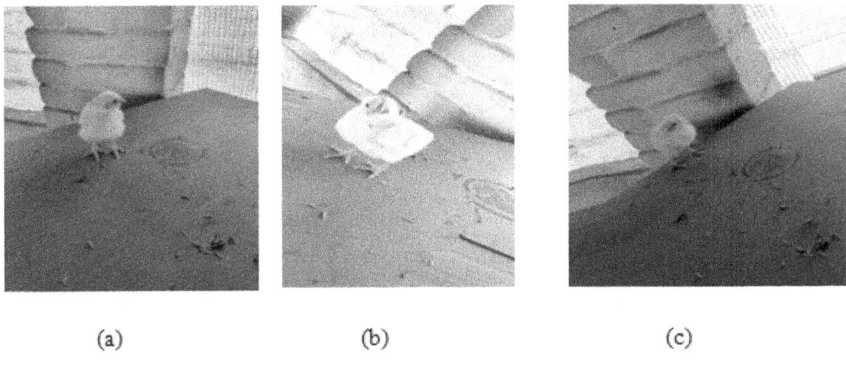

(a)   (b)   (c)

Fig. 4. (a) original image (b) Brighten Augmented Image (c) Rotated Augmented Image

the dataset, and its performance is assessed by monitoring the trends in training and validation accuracy.

The model used different hyper-parameters to achieve the best result of the CNN model and is shown in Table 6 and Table 7.

Table 6. The Results of Proposed Model Using Different Dropout Layer

Dropout	Epochs	Training Accuracy (%)	Validation Accuracy (%)	Training Loss (%)	Validation Loss (%)
0.6	25	87.31	89.56	28	26
0.5	25	89.73	87.85	24.8	27.9
0.4	25	91.71	89.06	19.25	29.46
0.2	25	91.46	88.55	20.48	25.65

Table 7. The Results of Proposed Model Using Different Epochs

Epochs	Training Accuracy (%)	Validation Accuracy (%)	Training Loss (%)	Validation Loss (%)
35	93.17	90.76	17.44	24.97
40	95.25	90.26	12.16	24.79
50	95.37	90.66	11.41	27.04
55	95.39	89.66	10.91	26.83
100	95.42	92.85	11.16	20.43

The metrics used to evaluate the model's effectiveness are precision, recall, and f1-score. The result of binary class achieved through the model is shown in the Table 8.

Table 8. The Results of Proposed CNN Model

Classes	Precision	Recall	F1-Score	Support
1	0.94	0.90	0.92	443
0	0.92	0.95	0.94	550
Accuracy			0.93	993
Macro Avg	0.93	0.93	0.93	993
Weighted Avg	0.93	0.93	0.93	993

The model achieved a training accuracy of 95.42% and a validation accuracy of 92.85% over 100 epochs. The accuracy and loss of the model are displayed in Figs. 5 and 6, respectively.

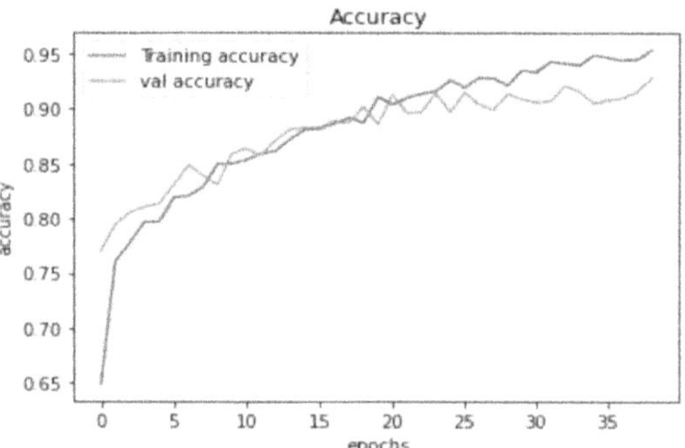

Fig. 5. Training and Validation Accuracy

Additionally, the model's performance is evaluated using five-fold cross-validation. In this process, the dataset is randomly shuffled, divided into 5 groups, and the test and train data are run across the folds to assess the model's robustness and generalization. In each run of the five-fold cross-validation, one fold is used for testing, while the remaining folds are used for training. The process progresses through iterations, with each fold serving as the test set once, ensuring a thorough evaluation of the model's performance. Therefore, one fold will be used for testing and the other folds for training ideally once through the complete the process. The accuracy score for each iteration is computed, and the average value for accuracy obtained is 95.68%. These results confirm that the model accuracy is better in case of cross-validation..

The CNN model employed in this study uses images to predict the lameness and achieves an accuracy of 95.42% and in comparison to the work described in the paper

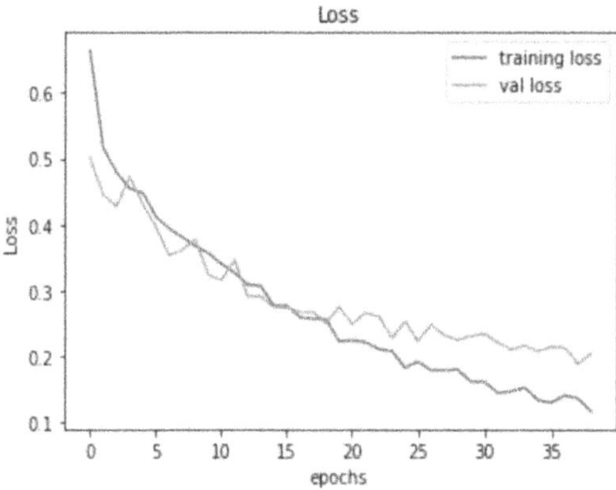

Fig. 6. Training and Validation Loss

[2] where decision tree were to predict the lameness in broiler chickens and achieved an accuracy of 91%. In this paper gait score is used to calculate the lameness in the chickens. The comparison is shown in Table 9.

Table 9. Comparison of proposed model with state-of-art method

Paper	Technique Used	Accuracy (%)
Proposed Model	CNN	95.42
Proposed Model (with cross-validation)	CNN	95.68
[2] (2021)	Decision Tree	91

5   Conclusion and Future Scope

Poultry sector provides significant support in country's economy. Stakeholders are worried about the safety measures adopted to protect the well-being of the birds given the poultry meat industry's rapid expansion. Early detection of escalating outbreaks of poultry disease is essential in the chicken industry. Chicken illnesses can be predicted and prevented using a variety of techniques. Images, videos, and sound analysis can all be utilized to identify infected birds, providing multiple methods for detecting and monitoring poultry health. The application of various machine learning algorithms helps in the early diagnosis of diseases in broilers, thereby reducing financial losses for poultry farms. Eliminating chickens with transmissible illnesses requires early detection. Chickens are susceptible to a number of illnesses, including CRD, lameness, fever, respiratory disease, and others. There hasn't been a lot of research done on predicting lameness in chicks. Disability has a detrimental effect on animal welfare and has significant economic consequences because of low growth, higher culling, and mortality, and undervalued and condemned corpses at slaughter.

This study aims to classify chickens into two groups—lame and healthy—using deep learning techniques. The dataset from the poultry farm is manually collected for this purpose. The data is split into training and testing groups before implementing the CNN model. Hyperparameter tuning is then performed to enhance the model's accuracy. The CNN model achieved a training accuracy of 95.42% and a testing accuracy of 92.85%. Furthermore, the model attained an accuracy of 95.68% with five-fold cross validation. The model is tested further by uploading an image of a healthy or lame chick, after which the model determines whether the image belongs to a healthy or lame chick. The proposed model for classifying lame chickens can be enhanced further. Here are a few potential future directions of this research; in this model, only a single chick is used; however, a group of chickens may be used in the future. In addition to the images utilized, work can be done on videos, sensor devices. Moreover, the model may be enhanced to provide multi-class classification so that one can detect multiple diseases. However, other techniques such as transfer learning technique can also be used. Also, it is feasible to create applications that are easy for end-users to use on their gadgets, including mobile phones and tablets, and support live monitoring.

References

1. Admassu, B., Teshome, M., Fentahunand, T.: Detection of sick broilers by digital image processing and deep learning. Biosyst. Eng. **179**, 106–116 (2019). https://doi.org/10.1016/j. biosystemseng.2019.01.003
2. de Alencar, N.I., da Silva Lima, N.D., Gonçalves, R.F., Antonio de Lima, L., Ungaro, H., Minoro Abe, J.: Lameness prediction in broiler chicken using a machine learning technique. Inf. Process. Agric. **8**, 409–418 (2021). https://doi.org/10.1016/j.inpa.2020.10.003
3. Astill, J., Fraser, E., Dara, R., Sharif, S.: Detecting and predicting emerging disease in poultry with the implementation of new technologies and big data: a focus on avian influenza virus. Front. Vet. Sci. **5**, 1–12 (2018). https://doi.org/10.3389/fvets.2018.00263
4. Aydin, A.: Leg weaknesses and lameness assessment methods in broiler chickens. Arch. Anim. Husb. Dairy Sci. **1**, 4–9 (2018). https://doi.org/10.33552/aahds.2018.01.000506
5. Fodor, I., van der Sluis, M., Jacobs, M., de Klerk, B., Bouwman, A.C., Ellen, E.D.: Automated pose estimation reveals walking characteristics associated with lameness in broilers. Poult. Sci. **102**, 1–11 (2023). https://doi.org/10.1016/j.psj.2023.102787
6. Huang, J., Wang, W., Zhang, T.: Method for detecting avian influenza disease of chickens based on sound analysis. Biosyst. Eng. **180**, 16–24 (2019). https://doi.org/10.1016/j.biosys temseng.2019.01.015
7. Vij, K., Singh, Y.: Enhancement of images using histogram processing techniques. Int. J. Comp. Tech. Appl. **2**, 309–313 (2011)
8. Li, L., Wang, Z., Hou, W., Zhou, Z., Xue, H.: A recognition method for aggressive chicken behavior based on machine learning. IEEE Access. **12**, 1–1 (2024). https://doi.org/10.1109/ access.2024.3365552
9. Mallick, S.: Shape Matching using Hu Moments (C++ / Python) | LearnOpenCV (2018). https://learnopencv.com/shape-matching-using-hu-moments-c-python/. Accessed 18 July 2022
10. Mbelwa, H., Machuve, D., Mbelwa, J.: Deep convolutional neural network for chicken diseases detection. Int. J. Adv. Comput. Sci. Appl. **12**, 759–765 (2021). https://doi.org/10.14569/ IJACSA.2021.0120295

11. Okinda, C. et al.: A machine vision system for early detection and prediction of sick birds: a broiler chicken model. Biosyst. Eng. **188**, 229–242 (2019). https://doi.org/10.1016/j.biosystemseng.2019.09.015
12. Okinda, C. et al.: A review on computer vision systems in monitoring of poultry: a welfare perspective. Artif. Intell. Agric. **4**, 184–208 (2020). https://doi.org/10.1016/j.aiia.2020.09.002

Author Index

GPSR Compliance
The European Union's (EU) General Product Safety Regulation (GPSR) is a set
of rules that requires consumer products to be safe and our obligations to
ensure this.

If you have any concerns about our products, you can contact us on

ProductSafety@springernature.com

In case Publisher is established outside the EU, the EU authorized
representative is:

Springer Nature Customer Service Center GmbH
Europaplatz 3
69115 Heidelberg, Germany